Paradise Lost

DOVER · THRIFT · EDITIONS

Paradise Lost

JOHN MILTON

Notes by
JOHN A. HIMES

DOVER PUBLICATIONS, INC.
Mineola, New York

DOVER GIANT THRIFT EDITIONS

GENERAL EDITOR: MARY CAROLYN WALDREP
EDITOR OF THIS VOLUME: SUSAN L. RATTINER

Bibliographical Note

This Dover edition, first published in 2005, is an unabridged republication of the poem and notes from *Paradise Lost, A Poem in Twelve Books, by John Milton; with an introduction and notes on its structure and meaning by John A. Himes,* as originally published by Harper & Brothers, New York and London, in 1898. A new introductory Note has been specially prepared for the present edition.

Library of Congress Cataloging-in-Publication Data

Milton, John, 1608–1674.
    Paradise lost / John Milton ; notes by John A. Himes.
        p. cm. — (Dover giant thrift editions)
    "This Dover edition, first published in 2005, is an unabridged republication of the poem and notes from Paradise lost, a poem in twelve books, by John Milton; with an introduction and notes on its structure and meaning by John A. Himes, as originally published by Harper & Brothers, New York and London, in 1898. A new introductory note has been specially prepared for the present edition"—T.p. verso.
    ISBN-13: 0-486-44287-7 (pbk.)
    ISBN-10: 0-486-44287-X (pbk.)
    1. Bible. O.T. Genesis—History of Biblical events—Poetry. 2. Adam (Biblical figure)—Poetry. 3. Eve (Biblical figure)—Poetry. 4. Fall of man—Poetry. I. Title. II. Series.

PR3560 2005
821'.4—dc22

2004061879

Manufactured in the United States by Courier Corporation
44287X03
www.doverpublications.com

Note

WITH THE publication of *Paradise Lost,* John Milton (1608–1674) had finally realized his long-standing ambition to write an epic poem based upon such classical models as the *Iliad* and the *Aeneid.* During the seventeenth century, the epic was considered the greatest creative achievement possible, and Milton sought to pen the definitive English epic, following conventions established by Homer and Virgil. Although he had originally planned his theme around the Arthurian legends, Milton decided to focus instead on the Book of Genesis in the Bible. Centering on the fall of Adam and Eve and their restoration to God's favor, the epic ranges over time from the rebellion of Satan and his followers in Heaven to Judgment Day. In his narration of the most significant biblical events, Milton offers a comprehensive account of Christian belief and values.

The son of a wealthy scrivener and accomplished composer of madrigals, John Milton had a privileged upbringing. His prosperous family was able to provide for him the very best of educations. After private tutoring, the young boy entered St. Paul's School and Christ's College, Cambridge, and was then supported through five years of independent study. Ultimately, he was sent on a two-year tour of Europe to further enhance his knowledge. During this period of his learning, Milton began writing his most famous poetry, including the masque *Comus* and the elegy *Lycidas,* as well as other poems in both English and Latin. He traveled extensively in France and Italy in the 1630s, meeting the jurist and theologian Hugo Grotius and the astronomer Galileo, who was then under house arrest by the Inquisition in Florence.

In 1642, he was wed—his first of three marriages—to a woman half his age, but she returned to her family after only one month. Her desertion encouraged him to compose *The Doctrine and Discipline of Divorce* (1643), in which he upheld the morality of divorce for incompatibility. The pair did eventually reconcile, but she died in childbirth in 1652. He married twice more, the last being the happiest.

Concerned with the Puritan cause, Milton wrote a series of pamphlets defending civil and religious rights. In 1649 he served as secretary to

Oliver Cromwell, for whom he handled correspondence with foreign
nations and was apologist to the Commonwealth. In 1652 Milton lost his
eyesight from his grueling work, and the poet Andrew Marvell became
his assistant. After the Restoration of Charles II in 1660, Milton was
arrested as a defender of the Commonwealth and massively fined, but
escaped imprisonment and death, due in part to Marvell's effusive
protests on his behalf. Now aging and blind, Milton recited his verse to
one of his two daughters, who wrote his poem down for him. He con-
tinued to dictate *Paradise Lost* for several more years before publishing his
masterpiece in 1667 in ten books. It was followed in 1671 by its sequel,
Paradise Regained. In 1674 Milton revised *Paradise Lost* into twelve books
(as the classical epics were divided), and published this second edition
with commendatory poems by seventeenth-century poet Samuel
Barrow and Andrew Marvell.

Milton's powerful prose and the eloquence of his poetry had an
immense influence on the development of eighteenth-century verse. His
blank-verse poem influenced many subsequent authors and artists,
including John Dryden, William Blake, and C. S. Lewis. Milton's success
from *Paradise Lost* stems not only from the sheer beauty of its language
and powerful characterization, but also endures in the high esteem in
which the poem is held to this day. The content of the poem itself,
which delves into universal questions on the nature of good and evil,
continues to enthrall generations of readers. In the conclusion to his crit-
ical essay on *Paradise Lost,* Samuel Johnson sums up Milton's stature as an
epic poet with the following:

> The highest praise of genius is original invention. Milton cannot be
> said to have contrived the structure of an epic poem, and therefore
> owes reverence to that vigor and amplitude of mind to which all gen-
> erations must be indebted for the art of poetical narration, for the
> texture of the fable, the variation of incidents, the interposition of
> dialogue, and all the stratagems that surprise and enchain attention.
> But, of all the borrowers from Homer, Milton is perhaps the least
> indebted. He was naturally a thinker for himself, confident of his own
> abilities, and disdainful of help or hindrance: he did not refuse admis-
> sion to the thoughts or images of his predecessors, but he did not seek
> them. From his contemporaries he neither courted nor received sup-
> port; there is in his writings nothing by which the pride of other
> authors might be gratified, or favor gained; no exchange of praise, nor
> solicitation of support. His great works were performed under dis-
> countenance, and in blindness, but difficulties vanished at his touch;
> he was born for whatever is arduous, and his work is not the greatest
> of heroic poems, only because it is not the first.

Contents

Contents

THE VERSE

THE measure is English heroic verse without rime, as that of Homer in Greek, and of Virgil in Latin—rime being no necessary adjunct or true ornament of poem or good verse, in longer works especially, but the invention of a barbarous age, to set off wretched matter and lame metre; graced indeed since by the use of some famous modern poets, carried away by custom, but much to their own vexation, hindrance, and constraint to express many things otherwise, and for the most part worse, than else they would have expressed them. Not without cause therefore some both Italian and Spanish poets of prime note have rejected rime both in longer and shorter works, as have also long since our best English tragedies, as a thing of itself, to all judicious ears, trivial and of no true musical delight; which consists only in apt numbers, fit quantity of syllables, and the sense variously drawn out from one verse into another, not in the jingling sound of like endings—a fault avoided by the learned ancients both in poetry and all good oratory. This neglect then of rime so little is to be taken for a defect, though it may seem so perhaps to vulgar readers, that it rather is to be esteemed an example set, the first in English, of ancient liberty recovered to heroic poem from the troublesome and modern bondage of riming.

BOOK I

THE ARGUMENT

THIS First Book proposes, first in brief, the whole subject—Man's disobe-
dience, and the loss thereupon of Paradise, wherein he was placed: then
touches the prime cause of his fall—the Serpent, or rather Satan in the
Serpent; who, revolting from God, and drawing to his side many legions of
Angels, was, by the command of God, driven out of Heaven, with all his
crew, into the great Deep. Which action passed over, the Poem hastens into
the midst of things; presenting Satan, with his Angels, now fallen into
Hell—described here not in the Centre (for heaven and earth may be sup-
posed as yet not made, certainly not yet accursed), but in a place of utter
darkness, fitliest called Chaos. Here Satan, with his Angels lying on the
burning lake, thunderstruck and astonished, after a certain space recovers, as
from confusion; calls up him who, next in order and dignity, lay by him: they
confer of their miserable fall. Satan awakens all his legions, who lay till then
in the same manner confounded. They rise: their numbers; array of battle;
their chief leaders named, according to the idols known afterwards in
Canaan and the countries adjoining. To these Satan directs his speech; com-
forts them with hope yet of regaining Heaven; but tells them, lastly, of a new
world and new kind of creature to be created, according to an ancient
prophecy, or report, in Heaven—for that Angels were long before this vis-
ible creation was the opinion of many ancient Fathers. To find out the truth
of this prophecy, and what to determine thereon, he refers to a full coun-
cil. What his associates thence attempt. Pandemonium, the palace of Satan,
rises suddenly built out of the Deep: the infernal Peers there sit in council.

> Of Man's first disobedience, and the fruit
> Of that forbidden tree whose mortal taste
> Brought death into the World, and all our woe,
> With loss of Eden, till one greater Man
> Restore us, and regain the blissful seat,
> Sing, Heavenly Muse, that, on the secret top

Of Oreb, or of Sinai, didst inspire
That shepherd who first taught the chosen seed
In the beginning how the heavens and earth
Rose out of Chaos: or, if Sion hill   10
Delight thee more, and Siloa's brook that flowed
Fast by the oracle of God, I thence
Invoke thy aid to my adventrous song,
That with no middle flight intends to soar
Above the Aonian mount, while it pursues
Things unattempted yet in prose or rhyme.
And chiefly thou, O Spirit, that dost prefer
Before all temples the upright heart and pure,
Instruct me, for Thou know'st; Thou from the first
Wast present, and, with mighty wings outspread,   20
Dove-like sat'st brooding on the vast Abyss,
And mad'st it pregnant: what in me is dark
Illumine, what is low raise and support;
That, to the highth of this great argument,
I may assert Eternal Providence,
And justify the ways of God to men.
    Say first—for Heaven hides nothing from thy view,
Nor the deep tract of Hell—say first what cause
Moved our grand Parents, in that happy state,
Favored of Heaven so highly, to fall off   30
From their Creator, and transgress his will
For one restraint, lords of the World besides.
Who first seduced them to that foul revolt?
    The infernal Serpent; he it was whose guile,
Stirred up with envy and revenge, deceived
The mother of mankind, what time his pride
Had cast him out from Heaven, with all his host
Of rebel Angels, by whose aid, aspiring
To set himself in glory above his peers,
He trusted to have equalled the Most High,   40
If he opposed, and, with ambitious aim
Against the throne and monarchy of God,
Raised impious war in Heaven and battle proud,
With vain attempt. Him the Almighty Power
Hurled headlong flaming from the ethereal sky,
With hideous ruin and combustion, down
To bottomless perdition, there to dwell
In adamantine chains and penal fire,
Who durst defy the Omnipotent to arms.

Nine times the space that measures day and night   50
To mortal men, he, with his horrid crew,
Lay vanquished, rolling in the fiery gulf,
Confounded, though immortal. But his doom
Reserved him to more wrath; for now the thought
Both of lost happiness and lasting pain
Torments him: round he throws his baleful eyes,
That witnessed huge affliction and dismay,
Mixed with obdurate pride and steadfast hate.
At once, as far as Angel's ken, he views
The dismal situation waste and wild.   60
A dungeon horrible, on all sides round,
As one great furnace flamed; yet from those flames
No light; but rather darkness visible
Served only to discover sights of woe,
Regions of sorrow, doleful shades, where peace
And rest can never dwell, hope never comes
That comes to all, but torture without end
Still urges, and a fiery deluge, fed
With ever-burning sulphur unconsumed.
Such place Eternal Justice had prepared   70
For those rebellious; here their prison ordained
In utter darkness, and their portion set,
As far removed from God and light of Heaven
As from the centre thrice to the utmost pole.
Oh how unlike the place from whence they fell!
There the companions of his fall, o'erwhelmed
With floods and whirlwinds of tempestuous fire,
He soon discerns; and, weltering by his side,
One next himself in power, and next in crime,
Long after known in Palestine, and named   80
BEËLZEBUB. To whom the Arch-Enemy,
And thence in Heaven called SATAN, with bold words
Breaking the horrid silence, thus began:—
     "If thou beest he—but O how fallen! how changed
From him!—who, in the happy realms of light,
Clothed with transcendent brightness, didst outshine
Myriads, though bright—if he whom mutual league,
United thoughts and counsels, equal hope
And hazard in the glorious enterprise,
Joined with me once, now misery hath joined   90
In equal ruin; into what pit thou seest
From what highth fallen: so much the stronger proved

He with his thunder: and till then who knew
The force of those dire arms? Yet not for those,
Nor what the potent Victor in his rage
Can else inflict, do I repent, or change,
Though changed in outward lustre, that fixed mind,
And high disdain from sense of injured merit,
That with the Mightiest raised me to contend,
And to the fierce contention brought along   100
Innumerable force of Spirits armed,
That durst dislike his reign, and, me preferring,
His utmost power with adverse power opposed
In dubious battle on the plains of Heaven,
And shook his throne. What though the field be lost?
All is not lost—the unconquerable will,
And study of revenge, immortal hate,
And courage never to submit or yield:
And what is else not to be overcome.
That glory never shall his wrath or might   110
Extort from me. To bow and sue for grace
With suppliant knee, and deify his power
Who, from the terror of this arm, so late
Doubted his empire—that were low indeed;
That were an ignominy and shame beneath
This downfall; since, by fate, the strength of Gods,
And this empyreal substance, cannot fail;
Since, through experience of this great event,
In arms not worse, in foresight much advanced,
We may with more successful hope resolve   120
To wage by force or guile eternal war,
Irreconcilable to our grand Foe,
Who now triumphs, and in the excess of joy
Sole reigning holds the tyranny of Heaven."
   So spake the apostate Angel, though in pain,
Vaunting aloud, but racked with deep despair;
And him thus answered soon his bold compeer:—
   "O Prince, O Chief of many thronèd Powers
That led the embattled Seraphim to war
Under thy conduct, and, in dreadful deeds   130
Fearless, endangered Heaven's perpetual King,
And put to proof his high supremacy,
Whether upheld by strength, or chance, or fate!
Too well I see and rue the dire event
That, with sad overthrow and foul defeat,

Hath lost us Heaven, and all this mighty host
In horrible destruction laid thus low,
As far as Gods and Heavenly Essences
Can perish: for the mind and spirit remains
Invincible, and vigor soon returns,   140
Though all our glory extinct, and happy state
Here swallowed up in endless misery.
But what if He our Conqueror (whom I now
Of force believe almighty, since no less
Than such could have o'erpowered such force as ours)
Have left us this our spirit and strength entire,
Strongly to suffer and support our pains,
That we may so suffice his vengeful ire
Or do him mightier service as his thralls
By right of war, whate'er his business be,   150
Here in the heart of Hell to work in fire,
Or do his errands in the gloomy Deep?
What can it then avail though yet we feel
Strength undiminished, or eternal being
To undergo eternal punishment?"
    Whereto with speedy words the Arch-Fiend replied:—
"Fallen Cherub, to be weak is miserable,
Doing or suffering: but of this be sure—
To do aught good never will be our task,
But ever to do ill our sole delight,   160
As being the contrary to His high will
Whom we resist. If then his providence
Out of our evil seek to bring forth good,
Our labor must be to pervert that end,
And out of good still to find means of evil;
Which ofttimes may succeed so as perhaps
Shall grieve him, if I fail not, and disturb
His inmost counsels from their destined aim.
But see! the angry Victor hath recalled
His ministers of vengeance and pursuit   170
Back to the gates of Heaven: the sulphurous hail,
Shot after us in storm, o'erblown hath laid
The fiery surge that from the precipice
Of Heaven received us falling; and the thunder,
Winged with red lightning and impetuous rage,
Perhaps hath spent his shafts, and ceases now
To bellow through the vast and boundless Deep.
Let us not slip the occasion, whether scorn

Or satiate fury yield it from our Foe.
Seest thou yon dreary plain, forlorn and wild,   180
The seat of desolation, void of light,
Save what the glimmering of these livid flames
Casts pale and dreadful? Thither let us tend
From off the tossing of these fiery waves;
There rest, if any rest can harbor there;
And, re-assembling our afflicted powers,
Consult how we may henceforth most offend
Our enemy, our own loss how repair,
How overcome this dire calamity,
What reinforcement we may gain from hope,   190
If not what resolution from despair."
   Thus Satan, talking to his nearest mate,
With head uplift above the wave, and eyes
That sparkling blazed; his other parts besides
Prone on the flood, extended long and large,
Lay floating many a rood, in bulk as huge
As whom the fables name of monstrous size,
Titanian or Earth-born, that warred on Jove,
Briareos or Typhon, whom the den
By ancient Tarsus held, or that sea-beast   200
Leviathan, which God of all his works
Created hugest that swim the ocean-stream.
Him, haply slumbering on the Norway foam,
The pilot of some small night-foundered skiff,
Deeming some island, oft, as seamen tell,
With fixèd anchor in his scaly rind,
Moors by his side under the lee, while night
Invests the sea, and wishèd morn delays.
So stretched out huge in length the Arch-Fiend lay,
Chained on the burning lake; nor ever thence   210
Had risen, or heaved his head, but that the will
And high permission of all-ruling Heaven
Left him at large to his own dark designs,
That with reiterated crimes he might
Heap on himself damnation, while he sought
Evil to others, and enraged might see
How all his malice served but to bring forth
Infinite goodness, grace, and mercy, shewn
On Man by him seduced, but on himself
Treble confusion, wrath, and vengeance poured.   220
   Forthwith upright he rears from off the pool

His mighty stature; on each hand the flames
Driven backward slope their pointing spires, and, rolled
In billows, leave i' the midst a horrid vale.
Then with expanded wings he steers his flight
Aloft, incumbent on the dusky air,
That felt unusual weight; till on dry land
He lights—if it were land that ever burned
With solid, as the lake with liquid fire,
And such appeared in hue as when the force   230
Of subterranean wind transports a hill
Torn from Pelorus, or the shattered side
Of thundering Ætna, whose combustible
And fuelled entrails, thence conceiving fire,
Sublimed with mineral fury, aid the winds,
And leave a singèd bottom all involved
With stench and smoke. Such resting found the sole
Of unblest feet. Him followed his next mate;
Both glorying to have scaped the Stygian flood
As gods, and by their own recovered strength,   240
Not by the sufferance of supernal power.
      "Is this the region, this the soil, the clime,"
Said then the lost Archangel, "this the seat
That we must change for Heaven?—this mournful gloom
For that celestial light? Be it so, since He
Who now is sovran can dispose and bid
What shall be right: farthest from Him is best,
Whom reason hath equalled, force hath made supreme
Above his equals. Farewell, happy fields,
Where joy for ever dwells! Hail, horrors! hail,   250
Infernal World! and thou, profoundest Hell,
Receive thy new possessor—one who brings
A mind not to be changed by place or time.
The mind is its own place, and in itself
Can make a Heaven of Hell, a Hell of Heaven.
What matter where, if I be still the same,
And what I should be, all but less than he
Whom thunder hath made greater? Here at least
We shall be free; the Almighty hath not built
Here for his envy, will not drive us hence: 260
Here we may reign secure; and, in my choice,
To reign is worth ambition, though in Hell:
Better to reign in Hell than serve in Heaven.
But wherefore let we then our faithful friends,

The associates and co-partners of our loss,
Lie thus astonished on the oblivious pool,
And call them not to share with us their part
In this unhappy mansion, or once more
With rallied arms to try what may be yet
Regained in Heaven, or what more lost in Hell?"   270
    So Satan spoke; and him Beëlzebub
Thus answered:—"Leader of those armies bright
Which, but the Omnipotent, none could have foiled!
If once they hear that voice, their liveliest pledge
Of hope in fears and dangers—heard so oft
In worst extremes, and on the perilous edge
Of battle, when it raged, in all assaults
Their surest signal—they will soon resume
New courage and revive, though now they lie
Grovelling and prostrate on yon lake of fire,   280
As we erewhile, astounded and amazed;
No wonder, fallen such a pernicious highth!"
    He scarce had ceased when the superior Fiend
Was moving toward the shore; his ponderous shield,
Ethereal temper, massy, large, and round,
Behind him cast. The broad circumference
Hung on his shoulders like the moon, whose orb
Through optic glass the Tuscan artist views
At evening, from the top of Fesolè,
Or in Valdarno, to descry new lands,   290
Rivers, or mountains, in her spotty globe.
His spear—to equal which the tallest pine
Hewn on Norwegian hills, to be the mast
Of some great ammiral, were but a wand—
He walked with, to support uneasy steps
Over the burning marle, not like those steps
On Heaven's azure; and the torrid clime
Smote on him sore besides, vaulted with fire.
Nathless he so endured, till on the beach
Of that inflamèd sea he stood, and called   300
His legions—Angel Forms, who lay entranced
Thick as autumnal leaves that strow the brooks
In Vallombrosa, where the Etrurian shades
High over-arched embower; or scattered sedge
Afloat, when with fierce winds Orion armed
Hath vexed the Red-Sea coast, whose waves o'erthrew
Busiris and his Memphian chivalry,

While with perfidious hatred they pursued
The sojourners of Goshen, who beheld
From the safe shore their floating carcases   310
And broken chariot-wheels. So thick bestrown,
Abject and lost, lay these, covering the flood,
Under amazement of their hideous change.
He called so loud that all the hollow deep
Of Hell resounded:—"Princes, Potentates,
Warriors, the Flower of Heaven—once yours; now lost,
If such astonishment as this can seize
Eternal Spirits! Or have ye chosen this place
After the toil of battle to repose
Your wearied virtue, for the ease you find   320
To slumber here, as in the vales of Heaven?
Or in this abject posture have ye sworn
To adore the Conqueror, who now beholds
Cherub and Seraph rolling in the flood
With scattered arms and ensigns, till anon
His swift pursuers from Heaven-gates discern
The advantage, and, descending, tread us down
Thus drooping, or with linkèd thunderbolts
Transfix us to the bottom of this gulf?—
Awake, arise, or be for ever fallen!"   330
    They heard, and were abashed, and up they sprung
Upon the wing, as when men wont to watch,
On duty sleeping found by whom they dread,
Rouse and bestir themselves ere well awake.
Nor did they not perceive the evil plight
In which they were, or the fierce pains not feel;
Yet to their General's voice they soon obeyed
Innumerable. As when the potent rod
Of Amram's son, in Egypt's evil day,
Waved round the coast, up-called a pitchy cloud   340
Of locusts, warping on the eastern wind,
That o'er the realm of impious Pharaoh hung
Like Night, and darkened all the land of Nile;
So numberless were those bad Angels seen
Hovering on wing under the cope of Hell,
'Twixt upper, nether, and surrounding fires;
Till, as a signal given, the uplifted spear
Of their great Sultan waving to direct
Their course, in even balance down they light
On the firm brimstone, and fill all the plain: 350

A multitude like which the populous North
Poured never from her frozen loins to pass
Rhene or the Danaw, when her barbarous sons
Came like a deluge on the South, and spread
Beneath Gibraltar to the Libyan sands.
Forthwith, from every squadron and each band,
The heads and leaders thither haste where stood
Their great Commander—godlike Shapes, and Forms
Excelling human; princely Dignities;
And Powers that erst in Heaven sat on thrones,   360
Though of their names in Heavenly records now
Be no memorial, blotted out and rased
By their rebellion from the Books of Life.
Nor had they yet among the sons of Eve
Got them new names, till, wandering o'er the earth,
Through God's high sufferance for the trial of man,
By falsities and lies the greatest part
Of mankind they corrupted to forsake
God their Creator, and the invisible
Glory of Him that made them to transform   370
Oft to the image of a brute, adorned
With gay religions full of pomp and gold,
And devils to adore for deities:
Then were they known to men by various names,
And various idols through the Heathen World.
    Say, Muse, their names then known, who first, who last,
Roused from the slumber on that fiery couch,
At their great Emperor's call, as next in worth
Came singly where he stood on the bare strand,
While the promiscuous crowd stood yet aloof.   380
    The chief were those who, from the pit of Hell
Roaming to seek their prey on Earth, durst fix
Their seats, long after, next the seat of God,
Their altars by His altar, gods adored
Among the nations round, and durst abide
Jehovah thundering out of Sion, throned
Between the Cherubim; yea, often placed
Within His sanctuary itself their shrines,
Abominations; and with cursed things
His holy rites and solemn feasts profaned,   390
And with their darkness durst affront his light.
First, *Moloch,* horrid king, besmeared with blood
Of human sacrifice, and parents' tears;

Though, for the noise of drums and timbrels loud,
Their children's cries unheard that passed through fire
To his grim idol. Him the Ammonite
Worshiped in Rabba and her watery plain,
In Argob and in Basan, to the stream
Of utmost Arnon. Nor content with such
Audacious neighborhood, the wisest heart   400
Of Solomon he led by fraud to build
His temple right against the temple of God
On that opprobrious hill, and made his grove
The pleasant valley of Hinnom, Tophet thence
And black Gehenna called, the type of Hell.
Next *Chemos,* the obscene dread of Moab's sons,
From Aroar to Nebo and the wild
Of southmost Abarim; in Hesebon
And Horonaim, Seon's realm, beyond
The flowery dale of Sibma clad with vines,   410
And Elealè to the Asphaltic Pool:
Peor his other name, when he enticed
Israel in Sittim, on their march from Nile,
To do him wanton rites, which cost them woe.
Yet thence his lustful orgies he enlarged
Even to that hill of scandal, by the grove
Of Moloch homicide, lust hard by hate,
Till good Josiah drove them thence to Hell.
With these came they who, from the bordering flood
Of old Euphrates to the brook that parts   420
Egypt from Syrian ground, had general names
Of *Baalim* and *Ashtaroth*—those male,
These feminine. For Spirits, when they please,
Can either sex assume, or both; so soft
And uncompounded is their essence pure,
Not tied or manacled with joint or limb,
Nor founded on the brittle strength of bones,
Like cumbrous flesh; but, in what shape they choose,
Dilated or condensed, bright or obscure,
Can execute their aery purposes,   430
And works of love or enmity fulfil.
For those the race of Israel oft forsook
Their Living Strength, and unfrequented left
His righteous altar, bowing lowly down
To bestial gods; for which their heads, as low
Bowed down in battle, sunk before the spear

Of despicable foes. With these in troop
Came *Astoreth,* whom the Phœnicians called
Astarte, queen of heaven, with crescent horns;
To whose bright image nightly by the moon⠀⠀⠀⠀⠀⠀⠀440
Sidonian virgins paid their vows and songs;
In Sion also not unsung, where stood
Her temple on the offensive mountain, built
By that uxorious king whose heart, though large,
Beguiled by fair idolatresses, fell
To idols foul. *Thammuz* came next behind,
Whose annual wound in Lebanon allured
The Syrian damsels to lament his fate
In amorous ditties all a summer's day,
While smooth Adonis from his native rock⠀⠀⠀⠀⠀⠀⠀450
Ran purple to the sea, supposed with blood
Of Thammuz yearly wounded: the love-tale
Infected Sion's daughters with like heat,
Whose wanton passions in the sacred porch
Ezekiel saw, when, by the vision led,
His eye surveyed the dark idolatries
Of alienated Judah. Next came one
Who mourned in earnest, when the captive ark
Maimed his brute image, head and hands lopt off,
In his own temple, on the grunsel-edge,⠀⠀⠀⠀⠀⠀⠀460
Where he fell flat and shamed his worshipers:
Dagon his name, sea-monster, upward man
And downward fish; yet had his temple high
Reared in Azotus, dreaded through the coast
Of Palestine, in Gath and Ascalon,
And Accaron and Gaza's frontier bounds.
Him followed *Rimmon,* whose delightful seat
Was fair Damascus, on the fertile banks
Of Abbana and Pharphar, lucid streams.
He also against the house of God was bold:⠀⠀⠀⠀⠀⠀⠀470
A leper once he lost, and gained a king—
Ahaz, his sottish conqueror, whom he drew
God's altar to disparage and displace
For one of Syrian mode, whereon to burn
His odious offerings, and adore the gods
Whom he had vanquished. After these appeared
A crew who, under names of old renown—
Osiris, Isis, Orus, and their train—
With monstrous shapes and sorceries abused

Fanatic Egypt and her priests to seek   480
Their wandering gods disguised in brutish forms
Rather than human. Nor did Israel scape
The infection, when their borrowed gold composed
The calf in Oreb; and the rebel king
Doubled that sin in Bethel and in Dan,
Likening his Maker to the grazèd ox—
Jehovah, who, in one night, when he passed
From Egypt marching, equalled with one stroke
Both her first-born and all her bleating gods.
Belial came last; than whom a spirit more lewd   490
Fell not from Heaven, or more gross to love
Vice for itself. To him no temple stood
Or altar smoked; yet who more oft than he
In temples and at altars, when the priest
Turns atheist, as did Eli's sons, who filled
With lust and violence the house of God?
In courts and palaces he also reigns,
And in luxurious cities, where the noise
Of riot ascends above their loftiest towers,
And injury and outrage; and, when night   500
Darkens the streets, then wander forth the sons
Of Belial, flown with insolence and wine.
Witness the streets of Sodom, and that night
In Gibeah, when the hospitable door
Exposed a matron, to avoid worse rape.
   These were the prime in order and in might:
The rest were long to tell; though far renowned
The Ionian gods—of Javan's issue held
Gods, yet confessed later than Heaven and Earth,
Their boasted parents;—*Titan,* Heaven's first-born,   510
With his enormous brood, and birthright seized
By younger *Saturn:* he from mightier Jove,
His own and Rhea's son, like measure found;
So *Jove* usurping reigned. These, first in Crete
And Ida known, thence on the snowy top
Of cold Olympus ruled the middle air,
Their highest heaven; or on the Delphian cliff,
Or in Dodona, and through all the bounds
Of Doric land; or who with Saturn old
Fled over Adria to the Hesperian fields,   520
And o'er the Celtic roamed the utmost Isles.
   All these and more came flocking; but with looks

Downcast and damp; yet such wherein appeared
Obscure some glimpse of joy to have found their Chief
Not in despair, to have found themselves not lost
In loss itself; which on his countenance cast
Like doubtful hue. But he, his wonted pride
Soon recollecting, with high words, that bore
Semblance of worth, not substance, gently raised
Their fainting courage, and dispelled their fears: 530
Then straight commands that, at the warlike sound
Of trumpets loud and clarions, be upreared
His mighty standard. That proud honor claimed
Azazel as his right, a Cherub tall:
Who forthwith from the glittering staff unfurled
The imperial ensign; which, full high advanced,
Shone like a meteor streaming to the wind,
With gems and golden lustre rich emblazed,
Seraphic arms and trophies; all the while
Sonorous metal blowing martial sounds: 540
At which the universal host up-sent
A shout that tore Hell's concave, and beyond
Frighted the reign of Chaos and old Night.
All in a moment through the gloom were seen
Ten thousand banners rise into the air,
With orient colors waving: with them rose
A forest huge of spears; and thronging helms
Appeared, and serried shields in thick array
Of depth immeasurable. Anon they move
In perfect phalanx to the Dorian mood   550
Of flutes and soft recorders—such as raised
To highth of noblest temper heroes old
Arming to battle, and instead of rage
Deliberate valor breathed, firm, and unmoved
With dread of death to flight or foul retreat;
Nor wanting power to mitigate and swage
With solemn touches troubled thoughts, and chase
Anguish and doubt and fear and sorrow and pain
From mortal or immortal minds. Thus they,
Breathing united force with fixèd thought,   560
Moved on in silence to soft pipes that charmed
Their painful steps o'er the burnt soil. And now
Advanced in view they stand—a horrid front
Of dreadful length and dazzling arms, in guise
Of warriors old, with ordered spear and shield,

Awaiting what command their mighty Chief
Had to impose. He through the armèd files
Darts his experienced eye, and soon traverse
The whole battalion views—their order due,
Their visages and stature as of gods;   570
Their number last he sums. And now his heart
Distends with pride, and, hardening in his strength,
Glories: for never, since created Man,
Met such embodied force as, named with these,
Could merit more than that small infantry
Warred on by cranes—though all the giant brood
Of Phlegra with the heroic race were joined
That fought at Thebes and Ilium, on each side
Mixed with auxiliar gods; and what resounds
In fable or romance of Uther's son,   580
Begirt with British and Armoric knights;
And all who since, baptized or infidel,
Jousted in Aspramont, or Montalban,
Damasco, or Marocco, or Trebisond,
Or whom Biserta sent from Afric shore
When Charlemain with all his peerage fell
By Fontarabia. Thus far these beyond
Compare of mortal prowess, yet observed
Their dread Commander. He, above the rest
In shape and gesture proudly eminent,   590
Stood like a tower. His form had yet not lost
All her original brightness, nor appeared
Less than Archangel ruined, and the excess
Of glory obscured: as when the sun new-risen
Looks through the horizontal misty air
Shorn of his beams, or, from behind the moon,
In dim eclipse, disastrous twilight sheds
On half the nations, and with fear of change
Perplexes monarchs. Darkened so, yet shone
Above them all the Archangel: but his face   600
Deep scars of thunder had intrenched, and care
Sat on his faded cheek, but under brows
Of dauntless courage, and considerate pride
Waiting revenge. Cruel his eye, but cast
Signs of remorse and passion, to behold
The fellows of his crime, the followers rather
(Far other once beheld in bliss), condemned
For ever now to have their lot in pain—

Millions of Spirits for his fault amerced
Of Heaven, and from eternal splendors flung   610
For his revolt—yet faithful how they stood,
Their glory withered; as, when heaven's fire
Hath scathed the forest oaks or mountain pines,
With singèd top their stately growth, though bare,
Stands on the blasted heath. He now prepared
To speak; whereat their doubled ranks they bend
From wing to wing, and half enclose him round
With all his peers: Attention held them mute.
Thrice he assayed, and thrice, in spite of scorn,
Tears, such as Angels weep, burst forth: at last   620
Words interwove with sighs found out their way:—
    "O myriads of immortal Spirits! O Powers
Matchless, but with the Almighty!—and that strife
Was not inglorious, though the event was dire,
As this place testifies, and this dire change,
Hateful to utter. But what power of mind,
Forseeing or presaging, from the depth
Of knowledge past or present, could have feared
How such united force of gods, how such
As stood like these, could ever know repulse?   630
For who can yet believe, though after loss,
That all these puissant legions, whose exile
Hath emptied Heaven, shall fail to re-ascend,
Self-raised, and re-possess their native seat?
For me, be witness all the host of Heaven,
If counsels different, or danger shunned
By me, have lost our hopes. But he who reigns
Monarch in Heaven till then as one secure
Sat on his throne, upheld by old repute,
Consent or custom, and his regal state   640
Put forth at full, but still his strength concealed—
Which tempted our attempt, and wrought our fall.
Henceforth his might we know, and know our own,
So as not either to provoke, or dread
New war provoked: our better part remains
To work in close design, by fraud or guile,
What force effected not; that he no less
At length from us may find, Who overcomes
By force hath overcome but half his foe.
Space may produce new Worlds; whereof so rife   650
There went a fame in Heaven that He ere long

Intended to create, and therein plant
A generation whom his choice regard
Should favor equal to the Sons of Heaven.
Thither, if but to pry, shall be perhaps
Our first eruption—thither, or elsewhere;
For this infernal pit shall never hold
Celestial Spirits in bondage, nor the Abyss
Long under darkness cover. But these thoughts
Full counsel must mature. Peace is despaired;   660
For who can think submission? War, then, war
Open or understood, must be resolved."
    He spake; and, to confirm his words, out-flew
Millions of flaming swords, drawn from the thighs
Of mighty Cherubim; the sudden blaze
Far round illumined Hell. Highly they raged
Against the Highest, and fierce with graspèd arms
Clashed on their sounding shields the din of war,
Hurling defiance toward the vault of Heaven.
    There stood a hill not far, whose grisly top   670
Belched fire and rolling smoke; the rest entire
Shone with a glossy scurf—undoubted sign
That in his womb was hid metallic ore,
The work of sulphur. Thither, winged with speed,
A numerous brigad hastened: as when bands
Of pioneers, with spade and pickaxe armed,
Forerun the royal camp, to trench a field,
Or cast a rampart. Mammon led them on—
Mammon, the least erected Spirit that fell
From Heaven; for even in Heaven his looks and thoughts   680
Were always downward bent, admiring more
The riches of Heaven's pavement, trodden gold,
Than aught divine or holy else enjoyed
In vision beatific. By him first
Men also, and by his suggestion taught,
Ransacked the Centre, and with impious hands
Rifled the bowels of their mother Earth
For treasures better hid. Soon had his crew
Opened into the hill a spacious wound,
And digged out ribs of gold. Let none admire   690
That riches grow in Hell; that soil may best
Deserve the precious bane. And here let those
Who boast in mortal things, and wondering tell
Of Babel, and the works of Memphian kings,

Learn how their greatest monuments of fame
And strength, and art, are easily outdone
By Spirits reprobate, and in an hour
What in an age they, with incessant toil
And hands innumerable, scarce perform.
Nigh on the plain, in many cells prepared,   700
That underneath had veins of liquid fire
Sluiced from the lake, a second multitude
With wondrous art founded the massy ore,
Severing each kind, and scummed the bullion-dross.
A third as soon had formed within the ground
A various mould, and from the boiling cells
By strange conveyance filled each hollow nook;
As in an organ, from one blast of wind,
To many a row of pipes the sound-board breathes.
Anon out of the earth a fabric huge   710
Rose like an exhalation, with the sound
Of dulcet symphonies and voices sweet—
Built like a temple, where pilasters round
Were set, and Doric pillars overlaid
With golden architrave; nor did there want
Cornice or frieze, with bossy sculptures graven:
The roof was fretted gold. Not Babylon
Nor great Alcairo such magnificence
Equalled in all their glories, to enshrine
Belus or Serapis their gods, or seat   720
Their kings, when Egypt with Assyria strove
In wealth and luxury. The ascending pile
Stood fixed her stately highth; and straight the doors,
Opening their brazen folds, discover, wide
Within, her ample spaces o'er the smooth
And level pavement: from the archèd roof,
Pendent by subtle magic, many a row
Of starry lamps and blazing cressets, fed
With naphtha and asphaltus, yielded light
As from a sky. The hasty multitude   730
Admiring entered; and the work some praise,
And some the architect. His hand was known
In Heaven by many a towered structure high,
Where sceptred Angels held their residence,
And sat as Princes, whom the supreme King
Exalted to such power, and gave to rule,
Each in his hierarchy, the Orders bright.

Nor was his name unheard or unadored
In ancient Greece; and in Ausonian land
Men called him Mulciber; and how he fell   740
From Heaven they fabled, thrown by angry Jove
Sheer o'er the crystal battlements: from morn
To noon he fell, from noon to dewy eve,
A summer's day, and with the setting sun
Dropt from the zenith, like a falling star,
On Lemnos, the Ægean isle. Thus they relate,
Erring; for he with this rebellious rout
Fell long before; nor aught availed him now
To have built in Heaven high towers; nor did he scape
By all his engines, but was headlong sent,   750
With his industrious crew, to build in Hell.
    Meanwhile the wingèd Heralds, by command
Of sovran power, with awful ceremony
And trumpet's sound, throughout the host proclaim
A solemn council forthwith to be held
At Pandemonium, the high capital
Of Satan and his peers. Their summons called
From every band and squarèd regiment
By place or choice the worthiest: they anon
With hundreds and with thousands trooping came   760
Attended. All access was thronged; the gates
And porches wide, but chief the spacious hall
(Though like a covered field, where champions bold
Wont ride in armed, and at the Soldan's chair
Defied the best of Panim chivalry
To mortal combat, or career with lance),
Thick swarmed, both on the ground and in the air,
Brushed with the hiss of rustling wings. As bees
In spring-time, when the Sun with Taurus rides.
Pour forth their populous youth about the hive   770
In clusters; they among fresh dews and flowers
Fly to and fro, or on the smoothèd plank,
The suburb of their straw-built citadel,
New rubbed with balm, expatiate, and confer
Their state affairs: so thick the aery crowd
Swarmed and were straitened; till, the signal given,
Behold a wonder! They but now who seemed
In bigness to surpass Earth's giant sons,
Now less than smallest dwarfs, in narrow room
Throng numberless—like that pygmean race   780

Beyond the Indian mount; or faery elves,
Whose midnight revels, by a forest-side
Or fountain, some belated peasant sees,
Or dreams he sees, while overhead the Moon
Sits arbitress, and nearer to the Earth
Wheels her pale course: they, on their mirth and dance
Intent, with jocund music charm his ear;
At once with joy and fear his heart rebounds.
Thus incorporeal Spirits to smallest forms
Reduced their shapes immense, and were at large,   790
Though without number still, amidst the hall
Of that infernal court. But far within,
And in their own dimensions like themselves,
The great Seraphic Lords and Cherubim
In close recess and secret conclave sat,
A thousand demi-gods on golden seats,
Frequent and full. After short silence then,
And summons read, the great consult began.

BOOK II

THE ARGUMENT

THE consultation begun, Satan debates whether another battle be to be hazarded for the recovery of Heaven: some advise it, others dissuade. A third proposal is preferred, mentioned before by Satan—to search the truth of that prophecy or tradition in Heaven concerning another world, and another kind of creature, equal, or not much inferior, to themselves, about this time to be created. Their doubt who shall be sent on this difficult search: Satan, their chief, undertakes alone the voyage; is honored and applauded. The council, thus ended, the rest betake them several ways and to several employments, as their inclinations lead them, to entertain the time till Satan return. He passes on his journey to Hell-gates; finds them shut, and who sat there to guard them; by whom at length they are opened, and discover to him the great gulf between Hell and Heaven. With what difficulty he passes through, directed by Chaos, the Power of that place, to the sight of this new World which he sought.

> High on a throne of royal state, which far
> Outshone the wealth of Ormus and of Ind,
> Or where the gorgeous East with richest hand
> Showers on her kings barbaric pearl and gold,
> Satan exalted sat, by merit raised
> To that bad eminence; and, from despair
> Thus high uplifted beyond hope, aspires
> Beyond thus high, insatiate to pursue
> Vain war with Heaven; and, by success untaught,
> His proud imaginations thus displayed:—   10
>   "Powers and Dominions, Deities of Heaven!—
> For, since no deep within her gulf can hold
> Immortal vigor, though oppressed and fallen,
> I give not Heaven for lost: from this descent

Celestial Virtues rising will appear
More glorious and more dread than from no fall,
And trust themselves to fear no second fate!—
Me though just right, and the fixed laws of Heaven,
Did first create your leader—next, free choice,
With what besides in council or in fight   20
Hath been achieved of merit—yet this loss,
Thus far at least recovered, hath much more
Established in a safe, unenvied throne,
Yielded with full consent. The happier state
In Heaven, which follows dignity, might draw
Envy from each inferior; but who here
Will envy whom the highest place exposes
Foremost to stand against the Thunderer's aim
Your bulwark, and condemns to greatest share
Of endless pain? Where there is, then, no good   30
For which to strive, no strife can grow up there
From faction: for none sure will claim in Hell
Precedence; none whose portion is so small
Of present pain that with ambitious mind
Will covet more! With this advantage, then,
To union, and firm faith, and firm accord,
More than can be in Heaven, we now return
To claim our just inheritance of old,
Surer to prosper than prosperity
Could have assured us; and by what best way,   40
Whether of open war or covert guile,
We now debate. Who can advise may speak."
    He ceased; and next him Moloch, sceptred king,
Stood up—the strongest and the fiercest Spirit
That fought in Heaven, now fiercer by despair.
His trust was with the Eternal to be deemed
Equal in strength, and rather than be less
Cared not to be at all; with that care lost
Went all his fear: of God, or Hell, or worse,
He recked not, and these words thereafter spake:—   50
    "My sentence is for open war. Of wiles,
More unexpert, I boast not: them let those
Contrive who need, or when they need; not now.
For, while they sit contriving, shall the rest—
Millions that stand in arms, and longing wait
The signal to ascend—sit lingering here,
Heaven's fugitives, and for their dwelling-place

Accept this dark opprobrious den of shame,
The prison of His tyranny who reigns
By our delay? No! let us rather choose,   60
Armed with Hell-flames and fury, all at once
O'er Heaven's high towers to force resistless way,
Turning our tortures into horrid arms
Against the Torturer; when, to meet the noise
Of his almighty engine, he shall hear
Infernal thunder, and, for lightning, see
Black fire and horror shot with equal rage
Among his Angels, and his throne itself
Mixed with Tartarean sulphur and strange fire,
His own invented torments. But perhaps   70
The way seems difficult, and steep to scale
With upright wing against a higher foe!
Let such bethink them, if the sleepy drench
Of that forgetful lake benumb not still,
That in our proper motion we ascend
Up to our native seat; descent and fall
To us is adverse. Who but felt of late,
When the fierce foe hung on our broken rear
Insulting, and pursued us through the Deep,
With what compulsion and laborious flight   80
We sunk thus low? The ascent is easy, then;
The event is feared! Should we again provoke
Our stronger, some worse way his wrath may find
To our destruction, if there be in Hell
Fear to be worse destroyed! What can be worse
Than to dwell here, driven out from bliss, condemned
In this abhorrèd deep to utter woe;
Where pain of unextinguishable fire
Must exercise us without hope of end
The vassals of his anger, when the scourge   90
Inexorably, and the torturing hour,
Calls us to penance? More destroyed than thus,
We should be quite abolished, and expire.
What fear we then? what doubt we to incense
His utmost ire? which, to the highth enraged,
Will either quite consume us, and reduce
To nothing this essential—happier far
Than miserable to have eternal being!—
Or, if our substance be indeed divine,
And cannot cease to be, we are at worst   100

On this side nothing; and by proof we feel
Our power sufficient to disturb his Heaven,
And with perpetual inroads to alarm,
Though inaccessible, his fatal throne:
Which, if not victory, is yet revenge."
   He ended frowning, and his look denounced
Desperate revenge, and battle dangerous
To less than gods. On the other side up rose
Belial, in act more graceful and humane.
A fairer person lost not Heaven; he seemed   110
For dignity composed, and high exploit.
But all was false and hollow; though his tongue
Dropt manna, and could make the worse appear
The better reason, to perplex and dash
Maturest counsels: for his thoughts were low—
To vice industrious, but to nobler deeds
Timorous and slothful. Yet he pleased the ear,
And with persuasive accent thus began:—
   "I should be much for open war, O Peers,
As not behind in hate, if what was urged   120
Main reason to persuade immediate war
Did not dissuade me most, and seem to cast
Ominous conjecture on the whole success;
When he who most excels in fact of arms,
In what he counsels and in what excels
Mistrustful, grounds his courage on despair
And utter dissolution, as the scope
Of all his aim, after some dire revenge.
First, what revenge? The towers of Heaven are filled
With armèd watch, that render all access   130
Impregnable: oft on the bordering Deep
Encamp their legions, or with obscure wing
Scout far and wide into the realm of Night,
Scorning surprise. Or, could we break our way
By force, and at our heels all Hell should rise
With blackest insurrection to confound
Heaven's purest light, yet our great Enemy,
All incorruptible, would on his throne
Sit unpolluted, and the ethereal mould,
Incapable of stain, would soon expel   140
Her mischief, and purge off the baser fire,
Victorious. Thus repulsed, our final hope
Is flat despair: we must exasperate

The Almighty Victor to spend all his rage;
And that must end us; that must be our cure—
To be no more. Sad cure! for who would lose,
Though full of pain, this intellectual being,
Those thoughts that wander through eternity,
To perish rather, swallowed up and lost
In the wide womb of uncreated Night,   150
Devoid of sense and motion? And who knows,
Let this be good, whether our angry Foe
Can give it, or will ever? How he can
Is doubtful; that he never will is sure.
Will He, so wise, let loose at once his ire,
Belike through impotence or unaware,
To give his enemies their wish, and end
Them in his anger whom his anger saves
To punish endless? 'Wherefore cease we, then?'
Say they who counsel war; 'we are decreed,   160
Reserved, and destined to eternal woe;
Whatever doing, what can we suffer more,
What can we suffer worse?' Is this, then, worst—
Thus sitting, thus consulting, thus in arms?
What when we fled amain, pursued and strook
With Heaven's afflicting thunder, and besought
The Deep to shelter us? This Hell then seemed
A refuge from those wounds. Or when we lay
Chained on the burning lake? That sure was worse.
What if the breath that kindled those grim fires,   170
Awaked, should blow them into sevenfold rage,
And plunge us in the flames; or from above
Should intermitted vengeance arm again
His red right hand to plague us? What if all
Her stores were opened, and this firmament
Of Hell should spout her cataracts of fire,
Impendent horrors, threatening hideous fall
One day upon our heads; while we perhaps,
Designing or exhorting glorious war,
Caught in a fiery tempest, shall be hurled,   180
Each on his rock transfixed, the sport and prey
Of racking whirlwinds, or for ever sunk
Under yon boiling ocean, wrapt in chains,
There to converse with everlasting groans,
Unrespited, unpitied, unreprieved,
Ages of hopeless end? This would be worse.

War, therefore, open or concealed, alike
My voice dissuades; for what can force or guile
With Him, or who deceive His mind, whose eye
Views all things at one view? He from Heaven's highth   190
All these our motions vain sees and derides,
Not more almighty to resist our might
Than wise to frustrate all our plots and wiles.
Shall we, then, live thus vile—the race of Heaven
Thus trampled, thus expelled, to suffer here
Chains and these torments? Better these than worse,
By my advice; since fate inevitable
Subdues us, and omnipotent decree,
The Victor's will. To suffer, as to do,
Our strength is equal; nor the law unjust   200
That so ordains. This was at first resolved,
If we were wise, against so great a foe
Contending, and so doubtful what might fall.
I laugh when those who at the spear are bold
And venturous, if that fail them, shrink, and fear
What yet they know must follow—to endure
Exile, or ignominy, or bonds, or pain,
The sentence of their conqueror. This is now
Our doom; which if we can sustain and bear,
Our Supreme Foe in time may much remit   210
His anger, and perhaps, thus far removed,
Not mind us not offending, satisfied
With what is punished; whence these raging fires
Will slacken, if his breath stir not their flames.
Our purer essence then will overcome
Their noxious vapor; or, inured, not feel;
Or, changed at length, and to the place conformed
In temper and in nature, will receive
Familiar the fierce heat; and, void of pain,
This horror will grow mild, this darkness light;   220
Besides what hope the never-ending flight
Of future days may bring, what chance, what change
Worth waiting—since our present lot appears
For happy though but ill, for ill not worst,
If we procure not to ourselves more woe."
    Thus Belial, with words clothed in reason's garb,
Counselled ignoble ease and peaceful sloth,
Not peace; and after him thus Mammon spake:—
    "Either to disenthrone the King of Heaven

We war, if war be best, or to regain   230
Our own right lost. Him to unthrone we then
May hope, when everlasting Fate shall yield
To fickle Chance, and Chaos judge the strife.
The former, vain to hope, argues as vain
The latter; for what place can be for us
Within Heaven's bound, unless Heaven's Lord Supreme
We overpower? Suppose he should relent,
And publish grace to all, on promise made
Of new subjection; with what eyes could we
Stand in his presence humble, and receive   240
Strict laws imposed, to celebrate his throne
With warbled hymns, and to his Godhead sing
Forced Halleluiahs, while he lordly sits
Our envied sovran, and his altar breathes
Ambrosial odors and ambrosial flowers,
Our servile offerings? This must be our task
In Heaven, this our delight. How wearisome
Eternity so spent in worship paid
To whom we hate! Let us not then pursue,
By force impossible, by leave obtained   250
Unacceptable, though in Heaven, our state
Of splendid vassalage; but rather seek
Our own good from ourselves, and from our own
Live to ourselves, though in this vast recess,
Free and to none accountable, preferring
Hard liberty before the easy yoke
Of servile pomp. Our greatness will appear
Then most conspicuous when great things of small,
Useful of hurtful, prosperous of adverse,
We can create, and in what place soe'er   260
Thrive under evil, and work ease out of pain
Through labor and endurance. This deep world
Of darkness do we dread? How oft amidst
Thick clouds and dark doth Heaven's all-ruling Sire
Choose to reside, his glory unobscured,
And with the majesty of darkness round
Covers his throne, from whence deep thunders roar.
Mustering their rage, and Heaven resembles Hell!
As He our darkness, cannot we His light
Imitate when we please? This desert soil   270
Wants not her hidden lustre, gems and gold;
Nor want we skill or art from whence to raise

Magnificence; and what can Heaven show more?
Our torments also may, in length of time,
Become our elements, these piercing fires
As soft as now severe, our temper changed
Into their temper; which must needs remove
The sensible of pain. All things invite
To peaceful counsels, and the settled state
Of order, how in safety best we may   280
Compose our present evils, with regard
Of what we are and where, dismissing quite
All thoughts of war. Ye have what I advise."
 He scarce had finished, when such murmur filled
The assembly as when hollow rocks retain
The sound of blustering winds, which all night long
Had roused the sea, now with hoarse cadence lull
Seafaring men o'erwatched, whose bark by chance,
Or pinnace, anchors in a craggy bay
After the tempest. Such applause was heard   290
As Mammon ended, and his sentence pleased,
Advising peace: for such another field
They dreaded worse than Hell; so much the fear
Of thunder and the sword of Michaël
Wrought still within them; and no less desire
To found this nether empire, which might rise,
By policy and long process of time,
In emulation opposite to Heaven.
Which when Beëlzebub perceived—than whom,
Satan except, none higher sat—with grave   300
Aspect he rose, and in his rising seemed
A pillar of state. Deep on his front engraven
Deliberation sat, and public care;
And princely counsel in his face yet shone,
Majestic, though in ruin. Sage he stood,
With Atlantean shoulders, fit to bear
The weight of mightiest monarchies; his look
Drew audience and attention still as night
Or summer's noontide air, while thus he spake:—
 "Thrones and Imperial Powers, Offspring of Heaven,   310
Ethereal Virtues! or these titles now
Must we renounce, and, changing style, be called
Princes of Hell? for so the popular vote
Inclines—here to continue, and build up here
A growing empire; doubtless! while we dream,

And know not that the King of Heaven hath doomed
This place our dungeon—not our safe retreat
Beyond his potent arm, to live exempt
From Heaven's high jurisdiction, in new league
Banded against his throne, but to remain   320
In strictest bondage, though thus far removed,
Under the inevitable curb, reserved
His captive multitude. For He, to be sure,
In highth or depth, still first and last will reign
Sole king, and of his kingdom lose no part
By our revolt, but over Hell extend
His empire, and with iron sceptre rule
Us here, as with his golden those in Heaven.
What sit we then projecting peace and war?
War hath determined us and foiled with loss   330
Irreparable; terms of peace yet none
Voutsafed or sought; for what peace will be given
To us enslaved, but custody severe,
And stripes and arbitrary punishment
Inflicted? and what peace can we return,
But, to our power, hostility and hate,
Untamed reluctance, and revenge, though slow,
Yet ever plotting how the Conqueror least
May reap his conquest, and may least rejoice
In doing what we most in suffering feel?   340
Nor will occasion want, nor shall we need
With dangerous expedition to invade
Heaven, whose high walls fear no assault or siege,
Or ambush from the Deep. What if we find
Some easier enterprise? There is a place
(If ancient and prophetic fame in Heaven
Err not)—another World, the happy seat
Of some new race, called Man, about this time
To be created like to us, though less
In power and excellence, but favored more   350
Of Him who rules above; so was His will
Pronounced among the gods, and by an oath
That shook Heaven's whole circumference confirmed.
Thither let us bend all our thoughts, to learn
What creatures there inhabit, of what mould
Or substance, how endued, and what their power
And where their weakness: how attempted best,
By force or subtlety. Though Heaven be shut,

And Heaven's high Arbitrator sit secure
In his own strength, this place may lie exposed,   360
The utmost border of his kingdom, left
To their defence who hold it: here, perhaps,
Some advantageous act may be achieved
By sudden onset—either with Hell-fire
To waste his whole creation, or possess
All as our own, and drive, as we are driven,
The puny habitants; or, if not drive,
Seduce them to our party, that their God
May prove their foe, and with repenting hand
Abolish his own works. This would surpass   370
Common revenge, and interrupt His joy
In our confusion, and our joy upraise
In His disturbance; when his darling sons,
Hurled headlong to partake with us, shall curse
Their frail original, and faded bliss—
Faded so soon! Advise if this be worth
Attempting, or to sit in darkness here
Hatching vain empires." Thus Beëlzebub
Pleaded his devilish counsel—first devised
By Satan, and in part proposed: for whence,   380
But from the author of all ill, could spring
So deep a malice, to confound the race
Of mankind in one root, and Earth with Hell
To mingle and involve, done all to spite
The great Creator? But their spite still serves
His glory to augment. The bold design
Pleased highly those Infernal States, and joy
Sparkled in all their eyes: with full assent
They vote: whereat his speech he thus renews:—
"Well have ye judged, well ended long debate,   390
Synod of Gods, and, like to what ye are,
Great things resolved, which from the lowest deep
Will once more lift us up, in spite of fate,
Nearer our ancient seat—perhaps in view
Of those bright confines, whence, with neighboring arms,
And opportune excursion, we may chance
Re-enter Heaven; or else in some mild zone
Dwell, not unvisited of Heaven's fair light,
Secure, and at the brightening orient beam
Purge off this gloom: the soft delicious air,   400
To heal the scar of these corrosive fires,

Shall breathe her balm. But, first, whom shall we send
In search of this new World? whom shall we find
Sufficient? who shall tempt with wandering feet
The dark, unbottomed, infinite Abyss,
And through the palpable obscure find out
His uncouth way, or spread his aery flight,
Upborne with indefatigable wings
Over the vast Abrupt, ere he arrive
The happy Isle? What strength, what art, can then   410
Suffice, or what evasion bear him safe
Through the strict senteries and stations thick
Of Angels watching round? Here he had need
All circumspection: and we now no less
Choice in our suffrage; for on whom we send
The weight of all, and our last hope, relies."
    This said, he sat; and expectation held
His look suspense, awaiting who appeared
To second, or oppose, or undertake
The perilous attempt. But all sat mute,   420
Pondering the danger with deep thoughts; and each
In other's countenance read his own dismay,
Astonished. None among the choice and prime
Of those Heaven-warring champions could be found
So hardy as to proffer or accept,
Alone, the dreadful voyage; till, at last,
Satan, whom now transcendent glory raised
Above his fellows, with monarchal pride
Conscious of highest worth, unmoved thus spake:—
    "O Progeny of Heaven! Empyreal Thrones!   430
With reason hath deep silence and demur
Seized us, though undismayed. Long is the way
And hard, that out of Hell leads up to Light.
Our prison strong, this huge convex of fire,
Outrageous to devour, immures us round
Ninefold; and gates of burning adamant,
Barred over us, prohibit all egress.
These passed, if any pass, the void profound
Of unessential Night receives him next,
Wide-gaping, and with utter loss of being   440
Threatens him, plunged in that abortive gulf.
If thence he scape, into whatever world,
Or unknown region, what remains him less
Than unknown dangers, and as hard escape?

But I should ill become this throne, O Peers,
And this imperial sovranty, adorned
With splendor, armed with power, if aught proposed
And judged of public moment in the shape
Of difficulty or danger, could deter
Me from attempting. Wherefore do I assume   450
These royalties, and not refuse to reign,
Refusing to accept as great a share
Of hazard as of honor, due alike
To him who reigns, and so much to him due
Of hazard more as he above the rest
High honored sits? Go, therefore, mighty Powers,
Terror of Heaven, though fallen; intend at home,
While here shall be our home, what best may ease
The present misery, and render Hell
More tolerable; if there be cure or charm   460
To respite, or deceive, or slack the pain
Of this ill mansion: intermit no watch
Against a wakeful foe, while I abroad
Through all the coasts of dark destruction seek
Deliverance for us all. This enterprise
None shall partake with me." Thus saying, rose
The Monarch, and prevented all reply;
Prudent lest, from his resolution raised,
Others among the chief might offer now,
Certain to be refused, what erst they feared,   470
And, so refused, might in opinion stand
His rivals, winning cheap the high repute
Which he through hazard huge must earn. But they
Dreaded not more the adventure than his voice
Forbidding; and at once with him they rose.
Their rising all at once was as the sound
Of thunder heard remote. Towards him they bend
With awful reverence prone, and as a God
Extol him equal to the Highest in Heaven.
Nor failed they to express how much they praised   480
That for the general safety he despised
His own: for neither do the Spirits damned
Lose all their virtue; lest bad men should boast
Their specious deeds on earth, which glory excites,
Or close ambition varnished o'er with zeal.
    Thus they their doubtful consultations dark
Ended, rejoicing in their matchless Chief:

As, when from mountain-tops the dusky clouds
Ascending, while the North-wind sleeps, o'erspread
Heaven's cheerful face, the louring element   490
Scowls o'er the darkened landscape snow or shower,
If chance the radiant sun, with farewell sweet,
Extend his evening beam, the fields revive,
The birds their notes renew, and bleating herds
Attest their joy, that hill and valley rings.
O shame to men! Devil with devil damned
Firm concord holds; men only disagree
Of creatures rational, though under hope
Of heavenly grace, and, God proclaiming peace,
Yet live in hatred, enmity, and strife   500
Among themselves, and levy cruel wars
Wasting the earth, each other to destroy:
As if (which might induce us to accord)
Man had not hellish foes enow besides,
That day and night for his destruction wait!
    The Stygian council thus dissolved; and forth
In order came the grand Infernal Peers:
Midst came their mighty Paramount, and seemed
Alone the antagonist of Heaven, nor less
Than Hell's dread Emperor, with pomp supreme,   510
And god-like imitated state: him round
A globe of fiery Seraphim enclosed
With bright emblazonry, and horrent arms.
Then of their session ended they bid cry
With trumpet's regal sound the great result:
Toward the four winds four speedy Cherubim
Put to their mouths the sounding alchymy,
By harald's voice explained; the hollow Abyss
Heard far and wide, and all the host of Hell
With deafening shout returned them loud acclaim.   520
Thence more at ease their minds, and somewhat raised
By false presumptuous hope, the rangèd Powers
Disband; and, wandering, each his several way
Pursues, as inclination or sad choice
Leads him perplexed, where he may likeliest find
Truce to his restless thoughts, and entertain
The irksome hours, till his great Chief return.
Part on the plain, or in the air sublime,
Upon the wing or in swift race contend,
As at the Olympian games or Pythian fields;   530

Part curb their fiery steeds, or shun the goal
With rapid wheels, or fronted brigads form:
As when, to warn proud cities, war appears
Waged in the troubled sky, and armies rush
To battle in the clouds; before each van
Prick forth the aery knights, and couch their spears,
Till thickest legions close; with feats of arms
From either end of heaven the welkin burns.
Others, with vast Typhœan rage, more fell,
Rend up both rocks and hills, and ride the air   540
In whirlwind; Hell scarce holds the wild uproar:—
As when Alcides, from Œchalia crowned
With conquest, felt the envenomed robe, and tore
Through pain up by the roots Thessalian pines,
And Lichas from the top of Œta threw
Into the Euboic sea. Others, more mild,
Retreated in a silent valley, sing
With notes angelical to many a harp
Their own heroic deeds, and hapless fall
By doom of battle, and complain that Fate   550
Free Virtue should enthrall to Force or Chance.
Their song was partial; but the harmony
(What could it less when Spirits immortal sing?)
Suspended Hell, and took with ravishment
The thronging audience. In discourse more sweet
(For Eloquence the Soul, Song charms the Sense)
Others apart sat on a hill retired,
In thoughts more elevate, and reasoned high
Of Providence, Foreknowledge, Will, and Fate—
Fixed fate, free will, foreknowledge absolute,   560
And found no end, in wandering mazes lost.
Of good and evil much they argued then,
Of happiness and final misery,
Passion and apathy, and glory and shame:
Vain wisdom all, and false philosophy!—
Yet, with a pleasing sorcery, could charm
Pain for a while or anguish, and excite
Fallacious hope, or arm the obdurèd breast
With stubborn patience as with triple steel.
Another part, in squadrons and gross bands,   570
On bold adventure to discover wide
That dismal world, if any clime perhaps
Might yield them easier habitation, bend

Four ways their flying march, along the banks
Of four infernal rivers, that disgorge
Into the burning lake their baleful streams—
Abhorrèd Styx, the flood of deadly hate;
Sad Acheron of sorrow, black and deep;
Cocytus, named of lamentation loud
Heard on the rueful stream; fierce Phlegeton,   580
Whose waves of torrent fire inflame with rage.
Far off from these, a slow and silent stream,
Lethe, the river of oblivion, rolls
Her watery labyrinth, whereof who drinks
Forthwith his former state and being forgets—
Forgets both joy and grief, pleasure and pain.
Beyond this flood a frozen continent
Lies dark and wild, beat with perpetual storms
Of whirlwind and dire hail, which on firm land
Thaws not, but gathers heap, and ruin seems   590
Of ancient pile; all else deep snow and ice,
A gulf profound as that Serbonian bog
Betwixt Damiata and Mount Casius old,
Where armies whole have sunk: the parching air
Burns frore, and cold performs the effect of fire.
Thither, by harpy-footed Furies haled,
At certain revolutions all the damned
Are brought; and feel by turns the bitter change
Of fierce extremes, extremes by change more fierce,
From beds of raging fire to starve in ice   600
Their soft ethereal warmth, and there to pine
Immovable, infixed, and frozen round
Periods of time,—thence hurried back to fire.
They ferry over this Lethean sound
Both to and fro, their sorrow to augment,
And wish and struggle, as they pass, to reach
The tempting stream, with one small drop to lose
In sweet forgetfulness all pain and woe,
All in one moment, and so near the brink;
But Fate withstands, and, to oppose the attempt,   610
Medusa with Gorgonian terror guards
The ford, and of itself the water flies
All taste of living wight, as once it fled
The lip of Tantalus. Thus roving on
In confused march forlorn, the adventurous bands,
With shuddering horror pale, and eyes aghast,

Viewed first their lamentable lot, and found
No rest. Through many a dark and dreary vale
They passed, and many a region dolorous,
O'er many a frozen, many a fiery Alp,   620
Rocks, caves, lakes, fens, bogs, dens, and shades of death—
A universe of death, which God by curse
Created evil, for evil only good;
Where all life dies, death lives, and Nature breeds,
Perverse, all monstrous, all prodigious things,
Abominable, inutterable, and worse
Than fables yet have feigned or fear conceived,
Gorgons, and Hydras, and Chimæras dire.
    Meanwhile the Adversary of God and Man,
Satan, with thoughts inflamed of highest design,   630
Puts on swift wings, and toward the gates of Hell
Explores his solitary flight: sometimes
He scours the right hand coast, sometimes the left;
Now shaves with level wing the deep, then soars
Up to the fiery concave towering high.
As when far off at sea a fleet descried
Hangs in the clouds, by equinoctial winds
Close sailing from Bengala, or the isles
Of Ternate and Tidore, whence merchants bring
Their spicy drugs; they on the trading flood,   640
Through the wide Ethiopian to the Cape,
Ply stemming nightly toward the pole: so seemed
Far off the flying Fiend. At last appear
Hell-bounds, high reaching to the horrid roof,
And thrice threefold the gates; three folds were brass,
Three iron, three of adamantine rock,
Impenetrable, impaled with circling fire,
Yet unconsumed. Before the gates there sat
On either side a formidable Shape.
The one seemed woman to the waist, and fair,   650
But ended foul in many a scaly fold,
Voluminous and vast—a serpent armed
With mortal sting. About her middle round
A cry of Hell-hounds never-ceasing barked
With wide Cerberean mouths full loud, and rung
A hideous peal; yet, when they list, would creep,
If aught disturbed their noise, into her womb,
And kennel there; yet there still barked and howled
Within unseen. Far less abhorred than these

Vexed Scylla, bathing in the sea that parts   660
Calabria from the hoarse Trinacrian shore;
Nor uglier follow the night-hag, when, called
In secret, riding through the air she comes,
Lured with the smell of infant blood, to dance
With Lapland witches, while the laboring moon
Eclipses at their charms. The other Shape—
If shape it might be called that shape had none
Distinguishable in member, joint, or limb;
Or substance might be called that shadow seemed,
For each seemed either—black it stood as Night,   670
Fierce as ten Furies, terrible as Hell,
And shook a dreadful dart: what seemed his head
The likeness of a kingly crown had on.
Satan was now at hand, and from his seat
The monster moving onward came as fast
With horrid strides; Hell trembled as he strode.
The undaunted Fiend what this might be admired—
Admired, not feared (God and his Son except,
Created thing naught valued he nor shunned),
And with disdainful look thus first began:—   680
    "Whence and what art thou, execrable Shape,
That dar'st, though grim and terrible, advance
Thy miscreated front athwart my way
To yonder gates? Through them I mean to pass,
That be assured, without leave asked of thee.
Retire; or taste thy folly, and learn by proof,
Hell-born, not to contend with Spirits of Heaven."
    To whom the Goblin, full of wrath, replied:—
"Art thou that Traitor-Angel, art thou he,
Who first broke peace in Heaven and faith, till then   690
Unbroken, and in proud rebellious arms
Drew after him the third part of Heaven's sons,
Conjured against the Highest—for which both thou
And they, outcast from God, are here condemned
To waste eternal days in woe and pain?
And reckon'st thou thyself with Spirits of Heaven,
Hell-doomed, and breath'st defiance here and scorn,
Where I reign king, and, to enrage thee more,
Thy king and lord? Back to thy punishment,
False fugitive; and to thy speed add wings,   700
Lest with a whip of scorpions I pursue
Thy lingering, or with one stroke of this dart

Strange horror seize thee, and pangs unfelt before."
    So spake the grisly Terror, and in shape,
So speaking and so threatening, grew tenfold
More dreadful and deform. On the other side,
Incensed with indignation, Satan stood
Unterrified, and like a comet burned,
That fires the length of Ophiuchus huge
In the arctic sky, and from his horrid hair   710
Shakes pestilence and war. Each at the head
Levelled his deadly aim; their fatal hands
No second stroke intend; and such a frown
Each cast at the other as when two black clouds,
With heaven's artillery fraught, come rattling on
Over the Caspian,—then stand front to front
Hovering a space, till winds the signal blow
To join their dark encounter in mid-air.
So frowned the mighty combatants that Hell
Grew darker at their frown; so matched they stood;   720
For never but once more was either like
To meet so great a foe. And now great deeds
Had been achieved, whereof all Hell had rung,
Had not the snaky Sorceress, that sat
Fast by Hell-gate and kept the fatal key,
Risen, and with hideous outcry rushed between.
    "O father, what intends thy hand," she cried,
"Against thy only son? What fury, O son,
Possesses thee to bend that mortal dart
Against thy father's head? And know'st for whom?   730
For Him who sits above, and laughs the while
At thee, ordained his drudge to execute
Whate'er his wrath, which he calls justice, bids—
His wrath, which one day will destroy ye both!"
    She spake, and at her words the hellish Pest
Forbore: then these to her Satan returned:—
    "So strange thy outcry, and thy words so strange
Thou interposest, that my sudden hand,
Prevented, spares to tell thee yet by deeds
What it intends, till first I know of thee   740
What thing thou art, thus double-formed, and why,
In this infernal vale first met, thou call'st
Me father, and that phantasm call'st my son.
I know thee not, nor ever saw till now
Sight more detestable than him and thee."

To whom thus the Portress of Hell-gate replied:—
"Hast thou forgot me, then; and do I seem
Now in thine eye so foul?—once deemed so fair
In Heaven, when at the assembly, and in sight
Of all the Seraphim with thee combined   750
In bold conspiracy against Heaven's King,
All on a sudden miserable pain
Surprised thee, dim thine eyes and dizzy swum
In darkness, while thy head flames thick and fast
Threw forth, till on the left side opening wide,
Likest to thee in shape and countenance bright,
Then shining heavenly fair, a goddess armed,
Out of thy head I sprung. Amazement seized
All the host of Heaven; back they recoiled afraid
At first, and called me *Sin*, and for a sign   760
Portentous held me; but, familiar grown,
I pleased, and with attractive graces won
The most averse—thee chiefly, who, full oft
Thyself in me thy perfect image viewing,
Becam'st enamoured; and such joy thou took'st
With me in secret that my womb conceived
A growing burden. Meanwhile war arose,
And fields were fought in Heaven: wherein remained
(For what could else?) to our Almighty Foe
Clear victory; to our part loss and rout   770
Through all the Empyrean. Down they fell,
Driven headlong from the pitch of Heaven, down
Into this Deep; and in the general fall
I also: at which time this powerful key
Into my hands was given, with charge to keep
These gates for ever shut, which none can pass
Without my opening. Pensive here I sat
Alone; but long I sat not, till my womb,
Pregnant by thee, and now excessive grown,
Prodigious motion felt and rueful throes.   780
At last this odious offspring, whom thou seest,
Thine own begotten, breaking violent way,
Tore through my entrails, that, with fear and pain
Distorted, all my nether shape thus grew
Transformed: but he my inbred enemy
Forth issued, brandishing his fatal dart,
Made to destroy. I fled, and cried out *Death!*
Hell trembled at the hideous name, and sighed

From all her caves, and back resounded *Death!*
I fled; but he pursued (though more, it seems,   790
Inflamed with lust than rage), and, swifter far,
Me overtook, his mother, all dismayed,
And, in embraces forcible and foul
Engendering with me, of that rape begot
These yelling monsters, that with ceaseless cry
Surround me, as thou saw'st—hourly conceived
And hourly born, with sorrow infinite
To me; for, when they list, into the womb
That bred them they return, and howl, and gnaw
My bowels, their repast; then, bursting forth   800
Afresh, with conscious terrors vex me round,
That rest or intermission none I find.
Before mine eyes in opposition sits
Grim Death, my son and foe, who sets them on,
And me, his parent, would full soon devour
For want of other prey, but that he knows
His end with mine involved, and knows that I
Should prove a bitter morsel, and his bane,
Whenever that shall be: so Fate pronounced.
But thou, O father, I forewarn thee, shun   810
His deadly arrow; neither vainly hope
To be invulnerable in those bright arms,
Though tempered heavenly; for that mortal dint,
Save He who reigns above, none can resist."
    She finished; and the subtle Fiend his lore
Soon learned, now milder, and thus answered smooth:—
    "Dear daughter—since thou claim'st me for thy sire,
And my fair son here show'st me, the dear pledge
Of dalliance had with thee in Heaven, and joys
Then sweet, now sad to mention, through dire change   820
Befallen us unforeseen, unthought-of—know,
I come no enemy, but to set free
From out this dark and dismal house of pain
Both him and thee, and all the Heavenly host
Of Spirits that, in our just pretences armed,
Fell with us from on high. From them I go
This uncouth errand sole, and one for all
Myself expose, with lonely steps to tread
The unfounded Deep, and through the void immense
To search, with wandering quest, a place foretold   830
Should be—and, by concurring signs, ere now

Created vast and round—a place of bliss
In the purlieus of Heaven; and therein placed
A race of upstart creatures, to supply
Perhaps our vacant room, though more removed,
Lest Heaven, surcharged with potent multitude,
Might hap to move new broils. Be this, or aught
Than this more secret, now designed, I haste
To know; and, this once known, shall soon return,
And bring ye to the place where thou and Death   840
Shall dwell at ease, and up and down unseen
Wing silently the buxom air, embalmed
With odors. There ye shall be fed and filled
Immeasurably; all things shall be your prey."
   He ceased; for both seemed highly pleased, and Death
Grinned horrible a ghastly smile, to hear
His famine should be filled, and blessed his maw
Destined to that good hour. No less rejoiced
His mother bad, and thus bespake her sire:—
   "The key of this infernal Pit, by due   850
And by command of Heaven's all-powerful King,
I keep, by Him forbidden to unlock
These adamantine gates; against all force
Death ready stands to interpose his dart,
Fearless to be o'ermatched by living might.
But what owe I to His commands above,
Who hates me, and hath hither thrust me down
Into this gloom of Tartarus profound,
To sit in hateful office here confined,
Inhabitant of Heaven and heavenly-born—   860
Here in perpetual agony and pain,
With terrors and with clamors compassed round
Of mine own brood, that on my bowels feed?
Thou art my father, thou my author, thou
My being gav'st me; whom should I obey
But thee? whom follow? Thou wilt bring me soon
To that new world of light and bliss, among
The gods who live at ease, where I shall reign
At thy right hand voluptuous, as beseems
Thy daughter and thy darling, without end."   870
    Thus saying, from her side the fatal key,
Sad instrument of all our woe, she took;
And, towards the gate rolling her bestial train,
Forthwith the huge portcullis high up-drew,

Which, but herself, not all the Stygian Powers
Could once have moved; then in the key-hole turns
The intricate wards, and every bolt and bar
Of massy iron or solid rock with ease
Unfastens. On a sudden open fly,
With impetuous recoil and jarring sound,   880
The infernal doors, and on their hinges grate
Harsh thunder, that the lowest bottom shook
Of Erebus. She opened; but to shut
Excelled her power: the gates wide open stood,
That with extended wings a bannered host,
Under spread ensigns marching, might pass through
With horse and chariots ranked in loose array;
So wide they stood, and like a furnace-mouth
Cast forth redounding smoke and ruddy flame.
Before their eyes in sudden view appear   890
The secrets of the hoary Deep—a dark
Illimitable ocean, without bound,
Without dimension; where length, breadth, and highth,
And time, and place, are lost; where eldest Night
And Chaos, ancestors of Nature, hold
Eternal anarchy, amidst the noise
Of endless wars, and by confusion stand.
For Hot, Cold, Moist, and Dry, four champions fierce,
Strive here for mastery, and to battle bring
Their embryon atoms: they around the flag   900
Of each his faction, in their several clans,
Light-armed or heavy, sharp, smooth, swift, or slow,
Swarm populous, unnumbered as the sands
Of Barca or Cyrene's torrid soil,
Levied to side with warring winds, and poise
Their lighter wings. To whom these most adhere
He rules a moment: Chaos umpire sits,
And by decision more embroils the fray
By which he reigns: next him, high arbiter,
Chance governs all. Into this wild Abyss,   910
The womb of Nature, and perhaps her grave,
Of neither Sea, nor Shore, nor Air, nor Fire,
But all these in their pregnant causes mixed
Confusedly, and which thus must ever fight,
Unless the Almighty Maker them ordain
His dark materials to create more worlds—
Into this wild Abyss the wary Fiend

Stood on the brink of Hell and looked a while,
Pondering his voyage; for no narrow frith
He had to cross. Nor was his ear less pealed   920
With noises loud and ruinous (to compare
Great things with small) than when Bellona storms
With all her battering engines, bent to rase
Some capital city; or less than if this frame
Of heaven were falling, and these elements
In mutiny had from her axle torn
The steadfast Earth. At last his sail-broad vans
He spread for flight, and, in the surging smoke
Uplifted, spurns the ground; thence many a league,
As in a cloudy chair, ascending rides   930
Audacious; but, that seat soon failing, meets
A vast vacuity. All unawares,
Fluttering his pennons vain, plumb-down he drops
Ten thousand fathom deep, and to this hour
Down had been falling, had not, by ill chance,
The strong rebuff of some tumultuous cloud,
Instinct with fire and nitre, hurried him
As many miles aloft. That fury stayed—
Quenched in a boggy Syrtis, neither sea,
Nor good dry land—nigh foundered, on he fares,   940
Treading the crude consistence, half on foot,
Half flying; behoves him now both oar and sail.
As when a gryphon through the wilderness
With wingèd course, o'er hill or moory dale,
Pursues the Arimaspian, who by stealth
Had from his wakeful custody purloined
The guarded gold; so eagerly the Fiend
O'er bog or steep, through strait, rough, dense, or rare,
With head, hands, wings, or feet, pursues his way,
And swims, or sinks, or wades, or creeps, or flies.   950
At length a universal hubbub wild
Of stunning sounds, and voices all confused,
Borne through the hollow dark, assaults his ear
With loudest vehemence. Thither he plies
Undaunted, to meet there whatever Power
Or Spirit of the nethermost Abyss
Might in that noise reside, of whom to ask
Which way the nearest coast of darkness lies
Bordering on light; when straight behold the throne
Of *Chaos,* and his dark pavilion spread   960

Wide on the wasteful Deep! With him enthroned
Sat sable-vested *Night,* eldest of things,
The consort of his reign; and by them stood
Orcus and Ades, and the dreaded name
Of Demogorgon; Rumor next, and Chance,
And Tumult, and Confusion, all embroiled,
And Discord, with a thousand various mouths.
   To whom Satan, turning boldly, thus:—"Ye Powers
And Spirits of this nethermost Abyss,
Chaos and ancient Night, I come no spy   970
With purpose to explore or to disturb
The secrets of your realm; but, by constraint
Wandering this darksome desert, as my way
Lies through your spacious empire up to light,
Alone and without guide, half lost, I seek,
What readiest path leads where your gloomy bounds
Confine with Heaven; or, if some other place,
From your dominion won, the Ethereal King
Possesses lately, thither to arrive
I travel this profound. Direct my course: 980
Directed, no mean recompense it brings
To your behoof, if I that region lost,
All usurpation thence expelled, reduce
To her original darkness and your sway
(Which is my present journey), and once more
Erect the standard there of ancient Night.
Yours be the advantage all, mine the revenge!"
   Thus Satan; and him thus the Anarch old,
With faltering speech and visage incomposed,
Answered:—"I know thee, stranger, who thou art—   990
That mighty leading Angel, who of late
Made head against Heaven's King, though overthrown.
I saw and heard; for such a numerous host
Fled not in silence through the frighted Deep,
With ruin upon ruin, rout on rout,
Confusion worse confounded; and Heaven-gates
Poured out by millions her victorious bands,
Pursuing. I upon my frontiers here
Keep residence; if all I can will serve
That little which is left so to defend,   1000
Encroached on still through our intestine broils
Weakening the sceptre of old Night: first, Hell,
Your dungeon, stretching far and wide beneath;

Now lately Heaven and Earth, another world
Hung o'er my realm, linked in a golden chain
To that side Heaven from whence your legions fell!
If that way be your walk, you have not far;
So much the nearer danger. Go, and speed;
Havoc, and spoil, and ruin, are my gain."
   He ceased; and Satan staid not to reply,   1010
But, glad that now his sea should find a shore,
With fresh alacrity and force renewed
Springs upward, like a pyramid of fire,
Into the wild expanse, and through the shock
Of fighting elements, on all sides round
Environed, wins his way; harder beset
And more endangered than when Argo passed
Through Bosporus betwixt the justling rocks,
Or when Ulysses on the larboard shunned
Charybdis, and by the other Whirlpool steered.   1020
So he with difficulty and labor hard
Moved on. With difficulty and labor he;
But, he once passed, soon after, when Man fell,
Strange alteration! Sin and Death amain,
Following his track (such was the will of Heaven)
Paved after him a broad and beaten way
Over the dark Abyss, whose boiling gulf
Tamely endured a bridge of wondrous length,
From Hell continued, reaching the utmost Orb
Of this frail World; by which the Spirits perverse   1030
With easy intercourse pass to and fro
To tempt or punish mortals, except whom
God and good Angels guard by special grace.
   But now at last the sacred influence
Of light appears, and from the walls of Heaven
Shoots far into the bosom of dim Night
A glimmering dawn. Here Nature first begins
Her farthest verge, and Chaos to retire,
As from her outmost works, a broken foe,
With tumult less and with less hostile din;   1040
That Satan, with less toil, and now with ease,
Wafts on the calmer wave by dubious light,
And, like a weather-beaten vessel, holds
Gladly the port, though shrouds and tackle torn;
Or in the emptier waste, resembling air,
Weighs his spread wings, at leisure to behold

Far off the empyreal Heaven, extended wide
In circuit, undetermined square or round,
With opal towers and battlements adorned
Of living sapphire, once his native seat;   1050
And, fast by, hanging in a golden chain,
This pendent World, in bigness as a star
Of smallest magnitude close by the moon.
Thither, full fraught with mischievous revenge,
Accurst, and in a cursed hour, he hies.

BOOK III

THE ARGUMENT

GOD, sitting on his throne, sees Satan flying towards this World, then newly created; shows him to the Son, who sat at his right hand; foretells the success of Satan in perverting mankind; clears his own justice and wisdom from all imputation, having created Man free, and able enough to have withstood his Tempter; yet declares his purpose of grace towards him, in regard he fell not of his own malice, as did Satan, but by him seduced. The Son of God renders praises to his Father for the manifestation of his gracious purpose towards Man: but God again declares that grace cannot be extended towards Man without the satisfaction of Divine Justice; Man hath offended the majesty of God by aspiring to Godhead, and therefore, with all his progeny, devoted to death, must die, unless some one can be found sufficient to answer for his offence, and undergo his punishment. The Son of God freely offers himself a ransom for Man: the Father accepts him, ordains his incarnation, pronounces his exaltation above all names in Heaven and Earth; commands all the Angels to adore him. They obey, and, hymning to their harps in full quire, celebrate the Father and the Son. Meanwhile Satan alights upon the bare convex of this World's outermost orb; where wandering he first finds a place since called the Limbo of Vanity; what persons and things fly up thither: thence comes to the gate of Heaven, described ascending by stairs, and the waters above the firmament that flow about it. His passage thence to the orb of the Sun: he finds there Uriel, the regent of that orb, but first changes himself into the shape of a meaner Angel, and, pretending a zealous desire to behold the new Creation, and Man whom God had placed here, inquires of him the place of his habitation, and is directed: Alights first on Mount Niphates.

Hail, holy Light, offspring of Heaven first-born!
Or of the Eternal coeternal beam
May I express thee unblamed? since God is light,
And never but in unapproachèd light
Dwelt from eternity—dwelt then in thee,
Bright effluence of bright essence increate!
Or hear'st thou rather pure Ethereal stream,
Whose fountain who shall tell? Before the Sun,
Before the Heavens, thou wert, and at the voice
Of God, as with a mantle, didst invest   10
The rising World of waters dark and deep,
Won from the void and formless Infinite!
Thee I revisit now with bolder wing,
Escaped the Stygian Pool, though long detained
In that obscure sojourn, while in my flight,
Through utter and through middle Darkness borne,
With other notes than to the Orphean lyre
I sung of Chaos and eternal Night,
Taught by the Heavenly muse to venture down
The dark descent, and up to re-ascend,   20
Though hard and rare. Thee I revisit safe,
And feel thy sovran vital lamp; but thou
Revisit'st not these eyes, that roll in vain
To find thy piercing ray, and find no dawn;
So thick a drop serene hath quenched their orbs,
Or dim suffusion veiled. Yet not the more
Cease I to wander where the Muses haunt
Clear spring, or shady grove, or sunny hill,
Smit with the love of sacred song; but chief
Thee, Sion, and the flowery brooks beneath,   30
That wash thy hallowed feet, and warbling flow,
Nightly I visit: nor sometimes forget
Those other two equalled with me in fate,
So were I equalled with them in renown,
Blind Thamyris and blind Mæonides,
And Tiresias and Phineus, prophets old:
Then feed on thoughts that voluntary move
Harmonious numbers; as the wakeful bird
Sings darkling, and, in shadiest covert hid,
Tunes her nocturnal note. Thus with the year   40
Seasons return; but not to me returns
Day, or the sweet approach of even or morn
Or sight of vernal bloom, or summer's rose,

Or flocks, or herds, or human face divine;
But cloud instead and ever-during dark
Surrounds me, from the cheerful ways of men
Cut off, and, for the book of knowledge fair,
Presented with a universal blank
Of Nature's works, to me expunged and rased,
And wisdom at one entrance quite shut out.   50
So much the rather thou, Celestial Light,
Shine inward, and the mind through all her powers
Irradiate; there plant eyes; all mist from thence
Purge and disperse, that I may see and tell
Of things invisible to mortal sight.
　　Now had the Almighty Father from above,
From the pure Empyrean where He sits
High throned above all highth, bent down his eye,
His own works and their works at once to view:
About him all the Sanctities of Heaven   60
Stood thick as stars, and from his sight received
Beatitude past utterance; on his right
The radiant image of his glory sat,
His only Son. On Earth he first beheld
Our two first parents, yet the only two
Of mankind, in the Happy Garden placed,
Reaping immortal fruits of joy and love,
Uninterrupted joy, unrivalled love,
In blissful solitude. He then surveyed
Hell and the gulf between, and Satan there   70
Coasting the wall of Heaven on this side Night,
In the dun air sublime, and ready now
To stoop, with wearied wings and willing feet,
On the bare outside of this World, that seemed
Firm land imbosomed without firmament,
Uncertain which, in ocean or in air.
Him God beholding from his prospect high,
Wherein past, present, future, he beholds,
Thus to His only Son foreseeing spake:—
　　"Only-begotten Son, seest thou what rage   80
Transports our Adversary? whom no bounds
Prescribed, no bars of Hell, nor all the chains
Heaped on him there, nor yet the main Abyss
Wide interrupt, can hold; so bent he seems
On desperate revenge, that shall redound
Upon his own rebellious head. And now,

Through all restraint broke loose, he wings his way
Not far off Heaven, in the precincts of light,
Directly towards the new-created World,
And Man there placed, with purpose to assay   90
If him by force he can destroy, or, worse,
By some false guile pervert: And shall pervert;
For Man will hearken to his glozing lies,
And easily transgress the sole command,
Sole pledge of his obedience: so will fall
He and his faithless progeny. Whose fault?
Whose but his own? Ingrate, he had of me
All he could have; I made him just and right,
Sufficient to have stood, though free to fall.
Such I created all the Ethereal Powers   100
And Spirits, both them who stood and them who failed;
Freely they stood who stood, and fell who fell.
Not free, what proof could they have given sincere
Of true allegiance, constant faith, or love,
Where only what they needs must do appeared,
Not what they would? What praise could they receive,
What pleasure I, from such obedience paid,
When Will and Reason (Reason also is Choice),
Useless and vain, of freedom both despoiled,
Made passive both, had served Necessity,   110
Not Me? They, therefore, as to right belonged
So were created, nor can justly accuse
Their Maker, or their making, or their fate,
As if Predestination overruled
Their will, disposed by absolute decree
Or high foreknowledge. They themselves decreed
Their own revolt, not I. If I foreknew,
Foreknowledge had no influence on their fault,
Which had no less proved certain unforeknown.
So without least impulse or shadow of fate,   120
Or aught by me immutably foreseen,
They trespass, authors to themselves in all,
Both what they judge and what they choose; for so
I formed them free, and free they must remain
Till they enthrall themselves: I else must change
Their nature, and revoke the high decree
Unchangeable, eternal, which ordained
Their freedom; they themselves ordained their fall.
The first sort by their own suggestion fell,

Self-tempted, self-depraved; Man falls, deceived   130
By the other first: Man, therefore, shall find grace;
The other, none. In mercy and justice both,
Through Heaven and Earth, so shall my glory excel;
But mercy, first and last, shall brightest shine."
   Thus while God spake ambrosial fragrance filled
All Heaven, and in the blessed Spirits elect
Sense of new joy ineffable diffused.
Beyond compare the Son of God was seen
Most glorious; in him all his Father shone
Substantially expressed; and in his face   140
Divine compassion visibly appeared,
Love without end, and without measure grace;
Which uttering, thus He to His father spake:—
   "O Father, gracious was that word which closed
Thy sovran sentence, that Man should find grace;
For which both Heaven and Earth shall high extol
Thy praises, with the innumerable sound
Of hymns and sacred songs, wherewith thy throne
Encompassed shall resound thee ever blest.
For, should Man finally be lost—should Man,   150
Thy creature late so loved, thy youngest son,
Fall circumvented thus by fraud, though joined
With his own folly—! That be from thee far,
That far be from thee, Father, who art judge
Of all things made, and judgest only right!
Or shall the Adversary thus obtain
His end, and frustrate thine? shall he fulfil
His malice, and thy goodness bring to naught
Or proud return, though to his heavier doom
Yet with revenge accomplished, and to Hell   160
Draw after him the whole race of mankind,
By him corrupted? Or wilt thou thyself
Abolish thy creation, and unmake,
For him, what for thy glory thou hast made?—
So should thy goodness and thy greatness both
Be questioned and blasphemed without defence."
   To whom the great Creator thus replied:—
"O Son, in whom my soul hath chief delight,
Son of my bosom, Son who art alone
My word, my wisdom, and effectual might,   170
All hast thou spoken as my thoughts are, all
As my eternal purpose hath decreed.

Man shall not quite be lost, but saved who will;
Yet not of will in him, but grace in me
Freely voutsafed. Once more I will renew
His lapsèd powers, though forfeit, and enthralled
By sin to foul exorbitant desires:
Upheld by me, yet once more he shall stand
On even ground against his mortal foe—
By me upheld, that he may know how frail   180
His fallen condition is, and to me owe
All his deliverance, and to none but me.
Some I have chosen of peculiar grace,
Elect above the rest; so is my will:
The rest shall hear me call, and oft be warned
Their sinful state, and to appease betimes
The incensèd Deity, while offered grace
Invites; for I will clear their senses dark
What may suffice, and soften stony hearts
To pray, repent, and bring obedience due.   190
To prayer, repentance, and obedience due,
Though but endeavored with sincere intent,
Mine ear shall not be slow, mine eye not shut.
And I will place within them as a guide
My umpire Conscience; whom if they will hear,
Light after light well used they shall attain,
And to the end persisting safe arrive.
This my long sufferance, and my day of grace,
They who neglect and scorn shall never taste;
But hard be hardened, blind be blinded more,   200
That they may stumble on, and deeper fall;
And none but such from mercy I exclude.—
But yet all is not done. Man disobeying,
Disloyal, breaks his fealty, and sins
Against the high supremacy of Heaven,
Affecting Godhead, and, so losing all,
To expiate his treason hath naught left,
But, to destruction sacred and devote,
He with his whole posterity must die;—
Die he or Justice must; unless for him   210
Some other, able, and as willing, pay
The rigid satisfaction, death for death.
Say, Heavenly Powers, where shall we find such love?
Which of ye will be mortal, to redeem
Man's mortal crime, and just, the unjust to save?

Dwells in all Heaven charity so dear?"
  He asked, but all the Heavenly Quire stood mute,
And silence was in Heaven: on Man's behalf
Patron or intercessor none appeared—
Much less that durst upon his own head draw   220
The deadly forfeiture, and ransom set.
And now without redemption all mankind
Must have been lost, adjudged to Death and Hell
By doom severe, had not the Son of God,
In whom the fulness dwells of love divine,
His dearest mediation thus renewed:—
  "Father, thy word is passed, Man shall find grace;
And shall Grace not find means, that finds her way,
The speediest of thy wingèd messengers,
To visit all thy creatures, and to all   230
Comes unprevented, unimplored, unsought?
Happy for Man, so coming! He her aid
Can never seek, once dead in sins and lost—
Atonement for himself, or offering meet,
Indebted and undone, hath none to bring.
Behold *me,* then: me for him, life for life,
I offer; on me let thine anger fall;
Account me Man: I for his sake will leave
Thy bosom, and this glory next to thee
Freely put off, and for him lastly die   240
Well pleased; on me let Death wreak all his rage.
Under his gloomy power I shall not long
Lie vanquished. Thou hast given me to possess
Life in myself for ever; by thee I live;
Though now to Death I yield, and am his due,
All that of me can die, yet, that debt paid,
Thou wilt not leave me in the loathsome grave
His prey, nor suffer my unspotted soul
For ever with corruption there to dwell;
But I shall rise victorious, and subdue   250
My vanquisher, spoiled of his vaunted spoil.
Death his death's wound shall then receive, and stoop
Inglorious, of his mortal sting disarmed;
I through the ample air in triumph high
Shall lead Hell captive maugre Hell, and show
The powers of Darkness bound. Thou, at the sight
Pleased, out of Heaven shalt look down and smile,
While, by thee raised, I ruin all my foes—

Death last, and with his carcase glut the grave;
Then, with the multitude of my redeemed,   260
Shall enter Heaven, long absent, and return.
Father, to see thy face, wherein no cloud
Of anger shall remain, but peace assured
And reconcilement: wrath shall be no more
Thenceforth, but in thy presence joy entire."
    His words here ended; but his meek aspéct
Silent yet spake, and breathed immortal love
To mortal men, above which only shone
Filial obedience: as a sacrifice
Glad to be offered, he attends the will   270
Of his great Father. Admiration seized
All Heaven, what this might mean, and whither tend,
Wondering; but soon the Almighty thus replied:—
    "O thou in Heaven and Earth the only peace
Found out for mankind under wrath, O thou
My sole complacence! well thou know'st how dear
To me are all my works; nor Man the least,
Though last created, that for him I spare
Thee from my bosom and right hand, to save,
By losing thee a while, the whole race lost!   280
Thou, therefore, whom thou only canst redeem,
Their nature also to thy nature join;
And by thyself Man among men on Earth,
Made flesh, when time shall be, of virgin seed,
By wondrous birth; be thou in Adam's room
The head of all mankind, though Adam's son.
As in him perish all men, so in thee,
As from a second root, shall be restored
As many as are restored; without thee, none.
His crime makes guilty all his sons; thy merit,   290
Imputed, shall absolve them who renounce
Their own both righteous and unrighteous deeds,
And live in thee transplanted, and from thee
Receive new life. So Man, as is most just,
Shall satisfy for Man, be judged and die,
And dying rise, and, rising, with him raise
His brethren, ransomed with his own dear life.
So Heavenly love shall outdo Hellish hate,
Giving to death, and dying to redeem,
So dearly to redeem what Hellish hate   300
So easily destroyed, and still destroys

In those who, when they may, accept not grace.
Nor shalt thou, by descending to assume
Man's nature, lessen or degrade thine own.
Because thou hast, though throned in highest bliss
Equal to God, and equally enjoying
God-like fruition, quitted all to save
A world from utter loss, and hast been found
By merit more than birthright Son of God,—
Found worthiest to be so by being good,   310
Far more than great or high; because in thee
Love hath abounded more than glory abounds;
Therefore thy humiliation shall exalt
With thee thy manhood also to this throne:
Here shalt thou sit incarnate, here shalt reign
Both God and Man, Son both of God and Man,
Anointed universal King. All power
I give thee; reign for ever, and assume
Thy merits; under thee, as Head Supreme,
Thrones, Princedoms, Powers, Dominions, I reduce: 320
All knees to thee shall bow of them that bide
In Heaven, or Earth, or, under Earth, in Hell.
When thou, attended gloriously from Heaven,
Shalt in the sky appear, and from thee send
The summoning Archangels to proclaim
Thy dread tribunal, forthwith from all winds
The living, and forthwith the cited dead
Of all past ages, to the general doom
Shall hasten; such a peal shall rouse their sleep.
Then, all thy Saints assembled, thou shalt judge   330
Bad men and Angels; they arraigned shall sink
Beneath thy sentence; Hell, her numbers full,
Thenceforth shall be for ever shut. Meanwhile
The World shall burn, and from her ashes spring
New Heaven and Earth, wherein the just shall dwell,
And, after all their tribulations long,
See golden days, fruitful of golden deeds,
With Joy and Love triumphing, and fair Truth.
Then thou thy regal sceptre shalt lay by;
For regal sceptre then no more shall need;   340
God shall be all in all. But all ye Gods,
Adore him who, to compass all this, dies;
Adore the Son, and honor him as me."
   No sooner had the Almighty ceased but—all

The multitude of Angels, with a shout
Loud as from numbers without number, sweet
As from blest voices, uttering joy—Heaven rung
With jubilee, and loud hosannas filled
The eternal regions. Lowly reverent
Towards either throne they bow, and to the ground   350
With solemn adoration down they cast
Their crowns, inwove with amarant and gold,—
Immortal amarant, a flower which once
In Paradise, fast by the Tree of Life,
Began to bloom, but, soon for Man's offence
To Heaven removed where first it grew, there grows
And flowers aloft, shading the Fount of Life,
And where the River of Bliss through midst of Heaven
Rolls o'er Elysian flowers her amber stream!
With these, that never fade, the Spirits elect   360
Bind their resplendent locks, inwreathed with beams.
Now in loose garlands thick thrown off, the bright
Pavement, that like a sea of jasper shone,
Impurpled with celestial roses smiled.
Then, crowned again, their golden harps they took—
Harps ever tuned, that glittering by their side
Like quivers hung; and with preamble sweet
Of charming symphony they introduce
Their sacred song, and waken raptures high:
No voice exempt, no voice but well could join   370
Melodious part; such concord is in Heaven.
     Thee, Father, first they sung, Omnipotent,
Immutable, Immortal, Infinite,
Eternal King; thee, Author of all being,
Fountain of light, thyself invisible
Amidst the glorious brightness where thou sitt'st
Throned inaccessible, but when thou shad'st
The full blaze of thy beams, and through a cloud
Drawn round about thee like a radiant shrine
Dark with excessive bright thy skirts appear,   380
Yet dazzle Heaven, that brightest Seraphim
Approach not, but with both wings veil their eyes.
Thee next they sang, of all creation first,
Begotten Son, Divine Similitude,
In whose conspicuous countenance, without cloud
Made visible, the Almighty Father shines,
Whom else no creature can behold: on thee

Impressed the effulgence of his glory abides;
Transfused on thee his ample Spirit rests.
He Heaven of Heavens, and all the Powers therein,   390
By thee created; and by thee threw down
The aspiring Dominations. Thou that day
Thy Father's dreadful thunder didst not spare,
Nor stop thy flaming chariot-wheels, that shook
Heaven's everlasting frame, while o'er the necks
Thou drov'st of warring Angels disarrayed.
Back from pursuit, thy Powers with loud acclaim
Thee only extolled, Son of thy Father's might,
To execute fierce vengeance on his foes.
Not so on Man: him, through their malice fallen,   400
Father of mercy and grace, thou didst not doom
So strictly, but much more to pity incline.
No sooner did thy dear and only Son
Perceive thee purposed not to doom frail Man
So strictly, but much more to pity inclined,
He, to appease thy wrath, and end the strife
Of mercy and justice in thy face discerned,
Regardless of the bliss wherein he sat
Second to thee, offered himself to die
For Man's offence. O unexampled love!   410
Love nowhere to be found less than Divine!
Hail, Son of God, Saviour of men! Thy name
Shall be the copious matter of my song
Henceforth, and never shall my harp thy praise
Forget, nor from thy Father's praise disjoin!
    Thus they in Heaven, above the Starry Sphere,
Their happy hours in joy and hymning spent.
Meanwhile, upon the firm opacous globe
Of this round World, whose first convex divides
The luminous inferior Orbs, enclosed   420
From Chaos and the inroad of Darkness old,
Satan alighted walks. A globe far off
It seemed; now seems a boundless continent,
Dark, waste, and wild, under the frown of Night
Starless exposed, and ever-threatening storms
Of Chaos blustering round, inclement sky,
Save on that side which from the wall of Heaven,
Though distant far, some small reflection gains
Of glimmering air less vexed with tempest loud.
Here walked the Fiend at large in spacious field.   430

As when a vulture, on Imaus bred,
Whose snowy ridge the roving Tartar bounds,
Dislodging from a region scarce of prey,
To gorge the flesh of lambs or yeanling kids
On hills where flocks are fed, flies toward the springs
Of Ganges or Hydaspes, Indian streams,
But in his way lights on the barren plains
Of Sericana, where Chineses drive
With sails and wind their cany waggons light;
So, on this windy sea of land, the Fiend   440
Walked up and down alone, bent on his prey:
Alone, for other creature in this place,
Living or lifeless, to be found was none;—
None yet; but store hereafter from the Earth
Up hither like aerial vapors flew
Of all things transitory and vain, when sin
With vanity had filled the works of men—
Both all things vain, and all who in vain things
Built their fond hopes of glory or lasting fame,
Or happiness in this or the other life.   450
All who have their reward on earth, the fruits
Of painful superstition and blind zeal,
Naught seeking but the praise of men, here find
Fit retribution, empty as their deeds;
All the unaccomplished works of Nature's hand,
Abortive, monstrous, or unkindly mixed,
Dissolved on Earth, fleet hither, and in vain,
Till final dissolution, wander here—
Not in the neighboring Moon, as some have dreamed:
Those argent fields more likely habitants,   460
Translated Saints, or middle Spirits hold,
Betwixt the angelical and human kind.
Hither, of ill-joined sons and daughters born,
First from the ancient world those Giants came,
With many a vain exploit, though then renowned:
The builders next of Babel on the plain
Of Sennaar, and still with vain design
New Babels, had they wherewithal, would build:
Others came single; he who, to be deemed
A god, leaped fondly into Ætna flames,   470
Empedocles; and he who, to enjoy
Plato's Elysium, leaped into the sea,
Cleombrotus; and many more, too long,

Embryos and idiots, eremites and friars,
White, black, and grey, with all their trumpery.
Here pilgrims roam, that strayed so far to seek
In Golgotha him dead who lives in Heaven;
And they who, to be sure of Paradise,
Dying put on the weeds of Dominic,
Or in Franciscan think to pass disguised.   480
They pass the planets seven, and pass the fixed,
And that crystalline sphere whose balance weighs
The trepidation talked, and that first moved;
And now Saint Peter at Heaven's wicket seems
To wait them with his keys, and now at foot
Of Heaven's ascent they lift their feet, when, lo!
A violent cross wind from either coast
Blows them transverse, ten thousand leagues awry,
Into the devious air. Then might ye see
Cowls, hoods, and habits, with their wearers, tost   490
And fluttered into rags; then reliques, beads,
Indulgences, dispenses, pardons, bulls,
The sport of winds: all these, upwhirled aloft,
Fly o'er the backside of the World far off
Into a Limbo large and broad, since called
The Paradise of Fools; to few unknown
Long after, now unpeopled and untrod.
    All this dark globe the Fiend found as he passed;
And long he wandered, till at last a gleam
Of dawning light turned thitherward in haste   500
His travelled steps. Far distant he descries,
Ascending by degrees magnificent
Up to the wall of Heaven, a structure high;
At top whereof, but far more rich, appeared
The work as of a kingly palace-gate,
With frontispiece of diamond and gold
Embellished; thick with sparkling orient gems
The portal shone, inimitable on Earth
By model, or by shading pencil drawn.
The stairs were such as whereon Jacob saw   510
Angels ascending and descending, bands
Of guardians bright, when he from Esau fled
To Padan-Aram, in the field of Luz
Dreaming by night under the open sky,
And waking cried, *This is the gate of Heaven*.
Each stair mysteriously was meant, nor stood

There always, but drawn up to Heaven sometimes
Viewless; and underneath a bright sea flowed
Of jasper, or of liquid pearl, whereon
Who after came from Earth sailing arrived   520
Wafted by Angels, or flew o'er the lake
Rapt in a chariot drawn by fiery steeds.
The stairs were then let down, whether to dare
The Fiend by easy ascent, or aggravate
His sad exclusion from the doors of bliss:
Direct against which opened from beneath,
Just o'er the blissful seat of Paradise,
A passage down to the Earth—a passage wide;
Wider by far than that of after-times
Over Mount Sion, and, though that were large,   530
Over the Promised Land to God so dear,
By which, to visit oft those happy tribes,
On high behests his Angels to and fro
Passed frequent, and his eye with choice regard
From Paneas, the fount of Jordan's flood,
To Beërsaba, where the Holy Land
Borders on Egypt and the Arabian shore.
So wide the opening seemed, where bounds were set
To darkness, such as bound the ocean wave.
Satan from hence, now on the lower stair,   540
That scaled by steps of gold to Heaven-gate,
Looks down with wonder at the sudden view
Of all this world at once. As when a scout,
Through dark and desert ways with peril gone
All night, at last by break of cheerful dawn
Obtains the brow of some high-climbing hill,
Which to his eye discovers unaware
The goodly prospect of some foreign land
First seen, or some renowned metropolis
With glistering spires and pinnacles adorned,   550
Which now the rising sun gilds with his beams;
Such wonder seized, though after Heaven seen,
The Spirit malign, but much more envy seized,
At sight of all this World beheld so fair.
Round he surveys (and well might, where he stood
So high above the circling canopy
Of Night's extended shade) from eastern point
Of Libra to the fleecy star that bears
Andromeda far off Atlantic seas

Beyond the horizon; then from pole to pole   560
He views in breadth—and, without longer pause,
Down right into the World's first region throws
His flight precipitant, and winds with ease
Through the pure marble air his oblique way
Amongst innumerable stars, that shone
Stars distant, but nigh-hand seemed other worlds.
Or other worlds they seemed, or happy isles,
Like those Hesperian Gardens famed of old,
Fortunate fields, and groves, and flowery vales;
Thrice happy isles! But who dwelt happy there   570
He staid not to inquire: above them all
The golden Sun, in splendor likest Heaven,
Allured his eye. Thither his course he bends,
Through the calm firmament (but up or down,
By centre or eccentric, hard to tell,
Or longitude) where the great luminary,
Aloof the vulgar constellations thick,
That from his lordly eye keep distance due,
Dispenses light from far. They, as they move
Their starry dance in numbers that compute   580
Days, months, and years, towards his all-cheering lamp
Turn swift their various motions, or are turned
By his magnetic beam, that gently warms
The Universe, and to each inward part
With gentle penetration, though unseen,
Shoots invisible virtue even to the Deep;
So wondrously was set his station bright.
There lands the Fiend, a spot like which perhaps
Astronomer in the Sun's lucent orb
Through his glazed optic tube yet never saw.   590
The place he found beyond expression bright,
Compared with aught on Earth, metal or stone—
Not all parts like, but all alike informed
With radiant light, as glowing iron with fire.
If metal, part seemed gold, part silver clear;
If stone, carbuncle most or chrysolite,
Ruby or topaz, to the twelve that shone
In Aaron's breast-plate, and a stone besides,
Imagined rather oft than elsewhere seen—
That stone, or like to that, which here below   600
Philosophers in vain so long have sought;
In vain, though by their powerful art they bind

Volatile Hermes, and call up unbound
In various shapes old Proteus from the sea,
Drained through a limbec to his native form.
What wonder then if fields and regions here
Breathe forth elixir pure, and rivers run
Potable gold, when, with one virtuous touch,
The arch-chemic Sun, so far from us remote,
Produces, with terrestrial humor mixed,   610
Here in the dark so many precious things
Of color glorious and effect so rare?
Here matter new to gaze the Devil met
Undazzled. Far and wide his eye commands;
For sight no obstacle found here, nor shade,
But all sunshine, as when his beams at noon
Culminate from the equator, as they now
Shot upward still direct, whence no way round
Shadow from body opaque can fall; and the air,
Nowhere so clear, sharpened his visual ray   620
To objects distant far, whereby he soon
Saw within ken a glorious Angel stand,
The same whom John saw also in the Sun.
His back was turned, but not his brightness hid;
Of beaming sunny rays a golden tiar
Circled his head, nor less his locks behind
Illustrious on his shoulders fledge with wings
Lay waving round: on some great charge employed
He seemed, or fixed in cogitation deep.
Glad was the Spirit impure, as now in hope   630
To find who might direct his wandering flight
To Paradise, the happy seat of Man,
His journey's end, and our beginning woe.
But first he casts to change his proper shape,
Which else might work him danger or delay:
And now a stripling Cherub he appears,
Not of the prime, yet such as in his face
Youth smiled celestial, and to every limb
Suitable grace diffused; so well he feigned.
Under a coronet his flowing hair   640
In curls on either cheek played; wings he wore
Of many a colored plume sprinkled with gold,
His habit fit for speed succinct, and held
Before his decent steps a silver wand.
He drew not nigh unheard; the Angel bright,

Ere he drew nigh, his radiant visage turned,
Admonished by his ear, and straight was known
The Archangel Uriel—one of the seven
Who in God's presence, nearest to his throne,
Stand ready at command, and are his eyes   650
That run through all the Heavens, or down to the Earth
Bear his swift errands over moist and dry,
O'er sea and land. Him Satan thus accosts:—
    "Uriel! for thou of those seven Spirits that stand
In sight of God's high throne, gloriously bright,
The first art wont his great authentic will
Interpreter through highest Heaven to bring,
Where all his Sons thy embassy attend,
And here art likeliest by supreme decree
Like honor to obtain, and as his eye   660
To visit oft this new Creation round—
Unspeakable desire to see and know
All these his wondrous works, but chiefly Man,
His chief delight and favor, him for whom
All these his works so wondrous he ordained,
Hath brought me from the quires of Cherubim
Alone thus wandering. Brightest Seraph, tell
In which of all these shining orbs hath Man
His fixèd seat—or fixèd seat hath none,
But all these shining orbs his choice to dwell—   670
That I may find him, and with secret gaze
Or open admiration him behold
On whom the great Creator hath bestowed
Worlds, and on whom hath all these graces poured;
That both in him and all things, as is meet,
The Universal Maker we may praise;
Who justly hath driven out his rebel foes
To deepest Hell, and, to repair that loss,
Created this new happy race of Men
To serve him better: Wise are all his ways!"   680
    So spake the false dissembler unperceived;
For neither man nor angel can discern
Hypocrisy—the only evil that walks
Invisible, except to God alone,
By his permissive will, through Heaven and Earth;
And oft, though Wisdom wake, Suspicion sleeps
At Wisdom's gate, and to Simplicity
Resigns her charge, while Goodness thinks no ill

Where no ill seems: which now for once beguiled
Uriel, though Regent of the Sun, and held   690
The sharpest-sighted Spirit of all in Heaven;
Who to the fraudulent impostor foul,
In his uprightness, answer thus returned:—
   "Fair Angel, thy desire, which tends to know
The works of God, thereby to glorify
The great Work-master, leads to no excess
That reaches blame, but rather merits praise
The more it seems excess, that led thee hither
From thy empyreal mansion thus alone,
To witness with thine eyes what some perhaps,   700
Contented with report, hear only in Heaven:
For wonderful indeed are all his works,
Pleasant to know, and worthiest to be all
Had in remembrance always with delight!
But what created mind can comprehend
Their number, or the wisdom infinite
That brought them forth, but hid their causes deep?
I saw when, at his word, the formless mass,
This World's material mould, came to a heap:
Confusion heard his voice, and wild Uproar   710
Stood ruled, stood vast Infinitude confined;
Till, at his second bidding, Darkness fled,
Light shone, and order from disorder sprung.
Swift to their several quarters hasted then
The cumbrous elements—Earth, Flood, Air, Fire;
And this ethereal quintessence of Heaven
Flew upward, spirited with various forms,
That rolled orbicular, and turned to stars
Numberless, as thou seest, and how they move:
Each had his place appointed, each his course;   720
The rest in circuit walls this Universe.
Look downward on that globe, whose hither side
With light from hence, though but reflected, shines:
That place is Earth, the seat of Man; that light
His day, which else, as the other hemisphere,
Night would invade; but there the neighboring Moon
(So call that opposite fair star) her aid
Timely interposes, and, her monthly round
Still ending, still renewing, through mid-heaven,
With borrowed light her countenance triform   730
Hence fills and empties, to enlighten the Earth,

And in her pale dominion checks the night.
That spot to which I point is Paradise,
Adam's abode; those lofty shades his bower.
Thy way thou canst not miss; me mine requires."
    Thus said, he turned; and Satan, bowing low,
As to superior Spirits is wont in Heaven,
Where honor due and reverence none neglects,
Took leave, and towards the coast of Earth beneath,
Down from the ecliptic, sped with hoped success,   740
Throws his steep flight in many an aery wheel,
Nor staid till on Niphates' top he lights.

BOOK IV

THE ARGUMENT

SATAN, now in prospect of Eden, and nigh the place where he must now attempt the bold enterprise which he undertook alone against God and Man, falls into many doubts with himself, and many passions—fear, envy, and despair; but at length confirms himself in evil; journeys on to Paradise, whose outward prospect and situation is described; overleaps the bounds; sits, in the shape of a cormorant, on the Tree of Life, as highest in the Garden, to look about him. The Garden described; Satan's first sight of Adam and Eve; his wonder at their excellent form and happy state, but with resolution to work their fall; overhears their discourse; thence gathers that the Tree of Knowledge was forbidden them to eat of under penalty of death, and thereon intends to found his temptation by seducing them to transgress; then leaves them a while, to know further of their state by some other means. Meanwhile Uriel, descending on a sunbeam, warns Gabriel, who had in charge the gate of Paradise, that some evil Spirit had escaped the Deep, and passed at noon by his Sphere, in the shape of a good Angel, down to Paradise, discovered after by his furious gestures in the mount. Gabriel promises to find him ere morning. Night coming on, Adam and Eve discourse of going to their rest: their bower described; their evening worship. Gabriel, drawing forth his bands of night-watch to walk the rounds of Paradise, appoints two strong Angels to Adam's bower, lest the evil Spirit should be there doing some harm to Adam or Eve sleeping: there they find him at the ear of Eve, tempting her in a dream, and bring him, though unwilling, to Gabriel; by whom questioned, he scornfully answers; prepares resistance; but, hindered by a sign from Heaven, flies out of Paradise.

> O for that warning voice, which he who saw
> The Apocalypse, heard cry in Heaven aloud,
> Then when the Dragon, put to second rout,

Came furious down to be revenged on men,
Woe to the inhabitants on Earth! that now,
While time was, our first parents had been warned
The coming of their secret foe, and scaped,
Haply so scaped, his mortal snare! For now
Satan, now first inflamed with rage, came down,
The tempter, ere the accuser, of mankind, 10
To wreak on innocent frail Man his loss
Of that first battle, and his flight to Hell.
Yet not rejoicing in his speed, though bold
Far off and fearless, nor with cause to boast,
Begins his dire attempt; which, nigh the birth
Now rolling, boils in his tumultuous breast,
And like a devilish engine back recoils
Upon himself. Horror and doubt distract
His troubled thoughts, and from the bottom stir
The hell within him; for within him Hell 20
He brings, and round about him, nor from Hell
One step, no more than from himself, can fly
By change of place. Now conscience wakes despair
That slumbered; wakes the bitter memory
Of what he was, what is, and what must be
Worse; of worse deeds worse sufferings must ensue!
Sometimes towards Eden, which now in his view
Lay pleasant, his grieved look he fixes sad;
Sometimes towards Heaven and the full-blazing Sun,
Which now sat high in his meridian tower: 30
Then, much revolving, thus in sighs began:—
   "O thou that, with surpassing glory crowned,
Look'st from thy sole dominion like the god
Of this new World—at whose sight all the stars
Hide their diminished heads—to thee I call,
But with no friendly voice, and add thy name,
O Sun, to tell thee how I hate thy beams,
That bring to my remembrance from what state
I fell, how glorious once above thy sphere,
Till pride and worse ambition threw me down, 40
Warring in Heaven against Heaven's matchless King!
Ah, wherefore? He deserved no such return
From me, whom he created what I was
In that bright eminence, and with his good
Upbraided none; nor was his service hard.
What could be less than to afford him praise,

The easiest recompence, and pay him thanks,
How due? Yet all his good proved ill in me,
And wrought but malice. Lifted up so high,
I sdained subjection, and thought one step higher   50
Would set me highest, and in a moment quit
The debt immense of endless gratitude,
So burdensome, still paying, still to owe;
Forgetful what from him I still received;
And understood not that a grateful mind
By owing owes not, but still pays, at once
Indebted and discharged—what burden then?
Oh, had his powerful destiny ordained
Me some inferior Angel, I had stood
Then happy; no unbounded hope had raised   60
Ambition. Yet why not? Some other Power
As great might have aspired, and me, though mean,
Drawn to his part. But other Powers as great
Fell not, but stand unshaken, from within
Or from without to all temptations armed!
Hadst thou the same free will and power to stand?
Thou hadst. Whom hast thou then, or what, to accuse,
But Heaven's free love dealt equally to all?
Be then his love accursed, since, love or hate,
To me alike it deals eternal woe.   70
Nay, cursed be thou; since against his thy will
Chose freely what it now so justly rues.
Me miserable! which way shall I fly
Infinite wrath and infinite despair?
Which way I fly is Hell; myself am Hell;
And, in the lowest deep, a lower deep
Still threatening to devour me opens wide,
To which the Hell I suffer seems a Heaven.
O, then, at last relent! Is there no place
Left for repentance, none for pardon left?   80
None left but by submission; and that word
Disdain forbids me, and my dread of shame
Among the Spirits beneath, whom I seduced
With other promises and other vaunts
Than to submit, boasting I could subdue
The Omnipotent. Ay me! they little know
How dearly I abide that boast so vain,
Under what torments inwardly I groan,
While they adore me on the throne of Hell.

With diadem and sceptre high advanced,   90
The lower still I fall, only supreme
In misery: such joy ambition finds!
But say I could repent, and could obtain,
By act of grace, my former state; how soon
Would highth recal high thoughts, how soon unsay
What feigned submission swore! Ease would recant
Vows made in pain, as violent and void
(For never can true reconcilement grow
Where wounds of deadly hate have pierced so deep);
Which would but lead me to a worse relapse   100
And heavier fall: so should I purchase dear
Short intermission, bought with double smart.
This knows my Punisher; therefore as far
From granting he, as I from begging, peace.
All hope excluded thus, behold, instead
Of us, outcast, exiled, his new delight,
Mankind, created, and for him this World!
So farewell hope, and, with hope, farewell fear,
Farewell remorse! All good to me is lost;
Evil, be thou my Good: by thee at least   110
Divided empire with Heaven's King I hold,
By thee, and more than half perhaps will reign;
As Man ere long, and this new World, shall know."
     Thus while he spake, each passion dimmed his face,
Thrice changed with pale—ire, envy, and despair;
Which marred his borrowed visage, and betrayed
Him counterfeit, if any eye beheld:
For Heavenly minds from such distempers foul
Are ever clear. Whereof he soon aware
Each perturbation smoothed with outward calm,   120
Artificer of fraud; and was the first
That practised falsehood under saintly show,
Deep malice to conceal, couched with revenge:
Yet not enough had practised to deceive
Uriel, once warned; whose eye pursued him down
The way he went, and on the Assyrian mount
Saw him disfigured, more than could befall
Spirit of happy sort: his gestures fierce
He marked and mad demeanor, then alone,
As he supposed, all unobserved, unseen.   130
     So on he fares, and to the border comes
Of Eden, where delicious Paradise,

Now nearer, crowns with her enclosure green,
As with a rural mound, the champain head
Of a steep wilderness, whose hairy sides
With thicket overgrown, grotesque and wild,
Access denied; and overhead up-grew
Insuperable highth of loftiest shade,
Cedar, and pine, and fir, and branching palm,
A sylvan scene, and, as the ranks ascend,   140
Shade above shade, a woody theatre
Of stateliest view. Yet higher than their tops
The verdurous wall of Paradise up-sprung;
Which to our general sire gave prospect large
Into his nether empire neighboring round.
And higher than that wall a circling row
Of goodliest trees, loaden with fairest fruit,
Blossoms and fruits at once of golden hue,
Appeared, with gay enamelled colors mixed;
On which the sun more glad impressed his beams   150
Than in fair evening cloud, or humid bow,
When God hath showered the earth: so lovely seemed
That landskip. And of pure now purer air
Meets his approach, and to the heart inspires
Vernal delight and joy, able to drive
All sadness but despair. Now gentle gales,
Fanning their odoriferous wings, dispense
Native perfumes, and whisper whence they stole
Those balmy spoils. As, when to them who sail
Beyond the Cape of Hope, and now are past   160
Mozambic, off at sea north-east winds blow
Sabean odors from the spicy shore
Of Araby the Blest, with such delay
Well pleased they slack their course, and many a league
Cheered with the grateful smell old Ocean smiles;
So entertained those odorous sweets the Fiend
Who came their bane, though with them better pleased
Than Asmodëus with the fishy fume
That drove him, though enamored, from the spouse
Of Tobit's son, and with a vengeance sent   170
From Media post to Egypt, there fast bound.
    Now to the ascent of that steep savage hill
Satan had journeyed on, pensive and slow;
But further way found none; so thick entwined,
As one continued brake, the undergrowth

Of shrubs and tangling bushes had perplexed
All path of man or beast that passed that way.
One gate there only was, and that looked east
On the other side. Which when the Arch-Felon saw,
Due entrance he disdained, and, in contempt,   180
At one slight bound high overleaped all bound
Of hill or highest wall, and sheer within
Lights on his feet. As when a prowling wolf,
Whom hunger drives to seek new haunt for prey,
Watching where shepherds pen their flocks at eve,
In hurdled cotes amid the field secure,
Leaps o'er the fence with ease into the fold;
Or as a thief, bent to unhoard the cash
Of some rich burgher, whose substantial doors,
Cross-barred and bolted fast, fear no assault,   190
In at the window climbs, or o'er the tiles;
So clomb this first grand Thief into God's fold:
So since into his Church lewd hirelings climb.
Thence up he flew, and on the Tree of Life,
The middle tree and highest there that grew,
Sat like a cormorant; yet not true life
Thereby regained, but sat devising death
To them who lived; nor on the virtue thought
Of that life-giving plant, but only used
For prospect what, well used, had been the pledge   200
Of immortality. So little knows
Any, but God alone, to value right
The good before him, but perverts best things
To worst abuse, or to their meanest use.
Beneath him, with new wonder, now he views,
To all delight of human sense exposed,
In narrow room Nature's whole wealth; yea, more!—
A Heaven on Earth; for blissful Paradise
Of God the garden was, by him in the east
Of Eden planted. Eden stretched her line   210
From Auran eastward to the royal towers
Of great Seleucia, built by Grecian kings,
Or where the sons of Eden long before
Dwelt in Telassar. In this pleasant soil
His far more pleasant garden God ordained.
Out of the fertile ground he caused to grow
All trees of noblest kind for sight, smell, taste;
And all amid them stood the Tree of Life,

High eminent, blooming ambrosial fruit
Of vegetable gold; and next to life,   220
Our death, the Tree of Knowledge, grew fast by—
Knowledge of good, bought dear by knowing ill.
Southward through Eden went a river large,
Nor changed his course, but through the shaggy hill
Passed underneath ingulfed; for God had thrown
That mountain, as his garden-mould, high raised
Upon the rapid current, which, through veins
Of porous earth with kindly thirst up-drawn,
Rose a fresh fountain, and with many a rill
Watered the garden; thence united fell   230
Down the steep glade, and met the nether flood,
Which from his darksome passage now appears,
And now, divided into four main streams,
Runs diverse, wandering many a famous realm
And country whereof here needs no account;
But rather to tell how, if Art could tell
How, from that sapphire fount the crispèd brooks,
Rolling on orient pearl and sands of gold,
With mazy error under pendant shades
Ran nectar, visiting each plant, and fed   240
Flowers worthy of Paradise, which not nice Art
In beds and curious knots, but Nature boon
Poured forth profuse on hill, and dale, and plain,
Both where the morning sun first warmly smote
The open field, and where the unpierced shade
Imbrowned the noontide bowers. Thus was this place,
A happy rural seat of various view:
Groves whose rich trees wept odorous gums and balm;
Others whose fruit, burnished with golden rind,
Hung amiable—Hesperian fables true,   250
If true, here only—and of delicious taste.
Betwixt them lawns, or level downs, and flocks
Grazing the tender herb, were interposed,
Or palmy hillock; or the flowery lap
Of some irriguous valley spread her store,
Flowers of all hue, and without thorn the rose.
Another side, umbrageous grots and caves
Of cool recess, o'er which the mantling vine
Lays forth her purple grape, and gently creeps
Luxuriant; meanwhile murmuring waters fall   260
Down the slope hills dispersed, or in a lake,

That to the fringèd bank with myrtle crowned
Her crystal mirror holds, unite their streams.
The birds their quire apply; airs, vernal airs,
Breathing the smell of field and grove, attune
The trembling leaves, while universal Pan,
Knit with the Graces and the Hours in dance,
Led on the eternal Spring. Not that fair field
Of Enna, where Proserpin gathering flowers,
Herself a fairer flower, by gloomy Dis   270
Was gathered—which cost Ceres all that pain
To seek her through the world—nor that sweet grove
Of Daphne, by Orontes, and the inspired
Castalian spring, might with this Paradise
Of Eden strive; nor that Nyseian isle,
Girt with the river Triton, where old Cham,
Whom Gentiles Ammon call and Libyan Jove,
Hid Amalthea, and her florid son,
Young Bacchus, from his stepdame Rhea's eye;
Nor, where Abassin kings their issue guard,   280
Mount Amara (though this by some supposed
True Paradise) under the Ethiop line
By Nilus' head, enclosed with shining rock,
A whole day's journey high, but wide remote
From this Assyrian garden, where the Fiend
Saw undelighted all delight, all kind
Of living creatures, new to sight and strange.
Two of far nobler shape, erect and tall,
God-like erect, with native honor clad
In naked majesty, seemed lords of all,   290
And worthy seemed; for in their looks divine
The image of their glorious Maker shone,
Truth, wisdom, sanctitude severe and pure—
Severe, but in true filial freedom placed,
Whence true authority in men: though both
Not equal, as their sex not equal seemed;
For contemplation he and valor formed,
For softness she and sweet attractive grace;
He for God only, she for God in him.
His fair large front and eye sublime declared   300
Absolute rule; and hyacinthine locks
Round from his parted forelock manly hung
Clustering, but not beneath his shoulders broad:
She, as a veil down to the slender waist,

Her unadornèd golden tresses wore
Dishevelled, but in wanton ringlets waved
As the vine curls her tendrils—which implied
Subjection, but required with gentle sway,
And by her yielded, by him best received
Yielded, with coy submission, modest pride,   310
And sweet, reluctant, amorous delay.
Nor those mysterious parts were then concealed;
Then was not guilty shame. Dishonest shame
Of Nature's works, honor dishonorable,
Sin-bred, how have ye troubled all mankind
With shows instead, mere shows of seeming pure,
And banished from man's life his happiest life,
Simplicity and spotless innocence!
So passed they naked on, nor shunned the sight
Of God or Angel; for they thought no ill: 320
So hand in hand they passed, the loveliest pair
That ever since in love's embraces met—
Adam the goodliest man of men since born
His sons; the fairest of her daughters Eve.
Under a tuft of shade that on a green
Stood whispering soft, by a fresh fountain-side,
They sat them down; and, after no more toil
Of their sweet gardening labor than sufficed
To recommend cool Zephyr, and make ease
More easy, wholesome thirst and appetite   330
More grateful, to their supper-fruits they fell—
Nectarine fruits, which the compliant boughs
Yielded them, sidelong as they sat recline
On the soft downy bank damasked with flowers.
The savory pulp they chew, and in the rind,
Still as they thirsted, scoop the brimming stream;
Nor gentle purpose, nor endearing smiles
Wanted, nor youthful dalliance, as beseems
Fair couple linked in happy nuptial league,
Alone as they. About them frisking played   340
All beasts of the earth, since wild, and of all chase
In wood or wilderness, forest or den.
Sporting the lion ramped, and in his paw
Dandled the kid; bears, tigers, ounces, pards,
Gambolled before them; the unwieldy elephant,
To make them mirth, used all his might, and wreathed
His lithe proboscis; close the serpent sly,

Insinuating, wove with Gordian twine
His braided train, and of his fatal guile
Gave proof unheeded. Others on the grass   350
Couched, and now filled with pasture, gazing sat,
Or bedward ruminating; for the sun,
Declined, was hastening now with prone career
To the Ocean Isles, and in the ascending scale
Of Heaven the stars that usher evening rose:
When Satan, still in gaze as first he stood,
Scarce thus at length failed speech recovered sad:—
    "O Hell! what do mine eyes with grief behold?
Into our room of bliss thus high advanced
Creatures of other mould—Earth-born perhaps,   360
Not Spirits, yet to Heavenly Spirits bright
Little inferior—whom my thoughts pursue
With wonder, and could love; so lively shines
In them divine resemblance, and such grace
The hand that formed them on their shape hath poured.
Ah! gentle pair, ye little think how nigh
Your change approaches, when all these delights
Will vanish, and deliver ye to woe—
More woe, the more your taste is now of joy:
Happy, but for so happy ill secured   370
Long to continue, and this high seat, your Heaven,
Ill fenced for Heaven to keep out such a foe
As now is entered; yet no purposed foe
To you, whom I could pity thus forlorn,
Though I unpitied. League with you I seek,
And mutual amity, so strait, so close,
That I with you must dwell, or you with me,
Henceforth. My dwelling, haply, may not please,
Like this fair Paradise, your sense; yet such
Accept your Maker's work; he gave it me,   380
Which I as freely give. Hell shall unfold,
To entertain you two, her widest gates,
And send forth all her kings; there will be room,
Not like these narrow limits, to receive
Your numerous offspring; if no better place,
Thank him who puts me, loath, to this revenge
On you, who wrong me not, for him who wronged.
And, should I at your harmless innocence
Melt, as I do, yet public reason just—
Honor and empire with revenge enlarged   390

By conquering this new World—compels me now
To do what else, though damned, I should abhor."
    So spake the Fiend, and with necessity,
The tyrant's plea, excused his devilish deeds.
Then from his lofty stand on that high tree
Down he alights among the sportful herd
Of those four-footed kinds, himself now one,
Now other, as their shape served best his end
Nearer to view his prey, and, unespied,
To mark what of their state he more might learn   400
By word or action marked. About them round
A lion now he stalks with fiery glare;
Then as a tiger, who by chance hath spied
In some purlieu two gentle fawns at play,
Straight crouches close; then, rising, changes oft
His couchant watch, as one who chose his ground,
Whence rushing he might surest seize them both
Griped in each paw: when Adam, first of men,
To first of women, Eve, thus moving speech,
Turned him all ear to hear new utterance flow:—   410
    "Sole partner and sole part of all these joys,
Dearer thyself than all, needs must the Power
That makes us, and for us this ample World,
Be infinitely good, and of his good
As liberal and free as infinite;
That raised us from the dust, and placed us here
In all this happiness, who at his hand
Have nothing merited, nor can perform
Aught whereof he hath need; he who requires
From us no other service than to keep   420
This one, this easy charge—of all the trees
In Paradise that bear delicious fruit
So various, not to taste that only Tree
Of Knowledge, planted by the Tree of Life;
So near grows Death to Life, whate'er Death is—
Some dreadful thing no doubt; for well thou know'st
God hath pronounced it Death to taste that Tree:
The only sign of our obedience left
Among so many signs of power and rule
Conferred upon us, and dominion given   430
Over all other creatures that possess
Earth, Air, and Sea. Then let us not think hard
One easy prohibition, who enjoy

Free leave so large to all things else, and choice
Unlimited of manifold delights;
But let us ever praise him, and extol
His bounty, following our delightful task,
To prune these growing plants, and tend these flowers;
Which, were it toilsome, yet with thee were sweet."
　　To whom thus Eve replied:—"O thou for whom   440
And from whom I was formed flesh of thy flesh,
And without whom am to no end, my guide
And head! what thou hast said is just and right.
For we to him, indeed, all praises owe,
And daily thanks—I chiefly, who enjoy
So far the happier lot, enjoying thee
Pre-eminent by so much odds, while thou
Like consort to thyself canst nowhere find.
That day I oft remember, when from sleep
I first awaked, and found myself reposed,   450
Under a shade, on flowers, much wondering where
And what I was, whence thither brought, and how.
Not distant far from thence a murmuring sound
Of waters issued from a cave, and spread
Into a liquid plain; then stood unmoved,
Pure as the expanse of Heaven. I thither went
With unexperienced thought, and laid me down
On the green bank, to look into the clear
Smooth lake, that to me seemed another sky.
As I bent down to look, just opposite   460
A shape within the watery gleam appeared,
Bending to look on me. I started back,
It started back; but pleased I soon returned,
Pleased it returned as soon with answering looks
Of sympathy and love. There I had fixed
Mine eyes till now, and pined with vain desire,
Had not a voice thus warned me: 'What thou seest,
What there thou seest, fair creature, is thyself;
With thee it came and goes: but follow me,
And I will bring thee where no shadow stays   470
Thy coming, and thy soft embraces—he
Whose image thou art, him thou shalt enjoy
Inseparably thine; to him shalt bear
Multitudes like thyself, and thence be called
Mother of human race.' What could I do,
But follow straight, invisibly thus led?

Till I espied thee, fair, indeed, and tall,
Under a platane; yet methought less fair,
Less winning soft, less amiably mild,
Than that smooth watery image. Back I turned;   480
Thou, following, cried'st aloud, 'Return, fair Eve;
Whom fliest thou? Whom thou fliest, of him thou art,
His flesh, his bone; to give thee being I lent
Out of my side to thee, nearest my heart,
Substantial life, to have thee by my side
Henceforth an individual solace dear:
Part of my soul I seek thee, and thee claim
My other half.' With that thy gentle hand
Seized mine: I yielded, and from that time see
How beauty is excelled by manly grace   490
And wisdom, which alone is truly fair."
   So spake our general mother, and, with eyes
Of conjugal attraction unreproved,
And meek surrender, half-embracing leaned
On our first father; half her swelling breast
Naked met his, under the flowing gold
Of her loose tresses hid. He, in delight
Both of her beauty and submissive charms,
Smiled with superior love, as Jupiter
On Juno smiles when he impregns the clouds   500
That shed May flowers, and pressed her matron lip
With kisses pure. Aside the Devil turned
For envy; yet with jealous leer malign
Eyed them askance, and to himself thus plained:—
   "Sight hateful, sight tormenting! Thus these two,
Imparadised in one another's arms,
The happier Eden, shall enjoy their fill
Of bliss on bliss; while I to Hell am thrust,
Where neither joy nor love, but fierce desire,
Among our other torments not the least,   510
Still unfulfilled, with pain of longing pines!
Yet let me not forget what I have gained
From their own mouths. All is not theirs, it seems;
One fatal tree there stands, of Knowledge called,
Forbidden them to taste. Knowledge forbidden?
Suspicious, reasonless! Why should their Lord
Envy them that? Can it be sin to know?
Can it be death? And do they only stand
By ignorance? Is that their happy state,

The proof of their obedience and their faith? 520
O fair foundation laid whereon to build
Their ruin! Hence I will excite their minds
With more desire to know, and to reject
Envious commands, invented with design
To keep them low, whom knowledge might exalt
Equal with gods. Aspiring to be such,
They taste and die: what likelier can ensue?
But first with narrow search I must walk round
This garden, and no corner leave unspied;
A chance but chance may lead where I may meet 530
Some wandering Spirit of Heaven, by fountain-side,
Or in thick shade retired, from him to draw
What further would be learned. Live while ye may,
Yet happy pair; enjoy, till I return,
Short pleasures; for long woes are to succeed!"
   So saying, his proud step he scornful turned,
But with sly circumspection, and began
Through wood, through waste, o'er hill, o'er dale, his roam.
Meanwhile in utmost longitude, where Heaven
With Earth and Ocean meets, the setting Sun 540
Slowly descended, and with right aspect
Against the eastern gate of Paradise
Levelled his evening rays. It was a rock
Of alabaster, piled up to the clouds,
Conspicuous far, winding with one ascent
Accessible from Earth, one entrance high;
The rest was craggy cliff, that overhung
Still as it rose, impossible to climb.
Betwixt these rocky pillars Gabriel sat,
Chief of the angelic guards, awaiting night; 550
About him exercised heroic games
The unarmed youth of Heaven; but nigh at hand
Celestial armory, shields, helms, and spears,
Hung high, with diamond flaming and with gold.
Thither came Uriel, gliding through the even
On a sunbeam, swift as a shooting star
In autumn thwarts the night, when vapors fired
Impress the air, and shows the mariner
From what point of his compass to beware
Impetuous winds. He thus began in haste:— 560
   "Gabriel, to thee thy course by lot hath given
Charge and strict watch that to this happy place

No evil thing approach or enter in.
This day at highth of noon came to my sphere
A Spirit, zealous, as he seemed, to know
More of the Almighty's works, and chiefly Man,
God's latest image. I described his way
Bent all on speed, and marked his aery gait,
But in the mount that lies from Eden north,
Where he first lighted, soon discerned his looks   570
Alien from Heaven, with passions foul obscured.
Mine eye pursued him still, but under shade
Lost sight of him. One of the banished crew,
I fear, hath ventured from the Deep, to raise
New troubles; him thy care must be to find."
    To whom the winged Warrior thus returned:—
"Uriel, no wonder if thy perfect sight,
Amid the Sun's bright circle where thou sitt'st,
See far and wide. In at this gate none pass
The vigilance here placed, but such as come   580
Well known from Heaven; and since meridian hour
No creature thence. If Spirit of other sort,
So minded, have o'erleaped these earthly bounds
On purpose, hard thou know'st it to exclude
Spiritual substance with corporeal bar.
But, if within the circuit of these walks,
In whatsoever shape, he lurk of whom
Thou tell'st, by morrow dawning I shall know."
    So promised he; and Uriel to his charge
Returned on that bright beam, whose point now raised   590
Bore him slope downward to the Sun, now fallen
Beneath the Azores; whether the Prime Orb,
Incredible how swift, had thither rolled
Diurnal, or this less volúbil Earth,
By shorter flight to the east, had left him there
Arraying with reflected purple and gold
The clouds that on his western throne attend.
    Now came still Evening on, and Twilight gray
Had in her sober livery all things clad;
Silence accompanied; for beast and bird,   600
They to their grassy couch, these to their nests
Were slunk, all but the wakeful nightingale.
She all night long her amorous descant sung:
Silence was pleased. Now glowed the firmament
With living sapphires; Hesperus, that led

The starry host, rode brightest, till the Moon,
Rising in clouded majesty, at length
Apparent queen, unveiled her peerless light,
And o'er the dark her silver mantle threw;
When Adam thus to Eve:—"Fair consort, the hour   610
Of night, and all things now retired to rest,
Mind us of like repose; since God hath set
Labor and rest, as day and night, to men
Successive, and the timely dew of sleep,
Now falling with soft slumberous weight, inclines
Our eye-lids. Other creatures all day long
Rove idle, unemployed, and less need rest;
Man hath his daily work of body or mind
Appointed, which declares his dignity,
And the regard of Heaven on all his ways;   620
While other animals unactive range,
And of their doings God takes no account.
To-morrow, ere fresh morning streak the east
With first approach of light, we must be risen,
And at our pleasant labor, to reform
Yon flowery arbors, yonder alleys green,
Our walk at noon, with branches overgrown,
That mock our scant manuring, and require
More hands than ours to lop their wanton growth.
Those blossoms also, and those dropping gums,   630
That lie bestrewn, unsightly and unsmooth,
Ask riddance, if we mean to tread with ease.
Meanwhile, as Nature wills, Night bids us rest."
    To whom thus Eve, with perfect beauty adorned:—
"My author and disposer, what thou bidd'st
Unargued I obey. So God ordains:
God is thy law, thou mine: to know no more
Is woman's happiest knowledge, and her praise.
With thee conversing, I forget all time,
All seasons, and their change; all please alike.   640
Sweet is the breath of Morn, her rising sweet,
With charm of earliest birds: pleasant the Sun,
When first on this delightful land he spreads
His orient beams, on herb, tree, fruit, and flower,
Glistering with dew, fragrant the fertile Earth
After soft showers; and sweet the coming-on
Of grateful Evening mild; then silent Night,
With this her solemn bird, and this fair Moon,

And these the gems of Heaven, her starry train;
But neither breath of Morn, when she ascends 650
With charm of earliest birds; nor rising Sun
On this delightful land; nor herb, fruit, flower,
Glistering with dew; nor fragrance after showers;
Nor grateful Evening mild; nor silent Night,
With this her solemn bird; nor walk by moon,
Or glittering star-light, without thee is sweet.
But wherefore all night long shine these? for whom
This glorious sight, when sleep hath shut all eyes?"
    To whom our general ancestor replied:—
"Daughter of God and Man, accomplished Eve, 660
Those have their course to finish round the Earth
By morrow evening, and from land to land
In order, though to nations yet unborn,
Ministering light prepared, they set and rise;
Lest total Darkness should by night regain
Her old possession, and extinguish life
In nature and all things; which these soft fires
Not only enlighten, but with kindly heat
Of various influence foment and warm,
Temper or nourish, or in part shed down 670
Their stellar virtue on all kinds that grow
On Earth, made hereby apter to receive
Perfection from the Sun's more potent ray.
These, then, though unbeheld in deep of night,
Shine not in vain. Nor think, though men were none,
That Heaven would want spectators, God want praise.
Millions of spiritual creatures walk the Earth
Unseen, both when we wake, and when we sleep:
All these with ceaseless praise his works behold
Both day and night. How often, from the steep 680
Of echoing hill or thicket, have we heard
Celestial voices to the midnight air,
Sole, or responsive each to other's note,
Singing their great Creator! Oft in bands
While they keep watch, or nightly rounding walk,
With heavenly touch of instrumental sounds
In full harmonic number joined, their songs
Divide the night, and lift our thoughts to Heaven."
    Thus talking, hand in hand alone they passed
On to their blissful bower. It was a place 690
Chosen by the sovran Planter, when he framed

All things to Man's delightful use. The roof
Of thickest covert was inwoven shade,
Laurel and myrtle, and what higher grew
Of firm and fragrant leaf; on either side
Acanthus, and each odorous bushy shrub,
Fenced up the verdant wall; each beauteous flower,
Iris all hues, roses, and jessamine,
Reared high their flourished heads between, and wrought
Mosaic; underfoot the violet,   700
Crocus, and hyacinth, with rich inlay
Broidered the ground, more colored than with stone
Of costliest emblem. Other creature here,
Beast, bird, insect, or worm, durst enter none;
Such was their awe of Man. In shadier bower
More sacred and sequestered, though but feigned,
Pan or Sylvanus never slept, nor Nymph
Nor Faunus haunted. Here, in close recess,
With flowers, garlands, and sweet-smelling herbs,
Espousèd Eve decked first her nuptial bed,   710
And heavenly choirs the hymenæan sung,
What day the genial Angel to our sire
Brought her, in naked beauty more adorned,
More lovely, than Pandora, whom the gods
Endowed with all their gifts; and, O! too like
In sad event, when, to the unwiser son
Of Japhet brought by Hermes, she ensnared
Mankind with her fair looks, to be avenged
On him who had stole Jove's authentic fire.
       Thus at their shady lodge arrived, both stood,   720
Both turned, and under open sky adored
The God that made both Sky, Air, Earth, and Heaven,
Which they beheld, the Moon's resplendent globe,
And starry Pole:—"Thou also madest the Night,
Maker Omnipotent; and thou the Day,
Which we, in our appointed work employed,
Have finished, happy in our mutual help
And mutual love, the crown of all our bliss
Ordained by thee; and this delicious place,
For us too large, where thy abundance wants   730
Partakers, and uncropt falls to the ground.
But thou hast promised from us two a race
To fill the Earth, who shall with us extol
Thy goodness infinite, both when we wake,

And when we seek, as now, thy gift of sleep."
  This said unanimous, and other rites
Observing none, but adoration pure,
Which God likes best, into their inmost bower
Handed they went; and, eased the putting-off
These troublesome disguises which we wear,   740
Straight side by side were laid; nor turned, I ween,
Adam from his fair spouse, nor Eve the rites
Mysterious of connubial love refused:
Whatever hypocrites austerely talk
Of purity, and place, and innocence,
Defaming as impure what God declares
Pure, and commands to some, leaves free to all.
Our Maker bids increase; who bids abstain
But our destroyer, foe to God and Man?
Hail, wedded Love, mysterious law, true source   750
Of human offspring, sole propriety
In Paradise of all things common else!
By thee adulterous lust was driven from men
Among the bestial herds to range; by thee,
Founded in reason, loyal, just, and pure,
Relations dear, and all the charities
Of father, son, and brother, first were known.
Far be it that I should write thee sin or blame,
Or think thee unbefitting holiest place,
Perpetual fountain of domestic sweets,   760
Whose bed is undefiled and chaste pronounced,
Present, or past, as saints and patriarchs used.
Here Love his golden shafts employs, here lights
His constant lamp, and waves his purple wings,
Reigns here and revels; not in the bought smile
Of harlots—loveless, joyless, unendeared,
Casual fruition; nor in court amours,
Mixed dance, or wanton mask, or midnight ball,
Or serenate, which the starved lover sings
To his proud fair, best quitted with disdain.   770
These, lulled by nightingales, embracing slept,
And on their naked limbs the flowery roof
Showered roses, which the morn repaired. Sleep on,
Blest pair! and, O! yet happiest, if ye seek
No happier state, and know to know no more!
  Now had Night measured with her shadowy cone
Half-way up-hill this vast sublunar vault,

And from their ivory port the Cherubim
Forth issuing, at the accustomed hour, stood armed
To their night-watches in warlike parade;   780
When Gabriel to his next in power thus spake:—
    "Uzziel, half these draw off, and coast the south
With strictest watch; these other wheel the north:
Our circuit meets full west." As flame they part,
Half wheeling to the shield, half to the spear.
From these, two strong and subtle Spirits he called
That near him stood, and gave them thus in charge:—
    "Ithuriel and Zephon, with winged speed
Search through this Garden; leave unsearched no nook;
But chiefly where those two fair creatures lodge,   790
Now laid perhaps asleep, secure of harm.
This evening from the Sun's decline arrived
Who tells of some infernal Spirit seen
Hitherward bent (who could have thought?) escaped
The bars of Hell, on errand bad, no doubt:
Such, where ye find, seize fast, and hither bring."
    So saying, on he led his radiant files,
Dazzling the moon; these to the bower direct
In search of whom they sought. Him there they found
Squat like a toad, close at the ear of Eve,   800
Assaying by his devilish art to reach
The organs of her fancy, and with them forge
Illusions as he list, phantasms and dreams;
Or if, inspiring venom, he might taint
The animal spirits, that from pure blood arise
Like gentle breaths from rivers pure, thence raise,
At least distempered, discontented thoughts,
Vain hopes, vain aims, inordinate desires,
Blown up with high conceits engendering pride.
Him thus intent Ithuriel with his spear   810
Touched lightly; for no falsehood can endure
Touch of celestial temper, but returns
Of force to its own likeness. Up he starts,
Discovered and surprised. As when a spark
Lights on a heap of nitrous powder, laid
Fit for the tun, some magazine to store
Against a rumored war, the smutty grain,
With sudden blaze diffused, inflames the air;
So started up, in his own shape, the Fiend.
Back stept those two fair Angels, half amazed   820

So sudden to behold the grisly King;
Yet thus, unmoved with fear, accost him soon:—
    "Which of those rebel Spirits adjudged to Hell
Com'st thou, escaped thy prison? and, transformed,
Why satt'st thou like an enemy in wait,
Here watching at the head of these that sleep?"
    "Know ye not, then," said Satan, filled with scorn,
"Know ye not me? Ye knew me once no mate
For you, there sitting where ye durst not soar!
Not to know me argues yourselves unknown,   830
The lowest of your throng; or, if ye know,
Why ask ye, and superfluous begin
Your message, like to end as much in vain?"
    To whom thus Zephon, answering scorn with scorn:—
"Think not, revolted Spirit, thy shape the same,
Or undiminished brightness, to be known
As when thou stood'st in Heaven upright and pure.
That glory then, when thou no more wast good,
Departed from thee; and thou resemblest now
Thy sin and place of doom obscure and foul.   840
But come; for thou, be sure, shalt give account
To him who sent us, whose charge is to keep
This place inviolable, and these from harm."
    So spake the Cherub; and his grave rebuke,
Severe in youthful beauty, added grace
Invincible. Abashed the Devil stood,
And felt how awful goodness is, and saw
Virtue in her shape how lovely—saw, and pined
His loss; but chiefly to find here observed
His lustre visibly impaired; yet seemed   850
Undaunted. "If I must contend," said he,
"Best with the best—the sender, not the sent;
Or all at once: more glory will be won,
Or less be lost." "Thy fear," said Zephon bold,
"Will save us trial what the least can do
Single against thee wicked, and thence weak."
    The Fiend replied not, overcome with rage;
But like a proud steed reined, went haughty on,
Champing his iron curb. To strive or fly
He held it vain; awe from above had quelled   860
His heart, not else dismayed. Now drew they nigh
The western point, where those half-rounding guards
Just met, and, closing, stood in squadron joined,

Awaiting next command. To whom their chief,
Gabriel, from the front thus called aloud:—
  "O friends, I hear the tread of nimble feet
Hasting this way, and now by glimpse discern
Ithuriel and Zephon through the shade;
And with them comes a third, of regal port,
But faded splendor wan, who by his gait   870
And fierce demeanor seems the Prince of Hell—
Not likely to part hence without contest.
Stand firm, for in his look defiance lours."
  He scarce had ended, when those two approached,
And brief related whom they brought, where found,
How busied, in what form and posture couched.
  To whom, with stern regard, thus Gabriel spake:—
"Why hast thou, Satan, broke the bounds prescribed
To thy transgressions, and disturbed the charge
Of others, who approve not to transgress   880
By thy example, but have power and right
To question thy bold entrance on this place;
Employed, it seems, to violate sleep, and those
Whose dwelling God hath planted here in bliss?"
  To whom thus Satan, with contemptuous brow:—
"Gabriel, thou hadst in Heaven the esteem of wise;
And such I held thee; but this question asked
Puts me in doubt. Lives there who loves his pain?
Who would not, finding way, break loose from Hell,
Though thither doomed? Thou wouldst thyself, no doubt, 890
And boldly venture to whatever place
Farthest from pain, where thou mightst hope to change
Torment with ease, and soonest recompense
Dole with delight; which in this place I sought:
To thee no reason, who know'st only good,
But evil hast not tried. And wilt object
His will who bound us? Let him surer bar
His iron gates, if he intends our stay
In that dark durance. Thus much what was asked:
The rest is true; they found me where they say;   900
But that implies not violence or harm."
  Thus he in scorn. The warlike Angel moved,
Disdainfully half smiling, thus replied:—
"O loss of one in Heaven to judge of wise,
Since Satan fell, whom folly overthrew,
And now returns him from his prison scaped,

Gravely in doubt whether to hold them wise
Or not who ask what boldness brought him hither
Unlicensed from his bounds in Hell prescribed!
So wise he judges it to fly from pain   910
However, and to scape his punishment!
So judge thou still, presumptuous, till the wrath,
Which thou incurr'st by flying, meet thy flight
Sevenfold, and scourge that wisdom back to Hell,
Which taught thee yet no better that no pain
Can equal anger infinite provoked.
But wherefore thou alone? Wherefore with thee
Came not all Hell broke loose? Is pain to them
Less pain, less to be fled? or thou than they
Less hardy to endure? Courageous chief,   920
The first in flight from pain, hadst thou alleged
To thy deserted host this cause of flight,
Thou surely hadst not come sole fugitive."
    To which the Fiend thus answered, frowning stern:—
"Not that I less endure, or shrink from pain,
Insulting Angel! well thou know'st I stood
Thy fiercest, when in battle to thy aid
The blasting volleyed thunder made all speed
And seconded thy else not dreaded spear.
But still thy words at random, as before,   930
Argue thy inexperience what behoves,
From hard assays and ill successes past,
A faithful leader—not to hazard all
Through ways of danger by himself untried.
I, therefore, I alone, first undertook
To wing the desolate Abyss, and spy
This new-created World, whereof in Hell
Fame is not silent, here in hope to find
Better abode, and my afflicted Powers
To settle here on Earth, or in mid Air;   940
Though for possession put to try once more
What thou and thy gay legions dare against;
Whose easier business were to serve their Lord
High up in Heaven, with songs to hymn his throne,
And practised distances to cringe, not fight."
    To whom the Warrior-Angel soon replied:—
"To say and straight unsay, pretending first
Wise to fly pain, professing next the spy,
Argues no leader, but a liar traced,

Satan; and couldst thou 'faithful' add? O name,   950
O sacred name of faithfulness profaned!
Faithful to whom? to thy rebellious crew?
Army of fiends, fit body to fit head!
Was this your discipline and faith engaged,
Your military obedience, to dissolve
Allegiance to the acknowledged Power Supreme:
And thou, sly hypocrite, who now wouldst seem
Patron of liberty, who more than thou
Once fawned, and cringed, and servilely adored
Heaven's awful Monarch? wherefore, but in hope   960
To dispossess him, and thyself to reign?
But mark what I areed thee now: Avaunt!
Fly thither whence thou fledd'st. If from this hour
Within these hallowed limits thou appear,
Back to the Infernal Pit I drag thee chained,
And seal thee so as henceforth not to scorn
The facile gates of Hell too slightly barred."
    So threatened he; but Satan to no threats
Gave heed, but waxing more in rage, replied:—
    "Then, when I am thy captive, talk of chains,   970
Proud limitary Cherub! but ere then
Far heavier load thyself expect to feel
From my prevailing arm, though Heaven's King
Ride on thy wings, and thou with thy compeers,
Used to the yoke, draw'st his triumphant wheels
In progress through the road of Heaven star-paved."
    While thus he spake, the angelic squadron bright
Turned fiery red, sharpening in moonèd horns
Their phalanx, and began to hem him round
With ported spears, as thick as when a field   980
Of Ceres ripe for harvest waving bends
Her bearded grove of ears which way the wind
Sways them; the careful ploughman doubting stands
Lest on the threshing-floor his hopeful sheaves
Prove chaff. On the other side, Satan, alarmed,
Collecting all his might, dilated stood,
Like Teneriff or Atlas, unremoved:
His stature reached the sky, and on his crest
Sat Horror plumed; nor wanted in his grasp
What seemed both spear and shield. Now dreadful deeds   990
Might have ensued; nor only Paradise,
In this commotion, but the starry cope

Of Heaven perhaps, or all the Elements
At least, had gone to wrack, disturbed and torn
With violence of this conflict, had not soon
The Eternal, to prevent such horrid fray,
Hung forth in Heaven his golden scales, yet seen
Betwixt Astræa and the Scorpion sign,
Wherein all things created first he weighed,
The pendulous round Earth with balanced air   1000
In counterpoise, now ponders all events,
Battles and realms. In these he put two weights,
The sequel each of parting and of fight:
The latter quick up flew, and kicked the beam;
Which Gabriel spying, thus bespake the Fiend:—
    "Satan, I know thy strength, and thou know'st mine,
Neither our own, but given; what folly then
To boast what arms can do! since thine no more
Than Heaven permits, nor mine, though doubled now
To trample thee as mire. For proof look up,   1010
And read thy lot in yon celestial sign,
Where thou art weighed, and shown how light, how weak
If thou resist." The Fiend looked up, and knew
His mounted scale aloft: nor more; but fled
Murmuring; and with him fled the shades of Night.

BOOK V

THE ARGUMENT

MORNING approached, Eve relates to Adam her troublesome dream; he
likes it not, yet comforts her: they come forth to their day labors: their
morning hymn at the door of their bower. God, to render Man inexcus-
able, sends Raphael to admonish him of his obedience, of his free estate,
of his enemy near at hand, who he is, and why his enemy, and whatever
else may avail Adam to know. Raphael comes down to Paradise; his
appearance described; his coming discerned by Adam afar off, sitting at
the door of his bower; he goes out to meet him, brings him to his lodge,
entertains him with the choicest fruits of Paradise, got together by Eve;
their discourse at table. Raphael performs his message, minds Adam of
his state and of his enemy; relates, at Adam's request, who that enemy is,
and how he came to be so, beginning from his first revolt in Heaven, and
the occasion thereof; how he drew his legions after him to the parts of
the North, and there incited them to rebel with him, persuading all but
only Abdiel, a seraph, who in argument dissuades and opposes him, then
forsakes him.

> Now Morn, her rosy steps in the eastern clime
> Advancing, sowed the earth with orient pearl,
> When Adam waked, so customed; for his sleep
> Was aery light, from pure digestion bred,
> And temperate vapors bland, which the only sound
> Of leaves and fuming rills, Aurora's fan,
> Lightly dispersed, and the shrill matin song
> Of birds on every bough. So much the more
> His wonder was to find unwakened Eve,
> With tresses discomposed, and glowing cheek,   10
> As through unquiet rest. He, on his side

Leaning half raised, with looks of cordial love
Hung over her enamoured, and beheld
Beauty, which, whether waking or asleep,
Shot forth peculiar graces; then, with voice
Mild, as when Zephyrus on Flora breathes,
Her hand soft touching, whispered thus:—"Awake,
My fairest, my espoused, my latest found,
Heaven's last, best gift, my ever-new delight!
Awake! the morning shines, and the fresh field   20
Calls us; we lose the prime to mark how spring
Our tended plants, how blows the citron grove,
What drops the myrrh, and what the balmy reed,
How Nature paints her colors, how the bee
Sits on the bloom extracting liquid sweet."
   Such whispering waked her, but with startled eye
On Adam; whom embracing, thus she spake:—
   "O sole in whom my thoughts find all repose,
My glory, my perfection! glad I see
Thy face, and morn returned; for I this night   30
(Such night till this I never passed) have dreamed,
If dreamed, not, as I oft am wont, of thee,
Works of day past, or morrow's next design;
But of offence and trouble, which my mind
Knew never till this irksome night. Methought
Close at mine ear one called me forth to walk
With gentle voice; I thought it thine. It said,
'Why sleep'st thou, Eve? now is the pleasant time,
The cool, the silent, save where silence yields
To the night-warbling bird, that now awake   40
Tunes sweetest his love-labored song; now reigns
Full-orbed the moon, and, with more pleasing light,
Shadowy sets off the face of things—in vain,
If none regard. Heaven wakes with all his eyes;
Whom to behold but thee, Nature's desire,
In whose sight all things joy, with ravishment
Attracted by thy beauty still to gaze?'
I rose as at thy call, but found thee not:
To find thee I directed then my walk;
And on, methought, alone I passed through ways   50
That brought me on a sudden to the tree
Of interdicted knowledge. Fair it seemed,
Much fairer to my fancy than by day;
And, as I wondering looked, beside it stood

One shaped and winged like one of those from Heaven
By us oft seen: his dewy locks distilled
Ambrosia. On that tree he also gazed;
And, 'O fair plant,' said he, 'with fruit surcharged,
Deigns none to ease thy load, and taste thy sweet,
Nor God nor Man? Is knowledge so despised?   60
Or envy, or what reserve forbids to taste?
Forbid who will, none shall from me withhold
Longer thy offered good, why else set here?'
This said, he paused not, but with venturous arm
He plucked, he tasted. Me damp horror chilled
At such bold words vouched with a deed so bold;
But he thus, overjoyed: 'O fruit divine,
Sweet of thyself, but much more sweet thus cropt,
Forbidden here, it seems, as only fit
For gods, yet able to make gods of men!   70
And why not gods of men, since good, the more
Communicated, more abundant grows,
The author not impaired, but honored more?
Here, happy creature, fair angelic Eve!
Partake thou also; happy though thou art,
Happier thou may'st be, worthier canst not be.
Taste this, and be henceforth among the gods
Thyself a goddess; not to Earth confined,
But sometimes in the Air, as we; sometimes
Ascend to Heaven, by merit thine, and see   80
What life the gods live there, and such live thou.'
So saying, he drew nigh, and to me held,
Even to my mouth of that same fruit held part
Which he had plucked: the pleasant savory smell
So quickened appetite that I, methought,
Could not but taste. Forthwith up to the clouds
With him I flew, and underneath beheld
The Earth outstretched immense, a prospect wide
And various. Wondering at my flight and change
To this high exaltation, suddenly   90
My guide was gone, and I, methought, sunk down,
And fell asleep; but, O, how glad I waked
To find this but a dream!" Thus Eve her night
Related, and thus Adam answered sad:—
    "Best image of myself, and dearer half,
The trouble of thy thoughts this night in sleep
Affects me equally; nor can I like

This uncouth dream—of evil sprung, I fear;
Yet evil whence? In thee can harbor none,
Created pure. But know that in the soul   100
Are many lesser faculties, that serve
Reason as chief. Among these Fancy next
Her office holds; of all external things,
Which the five watchful senses represent,
She forms imaginations, aery shapes,
Which Reason, joining or disjoining, frames
All what we affirm or what deny, and call
Our knowledge or opinion; then retires
Into her private cell when Nature rests.
Oft, in her absence, mimic Fancy wakes   110
To imitate her; but, misjoining shapes,
Wild work produces oft, and most in dreams,
Ill matching words and deeds long past or late.
Some such resemblances, methinks, I find
Of our last evening's talk in this thy dream,
But with addition strange. Yet be not sad:
Evil into the mind of God or Man
May come and go, so unapproved, and leave
No spot or blame behind; which gives me hope
That what in sleep thou didst abhor to dream   120
Waking thou never wilt consent to do.
Be not disheartened, then, nor cloud those looks,
That wont to be more cheerful and serene
Than when fair Morning first smiles on the world;
And let us to our fresh employments rise
Among the groves, the fountains, and the flowers,
That open now their choicest bosomed smells,
Reserved from night, and kept for thee in store."
        So cheered he his fair spouse; and she was cheered,
But silently a gentle tear let fall   130
From either eye, and wiped them with her hair:
Two other precious drops that ready stood,
Each in their crystal sluice, he, ere they fell,
Kissed as the gracious signs of sweet remorse
And pious awe, that feared to have offended.
        So all was cleared, and to the field they haste.
But first, from under shady arborous roof
Soon as they forth were come to open sight
Of day-spring, and the Sun—who, scarce uprisen,
With wheels yet hovering o'er the ocean-brim,   140

Shot parallel to the Earth his dewy ray,
Discovering in wide landskip all the east
Of Paradise and Eden's happy plains—
Lowly they bowed, adoring, and began
Their orisons, each morning duly paid
In various style; for neither various style
Nor holy rapture wanted they to praise
Their Maker, in fit strains pronounced, or sung
Unmeditated; such prompt eloquence
Flowed from their lips, in prose or numerous verse,   150
More tuneable than needed lute or harp
To add more sweetness: And they thus began:—
    "These are thy glorious works, Parent of good,
Almighty! thine this universal frame,
Thus wondrous fair: Thyself how wondrous then!
Unspeakable! who sitt'st above these heavens
To us invisible, or dimly seen
In these thy lowest works; yet these declare
Thy goodness beyond thought, and power divine.
Speak, ye who best can tell, ye Sons of Light,   160
Angels—for ye behold him, and with songs
And choral symphonies, day without night,
Circle his throne rejoicing—ye in Heaven;
On Earth join, all ye creatures, to extol
Him first, him last, him midst, and without end.
Fairest of Stars, last in the train of Night,
If better thou belong not to the Dawn,
Sure pledge of day, that crown'st the smiling morn
With thy bright circlet, praise him in thy sphere
While day arises, that sweet hour of prime.   170
Thou Sun, of this great World both eye and soul,
Acknowledge him thy greater; sound his praise
In thy eternal course, both when thou climb'st,
And when high noon hast gained, and when thou fall'st.
Moon, that now meet'st the orient Sun, now fliest,
With the fixed Stars, fixed in their orb that flies;
And ye five other wandering Fires, that move
In mystic dance, not without song, resound
His praise who out of Darkness called up Light.
Air, and ye Elements, the eldest birth   180
Of Nature's womb, that in quaternion run
Perpetual circle, multiform, and mix
And nourish all things, let your ceaseless change

Vary to our great Maker still new praise.
Ye Mists and Exhalations, that now rise
From hill or steaming lake, dusky or gray,
Till the sun paint your fleecy skirts with gold,
In honor to the World's great Author rise;
Whether to deck with clouds the uncolored sky,
Or wet the thirsty earth with falling showers,   190
Rising or falling, still advance his praise.
His praise, ye Winds, that from four quarters blow,
Breathe soft or loud; and wave your tops, ye Pines,
With every Plant, in sign of worship wave.
Fountains, and ye, that warble, as ye flow,
Melodious murmurs, warbling tune his praise.
Join voices, all ye living Souls. Ye Birds,
That, singing, up to Heaven-gate ascend,
Bear on your wings and in your notes his praise.
Ye that in waters glide, and ye that walk   200
The earth, and stately tread, or lowly creep,
Witness if *I* be silent, morn or even,
To hill or valley, fountain, or fresh shade,
Made vocal by my song, and taught his praise.
Hail, universal Lord! Be bounteous still
To give us only good; and, if the night
Have gathered aught of evil, or concealed,
Disperse it, as now light dispels the dark."
    So prayed they innocent, and to their thoughts
Firm peace recovered soon, and wonted calm.   210
On to their morning's rural work they haste,
Among sweet dews and flowers, where any row
Of fruit-trees, over-woody, reached too far
Their pampered boughs, and needed hands to check
Fruitless embraces: or they led the vine
To wed her elm; she, spoused, about him twines
Her marriageable arms, and with her brings
Her dower, the adopted clusters, to adorn
His barren leaves. Them thus employed beheld
With pity Heaven's high King, and to him called   220
Raphael, the sociable Spirit, that deigned
To travel with Tobias, and secured
His marriage with the seven-times-wedded maid.
    "Raphael," said he, "thou hear'st what stir on Earth
Satan, from Hell scaped through the darksome Gulf,
Hath raised in Paradise, and how disturbed

This night the human pair; how he designs
In them at once to ruin all mankind.
Go, therefore; half this day, as friend with friend,
Converse with Adam, in what bower or shade   230
Thou find'st him from the heat of noon retired
To respite his day-labor with repast
Or with repose; and such discourse bring on
As may advise him of his happy state—
Happiness in his power left free to will,
Left to his own free will, his will though free
Yet mutable. Whence warn him to beware
He swerve not, too secure: tell him withal
His danger, and from whom; what enemy,
Late fallen himself from Heaven, is plotting now   240
The fall of others from like state of bliss.
By violence? no, for that shall be withstood;
But by deceit and lies. This let him know,
Lest, wilfully transgressing, he pretend
Surprisal, unadmonished, unforewarned."
    So spake the Eternal Father, and fulfilled
All justice. Nor delayed the wingèd Saint
After his charge received; but from among
Thousand celestial Ardors, where he stood
Veiled with his gorgeous wings, upspringing light,   250
Flew through the midst of Heaven. The angelic quires,
On each hand parting, to his speed gave way
Through all the empyreal road, till, at the gate
Of Heaven arrived, the gate self-opened wide,
On golden hinges turning, as by work
Divine the sovran Architect had framed.
From hence—no cloud or, to obstruct his sight,
Star interposed, however small—he sees,
Not unconform to other shining globes,
Earth, and the Garden of God, with cedars crowned   260
Above all hills; as when by night the glass
Of Galileo, less assured, observes
Imagined lands and regions in the Moon;
Or pilot from amidst the Cyclades
Delos or Samos first appearing kens,
A cloudy spot. Down thither prone in flight
He speeds, and through the vast ethereal sky
Sails between worlds and worlds, with steady wing
Now on the polar winds; then with quick fan

Winnows the buxom air, till, within soar   270
Of towering eagles, to all the fowls he seems
A phœnix, gazed by all, as that sole bird,
When, to enshrine his relics in the Sun's
Bright temple, to Egyptian Thebes he flies.
At once on the eastern cliff of Paradise
He lights, and to his proper shape returns,
A Seraph winged. Six wings he wore, to shade
His lineaments divine: the pair that clad
Each shoulder broad came mantling o'er his breast
With regal ornament; the middle pair   280
Girt like a starry zone his waist, and round
Skirted his loins and thighs with downy gold
And colors dipt in heaven; the third his feet
Shadowed from either heel with feathered mail,
Sky-tinctured grain. Like Maia's son he stood,
And shook his plumes, that heavenly fragrance filled
The circuit wide. Straight knew him all the bands
Of Angels under watch, and to his state
And to his message high in honor rise;
For on some message high they guessed him bound.   290
Their glittering tents he passed, and now is come
Into the blissful field, through groves of myrrh,
And flowering odors, cassia, nard, and balm,
A wilderness of sweets; for Nature here
Wantoned as in her prime, and played at will
Her virgin fancies, pouring forth more sweet,
Wild above rule or art, enormous bliss.
Him, through the spicy forest onward come,
Adam discerned, as in the door he sat
Of his cool bower, while now the mounted Sun   300
Shot down direct his fervid rays, to warm
Earth's inmost womb, more warmth than Adam needs;
And Eve, within, due at her hour, prepared
For dinner savory fruits, of taste to please
True appetite, and not disrelish thirst
Of nectarous draughts between, from milky stream,
Berry or grape: to whom thus Adam called:—
     "Haste hither, Eve, and worth thy sight, behold
Eastward among those trees what glorious Shape
Comes this way moving; seems another morn   310
Risen on mid-noon. Some great behest from Heaven
To us perhaps he brings, and will voutsafe

This day to be our guest. But go with speed,
And what thy stores contain bring forth, and pour
Abundance fit to honor and receive
Our heavenly stranger; well we may afford
Our givers their own gifts, and large bestow
From large bestowed, where Nature multiplies
Her fertile growth, and by disburdening grows
More fruitful; which instructs us not to spare."   320
    To whom thus Eve:—"Adam, Earth's hallowed mould,
Of God inspired, small store will serve where store,
All seasons, ripe for use hangs on the stalk;
Save what, by frugal storing, firmness gains
To nourish, and superfluous moist consumes.
But I will haste, and from each bough and brake,
Each plant and juiciest gourd, will pluck such choice
To entertain our Angel-guest as he,
Beholding, shall confess that here on Earth
God hath dispensed his bounties as in Heaven."   330
    So saying, with dispatchful looks in haste
She turns, on hospitable thoughts intent
What choice to choose for delicacy best,
What order so contrived as not to mix
Tastes, not well joined, inelegant, but bring
Taste after taste upheld with kindliest change:
Bestirs her then, and from each tender stalk
Whatever Earth, all-bearing mother, yields
In India East or West, or middle shore
In Pontus or the Punic coast, or where   340
Alcinöus reigned, fruit of all kinds, in coat
Rough or smooth rined, or bearded husk, or shell,
She gathers, tribute large, and on the board
Heaps with unsparing hand. For drink the grape
She crushes, inoffensive must, and meaths
From many a berry, and from sweet kernels pressed
She tempers dulcet creams—nor these to hold
Wants her fit vessels pure; then strews the ground
With rose and odors from the shrub unfumed.
    Meanwhile our primitive great Sire, to meet   350
His godlike guest, walks forth, without more train
Accompanied than with his own complete
Perfections; in himself was all his state,
More solemn than the tedious pomp that waits
On princes, when their rich retinue long

Of horses led and grooms besmeared with gold
Dazzles the crowd and sets them all agape.
Nearer his presence, Adam, though not awed,
Yet with submiss approach and reverence meek,
As to a superior nature, bowing low,   360
Thus said:—"Native of Heaven (for other place
None can than Heaven such glorious Shape contain),
Since, by descending from the Thrones above,
Those happy places thou hast deigned a while
To want, and honor these, voutsafe with us,
Two only, who yet by sovran gift possess
This spacious ground, in yonder shady bower
To rest, and what the Garden choicest bears
To sit and taste, till this meridian heat
Be over, and the sun more cool decline."   370
      Whom thus the angelic Virtue answered mild:—
"Adam, I therefore came; nor art thou such
Created, or such place hast here to dwell,
As may not oft invite, though Spirits of Heaven,
To visit thee. Lead on, then, where thy bower
O'ershades; for these mid-hours, till evening rise,
I have at will." So to the sylvan lodge
They came, that like Pomona's arbor smiled,
With flowerets decked and fragrant smells. But Eve,
Undecked, save with herself, more lovely fair   380
Than wood-nymph, or the fairest goddess feigned
Of three that in Mount Ida naked strove,
Stood to entertain her guest from Heaven; no veil
She needed, virtue-proof; no thought infirm
Altered her cheek. On whom the Angel "Hail!"
Bestowed—the holy salutation used
Long after to blest Mary, second Eve:—
      "Hail, Mother of mankind, whose fruitful womb
Shall fill the world more numerous with thy sons
Than with these various fruits the trees of God   390
Have heaped this table!" Raised of grassy turf
Their table was, and mossy seats had round,
And on her ample square, from side to side,
All Autumn piled, though Spring and Autumn here
Danced hand-in-hand. A while discourse they hold—
No fear lest dinner cool—when thus began
Our Author:—"Heavenly Stranger, please to taste
These bounties, which our Nourisher, from whom

All perfect good, unmeasured out, descends,
To us for food and for delight hath caused   400
The Earth to yield: unsavory food perhaps,
To Spiritual Natures; only this I know,
That one Celestial Father gives to all."
   To whom the Angel:—"Therefore, what he gives
(Whose praise be ever sung) to Man, in part
Spiritual, may of purest Spirits be found
No ingrateful food: and food alike those pure
Intelligential substances require
As doth your Rational; and both contain
Within them every lower faculty   410
Of sense, whereby they hear, see, smell, touch, taste,
Tasting concoct, digest, assimilate,
And corporeal to incorporeal turn.
For know, whatever was created needs
To be sustained and fed. Of Elements
The grosser feeds the purer: Earth the Sea;
Earth and the Sea feed Air; the Air those Fires
Ethereal, and, as lowest, first the Moon;
Whence in her visage round those spots unpurged
Vapors not yet into her substance turned.   420
Nor doth the Moon no nourishment exhale
From her moist continent to higher Orbs.
The Sun, that light imparts to all, receives
From all his alimental recompense
In humid exhalations, and at even
Sups with the Ocean. Though in Heaven the trees
Of life ambrosial fruitage bear, and vines
Yield nectar—though from off the boughs each morn
We brush mellifluous dews and find the ground
Covered with pearly grain—yet God hath here   430
Varied his bounty so with new delights
As may compare with Heaven; and to taste
Think not I shall be nice." So down they sat,
And to their viands fell; nor seemingly
The Angel, nor in mist—the common gloss
Of theologians—but with keen dispatch
Of real hunger, and concoctive heat
To transubstantiate: what redounds transpires
Through Spirits with ease; nor wonder, if by fire
Of sooty coal the empiric alchemist   440
Can turn, or holds it possible to turn,

Metals of drossiest ore to perfect gold,
As from the mine. Meanwhile at table Eve
Ministered naked, and their flowing cups
With pleasant liquors crowned. O innocence
Deserving Paradise! If ever, then,
Then had the Sons of God excuse to have been
Enamoured at that sight. But in those hearts
Love unlibidinous reigned, nor jealousy
Was understood, the injured lover's hell.   450
    Thus when with meats and drinks they had sufficed,
Not burdened nature, sudden mind arose
In Adam not to let the occasion pass,
Given him by this great conference, to know
Of things above his world, and of their being
Who dwell in Heaven, whose excellence he saw
Transcend his own so far, whose radiant forms,
Divine effulgence, whose high power so far
Exceeded human; and his wary speech
Thus to the empyreal minister he framed:—   460
    "Inhabitant with God, now know I well
Thy favor, in this honor done to Man;
Under whose lowly roof thou hast voutsafed
To enter, and these earthly fruits to taste,
Food not of Angels, yet accepted so
As that more willingly thou couldst not seem
At Heaven's high feasts to have fed: yet what compare!"
    To whom the wingèd Hierarch replied:—
"O Adam, one Almighty is, from whom
All things proceed, and up to him return,   470
If not depraved from good, created all
Such to perfection; one first matter all,
Endued with various forms, various degrees
Of substance, and, in things that live, of life;
But more refined, more spiritous, and pure,
As nearer to him placed or nearer tending
Each in their several active spheres assigned,
Till body up to spirit work, in bounds
Proportioned to each kind. So from the root
Springs lighter the green stalk, from thence the leaves   480
More aery, last the bright consummate flower
Spirits odorous breathes: flowers and their fruit,
Man's nourishment, by gradual scale sublimed,
To vital spirits aspire, to animal,

To intellectual; give both life and sense,
Fancy and understanding; whence the Soul
Reason receives, and Reason is her being,
Discursive, or Intuitive: Discourse
Is oftest yours, the latter most is ours,
Differing but in degree, of kind the same.   490
Wonder not, then, what God for you saw good
If I refuse not, but convert, as you,
To proper substance. Time may come when Men
With Angels may participate, and find
No inconvenient diet, nor too light fare;
And from these corporal nutriments, perhaps,
Your bodies may at last turn all to spirit,
Improved by tract of time, and wing'd ascend
Ethereal, as we, or may at choice
Here or in heavenly paradises dwell,   500
If ye be found obedient, and retain
Unalterably firm his love entire
Whose progeny you are. Meanwhile enjoy,
Your fill, what happiness this happy state
Can comprehend, incapable of more."
　　To whom the Patriarch of Mankind replied:—
"O favorable Spirit, propitious guest,
Well hast thou taught the way that might direct
Our knowledge, and the scale of Nature set
From centre to circumference, whereon,   510
In contemplation of created things,
By steps we may ascend to God. But say,
What meant that caution joined, *If ye be found
Obedient?* Can we want obedience, then,
To him, or possibly his love desert,
Who formed us from the dust, and placed us here
Full to the utmost measure of what bliss
Human desires can seek or apprehend?"
　　To whom the Angel:—"Son of Heaven and Earth,
Attend! That thou art happy, owe to God;   520
That thou continuest such, owe to thyself,
That is, to thy obedience; therein stand.
This was that caution given thee; be advised.
God made thee perfect, not immutable;
And good he made thee; but to persevere
He left it in thy power—ordained thy will
By nature free, not over-ruled by fate

Inextricable, or strict necessity.
Our voluntary service he requires,
Not our necessitated. Such with him   530
Finds no acceptance, nor can find; for how
Can hearts not free be tried whether they serve
Willing or no, who will but what they must
By destiny, and can no other choose?
Myself, and all the Angelic Host, that stand
In sight of God enthroned, our happy state
Hold, as you yours, while our obedience holds.
On other surety none: freely we serve,
Because we freely love, as in our will
To love or not; in this we stand or fall.   540
And some are fallen, to disobedience fallen,
And so from Heaven to deepest Hell. O fall
From what high state of bliss into what woe!"
    To whom our great Progenitor:—"Thy words
Attentive, and with more delighted ear,
Divine instructor, I have heard, than when
Cherubic songs by night from neighboring hills
Aërial music send. Nor knew I not
To be, both will and deed, created free.
Yet that we never shall forget to love   550
Our Maker, and obey him whose command
Single is yet so just, my constant thoughts
Assured me, and still assure; though what thou tell'st
Hath passed in Heaven some doubt within me move,
But more desire to hear, if thou consent,
The full relation, which must needs be strange,
Worthy of sacred silence to be heard.
And we have yet large day, for scarce the Sun
Hath finished half his journey, and scarce begins
His other half in the great zone of heaven."   560
    Thus Adam made request; and Raphael,
After short pause assenting, thus began:—
    "High matter thou enjoin'st me, O prime of Men—
Sad task and hard: for how shall I relate
To human sense the invisible exploits
Of warring Spirits? how, without remorse,
The ruin of so many, glorious once
And perfect while they stood? how, last, unfold
The secrets of another world, perhaps
Not lawful to reveal? Yet for thy good   570

This is dispensed; and what surmounts the reach
Of human sense I shall delineate so,
By likening spiritual to corporal forms,
As may express them best—though what if Earth
Be but the shadow of Heaven, and things therein
Each to other like more than on Earth is thought!
   "As yet this World was not, and Chaos wild
Reigned where these heavens now roll, where Earth now rests
Upon her centre poised, when on a day
(For Time, though in Eternity, applied   580
To motion, measures all things durable
By present, past, and future), on such day
As Heaven's great year brings forth, the empyreal host
Of Angels, by imperial summons called,
Innumerable before the Almighty's throne
Forthwith from all the ends of Heaven appeared
Under their hierarchs in orders bright.
Ten thousand thousand ensigns high advanced,
Standards and gonfalons, 'twixt van and rear
Stream in the air, and for distinction serve   590
Of hierarchies, of orders, and degrees;
Or in their glittering tissues bear emblazed
Holy memorials, acts of zeal and love
Recorded eminent. Thus when in orbs
Of circuit inexpressible they stood,
Orb within orb, the Father Infinite,
By whom in bliss embosomed sat the Son,
Amidst, as from a flaming mount, whose top
Brightness had made invisible, thus spake:—
   "'Hear, all ye Angels, Progeny of Light,   600
Thrones, Dominations, Princedoms, Virtues, Powers,
Hear my decree, which unrevoked shall stand!
This day I have begot whom I declare
My only Son, and on this holy hill
Him have anointed, whom ye now behold
At my right hand. Your head I him appoint,
And by myself have sworn to him shall bow
All knees in Heaven, and shall confess him Lord.
Under his great vicegerent reign abide,
United as one individual soul,   610
For ever happy. Him who disobeys
Me disobeys, breaks union, and, that day,
Cast out from God and blessed vision, falls

Into utter darkness, deep engulfed, his place
Ordained without redemption, without end.'
   "So spake the Omnipotent, and with his words
All seemed well pleased; all seemed, but were not all.
That day, as other solemn days, they spent
In song and dance about the sacred hill—
Mystical dance, which yonder starry sphere   620
Of planets and of fixed in all her wheels
Resembles nearest; mazes intricate,
Eccentric, intervolved, yet regular
Then most when most irregular they seem;
And in their motions harmony divine
So smooths her charming tones that God's own ear
Listens delighted. Evening now approached
(For we have also our evening and our morn—
We ours for change delectable, not need),
Forthwith from dance to sweet repast they turn   630
Desirous: all in circles as they stood,
Tables are set, and on a sudden piled
With Angels' food; and rubied nectar flows
In pearl, in diamond, and massy gold,
Fruit of delicious vines, the growth of Heaven.
On flowers reposed, and with fresh flowerets crowned,
They eat, they drink, and in communion sweet
Quaff immortality and joy, secure
Of surfeit where full measure only bounds
Excess, before the all-bounteous King, who showered   640
With copious hand, rejoicing in their joy.
Now when ambrosial Night, with clouds exhaled
From that high mount of God whence light and shade
Spring both, the face of brightest Heaven had changed
To grateful twilight (for Night comes not there
In darker veil), and roseate dews disposed
All but the unsleeping eyes of God to rest,
Wide over all the plain, and wider far
Than all this globous Earth in plain outspread
(Such are the courts of God), the Angelic throng,   650
Dispersed in bands and files, their camp extend
By living streams among the trees of life—
Pavilions numberless and sudden reared,
Celestial tabernacles, where they slept,
Fanned with cool winds; save those who, in their course,
Melodious hymns about the sovran throne

Alternate all night long. But not so waked
Satan—so call him now; his former name
Is heard no more in Heaven. He, of the first,
If not the first Archangel, great in power,   660
In favor, and pre-eminence, yet fraught
With envy against the Son of God, that day
Honored by his great Father, and proclaimed
Messiah, King Anointed, could not bear,
Through pride, that sight, and thought himself impaired.
Deep malice thence conceiving and disdain,
Soon as midnight brought on the dusky hour
Friendliest to sleep and silence, he resolved
With all his legions to dislodge, and leave
Unworshiped, unobeyed, the Throne supreme,   670
Contemptuous, and, his next subordinate
Awakening, thus to him in secret spake:—
　　"'Sleep'st thou, companion dear? what sleep can close
Thy eyelids? and rememberest what decree,
Of yesterday, so late hath passed the lips
Of Heaven's Almighty? Thou to me thy thoughts
Wast wont, I mine to thee was wont, to impart;
Both waking we were one; how, then, can now
Thy sleep dissent? New laws thou seest imposed;
New laws from him who reigns new minds may raise   680
In us who serve—new counsels, to debate
What doubtful may ensue. More in this place
To utter is not safe. Assemble thou
Of all those myriads which we lead the chief;
Tell them that, by command, ere yet dim Night
Her shadowy cloud withdraws, I am to haste,
And all who under me their banners wave,
Homeward with flying march where we possess
The quarters of the North, there to prepare
Fit entertainment to receive our King,   690
The great Messiah, and his new commands,
Who speedily through all the Hierarchies
Intends to pass triumphant, and give laws.'
　　"So spake the false Archangel, and infused
Bad influence into the unwary breast
Of his associate. He together calls,
Or several one by one, the regent Powers,
Under him regent; tells, as he was taught,
That, the Most High commanding, now ere Night,

Now ere dim Night had disencumbered Heaven,   700
The great hierarchal standard was to move;
Tells the suggested cause, and casts between
Ambiguous words and jealousies, to sound
Or taint integrity. But all obeyed
The wonted signal, and superior voice
Of their great Potentate; for great indeed
His name, and high was his degree in Heaven;
His countenance, as the morning-star that guides
The starry flock, allured them, and with lies
Drew after him the third part of Heaven's host.   710
Meanwhile, the Eternal Eye, whose sight discerns
Abstrusest thoughts, from forth his holy mount,
And from within the golden lamps that burn
Nightly before him, saw without their light
Rebellion rising—saw in whom, how spread
Among the Sons of Morn, what multitudes
Were banded to oppose his high decree;
And, smiling, to his only Son thus said:—
    "'Son, thou in whom my glory I behold
In full resplendence, Heir of all my might,   720
Nearly it now concerns us to be sure
Of our omnipotence, and with what arms
We mean to hold what anciently we claim
Of deity or empire: such a foe
Is rising, who intends to erect his throne
Equal to ours, throughout the spacious North;
Nor so content, hath in his thought to try
In battle what our power is or our right.
Let us advise, and to this hazard draw
With speed what force is left, and all employ   730
In our defence, lest unawares we lose
This our high place, our sanctuary, our hill.'
    "To whom the Son, with calm aspéct and clear,
Lightening divine, ineffable, serene,
Made answer:—'Mighty Father, thou thy foes
Justly hast in derision, and secure
Laugh'st at their vain designs and tumults vain—
Matter to me of glory, whom their hate
Illustrates, when they see all regal power
Given me to quell their pride, and in event   740
Know whether I be dextrous to subdue
Thy rebels, or be found the worst in Heaven.'

"So spake the Son; but Satan with his Powers
Far was advanced on winged speed, an host
Innumerable as the stars of night,
Or stars of morning, dew-drops which the sun
Impearls on every leaf and every flower.
Regions they passed, the mighty regencies
Of Seraphim and Potentates and Thrones
In their triple degrees—regions to which   750
All thy dominion, Adam, is no more
Than what this garden is to all the earth
And all the sea, from one entire globose
Stretched into longitude; which having passed,
At length into the limits of the North
They came, and Satan to his royal seat
High on a hill, far-blazing, as a mount
Raised on a mount, with pyramids and towers
From diamond quarries hewn and rocks of gold—
The palace of great Lucifer (so call   760
That structure, in the dialect of men
Interpreted) which, not long after, he,
Affecting all equality with God,
In imitation of that mount whereon
Messiah was declared in sight of Heaven,
The Mountain of the Congregation called;
For thither he assembled all his train,
Pretending so commanded to consult
About the great reception of their King
Thither to come, and with calumnious art   770
Of counterfeited truth thus held their ears:—
    "'Thrones, Dominations, Princedoms, Virtues, Powers—
If these magnific titles yet remain
Not merely titular, since by decree
Another now hath to himself engrossed
All power, and us eclipsed under the name
Of King Anointed; for whom all this haste
Of midnight march, and hurried meeting here,
This only to consult, how we may best,
With what may be devised of honors new,   780
Receive him coming to receive from us
Knee-tribute yet unpaid, prostration vile!
Too much to one! but double how endured—
To one and to his image now proclaimed?
But what if better counsels might erect

Our minds, and teach us to cast off this yoke!
Will ye submit your necks, and choose to bend
The supple knee? Ye will not, if I trust
To know ye right, or if ye know yourselves
Natives and Sons of Heaven possessed before   790
By none, and, if not equal all, yet free,
Equally free; for orders and degrees
Jar not with liberty, but well consist.
Who can in reason, then, or right, assume
Monarchy over such as live by right
His equals—if in power and splendor less,
In freedom equal? or can introduce
Law and edict on us, who without law
Err not? much less for this to be our Lord,
And look for adoration, to the abuse   800
Of those imperial titles which assert
Our being ordained to govern, not to serve!'
    "Thus far his bold discourse without control
Had audience, when, among the Seraphim,
Abdiel, than whom none with more zeal adored
The Deity, and divine commands obeyed,
Stood up, and in a flame of zeal severe
The current of his fury thus opposed:—
    "'O argument blasphemous, false, and proud—
Words which no ear ever to hear in Heaven   810
Expected; least of all from thee, ingrate,
In place thyself so high above thy peers!
Canst thou with impious obloquy condemn
The just decree of God, pronounced and sworn,
That to his only Son, by right endued
With regal sceptre, every soul in Heaven
Shall bend the knee, and in that honor due
Confess him rightful King? Unjust, thou say'st,
Flatly unjust, to bind with laws the free,
And equal over equals to let reign,   820
One over all with unsucceeded power!
Shalt thou give law to God? shalt thou dispute
With Him the points of liberty, who made
Thee what thou art, and formed the Powers of Heaven
Such as he pleased, and circumscribed their being?
Yet, by experience taught, we know how good,
And of our good and of our dignity
How provident, he is—how far from thought

To make us less; bent rather to exalt
Our happy state, under one head more near   830
United. But—to grant it thee unjust
That equal over equals monarch reign—
Thyself, though great and glorious, dost thou count,
Of all angelic nature joined in one,
Equal to him, begotten Son, by whom,
As by his Word, the Mighty Father made
All things, even thee, and all the Spirits of Heaven
By him created in their bright degrees,
Crowned them with glory, and to their glory named
Thrones, Dominations, Princedoms, Virtues, Powers?—   840
Essential Powers; nor by his reign obscured,
But more illustrious made; since he, the head,
One of our number thus reduced becomes;
His laws our laws; all honor to him done
Returns our own. Cease, then, this impious rage,
And tempt not these; but hasten to appease
The incensèd Father and the incensèd Son
While pardon may be found, in time besought.'
    "So spake the fervent Angel; but his zeal
None seconded, as out of season judged,   850
Or singular and rash. Whereat rejoiced
The Apostate, and, more haughty, thus replied:—
    "'That we were formed, then, say'st thou? and the work
Of secondary hands, by task transferred
From Father to his Son? Strange point and new!
Doctrine which we would know whence learned. Who saw
When this creation was? Remember'st thou
Thy making, while the Maker gave thee being?
We know no time when we were not as now;
Know none before us, self-begot, self-raised   860
By our own quickening power when fatal course
Had circled his full orb, the birth mature
Of this our native Heaven, Ethereal Sons.
Our puissance is our own; our own right hand
Shall teach us highest deeds, by proof to try
Who is our equal. Then thou shalt behold
Whether by supplication we intend
Address, and to begirt the Almighty Throne
Beseeching or besieging. This report,
These tidings, carry to the Anointed King;   870
And fly, ere evil intercept thy flight.'

"He said; and, as the sound of waters deep,
Hoarse murmur echoed to his words applause
Through the infinite host. Nor less for that
The flaming Seraph, fearless, though alone,
Encompassed round with foes, thus answered bold:—
    "'O alienate from God, O Spirit accursed,
Forsaken of all good! I see thy fall
Determined, and thy hapless crew involved
In this perfidious fraud, contagion spread   880
Both of thy crime and punishment. Henceforth
No more be troubled how to quit the yoke
Of God's Messiah. Those indulgent laws
Will not be now voutsafed; other decrees
Against thee are gone forth without recall;
That golden sceptre which thou didst reject,
Is now an iron rod to bruise and break
Thy disobedience. Well thou didst advise;
Yet not for thy advice or threats I fly
These wicked tents devoted, lest the wrath   890
Impendent, raging into sudden flame,
Distinguish not: for soon expect to feel
His thunder on thy head, devouring fire.
Then who created thee lamenting learn
When who can uncreate thee thou shalt know.'
    "So spake the Seraph Abdiel, faithful found;
Among the faithless faithful only he;
Among innumerable false unmoved,
Unshaken, unseduced, unterrified,
His loyalty he kept, his love, his zeal;   900
Nor number nor example with him wrought
To swerve from truth, or change his constant mind,
Though single. From amidst them forth he passed,
Long way through hostile scorn, which he sustained
Superior, nor of violence feared aught;
And with retorted scorn his back he turned
On those proud towers, to swift destruction doomed."

BOOK VI

THE ARGUMENT

RAPHAEL continues to relate how Michael and Gabriel were sent forth
to battle against Satan and his Angels. The first fight described: Satan and
his Powers retire under night. He calls a council; invents devilish engines,
which, in the second day's fight, put Michael and his Angels to some dis-
order; but they at length, pulling up mountains, overwhelmed both the
force and machines of Satan. Yet, the tumult not so ending, God, on the
third day, sends Messiah his Son, for whom he had reserved the glory of
that victory. He, in the power of his Father, coming to the place, and
causing all his legions to stand still on either side, with his chariot and
thunder driving into the midst of his enemies, pursues them, unable to
resist, towards the wall of Heaven; which opening, they leap down with
horror and confusion into the place of punishment prepared for them in
the Deep. Messiah returns with triumph to his Father.

> "All night the dreadless Angel, unpursued,
> Through Heaven's wide champain held his way, till Morn,
> Waked by the circling Hours, with rosy hand
> Unbarred the gates of Light. There is a cave
> Within the Mount of God, fast by his throne,
> Where Light and Darkness in perpetual round
> Lodge and dislodge by turns—which makes through Heaven
> Grateful vicissitude, like day and night;
> Light issues forth, and at the other door
> Obsequious Darkness enters, till her hour   10
> To veil the heaven, though darkness there might well
> Seem twilight here. And now went forth the Morn
> Such as in highest heaven, arrayed in gold
> Empyreal; from before her vanished Night,

Shot through with orient beams; when all the plain
Covered with thick embattled squadrons bright,
Chariots, and flaming arms, and fiery steeds,
Reflecting blaze on blaze, first met his view.
War he perceived, war in procinct, and found
Already known what he for news had thought   20
To have reported. Gladly then he mixed
Among those friendly Powers, who him received
With joy and acclamations loud, that one,
That of so many myriads fallen yet one,
Returned not lost. On to the sacred hill
They led him, high applauded, and present
Before the seat supreme; from whence a voice,
From midst a golden cloud, thus mild was heard:—
    "'Servant of God, well done! Well hast thou fought
The better fight, who single hast maintained   30
Against revolted multitudes the cause
Of truth, in word mightier than they in arms,
And for the testimony of truth hast borne
Universal reproach, far worse to bear
Than violence; for this was all thy care—
To stand approved in sight of God, though worlds
Judged thee perverse. The easier conquest now
Remains thee—aided by this host of friends,
Back on thy foes more glorious to return
Than scorned thou didst depart; and to subdue   40
By force who reason for their law refuse—
Right reason for their law, and for their King
Messiah, who by right of merit reigns.
Go, Michael, of celestial armies prince,
And thou, in military prowess next,
Gabriel; lead forth to battle these my sons
Invincible; lead forth my armed Saints,
By thousands and by millions ranged for fight,
Equal in number to that godless crew
Rebellious. Them with fire and hostile arms   50
Fearless assault; and to the brow of Heaven
Pursuing, drive them out from God and bliss
Into their place of punishment, the gulf
Of Tartarus, which ready opens wide
His fiery chaos to receive their fall.'
    "So spake the Sovran Voice; and clouds began
To darken all the hill, and smoke to roll

In dusky wreaths reluctant flames, the sign
Of wrath awaked; nor with less dread the loud
Ethereal trumpet from on high gan blow.   60
At which command the Powers Militant
That stood for Heaven, in mighty quadrate joined
Of union irresistible, moved on
In silence their bright legions to the sound
Of instrumental harmony, that breathed
Heroic ardor to adventurous deeds
Under their godlike leaders, in the cause
Of God and his Messiah. On they move,
Indissolubly firm; nor obvious hill,
Nor straitening vale, nor wood, nor stream, divides   70
Their perfect ranks; for high above the ground
Their march was, and the passive air upbore
Their nimble tread. As when the total kind
Of birds, in orderly array on wing,
Came summoned over Eden to receive
Their names of thee; so over many a tract
Of Heaven they marched, and many a province wide,
Tenfold the length of this terrene. At last,
Far in the horizon, to the north, appeared
From skirt to skirt a fiery region, stretched   80
In battailous aspect; and nearer view,
Bristled with upright beams innumerable
Of rigid spears, and helmets thronged, and shields
Various, with boastful argument portrayed,
The banded Powers of Satan hasting on
With furious expedition: for they weened
That self-same day, by fight or by surprise,
To win the Mount of God, and on his throne
To set the envier of his state, the proud
Aspirer. But their thoughts proved fond and vain   90
In the mid-way; though strange to us it seemed
At first that Angel should with Angel war,
And in fierce hosting meet, who wont to meet
So oft in festivals of joy and love
Unanimous, as sons of one great Sire,
Hymning the Eternal Father. But the shout
Of battle now began, and rushing sound
Of onset ended soon each milder thought.
High in the midst, exalted as a God,
The Apostate in his sun-bright chariot sat,   100

Idol of majesty divine, enclosed
With flaming Cherubim and golden shields;
Then lighted from his gorgeous throne—for now
'Twixt host and host but narrow space was left,
A dreadful interval, and front to front
Presented stood, in terrible array
Of hideous length. Before the cloudy van,
On the rough edge of battle ere it joined,
Satan, with vast and haughty strides advanced,
Came towering, armed in adamant and gold.   110
Abdiel that sight endured not, where he stood
Among the mightiest, bent on highest deeds,
And thus his own undaunted heart explores:—
   "'O Heaven! that such resemblance of the Highest
Should yet remain, where faith and realty
Remain not! Wherefore should not strength and might
There fail where virtue fails, or weakest prove
Where boldest, though to sight unconquerable?
His puissance, trusting in the Almighty's aid,
I mean to try, whose reason I have tried   120
Unsound and false; nor is it aught but just
That he who in debate of truth had won
Should win in arms, in both disputes alike
Victor. Though brutish that contést and foul,
When reason hath to deal with force, yet so
Most reason is that reason overcome.'
   "So pondering, and from his armed peers
Forth-stepping opposite, half-way he met
His daring foe, at this prevention more
Incensed, and thus securely him defied:—   130
   "'Proud, art thou met? Thy hope was to have reached
The highth of thy aspiring unopposed—
The throne of God unguarded, and his side
Abandoned at the terror of thy power
Or potent tongue. Fool! not to think how vain
Against the Omnipotent to rise in arms;
Who, out of smallest things, could, without end
Have raised incessant armies to defeat
Thy folly; or with solitary hand,
Reaching beyond all limit, at one blow,   140
Unaided could have finished thee, and whelmed
Thy legions under darkness! But thou seest
All are not of thy train; there be who faith

Prefer, and piety to God, though then
To thee not visible when I alone
Seemed in thy world erroneous to dissent
From all: my Sect thou seest: now learn too late
How few sometimes may know when thousands err.'
   "Whom the grand Foe, with scornful eye askance,
Thus answered:—'Ill for thee, but in wished hour   150
Of my revenge, first sought for, thou return'st
From flight, seditious Angel, to receive
Thy merited reward, the first assay
Of this right hand provoked, since first that tongue,
Inspired with contradiction, durst oppose
A third part of the Gods, in synod met
Their deities to assert: who, while they feel
Vigor divine within them, can allow
Omnipotence to none. But well thou com'st
Before thy fellows, ambitious to win   160
From me some plume, that thy success may show
Destruction to the rest. This pause between
(Unanswered lest thou boast) to let thee know.—
At first I thought that Liberty and Heaven
To heavenly souls had been all one: but now
I see that most through sloth had rather serve,
Ministering Spirits, trained up in feast and song:
Such hast thou armed, the minstrelsy of heaven—
Servility with freedom to contend,
As both their deeds compared this day shall prove.'   170
   "To whom, in brief, thus Abdiel stern replied:—
'Apostate! still thou err'st, nor end wilt find
Of erring, from the path of truth remote.
Unjustly thou deprav'st it with the name
Of servitude, to serve whom God ordains,
Or Nature: God and Nature bid the same,
When he who rules is worthiest, and excels
Them whom he governs. This is servitude—
To serve the unwise, or him who hath rebelled
Against his worthier, as thine now serve thee,   180
Thyself not free, but to thyself enthralled;
Yet lewdly dar'st our ministering upbraid.
Reign thou in Hell, thy kingdom; let me serve
In Heaven God ever blest, and his divine
Behests obey, worthiest to be obeyed.
Yet chains in Hell, not realms, expect: meanwhile,

From me returned, as erst thou saidst, from flight,
This greeting on thy impious crest receive.'
   "So saying, a noble stroke he lifted high,
Which hung not, but so swift with tempest fell   190
On the proud crest of Satan that no sight,
Nor motion of swift thought, less could his shield,
Such ruin intercept. Ten paces huge
He back recoiled; the tenth on bended knee
His massy spear upstayed: as if, on earth,
Winds under ground, or waters forcing way,
Sidelong had pushed a mountain from his seat,
Half-sunk with all his pines. Amazement seized
The rebel Thrones, but greater rage, to see
Thus foiled their mightiest; ours joy filled, and shout,   200
Presage of victory, and fierce desire
Of battle: whereat Michaël bid sound
The Archangel trumpet. Through the vast of Heaven
It sounded, and the faithful armies rung
Hosannah to the Highest; nor stood at gaze
The adverse legions, nor less hideous joined
The horrid shock. Now storming fury rose,
And clamor such as heard in Heaven till now
Was never; arms on armor clashing brayed
Horrible discord, and the madding wheels   210
Of brazen chariots raged; dire was the noise
Of conflict; overhead the dismal hiss
Of fiery darts in flaming vollies flew,
And, flying, vaulted either host with fire.
So under fiery cope together rushed
Both battles main with ruinous assault
And inextinguishable rage. All Heaven
Resounded; and, had Earth been then, all Earth
Had to her centre shook. What wonder, when
Millions of fierce encountering Angels fought   220
On either side, the least of whom could wield
These elements, and arm him with the force
Of all their regions? How much more of power
Army against army numberless to raise
Dreadful combustion warring, and disturb,
Though not destroy, their happy native seat;
Had not the Eternal King Omnipotent
From his strong hold of Heaven high overruled
And limited their might, though numbered such

As each divided legion might have seemed   230
A numerous host, in strength each armed hand
A legion! Led in fight, yet leader seemed
Each warrior single as in chief; expert
When to advance, or stand, or turn the sway
Of battle, open when, and when to close
The ridges of grim war. No thought of flight,
None of retreat, no unbecoming deed
That argued fear; each on himself relied
As only in his arm the moment lay
Of victory. Deeds of eternal fame   240
Were done, but infinite; for wide was spread
That war, and various: sometimes on firm ground
A standing fight; then, soaring on main wing,
Tormented all the air; all air seemed then
Conflicting fire. Long time in even scale
The battle hung; till Satan, who that day
Prodigious power had shown, and met in arms
No equal, ranging through the dire attack
Of fighting Seraphim confused, at length
Saw where the sword of Michael smote, and felled   250
Squadrons at once: with huge two-handed sway
Brandished aloft, the horrid edge came down
Wide-wasting. Such destruction to withstand
He hasted, and opposed the rocky orb
Of tenfold adamant, his ample shield,
A vast circumference. At his approach
The great Archangel from his warlike toil
Surceased, and, glad, as hoping here to end
Intestine war in Heaven, the Arch-foe subdued,
Or captive dragged in chains, with hostile frown   260
And visage all inflamed, first thus began:—
    "'Author of Evil, unknown till thy revolt,
Unnamed in Heaven, now plenteous as thou seest
These acts of hateful strife—hateful to all,
Though heaviest, by just measure, on thyself
And thy adherents—how hast thou disturbed
Heaven's blessed peace, and into Nature brought
Misery, uncreated till the crime
Of thy rebellion! how hast thou instilled
Thy malice into thousands, once upright   270
And faithful, now proved false! But think not here
To trouble holy rest; Heaven casts thee out

From all her confines; Heaven, the seat of bliss,
Brooks not the works of violence and war.
Hence, then, and Evil go with thee along,
Thy offspring, to the place of Evil, Hell—
Thou and thy wicked crew! there mingle broils!
Ere this avenging sword begin thy doom,
Or some more sudden vengeance, winged from God,
Precipitate thee with augmented pain.'   280
    "So spake the Prince of Angels; to whom thus
The Adversary:—'Nor think thou with wind
Of airy threats to awe whom yet with deeds
Thou canst not. Hast thou turned the least of these
To flight—or, if to fall, but that they rise
Unvanquished—easier to transact with me
That thou shouldst hope, imperious, and with threats
To chase me hence? Err not that so shall end
The strife which thou call'st evil, but we style
The strife of glory; which we mean to win,   290
Or turn this Heaven itself into the Hell
Thou fablest; here, however, to dwell free,
If not to reign. Meanwhile, thy utmost force—
And join him named Almighty to thy aid—
I fly not, but have sought thee far and nigh.'
    "They ended parle, and both addressed for fight
Unspeakable; for who, though with the tongue
Of Angels, can relate, or to what things
Liken on Earth conspicuous, that may lift
Human imagination to such highth   300
Of godlike power? for likest gods they seemed,
Stood they or moved, in stature, motion, arms,
Fit to decide the empire of great Heaven.
Now waved their fiery swords, and in the air
Made horrid circles; two broad suns their shields
Blazed opposite, while Expectation stood
In horror; from each hand with speed retired,
Where erst was thickest fight, the Angelic throng,
And left large field, unsafe within the wind
Of such commotion: such as (to set forth   310
Great things by small) if, Nature's concord broke,
Among the constellations war were sprung,
Two planets, rushing from aspéct malign
Of fiercest opposition, in mid sky
Should combat, and their jarring spheres confound.

Together both, with next to almighty arm
Uplifted imminent, one stroke they aimed
That might determine, and not need repeat
As not of power, at once; nor odds appeared
In might or swift prevention. But the sword   320
Of Michael from the armory of God
Was given him tempered so that neither keen
Nor solid might resist that edge: it met
The sword of Satan, with steep force to smite
Descending, and in half cut sheer; nor stayed,
But, with swift wheel reverse, deep entering, shared
All his right side. Then Satan first knew pain,
And writhed him to and fro convolved; so sore
The griding sword with discontinuous wound
Passed through him. But the ethereal substance closed,   330
Not long divisible; and from the gash
A stream of nectarous humor issuing flowed
Sanguine, such as celestial Spirits may bleed,
And all his armor stained, erewhile so bright,
Forthwith, on all sides, to his aid was run
By Angels many and strong, who interposed
Defence, while others bore him on their shields
Back to his chariot where it stood retired
From off the files of war: there they him laid
Gnashing for anguish, and despite, and shame   340
To find himself not matchless, and his pride
Humbled by such rebuke, so far beneath
His confidence to equal God in power.
Yet soon he healed; for Spirits, that live throughout
Vital in every part—not, as frail Man,
In entrails, heart or head, liver or reins—
Cannot but by annihilating die;
Nor in their liquid texture mortal wound
Receive, no more than can the fluid air:
All heart they live, all head, all eye, all ear,   350
All intellect, all sense; and as they please
They limb themselves, and color, shape, or size
Assume, as likes them best, condense or rare.
    "Meanwhile, in other parts, like deeds deserved
Memorial, where the might of Gabriel fought,
And with fierce ensigns pierced the deep array
Of Moloch, furious king, who him defied,
And at his chariot-wheels to drag him bound

Threatened, nor from the Holy One of Heaven
Refrained his tongue blasphémous, but anon,   360
Down cloven to the waist, with shattered arms
And uncouth pain fled bellowing. On each wing
Uriel, and Raphaël his vaunting foe,
Though huge and in a rock of diamond armed,
Vanquished—Adramelech and Asmadai,
Two potent Thrones, that to be less than Gods
Disdained, but meaner thoughts learned in their flight,
Mangled with ghastly wounds through plate and mail.
Nor stood unmindful Abdiel to annoy
The atheist crew, but with redoubled blow   370
Ariel, and Arioch, and the violence
Of Ramiel, scorched and blasted, overthrew.
I might relate of thousands, and their names
Eternize here on Earth; but those elect
Angels, contented with their fame in Heaven,
Seek not the praise of men: the other sort,
In might though wondrous and in acts of war,
Nor of renown less eager, yet by doom
Cancelled from Heaven and sacred memory,
Nameless in dark oblivion let them dwell   380
For strength from truth divided, and from just,
Illaudable, nought merits but dispraise
And ignominy, yet to glory aspires,
Vain-glorious, and through infamy seeks fame:
Therefore eternal silence be their doom!
     "And now, their mightiest quelled, the battle swerved,
With many an inroad gored; deformed rout
Entered, and foul disorder; all the ground
With shivered armor strown, and on a heap
Chariot and charioter lay overturned,   390
And fiery foaming steeds; what stood recoiled
O'er-wearied, through the faint Satanic host,
Defensive scarce, or with pale fear surprised—
Then first with fear surprised and sense of pain—
Fled ignominious, to such evil brought
By sin of disobedience, till that hour
Not liable to fear, or flight, or pain.
Far otherwise the inviolable Saints
In cubic phalanx firm advanced entire,
Invulnerable, impenetrably armed;   400
Such high advantages their innocence

Gave them above their foes—not to have sinned,
Not to have disobeyed; in fight they stood
Unwearied, unobnoxious to be pained
By wound, though from their place by violence moved.
    "Now Night her course began, and, over Heaven
Inducing darkness, grateful truce imposed,
And silence on the odious din of war.
Under her cloudy covert both retired,
Victor and vanquished. On the foughten field   410
Michaël and his Angels, prevalent
Encamping, placed in guard their watches round,
Cherubic waving fires: on the other part,
Satan with his rebellious disappeared,
Far in the dark dislodged, and, void of rest,
His potentates to council called by night,
And in the midst thus undismayed began:—
    "'O now in danger tried, now known in arms
Not to be overpowered, companions dear,
Found worthy not of liberty alone—   420
Too mean pretence—but, what we more affect,
Honor, dominion, glory, and renown;
Who have sustained one day in doubtful fight
(And, if one day, why not eternal days?)
What Heaven's Lord had powerfullest to send
Against us from about his throne, and judged
Sufficient to subdue us to his will,
But proves not so: then fallible, it seems,
Of future we may deem him, though till now
Omniscient thought! True is, less firmly armed,   430
Some disadvantage we endured, and pain—
Till now not known, but, known, as soon contemned;
Since now we find this our empyreal form
Incapable of mortal injury,
Imperishable, and, though pierced with wound,
Soon closing, and by native vigor healed.
Of evil, then, so small as easy think
The remedy: perhaps more valid arms,
Weapons more violent, when next we meet,
May serve to better us and worse our foes,   440
Or equal what between us made the odds,
In nature none. If other hidden cause
Left them superior, while we can preserve
Unhurt our minds, and understanding sound,

Due search and consultation will disclose.'
   "He sat; and in the assembly next upstood
Nisroch, of Principalities the prime.
As one he stood escaped from cruel fight
Sore toiled, his riven arms to havoc hewn,
And, cloudy in aspéct, thus answering spake:—   450
   "'Deliverer from new Lords, leader to free
Enjoyment of our right as Gods! yet hard
For Gods, and too unequal work, we find
Against unequal arms to fight in pain,
Against unpained, impassive; from which evil
Ruin must needs ensue. For what avails
Valor or strength, though matchless, quelled with pain,
Which all subdues, and makes remiss the hands
Of mightiest? Sense of pleasure we may well
Spare out of life perhaps, and not repine,   460
But live content—which is the calmest life;
But pain is perfect misery, the worst
Of evils, and, excessive, overturns
All patience. He who, therefore, can invent
With what more forcible we may offend
Our yet unwounded enemies, or arm
Ourselves with like defence, to me deserves
No less than for deliverance what we owe.'
   "Whereto, with look composed, Satan replied:—
'Not uninvented that, which thou aright   470
Believ'st so main to our success, I bring.
Which of us who beholds the bright surfáce
Of this ethereous mould whereon we stand—
This continent of spacious Heaven, adorned
With plant, fruit, flower ambrosial, gems and gold—
Whose eye so superficially surveys
These things as not to mind from whence they grow
Deep under ground: materials dark and crude,
Of spiritous and fiery spume, till, touched
With Heaven's ray, and tempered, they shoot forth   480
So beauteous, opening to the ambient light?
These in their dark nativity the Deep
Shall yield us, pregnant with infernal flame;
Which, into hollow engines, long and round
Thick-rammed, at the other bore with touch of fire
Dilated and infuriate, shall send forth
From far, with thundering noise, among our foes

Such implements of mischief as shall dash
To pieces and o'erwhelm whatever stands
Adverse, that they shall fear we have disarmed   490
The Thunderer of his only dreaded bolt.
Nor long shall be our labor; yet ere dawn
Effect shall end our wish. Meanwhile revive;
Abandon fear; to strength and counsel joined
Think nothing hard, much less to be despaired.'
    "He ended; and his words their drooping cheer
Enlightened, and their languished hope revived.
The invention all admired, and each how he
To be the inventor missed; so easy it seemed
Once found, which yet unfound most would have thought   500
Impossible! Yet, haply, of thy race,
In future days, if malice should abound,
Some one, intent on mischief, or inspired
With devilish machination, might devise
Like instrument to plague the sons of men
For sin, on war and mutual slaughter bent.
Forthwith from council to the work they flew;
None arguing stood; innumerable hands
Were ready; in a moment up they turned
Wide the celestial soil, and saw beneath   510
The originals of Nature in their crude
Conception; sulphurous and nitrous foam
They found, they mingled, and, with subtle art
Concocted and adusted, they reduced
To blackest grain, and into store conveyed.
Part hidden veins digged up (nor hath this Earth
Entrails unlike) of mineral and stone,
Whereof to found their engines and their balls
Of missive ruin; part incentive reed
Provide, pernicious with one touch to fire.   520
So all ere day-spring, under conscious Night,
Secret they finished, and in order set,
With silent circumspection, unespied.
    "Now, when fair Morn orient in Heaven appeared,
Up rose the victor Angels, and to arms
The matin trumpet sung. In arms they stood
Of golden panoply, refulgent host,
Soon banded; others from the dawning hills
Looked round, and scouts each coast light-armèd scour,
Each quarter, to descry the distant foe,   530

Where lodged, or whither fled, or if for fight,
In motion or in halt. Him soon they met
Under spread ensigns moving nigh, in slow
But firm battalion: back with speediest sail
Zophiel, of Cherubim the swiftest wing,
Came flying, and in mid air aloud thus cried:—
   "'Arm, Warriors, arm for fight! The foe at hand,
Whom fled we thought, will save us long pursuit
This day; fear not his flight; so thick a cloud
He comes, and settled in his face I see   540
Sad resolution and secure. Let each
His adamantine coat gird well, and each
Fit well his helm, gripe fast his orbed shield,
Borne even or high; for this day will pour down,
If I conjecture aught, no drizzling shower,
But rattling storm of arrows barbed with fire.'
   "So warned he them, aware themselves, and soon
In order, quit of all impediment.
Instant, without disturb, they took alarm,
And onward moved embattled: when, behold,   550
Not distant far, with heavy pace the foe
Approaching gross and huge, in hollow cube
Training his devilish enginry, impaled
On every side with shadowing squadrons deep,
To hide the fraud. At interview both stood
A while; but suddenly at head appeared
Satan, and thus was heard commanding loud:—
   "'Vanguard, to right and left the front unfold,
That all may see who hate us how we seek
Peace and composure, and with open breast   560
Stand ready to receive them, if they like
Our overture, and turn not back perverse:
But that I doubt. However, witness Heaven!
Heaven, witness thou anon! while we discharge
Freely our part. Ye, who appointed stand,
Do as you have in charge, and briefly touch
What we propound, and loud that all may hear.'
   "So scoffing in ambiguous words, he scarce
Had ended, when to right and left the front
Divided, and to either flank retired;   570
Which to our eyes discovered, new and strange,
A triple mounted row of pillars laid
On wheels (for like to pillars most they seemed,

Or hollowed bodies made of oak or fir,
With branches lopt, in wood or mountain felled),
Brass, iron, stony mould, had not their mouths
With hideous orifice gaped on us wide,
Portending hollow truce. At each, behind,
A Seraph stood, and in his hand a reed
Stood waving tipt with fire; while we, suspense,   580
Collected stood within our thoughts amused.
Not long! for sudden all at once their reeds
Put forth, and to a narrow vent applied
With nicest touch. Immediate in a flame,
But soon obscured with smoke, all Heaven appeared,
From those deep-throated engines belched, whose roar
Embowelled with outrageous noise the air,
And all her entrails tore, disgorging foul
Their devilish glut, chained thunderbolts and hail
Of iron globes; which, on the victor host   590
Levelled, with such impetuous fury smote,
That whom they hit none on their feet might stand,
Though standing else as rocks, but down they fell
By thousands, Angel on Archangel rolled,
The sooner for their arms. Unarmed, they might
Have easily, as Spirits, evaded swift
By quick contraction or remove; but now
Foul dissipation followed, and forced rout;
Nor served it to relax their serried files.
What should they do? If on they rushed, repulse   600
Repeated, and indecent overthrow
Doubled, would render them yet more despised,
And to their foes a laughter—for in view
Stood ranked of Seraphim another row,
In posture to displode their second tire
Of thunder; back defeated to return
They worse abhorred. Satan beheld their plight,
And to his mates thus in derision called:—
    "'O friends, why come not on these victors proud?
Erewhile they fierce were coming; and, when we,   610
To entertain them fair with open front
And breast (what could we more?), propounded terms
Of composition, straight they changed their minds,
Flew off, and into strange vagaries fell,
As they would dance. Yet for a dance they seemed
Somewhat extravagant and wild; perhaps

For joy of offered peace. But I suppose,
If our proposals once again were heard,
We should compel them to a quick result.'
  "To whom thus Belial, in like gamesome mood:— 620
'Leader, the terms we sent were terms of weight,
Of hard contents, and full of force urged home,
Such as we might perceive amused them all,
And stumbled many. Who receives them right
Had need from head to foot well understand;
Not understood, this gift they have besides—
They show us when our foes walk not upright.'
  "So they among themselves in pleasant vein
Stood scoffing, highthened in their thoughts beyond
All doubt of victory; Eternal Might 630
To match with their inventions they presumed
So easy, and of his thunder made a scorn,
And all his host derided, while they stood
A while in trouble. But they stood not long;
Rage prompted them at length, and found them arms
Against such hellish mischief fit to oppose.
Forthwith (behold the excellence, the power,
Which God hath in his mighty Angels placed!)
Their arms away they threw, and to the hills
(For Earth hath this variety from Heaven 640
Of pleasure situate in hill and dale)
Light as the lightning-glimpse they ran, they flew;
From their foundations, loosening to and fro,
They plucked the seated hills, with all their load,
Rocks, waters, woods, and by the shaggy tops
Uplifting, bore them in their hands. Amaze,
Be sure, and terror, seized the rebel host,
When coming towards them so dread they saw
The bottom of the mountains upward turned,
Till on those cursed engines' triple row 650
They saw them whelmed, and all their confidence
Under the weight of mountains buried deep;
Themselves invaded next, and on their heads
Main promontories flung, which in the air
Came shadowing, and oppressed whole legions armed.
Their armor helped their harm, crushed in and bruised,
Into their substance pent—which wrought them pain
Implacable, and many a dolorous groan,
Long struggling underneath, ere they could wind

Out of such prison, though Spirits of purest light,   660
Purest at first, now gross by sinning grown.
The rest, in imitation, to like arms
Betook them, and the neighboring hills uptore;
So hills amid the air encountered hills,
Hurled to and fro with jaculation dire,
That underground they fought in dismal shade:
Infernal noise! war seemed a civil game
To this uproar; horrid confusion heaped
Upon confusion rose. And now all Heaven
Had gone to wrack, with ruin overspread,   670
Had not the Almighty Father, where he sits
Shrined in his sanctuary of Heaven secure,
Consulting on the sum of things, foreseen
This tumult, and permitted all, advised,
That his great purpose he might so fulfil,
To honor his Anointed Son, avenged
Upon his enemies, and to declare
All power on him transferred. Whence to his Son,
The assessor of his throne, he thus began:—
    "'Effulgence of my glory, Son beloved,   680
Son in whose face invisible is beheld
Visibly, what by Deity I am,
And in whose hand what by decree I do,
Second Omnipotence! two days are passed,
Two days, as we compute the days of Heaven,
Since Michael and his Powers went forth to tame
These disobedient. Sore hath been their fight,
As likeliest was when two such foes met armed:
For to themselves I left them; and thou know'st
Equal in their creation they were formed,   690
Save what sin hath impaired—which yet hath wrought
Insensibly, for I suspend their doom:
Whence in perpetual fight they needs must last
Endless, and no solution will be found.
War wearied hath performed what war can do,
And to disordered rage let loose the reins,
With mountains, as with weapons, armed; which makes
Wild work in Heaven, and dangerous to the main.
Two days are, therefore, passed; the third is thine:
For thee I have ordained it, and thus far   700
Have suffered, that the glory may be thine
Of ending this great war, since none but thou

Can end it. Into thee such virtue and grace
Immense I have transfused, that all may know
In Heaven and Hell thy power above compare,
And this perverse commotion governed thus,
To manifest thee worthiest to be Heir
Of all things—to be Heir, and to be King
By sacred unction, thy deserved right.
Go, then, thou Mightiest, in thy Father's might;   710
Ascend my chariot; guide the rapid wheels
That shake Heaven's basis; bring forth all my war;
My bow and thunder, my almighty arms,
Gird on, and sword upon thy puissant thigh;
Pursue these Sons of Darkness, drive them out
From all Heaven's bounds into the utter Deep;
There let them learn, as likes them, to despise
God, and Messiah his anointed King.'
    "He said, and on his Son with rays direct
Shone full. He all his Father full expressed   720
Ineffably into his face received;
And thus the Filial Godhead answering spake:—
    "'O Father, O Supreme of Heavenly Thrones,
First, Highest, Holiest, Best, thou always seek'st
To glorify thy Son; I always thee,
As is most just. This I my glory account,
My exaltation, and my whole delight,
That thou in me, well pleased, declar'st thy will
Fulfilled, which to fulfil is all my bliss.
Sceptre and power, thy giving, I assume,   730
And gladlier shall resign when in the end
Thou shalt be all in all, and I in thee
For ever, and in me all whom thou lov'st.
But whom thou hat'st I hate, and can put on
Thy terrors, as I put thy mildness on,
Image of thee in all things: and shall soon,
Armed with thy might, rid Heaven of these rebelled,
To their prepared ill mansion driven down,
To chains of darkness and the undying worm,
That from thy just obedience could revolt,   740
Whom to obey is happiness entire.
Then shall thy Saints, unmixed, and from the impure
Far separate, circling thy holy Mount,
Unfeigned halleluiahs to thee sing,
Hymns of high praise, and I among them chief.'

"So said, he, o'er his sceptre bowing, rose
From the right hand of Glory where he sat;
And the third sacred morn began to shine,
Dawning through Heaven. Forth rushed with whirlwind sound
The chariot of Paternal Deity,   750
Flashing thick flames, wheel within wheel; undrawn,
Itself instinct with spirit, but convoyed
By four cherubic Shapes. Four faces each
Had wondrous; as with stars, their bodies all
And wings were set with eyes; with eyes the wheels
Of beryl, and careering fires between;
Over their heads a crystal firmament,
Whereon a sapphire throne, inlaid with pure
Amber and colors of the showery arch.
He, in celestial panoply all armed   760
Of radiant Urim, work divinely wrought,
Ascended; at his right hand Victory
Sat eagle-winged; beside him hung his bow,
And quiver, with three-bolted thunder stored;
And from about him fierce effusion rolled
Of smoke and bickering flame and sparkles dire.
Attended with ten thousand thousand Saints,
He onward came; far off his coming shone;
And twenty thousand (I their number heard)
Chariots of God, half on each hand, were seen.   770
He on the wings of Cherub rode sublime
On the crystalline sky, in sapphire throned—
Illustrious far and wide, but by his own
First seen. Them unexpected joy surprised
When the great ensign of Messiah blazed
Aloft, by Angels borne, his sign in Heaven;
Under whose conduct Michael soon reduced
His army, circumfused on either wing,
Under their Head embodied all in one.
Before him Power Divine his way prepared;   780
At his command the uprooted hills retired
Each to his place; they heard his voice, and went
Obsequious; Heaven his wonted face renewed,
And with fresh flowerets hill and valley smiled.
    "This saw his hapless foes, but stood obdured,
And to rebellious fight rallied their Powers,
Insensate, hope conceiving from despair.
In Heavenly Spirits could such perverseness dwell?

But to convince the proud what signs avail,
Or wonders move the obdurate to relent?   790
They, hardened more by what might most reclaim,
Grieving to see his glory, at the sight
Took envy, and, aspiring to his highth,
Stood re-embattled fierce, by force or fraud
Weening to prosper, and at length prevail
Against God and Messiah, or to fall
In universal ruin last; and now
To final battle drew, disdaining flight,
Or faint retreat: when the great Son of God
To all his host on either hand thus spake:—   800
  "'Stand still in bright array, ye Saints; here stand,
Ye Angels armed; this day from battle rest.
Faithful hath been your warfare, and of God
Accepted, fearless in his righteous cause;
And, as ye have received, so have ye done,
Invincibly. But of this cursed crew
The punishment to other hand belongs;
Vengeance is his, or whose he sole appoints.
Number to this day's work is not ordained,
Nor multitude; stand only and behold   810
God's indignation on these godless poured
By me. Not you, but me, they have despised,
Yet envied; against me is all their rage,
Because the Father, to whom in Heaven supreme
Kingdom and power and glory appertains,
Hath honored me, according to his will.
Therefore to me their doom he hath assigned,
That they may have their wish, to try with me
In battle which the stronger proves—they all,
Or I alone against them; since by strength   820
They measure all, of other excellence
Not emulous, nor care who them excels;
Nor other strife with them do I voutsafe.'
  "So spake the Son, and into terror changed
His countenance, too severe to be beheld,
And full of wrath bent on his enemies.
At once the Four spread out their starry wings
With dreadful shade contiguous, and the orbs
Of his fierce chariot rolled, as with the sound
Of torrent floods, or of a numerous host.   830
He on his impious foes right onward drove,

Gloomy as Night. Under his burning wheels
The steadfast Empyrean shook throughout,
All but the throne itself of God. Full soon
Among them he arrived, in his right hand
Grasping ten thousand thunders, which he sent
Before him, such as in their souls infixed
Plagues. They, astonished, all resistance lost,
All courage; down their idle weapons dropt;
O'er shields, and helms, and helmed heads he rode   840
Of Thrones and mighty Seraphim prostráte,
That wished the mountains now might be again
Thrown on them, as a shelter from his ire.
Nor less on either side tempestuous fell
His arrows, from the fourfold-visaged Four,
Distinct with eyes, and from the living wheels
Distinct alike with multitude of eyes;
One spirit in them ruled, and every eye
Glared lightning, and shot forth pernicious fire
Among the accursed, that withered all their strength,   850
And of their wonted vigor left them drained,
Exhausted, spiritless, afflicted, fallen.
Yet half his strength he put not forth, but checked
His thunder in mid-volley; for he meant
Not to destroy, but root them out of Heaven.
The overthrown he raised, and as a herd
Of goats or timorous flock together thronged,
Drove them before him thunderstruck, pursued
With terrors and with furies to the bounds
And crystal wall of Heaven; which, opening wide,   860
Rolled inward, and a spacious gap disclosed
Into the wasteful Deep. The monstrous sight
Strook them with horror backward; but far worse
Urged them behind: headlong themselves they threw
Down from the verge of Heaven: eternal wrath
Burnt after them to the bottomless pit.
   "Hell heard the unsufferable noise; Hell saw
Heaven ruining from Heaven, and would have fled
Affrighted; but strict Fate had cast too deep
Her dark foundations, and too fast had bound.   870
Nine days they fell; confounded Chaos roared,
And felt tenfold confusion in their fall
Through his wild Anarchy; so huge a rout
Encumbered him with ruin. Hell at last,

Yawning, received them whole, and on them closed—
Hell, their fit habitation, fraught with fire
Unquenchable, the house of woe and pain.
Disburdened Heaven rejoiced, and soon repaired
Her mural breach, returning whence it rolled.
Sole victor, from the expulsion of his foes   880
Messiah his triumphal chariot turned.
To meet him all his Saints, who silent stood
Eye-witnesses of his almighty acts,
With jubilee advanced; and, as they went,
Shaded with branching palm, each order bright
Sung triumph, and him sung victorious King,
Son, Heir, and Lord, to him dominion given,
Worthiest to reign. He celebrated rode,
Triumphant through mid Heaven, into the courts
And temple of his mighty Father throned   890
On high; who into glory him received,
Where now he sits at the right hand of bliss.
   "Thus, measuring things in Heaven by things on Earth,
At thy request, and that thou may'st beware
By what is past, to thee I have revealed
What might have else to human race been hid—
The discord which befell, and war in Heaven
Among the Angelic Powers, and the deep fall
Of those too high aspiring who rebelled
With Satan: he who envies now thy state,   900
Who now is plotting how he may seduce
Thee also from obedience, that, with him
Bereaved of happiness, thou may'st partake
His punishment, eternal misery;
Which would be all his solace and revenge,
As a despite done against the Most High,
Thee once to gain companion of his woe.
But listen not to his temptations; warn
Thy weaker; let it profit thee to have heard,
By terrible example, the reward   910
Of disobedience. Firm they might have stood,
Yet fell. Remember, and fear to transgress."

BOOK VII

THE ARGUMENT

RAPHAEL, at the request of Adam, relates how and wherefore this World
was first created:—that God, after the expelling of Satan and his Angels
out of Heaven, declared his pleasure to create another World, and other
creatures to dwell therein; sends his Son with glory, and attendance of
Angels, to perform the work of creation in six days: the Angels celebrate
with hymns the performance thereof, and his reascension into Heaven.

Descend from Heaven, Urania, by that name
If rightly thou art called, whose voice divine
Following, above the Olympian hill I soar,
Above the flight of Pegasean wing!
The meaning, not the name, I call; for thou
Nor of the Muses nine, nor on the top
Of old Olympus dwell'st; but, heavenly-born,
Before the hills appeared or fountain flowed,
Thou with Eternal Wisdom didst converse,
Wisdom thy sister, and with her didst play   10
In presence of the Almighty Father, pleased
With thy celestial song. Up led by thee,
Into the Heaven of Heavens I have presumed,
An earthly guest, and drawn empyreal air,
Thy tempering. With like safety guided down,
Return me to my native element;
Lest, from this flying steed unreined (as once
Bellerophon, though from a lower clime)
Dismounted, on the Aleian field I fall,
Erroneous there to wander and forlorn.   20
Half yet remains unsung, but narrower bound

137

Within the visible Diurnal Sphere.
Standing on Earth, not rapt above the pole,
More safe I sing with mortal voice, unchanged
To hoarse or mute, though fallen on evil days,
On evil days though fallen, and evil tongues,
In darkness, and with dangers compassed round,
And solitude; yet not alone, while thou
Visit'st my slumbers nightly, or when Morn
Purples the East. Still govern thou my song,   30
Urania, and fit audience find, though few.
But drive far off the barbarous dissonance
Of Bacchus and his revellers, the race
Of that wild rout that tore the Thracian bard
In Rhodope, where woods and rocks had ears
To rapture, till the savage clamor drowned
Both harp and voice; nor could the Muse defend
Her son. So fail not thou who thee implores;
For thou art heavenly, she an empty dream.
    Say, Goddess, what ensued when Raphael,   40
The affable Archangel, had forewarned
Adam, by dire example, to beware
Apostasy, by what befell in Heaven
To those apostates, lest the like befall
In Paradise to Adam or his race,
Charged not to touch the interdicted Tree,
If they transgress, and slight that sole command,
So easily obeyed amid the choice
Of all tastes else to please their appetite,
Though wandering. He, with his consorted Eve,   50
The story heard attentive, and was filled
With admiration and deep muse, to hear
Of things so high and strange—things to their thought
So unimaginable as hate in Heaven,
And war so near the peace of God in bliss,
With such confusion; but the evil, soon
Driven back, redounded as a flood on those
From whom it sprung, impossible to mix
With blessedness. Whence Adam soon repealed
The doubts that in his heart arose; and, now   60
Led on, yet sinless, with desire to know
What nearer might concern him—how this World
Of heaven and earth conspicuous first began;
When, and whereof, created, for what cause;

What within Eden, or without, was done
Before his memory—as one whose drouth,
Yet scarce allayed, still eyes the current stream,
Whose liquid murmur heard new thirst excites,
Proceeded thus to ask his Heavenly Guest:—
    "Great things, and full of wonder in our ears,   70
Far differing from this World, thou hast revealed,
Divine Interpreter! by favor sent
Down from the Empyrean to forewarn
Us timely of what might else have been our loss,
Unknown, which human knowledge could not reach;
For which to the infinitely Good we owe
Immortal thanks, and his admonishment
Receive with solemn purpose to observe
Immutably his sovran will, the end
Of what we are. But, since thou hast voutsafed   80
Gently, for our instruction, to impart
Things above Earthly thought, which yet concerned
Our knowing, as to highest Wisdom seemed,
Deign to descend now lower, and relate
What may no less perhaps avail us known—
How first began this Heaven which we behold
Distant so high, with moving fires adorned
Innumerable; and this which yields or fills
All space, the ambient Air, wide interfused,
Embracing round this florid Earth; what cause   90
Moved the Creator, in his holy rest
Through all eternity, so late to build
In Chaos; and, the work begun, how soon
Absolved: if unforbid thou may'st unfold
What we not to explore the secrets ask
Of his eternal empire, but the more
To magnify his works the more we know.
And the great Light of Day yet wants to run
Much of his race, though steep. Suspense in heaven
Held by thy voice, thy potent voice he hears,   100
And longer will delay, to hear thee tell
His generation, and the rising birth
Of Nature from the unapparent Deep:
Or, if the Star of Evening and the Moon
Haste to thy audience, Night with her will bring
Silence, and Sleep listening to thee will watch;
Or we can bid his absence till thy song

End, and dismiss thee ere the morning shine."
    Thus Adam his illustrious guest besought;
And thus the godlike Angel answered mild:—   110
    "This also thy request, with caution asked,
Obtain; though to recount almighty works
What words or tongue of Seraph can suffice,
Or heart of man suffice to comprehend?
Yet what thou canst attain, which best may serve
To glorify the Maker, and infer
Thee also happier, shall not be withheld
Thy hearing. Such commission from above
I have received, to answer thy desire
Of knowledge within bounds; beyond abstain   120
To ask, nor let thine own inventions hope
Things not revealed, which the invisible King,
Only omniscient, hath suppressed in night;
To none communicable in Earth or Heaven.
Enough is left besides to search and know;
But Knowledge is as food, and needs no less
Her temperance over appetite, to know
In measure what the mind may well contain;
Oppresses else with surfeit, and soon turns
Wisdom to folly, as nourishment to wind.   130
    "Know then that, after Lucifer from Heaven
(So call him, brighter once amidst the host
Of Angels than that star the stars among)
Fell with his flaming legions through the Deep
Into his place, and the great Son returned
Victorious with his Saints, the Omnipotent
Eternal Father from his throne beheld
Their multitude, and to his Son thus spake:—
    "'At least our envious foe hath failed, who thought
All like himself rebellious; by whose aid   140
This inaccessible high strength, the seat
Of Deity supreme, us dispossessed,
He trusted to have seized, and into fraud
Drew many whom their place knows here no more.
Yet far the greater part have kept, I see,
Their station; Heaven, yet populous, retains
Number sufficient to possess her realms,
Though wide, and this high temple to frequent
With ministeries due and solemn rites.
But, lest his heart exalt him in the harm   150

Already done, to have dispeopled Heaven—
My damage fondly deemed—I can repair
That detriment, if such it be to lose
Self-lost, and in a moment will create
Another world; out of one man a race
Of men innumerable, there to dwell,
Not here, till, by degrees of merit raised,
They open to themselves at length the way
Up hither, under long obedience tried,
And Earth be changed to Heaven, and Heaven to Earth,   160
One kingdom, joy and union without end.
Meanwhile inhabit lax, ye Powers of Heaven;
And thou, my Word, begotten Son, by thee
This I perform; speak thou, and be it done!
My overshadowing Spirit and might with thee
I send along; ride forth, and bid the Deep
Within appointed bounds be heaven and earth.
Boundless the Deep, because I am who fill
Infinitude; nor vacuous the space,
Though I, uncircumscribed, myself retire,   170
And put not forth my goodness, which is free
To act or not. Necessity and Chance
Approach not me, and what I will is Fate.'
   "So spake the Almighty; and to what he spake
His Word, the Filial Godhead, gave effect.
Immediate are the acts of God, more swift
Than time or motion, but to human ears
Cannot without process of speech be told,
So told as earthly notion can receive.
Great triumph and rejoicing was in Heaven   180
When such was heard declared the Almighty's will.
Glory they sung to the Most High, good-will
To future men, and in their dwellings peace—
Glory to Him whose just avenging ire
Had driven out the ungodly from his sight
And the habitations of the just; to Him
Glory and praise whose wisdom had ordained
Good out of evil to create—instead
Of Spirits malign, a better race to bring
Into their vacant room, and thence diffuse   190
His good to worlds and ages infinite.
   "So sang the Hierarchies. Meanwhile the Son
On his great expedition now appeared,

Girt with omnipotence, with radiance crowned
Of majesty divine, sapience and love
Immense; and all his Father in him shone.
About his chariot numberless were poured
Cherub and Seraph, Potentates and Thrones,
And Virtues, winged Spirits, and chariots winged
From the armory of God, where stand of old   200
Myriads, between two brazen mountains lodged
Against a solemn day, harnessed at hand,
Celestial equipage; and now came forth
Spontaneous, for within them Spirit lived.
Attendant on their Lord. Heaven opened wide
Her ever-during gates, harmonious sound
On golden hinges moving, to let forth
The King of Glory, in his powerful Word
And Spirit coming to create new worlds.
On Heavenly ground they stood, and from the shore   210
They viewed the vast immeasurable Abyss,
Outrageous as a sea, dark, wasteful, wild.
Up from the bottom turned by furious winds
And surging waves, as mountains to assault
Heaven's highth, and with the centre mix the pole.
    " 'Silence, ye troubled waves, and thou Deep, peace!'
Said then the omnific Word: 'your discord end!'
Nor stayed; but, on the wings of Cherubim
Uplifted, in paternal glory rode
Far into Chaos and the World unborn;   220
For Chaos heard his voice. Him all his train
Followed in bright procession, to behold
Creation, and the wonders of his might.
Then stayed the fervid wheels, and in his hand
He took the golden compasses, prepared
In God's eternal store, to circumscribe
This Universe, and all created things.
One foot he centred, and the other turned
Round through the vast profundity obscure,
And said, 'Thus far extend, thus far thy bounds;   230
This be thy just circumference, O World!'
Thus God the Heaven created, thus the Earth,
Matter unformed and void. Darkness profound
Covered the Abyss; but on the watery calm
His brooding wings the Spirit of God outspread,
And vital virtue infused, and vital warmth,

Throughout the fluid mass, but downward purged
The black, tartareous, cold, infernal dregs,
Adverse to life; then founded, then conglobed,
Like things to like, the rest to several place   240
Disparted, and between spun out the Air,
And Earth, self-balanced, on her centre hung.
　"'Let there be Light!' said God; and forthwith Light
Ethereal, first of things, quintessence pure,
Sprung from the Deep; and from her native East
To journey through the aery gloom began,
Sphered in a radiant cloud—for yet the Sun
Was not; she in a cloudy tabernacle
Sojourned the while. God saw the Light was good;
And light from darkness by the hemisphere   250
Divided: Light the Day, and Darkness Night,
He named. Thus was the first Day even and morn;
Nor passed uncelebrated, nor unsung
By the celestial quires, when orient light
Exhaling first from darkness they beheld,
Birth-day of Heaven and Earth. With joy and shout
The hollow universal orb they filled,
And touched their golden harps, and hymning praised
God and his works; Creator him they sung,
Both when first evening was, and when first morn.   260
　"Again God said, 'Let there be firmament
Amid the waters, and let it divide
The waters from the waters!' And God made
The firmament, expanse of liquid, pure,
Transparent, elemental air, diffused
In circuit to the uttermost convex
Of this great round—partition firm and sure,
The waters underneath from those above
Dividing; for as Earth, so he the World
Built on circumfluous waters calm, in wide   270
Crystalline ocean, and the loud misrule
Of Chaos far removed, lest fierce extremes
Contiguous might distemper the whole frame:
And Heaven he named the Firmament. So even
And morning chorus sung the second Day.
　"The Earth was formed, but, in the womb as yet
Of waters, embryon immature, involved,
Appeared not; over all the face of Earth
Main ocean flowed, not idle, but, with warm

Prolific humor softening all her globe,   280
Fermented the great mother to conceive,
Satiate with genial moisture; when God said,
'Be gathered now, ye waters under heaven,
Into one place, and let dry land appear.'
Immediately the mountains huge appear
Emergent, and their broad bare backs upheave
Into the clouds; their tops ascend the sky.
So high as heaved the tumid hills, so low
Down sunk a hollow bottom broad and deep,
Capacious bed of waters. Thither they   290
Hasted with glad precipitance, uprolled,
As drops on dust conglobing, from the dry:
Part rise in crystal wall, or ridge direct,
For haste; such flight the great command impressed
On the swift floods. As armies at the call
Of trumpet (for of armies thou hast heard)
Troop to the standard, so the watery throng,
Wave rolling after wave, where way they found—
If steep, with torrent rapture, if through plain,
Soft-ebbing; nor withstood them rock or hill;   300
But they, or underground, or circuit wide
With serpent error wandering, found their way,
And on the washy ooze deep channels wore:
Easy, ere God had bid the ground be dry.
All but within those banks where rivers now
Stream, and perpetual draw their humid train.
The dry land Earth, and the great receptacle
Of congregated waters he called Seas;
And saw that it was good, and said, 'Let the Earth
Put forth the verdant grass, herb yielding seed,   310
And fruit-tree yielding fruit after her kind,
Whose seed is in herself upon the Earth!'
He scarce had said when the bare Earth, till then
Desert and bare, unsightly, unadorned,
Brought forth the tender grass, whose verdure clad
Her universal face with pleasant green;
Then herbs of every leaf, that sudden flowered,
Opening their various colors, and made gay
Her bosom, smelling sweet; and, these scarce blown,
Forth flourished thick the clustering vine, forth crept   320
The smelling gourd, up stood the corny reed
Embattled in her field: add the humble shrub,

And bush with frizzled hair implicit: last
Rose, as in dance, the stately trees, and spread
Their branches hung with copious fruit, or gemmed
Their blossoms. With high woods the hills were crowned,
With tufts the valleys and each fountain-side,
With borders long the rivers, that Earth now
Seemed like to Heaven, a seat where gods might dwell,
Or wander with delight, and love to haunt   330
Her sacred shades; though God had yet not rained
Upon the Earth, and man to till the ground
None was, but from the Earth a dewy mist
Went up and watered all the ground, and each
Plant of the field, which ere it was in the Earth
God made, and every herb before it grew
On the green stem. God saw that it was good;
So even and morn recorded the third Day.
    "Again the Almighty spake, 'Let there be Lights
High in the expanse of Heaven, to divide   340
The Day from Night; and let them be for signs,
For seasons, and for days, and circling years;
And let them be for lights, as I ordain
Their office in the firmament of heaven,
To give light on the Earth!' and it was so.
And God made two great Lights, great for their use
To Man, the greater to have rule by day,
The less by night, altern; and made the Stars,
And set them in the firmament of heaven
To illuminate the Earth, and rule the day   350
In their vicissitude, and rule the night,
And light from darkness to divide. God saw,
Surveying his great work, that it was good:
For, of celestial bodies, first the Sun
A mighty sphere he framed, unlightsome first,
Though of ethereal mould; then formed the Moon
Globose, and every magnitude of Stars,
And sowed with stars the heaven thick as a field.
Of light by far the greater part he took,
Transplanted from her cloudy shrine, and placed   360
In the Sun's orb, made porous to receive
And drink the liquid light, firm to retain
Her gathered beams, great palace now of Light.
Hither, as to their fountain, other stars
Repairing in their golden urns draw light,

And hence the morning planet gilds her horns;
By tincture or reflection they augment
Their small peculiar, though, from human sight
So far remote, with diminution seen.
First in his east the glorious lamp was seen,   370
Regent of day, and all the horizon round
Invested with bright rays, jocund to run
His longitude through heaven's high road; the grey
Dawn, and the Pleiades, before him danced,
Shedding sweet influence. Less bright the Moon,
But opposite in levelled west, was set,
His mirror, with full face borrowing her light
From him; for other light she needed none
In that aspect, and still that distance keeps
Till night; then in the east her turn she shines,   380
Revolved on heaven's great axle, and her reign
With thousand lesser lights dividual holds,
With thousand thousand stars, that then appeared
Spangling the hemisphere. Then first adorned
With their bright luminaries, that set and rose,
Glad evening and glad morn crowned the fourth Day.
    "And God said, 'Let the waters generate
Reptile with spawn abundant, living soul;
And let Fowl fly above the earth, with wings
Displayed on the open firmament of heaven!   390
And God created the great whales, and each
Soul living, each that crept, which plenteously
The waters generated by their kinds,
And every bird of wing after his kind,
And saw that it was good, and blessed them, saying,
'Be fruitful, multiply, and, in the seas,
And lakes, and running streams, the waters fill;
And let the fowl be multiplied on the earth!'
Forthwith the sounds and seas, each creek and bay,
With fry innumerable swarm, and shoals   400
Of fish that, with their fins and shining scales,
Glide under the green wave in sculls that oft
Bank the mid-sea. Part, single or with mate,
Graze the sea-weed, their pasture, and through groves
Of coral stray, or, sporting with quick glance,
Show to the sun their waved coats dropt with gold,
Or, in their pearly shells at ease, attend
Moist nutriment, or under rocks their food

In jointed armor watch; on smooth the seal
And bended dolphins play: part, huge of bulk,   410
Wallowing unwieldy, enormous in their gait,
Tempest the ocean. There leviathan,
Hugest of living creatures, on the deep
Stretched like a promontory, sleeps or swims,
And seems a moving land, and at his gills
Draws in, and at his trunk spouts out, a sea.
Meanwhile the tepid caves, and fens, and shores,
Their brood as numerous hatch from the egg, that soon,
Bursting with kindly rupture, forth disclosed
Their callow young; but feathered soon and fledge   420
They summed their pens, and, soaring the air sublime,
With clang despised the ground, under a cloud
In prospect. There the eagle and the stork
On cliffs and cedar-tops their eyries build.
Part loosely wing the region; part, more wise,
In common, ranged in figure, wedge their way,
Intelligent of seasons, and set forth
Their aery caravan, high over seas
Flying, and over lands, with mutual wing
Easing their flight: so steers the prudent crane   430
Her annual voyage, borne on winds; the air
Floats as they pass, fanned with unnumbered plumes.
From branch to branch the smaller birds with song
Solaced the woods, and spread their painted wings,
Till even; nor then the solemn nightingale
Ceased warbling, but all night tuned her soft lays.
Others, on silver lakes and rivers, bathed
Their downy breast; the swan, with arched neck
Between her white wings mantling proudly, rows
Her state with oary feet; yet oft they quit   440
The dank, and, rising on stiff pennons, tower
The mid aerial sky. Others on ground
Walked firm—the crested cock, whose clarion sounds
The silent hours, and the other, whose gay train
Adorns him, colored with the florid hue
Of rainbows and starry eyes. The waters thus
With Fish replenished, and the air with Fowl,
Evening and morn solemnized the fifth Day.
    "The sixth, and of Creation last, arose
With evening harps and matin; when God said,   450
'Let the Earth bring forth soul living in her kind,

Cattle, and creeping things, and beast of the earth,
Each in their kind!' The Earth obeyed, and, straight
Opening her fertile womb, teemed at a birth
Innumerous living creatures, perfect forms,
Limbed and full-grown. Out of the ground up rose,
As from his lair, the wild beast, where he wons
In forest wild, in thicket, brake, or den—
Among the trees in pairs they rose, they walked;
The cattle in the fields and meadows green: 460
Those rare and solitary, these in flocks
Pasturing at once and in broad herds, upsprung.
The grassy clods now calved; now half appeared
The tawny lion, pawing to get free
His hinder parts—then springs, as broke from bonds,
And rampant shakes his brinded mane; the ounce,
The libbard, and the tiger, as the mole
Rising, the crumbled earth above them threw
In hillocks; the swift stag from underground
Bore up his branching head; scarce from his mould   470
Behemoth, biggest born of earth, upheaved
His vastness; fleeced the flocks and bleating rose,
As plants; ambiguous between sea and land,
A river-horse and scaly crocodile.
At once came forth whatever creeps the ground,
Insect or worm. Those waved their limber fans
For wings, and smallest lineaments exact
In all the liveries decked of summer's pride,
With spots of gold and purple, azure and green;
These as a line their long dimension drew,   480
Streaking the ground with sinuous trace: not all
Minims of nature; some of serpent kind,
Wondrous in length and corpulence, involved
Their snaky folds, and added wings. First crept
The parsimonious emmet, provident
Of future, in small room large heart enclosed—
Pattern of just equality perhaps
Hereafter—joined in her popular tribes
Of commonalty. Swarming next appeared
The female bee, that feeds her husband drone   490
Deliciously, and builds her waxen cells
With honey stored. The rest are numberless,
And thou their natures know'st, and gav'st them names,
Needless to thee repeated; nor unknown

The serpent, subtlest beast of all the field,
Of huge extent sometimes, with brazen eyes
And hairy mane terrific, though to thee
Not noxious, but obedient at thy call.
   "Now Heaven in all her glory shone, and rolled
Her motions, as the great First Mover's hand   500
First wheeled their course; Earth, in her rich attire
Consummate, lovely smiled; Air, Water, Earth,
By fowl, fish, beast, was flown, was swum, was walked,
Frequent; and of the sixth Day yet remained.
There wanted yet the master-work, the end
Of all yet done—a creature, who, not prone
And brute as other creatures, but endued
With sanctity of reason, might erect
His stature, and, upright with front serene
Govern the rest, self-knowing, and from thence   510
Magnanimous to correspond with Heaven,
But grateful to acknowledge whence his good
Descends; thither with heart, and voice, and eyes
Directed in devotion, to adore
And worship God Supreme, who made him chief
Of all his works. Therefore the Omnipotent
Eternal Father (for where is not He
Present?) thus to his Son audibly spake:—
'Let us make now Man in our image, Man
In our similitude, and let them rule   520
Over the fish and fowl of sea and air,
Beast of the field, and over all the earth,
And every creeping thing that creeps the ground!'
This said, he formed thee, Adam, thee, O Man,
Dust of the ground, and in thy nostrils breathed
The breath of life; in his own image he
Created thee, in the image of God
Express, and thou becam'st a living soul.
Male he created thee, but thy consort
Female, for race; then blessed mankind, and said,   530
'Be fruitful, multiply, and fill the Earth;
Subdue it, and throughout dominion hold
Over fish of the sea, and fowl of the air,
And every living thing that moves on the Earth!'
Wherever thus created—for no place
Is yet distinct by name—thence, as thou know'st,
He brought thee into this delicious grove,

This Garden, planted with the trees of God,
Delectable both to behold and taste,
And freely all their pleasant fruit for food   540
Gave thee. All sorts are here that all the earth yields,
Variety without end; but of the tree
Which tasted works knowledge of good and evil
Thou may'st not; in the day thou eat'st, thou diest.
Death is the penalty imposed; beware,
And govern well thy appetite, lest Sin
Surprise thee, and her black attendant, Death.
    "Here finished He, and all that he had made
Viewed, and, behold! all was entirely good.
So even and morn accomplished the sixth Day: 550
Yet not till the Creator, from his work
Desisting, though unwearied, up returned,
Up to the Heaven of Heavens, his high abode,
Thence to behold this new-created World,
The addition of his empire, how it showed
In prospect from his throne, how good, how fair,
Answering his great idea. Up he rode,
Followed with acclamation, and the sound
Symphonious of ten thousand harps, that tuned
Angelic harmonies. The Earth, the Air   560
Resounded (thou remember'st, for thou heard'st),
The heavens and all the constellations rung,
The planets in their stations listening stood,
While the bright pomp ascended jubilant.
'Open, ye everlasting gates!' they sung:
'Open, ye Heavens! your living doors! let in
The great Creator, from his work returned
Magnificent, his six days' work, a World!
Open, and henceforth oft; for God will deign
To visit oft the dwellings of just men   570
Delighted, and with frequent intercourse
Thither will send his winged messengers
On errands of supernal grace.' So sung
The glorious train ascending. He through Heaven,
That opened wide her blazing portals, led
To God's eternal house direct the way—
A broad and ample road, whose dust is gold,
And pavement stars, as stars to thee appear
Seen in the Galaxy, that milky way
Which nightly as a circling zone thou seest   580

Powdered with stars. And now on Earth the seventh
Evening arose in Eden—for the sun
Was set, and twilight from the east came on,
Forerunning night—when at the holy mount
Of Heaven's high-seated top, the imperial throne
Of Godhead, fixed for ever firm and sure,
The Filial Power arrived, and sat him down
With his great Father; for he also went
Invisible, yet stayed (such privilege
Hath Omnipresence) and the work ordained,   590
Author and end of all things, and, from work
Now resting, blessed and hallowed the seventh Day,
As resting on that day from all his work;
But not in silence holy kept: the harp
Had work, and rested not; the solemn pipe
And dulcimer, all organs of sweet stop,
All sounds on fret by string or golden wire,
Tempered soft tunings, intermixed with voice
Choral or unison; of incense clouds,
Fuming from golden censers, hid the Mount.   600
Creation and the Six Days' acts they sung:—
'Great are thy works, Jehovah! infinite
Thy power! what thought can measure thee, or tongue
Relate thee—greater now in thy return
Than from the Giant-angels? Thee that day
Thy thunders magnified; but to create
Is greater than created to destroy.
Who can impair thee, Mighty King, or bound
Thy empire? Easily the proud attempt
Of Spirits apostate, and their counsels vain,   610
Thou hast repelled, while impiously they thought
Thee to diminish, and from thee withdraw
The number of thy worshippers. Who seeks
To lessen thee, against his purpose, serves
To manifest the more thy might; his evil
Thou usest, and from thence creat'st more good.
Witness this new-made World, another Heaven
From Heaven-gate not far, founded in view
On the clear hyaline, the glassy sea;
Of amplitude almost immense, with stars   620
Numerous, and every star perhaps a world
Of destined habitation—but thou know'st
Their seasons; among these the seat of men,

Earth, with her nether ocean circumfused,
Their pleasant dwelling-place. Thrice happy men,
And sons of men, whom God hath thus advanced,
Created in his image, there to dwell
And worship him, and in reward to rule
Over his works, on earth, in sea, or air,
And multiply a race of worshipers   630
Holy and just! thrice happy, if they know
Their happiness, and persevere upright!'
    "So sung they, and the Empyrean rung
With halleluiahs. Thus was Sabbath kept.
And thy request think now fulfilled, that asked
How first this World and face of things began,
And what before thy memory was done
From the beginning, that posterity,
Informed by thee, might know. If else thou seek'st
Aught, not surpassing human measure, say."   640

BOOK VIII

THE ARGUMENT

ADAM inquires concerning celestial motions; is doubtfully answered, and exhorted to search rather things more worthy of knowledge. Adam assents, and, still desirous to detain Raphael, relates to him what he remembered since his own creation—his placing in Paradise; his talk with God concerning solitude and fit society; his first meeting and nuptials with Eve. His discourse with the Angel thereupon; who, after admonitions repeated, departs.

The Angel ended, and in Adam's ear
So charming left his voice that he a while
Thought him still speaking, still stood fixed to hear;
Then, as new-waked, thus gratefully replied:—
    "What thanks sufficient, or what recompense
Equal, have I to render thee, divine
Historian, who thus largely hast allayed
The thirst I had of knowledge, and voutsafed
This friendly condescension to relate
Things else by me unsearchable—now heard   10
With wonder, but delight, and, as is due,
With glory attributed to the high
Creator? Something yet of doubt remains,
Which only thy solution can resolve.
When I behold this goodly frame, this World,
Of Heaven and Earth consisting, and compute
Their magnitudes—this Earth, a spot, a grain,
An atom, with the Firmament compared
And all her numbered stars, that seem to roll
Spaces incomprehensible (for such   20

Their distance argues, and their swift return
Diurnal) merely to officiate light
Round this opacous Earth, this punctual spot,
One day and night, in all their vast survey
Useless besides—reasoning, I oft admire
How Nature, wise and frugal, could commit
Such disproportions, with superfluous hand
So many nobler bodies to create,
Greater so manifold, to this one use
For aught appears, and on their Orbs impose   30
Such restless revolution day by day
Repeated, while the sedentary Earth,
That better might with far less compass move,
Served by more noble than herself, attains
Her end without least motion, and receives,
As tribute, such a sumless journey brought
Of incorporeal speed, her warmth and light;
Speed, to describe whose swiftness number fails."
    So spake our Sire, and by his countenance seemed
Entering on studious thoughts abstruse; which Eve   40
Perceiving, where she sat retired in sight,
With lowliness majestic from her seat,
And grace that won who saw to wish her stay,
Rose, and went forth among her fruits and flowers,
To visit how they prospered, bud and bloom,
Her nursery; they at her coming sprung,
And, touched by her fair tendance, gladlier grew.
Yet went she not as not with such discourse
Delighted, or not capable her ear
Of what was high. Such pleasure she reserved,   50
Adam relating, she sole auditress;
Her husband the relater she preferred
Before the Angel, and of him to ask
Chose rather; he, she knew, would intermix
Grateful digressions, and solve high dispute
With conjugal caresses: from his lip
Not words alone pleased her. Oh, when meet now
Such pairs, in love and mutual honor joined?
With goddess-like demeanor forth she went,
Not unattended; for on her as Queen   60
A pomp of winning Graces waited still,
And from about her shot darts of desire
Into all eyes, to wish her still in sight.

And Raphael now to Adam's doubt proposed
Benevolent and facile thus replied:—
    "To ask or search I blame thee not; for Heaven
Is as the Book of God before thee set,
Wherein to read his wondrous works, and learn
His seasons, hours, or days, or months, or years.
This to attain, whether Heaven move or Earth   70
Imports not, if thou reckon right; the rest
From Man or Angel the great Architect
Did wisely to conceal, and not divulge
His secrets, to be scanned by them who ought
Rather admire. Or, if they list to try
Conjecture, he his fabric of the Heavens
Hath left to their disputes—perhaps to move
His laughter at their quaint opinions wide
Hereafter, when they come to model Heaven,
And calculate the stars; how they will wield   80
The mighty frame; how build, unbuild, contrive
To save appearances; how gird the Sphere
With Centric and Eccentric scribbled o'er,
Cycle and Epicycle, Orb in Orb.
Already by thy reasoning this I guess,
Who art to lead thy offspring, and supposest
That bodies bright and greater should not serve
The less not bright, nor Heaven such journeys run,
Earth sitting still, when she alone receives
The benefit. Consider, first, that great   90
Or bright infers not excellence. The Earth,
Though, in comparison of Heaven, so small,
Nor glistering, may of solid good contain
More plenty than the Sun that barren shines,
Whose virtue on itself works no effect,
But in the fruitful Earth; there first received,
His beams, unactive else, their vigor find.
Yet not to Earth are those bright luminaries
Officious, but to thee, Earth's habitant.
And, for the Heaven's wide circuit, let it speak   100
The Maker's high magnificence, who built
So spacious, and his line stretched out so far,
That Man may know he dwells not in his own—
An edifice too large for him to fill,
Lodged in a small partition, and the rest
Ordained for uses to his Lord best known.

The swiftness of those Circles attribute,
Though numberless, to his omnipotence,
That to corporeal substances could add
Speed almost spiritual. Me thou think'st not slow,   110
Who since the morning-hour set out from Heaven
Where God resides, and ere mid-day arrived
In Eden—distance inexpressible
By numbers that have name. But this I urge,
Admitting motion in the Heavens, to show
Invalid that which thee to doubt it moved;
Not that I so affirm, though so it seem
To thee who hast thy dwelling here on Earth.
God, to remove his ways from human sense,
Placed Heaven from Earth so far, that earthly sight,   120
If it presume, might err in things too high,
And no advantage gain. What if the Sun
Be centre to the World; and other Stars,
By his attractive virtue and their own
Incited, dance about him various rounds?
Their wandering course, now high, now low, then hid,
Progressive, retrograde, or standing still,
In six thou seest; and what if, seventh to these,
The planet Earth, so steadfast though she seem,
Insensibly three different motions move?   130
Which else to several spheres thou must ascribe,
Moved contrary with thwart obliquities,
Or save the Sun his labor, and that swift
Nocturnal and diurnal rhomb supposed,
Invisible else above all stars, the wheel
Of Day and Night; which needs not thy belief,
If Earth, industrious of herself, fetch Day,
Travelling east, and with her part averse
From the Sun's beam meet Night, her other part
Still luminous by his ray. What if that light,   140
Sent from her through the wide transpicuous air,
To the terrestrial Moon be as a star,
Enlightening her by day, as she by night
This Earth—reciprocal, if land be there,
Fields and inhabitants? Her spots thou seest
As clouds, and clouds may rain, and rain produce
Fruits in her softened soil, for some to eat
Allotted there; and other Suns, perhaps,
With their attendant Moons, thou wilt descry,

Communicating male and female light—   150
Which two great sexes animate the World,
Stored in each Orb perhaps with some that live.
For such vast room in Nature unpossessed
By living soul, desert and desolate,
Only to shine, yet scarce to contribute
Each Orb a glimpse of light, conveyed so far
Down to this habitable, which returns
Light back to them, is obvious to dispute.
But whether thus these things, or whether not—
Whether the Sun, predominant in heaven,   160
Rise on the Earth; or Earth rise on the Sun;
He from the east his flaming road begin,
Or she from west her silent course advance
With inoffensive pace that spinning sleeps
On her soft axle, while she paces even,
And bears thee soft with the smooth air along—
Solicit not thy thoughts with matters hid;
Leave them to God above; him serve and fear.
Of other creatures as him pleases best,
Wherever placed, let him dispose; joy thou   170
In what he gives to thee, this Paradise
And thy fair Eve; Heaven is for thee too high
To know what passes there. Be lowly wise;
Think only what concerns thee and thy being;
Dream not of other worlds, what creatures there
Live, in what state, condition, or degree—
Contented that thus far hath been revealed
Not of Earth only, but of highest Heaven."
    To whom thus Adam, cleared of doubt, replied:—
"How fully hast thou satisfied me, pure   180
Intelligence of Heaven, Angel serene,
And, freed from intricacies, taught to live
The easiest way, nor with perplexing thoughts
To interrupt the sweet of life, from which
God hath bid dwell far off all anxious cares,
And not molest us, unless we ourselves
Seek them with wandering thoughts, and notions vain!
But apt the mind or fancy is to rove
Unchecked; and of her roving is no end,
Till, warned, or by experience taught, she learn   190
That not to know at large of things remote
From use, obscure and subtle, but to know

That which before us lies in daily life,
Is the prime wisdom: what is more is fume,
Or emptiness, or fond impertinence,
And renders us in things that most concern
Unpractised, unprepared, and still to seek.
Therefore from this high pitch let us descend
A lower flight, and speak of things at hand
Useful; whence, haply, mention may arise   200
Of something not unseasonable to ask,
By sufferance, and thy wonted favor, deigned.
Thee I have heard relating what was done
Ere my remembrance; now hear me relate
My story, which, perhaps, thou hast not heard.
And day is not yet spent; till then thou seest
How subtly to detain thee I devise,
Inviting thee to hear while I relate—
Fond, were it not in hope of thy reply.
For, while I sit with thee, I seem in Heaven;   210
And sweeter thy discourse is to my ear
Than fruits of palm-tree, pleasantest to thirst
And hunger both, from labor, at the hour
Of sweet repast. They satiate, and soon fill,
Though pleasant; but thy words, with grace divine
Imbued, bring to their sweetness no satiety."
    To whom thus Raphael answered, heavenly meek:—
"Nor are thy lips ungraceful, Sire of Men,
Nor tongue ineloquent; for God on thee
Abundantly his gifts hath also poured,   220
Inward and outward both, his image fair:
Speaking, or mute, all comeliness and grace
Attends thee, and each word, each motion, forms.
Nor less think we in Heaven of thee on Earth
Than of our fellow-servant, and inquire
Gladly into the ways of God with Man;
For God, we see, hath honored thee, and set
On Man his equal love. Say therefore on;
For I that day was absent, as befell,
Bound on a voyage uncouth and obscure,   230
Far on excursion toward the gates of Hell,
Squared in full legion (such command we had),
To see that none thence issued forth a spy
Or enemy, while God was in his work,
Lest he, incensed at such eruption bold,

Destruction with Creation might have mixed.
Not that they durst without his leave attempt;
But us he sends upon his high behests
For state, as sovran King, and to inure
Our prompt obedience. Fast we found, fast shut,   240
The dismal gates, and barricadoed strong,
But, long ere our approaching, heard within
Noise, other than the sound of dance or song—
Torment, and loud lament, and furious rage.
Glad we returned up to the coasts of Light
Ere Sabbath-evening; so we had in charge.
But thy relation now; for I attend,
Pleased with thy words no less than thou with mine."
    So spake the godlike Power, and thus our Sire:—
"For Man to tell how human life began   250
Is hard; for who himself beginning knew?
Desire with thee still longer to converse
Induced me. As new-waked from soundest sleep,
Soft on the flowery herb I found me laid,
In balmy sweat, which with his beams the Sun
Soon dried, and on the reeking moisture fed.
Straight toward Heaven my wondering eyes I turned,
And gazed a while the ample sky, till, raised
By quick instinctive motion, up I sprung,
As thitherward endeavoring, and upright   260
Stood on my feet. About me round I saw
Hill, dale, and shady woods, and sunny plains,
And liquid lapse of murmuring streams; by these,
Creatures that lived and moved, and walked or flew,
Birds on the branches warbling: all things smiled;
With fragrance and with joy my heart o'erflowed.
Myself I then perused, and limb by limb
Surveyed, and sometimes went, and sometimes ran
With supple joints, as lively vigor led;
But who I was, or where, or from what cause,   270
Knew not. To speak I tried, and forthwith spake;
My tongue obeyed, and readily could name
Whate'er I saw. 'Thou Sun,' said I, 'fair light,
And thou enlightened Earth, so fresh and gay,
Ye hills and dales, ye rivers, woods, and plains,
And ye that live and move, fair creatures, tell,
Tell, if ye saw, how I came thus, how here!
Not of myself, by some great Maker then,

In goodness and in power pre-eminent.
Tell me, how may I know him, how adore,   280
From whom I have that thus I move and live,
And feel that I am happier than I know!'
While thus I called, and strayed I knew not whither,
From where I first drew air, and first beheld
This happy light, when, answer none returned,
On a green shady bank, profuse of flowers,
Pensive I sat me down. There gentle sleep
First found me, and with soft oppression seized
My drowsed sense, untroubled, though I thought
I then was passing to my former state   290
Insensible, and forthwith to dissolve:
When suddenly stood at my head a dream.
Whose inward apparition gently moved
My fancy to believe I yet had being,
And lived. One came, methought, of shape divine,
And said, 'Thy mansion wants thee, Adam; rise,
First Man, of men innumerable ordained
First father! called by thee, I come thy guide
To the Garden of bliss, thy seat prepared.'
So saying, by the hand he took me, raised,   300
And over fields and waters, as in air
Smooth sliding without step, last led me up
A woody mountain, whose high top was plain,
A circuit wide, enclosed, with goodliest trees
Planted, with walks and bowers, that what I saw
Of Earth before scarce pleasant seemed. Each tree
Loaden with fairest fruit, that hung to the eye
Tempting, stirred in me sudden appetite
To pluck and eat; whereat I waked, and found
Before mine eyes all real, as the dream   310
Had lively shadowed. Here had new begun
My wandering, had not He who was my guide
Up hither from among the trees appeared,
Presence Divine. Rejoicing, but with awe,
In adoration at his feet I fell
Submiss. He reared me, and 'Whom thou sought'st I am,'
Said mildly, 'Author of all this thou seest
Above, or round about thee, or beneath.
This Paradise I give thee; count it thine
To till and keep, and of the fruit to eat.   320
Of every tree that in the Garden grows

Eat freely with glad heart; fear here no dearth.
But of the tree whose operation brings
Knowledge of good and ill, which I have set,
The pledge of thy obedience and thy faith,
Amid the garden by the Tree of Life—
Remember what I warn thee—shun to taste,
And shun the bitter consequence: for know,
The day thou eat'st thereof, my sole command
Transgressed, inevitably thou shalt die,   330
From that day mortal, and this happy state
Shalt lose, expelled from hence into a world
Of woe and sorrow.' Sternly he pronounced
The rigid interdiction, which resounds
Yet dreadful in mine ear, though in my choice
Not to incur; but soon his clear aspéct
Returned, and gracious purpose thus renewed:—
'Not only these fair bounds, but all the Earth
To thee and to thy race I give; as lords
Possess it, and all things that therein live,   340
Or live in sea or air, beast, fish, and fowl.
In sign whereof, each bird and beast behold
After their kinds; I bring them to receive
From thee their names, and pay thee fealty
With low subjection. Understand the same
Of fish within their watery residence,
Not hither summoned, since they cannot change
Their element to draw the thinner air.'
As thus he spake, each bird and beast behold
Approaching two and two—these cowering low   350
With blandishment; each bird stooped on his wing.
I named them as they passed, and understood
Their nature; with such knowledge God endued
My sudden apprehension. But in these
I found not what methought I wanted still,
And to the Heavenly Vision thus presumed:—
    "'O, by what name—for Thou above all these,
Above mankind, or aught than mankind higher,
Surpassest far my naming—how may I
Adore thee, Author of this Universe,   360
And all this good to Man, for whose well-being
So amply, and with hands so liberal,
Thou hast provided all things? But with me
I see not who partakes. In solitude

What happiness? who can enjoy alone,
Or, all enjoying, what contentment find?'
Thus I, presumptuous; and the Vision bright,
As with a smile more brightened, thus replied:—
    "'What call'st thou solitude? Is not the Earth
With various living creatures, and the Air,   370
Replenished, and all these at thy command
To come and play before thee? Know'st thou not
Their language and their ways? They also know,
And reason not contemptibly; with these
Find pastime, and bear rule; thy realm is large.'
So spake the Universal Lord, and seemed
So ordering. I, with leave of speech implored,
And humble deprecation, thus replied:—
    "'Let not my words offend thee, Heavenly Power;
My Maker, be propitious while I speak.   380
Hast thou not made me here thy substitute,
And these inferior far beneath me set?
Among unequals what society
Can sort, what harmony or true delight?
Which must be mutual, in proportion due
Given and received; but, in disparity,
The one intense, the other still remiss,
Cannot well suit with either, but soon prove
Tedious alike. Of fellowship I speak
Such as I seek, fit to participate   390
All rational delight, wherein the brute
Cannot be human consort. They rejoice
Each with their kind, lion with lioness;
So fitly them in pairs thou hast combined:
Much less can bird with beast, or fish with fowl,
So well converse, nor with the ox the ape;
Worse, then, can man with beast, and least of all.'
    "Whereto the Almighty answered, not displeased:—
'A nice and subtle happiness, I see,
Thou to thyself proposest, in the choice   400
Of thy associates, Adam, and wilt taste
No pleasure, though in pleasure, solitary.
What think'st thou, then, of me, and this my state?
Seem I to thee sufficiently possessed
Of happiness, or not, who am alone
From all eternity? for none I know
Second to me or like, equal much less.

How have I, then, with whom to hold converse,
Save with the creatures which I made, and those
To me inferior infinite descents   410
Beneath what other creatures are to thee?'
　　"He ceased. I lowly answered:—'To attain
The highth and depth of thy eternal ways
All human thoughts come short, Supreme of Things!
Thou in thyself art perfect, and in thee
Is no deficience found. Not so is Man,
But in degree—the cause of his desire
By conversation with his like to help
Or solace his defects. No need that thou
Should'st propagate, already infinite,   420
And through all numbers absolute, though One;
But Man by number is to manifest
His single imperfection, and beget
Like of his like, his image multiplied,
In unity defective; which requires
Collateral love, and dearest amity.
Thou, in thy secrecy although alone,
Best with thyself accompanied, seek'st not
Social communication—yet, so pleased,
Canst raise thy creature to what highth thou wilt   430
Of union or communion, deified;
I, by conversing, cannot these erect
From prone, nor in their ways complacence find.'
Thus I emboldened spake, and freedom used
Permissive, and acceptance found; which gained
This answer from the gracious Voice Divine:—
　　"'Thus far to try thee, Adam, I was pleased,
And find thee knowing not of beasts alone,
Which thou hast rightly named, but of thyself—
Expressing well the spirit within thee free,   440
My image, not imparted to the brute;
Whose fellowship, therefore, unmeet for thee,
Good reason was thou freely shouldst dislike.
And be so minded still. I, ere thou spak'st,
Knew it not good for Man to be alone,
And no such company as then thou saw'st
Intended thee—for trial only brought,
To see how thou couldst judge of fit and meet.
What next I bring shall please thee, be assured,
Thy likeness, thy fit help, thy other self,   450

Thy wish exactly to thy heart's desire.'
   "He ended, or I heard no more; for now
My earthly, by his heavenly overpowered,
Which it had long stood under, strained to the highth
In that celestial colloquy sublime,
As with an object that excels the sense,
Dazzled and spent, sunk down, and sought repair
Of sleep, which instantly fell on me, called
By Nature as in aid, and closed mine eyes.
Mine eyes he closed, but open left the cell   460
Of fancy, my internal sight; by which,
Abstract as in a trance, methought I saw,
Though sleeping, where I lay, and saw the Shape
Still glorious before whom awake I stood;
Who, stooping, opened my left side, and took
From thence a rib, with cordial spirits warm,
And life-blood streaming fresh; wide was the wound,
But suddenly with flesh filled up and healed.
The rib he formed and fashioned with his hands;
Under his forming hands a creature grew,   470
Man-like, but different sex, so lovely fair
That what seemed fair in all the world seemed now
Mean, or in her summed up, in her contained
And in her looks, which from that time infused
Sweetness into my heart unfelt before,
And into all things from her air inspired
The spirit of love and amorous delight.
She disappeared, and left me dark; I waked
To find her, or for ever to deplore
Her loss, and other pleasures all abjure: 480
When, out of hope, behold her not far off,
Such as I saw her in my dream, adorned
With what all Earth or Heaven could bestow
To make her amiable. On she came,
Led by her Heavenly Maker, though unseen
And guided by his voice, nor uninformed
Of nuptial sanctity and marriage rites.
Grace was in all her steps, heaven in her eye,
In every gesture dignity and love.
I, overjoyed, could not forbear aloud:—   490
   "'This turn hath made amends; thou hast fulfilled
Thy words, Creator bounteous and benign,
Giver of all things fair—but fairest this

Of all thy gifts!—nor enviest. I now see
Bone of my bone, flesh of my flesh, my Self
Before me. Woman is her name, of Man
Extracted: for this cause he shall forgo
Father and mother, and to his wife adhere,
And they shall be one flesh, one heart, one soul.'
    "She heard me thus; and, though divinely brought,   500
Yet innocence and virgin modesty,
Her virtue, and the conscience of her worth,
That would be wooed, and not unsought be won,
Not obvious, not obtrusive, but, retired,
The more desirable—or, to say all,
Nature herself, though pure of sinful thought—
Wrought in her so, that, seeing me, she turned.
I followed her; she what was honor knew,
And with obsequious majesty approved
My pleaded reason. To the nuptial bower   510
I led her blushing like the Morn; All Heaven,
And happy constellations, on that hour
Shed their selectest influence; the Earth
Gave sign of gratulation, and each hill;
Joyous the birds; fresh gales and gentle airs
Whispered it to the woods, and from their wings
Flung rose, flung odors from the spicy shrub,
Disporting, till the amorous bird of night
Sung spousal, and bid haste the Evening-star
On his hill-top to light the bridal lamp.   520
    "Thus have I told thee all my state, and brought
My story to the sum of earthly bliss
Which I enjoy, and must confess to find
In all things else delight indeed, but such
As, used or not, works in the mind no change,
Nor vehement desire—these delicacies
I mean of taste, sight, smell, herbs, fruits, and flowers,
Walks, and the melody of birds: but here,
Far otherwise, transported I behold,
Transported touch; here passion first I felt,   530
Commotion strange, in all enjoyments else
Superior and unmoved, here only weak
Against the charm of beauty's powerful glance.
Or Nature failed in me, and left some part
Not proof enough such object to sustain,
Or, from my side subducting, took perhaps

More than enough—at least on her bestowed
Too much of ornament, in outward show
Elaborate, of inward less exact.
For well I understand in the prime end   540
Of Nature her the inferior, in the mind
And inward faculties, which most excel;
In outward also her resembling less
His image who made both, and less expressing
The character of that dominion given
O'er other creatures. Yet when I approach
Her loveliness, so absolute she seems
And in herself complete, so well to know
Her own, that what she wills to do or say
Seems wisest, virtuousest, discreetest, best.   550
All higher Knowledge in her presence falls
Degraded; Wisdom in discourse with her
Loses, discountenanced, and like Folly shows;
Authority and Reason on her wait,
As one intended first, not after made
Occasionally: and, to consummate all,
Greatness of mind and nobleness their seat
Build in her loveliest, and create an awe
About her, as a guard angelic placed."
    To whom the Angel, with contracted brow:—   560
"Accuse not Nature! she hath done her part;
Do thou but thine! and be not diffident
Of Wisdom; she deserts thee not, if thou
Dismiss not her, when most thou need'st her nigh,
By attributing overmuch to things
Less excellent, as thou thyself perceiv'st.
For what admir'st thou, what transports thee so?
An outside—fair, no doubt, and worthy well
Thy cherishing, thy honoring, and thy love;
Not thy subjection. Weigh with her thyself;   570
Then value. Oft-times nothing profits more
Than self-esteem, grounded on just and right
Well managed. Of that skill the more thou know'st,
The more she will acknowledge thee her head,
And to realities yield all her shows—
Made so adorn for thy delight the more,
So awful, that with honor thou may'st love
Thy mate, who sees when thou art seen least wise.
But, if the sense of touch, whereby mankind

Is propagated, seem such dear delight   580
Beyond all other, think the same voutsafed
To cattle and each beast; which would not be
To them made common and divulged, if aught
Therein enjoyed were worthy to subdue
The soul of Man, or passion in him move.
What higher in her society thou find'st
Attractive, human, rational, love still:
In loving thou dost well; in passion not,
Wherein true Love consists not. Love refines
The thoughts, and heart enlarges—hath his seat   590
In Reason, and is judicious, is the scale
By which to Heavenly Love thou may'st ascend,
Not sunk in carnal pleasure; for which cause
Among the beasts no mate for thee was found."
    To whom thus, half abashed, Adam replied:—
"Neither her outside formed so fair, nor aught
In procreation, common to all kinds
(Though higher of the genial bed by far,
And with mysterious reverence, I deem),
So much delights me as those graceful acts,   600
Those thousand decencies, that daily flow
From all her words and actions, mixed with love
And sweet compliance, which declare unfeigned
Union of mind, or in us both one soul—
Harmony to behold in wedded pair
More grateful than harmonious sound to the ear.
Yet these subject not; I to thee disclose
What inward thence I feel, not therefore foiled,
Who meet with various objects, from the sense
Variously representing; yet, still free,   610
Approve the best, and follow what I approve.
To love thou blam'st me not—for Love, thou say'st,
Leads up to Heaven, is both the way and guide;
Bear with me, then, if lawful what I ask.
Love not the Heavenly Spirits, and how their love
Express they—by looks only, or do they mix
Irradiance, virtual or immediate touch?"
    To whom the Angel, with a smile that glowed
Celestial rosy-red, Love's proper hue,
Answered:—"Let it suffice thee that thou know'st   620
Us happy, and without Love no happiness.
Whatever pure thou in the body enjoy'st

(And pure thou wert created) we enjoy
In eminence, and obstacle find none
Of membrane, joint, or limb, exclusive bars.
Easier than air with air, if Spirits embrace,
Total they mix, union of pure with pure
Desiring, nor restrained conveyance need
As flesh to mix with flesh, or soul with soul.
But I can now no more: the parting Sun   630
Beyond the Earth's green Cape and verdant Isles
Hesperean sets, my signal to depart.
Be strong, live happy, and love! but, first of all
Him whom to love is to obey, and keep
His great command; take heed lest passion sway
Thy judgment to do aught which else free-will
Would not admit; thine and of all thy sons
The weal or woe in thee is placed; beware!
I in thy persevering shall rejoice,
And all the Blest. Stand fast; to stand or fall   640
Free in thine own arbitrement it lies.
Perfect within, no outward aid require;
And all temptation to transgress repel."
　　So saying, he arose; whom Adam thus
Followed with benediction:—"Since to part,
Go, Heavenly Guest, Ethereal Messenger,
Sent from whose sovran goodness I adore!
Gentle to me and affable hath been
Thy condescension, and shall be honored ever
With grateful memory. Thou to Mankind   650
Be good and friendly still, and oft return!"
　　So parted they, the Angel up to Heaven
From the thick shade, and Adam to his bower.

BOOK IX

THE ARGUMENT

SATAN, having compassed the Earth, with meditated guile returns as a mist by night into Paradise; enters into the Serpent sleeping. Adam and Eve in the morning go forth to their labors, which Eve proposes to divide in several places, each laboring apart: Adam consents not, alleging the danger lest that enemy of whom they were forewarned should attempt her found alone. Eve, loth to be thought not circumspect or firm enough, urges her going apart, the rather desirous to make trial of her strength; Adam at last yields. The Serpent finds her alone: his subtle approach, first gazing, then speaking, with much flattery extolling Eve above all other creatures. Eve, wondering to hear the Serpent speak, asks how he attained to human speech and such understanding not till now; the Serpent answers that by tasting of a certain tree in the Garden he attained both to speech and reason, till then void of both. Eve requires him to bring her to that tree, and finds it to be the Tree of Knowledge forbidden; the Serpent, now grown bolder, with many wiles and arguments induces her at length to eat. She, pleased with the taste, deliberates a while whether to impart thereof to Adam or not; at last brings him of the fruit; relates what persuaded her to eat thereof. Adam, at first amazed, but perceiving her lost, resolves, through vehemence of love, to perish with her, and, extenuating the trespass, eats also of the fruit. The effects thereof in them both; they seek to cover their nakedness; then fall to variance and accusation of one another.

> No more of talk where God or Angel Guest
> With Man, as with his friend, familiar used
> To sit indulgent, and with him partake
> Rural repast, permitting him the while
> Venial discourse unblamed. I now must change

Those notes to tragic—foul distrust, and breach
Disloyal, on the part of man, revolt
And disobedience: on the part of Heaven,
Now alienated, distance and distaste,
Anger and just rebuke, and judgment given,   10
That brought into this World a world of woe,
Sin and her shadow Death, and Misery,
Death's harbinger. Sad task! yet argument
Not less but more heroic than the wrath
Of stern Achilles on his foe pursued
Thrice fugitive about Troy wall; or rage
Of Turnus for Lavinia disespoused;
Or Neptune's ire, or Juno's, that so long
Perplexed the Greek, and Cytherea's son:
If answerable style I can obtain   20
Of my celestial Patroness, who deigns
Her nightly visitation unimplored,
And dictates to me slumbering, or inspires
Easy my unpremeditated verse,
Since first this subject for heroic song
Pleased me, long choosing and beginning late,
Not sedulous by nature to indite
Wars, hitherto the only argument
Heroic deemed, chief mastery to dissect
With long and tedious havoc fabled knights   30
In battles feigned (the better fortitude
Of patience and heroic martyrdom
Unsung), or to describe races and games,
Or tilting furniture, emblazoned shields,
Impresses quaint, caparisons and steeds,
Bases and tinsel trappings, gorgeous knights
At joust and tournament; then marshalled feast
Served up in hall with sewers and seneschals:
The skill of artifice or office mean;
Not that which justly gives heroic name   40
To person, or to poem! Me, of these
Nor skilled nor studious, higher argument
Remains, sufficient of itself to raise
That name, unless an age too late, or cold
Climate, or years, damp my intended wing
Depressed; and much they may if all be mine,
Not hers who brings it nightly to my ear.
    The Sun was sunk, and after him the Star

Of Hesperus, whose office is to bring
Twilight upon the Earth, short arbiter   50
'Twixt day and night, and now from end to end
Night's hemisphere had veiled the horizon round,
When Satan, who late fled before the threats
Of Gabriel out of Eden, now improved
In meditated fraud and malice, bent
On Man's destruction, maugre what might hap
Of heavier on himself, fearless returned.
By night he fled, and at midnight returned
From compassing the Earth—cautious of day
Since Uriel, Regent of the Sun, descried   60
His entrance, and forewarned the Cherubim
That kept their watch. Thence, full of anguish, driven,
The space of seven continued nights he rode
With darkness—thrice the equinoctial line
He circled, four times crossed the car of Night
From pole to pole, traversing each colure—
On the eighth returned, and on the coast averse
From entrance or cherubic watch by stealth
Found unsuspected way. There was a place
(Now not, though Sin, not Time, first wrought the change) 70
Where Tigris, at the foot of Paradise,
Into a gulf shot under ground, till part
Rose up a fountain by the Tree of Life.
In with the river sunk, and with it rose,
Satan, involved in rising mist; then sought
Where to lie hid. Sea he had searched and land
From Eden over Pontus, and the Pool
Mæotis, up beyond the river Ob;
Downward as far antarctic; and, in length,
West from Orontes to the ocean barred   80
At Darien, thence to the land where flows
Ganges and Indus. Thus the orb he roamed
With narrow search, and with inspection deep
Considered every creature, which of all
Most opportune might serve his wiles, and found
The Serpent subtlest beast of all the field.
Him, after long debate, irresolute
Of thoughts revolved, his final sentence chose
Fit vessel, fittest imp of fraud, in whom
To enter, and his dark suggestions hide   90
From sharpest sight; for in the wily snake

Whatever sleights none would suspicious mark,
As from his wit and native subtlety
Proceeding, which, in other beasts observed,
Doubt might beget of diabolic power
Active within beyond the sense of brute.
Thus he resolved, but first from inward grief
His bursting passion into plaints thus poured:—
    "O Earth, how like to Heaven, if not preferred
More justly, seat worthier of Gods, as built   100
With second thoughts, reforming what was old!
For what God, after better, worse would build?
Terrestrial Heaven, danced round by other Heavens,
That shine, yet bear their bright officious lamps,
Light above light, for thee alone, as seems,
In thee concentring all their precious beams
Of sacred influence! As God in Heaven
Is centre, yet extends to all, so thou
Centring receiv'st from all those orbs; in thee,
Not in themselves, all their known virtue appears,   110
Productive in herb, plant, and nobler birth
Of creatures animate with gradual life
Of growth, sense, reason, all summed up in Man.
With what delight could I have walked thee round,
If I could joy in aught—sweet interchange
Of hill and valley, rivers, woods, and plains,
Now land, now sea, and shores with forest crowned,
Rocks, dens, and caves! But I in none of these
Find place or refuge; and the more I see
Pleasures about me, so much more I feel   120
Torment within me, as from the hateful siege
Of contraries; all good to me becomes
Bane, and in Heaven much worse would be my state,
But neither here seek I, no, nor in Heaven,
To dwell, unless by mastering Heaven's Supreme;
Nor hope to be myself less miserable
By what I seek, but others to make such
As I, though thereby worse to me redound.
For only in destroying I find ease
To my relentless thoughts; and him destroyed,   130
Or won to what may work his utter loss,
For whom all this was made, all this will soon
Follow, as to him linked in weal or woe:
In woe then, that destruction wide may range!

To me shall be the glory sole among
The Infernal Powers, in one day to have marred
What he, Almighty styled, six nights and days
Continued making, and who knows how long
Before had been contriving? though perhaps
Not longer than since I in one night freed   140
From servitude inglorious well nigh half
The Angelic Name, and thinner left the throng
Of his adorers. He, to be avenged,
And to repair his numbers thus impaired—
Whether such virtue, spent of old, now failed
More Angels to create (if they at least
Are his created), or, to spite us more—
Determined to advance into our room
A creature formed of earth, and him endow,
Exalted from so base original,   150
With heavenly spoils, our spoils. What he decreed
He effected; Man he made, and for him built
Magnificent this World, and Earth his seat,
Him Lord pronounced, and, O indignity!
Subjected to his service Angel-wings
And flaming ministers, to watch and tend
Their earthly charge. Of these the vigilance
I dread, and to elude, thus wrapt in mist
Of midnight vapor, glide obscure, and pry
In every bush and brake, where hap may find   160
The Serpent sleeping, in whose mazy folds
To hide me, and the dark intent I bring.
O foul descent! that I, who erst contended
With Gods to sit the highest, am now constrained
Into a beast, and, mixed with bestial slime,
This essence to incarnate and imbrute,
That to the highth of deity aspired!
But what will not ambition and revenge
Descend to? Who aspires must down as low
As high he soared, obnoxious, first or last,   170
To basest things. Revenge, at first though sweet,
Bitter ere long back on itself recoils.
Let it; I reck not, so it light well aimed,
Since higher I fall short, on him who next
Provokes my envy, this new favorite
Of Heaven, this Man of Clay, son of despite,
Whom, us the more to spite, his Maker raised

From dust: spite then with spite is best repaid."
    So saying, through each thicket, dank or dry,
Like a black mist low-creeping, he held on   180
His midnight-search, where soonest he might find
The Serpent. Him fast-sleeping soon he found,
In labyrinth of many a round self-rolled,
His head the midst, well stored with subtle wiles:
Not yet in horrid shade or dismal den,
Nor nocent yet, but on the grassy herb,
Fearless, unfeared, he slept. In at his mouth
The Devil entered, and his brutal sense,
In heart or head, possessing soon inspired
With act intelligential; but his sleep   190
Disturbed not, waiting close the approach of morn.
    Now, whenas sacred light began to dawn
In Eden on the humid flowers, that breathed
Their morning incense, when all things that breathe
From the Earth's great altar send up silent praise
To the Creator, and his nostrils fill
With grateful smell, forth came the human pair,
And joined their vocal worship to the quire
Of creatures wanting voice; that done, partake
The season, prime for sweetest scents and airs;   200
Then commune how that day they best may ply
Their growing work—for much their work outgrew
The hands' dispatch of two gardening so wide:
And Eve first to her husband thus began:—
    "Adam, well may we labor still to dress
This Garden, still to tend plant, herb, and flower,
Our pleasant task enjoined; but, till more hands
Aid us, the work under our labor grows,
Luxurious by restraint: what we by day
Lop overgrown, or prune, or prop, or bind,   210
One night or two with wanton growth derides,
Tending to wild. Thou, therefore, now advise,
Or hear what to my mind first thoughts present.
Let us divide our labors—thou, where choice
Leads thee, or where most needs, whether to wind
The woodbine round this arbor, or direct
The clasping ivy where to climb; while I
In yonder spring of roses intermixed
With myrtle find what to redress till noon.
For, while so near each other thus all day   220

Our task we choose, what wonder if so near
Looks intervene and smiles, or objects new
Casual discourse draw on, which intermits
Our day's work, brought to little, though begun
Early, and the hour of supper comes unearned!"
    To whom mild answer Adam thus returned:—
"Sole Eve, associate sole, to me beyond
Compare above all living creatures dear!
Well hast thou motioned, well thy thoughts employed
How we might best fulfil the work which here   230
God hath assigned us, nor of me shalt pass
Unpraised; for nothing lovelier can be found
In woman than to study houshold good,
And good works in her husband to promote.
Yet not so strictly hath our Lord imposed
Labor as to debar us when we need
Refreshment, whether food, or talk between,
Food of the mind, or this sweet intercourse
Of looks and smiles; for smiles from reason flow
To brute denied, and are of love the food—   240
Love, not the lowest end of human life.
For not to irksome toil, but to delight,
He made us, and delight to reason joined.
These paths and bowers doubt not but our joint hands
Will keep from wilderness with ease, as wide
As we need walk, till younger hands ere long
Assist us. But, if much converse perhaps
Thee satiate, to short absence I could yield;
For solitude sometimes is best society,
And short retirement urges sweet return.   250
But other doubt possesses me, lest harm
Befall thee, severed from me; for thou know'st
What hath been warned us—what malicious foe,
Envying our happiness, and of his own
Despairing, seeks to work us woe and shame
By sly assault, and somewhere nigh at hand
Watches, no doubt, with greedy hope to find
His wish and best advantage, us asunder,
Hopeless to circumvent us joined, where each
To other speedy aid might lend at need.   260
Whether his first design be to withdraw
Our fealty from God, or to disturb
Conjugal love—than which perhaps no bliss

Enjoyed by us excites his envy more—
Or this, or worse, leave not the faithful side
That gave thee being, still shades thee and protects.
The wife, where danger or dishonor lurks,
Safest and seemliest by her husband stays,
Who guards her, or with her the worst endures."
    To whom the virgin majesty of Eve,   270
As one who loves, and some unkindness meets,
With sweet austere composure thus replied:—
    "Offspring of Heaven and Earth, and all Earth's lord!
That such an enemy we have, who seeks
Our ruin, both by thee informed I learn,
And from the parting Angel overheard,
As in a shady nook I stood behind,
Just then returned at shut of evening flowers.
But that thou shouldst my firmness therefore doubt
To God or thee, because we have a foe   280
May tempt it, I expected not to hear.
His violence thou fear'st not, being such
As we, not capable of death or pain,
Can either not receive, or can repel.
His fraud is, then, thy fear; which plain infers
Thy equal fear that my firm faith and love
Can by his fraud be shaken or seduced:
Thoughts, which how found they harbor in thy breast,
Adam! misthought of her to thee so dear?"
    To whom, with healing words, Adam replied:—   290
"Daughter of God and Man, immortal Eve!—
For such thou art, from sin and blame entire—
Not diffident of thee do I dissuade
Thy absence from my sight, but to avoid
The attempt itself, intended by our foe.
For he who tempts, though in vain, at least asperses
The tempted with dishonor foul, supposed
Not incorruptible of faith, not proof
Against temptation. Thou thyself with scorn
And anger wouldst resent the offered wrong,   300
Though ineffectual found; misdeem not, then,
If such affront I labor to avert
From thee alone, which on us both at once
The enemy, though bold, will hardly dare;
Or, daring, first on me the assault shall light.
Nor thou his malice and false guile contemn—

Subtle he needs must be who could seduce
Angels—nor think superfluous others' aid.
I from the influence of thy looks receive
Access in every virtue—in thy sight   310
More wise, more watchful, stronger, if need were
Of outward strength; while shame, thou looking on,
Shame to be overcome or overreached,
Would utmost vigor raise, and raised unite.
Why shouldst not thou like sense within thee feel
When I am present, and thy trial choose
With me, best witness of thy virtue tried?"
   So spake domestic Adam in his care
And matrimonial love; but Eve, who thought
Less attributed to her faith sincere,   320
Thus her reply with accent sweet renewed:—
   "If this be our condition, thus to dwell
In narrow circuit straitened by a foe,
Subtle or violent, we not endued
Single with like defence wherever met,
How are we happy, still in fear of harm?
But harm precedes not sin: only our foe
Tempting affronts us with his foul esteem
Of our integrity: his foul esteem
Sticks no dishonor on our front, but turns   330
Foul on himself; then wherefore shunned or feared
By us, who rather double honor gain
From his surmise proved false, find peace within,
Favor from Heaven, our witness, from the event?
And what is faith, love, virtue, unassayed
Alone, without exterior help sustained?
Let us not then suspect our happy state
Left so imperfect by the Maker wise
As not secure to single or combined.
Frail is our happiness, if this be so;   340
And Eden were no Eden, thus exposed."
   To whom thus Adam fervently replied:—
"O Woman, best are all things as the will
Of God ordained them; his creating hand
Nothing imperfect or deficient left
Of all that he created—much less Man,
Or aught that might his happy state secure,
Secure from outward force. Within himself
The danger lies, yet lies within his power;

Against his will he can receive no harm.   350
But God left free the Will; for what obeys
Reason is free; and Reason he made right,
But bid her well be ware, and still erect,
Lest, by some fair appearing good surprised,
She dictate false, and misinform the Will
To do what God expressly hath forbid.
Not then mistrust, but tender love, enjoins
That I should mind thee oft; and mind thou me.
Firm we subsist, yet possible to swerve,
Since Reason not impossibly may meet   360
Some specious object by the foe suborned,
And fall into deception unaware,
Not keeping strictest watch, as she was warned.
Seek not temptation, then, which to avoid
Were better, and most likely if from me
Thou sever not: trial will come unsought.
Wouldst thou approve thy constancy, approve
First thy obedience; the other who can know,
Not seeing thee attempted, who attest?
But, if thou think trial unsought may find   370
Us both securer than thus warned thou seem'st,
Go; for thy stay, not free, absents thee more.
Go in thy native innocence; rely
On what thou hast of virtue; summon all;
For God towards thee hath done his part: do thine."
   So spake the Patriarch of Mankind; but Eve
Persisted; yet submiss, though last, replied:—
   "With thy permission, then, and thus forewarned,
Chiefly by what thy own last reasoning words
Touched only, that our trial, when least sought,   380
May find us both perhaps far less prepared,
The willinger I go, nor much expect
A foe so proud will first the weaker seek;
So bent, the more shall shame him his repulse."
   Thus saying, from her husband's hand her hand
Soft she withdrew, and, like a wood-nymph light,
Oread or Dryad, or of Delia's train,
Betook her to the groves, but Delia's self
In gait surpassed and goddess-like deport,
Though not as she with bow and quiver armed,   390
But with such gardening tools as Art, yet rude,
Guiltless of fire had formed, or Angels brought.

To Pales, or Pomona, thus adorned,
Likest she seemed—Pomona when she fled
Vertumnus—or to Ceres in her prime,
Yet virgin of Proserpina from Jove.
Her long with ardent look his eye pursued
Delighted, but desiring more her stay.
Oft he to her his charge of quick return
Repeated; she to him as oft engaged   400
To be returned by noon amid the bower,
And all things in best order to invite
Noontide repast, or afternoon's repose.
O much deceived, much failing, hapless Eve,
Of thy presumed return! event perverse!
Thou never from that hour in Paradise
Found'st either sweet repast or sound repose;
Such ambush, hid among sweet flowers and shades,
Waited, with hellish rancor imminent,
To intercept thy way, or send thee back   410
Despoiled of innocence, of faith, of bliss.
For now, and since first break of dawn, the Fiend,
Mere serpent in appearance, forth was come,
And on his quest where likeliest he might find
The only two of mankind, but in them
The whole included race, his purposed prey.
In bower and field he sought, where any tuft
Of grove or garden-plot more pleasant lay,
Their tendance or plantation for delight;
By fountain or by shady rivulet   420
He sought them both, but wished his hap might find
Eve separate; he wished, but not with hope
Of what so seldom chanced, when to his wish,
Beyond his hope, Eve separate he spies,
Veiled in a cloud of fragrance, where she stood,
Half-spied, so thick the roses bushing round
About her glowed, oft stooping to support
Each flower of tender stalk, whose head, though gay
Carnation, purple, azure, or specked with gold,
Hung drooping unsustained. Them she upstays   430
Gently with myrtle band, mindless the while
Herself, though fairest unsupported flower,
From her best prop so far, and storm so nigh.
Nearer he drew, and many a walk traversed
Of stateliest covert, cedar, pine, or palm;

Then voluble and bold, now hid, now seen
Among thick-woven arborets, and flowers
Imbordered on each bank, the hand of Eve:
Spot more delicious than those gardens feigned
Or of revived Adonis, or renowned   440
Alcinous, host of old Laertes' son,
Or that, not mystic, where the sapient king
Held dalliance with his fair Egyptian spouse.
Much he the place admired, the person more.
As one who, long in populous city pent,
Where houses thick and sewers annoy the air,
Forth issuing on a summer's morn, to breathe
Among the pleasant villages and farms
Adjoined, from each thing met conceives delight—
The smell of grain, or tedded grass, or kine,   450
Or dairy, each rural sight, each rural sound—
If chance with nymph-like step fair virgin pass,
What pleasing seemed for her now pleases more,
She most, and in her look sums all delight:
Such pleasure took the Serpent to behold
This flowery plat, the sweet recess of Eve
Thus early, thus alone. Her heavenly form
Angelic, but more soft and feminine,
Her graceful innocence, her every air
Of gesture or least action, overawed   460
His malice, and with rapine sweet bereaved
His fierceness of the fierce intent it brought.
That space the Evil One abstracted stood
From his own evil, and for the time remained
Stupidly good, of enmity disarmed,
Of guile, of hate, of envy, of revenge.
But the hot hell that always in him burns,
Though in mid Heaven, soon ended his delight,
And tortures him now more, the more he sees
Of pleasure not for him ordained. Then soon   470
Fierce hate he recollects, and all his thoughts
Of mischief, gratulating, thus excites:—
    "Thoughts, whither have ye led me? with what sweet
Compulsion thus transported to forget
What hither brought us? hate, not love, nor hope
Of Paradise for Hell, hope here to taste
Of pleasure, but all pleasure to destroy,
Save what is in destroying; other joy

To me is lost. Then let me not let pass
Occasion which now smiles. Behold alone   480
The Woman, opportune to all attempts—
Her husband, for I view far round, not nigh,
Whose higher intellectual more I shun,
And strength, of courage haughty, and of limb
Heroic built, though of terrestrial mould;
Foe not informidable, exempt from wound—
I not; so much hath Hell debased, and pain
Enfeebled me, to what I was in Heaven.
She fair, divinely fair, fit love for Gods,
Not terrible, though terror be in love,   490
And beauty, not approached by stronger hate,
Hate stronger under show of love well feigned—
The way which to her ruin now I tend."
     So spake the Enemy of Mankind, enclosed
In serpent, inmate bad, and toward Eve
Addressed his way—not with indented wave,
Prone on the ground, as since, but on his rear,
Circular base of rising folds, that towered
Fold above fold, a surging maze; his head
Crested aloft, and carbuncle his eyes;   500
With burnished neck of verdant gold, erect
Amidst his circling spires, that on the grass
Floated redundant. Pleasing was his shape
And lovely; never since of serpent kind
Lovelier—not those that in Illyria changed
Hermione and Cadmus, or the god
In Epidaurus; nor to which transformed
Ammonian Jove, or Capitoline, was seen,
He with Olympias, this with her who bore
Scipio, the highth of Rome. With tract oblique   510
At first, as one who sought access but feared
To interrupt, sidelong he works his way.
As when a ship, by skilful steersmen wrought
Nigh river's mouth or foreland, where the wind
Veers oft, as oft so steers, and shifts her sail,
So varied he, and of his tortuous train
Curled many a wanton wreath in sight of Eve,
To lure her eye. She, busied, heard the sound
Of rustling leaves, but minded not, as used
To such disport before her through the field   520
From every beast, more duteous at her call

Than at Circean call the herd disguised.
He, bolder now, uncalled before her stood,
But as in gaze admiring. Oft he bowed
His turret crest and sleek enamelled neck,
Fawning, and licked the ground whereon she trod.
His gentle dumb expression turned at length
The eye of Eve to mark his play; he, glad
Of her attention gained, with serpent-tongue
Organic, or impulse of vocal air,   530
His fraudulent temptation thus began:—
    "Wonder not, sovran mistress (if perhaps
Thou canst who art sole wonder), much less arm
Thy looks, the heaven of mildness, with disdain,
Displeased that I approach thee thus, and gaze
Insatiate, I thus single, nor have feared
Thy awful brow, more awful thus retired.
Fairest resemblance of thy Maker fair,
Thee all things living gaze on, all things thine
By gift, and thy celestial beauty adore,   540
With ravishment beheld—there best beheld
Where universally admired. But here,
In this enclosure wild, these beasts among,
Beholders rude, and shallow to discern
Half what in thee is fair, one man except,
Who sees thee (and what is one?) who shouldst be seen
A Goddess among Gods, adored and served
By Angels numberless, thy daily train?"
    So glozed the Tempter, and his proem tuned.
Into the heart of Eve his words made way,   550
Though at the voice much marvelling; at length,
Not unamazed, she thus in answer spake:—
    "What may this mean? Language of Man pronounced
By tongue of brute, and human sense expressed!
The first at least of these I thought denied
To beasts, whom God, on their creation-day
Created mute to all articulate sound;
The latter I demur, for in their looks
Much reason, and in their actions, oft appears.
Thee, Serpent, subtlest beast of all the field   560
I knew, but not with human voice endued;
Redouble, then, this miracle, and say,
How cam'st thou speakable of mute, and how
To me so friendly grown above the rest

Of brutal kind that daily are in sight:
Say, for such wonder claims attention due."
  To whom the guileful Tempter thus replied:—
"Empress of this fair World, resplendent Eve!
Easy to me it is to tell thee all
What thou command'st, and right thou shouldst be obeyed.   570
I was at first as other beasts that graze
The trodden herb, of abject thoughts and low,
As was my food, nor aught but food discerned
Or sex, and apprehended nothing high:
Till on a day, roving the field, I chanced
A goodly tree far distant to behold,
Loaden with fruit of fairest colors mixed,
Ruddy and gold. I nearer drew to gaze;
When from the boughs a savory odor blown,
Grateful to appetite, more pleased my sense   580
Than smell of sweetest fennel, or the teats
Of ewe or goat dropping with milk at even,
Unsucked of lamb or kid, that tend their play.
To satisfy the sharp desire I had
Of tasting those fair apples, I resolved
Not to defer; hunger and thirst at once,
Powerful persuaders, quickened at the scent
Of that alluring fruit, urged me so keen.
About the mossy trunk I wound me soon;
For, high from ground, the branches would require   590
Thy utmost reach, or Adam's: round the tree
All other beasts that saw, with like desire
Longing and envying stood, but could not reach.
Amid the tree now got, where plenty hung
Tempting so nigh, to pluck and eat my fill
I spared not; for such pleasure till that hour
At feed or fountain never had I found.
Sated at length, ere long I might perceive
Strange alteration in me, to degree
Of Reason in my inward powers; and Speech   600
Wanted not long, though to this shape retained.
Thenceforth to speculations high or deep
I turned my thoughts, and with capacious mind
Considered all things visible in Heaven,
Or Earth, or Middle, all things fair and good.
But all that fair and good in thy divine
Semblance, and in thy beauty's heavenly ray,

United I beheld—no fair to thine
Equivalent or second; which compelled
Me thus, though importune perhaps, to come   610
And gaze, and worship thee of right declared
Sovran of creatures, universal Dame!"
   So talked the spirited sly Snake; and Eve,
Yet more amazed, unwary thus replied:—
   "Serpent, thy overpraising leaves in doubt
The virtue of that fruit, in thee first proved.
But say, where grows the tree? from hence how far?
For many are the trees of God that grow
In Paradise, and various, yet unknown
To us; in such abundance lies our choice   620
As leaves a greater store of fruit untouched,
Still hanging incorruptible, till men
Grow up to their provision, and more hands
Help to disburden Nature of her bearth."
   To whom the wily Adder, blithe and glad:—
"Empress, the way is ready, and not long—
Beyond a row of myrtles, on a flat,
Fast by a fountain, one small thicket past
Of blowing myrrh and balm. If thou accept
My conduct, I can bring thee thither soon."   630
   "Lead then," said Eve. He, leading, swiftly rolled
In tangles, and made intricate seem straight,
To mischief swift. Hope elevates, and joy
Brightens his crest. As when a wandering fire,
Compact of unctuous vapor, which the night
Condenses, and the cold environs round,
Kindled through agitation to a flame
(Which oft, they say, some evil spirit attends),
Hovering and blazing with delusive light,
Misleads the amazed night-wanderer from his way   640
To bogs and mires, and oft through pond or pool,
There swallowed up and lost, from succor far:
So glistered the dire Snake, and into fraud
Led Eve, our credulous mother, to the Tree
Of Prohibition, root of all our woe;
Which when she saw, thus to her guide she spake:—
   "Serpent, we might have spared our coming hither,
Fruitless to me, though fruit be here to excess,
The credit of whose virtue rest with thee—
Wondrous, indeed, if cause of such effects!   650

But of this tree we may not taste nor touch;
God so commanded, and left that command
Sole daughter of his voice: the rest, we live
Law to ourselves; our Reason is our Law."
　　To whom the Tempter guilefully replied:—
"Indeed! Hath God then said that of the fruit
Of all these garden-trees ye shall not eat,
Yet lords declared of all in Earth or Air?"
　　To whom thus Eve, yet sinless:—"Of the fruit
Of each tree in the garden we may eat;   660
But of the fruit of this fair tree, amidst
The Garden, God hath said, 'Ye shall not eat
Thereof, nor shall ye touch it, lest ye die.'"
　　She scarce had said, though brief, when now more bold
The Tempter, but, with show of zeal and love
To Man, and indignation at his wrong,
New part puts on, and, as to passion moved,
Fluctuates disturbed, yet comely, and in act
Raised, as of some great matter to begin.
As when of old some orator renowned   670
In Athens or free Rome, where eloquence
Flourished, since mute, to some great cause addressed,
Stood in himself collected, while each part,
Motion, each act, won audience ere the tongue
Sometimes in highth began, as no delay
Of preface brooking through his zeal of right:
So standing, moving, or to highth upgrown,
The Tempter, all impassioned, thus began:—
　　"O sacred, wise, and wisdom-giving Plant,
Mother of science! now I feel thy power   680
Within me clear, not only to discern
Things in their causes, but to trace the ways
Of highest agents, deemed however wise.
Queen of this Universe! do not believe
Those rigid threats of death. Ye shall not die.
How should ye? By the fruit? it gives you life
To knowledge. By the Threatener? look on me,
Me who have touched and tasted, yet both live,
And life more perfect have attained than Fate
Meant me, by venturing higher than my lot.   690
Shall that be shut to Man which to the Beast
Is open? or will God incense his ire
For such a petty trespass, and not praise

Rather your dauntless virtue, whom the pain
Of Death denounced, whatever thing Death be,
Deterred not from achieving what might lead
To happier life, knowledge of Good and Evil?
Of good, how just! of evil—if what is evil
Be real, why not known, since easier shunned?
God, therefore, cannot hurt ye, and be just;   700
Not just, not God; not feared then, nor obeyed:
Your fear itself of death removes the fear.
Why, then, was this forbid? Why but to awe,
Why but to keep ye low and ignorant,
His worshipers? He knows that in the day
Ye eat thereof your eyes, that seem so clear,
Yet are but dim, shall perfectly be then
Opened and cleared, and ye shall be as Gods,
Knowing both good and evil, as they know.
That ye should be as Gods, since I as Man,   710
Internal Man, is but proportion meet—
I, of brute, human; ye, of human, Gods.
So ye shall die perhaps, by putting off
Human, to put on Gods—death to be wished,
Though threatened, which no worse than this can bring!
And what are Gods, that Man may not become
As they, participating godlike food?
The Gods are first, and that advantage use
On our belief, that all from them proceeds.
I question it; for this fair Earth I see,   720
Warmed by the sun, producing every kind;
Them nothing. If they all things, who enclosed
Knowledge of good and evil in this tree,
That whoso eats thereof forthwith attains
Wisdom without their leave? and wherein lies
The offence, that Man should thus attain to know?
What can your knowledge hurt him, or this tree
Impart against his will, if all be his?
Or is it envy? and can envy dwell
In Heavenly breasts? These, these and many more   730
Causes import your need of this fair fruit.
Goddess humane, reach then, and freely taste!"
    He ended; and his words, replete with guile,
Into her heart too easy entrance won.
Fixed on the fruit she gazed, which to behold
Might tempt alone; and in her ears the sound

Yet rung of his persuasive words, impregned
With reason, to her seeming, and with truth.
Meanwhile the hour of noon drew on, and waked
An eager appetite, raised by the smell   740
So savory of that fruit, which with desire,
Inclinable now grown to touch or taste,
Solicited her longing eye; yet first,
Pausing a while, thus to herself she mused:—
    "Great are thy virtues, doubtless, best of fruits,
Though kept from Man, and worthy to be admired,
Whose taste, too long forborne, at first assay
Gave elocution to the mute, and taught
The tongue not made for speech to speak thy praise.
Thy praise he also who forbids thy use   750
Conceals not from us, naming thee the Tree
Of Knowledge, knowledge both of good and evil;
Forbids us then to taste. But his forbidding
Commends thee more, while it infers the good
By thee communicated, and our want;
For good unknown sure is not had, or, had
And yet unknown, is as not had at all.
In plain, then, what forbids he but to know?
Forbids us good, forbids us to be wise!
Such prohibitions bind not. But, if Death   760
Bind us with after-bands, what profits then
Our inward freedom? In the day we eat
Of this fair fruit, our doom is we shall die!
How dies the Serpent? He hath eaten, and lives,
And knows, and speaks, and reasons, and discerns,
Irrational till then. For us alone
Was death invented? or to us denied
This intellectual food, for beasts reserved?
For beasts it seems; yet that one beast which first
Hath tasted envies not, but brings with joy   770
The good befallen him, author unsuspect,
Friendly to Man, far from deceit or guile.
What fear I, then? rather, what know to fear
Under this ignorance of good and evil,
Of God or Death, of law or penalty?
Here grows the cure of all, this fruit divine,
Fair to the eye, inviting to the taste,
Of virtue to make wise. What hinders, then,
To reach, and feed at once both body and mind?"

So saying, her rash hand in evil hour   780
Forth-reaching to the fruit, she plucked, she eat.
Earth felt the wound, and Nature from her seat,
Sighing through all her works, gave signs of woe
That all was lost. Back to the thicket slunk
The guilty Serpent, and well might, for Eve,
Intent now only on her taste, naught else
Regarded; such delight till then, as seemed,
In fruit she never tasted, whether true,
Or fancied so through expectation high
Of knowledge; nor was Godhead from her thought.   790
Greedily she ingorged without restraint,
And knew not eating death. Satiate at length,
And hightened as with wine, jocund and boon,
Thus to herself she pleasingly began:—
    "O sovran, virtuous, precious of all trees
In Paradise! of operation blest
To sapience, hitherto obscured, infamed,
And thy fair fruit let hang, as to no end
Created! but henceforth my early care,
Not without song, each morning, and due praise,   800
Shall tend thee, and the fertile burden ease
Of thy full branches, offered free to all;
Till, dieted by thee, I grow mature
In knowledge, as the Gods who all things know.
Though others envy what they cannot give—
For, had the gift been theirs, it had not here
Thus grown! Experience next to thee I owe,
Best guide: not following thee, I had remained
In ignorance; thou open'st Wisdom's way,
And giv'st access, though secret she retire.   810
And I perhaps am secret: Heaven is high—
High, and remote to see from thence distinct
Each thing on Earth; and other care perhaps
May have diverted from continual watch
Our great Forbidder, safe with all his spies
About him. But to Adam in what sort
Shall I appear? Shall I to him make known
As yet my change, and give him to partake
Full happiness with me, or rather not,
But keep the odds of knowledge in my power   820
Without copartner? so to add what wants
In female sex, the more to draw his love,

And render me more equal, and perhaps—
A thing not undesirable—sometime
Superior; for, inferior, who is free?
This may be well; but what if God have seen,
And death ensue? Then I shall be no more;
And Adam, wedded to another Eve,
Shall live with her enjoying, I extinct!
A death to think! Confirmed then, I resolve   830
Adam shall share with me in bliss or woe.
So dear I love him that with him all deaths
I could endure, without him live no life."

   So saying, from the tree her step she turned,
But first low reverence done, as to the Power
That dwelt within, whose presence had infused
Into the plant sciential sap, derived
From nectar, drink of Gods. Adam the while,
Waiting desirous her return, had wove
Of choicest flowers a garland, to adorn   840
Her tresses, and her rural labors crown,
As reapers oft are wont their harvest-queen.
Great joy he promised to his thoughts, and new
Solace in her return, so long delayed;
Yet oft his heart, divine of something ill,
Misgave him. He the faltering measure felt,
And forth to meet her went, the way she took
That morn when first they parted. By the Tree
Of Knowledge he must pass; there he her met,
Scarce from the tree returning; in her hand   850
A bough of fairest fruit, that downy smiled,
New gathered, and ambrosial smell diffused.
To him she hasted; in her face excuse
Came prologue, and apology to prompt,
Which, with bland words at will, she thus addressed:—
   "Hast thou not wondered, Adam, at my stay?
Thee I have missed, and thought it long, deprived
Thy presence—agony of love till now
Not felt, nor shall be twice; for never more
Mean I to try, what rash untried I sought,   860
The pain of absence from thy sight. But strange
Hath been the cause, and wonderful to hear.
This tree is not, as we are told, a tree
Of danger tasted, nor to evil unknown
Opening the way, but of divine effect

To open eyes, and make them Gods who taste;
And hath been tasted such. The Serpent wise,
Or not restrained as we, or not obeying,
Hath eaten of the fruit, and is become
Not dead, as we are threatened, but thenceforth   870
Endued with human voice and human sense,
Reasoning to admiration, and with me
Persuasively hath so prevailed that I
Have also tasted, and have also found
The effects to correspond—opener mine eyes,
Dim erst, dilated spirits, ampler heart,
And growing up to Godhead; which for thee
Chiefly I sought, without thee can despise.
For bliss, as thou hast part, to me is bliss;
Tedious, unshared with thee, and odious soon.   880
Thou, therefore, also taste, that equal lot
May join us, equal joy, as equal love;
Lest, thou not tasting, different degree
Disjoin us, and I then too late renounce
Deity for thee, when fate will not permit."
    Thus Eve with countenance blithe her story told;
But in her cheek distemper flushing glowed.
On the other side, Adam, soon as he heard
The fatal trespass done by Eve, amazed,
Astonied stood and blank, while horror chill   890
Ran through his veins, and all his joints relaxed.
From his slack hand the garland wreathed for Eve
Down dropt, and all the faded roses shed.
Speechless he stood and pale, till thus at length
First to himself he inward silence broke:—
    "O fairest of Creation, last and best
Of all God's works, creature in whom excelled
Whatever can to sight or thought be formed,
Holy, divine, good, amiable, or sweet!
How art thou lost! how on a sudden lost,   900
Defaced, deflowered, and now to death devote!
Rather, how hast thou yielded to transgress
The strict forbiddance, how to violate
The sacred fruit forbidden? Some cursed fraud
Of enemy hath beguiled thee, yet unknown,
And me with thee hath ruined; for with thee
Certain my resolution is to die.
How can I live without thee? how forgo

Thy sweet converse, and love so dearly joined,
To live again in these wild woods forlorn? 910
Should God create another Eve, and I
Another rib afford, yet loss of thee
Would never from my heart. No, no! I feel
The link of Nature draw me: flesh of flesh,
Bone of my bone thou art, and from thy state
Mine never shall be parted, bliss or woe."
   So having said, as one from sad dismay
Recomforted, and, after thoughts disturbed,
Submitting to what seemed remediless,
Thus in calm mood his words to Eve he turned:— 920
   "Bold deed thou hast presumed, adventurous Eve,
And peril great provoked, who thus hast dared
Had it been only coveting to eye
That sacred food, sacred to abstinence;
Much more to taste it, under ban to touch.
But past who can recall, or done undo?
Not God Omnipotent, nor Fate! Yet so
Perhaps thou shalt not die; perhaps the fact
Is not so heinous now—foretasted fruit,
Profaned first by the Serpent, by him first 930
Made common and unhallowed ere our taste,
Nor yet on him found deadly. He yet lives—
Lives, as thou saidst, and gains to live, as Man,
Higher degree of life: inducement strong
To us, as likely, tasting, to attain
Proportional ascent; which cannot be
But to be Gods, or Angels, demi-gods.
Nor can I think that God, Creator wise,
Though threatening, will in earnest so destroy
Us, his prime creatures, dignified so high, 940
Set over all his works; which, in our fall,
For us created, needs with us must fail,
Dependent made. So God shall uncreate,
Be frustrate, do, undo, and labor lose—
Not well conceived of God; who, though his power
Creation could repeat, yet would be loth
Us to abolish, lest the Adversary
Triumph and say: 'Fickle their state whom God
Most favors; who can please him long? Me first
He ruined, now Mankind; whom will he next?'— 950
Matter of scorn not to be given the Foe.

However, I with thee have fixed my lot,
Certain to undergo like doom. If death
Consort with thee, death is to me as life;
So forcible within my heart I feel
The bond of Nature draw me to my own—
My own in thee; for what thou art is mine.
Our state cannot be severed; we are one,
One flesh; to lose thee were to lose myself."
   So Adam; and thus Eve to him replied:—   960
"O glorious trial of exceeding love,
Illustrious evidence, example high!
Engaging me to emulate; but, short
Of thy perfection, how shall I attain,
Adam? from whose dear side I boast me sprung,
And gladly of our union hear thee speak,
One heart, one soul in both; whereof good proof
This day affords, declaring thee resolved,
Rather than death, or aught than death more dread,
Shall separate us, linked in love so dear,   970
To undergo with me one guilt, one crime,
If any be, of tasting this fair fruit;
Whose virtue (for of good still good proceeds,
Direct, or by occasion) hath presented
This happy trial of thy love, which else
So eminently never had been known.
Were it I thought death menaced would ensue
This my attempt, I would sustain alone
The worst, and not persuade thee—rather die
Deserted than oblige thee with a fact   980
Pernicious to thy peace, chiefly assured
Remarkably so late of thy so true,
So faithful, love unequalled. But I feel
Far otherwise the event—not death, but life
Augmented, opened eyes, new hopes, new joys,
Taste so divine that what of sweet before
Hath touched my sense flat seems to this and harsh.
On my experience, Adam, freely taste,
And fear of death deliver to the winds."
   So saying, she embraced him, and for joy   990
Tenderly wept, much won that he his love
Had so ennobled as of choice to incur
Divine displeasure for her sake, or death.
In recompense (for such compliance bad

Such recompense best merits), from the bough
She gave him of that fair enticing fruit
With liberal hand. He scrupled not to eat,
Against his better knowledge, not deceived,
But fondly overcome with female charm.
Earth trembled from her entrails, as again   1000
In pangs, and Nature gave a second groan;
Sky loured, and, muttering thunder, some sad drops
Wept at completing of the mortal Sin
Original; while Adam took no thought,
Eating his fill, nor Eve to iterate
Her former trespass feared, the more to soothe
Him with her loved society; that now,
As with new wine intoxicated both,
They swim in mirth, and fancy that they feel
Divinity within them breeding wings   1010
Wherewith to scorn the Earth. But that false fruit
Far other operation first displayed,
Carnal desire inflaming. He on Eve
Began to cast lascivious eyes; she him
As wantonly repaid; in lust they burn,
Till Adam thus gan Eve to dalliance move:—
    "Eve, now I see thou art exact of taste
And elegant—of sapience no small part;
Since to each meaning savor we apply,
And palate call judicious. I the praise   1020
Yield thee; so well this day thou hast purveyed.
Much pleasure we have lost, while we abstained
From this delightful fruit, nor known till now
True relish, tasting. If such pleasure be
In things to us forbidden, it might be wished
For this one tree had been forbidden ten.
But come; so well refreshed, now let us play,
As meet is, after such delicious fare;
For never did thy beauty, since the day
I saw thee first and wedded thee, adorned   1030
With all perfections, so inflame my sense
With ardor to enjoy thee, fairer now
Than ever—bounty of this virtuous tree!"
    So said he, and forebore not glance or toy
Of amorous intent, well understood
Of Eve, whose eye darted contagious fire.
Her hand he seized, and to a shady bank,

Thick overhead with verdant roof embowered,
He led her, nothing loth; flowers were the couch,
Pansies, and violets, and asphodel,   1040
And hyacinth—Earth's freshest, softest lap.
There they their fill of love and love's disport
Took largely, of their mutual guilt the seal,
The solace of their sin, till dewy sleep
Oppressed them, wearied with their amorous play.
    Soon as the force of that fallacious fruit,
That with exhilarating vapor bland
About their spirits had played, and inmost powers
Made err, was now exhaled, and grosser sleep,
Bred of unkindly fumes, with conscious dreams   1050
Encumbered, now had left them, up they rose
As from unrest, and, each the other viewing,
Soon found their eyes how opened, and their minds
How darkened. Innocence, that as a veil
Had shadowed them from knowing ill, was gone;
Just confidence, and native righteousness,
And honor, from about them, naked left
To guilty Shame: he covered, but his robe
Uncovered more. So rose the Danite strong,
Herculean Samson, from the harlot-lap   1060
Of Philistean Dalilah, and waked
Shorn of his strength; they destitute and bare
Of all their virtue. Silent, and in face
Confounded, long they sat, as strucken mute;
Till Adam, though not less than Eve abashed,
At length gave utterance to these words constrained:—
    "O Eve, in evil hour thou didst give ear
To that false Worm, of whomsoever taught
To counterfeit Man's voice—true in our fall,
False in our promised rising; since our eyes   1070
Opened we find indeed, and find we know
Both good and evil, good lost, and evil got:
Bad fruit of knowledge, if this be to know,
Which leaves us naked thus, of honor void,
Of innocence, of faith, of purity,
Our wonted ornaments now soiled and stained,
And in our faces evident the signs
Of foul concupiscence; whence evil store,
Even shame, the last of evils; of the first
Be sure then. How shall I behold the face   1080

Henceforth of God or Angel, erst with joy
And rapture so oft beheld? Those Heavenly Shapes
Will dazzle now this earthly with their blaze
Insufferably bright. Oh, might I here
In solitude live savage, in some glade
Obscured, where highest woods, impenetrable
To star or sunlight, spread their umbrage broad,
And brown as evening! Cover me, ye pines!
Ye cedars, with innumerable boughs
Hide me, where I may never see them more!   1090
But let us now, as in bad plight, devise
What best may, for the present, serve to hide
The parts of each from other that seem most
To shame obnoxious, and unseemliest seen—
Some tree, whose broad smooth leaves, together sewed,
And girded on our loins, may cover round
Those middle parts, that this new comer, Shame,
There sit not, and reproach us as unclean."
　　So counselled he, and both together went
Into the thickest wood. There soon they chose   1100
The fig-tree—not that kind for fruit renowned,
But such as, at this day, to Indians known,
In Malabar or Decan spreads her arms
Branching so broad and long that in the ground
The bended twigs take root, and daughters grow
About the mother tree, a pillared shade
High overarched, and echoing walks between:
There oft the Indian herdsman, shunning heat,
Shelters in cool, and tends his pasturing herds
At loop-holes cut through thickest shade. Those leaves   1110
They gathered, broad as Amazonian targe,
And with what skill they had, together sewed,
To gird their waist—vain covering, if to hide
Their guilt and dreaded shame! O how unlike
To that first naked glory! Such of late
Columbus found the American, so girt
With feathered cincture, naked else, and wild,
Among the trees on isles and woody shores.
Thus fenced, and, as they thought, their shame in part
Covered, but not at rest or ease of mind,   1120
They sat them down to weep. Nor only tears
Rained at their eyes, but high winds worse within
Began to rise, high passions—anger, hate,

Mistrust, suspicion, discord—and shook sore
Their inward state of mind, calm region once
And full of peace, now tost and turbulent:
For Understanding ruled not, and the Will
Heard not her lore, both in subjection now
To sensual Appetite, who, from beneath
Usurping over sovran Reason, claimed   1130
Superior sway. From thus distempered breast
Adam, estranged in look and altered style,
Speech intermitted thus to Eve renewed:—
    "Would thou hadst hearkened to my words, and stayed
With me, as I besought thee, when that strange
Desire of wandering, this unhappy morn,
I know not whence possessed thee! We had then
Remained still happy—not, as now, despoiled
Of all our good, shamed, naked, miserable!
Let none henceforth seek needless cause to approve   1140
The faith they owe; when earnestly they seek
Such proof, conclude they then begin to fail."
    To whom, soon moved with touch of blame, thus Eve:—
"What words have passed thy lips, Adam severe?
Imput'st thou that to my default, or will
Of wandering, as thou call'st it, which who knows
But might as ill have happened thou being by,
Or to thyself perhaps? Hadst thou been there,
Or here the attempt, thou couldst not have discerned
Fraud in the Serpent, speaking as he spake;   1150
No ground of enmity between us known
Why he should mean me ill or seek to harm.
Was I to have never parted from thy side?
As good have grown there still, a lifeless rib.
Being as I am, why didst not thou, the head,
Command me absolutely not to go,
Going into such danger, as thou saidst?
Too facile then, thou didst not much gainsay,
Nay didst permit, approve, and fair dismiss.
Hadst thou been firm and fixed in thy dissent,   1160
Neither had I transgressed, nor thou with me."
    To whom, then first incensed, Adam replied:—
"Is this the love, is this the recompense
Of mine to thee, ingrateful Eve, expressed
Immutable when thou wert lost, not I—
Who might have lived, and joyed immortal bliss,

Yet willingly chose rather death with thee?
And am I now upbraided as the cause
Of thy transgressing? not enough severe,
It seems, in thy restraint! What could I more?   1170
I warned thee, I admonished thee, foretold
The danger, and the lurking enemy
That lay in wait; beyond this had been force,
And force upon free will hath here no place.
But confidence then bore thee on, secure
Either to meet no danger, or to find
Matter of glorious trial; and perhaps
I also erred in overmuch admiring
What seemed in thee so perfect that I thought
No evil durst attempt thee. But I rue   1180
That error now, which is become my crime,
And thou the accuser. Thus it shall befall
Him who, to worth in women overtrusting,
Lets her will rule: restraint she will not brook;
And, left to herself, if evil thence ensue,
She first his weak indulgence will accuse."
    Thus they in mutual accusation spent
The fruitless hours, but neither self-condemning;
And of their vain contest appeared no end.

BOOK X

THE ARGUMENT

MAN'S transgression known, the guardian Angels forsake Paradise, and
return up to Heaven to approve their vigilance, and are approved; God
declaring that the entrance of Satan could not be by them prevented. He
sends his Son to judge the transgressors; who descends, and gives sen-
tence accordingly; then, in pity, clothes them both, and reascends. Sin and
Death, sitting till then at the gates of Hell, by wondrous sympathy feel-
ing the success of Satan in this new World, and the sin by Man there
committed, resolve to sit no longer confined in Hell, but to follow Satan,
their sire, up to the place of Man: to make the way easier from Hell to
this World to and fro, they pave a broad highway or bridge over Chaos,
according to the track that Satan first made; then, preparing for Earth,
they meet him, proud of his success, returning to Hell; their mutual grat-
ulation. Satan arrives at Pandemonium; in full assembly relates, with
boasting, his success against Man; instead of applause is entertained with
a general hiss by all his audience, transformed, with himself also, suddenly
into Serpents, according to his doom given in Paradise; then, deluded
with a show of the Forbidden Tree springing up before them, they,
greedily reaching to take of the fruit, chew dust and bitter ashes. The
proceedings of Sin and Death: God foretells the final victory of his Son
over them, and the renewing of all things; but, for the present, commands
his Angels to make several alterations in the Heavens and Elements.
Adam, more and more perceiving his fallen condition, heavily bewails,
rejects the condolement of Eve; she persists, and at length appeases him:
then, to evade the curse likely to fall on their offspring, proposes to
Adam violent ways; which he approves not, but, conceiving better hope,
puts her in mind of the late promise made them, that her seed should be
revenged on the Serpent, and exhorts her, with him, to seek peace of the
offended Deity by repentance and supplication.

Meanwhile the heinous and despiteful act
Of Satan done in Paradise, and how
He, in the Serpent, had perverted Eve,
Her husband she, to taste the fatal fruit,
Was known in Heaven; for what can scape the eye
Of God all-seeing, or deceive his heart
Omniscient? who, in all things wise and just,
Hindered not Satan to attempt the mind
Of Man, with strength entire and free will armed
Complete to have discovered and repulsed   10
Whatever wiles of foe or seeming friend.
For still they knew, and ought to have still remembered,
The high injunction not to taste that fruit,
Whoever tempted; which they not obeying
Incurred (what could they less?) the penalty,
And, manifold in sin, deserved to fall.
Up into Heaven from Paradise in haste
The Angelic guards ascended, mute and sad
For Man; for of his state by this they knew,
Much wondering how the subtle Fiend had stolen   20
Entrance unseen. Soon as the unwelcome news
From Earth arrived at Heaven-gate, displeased
All were who heard; dim sadness did not spare
That time celestial visages, yet, mixed
With pity, violated not their bliss.
About the new-arrived, in multitudes,
The Ethereal people ran, to hear and know
How all befell. They towards the throne supreme,
Accountable, made haste, to make appear,
With righteous plea, their utmost vigilance   30
And easily approved; when the Most High,
Eternal Father, from his secret cloud
Amidst, in thunder uttered thus his voice:—

    "Assembled Angels, and ye Powers returned
From unsuccessful charge, be not dismayed
Nor troubled at these tidings from the Earth,
Which your sincerest care could not prevent,
Foretold so lately what would come to pass,
When first this Tempter crossed the gulf from Hell.
I told ye then he should prevail, and speed   40
On his bad errand—Man should be seduced,
And flattered out of all, believing lies
Against his Maker; no decree of mine,

Concurring to necessitate his fall,
Or touch with lightest moment of impulse
His free will, to her own inclining left
In even scale. But fallen he is; and now
What rests, but that the mortal sentence pass
On his transgression, Death denounced that day?
Which he presumes already vain and void,   50
Because not yet inflicted, as he feared,
By some immediate stroke, but soon shall find
Forbearance no acquittance ere day end.
Justice shall not return, as bounty, scorned.
But whom send I to judge them? whom but thee,
Vicegerent Son? To thee I have transferred
All judgment, whether in Heaven, or Earth, or Hell.
Easy it may be seen that I intend
Mercy colleague with justice, sending thee,
Man's friend, his Mediator, his designed   60
Both ransom and Redeemer voluntary,
And destined Man himself to judge Man fallen."
So spake the Father; and, unfolding bright
Toward the right hand his glory, on the Son
Blazed forth unclouded deity. He full
Resplendent all his Father manifest
Expressed, and thus divinely answered mild:—
   "Father Eternal, thine is to decree;
Mine both in Heaven and Earth to do thy will
Supreme, that thou in me, thy Son beloved,   70
May'st ever rest well pleased. I go to judge
On Earth these thy transgressors; but thou know'st,
Whoever judged, the worst on me must light,
When time shall be; for so I undertook
Before thee, and, not repenting, this obtain
Of right, that I may mitigate their doom
On me derived. Yet I shall temper so
Justice with mercy as may illustrate most
Them fully satisfied, and thee appease.
Attendance none shall need, nor train, where none   80
Are to behold the judgment but the judged,
Those two; the third best absent is condemned,
Convict by flight, and rebel to all law:
Conviction to the Serpent none belongs."
   Thus saying, from his radiant seat he rose
Of high collateral glory. Him Thrones, and Powers,

Princedoms, and Dominations ministrant,
Accompanied to Heaven-gate, from whence
Eden and all the coast in prospect lay.
Down he descended straight; the speed of Gods   90
Time counts not, though with swiftest minutes winged.
   Now was the Sun in western cadence low
From noon, and gentle airs due at their hour
To fan the Earth now waked, and usher in
The evening cool, when he, from wrath more cool,
Came, the mild judge, and intercessor both,
To sentence Man. The voice of God they heard
Now walking in the Garden, by soft winds
Brought to their ears, while day declined; they heard,
And from his presence hid themselves among   100
The thickest trees, both man and wife, till God,
Approaching, thus to Adam called aloud:—
   "Where art thou, Adam, wont with joy to meet
My coming, seen far off? I miss thee here,
Not pleased, thus entertained with solitude,
Where obvious duty erewhile appeared unsought.
Or come I less conspicuous, or what change
Absents thee, or what chance detains? Come forth!"
   He came, and with him Eve, more loth, though first
To offend, discountenanced both, and discomposed.   110
Love was not in their looks, either to God
Or to each other, but apparent guilt,
And shame, and perturbation, and despair,
Anger, and obstinacy, and hate, and guile.
Whence Adam, faltering long, thus answered brief:—
   "I heard thee in the Garden, and, of thy voice
Afraid, being naked, hid myself." To whom
The gracious Judge, without revile, replied:—
   "My voice thou oft hast heard, and hast not feared,
But still rejoiced; how is it now become   120
So dreadful to thee? That thou art naked who
Hath told thee? Hast thou eaten of the tree
Whereof I gave thee charge thou shouldst not eat?"
To whom thus Adam, sore beset, replied:—
   "O Heaven! in evil strait this day I stand
Before my Judge—either to undergo
Myself the total crime, or to accuse
My other self, the partner of my life,
Whose failing, while her faith to me remains,

I should conceal, and not expose to blame   130
By my complaint. But strict necessity
Subdues me, and calamitous constraint,
Lest on my head both sin and punishment,
However insupportable, be all
Devolved; though, should I hold my peace, yet thou
Wouldst easily detect what I conceal.
This Woman, whom thou mad'st to be my help,
And gav'st me as thy perfect gift, so good,
So fit, so acceptable, so divine,
That from her hand I could suspect no ill,   140
And what she did, whatever in itself,
Her doing seemed to justify the deed—
She gave me of the tree, and I did eat."
To whom the Sovran Presence thus replied:—
    "Was she thy God, that her thou didst obey
Before his voice? or was she made thy guide,
Superior, or but equal, that to her
Thou didst resign thy manhood, and the place
Wherein God set thee above her, made of thee
And for thee, whose perfection far excelled   150
Hers in all real dignity? Adorned
She was indeed, and lovely, to attract
Thy love, not thy subjection; and her gifts
Were such, as under government well seemed—
Unseemly to bear rule; which was thy part
And person, hadst thou known thyself aright."
    So having said, he thus to Eve in few:—
"Say, Woman, what is this which thou hast done?"
    To whom said Eve, with shame nigh overwhelmed,
Confessing soon, yet not before her Judge   160
Bold or loquacious, thus abashed replied:—
"The Serpent me beguiled, and I did eat."
    Which when the Lord God heard, without delay
To judgment he proceeded on the accused
Serpent, though brute, unable to transfer
The guilt on him who made him instrument
Of mischief, and polluted from the end
Of his creation—justly then accursed,
As vitiated in nature. More to know
Concerned not Man (since he no further knew),   170
Nor altered his offence; yet God at last
To Satan, first in sin, his doom applied,

Though in mysterious terms, judged as then best;
And on the Serpent thus his curse let fall:—
    "Because thou hast done this, thou art accursed
Above all cattle, each beast of the field;
Upon thy belly grovelling thou shalt go,
And dust shalt eat all the days of thy life.
Between thee and the Woman I will put
Enmity, and between thine and her seed;   180
Her seed shall bruise thy head, thou bruise his heel."
    So spake this oracle—then verified
When Jesus, son of Mary, second Eve,
Saw Satan fall like lightning down from Heaven,
Prince of the Air; then, rising from his grave,
Spoiled Principalities and Powers, triumphed
In open show, and, with ascension bright,
Captivity led captive through the Air,
The realm itself of Satan, long usurped,
Whom he shall tread at last under our feet;   190
Even he who now foretold his fatal bruise,
And to the Woman thus his sentence turned:—
    "Thy sorrow I will greatly multiply
By thy conception; children thou shalt bring
In sorrow forth, and to thy husband's will
Thine shall submit; he over thee shall rule."
    On Adam last thus judgment he pronounced:—
"Because thou hast hearkened to the voice of thy wife,
And eaten of the tree concerning which
I charged thee, saying, *Thou shalt not eat thereof,*   200
Curs'd is the ground for thy sake; thou in sorrow
Shalt eat thereof all the days of thy life;
Thorns also and thistles it shall bring thee forth
Unbid; and thou shalt eat the herb of the field;
In the sweat of thy face shalt thou eat bread,
Till thou return unto the ground; for thou
Out of the ground wast taken: know thy birth,
For dust thou art, and shalt to dust return."
    So judged he Man, both Judge and Saviour sent,
And the instant stroke of death, denounced that day,   210
Removed far off; then, pitying how they stood
Before him naked to the air, that now
Must suffer change, disdained not to begin
Thenceforth the form of servant to assume.
As when he washed his servants' feet, so now,

As father of his family, he clad
Their nakedness with skins of beasts, or slain,
Or, as the snake, with youthful coat repaid;
And thought not much to clothe his enemies.
Nor he their outward only with the skins   220
Of beasts, but inward nakedness, much more
Opprobrious, with his robe of righteousness
Arraying, covered from his Father's sight.
To him with swift ascent he up returned,
Into his blissful bosom reassumed
In glory as of old; to him, appeased,
All, though all-knowing, what had passed with Man
Recounted, mixing intercession sweet.
    Meanwhile, ere thus was sinned and judged on Earth,
Within the gates of Hell sat Sin and Death,   230
In counterview within the gates, that now
Stood open wide, belching outrageous flame
Far into Chaos, since the Fiend passed through,
Sin opening; who thus now to Death began:—
    "O Son, why sit we here, each other viewing
Idly, while Satan, our great author, thrives
In other worlds, and happier seat provides
For us, his offspring dear? It cannot be
But that success attends him; if mishap,
Ere this he had returned, with fury driven   240
By his avengers, since no place like this
Can fit his punishment, or their revenge.
Methinks I feel new strength within me rise,
Wings growing, and dominion given me large
Beyond this Deep—whatever draws me on,
Or sympathy, or some connatural force,
Powerful at greatest distance to unite
With secret amity things of like kind
By secretest conveyance. Thou, my shade
Inseparable, must with me along;   250
For Death from Sin no power can separate.
But, lest the difficulty of passing back
Stay his return perhaps over this gulf
Impassable, impervious, let us try
(Adventurous work, yet to thy power and mine
Not unagreeable!) to found a path
Over this main from Hell to that new World
Where Satan now prevails—a monument

Of merit high to all the infernal host,
Easing their passage hence, for intercourse   260
Or transmigration, as their lot shall lead.
Nor can I miss the way, so strongly drawn
By this new-felt attraction and instinct."
　　Whom thus the meagre Shadow answered soon:—
"Go whither fate and inclination strong
Leads thee; I shall not lag behind, nor err
The way, thou leading: such a scent I draw
Of carnage, prey innumerable, and taste
The savor of death from all things there that live.
Nor shall I to the work thou enterprisest   270
Be wanting, but afford thee equal aid."
　　So saying, with delight he snuffed the smell
Of mortal change on Earth. As when a flock
Of ravenous fowl, though many a league remote,
Against the day of battle, to a field
Where armies lie encamped come flying, lured
With scent of living carcasses designed
For death the following day in bloody fight;
So scented the grim Feature, and upturned
His nostril wide into the murky air,   280
Sagacious of his quarry from so far.
Then both, from out Hell-gates, into the waste
Wide anarchy of Chaos, damp and dark,
Flew diverse, and, with power (their power was great)
Hovering upon the waters, what they met
Solid or slimy, as in raging sea
Tossed up and down, together crowded drove,
From each side shoaling, towards the mouth of Hell;
As when two polar winds, blowing adverse
Upon the Cronian sea, together drive   290
Mountains of ice, that stop the imagined way
Beyond Petsora eastward to the rich
Cathaian coast. The aggregated soil
Death with his mace petrific, cold and dry,
As with a trident smote, and fixed as firm
As Delos, floating once; the rest his look
Bound with Gorgonian rigor not to move,
And with asphaltic slime; broad as the gate,
Deep to the roots of Hell the gathered beach
They fastened, and the mole immense wrought on   300
Over the foaming Deep high-arched, a bridge

Of length prodigious, joining to the wall
Immovable of this now fenceless World,
Forfeit to Death—from hence a passage broad,
Smooth, easy, inoffensive, down to Hell.
So if great things to small may be compared,
Xerxes, the liberty of Greece to yoke,
From Susa, his Memnonian palace high,
Came to the sea, and, over Hellespont
Bridging his way, Europe with Asia joined,   310
And scourged with many a stroke the indignant waves.
Now had they brought the work by wondrous art
Pontifical—a ridge of pendant rock
Over the vexed Abyss, following the track
Of Satan, to the self-same place where he
First lighted from his wing and landed safe
From out of Chaos—to the outside bare
Of this round World. With pins of adamant
And chains they made all fast, too fast they made
And durable; and now in little space   320
The confines met of empyrean Heaven
And of this World, and, on the left hand Hell,
With long reach interposed; three several ways
In sight to each of these three places led.
And now their way to Earth they had descried,
To Paradise first tending, when, behold
Satan, in likeness of an Angel bright,
Betwixt the Centaur and the Scorpion steering
His zenith, while the Sun in Aries rose!
Disguised he came; but those his children dear   330
Their parent soon discerned, though in disguise.
He, after Eve seduced, unminded slunk
Into the wood fast by, and, changing shape
To observe the sequel, saw his guileful act
By Eve, though all unweeting, seconded
Upon her husband—saw their shame that sought
Vain covertures; but, when he saw descend
The Son of God to judge them, terrified
He fled, not hoping to escape, but shun
The present—fearing, guilty, what his wrath   340
Might suddenly inflict; that past, returned
By night, and, listening where the hapless pair
Sat in their sad discourse and various plaint,
Thence gathered his own doom; which understood

Not instant, but of future time, with joy
And tidings fraught, to Hell he now returned,
And at the brink of Chaos, near the foot
Of this new wondrous pontifice, unhoped
Met who to meet him came, his offspring dear.
Great joy was at their meeting, and at sight   350
Of that stupendious bridge his joy increased.
Long he admiring stood, till Sin, his fair
Enchanting daughter, thus the silence broke:—
    "O Parent, these are thy magnific deeds,
Thy trophies! which thou view'st as not thine own;
Thou art their author, and prime architect.
For I no sooner in my heart divined
(My heart, which by a secret harmony
Still moves with thine, joined in connexion sweet)
That thou on Earth hadst prospered, which thy looks   360
Now also evidence, but straight I felt—
Though distant from thee worlds between, yet felt—
That I must after thee with this thy son;
Such fatal consequence unites us three.
Hell could no longer hold us in her bounds,
Nor this unvoyageable gulf obscure
Detain from following thy illustrious track.
Thou hast achieved our liberty, confined
Within Hell-gates till now; thou us empowered
To fortify thus far, and overlay   370
With this portentous bridge the dark Abyss.
Thine now is all this World; thy virtue hath won
What thy hands builded not; thy wisdom gained,
With odds, what war hath lost, and fully avenged
Our foil in Heaven. Here thou shalt monarch reign,
There didst not; there let him still victor sway,
As battle hath adjudged, from this new World
Retiring, by his own doom alienated,
And henceforth monarchy with thee divide
Of all things, parted by the empyreal bounds,   380
His quadrature, from thy orbicular World,
Or try thee now more dangerous to his throne."
    Whom thus the Prince of Darkness answered glad:—
"Fair Daughter, and thou, son and grandchild both,
High proof ye now have given to be the race
Of Satan (for I glory in the name,
Antagonist of Heaven's Almighty King),

Amply have merited of me, of all
The Infernal Empire, that so near Heaven's door
Triumphal with triumphal act have met,   390
Mine with this glorious work, and made one realm
Hell and this World—one realm, one continent
Of easy thoroughfare. Therefore, while I
Descend through Darkness, on your road with ease,
To my associate Powers, them to acquaint
With these successes, and with them rejoice,
You two this way, among these numerous orbs,
All yours, right down to Paradise descend;
There dwell, and reign in bliss; thence on the Earth
Dominion exercise and in the air,   400
Chiefly on Man, sole lord of all declared;
Him first make sure your thrall, and lastly kill.
My substitutes I send ye, and create
Plenipotent on Earth, of matchless might
Issuing from me. On your joint vigor now
My hold of this new kingdom all depends,
Through Sin to Death exposed by my exploit.
If your joint power prevail, the affairs of Hell
No detriment need fear; go, and be strong."
        So saying, he dismissed them; they with speed   410
Their course through thickest constellations held,
Spreading their bane; the blasted stars looked wan,
And planets, planet-strook, real eclipse
Then suffered. The other way Satan went down
The causey to Hell-gate; on either side
Disparted Chaos overbuilt exclaimed,
And with rebounding surge the bars assailed,
That scorned his indignation. Through the gate,
Wide open and unguarded, Satan passed,
And all about found desolate; for those   420
Appointed to sit there had left their charge,
Flown to the upper World; the rest were all
Far to the inland retired, about the walls
Of Pandemonium; city and proud seat
Of Lucifer, so by allusion called
Of that bright star to Satan paragoned.
There kept their watch the legions, while the Grand
In council sat, solicitous what chance
Might intercept their Emperor sent; so he
Departing gave command, and they observed.   430

As when the Tartar from his Russian foe,
By Astracan, over the snowy plains,
Retires, or Bactrian Sophi, from the horns
Of Turkish crescent, leaves all waste beyond
The realm of Aladule, in his retreat
To Tauris or Casbeen; so these, the late
Heaven-banished host, left desert utmost Hell
Many a dark league, reduced in careful watch
Round their metropolis, and now expecting
Each hour their great Adventurer from the search   440
Of foreign worlds. He through the midst unmarked,
In show plebeian Angel militant
Of lowest order, passed, and, from the door
Of that Plutonian hall, invisible
Ascended his high throne, which, under state
Of richest texture spread, at the upper end
Was placed in regal lustre. Down a while
He sat, and round about him saw, unseen.
At last, as from a cloud, his fulgent head
And shape star-bright appeared, or brighter, clad   450
With what permissive glory since his fall
Was left him, or false glitter. All amazed
At that so sudden blaze, the Stygian throng
Bent their aspect, and whom they wished beheld,
Their mighty Chief returned: loud was the acclaim.
Forth rushed in haste the great consulting Peers,
Raised from their dark Divan, and with like joy
Congratulant approached him, who with hand
Silence, and with these words attention, won:—
    "Thrones, Dominations, Princedoms, Virtues, Powers!—   460
For in possession such, not only of right,
I call ye, and declare ye now, returned,
Successful beyond hope, to lead ye forth
Triumphant out of this infernal pit
Abominable, accursed, the house of woe,
And dungeon of our tyrant! Now possess,
As lords, a spacious World, to our native Heaven
Little inferior, by my adventure hard
With peril great achieved. Long were to tell
What I have done, what suffered, with what pain   470
Voyaged the unreal, vast, unbounded Deep
Of horrible confusion—over which
By Sin and Death a broad way now is paved,

To expedite your glorious march; but I
Toiled out my uncouth passage, forced to ride
The untractable Abyss, plunged in the womb
Of unoriginal Night and Chaos wild,
That, jealous of their secrets, fiercely opposed
My journey strange, with clamorous uproar
Protesting Fate supreme; thence how I found   480
The new-created World, which fame in Heaven
Long had foretold, a fabric wonderful,
Of absolute perfection; therein Man
Placed in a paradise, by our exile
Made happy. Him by fraud I have seduced
From his Creator, and, the more to increase
Your wonder, with an apple! He, thereat
Offended—worth your laughter!—hath given up
Both his beloved Man and all his World
To Sin and Death a prey, and so to us,   490
Without our hazard, labor, or alarm,
To range in, and to dwell, and over Man
To rule, as over all he should have ruled.
True is, me also he hath judged; or rather
Me not, but the brute Serpent, in whose shape
Man I deceived. That which to me belongs
Is enmity, which he will put between
Me and Mankind: I am to bruise his heel;
His seed—when is not set—shall bruise my head!
A world who would not purchase with a bruise,   500
Or much more grievous pain? Ye have the account
Of my performance; what remains, ye Gods,
But up and enter now into full bliss?"
    So having said, a while he stood, expecting
Their universal shout and high applause
To fill his ear; when, contrary, he hears,
On all sides, from innumerable tongues
A dismal universal hiss, the sound
Of public scorn. He wondered, but not long
Had leisure, wondering at himself now more.   510
His visage drawn he felt to sharp and spare,
His arms clung to his ribs, his legs entwining
Each other, till, supplanted, down he fell,
A monstrous serpent on his belly prone,
Reluctant, but in vain; a greater power
Now ruled him, punished in the shape he sinned,

According to his doom. He would have spoke,
But hiss for hiss returned with forked tongue
To forked tongue; for now were all transformed
Alike, to serpents all, as accessories   520
To his bold riot. Dreadful was the din
Of hissing through the hall, thick-swarming now
With complicated monsters, head and tail—
Scorpion, and Asp, and Amphisbæna dire,
Cerastes horned, Hydrus, and Ellops drear,
And Dipsas (not so thick swarmed once the soil
Bedropt with blood of Gorgon, or the isle
Ophiusa); but still greatest he the midst,
Now Dragon grown, larger than whom the Sun
Engendered in the Pythian vale on slime,   530
Huge Python; and his power no less he seemed
Above the rest still to retain. They all
Him followed, issuing forth to the open field,
Where all yet left of that revolted rout,
Heaven-fallen, in station stood or just array,
Sublime with expectation when to see
In triumph issuing forth their glorious Chief.
They saw, but other sight instead—a crowd
Of ugly serpents! Horror on them fell,
And horrid sympathy; for what they saw   540
They felt themselves now changing. Down their arms,
Down fell both spear and shield; down they as fast,
And the dire hiss renewed, and the dire form
Catched by contagion, like in punishment
As in their crime. Thus was the applause they meant
Turned to exploding hiss, triumph to shame
Cast on themselves from their own mouths. There stood
A grove hard by, sprung up with this their change,
His will who reigns above, to aggravate
Their penance, laden with fair fruit, like that   550
Which grew in Paradise, the bait of Eve
Used by the Tempter. On that prospect strange
Their earnest eyes they fixed, imagining
For one forbidden tree a multitude
Now risen, to work them further woe or shame;
Yet, parched with scalding thirst and hunger fierce,
Though to delude them sent, could not abstain,
But on they rolled in heaps, and, up the trees
Climbing, sat thicker than the snaky locks

That curled Megæra. Greedily they plucked   560
The fruitage fair to sight, like that which grew
Near that bituminous lake where Sodom flamed;
This, more delusive, not the touch, but taste
Deceived; they, fondly thinking to allay
Their appetite with gust, instead of fruit
Chewed bitter ashes, which the offended taste
With spattering noise rejected. Oft they assayed,
Hunger and thirst constraining; drugged as oft,
With hatefulest disrelish writhed their jaws
With soot and cinders filled; so oft they fell   570
Into the same illusion, not as Man
Whom they triumphed once lapsed. Thus were they plagued,
And, worn with famine, long and ceaseless hiss,
Till their lost shape, permitted, they resumed—
Yearly enjoined, some say, to undergo
This annual humbling certain numbered days,
To dash their pride, and joy for Man seduced.
However, some tradition they dispersed
Among the Heathen of their purchase got,
And fabled how the Serpent, whom they called   580
Ophion, with Eurynome (the wide-
Encroaching Eve perhaps), had first the rule
Of high Olympus, thence by Saturn driven
And Ops, ere yet Dictæan Jove was born.
    Meanwhile in Paradise the Hellish pair
Too soon arrived—Sin, there in power before
Once actual, now in body, and to dwell
Habitual habitant; behind her Death,
Close following pace for pace, not mounted yet
On his pale horse; to whom Sin thus began:—   590
    "Second of Satan sprung, all-conquering Death!
What think'st thou of our empire now? though earned
With travail difficult, not better far
Than still at Hell's dark threshold to have sat watch,
Unnamed, undreaded, and thyself half-starved?"
    Whom thus the Sin-born Monster answered soon:—
"To me, who with eternal famine pine,
Alike is Hell, or Paradise, or Heaven—
There best where most with ravin I may meet:
Which here, though plenteous, all too little seems   600
To stuff this maw, this vast unhide-bound corpse."
    To whom the incestuous Mother thus replied:—

"Thou, therefore, on these herbs, and fruits, and flowers,
Feed first; on each beast next, and fish, and fowl—
No homely morsels; and whatever thing
The scythe of Time mows down devour unspared;
Till I, in Man residing through the race,
His thoughts, his looks, words, actions, all infect,
And season him thy last and sweetest prey."
   This said, they both betook them several ways,   610
Both to destroy, or unimmortal make
All kinds, and for destruction to mature
Sooner or later; which the Almighty seeing,
From his transcendent seat the Saints among,
To those bright Orders uttered thus his voice:—
   "See with what heat these dogs of Hell advance
To waste and havoc yonder World, which I
So fair and good created, and had still
Kept in that state, had not the folly of Man
Let in these wasteful furies, who impute   620
Folly to me (so doth the Prince of Hell
And his adherents), that with so much ease
I suffer them to enter and possess
A place so heavenly, and, conniving, seem
To gratify my scornful enemies,
That laugh, as if, transported with some fit
Of passion, I to them had quitted all,
At random yielded up to their misrule;
And know not that I called and drew them thither,
My Hell-hounds, to lick up the draff and filth   630
Which Man's polluting sin with taint hath shed
On what was pure; till, crammed and gorged, nigh burst
With sucked and glutted offal, at one sling
Of thy victorious arm, well-pleasing Son,
Both Sin and Death, and yawning Grave, at last
Through Chaos hurled, obstruct the mouth of Hell
For ever, and seal up his ravenous jaws.
Then Heaven and Earth, renewed, shall be made pure
To sanctity that shall receive no stain:
Till then the curse pronounced on both precedes."   640
   He ended, and the Heavenly audience loud
Sung Halleluiah, as the sound of seas,
Through multitude that sung:—"Just are thy ways,
Righteous are thy decrees on all thy works;
Who can extenuate thee? Next, to the Son,

Destined Restorer of Mankind, by whom
New Heaven and Earth shall to the ages rise,
Or down from Heaven descend." Such was their song,
While the Creator, calling forth by name
His mighty Angels, gave them several charge,   650
As sorted best with present things. The Sun
Had first his precept so to move, so shine,
As might affect the Earth with cold and heat
Scarce tolerable, and from the north to call
Decrepit winter, from the south to bring
Solstitial summer's heat. To the blanc Moon
Her office they prescribed; to the other five
Their planetary motions and aspécts,
In sextile, square, and trine, and opposite,
Of noxious efficacy, and when to join   660
In synod unbenign; and taught the fixed
Their influence malignant when to shower—
Which of them, rising with the Sun or falling,
Should prove tempestuous. To the winds they set
Their corners, when with bluster to confound
Sea, air, and shore; the thunder when to roll
With terror through the dark aerial hall.
Some say he bid his Angels turn askance
The poles of Earth twice ten degrees and more
From the Sun's axle; they with labor pushed   670
Oblique the centric Globe: some say the Sun
Was bid turn reins from the equinoctial road
Like distant breadth—to Taurus with the seven
Atlantic Sisters, and the Spartan Twins,
Up to the Tropic Crab; thence down amain
By Leo, and the Virgin, and the Scales,
As deep as Capricorn; to bring in change
Of seasons to each clime. Else had the spring
Perpetual smiled on Earth with vernant flowers,
Equal in days and nights, except to those   680
Beyond the polar circles; to them day
Had unbenighted shone, while the low Sun,
To recompense his distance, in their sight
Had rounded still the horizon, and not known
Or east or west—which had forbid the snow
From cold Estotiland, and south as far
Beneath Magellan. At that tasted fruit,
The Sun, as from Thyestean banquet, turned

His course intended; else, how had the world
Inhabited, though sinless, more than now   690
Avoided pinching cold and scorching heat?
These changes in the heavens, though slow, produced
Like change on sea and land—sideral blast,
Vapor, and mist, and exhalation hot,
Corrupt and pestilent. Now from the north
Of Norumbega, and the Samoed shore,
Bursting their brazen dungeon, armed with ice,
And snow, and hail, and stormy gust and flaw,
Boreas and Cæcias and Argestes loud
And Thrascias rend the woods, and seas upturn;   700
With adverse blast upturns them from the south
Notus and Afer, black with thundrous clouds
From Serraliona; thwart of these, as fierce
Forth rush the Levant and the Ponent winds,
Eurus and Zephyr, with their lateral noise,
Sirocco and Libecchio. Thus began
Outrage from lifeless things; but Discord first,
Daughter of Sin, among the irrational
Death introduced through fierce antipathy.
Beast now with beast 'gan war, and fowl with fowl,   710
And fish with fish. To graze the herb all leaving
Devoured each other; nor stood much in awe
Of Man, but fled him, or with countenance grim
Glared on him passing. These were from without
The growing miseries; which Adam saw
Already in part, though hid in gloomiest shade,
To sorrow abandoned, but worse felt within,
And, in a troubled sea of passion tost,
Thus to disburden sought with sad complaint:—
    "O miserable of happy! Is this the end   720
Of this new glorious World, and me so late
The glory of that glory? who now, become
Accursed of blessed, hide me from the face
Of God, whom to behold was then my highth
Of happiness! Yet well, if here would end
The misery! I deserved it, and would bear
My own deservings. But this will not serve:
All that I eat or drink, or shall beget,
Is propagated curse. O voice, once heard
Delightfully, *Increase and multiply;'*   730
Now death to hear! for what can I increase

Or multiply but curses on my head?
Who, of all ages to succeed, but, feeling
The evil on him brought by me, will curse
My head? 'Ill fare our Ancestor impure!
For this we may thank Adam!' but his thanks
Shall be the execration. So, besides
Mine own that bide upon me, all from me
Shall with a fierce reflux on me redound—
On me, as on their natural centre, light;   740
Heavy, though in their place. O fleeting joys
Of Paradise, dear bought with lasting woes!
Did I request thee, Maker, from my clay
To mould me Man? Did I solicit thee
From darkness to promote me, or here place
In this delicious Garden? As my will
Concurred not to my being, it were but right
And equal to reduce me to my dust,
Desirous to resign and render back
All I received, unable to perform   750
Thy terms too hard, by which I was to hold
The good I sought not. To the loss of that,
Sufficient penalty, why hast thou added
The sense of endless woes? Inexplicable
Thy justice seems. Yet, to say truth, too late
I thus contest; then should have been refused
Those terms, whatever, when they were proposed.
Thou didst accept them: wilt thou enjoy the good,
Then cavil the conditions? And, though God
Made thee without thy leave, what if thy son   760
Prove disobedient, and, reproved, retort,
'Wherefore didst thou beget me? I sought it not!'
Wouldst thou admit for his contempt of thee
That proud excuse? yet him not thy election,
But natural necessity, begot.
God made thee of choice his own, and of his own
To serve him; thy reward was of his grace;
Thy punishment, then, justly is at his will.
Be it so, for I submit; his doom is fair,
That dust I am, and shall to dust return.   770
O welcome hour whenever! Why delays
His hand to execute what his decree
Fixed on this day? Why do I overlive?
Why am I mocked with death, and lengthened out

To deathless pain? How gladly would I meet
Mortality, my sentence, and be earth
Insensible! how glad would lay me down
As in my mother's lap! There I should rest,
And sleep secure; his dreadful voice no more
Would thunder in my ears; no fear of worse   780
To me and to my offspring, would torment me
With cruel expectation. Yet one doubt
Pursues me still—lest all I cannot die;
Lest that pure breath of life, the Spirit of Man
Which God inspired, cannot together perish
With this corporeal clod. Then, in the grave,
Or in some other dismal place, who knows
But I shall die a living death? O thought
Horrid, if true! Yet why? It was but breath
Of life that sinned: what dies but what had life   790
And sin? The body properly hath neither.
All of me, then, shall die: let this appease
The doubt, since human reach no further knows.
For, though the Lord of all be infinite,
Is his wrath also? Be it, Man is not so,
But mortal doomed. How can he exercise
Wrath without end on Man, whom death must end?
Can he make deathless death? That were to make
Strange contradiction; which to God himself
Impossible is held, as argument   800
Of weakness, not of power. Will he draw out,
For anger's sake, finite to infinite
In punished Man, to satisfy his rigor
Satisfied never? That were to extend
His sentence beyond dust and Nature's law;
By which all causes else according still
To the reception of their matter act,
Not to the extent of their own sphere. But say
That death be not one stroke, as I supposed,
Bereaving sense, but endless misery   810
From this day onward, which I feel begun
Both in me and without me, and so last
To perpetuity—Ay me! that fear
Comes thundering back with dreadful revolution
On my defenceless head! Both Death and I
Am found eternal, and incorporate both:
Nor I on my part single; in me all

Posterity stands cursed. Fair patrimony
That I must leave ye, sons! Oh, were I able
To waste it all myself, and leave ye none!   820
So disinherited, how would ye bless
Me, now your curse! Ah, why should all Mankind,
For one man's fault, thus guiltless be condemned?
If guiltless! But from me what can proceed
But all corrupt—both mind and will depraved
Not to do only, but to will the same
With me? How can they, then, acquitted stand
In sight of God? Him, after all disputes,
Forced I absolve. All my evasions vain
And reasonings, though through mazes, lead me still   830
But to my own conviction: first and last
On me, me only, as the source and spring
Of all corruption, all the blame lights due.
So might the wrath! Fond wish! couldst thou support
That burden, heavier than the Earth to bear—
Than all the world much heavier, though divided
With that bad Woman? Thus, what thou desir'st,
And what thou fear'st, alike destroys all hope
Of refuge, and concludes thee miserable
Beyond all past example and future—   840
To Satan only like, both crime and doom.
O Conscience! into what abyss of fears
And horrors hast thou driven me; out of which
I find no way, from deep to deeper plunged!"
    Thus Adam to himself lamented loud
Through the still night—not now, as ere Man fell,
Wholesome and cool and mild, but with black air
Accompanied, with damps and dreadful gloom;
Which to his evil conscience represented
All things with double terror. On the ground   850
Outstretched he lay, on the cold ground, and oft
Cursed his creation; Death as oft accused
Of tardy execution, since denounced
The day of his offence. "Why comes not Death,"
Said he, "with one thrice-acceptable stroke
To end me? Shall Truth fail to keep her word,
Justice divine not hasten to be just?
But Death comes not at call; Justice divine
Mends not her slowest pace for prayers or cries.
O woods, O fountains, hillocks, dales, and bowers!   860

With other echo late I taught your shades
To answer, and resound far other song."
Whom thus afflicted when sad Eve beheld,
Desolate where she sat, approaching nigh,
Soft words to his fierce passion she assayed;
But her, with stern regard, he thus repelled:—
  "Out of my sight, thou serpent! That name best
Befits thee, with him leagued, thyself as false
And hateful: nothing wants, but that thy shape
Like his, and color serpentine, may show   870
Thy inward fraud, to warn all creatures from thee
Henceforth, lest that too heavenly form, pretended
To hellish falshood, snare them. But for thee
I had persisted happy, had not thy pride
And wandering vanity, when least was safe,
Rejected my forewarning, and disdained
Not to be trusted—longing to be seen,
Though by the Devil himself; him overweening
To overreach; but, with the Serpent meeting,
Fooled and beguiled; by him thou, I by thee,   880
To trust thee from my side, imagined wise,
Constant, mature, proof against all assaults,
And understood not all was but a show,
Rather than solid virtue, all but a rib
Crooked by nature—bent, as now appears,
More to the part sinister—from me drawn;
Well if thrown out, as supernumerary
To my just number found! Oh, why did God,
Creator wise, that peopled highest Heaven
With Spirits masculine, create at last   890
This novelty on Earth, this fair defect
Of Nature, and not fill the World at once
With men as Angels, without feminine;
Or find some other way to generate
Mankind? This mischief had not then befallen,
And more that shall befall—innumerable
Disturbances on Earth through female snares,
And strait conjunction with this sex. For either
He never shall find out fit mate, but such
As some misfortune brings him, or mistake;   900
Or whom he wishes most shall seldom gain,
Through her perverseness, but shall see her gained
By a far worse, or, if she love, withheld

By parents; or his happiest choice too late
Shall meet, already linked and wedlock-bound
To a fell adversary, his hate or shame:
Which infinite calamity shall cause
To human life, and houshold peace confound."
    He added not, and from her turned; but Eve,
Not so repulsed, with tears that ceased not flowing,   910
And tresses all disordered, at his feet
Fell humble, and, embracing them, besought
His peace, and thus proceeded in her plaint:—
    "Forsake me not thus, Adam! witness Heaven
What love sincere and reverence in my heart
I bear thee, and unweeting have offended,
Unhappily deceived! Thy suppliant
I beg, and clasp thy knees; bereave me not
Whereon I live, thy gentle looks, thy aid,
Thy counsel in this uttermost distress,   920
My only strength and stay. Forlorn of thee,
Whither shall I betake me, where subsist?
While yet we live, scarce one short hour perhaps,
Between us two let there be peace; both joining,
As joined in injuries, one enmity
Against a foe by doom express assigned us,
That cruel Serpent. On me exercise not
Thy hatred for this misery befallen—
On me already lost, me than thyself
More miserable. Both have sinned; but thou   930
Against God only; I against God and thee,
And to the place of judgment will return,
There with my cries importune Heaven, that all
The sentence, from thy head removed, may light
On me, sole cause to thee of all this woe,
Me, me only, just object of His ire."
    She ended, weeping; and her lowly plight,
Immovable till peace obtained from fault
Acknowledged and deplored, in Adam wrought
Commiseration. Soon his heart relented   940
Towards her, his life so late, and sole delight,
Now at his feet submissive in distress—
Creature so fair his reconcilement seeking,
His counsel whom she had displeased, his aid.
As one disarmed, his anger all he lost,
And thus with peaceful words upraised her soon:—

"Unwary, and too desirous, as before
So now, of what thou know'st not, who desir'st
The punishment all on thyself! Alas!
Bear thine own first, ill able to sustain   950
His full wrath whose thou feel'st as yet least part,
And my displeasure bear'st so ill. If prayers
Could alter high decrees, I to that place
Would speed before thee, and be louder heard,
That on my head all might be visited,
Thy frailty and infirmer sex forgiven,
To me committed, and by me exposed.
But rise; let us no more contend, nor blame
Each other, blamed enough elsewhere, but strive
In offices of love how we may lighten   960
Each other's burden in our share of woe;
Since this day's death denounced, if aught I see,
Will prove no sudden, but a slow-paced evil,
A long day's dying, to augment our pain,
And to our seed (O hapless seed!) derived."
    To whom thus Eve, recovering heart, replied:—
"Adam, by sad experiment I know
How little weight my words with thee can find,
Found so erroneous, thence by just event
Found so unfortunate. Nevertheless,   970
Restored by thee, vile as I am, to place
Of new acceptance, hopeful to regain
Thy love, the sole contentment of my heart,
Living or dying, from thee I will not hide
What thoughts in my unquiet breast are risen,
Tending to some relief of our extremes,
Or end, though sharp and sad, yet tolerable,
As in our evils, and of easier choice.
If care of our descent perplex us most,
Which must be born to certain woe, devoured   980
By Death at last (and miserable it is
To be to others cause of misery,
Our own begotten, and of our loins to bring
Into this cursed world a woeful race,
That, after wretched life, must be at last
Food for so foul a monster), in thy power
It lies, yet ere conception, to prevent
The race unblest, to being yet unbegot.
Childless thou art; childless remain. So Death

Shall be deceived his glut, and with us two   990
Be forced to satisfy his ravenous maw.
But, if thou judge it hard and difficult,
Conversing, looking, loving, to abstain
From love's due rights, nuptial embraces sweet,
And with desire to languish without hope
Before the present object languishing
With like desire—which would be misery
And torment less than none of what we dread—
Then, both our selves and seed at once to free
From what we fear for both, let us make short;   1000
Let us seek Death, or, he not found, supply
With our own hands his office on ourselves.
Why stand we longer shivering under fears
That show no end but death, and have the power,
Of many ways to die the shortest choosing,
Destruction with destruction to destroy?"
    She ended here, or vehement despair
Broke off the rest; so much of death her thoughts
Had entertained as dyed her cheeks with pale.
But Adam, with such counsel nothing swayed,   1010
To better hopes his more attentive mind
Laboring had raised, and thus to Eve replied:—
    "Eve, thy contempt of life and pleasure seems
To argue in thee something more sublime
And excellent than what thy mind contemns:
But self-destruction therefore sought refutes
That excellence thought in thee, and implies
Not thy contempt, but anguish and regret
For loss of life and pleasure overloved.
Or, if thou covet death, as utmost end   1020
Of misery, so thinking to evade
The penalty pronounced, doubt not but God
Hath wiselier armed his vengeful ire than so
To be forestalled. Much more I fear lest death
So snatched will not exempt us from the pain
We are by doom to pay; rather such acts
Of contumacy will provoke the Highest
To make death in us live. Then let us seek
Some safer resolution—which methinks
I have in view, calling to mind with heed   1030
Part of our sentence, that thy seed shall bruise
The Serpent's head. Piteous amends! unless

Be meant whom I conjecture, our grand foe,
Satan, who in the Serpent hath contrived
Against us this deceit. To crush his head
Would be revenge indeed—which will be lost
By death brought on ourselves, or childless days
Resolved as thou proposest; so our foe
Shall scape his punishment ordained, and we
Instead shall double ours upon our heads.   1040
No more be mentioned, then, of violence
Against ourselves, and wilful barrenness
That cuts us off from hope, and savors only
Rancor and pride, impatience and despite,
Reluctance against God and his just yoke
Laid on our necks. Remember with what mild
And gracious temper he both heard and judged,
Without wrath or reviling. We expected
Immediate dissolution, which we thought
Was meant by death that day; when, lo! to thee   1050
Pains only in child-bearing were foretold,
And bringing forth, soon recompensed with joy,
Fruit of thy womb. On me the curse aslope
Glanced on the ground. With labor I must earn
My bread; what harm? Idleness had been worse;
My labor will sustain me; and, lest cold
Or heat should injure us, his timely care
Hath, unbesought, provided, and his hands
Clothed us unworthy, pitying while he judged.
How much more, if we pray him, will his ear   1060
Be open, and his heart to pity incline,
And teach us further by what means to shun
The inclement seasons, rain, ice, hail, and snow!
Which now the sky, with various face, begins
To show us in this mountain, while the winds
Blow moist and keen, shattering the graceful locks
Of these fair spreading trees; which bids us seek
Some better shroud, some better warmth to cherish
Our limbs benumbed—ere this diurnal star
Leave cold the night, how we his gathered beams   1070
Reflected may with matter sere foment,
Or by collision of two bodies grind
The air attrite to fire; as late the clouds,
Justling, or pushed with winds, rude in their shock,
Tine the slant lightning, whose thwart flame, driven down,

Kindles the gummy bark of fir or pine,
And sends a comfortable heat from far,
Which might supply the Sun. Such fire to use,
And what may else be remedy or cure
To evils which our own misdeeds have wrought,   1080
He will instruct us praying, and of grace
Beseeching him; so as we need not fear
To pass commodiously this life, sustained
By him with many comforts, till we end
In dust, our final rest and native home.
What better can we do than, to the place
Repairing where he judged us, prostrate fall
Before him reverent, and there confess
Humbly our faults, and pardon beg, with tears
Watering the ground, and with our sighs the air   1090
Frequenting, sent from hearts contrite, in sign
Of sorrow unfeigned and humiliation meek?
Undoubtedly he will relent, and turn
From his displeasure, in whose look serene,
When angry most he seemed and most severe,
What else but favor, grace, and mercy shone?"
    So spake our Father penitent; nor Eve
Felt less remorse. They, forthwith to the place
Repairing where he judged them, prostrate fell
Before him reverent, and both confessed   1100
Humbly their faults, and pardon begged, with tears
Watering the ground, and with their sighs the air
Frequenting, sent from hearts contrite, in sign
Of sorrow unfeigned and humiliation meek.

BOOK XI

THE ARGUMENT

THE Son of God presents to his Father the prayers of our first parents
now repenting, and intercedes for them. God accepts them, but declares
that they must no longer abide in Paradise; sends Michael with a band of
Cherubim to dispossess them, but first to reveal to Adam future things:
Michael's coming down. Adam shows to Eve certain ominous signs: he
discerns Michael's approach; goes out to meet him: the Angel denounces
their departure. Eve's lamentation. Adam pleads, but submits: the Angel
leads him up to a high hill; sets before him in vision what shall happen
till the Flood.

> Thus they, in lowliest plight, repentant stood
> Praying; for from the mercy-seat above
> Prevenient grace descending had removed
> The stony from their hearts, and made new flesh
> Regenerate grow instead, that sighs now breathed
> Unutterable, which the Spirit of prayer
> Inspired, and winged for Heaven with speedier flight
> Than loudest oratory. Yet their port
> Not of mean suitors; nor important less
> Seemed their petition than when the ancient pair   10
> In fables old, less ancient yet than these,
> Deucalion and chaste Pyrrha, to restore
> The race of mankind drowned, before the shrine
> Of Themis stood devout. To Heaven their prayers
> Flew up, nor missed the way, by envious winds
> Blown vagabond or frustrate: in they passed
> Dimensionless through heavenly doors; then, clad
> With incense, where the golden altar fumed,

By their great Intercessor, came in sight
Before the Father's throne. Them the glad Son   20
Presenting thus to intercede began:—
    "See, Father, what first-fruits on Earth are sprung
From thy implanted grace in Man—these sighs
And prayers, which in this golden censer, mixed
With incense, I, thy priest, before thee bring;
Fruits of more pleasing savor, from thy seed
Sown with contrition in his heart, than those
Which, his own hand manuring, all the trees
Of Paradise could have produced, ere fallen
From innocence. Now, therefore, bend thine ear   30
To supplication: hear his sighs, though mute;
Unskilful with what words to pray, let me
Interpret for him, me his advocate
And propitiation; all his works on me,
Good or not good, ingraft; my merit those
Shall perfect, and for these my death shall pay.
Accept me, and, in me, from these receive
The smell of peace toward Mankind: let him live,
Before thee reconciled, at least his days
Numbered, though sad, till death, his doom (which I   40
To mitigate thus plead, not to reverse),
To better life shall yield him, where with me
All my redeemed may dwell in joy and bliss,
Made one with me, as I with thee am one."
    To whom the Father, without cloud, serene:—
"All thy request for Man, accepted Son,
Obtain; all thy request was my decree.
But longer in that Paradise to dwell
The law I gave to Nature him forbids;
Those pure immortal elements, that know   50
No gross, no unharmonious mixture foul,
Eject him, tainted now, and purge him off,
As a distemper, gross, to air as gross,
And mortal food, as may dispose him best
For dissolution wrought by sin, that first
Distempered all things, and of incorrupt
Corrupted. I, at first, with two fair gifts
Created him endowed—with Happiness
And Immortality; that fondly lost,
This other served but to eternize woe,   60
Till I provided Death: so Death becomes

His final remedy, and, after life
Tried in sharp tribulation, and refined
By faith and faithful works, to second life,
Waked in the renovation of the just,
Resigns him up with Heaven and Earth renewed.
But let us call to synod all the Blest
Through Heaven's wide bounds; from them I will not hide
My judgments—how with Mankind I proceed,
As how with peccant Angels late they saw,   70
And in their state, though firm, stood more confirmed."
    He ended, and the Son gave signal high
To the bright Minister that watched. He blew
His trumpet, heard in Oreb since perhaps
When God descended, and perhaps once more
To sound at general doom. The angelic blast
Filled all the regions: from their blisful bowers
Of amarantine shade, fountain or spring,
By the waters of life, where'er they sat
In fellowships of joy, the Sons of Light   80
Hasted, resorting to the summons high,
And took their seats, till from his throne supreme
The Almighty thus pronounced his sovran will:—
    "O Sons, like one of us Man is become
To know both good and evil, since his taste
Of that defended fruit; but let him boast
His knowledge of good lost and evil got,
Happier had it sufficed him to have known
Good by itself and evil not at all.
He sorrows now, repents, and prays contrite—   90
My motions in him; longer than they move,
His heart I know how variable and vain,
Self-left. Lest, therefore, his now bolder hand
Reach also of the Tree of Life, and eat,
And live for ever, dream at least to live
For ever, to remove him I decree,
And send him from the Garden forth, to till
The ground whence he was taken, fitter soil.
Michael, this my behest have thou in charge:
Take to thee from among the Cherubim   100
Thy choice of flaming warriors, lest the Fiend,
Or in behalf of Man, or to invade
Vacant possession, some new trouble raise;
Haste thee, and from the Paradise of God

Without remorse drive out the sinful pair,
From hallowed ground the unholy, and denounce
To them, and to their progeny, from thence
Perpetual banishment. Yet, lest they faint
At the sad sentence rigorously urged
(For I behold them softened, and with tears   110
Bewailing their excess), all terror hide.
If patiently thy bidding they obey,
Dismiss them not disconsolate; reveal
To Adam what shall come in future days,
As I shall thee enlighten; intermix
My covenant in the Woman's seed renewed.
So send them forth, though sorrowing, yet in peace;
And on the east side of the Garden place,
Where entrance up from Eden easiest climbs,
Cherubic watch, and of a sword the flame   120
Wide-waving, all approach far off to fright,
And guard all passage to the Tree of Life;
Lest Paradise a receptacle prove
To Spirits foul, and all my trees their prey,
With whose stolen fruit Man once more to delude."
    He ceased; and the Archangelic Power prepared
For swift descent; with him the cohort bright
Of watchful Cherubim. Four faces each
Had, like a double Janus; all their shape
Spangled with eyes more numerous than those   130
Of Argus, and more wakeful than to drowse,
Charmed with Arcadian pipe, the pastoral reed
Of Hermes, or his opiate rod. Meanwhile,
To resalute the World with sacred light,
Leucothea waked, and with fresh dews embalmed
The Earth, when Adam and first matron Eve
Had ended now their orisons, and found
Strength added from above, new hope to spring
Out of despair, joy, but with fear yet linked;
Which thus to Eve his welcome words renewed:—   140
    "Eve, easily my faith admit that all
The good which we enjoy from Heaven descends;
But that from us aught should ascend to Heaven
So prevalent as to concern the mind
Of God high-blest, or to incline his will,
Hard to belief may seem. Yet this will prayer,
Or one short sigh of human breath, upborne

Even to the seat of God. For, since I sought
By prayer the offended Deity to appease,
Kneeled and before him humbled all my heart,   150
Methought I saw him placable and mild,
Bending his ear; persuasion in me grew
That I was heard with favor; peace returned
Home to my breast, and to my memory
His promise that thy seed shall bruise our Foe;
Which, then not minded in dismay, yet now
Assures me that the bitterness of death
Is past, and we shall live. Whence hail to thee!
Eve rightly called, Mother of all Mankind,
Mother of all things living, since by thee   160
Man is to live, and all things live for Man."
    To whom thus Eve with sad demeanor meek:—
"Ill-worthy I such title should belong
To me transgressor, who, for thee ordained
A help, became thy snare; to me reproach
Rather belongs, distrust and all dispraise.
But infinite in pardon was my Judge,
That I, who first brought death on all, am graced
The source of life; next favorable thou,
Who highly thus to entitle me voutsaf'st,   170
Far other name deserving. But the field
To labor calls us, now with sweat imposed,
Though after sleepless night; for see! the Morn,
All unconcerned with our unrest, begins
Her rosy progress smiling. Let us forth,
I never from thy side henceforth to stray,
Where'er our day's work lies, though now enjoined
Laborious, till day droop. While here we dwell,
What can be toilsome in these pleasant walks?
Here let us live, though in fallen state, content."   180
    So spake, so wished, much-humbled Eve; but Fate
Subscribed not. Nature first gave signs, impressed
On bird, beast, air—air suddenly eclipsed,
After short blush of morn. Nigh in her sight
The bird of Jove, stooped from his aery tour,
Two birds of gayest plume before him drove;
Down from a hill the beast that reigns in woods,
First hunter then, pursued a gentle brace,
Goodliest of all the forest, hart and hind;
Direct to the eastern gate was bent their flight.   190

Adam observed, and, with his eye the chase
Pursuing, not unmoved, to Eve thus spake:—
    "O Eve, some further change awaits us nigh,
Which Heaven by these mute signs in Nature shows,
Forerunners of his purpose, or to warn
Us, haply too secure of our discharge
From penalty because from death released
Some days: how long, and what till then our life,
Who knows, or more than this, that we are dust,
And thither must return, and be no more?   200
Why else this double object in our sight,
Of flight pursued in the air and o'er the ground
One way the self-same hour? Why in the east
Darkness ere day's mid-course, and morning-light
More orient in yon western cloud, that draws
O'er the blue firmament a radiant white,
And slow descends, with something Heavenly fraught?"
    He erred not; for, by this, the Heavenly bands
Down from a sky of jasper lighted now
In Paradise, and on a hill made halt—   210
A glorious apparition, had not doubt
And carnal fear that day dimmed Adam's eye.
Not that more glorious, when the Angels met
Jacob in Mahanaim, where he saw
The field pavilioned with his guardians bright;
Nor that which on the flaming mount appeared
In Dothan, covered with a camp of fire,
Against the Syrian king, who, to surprise
One man, assassin-like, had levied war,
War unproclaimed. The princely Hierarch   220
In their bright stand there left his Powers to seize
Possession of the Garden; he alone,
To find where Adam sheltered, took his way,
Not unperceived of Adam; who to Eve,
While the great visitant approached, thus spake:—
    "Eve, now expect great tidings, which, perhaps,
Of us will soon determine, or impose
New laws to be observed; for I descry,
From yonder blazing cloud that veils the hill,
One of the Heavenly host, and, by his gait,   230
None of the meanest—some great Potentate
Or of the Thrones above, such majesty
Invests him coming; yet not terrible,

That I should fear, nor sociably mild,
As Raphael, that I should much confide,
But solemn and sublime; whom, not to offend,
With reverence I must meet, and thou retire."
     He ended; and the Archangel soon drew nigh,
Not in his shape celestial, but as man
Clad to meet man. Over his lucid arms   240
A military vest of purple flowed,
Livelier than Melibœan, or the grain
Of Sarra, worn by kings and heroes old
In time of truce; Iris had dipt the woof.
His starry helm unbuckled showed him prime
In manhood where youth ended; by his side,
As in a glistering zodiac, hung the sword,
Satan's dire dread, and in his hand the spear.
Adam bowed low; he, kingly, from his state
Inclined not, but his coming thus declared:—   250
     "Adam, Heaven's high behest no preface needs.
Sufficient that thy prayers are heard, and Death,
Then due by sentence when thou didst transgress,
Defeated of his seizure many days,
Given thee of grace, wherein thou may'st repent,
And one bad act with many deeds well done
May'st cover. Well may then thy Lord, appeased,
Redeem thee quite from Death's rapacious claim;
But longer in this Paradise to dwell
Permits not. To remove thee I am come,   260
And send thee from the Garden forth, to till
The ground whence thou wast taken, fitter soil."
He added not; for Adam, at the news
Heart-strook, with chilling gripe of sorrow stood,
That all his senses bound; Eve, who unseen
Yet all had heard, with audible lament
Discovered soon the place of her retire:—
     "O unexpected stroke, worse than of Death!
Must I thus leave thee, Paradise? thus leave
Thee, native soil? these happy walks and shades,   270
Fit haunt of Gods, where I had hope to spend,
Quiet, though sad, the respite of that day
That must be mortal to us both? O flowers,
That never will in other climate grow,
My early visitation, and my last
At even, which I bred up with tender hand

From the first opening bud, and gave ye names,
Who now shall rear ye to the Sun, or rank
Your tribes, and water from the ambrosial fount?
Thee, lastly, nuptial bower, by me adorned   280
With what to sight or smell was sweet, from thee
How shall I part, and whither wander down
Into a lower world, to this obscure
And wild? How shall we breathe in other air
Less pure, accustomed to immortal fruits?"
    Whom thus the Angel interrupted mild:—
"Lament not, Eve, but patiently resign
What justly thou hast lost; nor set thy heart,
Thus over-fond, on that which is not thine.
Thy going is not lonely; with thee goes   290
Thy husband; him to follow thou art bound;
Where he abides, think there thy native soil."
    Adam, by this from the cold sudden damp
Recovering, and his scattered spirits returned,
To Michael thus his humble words addressed:—
    "Celestial, whether among the Thrones, or named
Of them the highest—for such of shape may seem
Prince above princes—gently hast thou told
Thy message, which might else in telling wound,
And in performing end us. What besides   300
Of sorrow, and dejection, and despair,
Our frailty can sustain, thy tidings bring—
Departure from this happy place, our sweet
Recess, and only consolation left
Familiar to our eyes; all places else
Inhospitable appear, and desolate,
Nor knowing us, nor known. And, if by prayer
Incessant I could hope to change the will
Of him who all things can, I would not cease
To weary him with my assiduous cries;   310
But prayer against his absolute decree
No more avails than breath against the wind,
Blown stifling back on him that breathes it forth:
Therefore to his great bidding I submit.
This most afflicts me—that, departing hence,
As from his face I shall be hid, deprived
His blessed countenance. Here I could frequent,
With worship, place by place where he voutsafed
Presence Divine, and to my sons relate,

'On this mount He appeared; under this tree   320
Stood visible; among these pines his voice
I heard; here with him at this fountain talked.'
So many grateful altars I would rear
Of grassy turf, and pile up every stone
Of lustre from the brook, in memory
Or monument to ages, and theron
Offer sweet-smelling gums, and fruits, and flowers.
In yonder nether world where shall I seek
His bright appearances, or footstep trace?
For, though I fled him angry, yet, recalled   330
To life prolonged and promised race, I now
Gladly behold though but his utmost skirts
Of glory, and far off his steps adore."
     To whom thus Michael, with regard benign:—
"Adam, thou know'st Heaven his, and all the Earth,
Not this rock only; his omnipresence fills
Land, sea, and air, and every kind that lives,
Fomented by his virtual power and warmed.
All the Earth he gave thee to possess and rule,
No despicable gift; surmise not, then,   340
His presence to these narrow bounds confined
Of Paradise or Eden. This had been
Perhaps thy capital seat, from whence had spread
All generations, and had hither come,
From all the ends of the Earth, to celebrate
And reverence thee their great progenitor.
But this pre-eminence thou hast lost, brought down
To dwell on even ground now with thy sons:
Yet doubt not but in valley and in plain
God is, as here, and will be found alike   350
Present, and of his presence many a sign
Still following thee, still compassing thee round
With goodness and paternal love, his face
Express, and of his steps the track divine.
Which that thou may'st believe, and be confirmed
Ere thou from hence depart, know I am sent
To show thee what shall come in future days
To thee and to thy offspring. Good with bad
Expect to hear, supernal grace contending
With sinfulness of men—thereby to learn   360
True patience, and to temper joy with fear
And pious sorrow, equally inured

By moderation either state to bear,
Prosperous or adverse: so shalt thou lead
Safest thy life, and best prepared endure
Thy mortal passage when it comes. Ascend
This hill; let Eve (for I have drenched her eyes)
Here sleep below while thou to foresight wak'st,
As once thou slept'st while she to life was formed."
    To whom thus Adam gratefully replied:—   370
"Ascend; I follow thee, safe guide, the path
Thou lead'st me, and to the hand of Heaven submit,
However chastening—to the evil turn
My obvious breast, arming to overcome
By suffering, and earn rest from labor won,
If so I may attain." So both ascend
In the visions of God. It was a hill,
Of Paradise the highest, from whose top
The hemisphere of Earth in clearest ken
Stretched out to the amplest reach of prospect lay.   380
Not higher that hill, nor wider looking round,
Whereon for different cause the Tempter set
Our second Adam, in the wilderness,
To show him all Earth's kingdoms and their glory.
His eye might there command wherever stood
City of old or modern fame, the seat
Of mightiest empire, from the destined walls
Of Cambalu, seat of Cathaian Can,
And Samarchand by Oxus, Temir's throne,
To Paquin, of Sinæan kings, and thence   390
To Agra and Lahor of Great Mogul,
Down to the golden Chersonese, or where
The Persian in Ecbatan sat, or since
In Hispahan, or where the Russian Ksar
In Mosco, or the Sultan in Bizance,
Turchestan-born; nor could his eye not ken
The empire of Negus to his utmost port
Ercoco, and the less maritime kings,
Mombaza, and Quiloa, and Melind,
And Sofala (thought Ophir), to the realm   400
Of Congo, and Angola farthest south,
Or thence from Niger flood to Atlas mount,
The kingdoms of Almansor, Fez and Sus,
Marocco, and Algiers, and Tremisen;
On Europe thence, and where Rome was to sway

The world: in spirit perhaps he also saw
Rich Mexico, the seat of Montezume,
And Cusco in Peru, the richer seat
Of Atabalipa; and yet unspoiled
Guiana, whose great city Geryon's sons   410
Call El Dorado. But to nobler sights
Michael from Adam's eyes the film removed
Which that false fruit that promised clearer sight
Had bred; then purged with euphrasy and rue
The visual nerve, for he had much to see,
And from the well of life three drops instilled.
So deep the power of these ingredients pierced,
Even to the inmost seat of mental sight,
That Adam, now enforced to close his eyes,
Sunk down, and all his spirits became entranced.   420
But him the gentle Angel by the hand
Soon raised, and his attention thus recalled:—
    "Adam, now ope thine eyes, and first behold
The effects which thy original crime hath wrought
In some to spring from thee, who never touched
The excepted tree, nor with the Snake conspired
Nor sinned thy sin, yet from that sin derive
Corruption to bring forth more violent deeds."
    His eyes he opened, and beheld a field,
Part arable and tilth, whereon were sheaves   430
New-reaped, the other part sheep-walks and folds;
I' the midst an altar as the landmark stood,
Rustic, of grassy sord. Thither anon
A sweaty reaper from his tillage brought
First-fruits, the green ear and the yellow sheaf,
Unculled, as came to hand. A shepherd next,
More meek, came with the firstlings of his flock,
Choicest and best; then, sacrificing, laid
The inwards and their fat, with incense strewed,
On the cleft wood, and all due rites performed.   440
His offering soon propitious fire from Heaven
Consumed, with nimble glance, and grateful steam;
The other's not, for his was not sincere:
Whereat he inly raged, and, as they talked,
Smote him into the midriff with a stone
That beat out life; he fell, and, deadly pale,
Groaned out his soul, with gushing blood effused.
Much at that sight was Adam in his heart

Dismayed, and thus in haste to the Angel cried:—
   "O Teacher, some great mischief hath befallen   450
To that meek man, who well had sacrificed:
Is piety thus and pure devotion paid?"
   To whom Michael thus, he also moved, replied:—
"These two are brethren, Adam, and to come
Out of thy loins. The unjust the just hath slain,
For envy that his brother's offering found
From Heaven acceptance; but the bloody fact
Will be avenged, and the other's faith approved
Lose no reward, though here thou see him die,
Rolling in dust and gore." To which our Sire:—   460
   "Alas! both for the deed and for the cause!
But have I now seen Death? Is this the way
I must return to native dust? O sight
Of terror, foul and ugly to behold!
Horrid to think, how horrible to feel!"
   To whom thus Michael:—"Death thou hast seen
In his first shape on Man; but many shapes
Of Death, and many are the ways that lead
To his grim cave—all dismal, yet to sense
More terrible at the entrance than within.   470
Some, as thou saw'st, by violent stroke shall die,
By fire, flood, famine; by intemperance more
In meats and drinks, which on the Earth shall bring
Diseases dire, of which a monstrous crew
Before thee shall appear, that thou may'st know
What misery the inabstinence of Eve
Shall bring on men." Immediately a place
Before his eyes appeared, sad, noisome, dark:
A lazar-house it seemed, wherein were laid
Numbers of all diseased—all maladies   480
Of ghastly spasm, or racking torture, qualms
Of heart-sick agony, all feverous kinds,
Convulsions, epilepsies, fierce catarrhs,
Intestine stone and ulcer, colic pangs,
Demoniac phrenzy, moping melancholy,
And moon-struck madness, pining atrophy,
Marasmus, and wide-wasting pestilence,
Dropsies and asthmas, and joint-racking rheums.
Dire was the tossing, deep the groans; Despair
Tended the sick, busiest from couch to couch;   490
And over them triumphant Death his dart

Shook, but delayed to strike, though oft invoked
With vows, as their chief good and final hope.
Sight so deform what heart of rock could long
Dry-eyed behold? Adam could not, but wept,
Though not of woman born: compassion quelled
His best of man, and gave him up to tears
A space, till firmer thoughts restrained excess,
And, scarce recovering words, his plaint renewed:—
   "O miserable Mankind, to what fall   500
Degraded, to what wretched state reserved!
Better end here unborn. Why is life given
To be thus wrested from us? rather why
Obtruded on us thus? who, if we knew
What we receive, would either not accept
Life offered, or soon beg to lay it down,
Glad to be so dismissed in peace. Can thus
The image of God in Man, created once
So goodly and erect, though faulty since,
To such unsightly sufferings be debased   510
Under inhuman pains? Why should not Man,
Retaining still divine similitude
In part, from such deformities be free,
And for his Maker's image' sake, exempt?"
   "Their Maker's image," answered Michael, "then
Forsook them, when themselves they vilified
To serve ungoverned Appetite, and took
His image whom they served—a brutish vice,
Inductive mainly to the sin of Eve.
Therefore so abject is their punishment,   520
Disfiguring not God's likeness, but their own;
Or, if his likeness, by themselves defaced
While they pervert pure Nature's healthful rules
To loathsome sickness—worthily, since they
God's image did not reverence in themselves."
   "I yield it just," said Adam, "and submit.
But is there yet no other way, besides
These painful passages, how we may come
To death, and mix with our connatural dust?"
   "There is," said Michael, "if thou well observe   530
The rule of *Not too much,* by temperance taught
In what thou eat'st and drink'st, seeking from thence
Due nourishment, not gluttonous delight,
Till many years over thy head return.

So may'st thou live, till, like ripe fruit, thou drop
Into thy mother's lap, or be with ease
Gathered, nor harshly plucked, for death mature.
This is old age; but then, thou must outlive
Thy youth, thy strength, thy beauty, which will change
To withered, weak, and grey; thy senses then,   540
Obtuse, all taste of pleasure must forgo
To what thou hast; and, for the air of youth,
Hopeful and cheerful, in thy blood will reign
A melancholy damp of cold and dry,
To weigh thy spirits down, and last consume
The balm of life." To whom our Ancestor:—

    "Henceforth I fly not death, nor would prolong
Life much—bent rather how I may be quit,
Fairest and easiest, of this cumbrous charge,
Which I must keep till my appointed day   550
Of rendering up, and patiently attend
My dissolution." Michael replied:—

    "Nor love thy life, nor hate; but what thou liv'st
Live well; how long or short permit to Heaven.
And now prepare thee for another sight."

    He looked, and saw a spacious plain, whereon
Were tents of various hue: by some were herds
Of cattle grazing: others whence the sound
Of instruments that made melodious chime
Was heard, of harp and organ, and who moved   560
Their stops and chords was seen: his volant touch
Instinct through all proportions low and high
Fled and pursued transverse the resonant fugue.
In other part stood one who, at the forge
Laboring, two massy clods of iron and brass
Had melted (whether found where casual fire
Had wasted woods, on mountain or in vale,
Down to the veins of earth, thence gliding hot
To some cave's mouth, or whether washed by stream
From underground); the liquid ore he drained   570
Into fit moulds prepared; from which he formed
First his own tools, then what might else be wrought
Fusil or graven in metal. After these,
But on the hither side, a different sort
From the high neighboring hills, which was their seat,
Down to the plain descended; by their guise
Just men they seemed, and all their study bent

To worship God aright, and know his works
Not hid; nor those things last which might preserve
Freedom and peace to men. They on the plain   580
Long had not walked, when from the tents behold
A bevy of fair women, richly gay
In gems and wanton dress! to the harp they sung
Soft amorous ditties, and in dance came on.
The men, though grave, eyed them, and let their eyes
Rove without rein, till, in the amorous net
Fast caught, they liked, and each his liking chose.
And now of love they treat, till the evening-star,
Love's harbinger, appeared; then, all in heat,
They light the nuptial torch, and bid invoke   590
Hymen, then first to marriage rites invoked:
With feast and music all the tents resound.
Such happy interview, and fair event
Of love and youth not lost, songs, garlands, flowers,
And charming symphonies, attached the heart
Of Adam, soon inclined to admit delight,
The bent of Nature; which he thus expressed:—
    "True opener of mine eyes, prime Angel blest,
Much better seems this vision, and more hope
Of peaceful days portends, than those two past: 600
Those were of hate and death, or pain much worse;
Here Nature seems fulfilled in all her ends."
    To whom thus Michael:—"Judge not what is best
By pleasure, though to Nature seeming meet,
Created, as thou art, to nobler end,
Holy and pure, conformity divine.
Those tents thou saw'st so pleasant were the tents
Of wickedness, wherein shall dwell his race
Who slew his brother: studious they appear
Of arts that polish life, inventors rare;   610
Unmindful of their Maker, though his Spirit
Taught them; but they his gifts acknowledged none.
Yet they a beauteous offspring shall beget;
For that fair female troop thou saw'st, that seemed
Of goddesses, so blithe, so smooth, so gay,
Yet empty of all good wherein consists
Woman's domestic honor and chief praise;
Bred only and completed to the taste
Of lustful appetence, to sing, to dance,
To dress, and troll the tongue, and roll the eye;—   620

To these that sober race of men, whose lives
Religious titled them the Sons of God,
Shall yield up all their virtue, all their fame,
Ignobly, to the trains and to the smiles
Of these fair atheists, and now swim in joy
(Erelong to swim at large) and laugh; for which
The world erelong a world of tears must weep."

    To whom thus Adam, of short joy bereft:—
"O pity and shame, that they who to live well
Entered so fair should turn aside to tread   630
Paths indirect, or in the midway faint!
But still I see the tenor of Man's woe
Holds on the same, from Woman to begin."

    "From Man's effeminate slackness it begins,"
Said the Angel, "who should better hold his place
By wisdom, and superior gifts received.
But now prepare thee for another scene."

    He looked, and saw wide territory spread
Before him—towns, and rural works between,
Cities of men with lofty gates and towers,   640
Concourse in arms, fierce faces threatening war,
Giants of mighty bone and bold emprise.
Part wield their arms, part curb the foaming steed,
Single or in array of battle ranged
Both horse and foot, nor idly mustering stood.
One way a band select from forage drives
A herd of beeves, fair oxen and fair kine,
From a fat meadow-ground, or fleecy flock,
Ewes and their bleating lambs, over the plain,
Their booty; scarce with life the shepherds fly,   650
But call in aid, which makes a bloody fray:
With cruel tournament the squadrons join;
Where cattle pastured late, now scattered lies
With carcasses and arms the ensanguined field
Deserted. Others to a city strong
Lay siege, encamped, by battery, scale, and mine,
Assaulting; others from the wall defend
With dart and javelin, stones, and sulphurous fire;
On each hand slaughter and gigantic deeds.
In other part the sceptred haralds call   660
To council in the city-gates: anon
Grey-headed men and grave, with warriors mixed,
Assemble, and harangues are heard; but soon

In factious opposition, till at last
Of middle age one rising, eminent
In wise deport, spake much of right and wrong,
Of justice, of religion, truth, and peace,
And judgment from above: him old and young
Exploded, and had seized with violent hands,
Had not a cloud descending snatched him thence,   670
Unseen amid the throng. So violence
Proceeded, and oppression, and sword-law,
Through all the plain, and refuge none was found.
Adam was all in tears, and to his guide
Lamenting turned full sad:—"Oh, what are these?
Death's ministers, not men! who thus deal death
Inhumanly to men, and multiply
Ten thousandfold the sin of him who slew
His brother; for of whom such massacre
Make they but of their brethren, men of men?   680
But who was that just man, whom had not Heaven
Rescued, had in his righteousness been lost?"
    To whom thus Michael:—"These are the product
Of those ill-mated marriages thou saw'st,
Where good with bad were matched; who of themselves
Abhor to join, and, by imprudence mixed,
Produce prodigious births of body or mind.
Such were these Giants, men of high renown;
For in those days might only shall be admired,
And valor and heroic virtue called.   690
To overcome in battle, and subdue
Nations, and bring home spoils with infinite
Manslaughter, shall be held the highest pitch
Of human glory, and, for glory done,
Of triumph to be styled great conquerors,
Patrons of mankind, gods, and sons of gods—
Destroyers rightlier called, and plagues of men.
Thus fame shall be achieved, renown on earth,
And what most merits fame in silence hid.
But he, the seventh from thee, whom thou beheld'st   700
The only righteous in a world perverse,
And therefore hated, therefore so beset
With foes, for daring single to be just,
And utter odious truth, that God would come
To judge them with his Saints—him the Most High,
Rapt in a balmy cloud, with winged steeds,

Did, as thou saw'st, receive, to walk with God
High in salvation and the climes of bliss,
Exempt from death, to show thee what reward
Awaits the good, the rest what punishment;   710
Which now direct thine eyes and soon behold."
    He looked, and saw the face of things quite changed.
The brazen throat of war had ceased to roar;
All now was turned to jollity and game,
To luxury and riot, feast and dance,
Marrying or prostituting, as befell,
Rape or adultery, where passing fair
Allured them; thence from cups to civil broils.
At length a reverend sire among them came,
And of their doings great dislike declared,   720
And testified against their ways. He oft
Frequented their assemblies, whereso met,
Triumphs or festivals, and to them preached
Conversion and repentance, as to souls
In prison, under judgments imminent;
But all in vain. Which when he saw, he ceased
Contending, and removed his tents far off;
Then, from the mountain hewing timber tall,
Began to build a vessel of huge bulk,
Measured by cubit, length, and breadth, and highth,   730
Smeared round with pitch, and in the side a door
Contrived, and of provisions laid in large
For man and beast: when lo! a wonder strange!
Of every beast, and bird, and insect small,
Came sevens and pairs, and entered in, as taught
Their order; last, the sire and his three sons,
With their four wives; and God made fast the door.
Meanwhile the South-wind rose, and, with black wings
Wide-hovering, all the clouds together drove
From under heaven; the hills to their supply   740
Vapor, and exhalation dusk and moist,
Sent up amain; and now the thickened sky
Like a dark ceiling stood: down rushed the rain
Impetuous, and continued till the earth
No more was seen. The floating vessel swum
Uplifted, and secure with beaked prow
Rode tilting o'er the waves; all dwellings else
Flood overwhelmed, and them with all their pomp
Deep under water rolled; sea covered sea,

Sea without shore: and in their palaces,   750
Where luxury late reigned, sea-monsters whelped
And stabled: of mankind, so numerous late,
All left in one small bottom swum embarked.
How didst thou grieve then, Adam, to behold
The end of all thy offspring, end so sad,
Depopulation! Thee another flood,
Of tears and sorrow a flood, thee also drowned,
And sunk thee as thy sons; till, gently reared
By the Angel, on thy feet thou stood'st at last,
Though comfortless, as when a father mourns   760
His children, all in view destroyed at once,
And scarce to the Angel utter'dst thus thy plaint:—
     "O visions ill foreseen! Better had I
Lived ignorant of future—so had borne
My part of evil only, each day's lot
Enough to bear. Those now that were dispensed
The burden of many ages on me light
At once, by my foreknowledge gaining birth
Abortive, to torment me, ere their being,
With thought that they must be. Let no man seek   770
Henceforth to be foretold what shall befall
Him or his children—evil, he may be sure,
Which neither his foreknowing can prevent,
And he the future evil shall no less
In apprehension than in substance feel
Grievous to bear. But that care now is past;
Man is not whom to warn; those few escaped
Famine and anguish will at last consume,
Wandering that watery desert. I had hope,
When violence was ceased and war on Earth,   780
All would have then gone well, peace would have crowned
With length of happy days the race of Man;
But I was far deceived, for now I see
Peace to corrupt no less than war to waste.
How comes it thus? Unfold, Celestial Guide,
And whether here the race of Man will end."
     To whom thus Michael:—"Those, whom last thou saw'st
In triumph and luxurious wealth are they
First seen in acts of prowess eminent
And great exploits, but of true virtue void,   790
Who, having spilt much blood, and done much waste,
Subduing nations, and achieved thereby

Fame in the world, high titles, and rich prey,
Shall change their course to pleasure, ease, and sloth,
Surfeit, and lust, till wantonness and pride
Raise out of friendship hostile deeds in peace.
The conquered, also, and enslaved by war,
Shall, with their freedom lost, all virtue lose,
And fear of God—from whom their piety feigned
In sharp contest of battle found no aid   800
Against invaders; therefore, cooled in zeal,
Thenceforth shall practise how to live secure,
Worldly or dissolute, on what their lords
Shall leave them to enjoy; for the Earth shall bear
More than enough, that temperance may be tried.
So all shall turn degenerate, all depraved,
Justice and temperance, truth and faith, forgot;
One man except, the only son of light
In a dark age, against example good,
Against allurement, custom, and a world   810
Offended. Fearless of reproach and scorn,
Or violence, he of their wicked ways
Shall them admonish, and before them set
The paths of righteousness, how much more safe
And full of peace, denouncing wrath to come
On their impenitence, and shall return
Of them derided, but of God observed
The one just man alive: by his command
Shall build a wondrous ark, as thou beheld'st,
To save himself and household from amidst   820
A world devote to universal wrack.
No sooner he, with them of man and beast
Select for life, shall in the ark be lodged
And sheltered round, but all the cataracts
Of Heaven set open on the Earth shall pour
Rain day and night; all fountains of the deep,
Broke up, shall heave the ocean to usurp
Beyond all bounds, till inundation rise
Above the highest hills. Then shall this Mount
Of Paradise by might of waves be moved   830
Out of his place, pushed by the horned flood,
With all his verdure spoiled, and trees adrift,
Down the great river to the opening Gulf,
And there take root, an island salt and bare,
The haunt of seals, and orcs, and sea-mews' clang—

To teach thee that God attributes to place
No sanctity, if none be thither brought
By men who there frequent or therein dwell.
And now what further shall ensue behold."
    He looked, and saw the ark hull on the flood,   840
Which now abated; for the clouds were fled,
Driven by a keen North-wind, that, blowing dry,
Wrinkled the face of deluge, as decayed;
And the clear sun on his wide watery glass
Gazed hot, and of the fresh wave largely drew,
As after thirst; which made their flowing shrink
From standing lake to tripping ebb, that stole
With soft foot towards the deep, who now had stopt
His sluices, as the heaven his windows shut.
The ark no more now floats, but seems on ground,   850
Fast on the top of some high mountain fixed.
And now the tops of hills as rocks appear;
With clamor thence the rapid currents drive
Towards the retreating sea their furious tide.
Forthwith from out the ark a raven flies,
And, after him, the surer messenger,
A dove, sent forth once and again to spy
Green tree or ground whereon his foot may light;
The second time returning, in his bill
An olive-leaf he brings, pacific sign.   860
Anon dry ground appears, and from his ark
The ancient sire descends, with all his train;
Then, with uplifted hands and eyes devout,
Grateful to Heaven, over his head beholds
A dewy cloud, and in the cloud a bow
Conspicuous with three lifted colors gay,
Betokening peace from God, and covenant new.
Whereat the heart of Adam, erst so sad,
Greatly rejoiced; and thus his joy broke forth:—
    "O thou, who future things canst represent   870
As present, Heavenly Instructor, I revive
At this last sight, assured that Man shall live,
With all the creatures, and their seed preserve.
Far less I now lament for one whole world
Of wicked sons destroyed than I rejoice
For one man found so perfect and so just
That God voutsafes to raise another world
From him, and all his anger to forget.

But say what mean those colored streaks in Heaven:
Distended as the brow of God appeased?   880
Or serve they as a flowery verge to bind
The fluid skirts of that same watery cloud,
Lest it again dissolve and shower the Earth?"
    To whom the Archangel:—"Dextrously thou aim'st.
So willingly doth God remit his ire:
Though late repenting him of Man depraved,
Grieved at his heart, when, looking down, he saw
The whole Earth filled with violence, and all flesh
Corrupting each their way; yet, those removed,
Such grace shall one just man find in his sight   890
That he relents, not to blot out mankind,
And makes a covenant never to destroy
The Earth again by flood, nor let the sea
Surpass his bounds, nor rain to drown the world
With man therein or beast; but, when he brings
Over the Earth a cloud, will therein set
His triple-colored bow, whereon to look
And call to mind his covenant. Day and night,
Seed-time and harvest, heat and hoary frost,
Shall hold their course, till fire purge all things new.   900
Both Heaven and Earth, wherein the just shall dwell."

BOOK XII

THE ARGUMENT

THE Angel Michael continues, from the Flood, to relate what shall suc-
ceed; then, in the mention of Abraham, comes by degrees to explain who
that Seed of the Woman shall be which was promised Adam and Eve in
the Fall: his incarnation, death, resurrection, and ascension; the state of
the Church till his second coming. Adam, greatly satisfied and recom-
forted by these relations and promises, descends the hill with Michael;
wakens Eve, who all this while had slept, but with gentle dreams com-
posed to quietness of mind and submission. Michael in either hand leads
them out of Paradise, the fiery sword waving behind them, and the
Cherubim taking their stations to guard the place.

> As one who, in his journey, bates at noon,
> Though bent on speed, so here the Archangel paused
> Betwixt the world destroyed and world restored,
> If Adam aught perhaps might interpose;
> Then, with transition sweet, new speech resumes:—
>   "Thus thou hast seen one world begin and end,
> And Man as from a second stock proceed.
> Much thou hast yet to see; but I perceive
> Thy mortal sight to fail; objects divine
> Must needs impair and weary human sense.   10
> Henceforth what is to come I will relate;
> Thou, therefore, give due audience, and attend.
>   "This second source of men, while yet but few,
> And while the dread of judgment past remains
> Fresh in their minds, fearing the Deity,
> With some regard to what is just and right
> Shall lead their lives, and multiply apace,

247

Laboring the soil, and reaping plenteous crop,
Corn, wine, and oil; and, from the herd or flock
Oft sacrificing bullock, lamb, or kid,   20
With large wine-offerings poured, and sacred feast,
Shall spend their days in joy unblamed, and dwell
Long time in peace, by families and tribes,
Under paternal rule, till one shall rise,
Of proud, ambitious heart, who, not content
With fair equality, fraternal state,
Will arrogate dominion undeserved
Over his brethren, and quite dispossess
Concord and law of Nature from the Earth—
Hunting (and men, not beasts, shall be his game)   30
With war and hostile snare such as refuse
Subjection to his empire tyrannous.
A mighty hunter thence he shall be styled
Before the Lord, as in despite of Heaven,
Or from Heaven claiming second sovranty,
And from rebellion shall derive his name,
Though of rebellion others he accuse.
He, with a crew, whom like ambition joins
With him or under him to tyrannize,
Marching from Eden towards the west, shall find   40
The plain, wherein a black bituminous gurge
Boils out from under ground, the mouth of Hell.
Of brick, and of that stuff, they cast to build
A city and tower, whose top may reach to Heaven;
And get themselves a name, lest, far dispersed
In foreign lands, their memory be lost—
Regardless whether good or evil fame.
But God, who oft descends to visit men
Unseen, and through their habitations walks,
To mark their doings, them beholding soon,   50
Comes down to see their city, ere the tower
Obstruct Heaven-towers, and in derision sets
Upon their tongues a various spirit, to rase
Quite out their native language; and, instead,
To sow a jangling noise of words unknown.
Forthwith a hideous gabble rises loud
Among the builders; each to other calls,
Not understood—till, hoarse and all in rage,
As mocked they storm. Great laughter was in Heaven,
And looking down to see the hubbub strange   60

And hear the din. Thus was the building left
Ridiculous, and the work *Confusion* named."
　　Whereto thus Adam, fatherly displeased:—
"O execrable son, so to aspire
Above his brethren, to himself assuming
Authority usurped, from God not given!
He gave us only over beast, fish, fowl,
Dominion absolute: that right we hold
By his donation: but man over men
He made not lord—such title to himself   70
Reserving, human left from human free.
But this usurper his encroachment proud
Stays not on Man; to God his tower intends
Siege and defiance. Wretched man! what food
Will he convey up thither, to sustain
Himself and his rash army, where thin air
Above the clouds will pine his entrails gross,
And famish him of breath, if not of bread?"
　　To whom thus Michael:—"Justly thou abhorr'st
That son, who on the quiet state of men   80
Such trouble brought, affecting to subdue
Rational liberty; yet know withal,
Since thy original lapse, true liberty
Is lost, which always with right reason dwells
Twinned, and from her hath no dividual being.
Reason in Man obscured, or not obeyed,
Immediately inordinate desires
And upstart passions catch the government
From Reason, and to servitude reduce
Man, till then free. Therefore, since he permits   90
Within himself unworthy powers to reign
Over free reason, God, in judgment just,
Subjects him from without to violent lords,
Who oft as undeservedly enthral
His outward freedom. Tyranny must be,
Though to the tyrant thereby no excuse.
Yet sometimes nations will decline so low
From virtue, which is reason, that no wrong,
But justice and some fatal curse annexed,
Deprives them of their outward liberty,   100
Their inward lost: witness the irreverent son
Of him who built the ark, who, for the shame
Done to his father, heard this heavy curse,

Servant of servants, on his vicious race.
Thus will this latter, as the former world,
Still tend from bad to worse, till God at last,
Wearied with their iniquities, withdraw
His presence from among them, and avert
His holy eyes, resolving from thenceforth
To leave them to their own polluted ways,   110
And one peculiar nation to select
From all the rest, of whom to be invoked—
A nation from one faithful man to spring.
Him on this side Euphrates yet residing,
Bred up in idol-worship—Oh, that men
(Canst thou believe?) should be so stupid grown,
While yet the patriarch lived who scaped the Flood,
As to forsake the living God, and fall
To worship their own work in wood and stone
For gods!—yet him God the Most High voutsafes   120
To call by vision from his father's house,
His kindred, and false gods, into a land
Which he will show him, and from him will raise
A mighty nation, and upon him shower
His benediction so that in his seed
All nations shall be blest. He straight obeys;
Not knowing to what land, yet firm believes.
I see him, but thou canst not, with what faith
He leaves his gods, his friends, and native soil,
Ur of Chaldæa, passing now the ford   130
To Haran—after him a cumbrous train
Of herds and flocks, and numerous servitude—
Not wandering poor, but trusting all his wealth
With God, who called him, in a land unknown.
Canaan he now attains; I see his tents
Pitched about Sechem, and the neighboring plain
Of Moreh. There, by promise, he receives
Gift to his progeny of all that land,
From Hamath northward to the Desert south
(Things by their names I call, though yet unnamed),   140
From Hermon east to the great western sea;
Mount Hermon, yonder sea, each place behold
In prospect, as I point them: on the shore,
Mount Carmel; here, the double-founted stream,
Jordan, true limit eastward; but his sons
Shall dwell to Senir, that long ridge of hills.

This ponder, that all nations of the Earth
Shall in his seed be blessed. By that seed
Is meant thy great Deliverer, who shall bruise
The Serpent's head; whereof to thee anon   150
Plainlier shall be revealed. This patriarch blest,
Whom *faithful Abraham* due time shall call,
A son, and of his son a grandchild, leaves,
Like him in faith, in wisdom, and renown.
The grandchild, with twelve sons increased, departs
From Canaan to a land hereafter called
Egypt, divided by the river Nile;
See where it flows, disgorging at seven mouths
Into the sea. To sojourn in that land
He comes, invited by a younger son   160
In time of dearth—a son whose worthy deeds
Raise him to be the second in that realm
Of Pharaoh. There he dies, and leaves his race
Growing into a nation, and now grown
Suspected to a sequent king, who seeks
To stop their overgrowth, as inmate guests
Too numerous; whence of guests he makes them slaves
Inhospitably, and kills their infant males:
Till, by two brethren (those two brethren call
Moses and Aaron) sent from God to claim   170
His people from enthralment, they return,
With glory and spoil, back to their promised land.
But first the lawless tyrant, who denies
To know their God, or message to regard,
Must be compelled by signs and judgments dire;
To blood unshed the rivers must be turned;
Frogs, lice, and flies must all his palace fill
With loathed intrusion, and fill all the land;
His cattle must of rot and murrain die;
Botches and blains must all his flesh emboss,   180
And all his people; thunder mixed with hail,
Hail mixed with fire, must rend the Egyptian sky,
And wheel on the earth, devouring where it rolls;
What it devours not, herb, or fruit, or grain,
A darksome cloud of locusts swarming down
Must eat, and on the ground leave nothing green;
Darkness must overshadow all his bounds,
Palpable darkness, and blot out three days;
Last, with one midnight-stroke, all the first-born

Of Egypt must lie dead. Thus with ten wounds   190
The river-dragon tamed at length submits
To let his sojourners depart, and oft
Humbles his stubborn heart, but still as ice
More hardened after thaw; till, in his rage
Pursuing whom he late dismissed, the sea
Swallows him with his host, but them lets pass,
As on dry land, between two crystal walls,
Awed by the rod of Moses so to stand
Divided till his rescued gain their shore:
Such wondrous power God to his Saint will lend,   200
Though present in his Angel, who shall go
Before them in a cloud, and pillar of fire—
By day a cloud, by night a pillar of fire—
To guide them in their journey, and remove
Behind them, while the obdurate king pursues.
All night he will pursue, but his approach
Darkness defends between till morning-watch;
Then through the fiery pillar and the cloud
God looking forth will trouble all his host,
And craze their chariot-wheels: when, by command,   210
Moses once more his potent rod extends
Over the sea; the sea his rod obeys;
On their embattled ranks the waves return,
And overwhelm their war. The race elect
Safe toward Canaan, from the shore, advance
Through the wild Desert—not the readiest way,
Lest, entering on the Canaanite alarmed,
War terrify them inexpert, and fear
Return them back to Egypt, choosing rather
Inglorious life with servitude; for life   220
To noble and ignoble is more sweet
Untrained in arms, where rashness leads not on.
This also shall they gain by their delay
In the wide wilderness: there they shall found
Their government, and their great Senate choose
Through the twelve tribes, to rule by laws ordained.
God, from the Mount of Sinai, whose grey top
Shall tremble, he descending, will himself,
In thunder, lightning, and loud trumpet's sound,
Ordain them laws—part, such as appertain   230
To civil justice; part, religious rites
Of sacrifice, informing them, by types

And shadows, of that destined Seed to bruise
The Serpent, by what means he shall achieve
Mankind's deliverance. But the voice of God
To mortal ear is dreadful: they beseech
That Moses might report to them his will,
And terror cease; he grants what they besought,
Instructed that to God is no access
Without Mediator, whose high office now   240
Moses in figure bears, to introduce
One greater, of whose day he shall foretell,
And all the Prophets, in their age, the times
Of great Messiah shall sing. Thus, laws and rites
Established, such delight hath God in men
Obedient to his will that he voutsafes
Among them to set up his tabernacle—
The Holy One with mortal men to dwell.
By his prescript a sanctuary is framed
Of cedar, overlaid with gold; therein   250
An ark, and in the ark his testimony,
The records of his covenant; over these
A mercy-seat of gold, between the wings
Of two bright Cherubim; before him burn
Seven lamps, as in a zodiac representing
The heavenly fires. Over the tent a cloud
Shall rest by day, a fiery gleam by night,
Save when they journey; and at length they come,
Conducted by his Angel, to the land
Promised to Abraham and his seed. The rest   260
Were long to tell—how many battles fought;
How many kings destroyed, and kingdoms won;
Or how the sun shall in mid-heaven stand still
A day entire, and night's due course adjourn,
Man's voice commanding, 'Sun, in Gibeon stand,
And thou Moon, in the vale of Aialon,
Till *Israel* overcome!'—so call the third
From Abraham, son of Isaac, and from him
His whole descent, who thus shall Canaan win."
    Here Adam interposed:—"O sent from Heaven,   270
Enlightener of my darkness, gracious things
Thou hast revealed, those chiefly which concern
Just Abraham and his seed. Now first I find
Mine eyes true opening, and my heart much eased,
Erewhile perplexed with thoughts, what would become

Of me and all mankind; but now I see
His day, in whom all nations shall be blest—
Favor unmerited by me, who sought
Forbidden knowledge by forbidden means.
This yet I apprehend not—why to those   280
Among whom God will deign to dwell on Earth
So many and so various laws are given.
So many laws argue so many sins
Among them; how can God with such reside?"
    To whom thus Michael:—"Doubt not but that sin
Will reign among them, as of thee begot;
And therefore was law given them, to evince
Their natural pravity, by stirring up
Sin against Law to fight, that, when they see
Law can discover sin, but not remove,   290
Save by those shadowy expiations weak,
The blood of bulls and goats, they may conclude
Some blood more precious must be paid for Man,
Just for unjust, that, in such righteousness,
To them by faith imputed, they may find
Justification towards God, and peace
Of conscience, which the law by ceremonies
Cannot appease, nor man the moral part
Perform, and not performing cannot live.
So Law appears imperfect, and but given   300
With purpose to resign them, in full time,
Up to a better covenant, disciplined
From shadowy types to truth, from flesh to spirit,
From imposition of strict laws to free
Acceptance of large grace, from servile fear
To filial, works of law to works of faith.
And therefore shall not Moses, though of God
Highly beloved, being but the minister
Of Law, his people into Canaan lead;
But Joshua, whom the Gentiles Jesus call,   310
His name and office bearing who shall quell
The adversary Serpent, and bring back
Through the world's wilderness long-wandered Man
Safe to eternal Paradise of rest.
Meanwhile they, in their earthly Canaan placed,
Long time shall dwell and prosper, but when sins
National interrupt their public peace,
Provoking God to raise them enemies—

From whom as oft he saves them penitent,
By Judges first, then under Kings; of whom   320
The second, both for piety renowned
And puissant deeds, a promise shall receive
Irrevocable, that his regal throne
For ever shall endure. The like shall sing
All Prophecy—that of the royal stock
Of David (so I name this king) shall rise
A son, the Woman's Seed to thee foretold,
Foretold to Abraham as in whom shall trust
All nations, and to kings foretold of kings
The last, for of his reign shall be no end.   330
But first a long succession must ensue;
And his next son, for wealth and wisdom famed,
The clouded ark of God, till then in tents
Wandering, shall in a glorious temple enshrine.
Such follow him as shall be registered
Part good, part bad; of bad the longer scroll:
Whose foul idolatries and other faults,
Heaped to the popular sum, will so incense
God, as to leave them, and expose their land,
Their city, his temple, and his holy ark,   340
With all his sacred things, a scorn and prey
To that proud city whose high walls thou saw'st
Left in confusion, Babylon thence called.
There in captivity he lets them dwell
The space of seventy years; then brings them back,
Remembering mercy, and his covenant sworn
To David, stablished as the days of Heaven.
Returned from Babylon by leave of kings,
Their lords, whom God disposed, the house of God
They first re-edify, and for a while   350
In mean estate live moderate, till, grown
In wealth and multitude, factious they grow.
But first among the priests dissension springs—
Men who attend the altar, and should most
Endeavor peace: their strife pollution brings
Upon the temple itself; at last they seize
The sceptre, and regard not David's sons;
Then lose it to a stranger, that the true
Anointed King Messiah might be born
Barred of his right. Yet at his birth a star,   360
Unseen before in heaven, proclaims him come,

And guides the eastern sages, who inquire
His place, to offer incense, myrrh, and gold:
His place of birth a solemn Angel tells
To simple shepherds, keeping watch by night;
They gladly thither haste, and by a quire
Of squadroned Angels hear his carol sung.
A Virgin is his mother, but his sire
The Power of the Most High. He shall ascend
The throne hereditary, and bound his reign   370
With Earth's wide bounds, his glory with the Heavens."
   He ceased, discerning Adam with such joy
Surcharged as had, like grief, been dewed in tears,
Without the vent of words; which these he breathed:—
   "O prophet of glad tidings, finisher
Of utmost hope! now clear I understand
What oft my steadiest thoughts have searched in vain—
Why our great Expectation should be called
The Seed of Woman. Virgin Mother, hail!
High in the love of Heaven, yet from my loins   380
Thou shalt proceed, and from thy womb the Son
Of God Most High; so God with Man unites.
Needs must the Serpent now his capital bruise
Expect with mortal pain. Say where and when
Their fight, what stroke shall bruise the Victor's heel."
   To whom thus Michael:—"Dream not of their fight
As of a duel, or the local wounds
Of head or heel. Not therefore joins the Son
Manhood to Godhead, with more strength to foil
Thy enemy; nor so is overcome   390
Satan, whose fall from Heaven, a deadlier bruise,
Disabled not to give thee thy death's wound;
Which he who comes thy Saviour shall recure,
Not by destroying Satan, but his works
In thee and in thy seed. Nor can this be,
But by fulfilling that which thou didst want,
Obedience to the law of God, imposed
On penalty of death, and suffering death,
The penalty to thy transgression due,
And due to theirs which out of thine will grow: 400
So only can high justice rest appaid.
The Law of God exact he shall fulfil
Both by obedience and by love, though love
Alone fulfil the Law; thy punishment

He shall endure, by coming in the flesh
To a reproachful life and cursed death,
Proclaiming life to all who shall believe
In his redemption, and that his obedience
Imputed becomes theirs by faith—his merits
To save them, not their own, though legal, works.   410
For this he shall live hated, be blasphemed,
Seized on by force, judged, and to death condemned
A shameful and accursed, nailed to the cross
By his own nation, slain for bringing life;
But to the cross he nails thy enemies—
The Law that is against thee, and the sins
Of all mankind, with him there crucified,
Never to hurt them more who rightly trust
In this his satisfaction. So he dies,
But soon revives; Death over him no power   420
Shall long usurp. Ere the third dawning light
Return, the stars of morn shall see him rise
Out of his grave, fresh as the dawning light,
Thy ransom paid, which Man from Death redeems—
His death for Man, as many as offered life
Neglect not, and the benefit embrace
By faith not void of works. This godlike act
Annuls thy doom, the death thou shouldst have died,
In sin forever lost from life; this act
Shall bruise the head of Satan, crush his strength,   430
Defeating Sin and Death, his two main arms,
And fix far deeper in his head their stings
Than temporal death shall bruise the Victor's heel,
Or theirs whom he redeems—a death, like sleep,
A gentle wafting to immortal life.
Nor after resurrection shall he stay
Longer on Earth than certain times to appear
To his disciples—men who in his life
Still followed him; to them shall leave in charge
To teach all nations what of him they learned   440
And his salvation, them who shall believe
Baptizing in the profluent stream—the sign
Of washing them from guilt of sin to life
Pure, and in mind prepared, if so befall,
For death like that which the Redeemer died.
All nations they shall teach; for from that day
Not only to the sons of Abraham's loins

Salvation shall be preached, but to the sons
Of Abraham's faith wherever through the world;
So in his seed all nations shall be blest.   450
Then to the Heaven of Heavens he shall ascend
With victory, triumphing through the air
Over his foes and thine; there shall surprise
The Serpent, Prince of Air, and drag in chains
Through all his realm, and there confounded leave;
Then enter into glory, and resume
His seat at God's right hand, exalted high
Above all names in Heaven; and thence shall come,
When this World's dissolution shall be ripe,
With glory and power, to judge both quick and dead—   460
To judge the unfaithful dead, but to reward
His faithful, and receive them into bliss,
Whether in Heaven or Earth; for then the Earth
Shall be all Paradise, far happier place
Than this of Eden, and far happier days."
  So spake the Archangel Michael; then paused,
As at the World's great period; and our Sire,
Replete with joy and wonder, thus replied:—
  "O Goodness infinite, Goodness immense,
That all this good of evil shall produce,   470
And evil turn to good—more wonderful
Than that which by creation first brought forth
Light out of darkness! Full of doubt I stand,
Whether I should repent me now of sin
By me done and occasioned, or rejoice
Much more that much more good thereof shall spring—
To God more glory, more good-will to men
From God—and over wrath grace shall abound.
But say, if our Deliverer up to Heaven
Must reascend, what will betide the few,   480
His faithful, left among the unfaithful herd,
The enemies of truth. Who then shall guide
His people, who defend? Will they not deal
Worse with his followers than with him they dealt?"
  "Be sure they will," said the Angel; "but from Heaven
He to his own a Comforter will send,
The promise of the Father, who shall dwell,
His Spirit, within them, and the law of faith
Working through love upon their hearts shall write,
To guide them in all truth, and also arm   490

With spiritual armor, able to resist
Satan's assaults, and quench his fiery darts—
What man can do against them not afraid,
Though to the death; against such cruelties
With inward consolations recompensed,
And oft supported so as shall amaze
Their proudest persecutors. For the Spirit,
Poured first on his Apostles, whom he sends
To evangelize the nations, then on all
Baptized, shall them with wondrous gifts endue   500
To speak all tongues, and do all miracles,
As did their Lord before them. Thus they win
Great numbers of each nation to receive
With joy the tidings brought from Heaven: at length,
Their ministry performed, and race well run,
Their doctrine and their story written left,
They die; but in their room, as they forewarn,
Wolves shall succeed for teachers, grievous wolves,
Who all the sacred mysteries of Heaven
To their own vile advantages shall turn   510
Of lucre and ambition, and the truth
With superstitions and traditions taint,
Left only in those written records pure,
Though not but by the Spirit understood.
Then shall they seek to avail themselves of names,
Places, and titles, and with these to join
Secular power, though feigning still to act
By spiritual; to themselves appropriating
The Spirit of God, promised alike and given
To all believers; and, from that pretence,   520
Spiritual laws by carnal power shall force
On every conscience—laws which none shall find
Left them enrolled, or what the Spirit within
Shall on the heart engrave. What will they then
But force the Spirit of Grace itself, and bind
His consort, Liberty? what but unbuild
His living temples, built by faith to stand—
Their own faith, not another's? for, on Earth,
Who against faith and conscience can be heard
Infallible? Yet many will presume: 530
Whence heavy persecution shall arise
On all who in the worship persevere
Of Spirit and Truth; the rest, far greater part,

Will deem in outward rites and specious forms
Religion satisfied; Truth shall retire
Bestuck with slanderous darts, and works of Faith
Rarely be found. So shall the World go on,
To good malignant, to bad men benign,
Under her own weight groaning, till the day
Appear of respiration to the just   540
And vengeance to the wicked, at return
Of Him so lately promised to thy aid,
The Woman's Seed—obscurely then foretold,
Now amplier known thy Saviour and thy Lord;
Last in the clouds from Heaven to be revealed
In glory of the Father, to dissolve
Satan with his perverted World; then raise
From the conflagrant mass, purged and refined,
New Heavens, new Earth, Ages of endless date
Founded in righteousness and peace and love,   550
To bring forth fruits, joy and eternal bliss."
     He ended; and thus Adam last replied:—
"How soon hath thy prediction, Seer blest,
Measured this transient World, the race of Time,
Till Time stand fixed! Beyond is all abyss—
Eternity, whose end no eye can reach.
Greatly instructed I shall hence depart,
Greatly in peace of thought, and have my fill
Of knowledge, what this vessel can contain;
Beyond which was my folly to aspire.   560
Henceforth I learn that to obey is best,
And love with fear the only God, to walk
As in his presence, ever to observe
His providence, and on him sole depend,
Merciful over all his works, with good
Still overcoming evil, and by small
Accomplishing great things—by things deemed weak
Subverting worldly-strong, and worldly-wise
By simply meek; that suffering for Truth's sake
Is fortitude to highest victory,   570
And to the faithful death the gate of life—
Taught this by his example whom I now
Acknowledge my Redeemer ever blest."
     To whom thus also the Angel last replied:—
"This having learned, thou hast attained the sum
Of wisdom; hope no higher, though all the stars

Thou knew'st by name, and all the ethereal powers,
All secrets of the Deep, all Nature's works,
Or works of God in heaven, air, earth, or sea,
And all the riches of this world enjoy'dst,   580
And all the rule, one empire. Only add
Deeds to thy knowledge answerable; add faith;
Add virtue, patience, temperance; add love,
By name to come called Charity, the soul
Of all the rest: then wilt thou not be loth
To leave this Paradise, but shalt possess
A Paradise within thee, happier far.
Let us descend now, therefore, from this top
Of speculation; for the hour precise
Exacts our parting hence; and, see! the guards,   590
By me encamped on yonder hill, expect
Their motion, at whose front a flaming sword,
In signal of remove, waves fiercely round.
We may no longer stay. Go, waken Eve;
Her also I with gentle dreams have calmed,
Portending good, and all her spirits composed
To meek submission: thou, at season fit,
Let her with thee partake what thou hast heard—
Chiefly what may concern her faith to know,
The great deliverance by her seed to come   600
(For by the Woman's Seed) on all mankind—
That ye may live, which will be many days,
Both in one faith unanimous; though sad
With cause for evils past, yet much more cheered
With meditation on the happy end."
     He ended, and they both descend the hill.
Descended, Adam to the bower where Eve
Lay sleeping ran before, but found her waked;
And thus with words not sad she him received:—
     "Whence thou return'st and whither went'st, I know;   610
For God is also in sleep, and dreams advise,
Which he hath sent propitious, some great good
Presaging, since, with sorrow and heart's distress
Wearied, I fell asleep. But now lead on;
In me is no delay; with thee to go
Is to stay here; without thee here to stay
Is to go hence unwilling; thou to me
Art all things under Heaven, all places thou,
Who for my wilful crime art banished hence.

This further consolation yet secure   620
I carry hence: though all by me is lost,
Such favor I unworthy am voutsafed,
By me the Promised Seed shall all restore."
  So spake our mother Eve; and Adam heard
Well pleased, but answered not: for now too nigh
The Archangel stood, and from the other hill
To their fixed station, all in bright array,
The Cherubim descended, on the ground
Gliding meteorous, as evening mist
Risen from a river o'er the marish glides,   630
And gathers ground fast at the laborer's heel
Homeward returning. High in front advanced,
The brandished sword of God before them blazed,
Fierce as a comet; which with torrid heat,
And vapor as the Libyan air adust,
Began to parch that temperate clime; whereat
In either hand the hastening Angel caught
Our lingering parents, and to the eastern gate
Led them direct, and down the cliff as fast
To the subjected plain—then disappeared.   640
They, looking back, all the eastern side beheld
Of Paradise, so late their happy seat,
Waved over by that flaming brand; the gate
With dreadful faces thronged and fiery arms.
Some natural tears they dropped, but wiped them soon;
The world was all before them, where to choose
Their place of rest, and Providence their guide.
They, hand in hand, with wandering steps and slow,
Through Eden took their solitary way.

NOTES

BOOK I

1–26. THE SUBJECT

Paradise Lost differs in its opening from its ancient models, the *Iliad,* the *Odyssey,* and the *Æneid,* in having a double invocation. The first is to the Genius of Sacred Song, elsewhere called Urania, who is the inspirer of the rhythmical language in versified portions of the Holy Scriptures, who appears in Heaven as the sister and companion of eternal Wisdom, and who gives to the speech of the blessed that prompt eloquence and musical sweetness by which it is characterized. She has to do with expression.

The Holy Spirit, who is next invoked for enlightenment and instruction, has to do with substance rather than with form. To Him the poet prays for knowledge and ability to set forth the truth. This implies an intention to hold fancy in check and to subordinate everything to the correct presentation of great spiritual facts. They make a radical mistake who say that certain things in the poem may be poetry but are not theology.

1. *Disobedience.* This is the principal word of the subject. It prepares us for a certain sternness of sentiment, especially in the words of the offended Deity. Justice rather than love is the keynote; and the poet's main purpose is to show the righteousness of God's dealings.

1–5. The subject is not fully stated until the end of the fifth line. Landor's idea that the fourth and fifth lines might be advantageously omitted is erroneous; they are needed to mark out exactly the scope of the poem. Milton carries us forward to the period of the restored earth and the establishment of the saved in it (xii. 463–465).

6. *Secret* means "separate," "retired," "apart." The loneliness of the desert retreat is contrasted with the publicity of Mount Zion, its kingly palace, its architectural beauty, and its tides of human life. The Heavenly Muse visits her votaries not only in remote solitudes but also in crowded cities.

8. *That shepherd.* Moses had been literally a shepherd in the district about Horeb and Sinai (*Exod.* iii. I); he is called a shepherd metaphorically as the leader of the Israelites out of Egypt (*Isa.* lxiii. II); he is so designated here in allusion to his poetical character. The peculiar fitness in this early mention of Moses appears from the fact that to him chiefly Milton is indebted for the knowledge of "man's first disobedience."

10. *Zion hill.* The names of David and Isaiah, true poets, are associated with this spot, which may well, therefore, be regarded as a haunt of the Muses.

13. *Adventrous.* "Now of the Heaven which is above the heavens no earthly poet has sung, or ever will sing, in a worthy manner."—Plato's *Phædrus.* The task, impracticable to the Pagan world, Milton was able to undertake with the aid of Divine revelation.

14. *No middle flight.* He celebrates the very throne of God, "high above all height." Since there is no summit beyond that to which he aspires, the word "middle" is used in its exact sense and not in the vague sense of "mediocre" or "mean."

16. *Unattempted.* What does this mean? The War in Heaven, the Fall of Lucifer, the Creation of the World, and the Fall of Man had been subjects frequently treated by poets of almost every Christian nation. But in the grandeur of his scope and method Milton had no predecessor or model. His is a universal poem, not bounded by the ordinary limits of space and time.

18. *Before all temples.* Whatever mountain or spring may be the haunt of the tuneful Nine or the Heavenly Muse, the Holy Spirit does not favor any particular spot of earth, but dwells everywhere in pious hearts. "Temple" here does not mean a building erected by human hands, but any precinct, whether hill, or grove, or spring hallowed by the presence of a deity.

19. *Instruct me.* This invocation is not a mere form. It results from a conviction deeply felt and long before expressed (*Reason of Church Government,* Introd. to Book II., 1641) that in the work which he owed to the world he must rely not upon "dame Memory and her siren daughters," but upon "devout prayer to that eternal Spirit who can enrich with all utterance and knowledge and send out his seraphim with the hallowed fire of his altar, to touch and purify the lips of whom he pleases."

21. *Dove-like.* "The comparison 'dove-like,' to illustrate the meaning of 'brooding,' occurs in the Talmudists or Jewish commentators on the Bible. There may also be a recollection of *Luke* iii. 22."—*Masson.* "Brooded" is said to be a better translation of the Hebrew word in *Gen.* i, 2, rendered "moved."

Abyss. Chaos, out of a portion of which our universe was formed.

24. *To the highth,* as much as the proposed subject demands or will bear.

25, 26. "As to the *Paradise Lost,* it happens that there is—whether there ought to be or not—a pure golden moral, distinctly announced, separately contemplated, and the very weightiest ever uttered by man or realized by fable. It is a moral rather for the drama of a world than for a human poem."—(De Quincey, in the *Opium-Eater*).

27–33. THE QUESTION

Next to the announcement of the subject and the invocation of the Muse, each of the great epics of antiquity has a question, the answer to which names at once the chief hostile agent and states the motives of the struggles and sufferings to be told. The answer in detail is the whole epic narrative. The introduction of this question, then, is essential to the rhetorical completeness of the poem.

27. *Heaven hides nothing,* etc. See 1 *Cor.* ii, 10; *Ps.* cxxxix. 7, 8.

34–49. THE STATUS

This is another essential part of the epic, which contains in the most general terms a statement of the motives that animate the chief actor in his malignant course.

34. *Serpent.* The first Scriptural designation of the devil as well as Milton's first, and perhaps the most general term that could have been chosen to denote the power of evil. *Rev.* xii. 9.

In the *Iliad,* Apollo is the offended divinity; in the *Odyssey,* Neptune; in the *Æneid,* Juno; and in *Paradise Lost,* Satan, who, as we shall see, is identified with Apollo. This means that the *Iliad* and *Paradise Lost* describe the operation of the same malignant principle.

35. *Envy and revenge.* His hostility was against both man and God (*Rev.* xii. 12, 13).

36. *What time.* Commonly regarded as a Latinism, but found by Professor Cook in the *Ormulum,* and believed by him to be of "Northern origin."

41. *Ambitious.* This word summarizes the motives of Satan. He is the origin and inspiration of all evil, positive and negative, but the mainspring of his deeds and thoughts is the purpose to make himself supreme. He is selfish, but it is not so much possession as rule that he covets.

46. *Ruin and combustion.* These are general terms, fitting their place, for what are further on specified as "sulphurous hail" (171) and "red lightning" (175); ruin (Lat. *ruina,* a precipitate fall) referring to the former, and *combustion* to the latter. The conception originates in *Rev.* viii. 7.

50–191. THE DRAGON BOUND

There was a time at the beginning of this world when there was no evil in the universe, and all things were pronounced "very good" (*Gen.* i. 31). During this period the devils were lying in a state of inertness, destruction, or death upon the burning lake (*Rev.* viii. 9). Their condition was that of the great dragon when he was bound in the bottomless pit (*Rev.* xx. 1–3). The opening scene of the poem shows the place of punishment and the effect of torment upon the Satanic nature, making it more stubborn and vindictive. Prometheus bound in adamantine chains on Mount Caucasus affords a parallel from classic fable, and the defiant speeches of the Titan have a recognized resemblance to those of Satan.

50. *Nine times,* etc. This period is made up of the triumphal sabbath before Creation, the six days, the sabbath after, and the next day, on which the commandment to abstain from the tree of Knowledge was given to Adam. While there was no law, there could be no transgression; "but when the commandment came sin revived" (*Rom.* vii. 9). The doings on earth have instantaneous effect in Hell.

Already the poet introduces us to a series of events in the career of Apollo, with whom St. John identifies Satan (*Rev.* ix.11). The myth of the nine days' and nights' labor of Latona (Αητώ, Death) at the birth of her children, Apollo and Artemis, is here satisfied. When every other place had refused to receive Latona, Delos, which had been floating about in the sea, was moored by Jupiter for this purpose. In like manner Hell had been prepared for the apostates, but would have fled affrighted had not its foundation, at their fall, been fixed too fast and deep (vi. 867–870).

53. *Confounded though immortal.* The confusion is opposed to the immortality and answers to death in spiritual creatures.

57. *Witnessed.* His baleful eyes *showed* his affliction and dismay (*Luke* xvi. 23).

63. *Darkness visible.* Job (x. 22) describes the realm of death as "a land of darkness as darkness itself, without any order, and *where the light is as darkness.*" Gregory the Great, commenting on this passage in Job, says: "Though there the fire gives no light for comfort, yet that it may torment the more, it does give light for a purpose. For the damned shall see by the flame lighting them all their followers along with themselves in torment for the love of whom they transgressed, that . . . the destruction of those very persons may also afflict them for the increase of their own condemnation."

66. *Hope never comes,* etc. Every one is reminded here of the inscription over the gate of Dante's Hell, "All hope abandon, ye who enter here"; but the thought is more fully contained in *Eccl.* ix. 4.

73. *As far removed,* etc. Landor thinks that this "is not very far for crea-
tures who could have measured all that and a much greater distance by a
single act of the will." No matter; that is the distance, on the authority
of *Ps.* ciii. 11, 12, between blessedness and despair.

The remarks of Bishop Newton on these lines have misled many. He
says: "It is observable that Homer makes the seat of Hell as far beneath
the deepest pit of earth as Heaven is above the earth. Virgil makes it
twice as far, and Milton thrice as far, as if the three great poets had
stretched their utmost genius and vied with each other in extending his
idea of Hell farthest." A little reflection will satisfy any one that such
petty artifice by Homer's successors to outrival their master would be
worthy only of contempt, and that Virgil and Milton would have been
the last in the world to be guilty of such irreverence. On the contrary,
they took pains to conform to his ideas while varying from his manner
of expressing them. Each of the poets recognizes below the Empyrean
three regions, one under the other and of equal depth: first, the Earth;
second, Hades; and third, Tartarus. Homer, speaking of the location of
Tartarus, teaches that it extends "as far below Hades as the distance from
heaven to earth" (*Il.* viii. 16). Virgil, measuring from the surface of the
earth, and of course including Hades, says: "Then Tartarus itself sinks
deep down and extends towards the shades twice as far as is the prospect
upward to the ethereal throne of heaven" (*Æn.* vi. 577–579). Milton
confirms both with the statement that the whole distance from Heaven
to Hell is three times as far as from Heaven to Earth.

"Hell appears to be situated beyond the limits of this universe. . . . Nor
are reasons wanting for this locality; for as the place of the damned is the
same as that prepared for the devil and his angels (*Matt.* xxv. 41) in pun-
ishment of their apostasy, which occurred before the Fall of Man, it does
not seem probable that Hell should have been prepared within the lim-
its of this world, in the bowels of the earth on which the curse had not
yet passed. This is said to have been the opinion of Chrysostom, as like-
wise of Luther and some later divines" (Milton: *Chris. Doct.,* xxxiii.).

78. *Weltering,* rolling, especially in blood, in allusion to *Rev.* viii. 8, 9.

80. *Palestine* here has the narrower meaning of Philistia, in one of
the cities of which (Ekron) Beelzebub was specially worshipped (2 *Kings*
i. 3).

81. BEELZEBUB, the god of *Reason,* is distinguished from the other
devils by his superior wisdom. He is also the lunar divinity and con-
nected in the Bible with divination and sorcery (2 *Kings* i. 2, *et seq.; Matt.*
xii. 24–27). Many of his characteristics, as drawn by Milton, are taken
from the Homeric Ulysses, who was a favorite of the goddess Athene
and had his home in Ithaca, an island of the Ionian Sea. The name
Beelzebub, meaning "God of Flies," suggests the mastery of reason over

the fancies that flit through the mind (Compare note on v. 102), and also the mental torment caused by an unruly fancy as figured by the *æstrus*-driven Io, from whom the Ionian Sea was named.

82. SATAN (*Hebr.* Adversary). The name reveals *Self-will* as the core of this leading spirit's character. *Ambition* is his peculiar quality, though he is not specialized like the rest. They are limited each to his particular vice, but Satan is present in all and may do the work of Moloch, Belial, and the others as occasion calls. In his appropriate activity he resembles Apollo and the gods and men whom that deity inspires. He is the solar divinity and bears the name Lucifer in common with the King of Babylon. He enters the haughty spirit of this ruler and many others, and then their acts become his own.

The dialogue that follows has many points of likeness to the one between Prometheus (surnamed Πυρφόρος, Fire-bringer) and Io in the drama of Æschylus. The speeches of Beelzebub contain a weak protest of Reason against the rash ventures of Ambition.

84. *How changed!* Io complains of the terrible distortion of her person and mind (*Prom. Vinct.* 673).

86. *Didst outshine myriads.* Being the lunar divinity, he outshone the rest as the moon does the stars. Professor Cook aptly quotes *Odys.* vi. 107, 108: "High over all she [Artemis] rears her head and brows, and easily may she be known—but all are fair."

93, 94. *He with his thunder,* etc. See note on iv. 928. Compare *Prom. Vinct.* 1080–1085, 992–997.

102. *Durst dislike,* etc. The implication is that even their feelings were not free. In an important sense this was true, but it does not involve the idea of tyranny in Heaven (*Matt.* xxii. 37).

105. *What though,* etc. The *Cambridge* edition on this point is important: "The second edition has at the end of 108 a colon; of 109 a note of interrogation. . . . The line [109] is an interrogation, and Satan asks, 'To retain one's hate, one's courage, etc., is not that to be still unsubdued: in what else but this lies the test of not being overcome?' "

116. *Fate* literally means "that which is spoken." When God declares his will, that is fate. Since God cannot change or repent, it is always true that what he wills is fate (vii. 173). Satan considers fate as something above the will of God, limiting him as Jupiter was supposed to be limited (*Prom. Vinct.* 1053).

126. *Vaunting,* etc., like the King of Assyria (*Isa.* x. 8–14). This throws its light back upon what precedes. Satan did not shake God's throne, or call out Heaven's utmost power, or gain foresight from experience, or even maintain an inflexible will. Yet these are not gross lies; to a narrow vision they might even seem like truths.

127. *Compeer.* The authority for treating Beelzebub as equal with Satan

comes from *Matt.* xii, 26, 27, where the names of the two are used synonymously.

128. *O Prince,* etc. The King of Babylon, bearing in common with Satan the surname Lucifer, was like him in ambition and coveted the title of "king of kings" (*Dan.* ii. 37).

129. *Seraphim.* See note on l. 157.

131. *Endangered.* Nimrod, the first king of Babylon (*Gen.* x. 10), in building the Tower of Babel, tried to usurp the authority of God on earth, and would have succeeded but for miraculous interference from Heaven (*Gen.* xi. 6).

134. *I see and rue,* etc. The prudence of Beelzebub causes him, like his worshippers of Ekron, to cry out the sooner in the presence of calamities (1 *Sam,* v. 10–12).

138. *Gods* is a title which belongs to them of right. "The name of god is not unfrequently ascribed by the will and concession of God the Father even to angels and to men" (*Christ. Doct.* v). In the Bible the evil spirits are sometimes spoken of as "strange gods."

144. *Believe almighty. James* ii. 19. Probably the highest attainment of infernal wisdom.

147. *Strongly to suffer,* etc. Ulysses, "the much-enduring," and Atlas, "the sufferer," this spirit's prototypes, also suffer and are silent.

149. *Mightier service,* etc. Like delinquent debtors, the evil spirits are cast into prison to toil as slaves until the last mite is paid (*Luke* xii. 58, 59).

151. *Heart of Hell,* etc. The lake of Fire in the centre of Hell was the special place of torment which the devils feared when about to be cast out by Jesus (*Matt.* viii. 29). They also feared the "gloomy Deep" (*Luke* viii. 31).

153. *What can it then avail?* Nonentity is better than existence under eternal torment (*Matt.* xxvi. 24).

156. *Speedy words.* Not a meaningless echo of Homer's "winged words." The wisdom and faith of Beelzebub must not be long entertained, or Satan's whole infernal scheme will fall.

157. *Cherub.* "Some of the rabbins tell us that the cherubim are a set of angels who know most, and the seraphim a set of angels who love most."—*Addison*. This statement, though not very precise, will serve to suggest the interior distinction between cherubim and seraphim. The exterior, or physical, distinction corresponds to this; spirits of light and heat being seraphim and spirits of air and water cherubim. Beelzebub is eminently a cherub, because of his wisdom and also because of his association with the moon, which shines only by reflected light and rules the night, the air, and the sea. Satan, on the other hand, is the leader of the seraphim because of his fiery ambition and also because of his association with the sun.

170. *His ministers.* "Bentley points out a contradiction between Satan's apparent assumption on the one hand, that the good angels pursued the bad to the verge of Hell (confirmed by Moloch, Book ii. 78, 79) and the statement by Raphael on the other hand, that all the holy angels stood silent witnesses of the almighty acts of the Messiah in vanquishing, single-handed, his foes (vi. 882, 883). Bentley cites the testimony of Chaos, that Heaven 'poured forth by millions her victorious bands pursuing.'"—*Sprague.* Newton and Sprague have furnished explanations of the apparent inconsistency. The fact is, however, that Milton is only introducing one of those paradoxes so frequently found in the Scriptures. In *Matt.* xiii. 49, 50, it is said that at the judgment the angels shall "sever the wicked from among the just and shall cast them into the furnace of fire." In 2 *Thess.* i. 7, 8, Christ himself is designated as the one who on the same occasion in flaming fire will take vengeance on them that know not God. The true sense is that the angels were active as instruments through the whole struggle; their clear faith enabled them to see Messiah as the real victor who gave his servants strength to overcome, while the devils with dimmer spiritual vision, though they could not fail to recognize his presence, saw prominently the immediate instruments of their defeat. Raphael attributes all success to the Messiah; Satan and his associates divide it between him and his followers. During the Saviour's incarnation the disciples were at first unable to cast out devils, but afterwards succeeded through the name of Christ—evidence that the power lay not with them but with their Lord (*Luke* ix. 38–42).

172. *O'erblown,* etc. Compare *Isa.* xxx. 33.

180. *Yon dreary plain,* etc. The plain of Dura, where Babylon stood, is, in its desolation, typical of Hell, just as the ambitious King of Babylon is sometimes put for Satan. After the Divine curse had fallen upon the land, it was prophetically described as a desolation, a dry land, a wilderness, and a land wherein no man dwelleth. It also became, like this plain of Hell, "a dwelling-place for dragons," "the habitation of devils," etc. (*Jer.* li. 37, 43; *Rev.* xviii. 2).

191. *If not.* Bentley suggests, "if none"; Sprague says, "supply 'any.'"

192–282. THE DRAGON LOOSED

The present scene, based on *Rev.* xx. 3, 7, shows the loosing of Satan, the great dragon, from the chains of his inertness.

195. *Sparkling blazed.* Of the leviathan it is said, "His eyes are like the eyelids of the morning" (*Job* xli. 18). Spenser, describing the old dragon, says (*Faerie Queene,* l. xi. 14):

"His blazing eyes, like two bright shining shields,
Did burn with wrath, and sparkled living fire."

197. *As whom the fables,* etc. The list of gigantic beings to whom Satan is compared contains one Titan, Uranid, or heaven-born (Briareus), one giant or earth-born (Typhon), and one sea-beast (Leviathan). When Satan flies he is the largest creature in the air, like the eagle; when he walks, the largest on the land, like the behemoth; when he floats, the largest in the sea, like the leviathan. These creatures are described in succession in the Book of *Job* (xxxix.–xli.); and Milton, without much doubt, means Job's eagle (the feathers of which are its hundred hands) and behemoth, when he names Briareus and Typhon.

203. *Him haply,* etc. This means that the mysterious monster of which sailors speak is probably the leviathan (*Ps.* civ. 25, 26). Nothing is said or hinted about the whale, as commentators usually assume.

205. *As seamen tell.* The stories of Olaus Magnus are hardly of sufficient standing for even an allusion in this poem. But the experience of St. Paul (*Acts* xxvii. 20 *et seq.*) and the remarkably similar adventures of Ulysses in apparently the same seas (*Odys.* v. 286 *et seq.*), together with suggestions in *Job* xli., are perhaps enough to account for this passage.

296. *Scaly.* Critics generally agree that whales have no scales, and Milton does not say that they have, but the leviathan, which he is describing, has (*Job* xli. 15). The poet follows *Isaiah* (xxvii. 1) in comparing Satan to this sea-beast, who is "king over all the children of pride" (*Job* xli. 34).

210. *Chained.* "We are not told how he loosed himself."—*Keightley.* Compare "ychained in sleep" in the *Hymn on the Nativity,* 156. The chains are stupor and inertia, and it is hardly worth while to look for the pieces after they are broken.

214. *That with,* etc. For similar statements of the Divine purpose see *Exod.* ix. 16; xiv. 4; *Rom.* ix. 15–18.

221. *Pool.* The lake shrinks to a "pool" as the ocean to a stream compared with the bulk of the leviathan (*Job* xli. 30–32).

227. *Felt unusual weight.* Many have recognized the close resemblance of this to *Faerie Queene* I. ix. 18, where the air is "nigh too feeble" to bear the weight of the flying dragon. In *Job* iii. 8, R. V., and xli. 25, the rousing of the leviathan means danger.

230. *Hue.* The color of the burning land is red, like flame or blood, or like the hills of cinders and ashes about the principal cone of Ætna (*Æn.* iii. 571–574). Compare Aceldama, the "field of blood," purchased by Judas Iscariot (*Acts* i. 19).

231. *Transports a hill,* etc. *Rev.* viii. 8; *Jer.* li. 25.

232. *Pelorus.* The name itself (πέλωρος, monstrous, prodigious) is an epithet of the Cyclops, and the whole region about Pelorus and Ætna was the haunt of this monster race.

235. *Sublimed,* used in its etymological sense, "raised aloft."

239. *Scaped,* directly from the Italian *scappare,* does not need the apostrophe.

252. *Possessor.* Judas went "to his own place" (*Acts* i. 25). But the name Hector ("Εκτωρ) also means "possessor," and Satan's fortunes resemble in many respects those of the warlike Trojan.

254. *The mind is its own place,* etc. These lines are always quoted as peculiarly Miltonic rather than diabolic in their sentiment; but no doctrine is taught more consistently in the poem than that disobedience to God causes misery, and that no stoicism can expel from the wicked the inner feeling of wretchedness and despair. The Stoic doctrine, that the wise man is king of circumstances and perfect in himself, is shown by Christ (*Par. Reg.* iv. 300–308) to be the offspring of philosophic pride and delusion.

256. *All but less,* etc. This is interpreted as meaning "nearly equal to." But does Satan think that he "should be," even in the least degree, inferior to the Almighty? Does he not mean that in Hell he retains all that he had in Heaven, except that his inferiority to the Thunderer has been thrown off? In Hell he is first, not second.

261. *And in my choice,* etc. The notorious William Lauder, bent on fixing upon Milton the stigma of plagiarism, turned these lines into Latin about 1750 and falsely represented them as taken from the *Adamus Exul* (1601) of Grotius. Lauder's Latin is as follows:

> "Nam, me judice,
> Regnare dignum est ambitu, etsi in Tartaro;
> Alto praeesse Tartaro siquidem juvat,
> Coelis quam in ipsis servi obire munia."

It is important to be explicit here, for though the forgeries were long since exposed, recent editions of Milton still repeat the error of Bishop Newton in accepting the Latin as a genuine product of Grotius.

272. *Thus answered.* Beelzebub, with all his prudence, is less wise than Gamaliel before the Sanhedrim (*Acts* v. 34 *et seq.*). The latter asserted the folly of fighting against God, and the weakness of any cause not supported by truth.

274. *That voice.* The voice of boasting gained adherents to Theudas and Judas, with whose story Gamaliel pointed his speech. Satan proposes to use the same means to rouse his partisans.

276. *Edge* (Lat. *acies*), the forefront. Here perished the adventurers just referred to. Hector, whose name is synonymous with "boaster" and "blusterer," fought among the foremost of the Trojans (*Il.* vi. 445).

282. *Highth,* an accusative of extent of space.

283–375. COLLECTION OF FORCES

No sooner is Satan released than he goes forth "to deceive the nations" and summon them to battle (*Rev.* xx. 8). His strategy for the purpose consists in boasting, and equals him in this respect with those typical braggarts, Hector and the giant Polyphemus (πολύς+φήμη, much-speaking).

284. *Ethereal temper.* How Hector and Satan came to have divinely wrought armor may be understood from the note on vi. 301.

285. *Behind him cast.* Hector carried his shield on his back when, fearing defeat, he left the field of conflict to solicit the prayers of the women in Troy (*Il.* vi. 116–118). The boaster appears as a coward.

287. *Like the moon.* The shield of Achilles, and hence its double possessed by Hector, was like the moon in splendor (*Il.* xix. 373 *et seq.*).

289. "*The Tuscan artist* is Galileo, who first employed the telescope for astronomical purposes, about 1609; Fesolè is a height close to Florence; Valdarno is the valley of the Arno, in which Florence lies."—*Masson.* Satan is enlarged to the natural eye by his boastful spirit.

292. *His spear,* etc. Hector, whose spear was eleven cubits in length, also used it to lean upon (*Il.* viii. 493–496). Homer compares the spear of Polyphemus to the mast of a ship (*Odys.* ix. 322), Virgil likens it to a pine (*Æn.* iii. 659), while Milton unites both ideas, and at the same time enlarges the conception of the spear as before he did that of the shield. The Greek word δόρυ has the two meanings of "timber for a ship," and also "a spear."

294. *Ammiral,* a flag-ship. Compare this with ii. 636 and 1043, and with *Rev.* viii. 9.

296. *Marle* denotes fertility. Polyphemus lived by Mount Ætna, at the foot of which the soil is very rich. Among our references to this boastful monster it may be well to observe the significant fact that Ulysses escaped from him by pretending to be Nobody (Οὖτις) (*Odys.* ix. 366).

301. *Angel forms.* A reminiscence, perhaps, of the other Cyclopes who inhabited the shore with Polyphemus, huge in stature though less than he.

303. *Vallombrosa (vallis + umbrosa),* shady valley. An earlier name of the whole district in which the Etruscans settled was Umbria, the land of

shade, of which Vallombrosa is part. Milton visited this valley, eighteen miles from Florence, in September, 1638.

304. *Sedge.* The comparison of the apostates to fallen leaves and to sedge tossed by waves and winds gives a hint of the fickleness of such as distrust God and confide in a boaster (*James* i. 6).

305. *Orion.* The mighty Bœotian hunter at his death became a constellation, whose setting in November was attended with storms. He appears in the heavens as a giant *armed* with a sword and a club (*Æn.* iii. 517).—*Clar. Press.*

307. *Busiris,* a mythical king of Egypt who sacrificed strangers, and was slain by Hercules for his cruelty. The individual name is used in a general sense suggestive of the sufferings endured by the Israelites as "strangers in Egypt."

Chivalry. Keightley and others say that the word is here used in the sense of "cavalry"; but the ordinary sense is better, for Pharaoh's host was one of *picked* men (*Exod.* xiv. 7; xv. 4).

314. *Deep . . . resounded.* The voice of Polyphemus was similarly resonant and powerful (*Æn.* iii. 672–674; *Odys.* ix. 395–400).

318. *Have ye chosen,* etc. Freedom is the principal boast of an ambitious spirit, and Satan's call contains the taunt, Are you any longer free or not? Compare 2 *Pet.* ii. 18, 19.

327. *Tread us down . . . transfix.* The punishment inflicted by the Messiah upon his enemies (*Rev.* xix. 15, 21), also the mocking and laughter of Wisdom at those who reject her counsel (*Prov.* i. 26, 27). The same lesson was taught where Minerva transfixed Ajax Oileus (*Æn.* i. 42–45).

332. *As when men,* etc. The fickle multitudes respond promptly to the voice of the boaster.

338. *As when the potent rod,* etc. *Exod.* x. 10–15. The plague of locusts came in response to an extraordinary outburst of insolence on the part of Pharaoh. The locusts of *Rev.* ix. 3 represent the curses that follow contemners of the Divine Law. Like the mythical Nemesis, the curse comes particularly upon boasters.

341. *Warping.* I can see no reason for inventing a new definition for this word, as Keightley does, to meet the present case. The east wind blowing unevenly, stronger in the middle than on the edges, against the side of the cloud of locusts, makes it bend or warp towards the east.

345. *Cope.* The covering, or roof, of Hell is a hollow hemisphere, like our sky.

348. *Sultan.* In Dunbar's *Dance of the Seven Deadly Sins* Mahoun, or Mohammed, is represented as directing the motions of the evil spirits. He is usually understood to be the "false prophet" of the *Apocalypse.* The Sultan is the chief magistrate of Mohammedan countries.

351. *The populous North,* etc. The barbarian nations of the North, supposed to be referred to in prophecy under the names of Gog and Magog, form the armies of the great Enemy of God's people (*Rev.* xx. 8; *Ezek.* xxxviii. and xxxix.). The comparison of their incursions to a flood comes from *Rev.* xvii. 15.

355. *Beneath Gibraltar.* In 429 A.D. the Vandals passed from Spain over into Africa, where the desert sands were a shore to stop the progress of the human flood.

358. *Godlike shapes,* etc. Like the Cyclopes, gathered at the call of Polyphemus (*Æn.* iii. 678–681).

365. *New names.* The Scriptures speak of the idols worshipped by the heathen nations as "devils." St. Augustine says: "The only true religion has alone been able to manifest that the gods of the nations are most impure demons who desire to be thought gods" (*De Civ. Dei,* vii. 33). Milton bridges the chasm between these and our modern notions of angels and devils.

376–521. THE CATALOGUE OF FORCES

Milton, following the example of Homer and Virgil in their catalogues of ships and forces, makes a register of the chief devils. The seven who are distinguished by a separate description represent the "Seven Deadly Sins" so much celebrated in English literature—prominently in Langland, Chaucer, Gower, Dunbar, and Spenser. Compare *Matt.* xii. 45.

376. *Muse.* Both Homer and Virgil have special invocations to the Muse at the beginning of their catalogues of forces.

378. *Emperor.* Of the four designations of Satan within about forty lines *General* and *Emperor* apparently contain allusions to the Roman power, *Sultan* and *Commander* to the Mohammedan.

392. *First* MOLOCH (Heb. *Molech,* king). He is the spirit of the North wind and personifies *Murder* among the deadly sins. As the only divinity among those mentioned whose worship required human sacrifices, he becomes the war-god of the infernal hosts and is identical with the Mars of Olympus. His impetuous and reckless temper would be reason enough for his priority here and in the subsequent council, but he also inspired the first recorded sinful act on earth after the Fall, the murder of Abel.

393. *Parents' tears.* "In peace, children bury their parents; in war, parents bury their children."

394. *Drums and timbrels,* instruments of martial music.

395. *Passed through fire,* etc. Whatever the rite in which he was wor-

shipped may have been, it symbolized passing through the heat of battle to the cold of death.

396–399. The proper names in this sentence are suggestive of war and strife; Rabbath (Contentious), the capital of Ammon, is especially memorable for its sieges and destruction.

403. *Opprobrious hill,* the Mount of Corruption spoken of in 2 *Kings* xxiii. 13, more recently known as the Mount of Offence. The vengeful Moloch made the hill "opprobrious"; the impure Chemosh made it "scandalous"; the proud Astoreth made it "offensive" (*Prov.* viii. 13).

404. *Tophet,* the valley of slaughter" in *Jer.* vii. 32. Aceldama was part of it.

405. *Gehenna,* or the valley of Hinnom, is a deep narrow glen a mile and a half in length to the southwest of Jerusalem. It derived its evil associations from the horrid rites of idolatry there practised in Solomon's time and later, and from its subsequent use as a public burying-ground.

406. CHEMOS personifies *Lust* among the deadly sins. Of the classical divinities he has much in common with Bacchus, whom he resembles in dwelling amidst vineyards, in having his worshippers wear upon their heads crowns like the vine-leaf and ivy crowns of Bacchanalians, and in being honored with the same tumultuous and "lustful orgies." Possibly a tradition about the origin of the Moabites may have aided in giving character to the people and their worship (*Gen.* xix. 30–37).

407–411. The proper names mark out pretty definitely the extent of Moab—the first set from north to south, the second from east to west. They are representative names and are all associated with the worship of Chemosh in prophetic denunciations (*Jer.* xlviii. 32–34).

409. *Seon's realm.* Sihon, king of the Amorites, had conquered the northern portion of Moab, before the Israelites had reached that neighborhood on the way to Canaan.

411. *Asphaltic pool (lacus Asphaltitus).* The Dead Sea with its memorials of Sodom fitly closes this list of places where the god of Lust is worshipped.

417. *Lust hard by fate.* 2 *Sam.* xiii. 15.

419. *Bordering flood,* etc. The Euphrates is so called because it formed the eastern boundary of the Promised Land (*Gen.* xv. 18), as the river of Egypt or Sihor (probably the present Wady-el-Arish) formed the western boundary.

422. *Baalim and Ashtaroth.* These are both plurals, or "general names," and together make up what Scriptural writers call "the host of heaven" (2 *Kings* xxiii. 5, etc.). They are spirits of direct and reflected light, of fixed stars and planets, the former being regarded as masculine, the latter as feminine (viii. 148–150).

429. *Dilated or condensed,* etc. This description applies specifically to

those spirits who are included under the title, "the host of heaven"; they follow the fortunes of those celestial lights with which they are associated. As a mere suggestion, I venture to say that comets are dilatations and eclipses obscurations, and according to the old astrologic faith stellar influence may be either auspicious or malign (*Judg.* v. 20).

435. *Bestial gods.* The constellations into which the stars have been grouped are generally bounded by the outline of some animal.

437. *In troop,* in company without any order, like the stars in the sky.

438. ASTORETH is the Venus of the Romans, and personifies *Pride* among the deadly sins. Her Greek name, Aphrodite (from ἀφρός, foam), is strikingly suggestive of vanity. Her symbol is the planet Venus.

Phœnicians (Φοίνιξ, purple, or crimson). The country and the people have taken their name from the discovery and earliest use of the color which has become the symbol and synonym of pomp and display. The two chief cities of Phœnicia, Tyre and Sidon, are denounced in prophecy for their pride (*Ezek.* xxviii. 17). The daughters of Zion fall under the same condemnation (*Isa.* iii. 16–23).

439. *Queen of Heaven,* etc., *Jer.* xliv. 17, 25. Venus is surnamed Urania, on account of her derivation from Uranus. She is the mistress of Adonis (see Thammuz) and the mother of Cupid (compare the notion of cupidity found in Dagon). The pride of Sidonian Jezebel, the envy of Ahab, his covetousness and theft form a connected series of sins (1 *Kings* xvi. 31; xxi. 2, 4, 16).

444. *Whose heart though large,* etc. With all his wisdom (which fosters humility) Solomon yielded to pride (1 *Kings* iv. 29–34).

446. THAMMUZ *came next.* After pride naturally comes *Envy,* here personified by Thammuz. His symbol is snow, which melts away, as if in tears and sorrow, under the heat that brings joy and life to nature. Thammuz is identified by St. Jerome with Adonis slain by a boar in Lebanon. Lucian tells of the red soil tinging the waters of the river Adonis.

448. *Lament his fate.* This absurd superstition was celebrated about the time of the summer solstice, during the month Thammuz, when the river Adonis was swollen with the melting snow of Lebanon (White Mountain). All the conditions of true sorrow are reversed, and the groundlessness of any real grief appears in the use of the word "supposed." In like manner Spenser's Envy (*Faerie Queene,* I. iv. 30):

> "Inwardly chawed his owne mawe
>   At neibors welth, that made him ever sad;
>   For death it was when any good he saw;
>   And wept, that cause of weeping none he had;
> But when he heard of harme, he wexed wondrous glad."

452. *Wounded,* reminding us of the secret pain ever cherished by Envy (1 *Kings* xxi. 4).

455. *Ezekiel saw.* Referring to the vision of "women weeping for Thammuz" and of the "image of Jealousy" (*Ezek.* viii.). The word here translated Jealousy is often rendered Envy, and the image referred to is thought to be that of Thammuz.

457. *Next came one,* etc. A natural sequel to envy is *Covetousness,* which grasps for itself the good things belonging rightfully to others. This vice is represented by a god of the Philistines, who in the very earliest times are on record for their disregard of the rights of others (*Gen.* xxi. 25; xxvi. 14–21).

462. DAGON (*dag,* a fish). The fish was worshipped as a symbol of fertility, or of the gain accruing from maritime traffic (*Encyc. Brit.* vi. 761). Dagon resembles Triton, a sea-monster, of fish-like form, with a head human except the beast-like teeth, who was noted for his thefts, and had his head cut off on account of them. The sea, which receives all the rivers and yet is not full, is a suitable type of covetousness.

463. *His temple . . . in Azotus.* Azotus, or Ashdod, means *Theft.* Covetousness is the inspiration to theft; theft is a sacrifice to covetousness.

467. *Him followed* RIMMON. When covetousness has been satisfied, *Gluttony* begins (see parable, *Luke* xii. 15–19). Rimmon is mentioned but once in the Scriptures (2 *Kings* v. 18), but his nature is evident from several facts: *First,* the name signifies *pomegranate,* a delicious fruit; and to exalt it into an object of worship is in a very literal sense to make a god of the belly. *Secondly,* the myth of Ceres and Proserpina makes the pomegranate a representative of the fruits of the earth, and Rimmon seems to have been worshipped as a god of agriculture with meat (*i.e.,* fruit) and drink offerings, very much as Ceres was (2 *Kings* xvi. 15). *Thirdly,* Damascus, the seat of Rimmon's worship, lies in a plain of wonderful fertility; but in the days of the disgraceful alliance between Ahaz and Syria, Isaiah foretold a time of great scarcity to the devotees of Rimmon in both countries (*Isa.* xvii. 4–6, 10, 11). A famine upon the worshippers of the god of agriculture would be the fittest kind of retribution.

471. *Leper . . . king.* See 2 *Kings* v. and xvi.

472. *Sottish* implies stupidity, like that which comes from overburdening the system with food and drink.

478. *Osiris, Isis, Orus.* These divinities appear to have exercised special influence over agriculture in the land of the Nile, and are, therefore, of the same class as Rimmon. Their brutish forms suggest that their worshippers have degenerated through gluttony into *Bestiality* (*Exod.* xvi. 3).

481. *Disguised.* Greek tradition represents the gods as having fled from the giants and hidden in Egypt under the form of beasts.

490. BELIAL *came last.* Belial, whose name means "worthless," is the spirit of *Idleness,* the last of the seven deadly sins. There is only one "fleshlier incubus," the unfeeling Asmadai, the spirit of stolid *Indolence* (*Par. Reg.* ii. 150–152). See note on ii. 109.

494. *In temples,* etc. When men appointed to instruct and rule in the church neglect their duties, evils creep in and corrupt. The lack of restraint by proper authority led to the violent acts of Eli's sons (1 *Sam.* ii. 12 *et seq.*).

497. *In courts,* etc. Civil as well as ecclesiastical rulers may be negligent; kings and judges may seek their own ease instead of the establishment of justice and morality. Riot, injury, and outrage then prevail unchecked, chiefly in cities where wealth and luxury remove the necessity for toil. Labor itself is a restraint, but idleness engenders the vices of the sons of Belial.

502. *Flown,* perhaps "set in motion," like a sluggish stream. The usual explanation is "inflated," "flushed."

503. *Sodom.* Idleness is called the sin of Sodom and her daughters (*Ezek.* xvi. 49).

504. *Gibeah.* It is significant that the hospitality was shown by a laboring man (*Judg.* xix. 16), and that the outrage occurred at a time when "there was no king in Israel," but "every man did that which was right in his own eyes."

509. *Gods, yet confessed later,* etc. The function of godhead is creative or causative, and is needed to account for the existence of the world; but the myth-writers represent Heaven and Earth (Uranus and Gæa) as existing before the gods, and producing them instead of being produced by them (*Acts* xvii. 24 *et seq.*).

510. *Titan,* etc. The Titans have the air as their element, and, therefore, I take the word here to mean the primeval water (Oceanus) surrounding the earth in the condition of vapor (*Job* xxxviii. 9). Primeval darkness associated with *Saturn* (Κρόνος, Time) coexisted with this cloud and continued into the first night after the cloud had passed. The darkness was afterwards dispossessed by *Jove,* the god of the sky, or day (*Gen.* i. 1–5). These deities were worshipped at Athens, and impressed their nature upon the character of the people (*Acts* xvii. 16–32).

515. *Ida,* a mountain in Crete (Candia) where Jupiter was born and reared.

516. *Olympus,* a mountain in Thessaly covered with perpetual snow, and fabled to be the residence of the gods.

Middle air, probably the stratum which the clouds frequent. Satan is "prince of the power of the air" (*Eph.* ii. 2). The *Cambridge ed.* has an interesting discussion of this point.

517. *Delphian cliff.* Delphi, with its celebrated oracle of Apollo, was on a steep declivity of Parnassus.

518. *Dodona,* in Epirus, was the seat of a very ancient oracle of Jupiter.

519–520. *Doric land,* Greece; *Adria,* the sea between Greece and Italy; *Hesperian,* Italian, with the significance of "the sunset land."

522–669. THE ARMY OF APOLLYON

The present scene, like some of the preceding, has its origin in the *Apocalypse.* The demon army of the ninth chapter has for its commander Apollyon, the Apollo or sun-god of the Greeks, whom we have already seen identified with Milton's Satan, or Lucifer. In its material aspect the scene consists of a climax whose steps are the degrees of light in a sunrise from the dimmest dawn to the full-orbed day. First, there is a faint and uncertain prophecy (524); then a more decided promise of day (537); then the rosy flush of morning about the horizon (546); then the brightness of the moment before sunrise (564); then the sun itself "shorn of his beams" in the impressive simile of line 594; lastly, the blaze of light at the close of the scene (665). The idea is carried over into the comparisons of the next book (1–5; 488–493), and indeed is never lost sight of throughout the poem.

But, besides, Apollo was the god of fame, poetry, eloquence, music, medicine, number, romance, and augury; all of which, as will appear, enter into this remarkable scene.

524. *Glimpse of joy. Job* xli. 22.

534. *Azazel* is the name of the scape-goat appointed to bear away the sins of God's people into the wilderness (*Lev.* xvi. 10, 21, 22). In Hell he represents *Fame,* the power that commemorates and displays what Heaven would have forgotten, the triumphs of falsehood and wrong. He is tall, indicating his haughtiness; and his standard shows like a meteor, suggesting how short-lived is the glory that he confers. His essence is but the breath that conveys his stories from mouth to mouth, and hence the sounding trumpets and clarions and the banner "streaming to the wind." He is the Æolus (Changeable), the god of the winds, among the infernal spirits.

542. *Shout that tore,* etc. Fame invades the realm of Chaos and Night when the report of evil deeds survives their doers.

545. *Ten thousand banners,* etc. A speedy response comes from all quarters to the example set by Fame. The "orient colors" suggest the poetry, oratory, and rhetoric devoted to the service of this power.

550. *Phalanx.* This allusion to the Spartans and their array in battle has not escaped the notice of commentators. But I am not aware that any one has found a reason for the allusion in the name Lacedæmon (λάκ(κ)ος + δαίμων, deity, or demon of the pit), or Spartan (σπείρω,

to sow; Σπαρτόι, the Sown-men, those who claimed descent from the *Dragon's* teeth sowed by Cadmus).

Dorian, "grave; as the Lydian was soft and the Phrygian sprightly. The Spartans were of Dorian descent."—*Sprague.* Grave notes are suited to the dignity of Fame.

556. *Nor wanting power,* etc. Pæan (Παιάν) was the physician of the gods, and his name has come to mean a triumphal song. "If any one, having sadness in his fresh-grieving mind, suffers, being pained in heart, Song, a Servant of the Muses, may hymn the illustrious deeds of former men and the blessed gods who possess Olympus, and soon he is eased of his uncomfortable thoughts and does not remember any of his cares" (Hesiod, *Theog.* 98–103). Compare I *Sam.* xvi. 14–23; *Il.* v. 899–906.

560–563. Compare the array, the temper, and the condition of the Greek army on the plain of Troy marching to the first of Homer's battles (*Il.* ii. end and iii. beginning).

571. *Their number.* St. John, after giving the sum of Apollyon's army, adds, "And I heard the number of them," as though it had been matter of amazed report (*Rev.* ix. 16).

572. *His heart distends,* etc. Pride was the sin for which David was punished, when, at Satan's instigation, he numbered Israel (1 Chron. xxi.).

575. *That small infantry,* etc. A comparison in Homer's description of the embattled hosts on the plain of Troy (*Il.* iii. 3).

Professor Jebb (*Homer,* p. 16) sums up the following passage: "A large range of literature is laid under contribution—the classical poets, the Arthurian cycle, the Italian romances of chivalry, the French legends of Charlemagne. The lost angels are measured against the Giants, the Greek heroes, the Knights of the Round Table, the champions of the Cross or the Crescent, and the paladins slain at Roncesvalles. Every name is a literary reminiscence." The conclusion is drawn that *Paradise Lost* is a "literary epic" as distinguished from the natural "Homeric epic." This may be, though I cannot help thinking Professor Jebb unfortunate in the selection of his illustration. Romance is consciously and purposely introduced as an element in the thought, like fame, music, and number. May not the dragon's teeth sowed by Cadmus have some important relation to the letters he brought into Greece?

577. *Phlegra* (φλέγω, to burn), the earlier name of the peninsula of Pallene in Thrace, where the giants fought against the gods (*Il.* ii. 781–785).

Heroic race. The heroic age of Hesiod appears to have terminated with the immediate descendants of the Greeks who returned from Troy.

580. *Uther's son.* King Arthur, son of Uther Pendragon, flourished about the beginning of the sixth century. He and his Knights of the Round Table are represented in romance as performing the most impos-

sible feats of strength and daring.

581. *Armoric.* Armorica was the Celtic, or western, part of what is now France.

582. *Baptized or infidel.* "Baptized," usually explained as equivalent to Christian, has rather the meaning of "nominally Christian." Milton's Christianity had no room for the old chivalry with its affairs of honor and deeds of violence.

583. *Aspramont,* in Limburg, Netherlands; *Montalban,* on the borders of Languedoc; *Trebisond,* a city of Cappadocia—all famous in romance for jousting.

585. *Biserta,* a town of Tunis, the ancient Utica.

587. *Fontarabia.* Milton prefers the romantic to the true account of the affair at Roncesvalles, near Fontarabia, 778: "On Charlemagne's return from the conquest of Spain the rear-guard was assailed and cut off by the mountaineers in the pass of Roncesvalles; Roland, their leader, was slain, and the overthrow of the Franks, transformed and wrought up in every possible way, became one of the great themes of song and romance. Charlemagne lived until 814" (*Encyc. Brit.* v. 403).

591. *Stood like a tower.* The conception of the sky as filled with towers in which the stars sit as deities is quite classical. The towered crown of Cybele, mother of the gods, embodies the idea in mythology. This comparison, therefore, prepared the way for the next one.

597. *Disastrous twilight,* etc. In *Isa.* viii. 21, 22, unnatural darkness, suffering, and famine are said to drive the people to curse their king, and consequently to render his throne insecure. There is a tradition through Toland that the world "had like to be eternally deprived of this treasure by the ignorance or malice of the licenser who, among other frivolous exceptions, would needs suppress the whole poem for imaginary treason" in these words.

600. *But his face,* etc. As if to remind us of where we are and to prepare us for a coming change of scene, the poet recurs to features suggestive again of Polyphemus and his monstrous brethren about Mount Ætna. Not far from Ætna with its giant race is Cumæ with its oracle of Apollo. Satan presently undertakes the function of Apollo as the god of augury.

605. *Remorse and passion.* These words imply nothing so divine as pity, but only the guilty feeling that comes from the consciousness of being the cause of others' misery (*Luke* xvi. 27–31).

613. *Oaks, pines.* The Cyclopes, standing about their angry chief, are by Virgil compared to "lofty oaks or cone-bearing cypresses" (*Æn.* iii. 680). The comparison affords Milton an admirable means of transition, for trees are also associated with augury. The oracle of Apollo at Cumæ is established in the neighborhood of a dense forest of pine and oak (*Æn.*

vi. 180). The "singed top" implies loss of intellectual power and prophetic insight (Compare *Rev.* viii. 7; *Jude* 12).

616. *Doubled.* "To double upon" is, in military phrase, to enclose between two fires; the wings move so as to look upon their leader from opposite directions—they double upon him. The figure formed by the troops is semicircular, for the ranks are bent at every point, "from wing to wing."

620. *Tears.* St. Augustine says that the weakness of the gods "is confessed in the story of the Cuman Apollo, who is said to have wept four days during the war with the Achæans and King Aristonicus.... Shortly afterwards it was reported that King Aristonicus was defeated and made a prisoner—a defeat certainly opposed to the will of Apollo; and this he indicated by even shedding tears from his marble image" (*De Civ. Dei* iii. II). See *Hymn on the Nativity,* 195. Compare also the behavior of Ahab (1 *Kings* xxi. 18–29) and of Agamemnon (*Il.* ix. 14–16) under the shadow of adverse fate.

622. *O myriads,* etc. The depression of Agamemnon after being deceived and defeated and the confidence of Hector in opposition to the advice of the prudent Polydamus, the seer (*Il.* xviii. 285–309) are united in this speech.

633. *Emptied Heaven.* All the prophets but one were on the side of Ahab (1. *Kings* xxii. 6–8).

641. *Strength concealed.* Satan before (ll. 92–94) placed it in the thunder (*Hab.* iii. 4). Agamemnon saw the folly of fighting against love, whose might is superior to all other might (*Il.* ix. 18–25).

645. *Our better part,* etc. Ahab tried by disguising himself to escape the doom foretold by Micaiah (1 *Kings* xxii. 30–37). The Greeks having found Jove to be against them in battle, resorted to spies and wiles, so that from this fact the name Δολώνεια has been given to the tenth book of the *Iliad.*

650. *Space may produce,* etc. Satan is a fatalist and does not credit God with the creation of anything either spiritual or material.

651. *Fame. Job* xxviii. 22. There was a similar expectation of Christ, the second Adam, prior to his advent, and in this expectation the pagan world shared.

653. *A generation,* etc. At the entrance to the sanctuary of Apollo at Cumæ there was a representation of the death of Androgeus (Man of the Earth) slain by fire-breathing bulls. This naturally suggests the fall of man through the agency of the devils.

663. *To confirm,* etc. The Trojans noisily applauded Hector (*Il.* xviii. 310) and the prophets Ahab (1 *Kings* xxii. 12) in their defiance of divine auguries.

665. *Cherubim* are cloud spirits and the scene which they help with

their lord to form is like that formed by masses of cloud lighted along their edges by the glory of the sun. They are cherubim (knowing ones) rather than seraphim, probably because the poet designed them to sustain the relation of the false prophets that encouraged Ahab in his impiety. At all events we have here the double climax of the passage, where Satan (Apollo) touches his greatest natural brilliancy as the sun-god and his highest intellectual elevation as an augur forecasting the future.

670–798. THE SPIRITUAL BABYLON

The scene widens from Cumæ, first south to Vesuvius, then north into the Campania, until in the erection of the infernal Capital it reaches Rome. This city was believed by the Reformers to be the Babylon and Egypt of the *Apocalypse* and the seat of Satan or Antichrist on earth. Milton fully accepts the idea, and develops it here and in other parts of the poem. This spiritual Babylon has three leading characteristics exploited by the poet—its devotion to *Wealth,* to *Art,* and to the business of *Government.*

670. *There stood a hill,* etc. This corresponds to Vesuvius, a short distance from Cumæ. Milton went as far south as Naples in 1638.

674. *The work of sulphur.* The combination of sulphur with iron forms iron pyrites, or "fools' gold"—a substance entirely different from "gold tried in the fire" (*James* v. 3).

678. *Cast a rampart.* "Money is a defence" (*Eccl.* vii. 12).

MAMMON (Syriac, *Riches*) is the spirit of *Worldliness* (*Faerie Queene* II. vii. 8) as manifested in the acquisition of material comforts and luxuries to the exclusion of spiritual good. See note on ii. 228.

682. *Pavement,* etc. *Rev.* xxi. 21. "Trodden" added to "gold" indicates its purity, and distinguishes it widely from that hard and brittle counterfeit which is "the work of sulphur." But it indicates also that in Heaven material good is lightly esteemed, as the mere vantage-ground from which to reach for spiritual excellence.

694. *Babel . . . Memphian.* Mulciber, or Vulcan, the architect of Pandemonium, had also, under the name of Serapis (?) a temple at Memphis, and under the name of Belus, or Baal, at Babylon. The temple of Belus is ascribed to Semiramis; that of Ptah (Serapis?) to Menes. "Memphian" suggests the pyramids, and properly enough, for there is an intimate relationship between Vulcan, the god of fire, and the pyramids (see note on ii. 1013).

700. *Nigh on the plain,* etc. The founders symbolize the manufacturing and trading classes in a social state. The plain of Campania well illustrates the processes of industry and the operations of trade. The natural advan-

tages of this garden of Italy, its genial climate, its fertile soil rich in various productions, and its excellent harbors, are a favorite theme with the Latin writers, and elicit from them many an eloquent tribute of admiration.

702. *Sluiced from the lake.* Lake Avernus, in Campania, on account of its noxious exhalations and gloomy surroundings, was fabled by the ancients to be the inlet to the infernal regions. In the course of time M. Vipsanius Agrippa converted the lake into a harbor by opening a communication with the sea and the Lucrine basin. It was thus made to serve the commercial prosperity of the district. Compare *Faerie Queene* II. vii. 17.

704. *Scummed the bullion dross. Faerie Queene* II. vii. 36. A few sentences of Milton's prose will throw light upon the meaning. He speaks of the "alchemy that the pope uses to extract heaps of gold and silver out of the drossy bullion of the people's sins;" and in close proximity: "Believe it, sir, right truly may it be said that Antichrist is Mammon's son. . . . If the splendor of gold and silver begin to lord it once again in the Church of England, we shall see Antichrist shortly wallow here, though his chief kennel be at Rome" (*Ref. in Eng.* ii.). This is the language not of a religious partisan but a stern, impartial censor of morals.

705. *Within the ground,* like Mulciber's house of Ambition (*Faerie Queene* II. vii. 43).

708. *As in an organ,* etc. Possibly to suggest the atmosphere of flattery in which the wealthy and powerful live (1 *Kings* xxii. 13).

711. *Like an exhalation.* The articles formed by Hephæstus (Mulciber) were frequently endowed with automatism. The fleeting nature of riches is involved in the comparison (*Prov.* xxiii. 5).

712. *Symphonies,* etc. Babylon was well provided with music (*Rev.* xviii. 22).

713. *Built like a temple,* etc. With one exception every part of this descriŢtion applies to the Roman *Pantheon,* erected doubtless of the wealth won from commerce and the industries of the Campania. The Pantheon is a *temple,* of a *round* shape, encircled with two rows of *pilasters,* magnificent in its *architrave,* its *cornice,* its *frieze,* its *statuary,* or "bossy sculptures," its roof covered with plates of *gilded bronze.*

714. *Doric pillars.* The Pantheon has Corinthian pillars, but the Doric order is more consistent (see notes on l. 550) and also more suitable for a council-hall. Though Milton used the works of the ancients as models, yet he dared to criticise them.

720. *Belus or Serapis,* Babylonian and Egyptian for Vulcan, the god of fire and art. The image on the plain of Dura seems to have been his, both from the character of the king, his worshipper, and from the punishment appointed for those who refused to worship (*Dan.* iv. 30; iii. 6).

721. *Egypt with Assyria strove.* The rivalry is described in *Ezek.* xxxi.

723. *Stood fixed,* when the whole of *her stately highth* was above ground. The entrance and the interior of the structure now show its likeness to the Pantheon in another series of particulars. The extraordinary *air of majesty* still impresses all who behold the interior of the Pantheon. Its doors are of *bronze.* By far the largest structure of ancient times and having an external diameter of 188 feet, it was celebrated for its *ample spaces,* its wonderful *pavement,* and its *vaulted roof* lined with silver, representing the firmament, but beyond all for its being lighted with *magical* effect directly *from the sky* through a circular opening of twenty-six feet in diameter in the centre of the roof.

729. *Naphtha and asphaltus.* Products of the land of Babylon (*Isa.* xxxiv. 9).

730. *Hasty multitude.* The devotees of ambition are always eager and hurried.

733. *In Heaven,* etc. The temple of the Lord on Mount Moriah, built after the pattern revealed from above (1 *Chron.* xxviii, 11–13) and the "towered structures" of Jerusalem furnish sufficient reasons for declaring art to have originated in Heaven.

739. *Greece . . . Ausonian land.* These lands were supreme in art. Ausonia is the name especially of that part of Italy where art had its highest development.

740. MULCIBER (*mulceo,* to soften), Vulcan, or Hephæstus, the god of fire who became the god of *Art,* because fire is the great agent in reducing and working the metals. Masson and others certainly err in identifying this spirit with Mammon. The two are clearly distinguished in *Faerie Queene* II. vii.

741. *They fabled,* etc. *Il.* i. 591–593. Baal, the Oriental Vulcan, in the contest at Mount Carmel between his priests and the prophet of the true God, to determine who had power over fire, fell "from morning even until noon" and from noon "until the time of the offering of the evening sacrifice." There are indications that this fall occurred on "a summer's day," when, on account of the heat, the false god's power should have been greatest. Vulcan's lameness finds its parallel in the limping of Baal's worshippers (1 *Kings* xviii. 21–29).

746. *Lemnos, the Ægean isle.* Ægean is derived from αἰγίς, or αἴξ, a rushing storm or hurricane. Baal's discomfiture was complete when in the very midst of the dry season, after a drought of three and a half years, the power of God was shown in sending "a great rain" upon the parched earth (1 *Kings* xviii. 45).

747. *Rout.* In allusion to the noises of industrial operations (*Faerie Queene* II. vii. 44).

748. *Nor aught availed,* etc. This recalls the fate of King Uzziah, who, though very active in fortifying his kingdom, and especially the holy city,

was punished with leprosy and expulsion from the sanctuary for an act of daring impiety (2 *Chron.* xxvi. 9–21).

751. *Industrious crew.* Landor censures Milton for using these words in a passion, but the epithet "industrious" properly characterizes the devotees of art.

755. PANDEMONIUM. "Some think Milton the inventor of this word formed on the analogy of Pantheon."—*Masson.* The Pantheon of the Pagan *is* the Pandemonium of the Christian (*Rev.* xviii. 2). The *government* of the spiritual Babylon is a monarchy supported by a peerage of the worst.

759. *They anon.* It is uncertain whether the pronoun refers to the heralds or those who were summoned. Even if the latter, it does not follow that Hell was deserted except in and about Pandemonium. Johnson and Addison speak of the "multitude and rabble" of spirits shrinking themselves into a small compass and of the "vulgar" among them contracting their forms, as though *all* the fallen spirits were admitted to the council. This is certainly a mistake (compare ii. 515–520).

763. *Like a covered field,* etc. Spenser describes such a field (*Faerie Queene* I. v. 5), and also furnishes the hint for the whole parenthesis. Pandemonium is a place where the Christian faith may be defended for amusement and under hostile conditions, and where to win is as fatal as to lose. Spenser speaks at length of such contests with paynims (pagans) under the patronage of "proud Lucifera," by whom he means the Apocalyptic Babylon.

768. *As bees,* etc. Organization under a leader, especially in the work of government, is symbolized by bees (*Il.* ii. 87–97; *Æn.* i. 430, 437). Milton himself has several remarkable utterances bearing on this point: "In your introduction to your discourse of the Pope's supremacy, you say that some divines in the Council of Trent made use of the government that is said to be amongst bees to prove the Pope's supremacy.... 'The bees,' say you, 'are a state, and so natural philosophers call them; they have a king, but a harmless one; he is a leader or captain, rather than a king; he never beats, nor pulls, nor kills his subject bees'" (*Pro Pop. Ang. Def.* ii.).

773. *Straw-built citadel.* In shape the Pantheon closely resembles the ordinary straw-built hive whose inflammability suggests the insecurity of material wealth and glory (*Dan.* iv. 31; *Rev.* xvii. 16).

774. *Expatiate and confer,* etc. The capital of a kingdom is the place from which laws issue and to which their operation is reported.

777. *Behold a wonder!* It was the sight at which St. John "wondered with great admiration" (*Rev.* xvii. 6). The matter of wonder was that the spirits submitted to the reduction. In the Bible, Homer, and Plato the bees are symbolical of nations. Angels, too, represent nations: "It appears also probable that there are certain angels appointed to preside over

ARADISE LOST

nations, kingdoms, and particular districts" (*Christ. Doct.* ix.; *Dan.* x. and xii.). The idea of a tutelary divinity expressing the genius of a nation is very prominent in the classical writings. The spirits summoned by the heralds are such tutelary divinities, and their treatment here sets forth the treatment of nations on earth by some predominant power. The authority assumed by Rome is the diminishing wand which reduces heroic forms to pygmies, the national gods to trickish elves, and bold independencies to degraded apes (*Rev.* xvii. 18).

781. *Indian mount.* Mount Ophir, formerly located in the peninsula of Farther India, is the easternmost point reached by the ships of Solomon (1 *Kings* x. 11, 22). Among the treasures and curiosities brought to the king by this eastern trade were "apes." These were probably the Pygmean race referred to; old superstitions recognized a close affinity between apes and devils; and the degrading image well suits the poet's purpose.

Faery elves. The belief in fairies arose in Europe during the Middle Ages, near the time when the popes began to assume secular as well as spiritual lordship over Christendom. Germany in the person of Henry IV., France in the person of Philip Augustus, and England in the person of John felt the power of the diminishing wand.

784. *The moon,* etc. Referring to the sorceries of the spiritual Babylon (*De Civ. Dei* x. 16; *Rev.* xviii. 23).

787. *Jocund . . . joy and fear.* The princes in pursuit of their pleasures and ambitions did not feel their humiliation. The peasants were glad at the limitation of the secular power, but dreaded the worse forms of priestly tyranny.

795. *Conclave.* These spirits, like the College of Cardinals convened to elect a pope who is to set up and pull down whatever potentate he pleases, represent organized hostility to human as well as divine law, and seem to be treated by St. Jude as a distinct class of devils opposed to the Archangel Michael, the spirit of law and justice. The real as well as the mystical Babylon undertook the humiliation of rulers (*Dan.* iii. 1–7). For the number, "a thousand," see *Dan.* v. 1.

BOOK II

1–505. AN INFERNAL COUNCIL

THE second book of the *Iliad* opens with a council in which the subject of debate—to abandon or continue war—much resembles the question here.

1–4. Commentators have noticed the likeness of this to Ovid's description of the palace of the Sun (*Met.* ii. 1) and to Spenser's of the house of Pride (*Faerie Queene* I. iv. 8). The Sun's palace, the house of Pride, and Pandemonium are properly identical with each other through Satan's identity with Apollo. Antetype of the Pantheon, the spiritual centre of Rome and symbol of her sway over the nations, the infernal capitol has its throne of power adorned with the royal colors, "the gold, the precious stones, and the pearls" with which the great city, the seat of Satan, is decked (*Rev.* xviii. 16).

2. *Ormus . . . Ind.* "The former was noted for its diamond mart, the latter for its diamond mines. An eastern coronation ceremony was the sprinkling of the monarch with gold-dust and seed-pearl."—*Clar. Press.*

7. *Uplifted beyond hope.* Unexpectedly uplifted, for hope has no place in Hell.

11. *Powers and dominions.* Only the dignitaries are addressed. The "warriors" of i. 316 are not present in the assembly.

16. *More glorious.* Color of truth is given to this assertion by the admiration felt for those who exhibit fortitude in suffering.

18. *Just right and fixed laws.* In Heaven these two coincide. Each rules by the free consent of the rest in that wherein he excels. Satan was leader in Heaven because of his superior endowments, the only reason for leadership which is founded in absolute justice. In Hell he finds the firmest title to his throne in the fact that it is unenviable and to be shunned.

29. *Your bulwark,* as Hector of the Trojans (*Il.* xxiv. 729, 730).

37. *More than can be,* etc. The argument is that envy and ambition, to which there is constant inducement, may raise new broils in Heaven,

hence new secessions and expulsions, until there shall not be enough left for successful defence. Had we (the defeated) won we should have been exposed to those rebellions and revolts which must now vex our enemy and divide his forces. But we shall be united by misfortune, while the disintegration of the heavenly kingdom goes on.

43. MOLOCH. See note on i. 392.

44. *Strongest.* After Achilles, Ajax Telamon was the strongest warrior in the Grecian army (*Il.* ii. 768). See note on l. 94.

46–50. Mars threatens to avenge the death of his son, even if he himself falls under Jove's thunderbolt (*Il.* xv. 115–118). This is the spirit of professional warriors.

52, 53. *Those who need,* weaklings; *when they need,* when they are unarmed.

55. *Opprobrious den of shame.* Professional murderers are sensitive about their honor. Moloch works himself into a fury over his disgrace; Mars, wounded by Diomed, shows the same temper (*Il.* v. 872 *et seq.*).

60–69. These vigorous lines are based on *Rev.* ix. 17, 18. Even the thrice-repeated mention of the weapons proposed by Moloch is there suggested. The *"almighty engine"* is apparently *Divine law,* and *"infernal thunder,"* scorn.

73. *If the sleepy drench,* etc. If not more dead than alive; if not spiritless.

75. *In our proper motion,* etc. The murderous Jews claimed to be Abraham's children and entitled by virtue of their birth to a place in the kingdom of God. Jesus rebuked the presumption (*John* viii. 39, 40).

81, 82. *The ascent is easy.* The wicked husbandmen expected to gain the inheritance for themselves by killing the "heir," but the "event" to them was destruction (*Luke* xx. 14, 16). The Jews expected to secure their hierarchy by killing Christ (*John* xi. 50).

90. *Vassals.* Bentley suggests "vessels," as in *Rom.* ix. 22—an absurdity. The word is sufficiently explained by the parable of the husbandmen who rebelled against being slaves or underlings.

94. *What doubt we (Quid dubitamus),* why hesitate we? Commentators have seen in these lines some resemblances to a speech of Ajax (*Il.* xv. 511–513), the Mars of the Grecian forces (*Il.* vii. 208). Ajax resembles Moloch in his superior size and strength, in his mad impetuosity, in his boast of warlike experience (*Il.* xiii. 811), in his gain of new strength from despair (*Il.* xv. 733–741), and in his appeal to the sense of shame and the love of glory among his companions (*Il.* xv. 661).

102. *To alarm,* etc. This savage and truculent spirit is one of those who at Rome give counsel against the kingdom of God on earth. His influence may be seen in the persecutions of Christians under the pagan emperors, in the barbarous cruelties of the Inquisition, in the wars and massacres instigated from the Vatican. Milton, at least, had no doubt as to

the identity of the great city in which "was found the blood of prophets, and of saints, and of all that were slain upon the earth" (*Rev.* xviii. 24).

106. *Frowning,* like Shakespeare's "grim-visaged war" with "his wrinkled front."

107. *Dangerous to less than gods.* Diomed, having wounded Venus and turned upon Apollo, was warned by the latter not to make himself the equal of a god; for "the deathless race of gods is not as those who walk the earth." Disdaining himself to engage a mortal, Apollo called upon Mars, "the slayer of men," to drive Diomed off the field, as though that were a more equal match. Mars, notwithstanding his physical strength, has a mean reputation among the gods.

109. BELIAL (see note on i. 490) is a pseudo Mercury, resembling that god in oratorical skill, in dishonest sophistry, in giving peaceful counsels, and in warning against the wrath of Jove. He has some of the characteristics of Juno, guardian of indolent Argos (ἀεργός), whose obstructive policy against leaders and rulers was exercised sometimes with the aid of Æolus (*Æn.* i. 64 *et seq.*) and sometimes with the help of Venus and Sleep (*Il.* xiv. 188, *et seq.*; *Æn.* iv. 92 *et seq.*). Deceived by this false Mercury in a treacherous dream (*Il.* ii. 6 *et seq.*) and weakened by his tutelary divinity, Agamemnon, king of Argos and commander of the Greeks, manifested his lack of energy in three times proposing to abandon the siege of Troy.

More graceful, etc. War is abhorrent and peace agreeable to our natural feelings.

110. *A fairer person,* etc. Idleness promises well but delays performance, finds plausible excuses for delay, waits for convenient seasons, and lets opportunity pass.

113. *Make the worse,* etc. This, according to Plato, was the charge brought against the Sophists.

115. *To vice industrious. Gen.* xix. 11; 1 *Sam.* ii. 12–17.

120. *Not behind in hate.* That Belial is as cruel as Moloch is shown in the fate of one of his victims (*Judg.* xix. 25–29).

128. *After some dire revenge,* etc. When the Jews manifested similar recklessness in demanding the crucifixion of Christ, Pilate, like Belial, advised against the rashness (*Matt.* xxvii. 24, 25).

131. *On the bordering Deep,* on the borders of Chaos, where it confines with Heaven. The true Mercury describes what is heard in Chaos where it confines with Hell (viii. 240–244).

134. *Scorning surprise.* The kingdom of God on earth is guarded against surprise by prophetic signs that light up the future (*Luke* xxi.). The sons of Belial may be "overcharged with surfeiting and drunkenness" and taken unawares, but not so the faithful servants of the Messiah.

146. *To be no more,* etc. Having shown that effective revenge is imprac-

ticable, Belial considers annihilation. He denies first that it is desirable, next that it is attainable.

148. *Those thoughts,* etc. The supposed "pathos" of this sentiment is much diminished by the character of the thoughts. Belial is a spirit of drunkenness and lust, one of the "filthy dreamers" mentioned by St. Jude—a fool whose eyes [thoughts] "are in the ends of the earth" (*Prov.* xvii. 24). Juno proposes a journey to the "far end of this green earth," to establish household peace between Oceanus and Tethys (*Il.* xiv. 200–205); her fleetness is thus described (*Il.* xv. 80–84):

> "As the thought of man
> Flies rapidly, when, having travelled far,
> He thinks, 'Here would I be, I would be there,'
> And flits from place to place, so swiftly flew
> Imperial Juno to the Olympian mount."

Mercury is also compared for fleetness to the wind (*Il.* xxiv. 342).

156. *Belike through impotence,* as if unable to control himself for passion, like Moloch.

165. *Amain,* with all our might, like the murderer fleeing from the avenger of blood.

171. *Sevenfold* has special application to Moloch. The vengeance that lighted upon the first murderer was to be visited sevenfold upon the second (*Gen.* iv. 15). See note on iv. 76.

174. *Red right hand* (Horace, *Odes* I. ii. 2, *rubente dextera*) suits the idea of avenging murder.

175–178. These *impendent horrors* did fall in due time upon Belial and his followers in his own city of Sodom (*Gen.* xix. 24).

180. *Caught in a fiery tempest,* etc. *Æn.* i. 44, 45.

182. *Sunk under,* etc. Satan as well as Moloch was in favor of war, and his doom is here foreshadowed. He should sink like the sun, but forever, into the western waves.

196. *Better these,* etc. So Juno in her fear counsels submission to Jupiter (*Il.* xv. 104–109).

204. *I laugh,* etc. His laugh is full of satire and bitterness like that of Juno who smiled with her lips while her brow was contracted in anger (*Il.* xv. 101–103).

212. *Not mind us not offending.* The mistake of the slothful servant (*Matt.* xxv. 24–30).

215. *Our purer essence,* etc. Their moral nature as yet remains; but they may either forget their guilt, if not reminded of it, or become hardened to its contemplation, or gradually lose the sense of right and wrong.

216. *Noxious vapor,* the sulphurous fumes, the "smoke of the torment"

of Babylon (*Rev.* xiv. 11).

219. *Void of pain.* Conscience eliminated, environment might become a matter of indifference. The Stoical doctrine is that pain which does not belong to the mind is no evil, and that the wise man will be happy in the midst of torture. Many other sentiments of Belial, particularly those inculcating a negative sort of virtue, resemble maxims of the Stoics, though he was in practice an Epicurean.

224. Professor Sprague aptly quotes from "*Theognis* (of Megara, 583–495 B.C.) 510: Ὡς εὖ μὲν, χαλεπῶς· ὡς χαλεπῶς δὲ, μαλ' εὖ.

227. Mercury with his wand is still accepted as the symbol of peace and commercial prosperity.

228. MAMMON. See note on i 678. He is identical with Jupiter and is called "the god of this world" (2 *Cor.* iv. 4). His special devotee is the aged Nestor who, like his tutelary divinity, overcame Saturn (Κρόνος, Time) in surviving three generations, who dwelt at Pylos in Elis, where at Olympia Jupiter had a famous temple, and who was bent with age as Mammon with his contemplation of the earth.

229. *To disenthrone,* etc. Jupiter dethroned his father Saturn and ruled in his stead. He is not constitutionally averse to war, as is Mercury, or constitutionally dependent upon it, as Mars. Both these divinities are his sons, and he inclines to one or the other as his advantage prompts. He professes to be the dispenser of justice, but justice with him is merely his own honor and advantage.

232. *Fate.* Jupiter professes to personate Fate and Nestor encourages the Greeks with reminders of what is fated (*Il.* ii. 346–353).

235. *What place,* etc. To escape being devoured by Saturn, Jupiter, until he grew strong enough to overpower his crafty sire, was removed from the light of day and concealed "in a sunless cave under the depths of the majestic earth" (Hesiod, *Theogony*). He cannot coexist in any human soul with the world's rightful Ruler (*Matt.* vi. 24).

239. *With what eyes,* etc. The Mammon-worshipper is very sensitive to shame. Compare *Il.* xv. 657–666 and *Luke* xvi. 3.

242. Apollo and the Muses sang at the banquet of Jove, though at the same time the gods were all "inly grieved" at the tyrannical behavior of their ruler (*Il.* i. 568–570, 603, 604).

244. *His altar.* After a new outburst of dictatorial pride, which angered the gods, Jove went to the height of Gargarus, where his "fragrant altar fumed" (*Il.* viii. 48) and sat there "exulting in the fulness of his might." See note on ix. 195.

252. *Seek our own good,* etc. Contrary to the admonition of Christ (*Matt.* vi. 19–34).

263. *How oft,* etc. See *Ps.* xviii. 11–13 and elsewhere. The special propriety of assigning these words to Mammon appears from his aspiring to

be himself the Thunderer. Wielding the thunderbolt was eminently the prerogative of Jove, the god of Elis (*elicere*, to draw down, as lightning from the skies), and Nestor, his worshipper, seems to some extent to have shared it, in pursuing his enemies "like a black tempest" (*Il*. xi. 747).

270. *Imitate.* Salmoneus, a king of Elis, wishing to receive divine honors, imitated the thunder, and was struck by a bolt from Jove for his impiety.

273. *What can Heaven,* etc. Mammon had contemplated material glory until he became blind to spiritual things and even skeptical as to their existence (2 *Cor*. iv. 4).

275. *Become our elements.* This seems an echo of Belial's suggestion (l. 217), but is to be understood in a more gross and bodily sense. Conscience is still active in Belial, but dead or dormant in Mammon.

278. *Sensible of pain.* The devotees of Mammon are extremely sensitive to bodily discomfort. Nestor's sumptuous halls and couches and soft, warm blankets and mantles will not be forgotten by readers of the *Odyssey*.

279. *Settled state.* Peace is the condition of society most conducive to material well-being. Jupiter professes to like Mars least of all the dwellers on Olympus (*Il*. v. 890), but honors Themis (Custom or Precedent) by giving her a place near his throne and taking her counsels.

284. *Such murmur,* etc. Critics cite *Il*. ii. 144, but the true foundation of the passage is in the description of the landing of Æneas and his companions in Queen Dido's realm, or what from a moral point of view is the same—the landing of Ulysses and his men on the island of Circe, the goddess of luxury and pleasure (*Æn*. i. 157–173; *Odys*. x. 87–94). After a night of tempest, Æneas and his followers, at daybreak, when the sea had been calmed by Neptune, came by chance to a "craggy bay," anchored within a grotto, where the waters rose and fell with a soft murmur, "and laid their drenched limbs down to repose upon the shore." The experience of Ulysses and his band in the neighborhood of Circe's isle was much the same, and when they had landed on a like rocky shore they "gave two days and nights to rest."

294. *Sword of Michael.* See note on vi. 44.

296. *Nether empire.* The Babylonian policy is received with favor (*Gen*. xi. 4).

The three spirits, Moloch, Belial, and Mammon, under Latin names, follow each other in the poet's order in the names of the days of the week: Tuesday = *dies Martis;* Wednesday = *dies Mercurii;* Thursday = *dies Jovis.*

The seer of Patmos, standing on the sand of the sea-shore, saw two beasts rising, one out of the sea, the other out of the earth (*Rev*. xiii.), as Moloch and Belial here rise from different sides of the assembly. The first beast was a combination of three strong, fierce, and cruel animals, wore many crowns, had received a deadly wound which was healed, had invincible power in war, spoke boastfully and blasphemously, made war against the saints, and was worshipped by all who were not eminent in faith and patience. The beast resembles in every point the fierce Moloch, the "sceptred king," who was wounded by Gabriel, had spoken blasphemies (vi. 357–362), and was now eager for a renewal of the war. The second beast was like a lamb, spake as a dragon, brought worshippers to the first beast, miraculously drew fire from heaven, and prevented all who had not the mark of the beast from buying and selling. The lamb represents Peace, and its two horns are the two spirits—Belial (idleness) and Mammon (industry). Both give utterance to their hate of the Almighty, and so speak like a dragon; the hate thus kindled leads to war, a worship of Moloch. Mammon is Jupiter who brings down false lightning. True lightning is the scorn of Wisdom towards Folly. Mammon's lightning is the laughter of the world at those who despise its rewards. The latter often deceives men, or, in the language of St. Paul, blinds them (2 *Cor.* iv. 4), as the lightning of Jupiter blinded those whom it struck (*Il.* vi. 139). Peaceful industry, too, supplies the "sinews of war" and thus gives power to the image of the beast. The assumption of control over buying and selling further identifies the second beast as the spirit of avaricious worldliness.

299. BEELZEBUB. See note on i. 81.

300. *With grave aspect.* So Ulysses rose to reprove Agamemnon for proposing to abandon Troy (*Il.* xiv. 82).

302. *A pillar of state.* Ulysses is often characterized by the same epithets—"much-enduring" and "wise-thinking"—that belong to Atlas, "who knows all the depths of the sea, and keeps the long pillars which hold heaven and earth asunder" (*Odys.* i. 52).

303. *Deliberation,* etc. Consult *Il.* iii. 216–219 and *Odys.* x. 373–387 for similar marks in Ulysses.

305. *Majestic though in ruin.* When Ulysses is disguised by Pallas as a beggar, his rags do not hide his nobility, but he impresses men as "Unhappy seemingly, yet like a king in person" (*Odys.* xx. 194).

306. *Atlantean shoulders.* Ulysses is "Less tall than Agamemnon, yet more broad in chest and shoulders" (*Il.* iii. 193, 194).

308. *Still as night.* Pallas commands silence when Ulysses rises to speak (*Il.* ii. 280).

310–315. This admonition resembles that given to Ulysses too well content with the pleasures of Circe's sumptuous couches to depart for Ithaca (*Odys.* x. 472–474) and that given to Æneas in the palaces of Dido, forgetful of his destined Italy (*Æn.* iv. 265–267). Mercury who bears the admonition to Æneas lights on his way on the top of Atlas.

322. *Curb*. See note on iv. 858.

334. *Stripes,* etc. Indifference as well as active hostility is punished (*Luke* xii. 47, 48).

346. *Ancient and prophetic fame.* Compare notes on i. 651 and ii. 831. While yet obedient, Beelzebub possessed that wisdom which rejoiced by anticipation in the works of God before they were made (*Prov.* viii. 22–31; *John* viii. 56).

353. *That shook,* etc. The things shaken are transitory; those that remain firm are permanent (*Heb.* xii. 27). Though earth and heaven pass away, Jehovah's word shall not fail (*Matt.* v. 18).

356. *How endued,* with what faculties of soul or thought.

364. *Either with Hell-fire,* etc. The work of Moloch, actually undertaken in the days before the Flood, when giants filled the earth with violence.

368. *Seduce,* etc. The work of Belial and Mammon, performed when the sons of God took wives of the daughters of men and gave way to luxury (*Gen.* vi.).

378. *Hatching,* etc. The figure seems to be drawn from *Jer.* xvii. ii.

387. *Pleased highly. Il.* ii. 333–335. Mammon's peaceful counsel satisfied a majority, but Beelzebub's ingenious plan provided employment in their respective preferences for all.

391. *Synod and States,* used so near together, imply an assumption of both spiritual and secular authority in this infernal government.

395. *With neighboring arms,* etc. Beelzebub was the god of Ekron on the border of Israel. The chosen people suffered much from the Philistines who, better than any other enemies of Israel, knew their opportunity.

399. *Secure.* Neighborhood to God's people wins some of their blessings and avoids some Divine judgments (*Matt.* xiii. 30; *Gen.* xviii. 23–26).

405. *Abyss.* Chaos, including Hell. Just outside of Hell-gates is a chasm which is bottomless; in length, breadth, and depth the region is infinite.

406. *Palpable obscure,* darkness that may be felt, as in *Exod.* x. 21.

407. *Uncouth way.* It lies through Death's "undiscovered country."

409. *Abrupt.* The whole perpendicular height between the two planes of Heaven and Hell, especially the precipice beyond the chasm outside of Hell-gates.

410. *Isle.* The commentators have had unreasonable trouble with this designation. Newton, Keightley, and others take it to signify "the earth hanging in the sea of air." Masson and Sprague correctly understand it to mean the whole world, or starry universe. But Masson goes too far in saying that the devils fancy it "an azure sphere or round, insulated between Heaven and Chaos." Of such a world they have had no experience; but they know Heaven as a vast continent rising out of the ocean of Chaos (vii. 210), and the World, being smaller in size, is thought of as

an island lying in some neighboring part of the same ocean. The epithet "happy" suggests the Atlantis of political philosophy and table. The conception comes fitly from Beelzebub, chief pillar of the infernal commonwealth and largely identified with the god Atlas from whom Atlantis gets its name.

418. *Suspense,* as in Belshazzar's palace, while the lords were waiting for some wise man to interpret the handwriting on the wall (*Dan.* v. 5–9).

426. *The dreadful voyage.* It was to be through the region of Hades or death. Ulysses and his companions wept and trembled at the prospect when he was called upon to enter the gloomy realm (*Odys.* x. 562–570). Æneas and his followers were chilled with fear under similar conditions (*Æn.* vi. 54, 55). The writing on the wall was a summons to Belshazzar, for on that night he was slain (*Dan.* v. 30).

432. *Long is the way,* etc. *Æn.* vi. 128, 129, 549–554.

438. *Void profound,* the *inane profundum* of Lucretius. This chasm, entirely empty, just outside of Hell-gates, is not the whole of Chaos. See note on l. 918.

441. *Abortive* (*aborior,* opposed to *exorior,* and so used primarily of the heavenly bodies, to set, to disappear). Compare l. 933.

445–456. Sarpedon, king of Lycia (Λύκη, light), where Apollo had an oracle, in like manner recognizes the obligations imposed by sovereignty (*Il.* xii. 310–328).

457. *Terror of Heaven.* Like the slain of Asshur (Assyria, the realm of Babylon) who, when alive, "caused terror in the land of the living" (*Ezek.* xxxii. 22, 23).

464. *Seek deliverance.* Apollo, it was fabled, could restore from the realm of death to the light of day; and he or his priest was invoked for a safe return from Hades (*Odys.* xi. 32; *Æn.* vi. 56; *Alcestis* 29, etc.).

466. *None shall partake.* Turnus, king of the Rutuli, the Virgilian Hector, forbids his followers to attack Pallas, whom he wishes himself to slay (*Æn.* x. 441–444).

474. *Dreaded . . . his voice.* The representative powers were ruled like those of Babylon whose king "made the earth to tremble and did shake kingdoms."

477. *Thunder heard remote;* that is, like the rumble of an earthquake. It was a political earthquake throughout the dependencies when a change occurred in the government of Babylon. When Belshazzar perished the kingdom was divided and new rulers were set up (*Dan.* v. 28–vi. 2).

481. *For the general safety,* etc. This clearly suggests the self-sacrifice of Marcus Curtius and the Decii, who devoted themselves to the infernal gods for the deliverance of Rome. According to Livy (vii. 6) a deep chasm was formed by an earthquake or some other means near the middle of the Forum and could not be filled up, so the soothsayers said,

unless the Romans should devote to it what constituted their principal strength. Curtius interpreted this to mean their arms and courage, and having arrayed himself in full armor, mounted his horse and rode into the gulf.

484. *Specious deeds,* deeds that seem generous and self-sacrificing, but are incited by a selfish love of glory. Virgil testifies that some of the Roman virtues had this origin (*Æn.* vi. 823).

490. *Louring element.* Water as clouds, not the air or sky, as some have thought.

492. *The radiant sun,* etc. However gloomily the day opened it ends in brightness. "Sorrow is turned into joy" before the mighty spirit that leads the fallen hosts (*Job* xli. 22).

497. *Firm concord.* Mark iii. 22–26.

506–628. MEMORIAL GAMES

The memorial games in honor of Patroclus (*Il.* xxiii.) and Anchises (*Æn.* v.) are the originals of these; but here the fallen spirits commemorate their own doom, not the loss of a friend. In each of the three cases, however, the activities immediately precede the departure of a leader— Achilles, Æneas, Satan—into the realm of Hades. The passions, memories, and speculations here indulged give no permanent relief to pain and remorse, but rather intensify them, so that finally not memory but oblivion is coveted. The division of the spirits on the basis of their physical distinctions is a feature of the passage. The scene of action changes from Italy to Greece.

507. *In order,* according to rank or precedence.

508. *Midst came,* etc. Reproduced from Virgil's description of Turnus, an Apollonean chief from Ardea (*ardeo,* to glow, burn) (*Æn.* vii. 783–793).

512. *A globe.* From the description of Turnus. Satan has just been compared to the sun in a clear sky, and the fiery seraphim with "horrent arms" represent the play of light about the grand luminary.

515. *Trumpets' regal sound.* The Latin Senate, after having decided on war, was accustomed to announce it in this way (*Æn.* vii. 611–615).

516. *Cherubim,* spirits of air, by whom tidings are conveyed as in speech.

523. *Disband.* Referring to those who had stood under arms outside of the council-hall during the deliberations. The activities and the scenery now become those of Thessaly and its neighborhood.

528. PART *on the plain,* etc. These are spirits of *Water.* Clouds and mists are the great racers. The order in the next line reverses the order in this.

530. *Olympian games,* etc. The Olympian and Pythian games were celebrated every fifth year—the former at Olympia in Elis, the latter on the Crissean plain, near Delphi. The first name suggests the races in the air; the second those on the ground.

531. PART *curb,* etc. These are spirits of *Fire.* The horses of the sun were Pyroeis, Eous, Æthon, and Phlegon, the significance of whose names is easy to see (Ovid, *Met.* ii. 153, 154). Compare the names of Hector's steeds (*Il.* viii. 185).

Shun the goal. The places where the heavenly bodies rise and set are by Ovid called "goals" (*Met.* iii. 145). In the *Iliad* (xxiii. 327–331) the goal stands

> "An ell above the ground, a sapless post
> Of oak or larch—a wood of slow decay
> By rain, and at its foot on either side
> Lies a white stone; there narrow is the way
> But level is the race-course all around.
> A monument it is of one long dead."

535. *Battle in the clouds.* A prodigy like that which portended the fall of Rome (Virgil, *Georg.* i. 474) and Jerusalem (*Luke* xxi. 5–11).

540. *Rend up both rocks and hills,* etc. This is suggested by the contests of the Lapithæ (Stone-Hurlers?) and the Centaurs (who used pine clubs) in Thessaly. The quoit or discus, or as in the *Iliad* (xxiii. 836–849) the heavy mass of iron was used in human contests instead of the rocks and hills in the games of the gods. In the games established by Achilles, Polypœtes, the Thessalian, son of Pirithous, king of the Lapithæ, won the prize in this contest.

542. *Alcides.* Hercules, the grandson of Alcæus, was returning from the conquest of Eurytus, king of Œchalia in Thessaly, and wishing to offer sacrifice, sent to Ceyx for a splendid robe to wear. Deianira, his wife, desiring to win back her husband's affection, tinged the tunic that was sent him with a philtre furnished by the Centaur Nessus, and unwittingly poisoned Hercules. The effects of Honor and Shame appear to be symbolized in the myth.

545. *Lichas* (Λίχας = λισσός, a steep cliff) was the bearer of the poisoned robe to Hercules. He was changed, through the pity of the gods, into a small island.

547. *A silent valley.* The charming Thessalian vale of Tempe was the first seat of the Muses and of the Pierides who challenged them to a contest of skill in song.

549. *Heroic deeds.* Achilles drew solace from the music of his harp and from singing the deeds of heroes, while his friend Patroclus sat in silence

by him till the song should cease (*Il.* ix. 186–191).

551. *Virtue should enthrall,* etc. Courage and Freedom are the subjects with which the poet Alcæus charms the thronging shades in Hades (Hor. *Odes* II. xiii. 30 *et seq.*).

554. *Suspended Hell.* In the contest of the Pierides with the Muses, at the song of the Pierides the sky became dark and all nature was put out of harmony. But at the song of the Muses the heavens themselves, the stars, the sea and the rivers stood motionless and Helicon swelled up with delight. Those eminent disciples of the Muses, Orpheus and Musæus, produced narrower effects of the same kind in Hell.

557. *On a hill.* The temple of Minerva (the Parthenon) at Athens was on the highest point of the Acropolis, and the colossal statue of the goddess overlooked the whole city. At the festival of this divinity celebrated at Athens only light-producing deities were honored. The most popular ceremony of the festival was the torch-race, which symbolized the diffusion of knowledge. Under the care of the goddess was a building called the Athenæum, where poets, philosophers, and literary men in general were accustomed to assemble and recite their compositions.

559. These are the topics, connected with Death and Immortality, on which in the time of Socrates the so-called philosophers of Athens were teaching their refined speculations. The tragedians, too, taught precepts of moral wisdom on the subjects, "Of fate and chance and change in human life" (*Par. Reg.* iv. 265). To show the vanity of all these high speculations and moral precepts, Socrates, the wisest and most honest man of the time, professed "to know only this, that he knew nothing."

561. *Wandering mazes.* In prehistoric times Athenian youths and maidens were shut into the Cretan labyrinth to be devoured of the Minotaur. The story aptly sets forth the fate of those who attempt a philosophy not of God.

562. *Good and evil,* etc. After the earlier philosophers and sophists came the sects of the Epicureans and Stoics, whose subjects of discussion were precisely those here given.

568. *Hope* based upon changes of fortune was encouraged by Epicureanism.

569. *Stubborn patience* was the aim of Stoicism.

570. *Another* PART. These are the spirits of *Air.* The use of the word "part" marks out three general divisions of the demons on a physical basis of classification. See lines 528, 531.

Squadrons and gross bands. The former implies concert in movement; the latter, absence of concert. "Squadron" was probably suggested by Virgil's *velut agmine facto* (*Æn.* i. 82).

574. *Four ways.* Homer and Hesiod mention four winds—Boreas, Eurus, Notus, and Zephyrus, from the four points of the compass. *Flying*

march expresses the motion of the winds—through the air, but also along the ground.

575–581. *Odys.* x. 513, 514. The four rivers of Hell, whose names the poet translates, signify, respectively, Hate and Sorrow, and their external manifestations, Rage and Lamentation. Christ speaks of Hell as a place where there is wailing and gnashing of teeth (*Luke* xiii. 28), the former caused in the inhabitants by a contemplation of their own loss, the latter by a view of the happiness of the good. The elements of punishment, then, are Sorrow and Hate augmented by personal sympathy with the manifestations of these in others.

583. *Lethe* (Λήθη, Oblivion) sustains in Hell the same relation that Sleep does in our earthly life. The mysterious action of the mind in sleep may have induced the poet to speak of the stream as a "labyrinth." Oblivion is naturally "far off" from pain and passion. Professor Cook remarks that "Plato (*Rep.* 10: 621) is perhaps the first to mention Lethe." If so, we have an explanation of the fact that Milton connects with Lethe certain characteristics that Homer and the myth-makers associate with the "ocean stream."

585. *State and being.* The first of these refers to the environment, the second to the spirit itself. Similarly in the next line, joy and grief are conditions of the soul, pleasure and pain effects of circumstances.

587. FROZEN CONTINENT. This is the land of Despair, the destiny of those who can get no relief from Lethe. It consists of two parts—one terra firma, presenting the ruin of past hopes; the rest a slough of Despond oppressing with fear of the future. It is Hell's borderland, is beaten with the "dire hail" of God's vengeance, and contains very many of the evils enumerated by Virgil (*Æn.* vi. 273–289) as having their place in the "jaws of Orcus." The superior art of Milton, however, is exhibited in avoiding a mere catalogue of personified evils and in showing their forces in operation. Thus instead of a capitalized Hunger, Milton's spirits "starve in ice"; Fear chills and freezes them; the Harpies and Furies become their jailers; Dreams torment them; Medusa guards the water against them; Death defends the gateway; Sin keeps the key.

592. *Serbonian bog.* The bog lies between Damietta (the ancient Pelusium, city of mud) and Mount Casius (a mound of sand). It is "surrounded by knolls of shifting sand, which in high winds was swept into the lake, till the water was hardly distinguishable from the land." "Many of those ignorant of the peculiarity of the region have disappeared [here] with whole armies." (*Diod. Sic.* I. 35).

595. *Burns frore,* etc. This makes it more like the seventh plague of Egypt in which fire was mingled with the hail (*Exod.* ix. 23).

596. *Harpy-footed furies.* The Eumenides, Erinnyes or Furies of the ancients were Alecto (Relentless Hatred), Megæra (Jealousy), and

Tisiphone (Revenge), and they were the special avengers of iniquity. The names of some of the Harpies are Aello (Storm-swift), Ocypete (Swift-flying), Podarge (White-foot), and Celæno (Darkness). Their most important function was to snatch away mortals to the other world, and surrender them to the Furies or bring them to the banks of Oceanus (*Odys.* xx. 66 *et seq.*).

597. *At certain revolutions.* Apparently a partial union of *Rev.* ix. 15 with *Æn.* vi. 745–751. Euphrates is the biblical name of Lethe. Dante connects the two in *Purgatorio* xxxiii. The "revolutions" are perhaps those that mark the hour, the day, the month, and the year of the evangelist. Milton recognizes no purgatorial punishments—only those of Hell.

607. *One small drop.* Such as Dives in torment craved from Lazarus (*Luke* xvi. 24).

611. *Medusa* (μέδομαι, to think on, care for) personifies Care, which, according to Spenser, is an enemy that often troubles sleep (*Faerie Queene* I. i. 40).

614. *Tantalus* (θάλλω, to flourish) is a man *flourishing* and abounding in wealth. Milton seems to identify him with the rich man of the parable. Care is peculiarly the enemy of the rich (*Eccl.* v. 12).

615. *Confused march.* Dreams are a means of punishment (*Job* vii. 12–14). The spirits, though in the neighborhood of Oblivion, did not taste it; like men who sleep but have their repose broken by horrible visions. The "confused march" typifies the incoherency of thought in dreams.

616. *Shuddering horror,* etc. Compare the experience of Eliphaz in a dream (*Job* iv. 14).

621. *Rocks, caves,* etc. These are the haunts of monsters, some of which are specified in l. 628, and a fuller catalogue of which is found in Virgil (*Æn.* vi. 285–289). The Chimæra dwelt on a mountain with a summit of flame, the Hydra in a marsh, the Gorgons on the border of the ocean. Typhon, the sire of some of these, lay in the Serbonian bog; Cerberus, whom Virgil puts in the same neighborhood, in a cave; Scylla on a rock. Burke cites this line as an example of "a very great degree of the sublime, which is raised yet higher by what follows, A UNIVERSE OF DEATH."

624. *Nature breeds perverse,* etc. All this brood is in the vicinity of Lethe and consists of the embodied visions of unhealthy slumber—strange and monstrous combinations, wrought by nature yet most unnatural, grotesque beyond the power of Fancy in her wildest moods to conjure up in waking moments, the essence of unreality in themselves but productive of real terror. The efficiency of dreams as a means of torture is demonstrated in some of Shakespeare's plays.

625. *Prodigious* (*prodigium,* a prodigy), portentous. The prophetic character of dreams as boding good or ill is widely recognized by poets, and

seems to be taken for granted in the Scriptures. An instance may be found in a dream of Pilate's wife before the crucifixion of Christ (*Matt.* xxvii. 19).

629–870. SATAN'S ENCOUNTER WITH DEATH

The foregoing general description of Hell enables us partly to anticipate some of the adventures of Satan in his outward progress. We know that he must traverse the dry land outside of Pandemonium, cross Lethe, and find his way over the "frozen continent."

635. *Sometimes,* etc. Satan exemplifies the crookedness of an evil-doer's way by appearing now on one hand and now on the other; at one moment on the deep, the next in the air.

636–643. This simile contains three prominent thoughts: Satan is compared to a fleet; to a fleet laden with spices; to a fleet moving southward. As the devils are spoken of in the *Apocalypse* under the figure of ships, the comparison is fitly applied to the Fiend when passing over Lethe, the ocean of the lower world. The "spicy drugs" are associated with this crossing of Lethe because of their agency among men in dissipating or inducing sleep, and thereby repelling or inviting oblivion. The motion of the fleet towards the pole indicates the general course of Satan, which is southward until he reaches the World.

637. *Equinoctial winds,* etc. At the autumnal equinox the ocean currents are aided by the northeast monsoons in propelling southern-bound vessels rapidly on their course (*Encyc. Brit.* xii. 822).

638. *From Bengala,* etc. The drug of Bengal is opium; cloves and other spices come from the Moluccas.

642. *Nightly.* Satan's course, like that of the fleet at night, was through darkness.

644. *Hell-bounds . . . roof.* A reason for this peculiar form of expression may be found in the meaning of a few words. One of the commonest names of the world of darkness is Erebus. "Erebus is from ἐρέφω, to cover, and is allied to ὀροφή, a roof" (*Encyc. Brit.* viii. 520). Gog and Magog are scriptural names to designate the enemies of God's people, or the country from which those enemies come. St. Augustine finds these names to mean—"Gog, a roof; Magog, from a roof" (*De Civ. Dei* xx. II).

645. *Thrice threefold the gates,* etc. Compare *Æn.* vi. 549–554. The allegory here becomes too complicated to interpret with any degree of confidence.

650. *One seemed woman,* etc. As sources of suggestions for this description of Sin have been cited Spenser's *Error,* Fletcher's *Hamartia,* Hesiod's *Echidna,* etc. But Sin, as here depicted, is chiefly the strange, flattering,

and foolish woman of *Proverbs* and the "scarlet woman" of *Revelation*. She combines the characteristics of many of the female creations of mythology, but is most like Hecate.

652. *A serpent armed with mortal sting.* Corresponding to the Hydra within the gates of Tartarus (*Æn.* vi. 576). Compare *James* i. 15; I *Cor.* xv. 56.

660. *Scylla* is by her dogs, by her descent from Hecate (according to some accounts), and through her transformation by Circe associated with sorcery, probably with the professional kind which is much less dangerous than that of Sin, the arch-sorceress (*Isa.* lvii. 3, 4).

662. *Night-hag.* The ancient Hecate, the goddess of witchcraft, also named Brimo (βρέμω, to roar) because of her terrific appearance when summoned by magic arts. She was accompanied by a howling pack of infernal dogs with which Milton here equals the whelps of Sin in ugliness. Hecate was the arch-sorceress of the ancients.

664. *Infant blood.* Horace, *Epod.* v.

665. *Laboring moon,* etc. Virgil calls eclipses *lunæ labores.* The sorceress Canidia professes to be able to snatch the moon from the sky with her charms (incantations) (Hor. *Epod.* xvii. 65–69).

666. *The other Shape,* etc. Corresponding to Virgil's impressively vague *Forma tricorporis umbræ* (*Æn.* vi. 289). In this Milton discovered a suggestion of the unique and indescribable power that has its seat under the tiara (triple crown) of the Papacy (see note on x. 294).

673. *Likeness of a kingly crown.* "As it were crowns" (*Rev.* ix. 7). Death is called the "King of Terrors" (*Job* xviii. 14) and rules over transgressors (*Rom.* v. 12–14). Many of his features are taken from the dark-haired ruler of the seas whom Homer constantly speaks of as "King Neptune." "Peoples and multitudes and nations and tongues" are the "waters" over which Death rules (*Rev.* xvii. 15), and it is noticeable that Neptune calms the seas as a man "revered for piety and public services" allays the excited feelings of a mob (*Æn.* i. 148–153). Death uses his mace as Neptune his trident (x. 295) and carries a scourge like the god's (compare x. 311 with *Il.* xiii. 25). The celebrated horses of Neptune (*Il.* xiii. 23; *Æn.* i. 156) correspond to the horses of Death (*Rev.* vi. 2–8; *Par. Lost* x. 590). Neptune also dwells in a shadow (*Il.* xx. 150).

676. *Horrid strides,* etc. Neptune hastening against the Trojans descended from his seat (*Il.* xiii. 17–19)

> "And trod the earth with rapid strides; the hills
> And forests quaked beneath the immortal feet
> Of Neptune as he walked."

681. *Execrable.* Death was the curse denounced against disobedience.

684. *To yonder gates.* In front of Troy Apollo was opposed to Neptune, but agreed with the grim monarch to refrain from an encounter. Afterwards, however, Achilles, son of the marine goddess Thetis, encountered successively two Trojan heroes under the protection of Apollo. Agenor first defied Achilles and threatened him with death, fear-inspiring and terrible as he was (*Il.* xxi. 588, 589). Hector next met the Grecian in his path to the gates of Troy, and was there slain by his pitiless antagonist.

687. *Spirits of Heaven.* Achilles was once deceived into a pursuit of Apollo himself, and was reproved by the god for his folly in attacking an immortal.

689. *Traitor-angel.* Like Achilles (the son of Thetis, or Law), Death pursues men and spirits who have broken faith with Heaven. Neptune reproaches Apollo for assisting the Trojans, whose king, Laomedon, faithlessly withheld from the two deities the promised reward for building the walls of Troy (*Il.* xxi. 450–460).

692, 694. *Third part,* etc. *Rev.* xii. 4; viii. 7–12; xii. 9.

698. *Where I reign,* etc. Neptune manifests like jealousy of trespass upon his realm (*Æn.* i. 138).

701. *Whip of scorpions.* Neptune uses a scourge (*Il.* xiii. 25), and Tisiphone at the gates of Tartarus wields a lash of snakes (*Æn.* vi. 570–572).

708. *Like a comet.* Sickness is the menace of Death. Certain fevers were known to the ancients as πλάνητες πυρετόι—a phrase also perfectly descriptive of comets. Comets seem to have been regarded by former ages as diseased stars, evidences of derangement in nature and precursors of pestilence and war. Compare *Jude* 13.

709. *Ophiuchus* (ὄφις + ἔχειν, serpent-holder), Serpentarius, a northern constellation forty degrees in length, directly over against Scorpio. The serpent-bearer, the son of Apollo, named Æsculapius among men and Pæan among the gods, is the god of Medicine. Hygeia, the goddess of Health, appears with a serpent in her hand. Compare *Numb.* xxi 8, 9; *John* iii. 14, 15.

714. *Two black clouds.* When Apollo descended in anger from Olympus, he came as the night and his arrows rattled upon his shoulders (*Il.* i 46, 47). Apollo and Neptune envelop their favorites, when endangered, in a cloud.

716. *Caspian.* Noted for its tempests, and important here apparently as separating those two barbarian races, Gog and Magog, hostile to each other, but united in enmity to God and his people.

717. *Winds the signal blow.* The trumpet used to call warriors of old to battle, and trumpeters were called Æolides, or sons of Æolus, god of the winds.

721. *Once more,* etc. All commentators refer to 1 *Cor.* xv. 26 and *Heb.* ii. 14. I add *Rev.* xvii. 14.

723. *All Hell had rung,* with joy and wonder at a victory over Death (*Matt.* ix. 26; *Luke* vii. 17).

726. *Outcry.* Wounded Venus shrieked when interposing in behalf of her son Æneas (*Il.* v. 343).

727. *Father . . . son.* The heroes under the inspiration of Apollo have generally each a wife and a son. This is true of Hector, Sarpedon, Æneas, and Hercules. The case of Hector is especially noteworthy. The name of his wife, the "white-armed" Andromache (Fighting with Men) suggests the twofold nature of Sin, while that of his son Astyanax (King of the City) points to the King of Terrors. Strangely enough, Andromache regards Hector as parents, husband, and brother, all in one (*Il.* vi. 429, 430).

741. *Double-formed.* A similar epithet is by Virgil applied to Scylla. It suggests duplicity and falsehood, like the name of Spenser's Duessa.

744. *I know thee not.* When David saw his sin in the parable of Nathan his "anger was greatly kindled," and he did not recognize it as his own (2 *Sam.* xi. xii.). That such blindness is common appears from *Matt.* xxv. 41–46.

749. *At the assembly,* etc. The King of Babylon has a similar experience (*Isa.* xiii. 7, 8). It includes the faintness ("dizzy swum in darkness"), the appearance of flames in the face, and the general amazement of beholders. The flames are the *Shame* which comes from the exposure of sin. Vulcan, the god of Fire, was fabled to have assisted at the birth of Athene (Minerva) from the brain of Jupiter. There is a false as well as a true Wisdom. The origin of Sin from Satan's *left* side is significant.

757. *A goddess armed.* The true Wisdom is armed with a threat; the false with an excuse.

760. *A sign portentous.* When Pallas Athene, like a meteor, lighted on the earth between the Trojans and the Greeks it was taken as a sign of wasting war and stubborn combats (*Il.* iv. 73–84). Her mission on that occasion was one of falsehood and deceit.

762. *With attractive graces,* etc. Pallas in disguise lured Hector to his death at the hand of Achilles (*Il.* xxii. 226–247). The "strange woman" likewise fools the "simple ones" to destruction (*Prov.* vii. 21, 22).

764. *Perfect image.* The devil is "a liar and the father of it," (*John* viii. 44). An image of the pseudo Athene, called the Palladium, was thrown from Heaven and taken up and placed within the walls of "treaty-breaking" Troy. It received the devotion of the Trojans, and often inspired them, but always to their harm. Troy was secure from capture while the image remained within the walls, but it was stolen and carried off by Ulysses and Diomed, the wisest of the Greeks.

770. *Clear victory.* Pallas Athene had the surname of Νίκη, Victory.

784. *Distorted,* etc. According to one of the myths, the transformation of Scylla was wrought in consequence of her intimacy with Neptune.

787. *I fled,* etc. So Amphitrite fled from the embraces of Neptune.

789. *Back resounded Death.* When Patroclus had been slain by Hector and Apollo, Achilles in distraction wept aloud; the maidens whom he had captured in war smote their breasts and swooned; Antilochus mourned; Thetis heard in her cavern the cry of her son and raised a wail of sorrow; the nymphs of ocean in concourse thronged the glimmering cave and moaned responsive (*Il.* xviii. 30–66). The Trojans similarly bewailed Hector.

790. *More . . . with lust,* etc. Milton, like the divines, reckons up in his *Christian Doctrine* four degrees of death: (1) all those evils which it is agreed came into the world immediately after the fall of man; (2) spiritual death, which means a loss of divine grace and innate righteousness; (3) the death of the body; (4) the punishment of the damned. Milton's personification includes all these degrees. In the second sense Death is in harmony with Sin, who thus brings forth "fruit unto death."

799. *Gnaw my bowels,* etc. *Rev.* xvii. 16.

807. *His end with mine involved.* Death came as a punishment for sin; when sin ends, punishment must cease. When Achilles had slain Hector, leader of the "treaty-breaking" Trojans, his own death soon followed—according to some, the next day.

808. *A bitter morsel.* The star called Wormwood represents Sin in the *Apocalypse* (*Rev.* viii. 10, 11). The end of the strange woman is "bitter as wormwood" (*Prov.* v. 4).

814. *None can resist,* etc. The husband of Thetis was fated to beget a son stronger than his sire. Death, like Achilles, represents retribution, and is stronger than Satan, his sire.

817. *Dear daughter.* Thus Jove commonly addresses Athene (*Il.* viii. 39; xxii. 183).

829. *Unfounded* (*fundus,* bottom), bottomless. Though itself unfounded, it is the foundation of the world (*Ps.* xxiv. 2).

831. *Concurring signs.* When Christ, the second Adam, was born there were signs in the heavens leading to a universal expectancy that a new era was about to begin. Chaldæa and Rome, the astrologers of the East and the Sibyl of the West, were predicting the appearance of a new head of the human race, the return of Saturnian times (Virgil's *Pollio*). According to calculations of Kepler, there was a conjunction of at least three planets—Jupiter, Saturn, and Mars—about the time of Christ's birth, as though to set out anew on their course from their original goal. It is a suggestive fact that Milton makes the five speakers in Pandemonium correspond to five of the planets—the Sun (Satan), the

Moon (Beelzebub), Mars (Moloch), Mercury (Belial), and Jupiter (Mammon), who likewise give names to the first five days of the week. Sin (Venus, after whom the sixth day is named) is now before us, and Chaos (Saturn, the planet and god of Saturday) is met with presently. May not these be regarded as the seven kings of *Rev.* xvii. 10, 11, and Death, the beast, making the eighth?

833. *Purlieus,* places for walking, as a garden near a house (*Gen.* iii. 8).

843. *Imbalmed with odors.* As the "strange woman" (*Prov.* vii. 17) and "scarlet woman" (*Rev.* xviii. 13).

846. *Grinned,* etc. Alluding to Cerberus, the fierce watch-dog of Hell, who subsided for Æneas upon being fed with a cake steeped in soporific drugs. The word "maw" used soon after confirms this idea.

850. *Key. Rev.* ix. 1. Hecate, the witch-goddess, is represented with a key (*Encyc. Brit.* xi. 609). The key is knowledge (*Luke* xi. 52).

857. *Thrust me down,* etc. As in the fall of Babylon (*Rev.* xviii. 21).

868. *Gods who live at ease.* θεοὶ ῥεῖα ζώοντες (*Il.* vi. 138). Babylon lived "deliciously" and voluptuously with the kings of the earth (*Rev.* xviii. 7).

869. *At thy right hand.* Compare *Ps.* cxliv. 8 and *Isa.* xliv. 20. The right hand is the place usually assigned to counsellors. Bathsheba, the temptress of David, sat after his death upon the right hand of Solomon and may have had more to do than is commonly supposed with turning the heart of the wise king to folly.

We are prepared, I think, to refer to *Rev.* xvii. as the true origin of this passage. The "scarlet woman" becomes Sin; the beast upon which she sits becomes Death; the seven kings are the seven deities associated with the seven planets, ruling over the days of the week; the ten kings that have power with the beast for one hour each are the ten hours (excluding morning and evening twilight) of the "black and dark night" when the scarlet woman exercises her sorcery (*Prov.* vii. 9). Since the bright hours of day guard the gates of Heaven, there is a fitness—almost a necessity—that the hours of night should be the gate-keepers of Hell. Besides, there is as little doubt that Sin represents the depravity of the spiritual Babylon, or Rome, and her son, "the man of sin," or the Papacy. Milton admitted a "power of the keys" very different from that which was claimed.

871–1055. SATAN IN HADES

Chaos is the Hades of both profane and sacred writers. Satan's journey through it is like those of Ulysses and Æneas through the Underworld. The way is crooked, but its trend is southward and upward to the entrance of the World. The conditions befit a place of uncreated matter and spiritual non-existence.

874. *Portcullis,* a heavy, harrow-like grating made to slide up and down before a castle gate. Spenser speaks of the human lips as a portcullis (*Faerie Queene* II. ix. 24). The gate is also the mouth of Hell.

876. *Could once have moved.* Virgil says that the gates of Hell cannot be broken through by all the force of men or gods, though apparently opened with ease by the guarding Hydra (*Æn.* vi. 552–577).

880. *Recoil.* After long detention in the "iron furnace" of Egypt, the children of Israel were thrust out (*Exod.* xi. 1). The recoil of Hell-gates is like the sudden urgency of the Egyptians after their sullen resistance.

882. *Lowest bottom shook.* The judgment that delivered the Israelites shook Egypt from top to bottom (*Exod.* xi. 5).

884. *Excelled her power.* It is Gabriel, the angel of Divine Wisdom, who closes the gates of Hell (compare iv. 965–967 with *Rev.* xx. 1–3).

885. *A bannered host,* etc. This should, it seems to me, refer to *Rev.* ix. 15–17, which, however, provides only obscurely, or by implication, for the banners and ensigns.

891. *Secrets of the hoary Deep.* The epithet "hoary" (Lat. *canus*) is often applied to foamy waters (see *Job* xli. 32). It belongs with special fitness to those ante-mundane waters which constitute the realm of old Father Time himself (Chaos = Saturn = Κρόνος = Time). Saturn was noted for his secrets and concealments; after his banishment by Jupiter he fled for safety to Latium (*lateo,* to lie concealed). His son, Pluto, who has rule over the shades of the dead, no less jealously guards the secrets of his gloomy realm. When the gods took part in the war before Troy, Pluto leaped from his seat in terror lest the horrible abodes beneath should be laid open to gods and mortals (*Il.* xx. 61–65). Isaiah (xlv. 2, 3) mentions "treasures of darkness and hidden riches of secret places" as lying beyond certain gates of brass and bars of iron. The treasures of Pluto (possibly the same as Plutus) seem to consist in events of the future of which we know not "what a day may bring forth."

892. *Illimitable ocean,* etc. Chaos is the lower of two primal infinities (*Gen.* i, 1, 2). It is bounded above by the Empyrean, and in one small sphere of space and time by our World. In other directions it is "without bound" (circumference) and "without dimension" (diameter).

893. *Length, breadth,* etc. Those who are in Chaos, the region of physical death, know nothing of the things which are the primary conditions of all knowledge. Milton cites Aristotle as saying that those who slept in the temples of the heroes on awaking "imagined that the moment in which they awoke had succeeded without an interval to that in which they fell asleep." "How much more," the poet adds, "must intervening time be annihilated to the departed, so that to them to die and to be with Christ will seem to take place at the same moment" (*Christ. Doct.* xiii.).

895. *Ancestors of nature.* Night and Chaos preceded the Creation and furnished materials for it (*Gen.* i. 2).

898. *Hot, Cold,* etc. Ovid, describing the same primitive Chaos, says: "Cold contended with warm, moist with dry, soft with hard, heavy with light" (*Met.* i. 19, 20). Lucretius also furnishes in the second book of his *De Rerum Natura* many of the features of this Chaos.

901. *Faction . . . clans.* "Faction" emphasizes the repulsions and diversities subsisting among the atoms; "clans," the attractions and kinships.

904. *Barca or Cyrene,* etc. The syrtes or quicksands of the coast and the sand-storms of the interior make this district a fit earthly type of Chaos. The Argonauts were driven on the syrtes after leaving Scylla and Charybdis. Æneas had the same experience.

905. *Poise their lighter wings,* give weight to the winds, which would be lighter without this ballast of sand.

907. *Umpire.* What Chance does not decide, Time, the judge of appeals, will pass upon. Solomon opposes the decisions of time and chance to those of reason and justice (*Eccl.* ix. 11).

910. *Chance.* As Chaos is the Saturn so Chance is the Minos of Milton. In the realm of the dead, where Minos judged, everything was decided by lot.

912. The four elements of ancient physics. Their order, as regards weight, beginning below with the heaviest, is earth, water, air, and fire. Though much intermixed in Chaos, they form recognizable strata in the order of their weight. The lowest stratum is chiefly earth; the second, chiefly water; the third, chiefly air; the fourth, pure air and fire, is the Empyrean and is no part of Chaos.

918. *Brink of Hell.* Since a brink is the margin of a steep descent, it is hard to see how such a thing can be outside of Hell-gates, if with Masson we suppose the gates to be at the zenith of the roof of Hell. But if we put them in the wall, where the gates ought to be, nothing is easier than to conceive of the chasm outside of the threshold. Here begins the "void profound" of Lucretius; here is the "gulf" or chasm (χάσμα) mentioned by St. Luke (xvi. 26) and by Hesiod (*Theog.* 740). Hesiod is very precise: "Neptune has fixed brazen gates, and a wall lies about it [the place where the Titans are punished] on every side. . . . There are the beginnings and ends of all things—of the murky earth and dark Tartarus and the starry heavens—places hard to be passed over and hateful even to the gods—a great chasm. No one in all time would reach a footing unless he were first within the gates, but here and there he would encounter storms upon storms. And gloomy Night stands at the terrible threshold concealed with dark clouds."

922. *Bellona* is the war-goddess and is represented sometimes as the sister and sometimes as the wife of Mars. She has *water* for her element,

while Mars has *air* for his; and her "battering engines" are rain, hail, sleet, and snow. She is outside of Hell-gates, as at Rome her temple was outside of the city walls. Spenser gives the goddess prominence in his cantos on *Mutabilitie.*

924. *Rase some capital city.* The Homeric epithet of Bellona is "city-wasting." The weather ruins the firmest structures of man, but cannot reach Heaven.

925. *Frame of Heaven,* etc. The noise attending the fall of this universal frame into confusion again is much dwelt upon in eschatology (2 *Pet.* iii. 10).

927. *Sail-broad vans,* like the wings of the dragon in *Faerie Queene* I. xi. 10. In this line the *general* description of Chaos ends, and the account of Satan's *particular* adventures begins. It is Milton's custom thus to put the general before the particular.

930. *As in a cloudy chair.* Satan in crossing this chasm has a series of adventures that strongly suggest those of Bellerophon. The Fiend, like the slayer of Bellerus (monster), has just escaped the "beast" called Death. He "spurns the ground" and rides audaciously upon a "cloudy chair," as Bellerophon rode upon Pegasus (Πήγασος, born of Neptune and Medusa near the sources, πηγάι, of the Ocean). He likewise falls from his seat and encounters a "tumultuous cloud instinct with fire and nitre" resembling the fire-breathing Chimæra which Bellerophon overcame. Milton puts the Chimæra in this neighborhood (l. 628), and no more fitting place could be devised for the embodiment of vanity and absurdity than this "vast vacuity." Compare *Job* xxvi. 7.

938. *Aloft.* Observe the direction indicated by "uplifted," "ascending," "aloft."

941. *Treading the crude consistence,* etc. The words now imply horizontal motion. Satan having ascended the first stratum of Chaos now moves along its surface. It is the stratum of *Earth,* the particles of which cohere and form a crude (disorderly) consistence, but the upper side of it blends with the water above it, forming bogs and quicksands.

942. *Oar and sail.* Satan needs both wings and feet in his progress, and, because the stratum through which he moves is a mixture of water and air, the wings serve the purpose of sails set to the air and of oars used in water. He moves *on* one element and *through* two.

943. *As when a gryphon,* etc. Æschylus speaks of "the keen-fanged hounds of Jupiter that never bark, the gryphons, and the cavalry host of one-eyed Arimaspians, who dwell on the banks of the gold-gushing fount, the stream of Pluto" (*Prom. Vinct.* 803–806). The gryphons having lived north of the Arimaspi, the pursuit must have been southward, the direction of Satan's journey.

948. *O'er bog or steep,* etc. The gryphon pursued the one-eyed

Arimaspian as Apollo pursued the one-eyed Cyclops. The Cyclopes, children of Neptune, are without government, subsisting upon human flesh and blood and upon the uncultivated products of the animal and vegetable world. The soil of their land is extremely fertile, nourishing dense and shaggy woods. The straits of Charybdis and Scylla, the bog of Camarine, the height of Etna and the plains of Gela are near by. These features are enumerated in connection with the account of the adventures of Ulysses (*Odys.* ix.) and Æneas (*Æn.* iii.) among the Cyclopes.

951. *A universal hubbub,* etc. Ulysses, after his escape from the Cyclopes, came to another uncultivated land with a city and sent messengers to find out who dwelt there. They found the Læstrigonians (λαός + τρυγάω, harvesters of men; or λαλέω + τρύζω, to talk excessively), a man-eating race, who attacked them with great clamor and destroyed many of them. Their king was named Antiphates (αντίφημι, to speak against; hence *Contradiction.*)

960. CHAOS, the Anarch, is the ancient Saturn (Κρόνος), resembling him in apprehensiveness, anarchical sway, alliance to darkness, propensity to devour his own offspring, and unfriendliness to order and stability. In Homer and Virgil the king of Hades is Aidoneus, or Pluto, the youngest son of Saturn. In Milton, Pluto (Ades) is a subordinate.

Pavilion (*Ps.* xviii. 11) is a shifting or movable dwelling, such as suits the ever-varying moods of Chance and Time.

962. *Sable-vested* NIGHT. Nox (Night), one of the oldest deities, is represented in mythology as covered with a black veil, and sometimes as approaching the earth to extinguish a flaming torch which she carries in her hand. The oldest Night had not a starry crown like the one who holds in the world divided rule with Day, but coexisted with Chaos, unrelieved by sun or starlight (Ovid, *Met.* i. 10, 11). Pluto's consort is Proserpina or Persephone (Light-destroyer).

964. ORCUS (ορκος, an oath), the divinity who punishes the false or perjured. The punishment of celestial perjury consisted in compelling the offending deity to swallow a noxious draught from the Styx, and thereupon lie outstretched for one whole year devoid of sense and motion and deprived of nectar and ambrosia (Hesiod, *Theog.* 783 *et seq.*). In brief, Orcus was the divinity who brought spirits under the dominion of death. The three of the inner circle about the seat of Chaos are distinguished by the powers which they exercised over the dead.

ADES (α + ιδεῖν, not to see) appears to personify the darkness of the grave, and is the divinity who rules the spirits brought by Orcus into the region of the dead.

965. DEMOGORGON. *Faerie Queene* IV. ii. 47. Associated with fate and witchcraft this power is specially invoked in the bringing up of ghosts (1 *Sam.* xxviii. 7–14). The terror of his prerogative is described by Eliphaz

and is manifested by the disciples of Christ (*Job* iv. 13–16; *Matt.* xiv. 26).

970. *I come no spy,* etc. The Sibyl guiding Æneas through the Underworld gives like assurance to the apprehensive Charon, explains the presence of the living man among the shades, shows the golden bough for Proserpina (*Æn.* vi. 399–407), and at last inquires of Musæus the way to Elysium {*Æn.* vi. 669–671).

981. *No mean recompense.* His gift to Proserpina (Night) is the reduction of the *whole World* to Chaos (2 *Pet.* iii. 10–12).

986. *Standard of ancient Night,* the "black flag" under which no quarter is given (*Eccl.* viii. 8).

988. *Anarch old,* etc. Saturn had sway in the first or Golden Age, when every man did as he wished. He is an old and infirm god with a gloomy countenance that has given us the epithet "saturnine." The word "anarch" is supposed to be Milton's own invention.

998. *Frontiers.* The nearness of his pavilion implies the speedy reduction of nature again to confusion—the passing away of the fashion of this world.

1001. *Intestine broils.* The family quarrels in which old Saturn was involved are well known. He made it his rule to devour his male children as soon as they were born, but was outwitted by his wife, who concealed Jupiter, Neptune, and Pluto until they were grown.

1005. *Linked in a golden chain.* Spenser speaks of the virtues as "a golden chayne," and St. Peter enumerates the component links of this chain that binds the World to Heaven. See note on iii. 516.

1009. *Havoc and spoil,* etc. How familiar are the phrases, "the spoils of Time," "the ruins of Time," and the decrepit figure of scythe-bearing Saturn!

1013. *Springs upward.* Note the change of direction at this point.

Like a pyramid of fire. The dissolving forces of Hades have reduced Satan to simple fire, and in the form of the primitive element of fire he rises out of Chaos. "The solid form of the pyramid is the original element and seed of fire" (Plato's *Timæus*). Compare Varro, quoted by St. Augustine, *De Civ. Dei* vi. 5.

1015. *Fighting elements.* In the middle stratum of Chaos the elements of earth, water, and air are contending. The elements of earth and water are destructive to the element of fire in which Satan rose, and would extinguish it, if brought in contact. To avoid these hostile elements was the difficulty.

1018. *Justling rocks.* The Cyaneæ, Symplegades, or Wandering Islands, floated about and sometimes united to crush the ships passing through the Bosporus. The Argo had a narrow escape and lost the extremity of her stern in passing between them. Pindar says that they were alive and moved to and fro more swiftly than the blasts, until, after the passage of the Argo, Fate "rooted them to the deep."

1020. *Charybdis,* etc. Satan's peril was like that of the Argo sailing between the rocks, or like that of Ulysses sailing between rock and whirlpool. The fiery essence was in danger of extinction from the justling atoms of earth and the storm-whirled atoms of water.

The three famous voyages of Jason, Ulysses, and Æneas were conceived on the same plan, had nearly the same adventures and in the same succession. The monsters, tempests, and hardships encountered have an allegorical significance which Milton closely studied and interpreted into the language of Christian symbolism.

1028. *Bridge* is the proper name for the structure considered in its relation to the ocean of Chaos; regarded in itself, it is a "causey" or footwalk (x. 415; *Matt.* vii. 13). The bridge is fastened to Hell at the gates and to the spherical shell of our World at the point farthest to the left.

1034. *Now at last,* etc. Satan has reached the uppermost of the three strata of Chaos, where the element of earth disappears and the element of fire takes its part in the chaotic strife.

Sacred. It is the light of heaven that makes a dawn in this part of space.

1036. *Shoots far,* etc. Suggested by Hecate ('Εκάτη, far-shooting), the name of the moon-goddess in the Underworld (*Æn.* iv. 511). Satan is near the world-ward entrance to Hades, where the way lies under, as it were, a treacherous moonlight (*Æn.* vi. 270). Heaven is presently compared to the moon (l. 1053). A title of the moon-goddess, Trivia, is explained in this region by the fact that it is the point of divergence of the *three roads,* to Heaven, Earth, and Hell (x. 322, 323).

1037. *Nature first begins.* Nature means order, organization, and life. In what sense it begins within the domain of chaos becomes clear when we think of the embryonic state in which living creatures exist before their birth into the World.

1043. *Like a weather-beaten vessel.* Satan is moving along the surface of the middle or watery stratum of Chaos, and, as when he crossed Lethe, he is compared to a ship. He rises at times into the third stratum "resembling air" and has need of wings. The motion is now again in a horizontal direction.

1047. *The empyreal Heaven,* or Heaven in the Empyrean, as distinguished from the intra-mundane heaven, is the place where the holy angels dwell. As the dwelling-place of finite beings it has limits, but the Empyrean, in which it is situated, has not.

1048. *Square or round.* The walls of Heaven are like our own horizon wall. The spontaneous opening and closing of the gates, the blue of the battlements aloft, the paler opal of the towers below and the impossibility of fixing their shape, all establish the fact. We speak indifferently of the "four corners of the earth" and the "circle of the earth" (*Isa.* xi. 12;

xl. 22); our horizon wall adapts itself to either conception. The appearance, however, of the walls from a given point within is always that of a quadrature, or half sphere, of which we are the centre (x. 381).

1052. *World.* Not the earth, as so many have thought, but our whole starry universe.

In bigness, etc. The two worlds are compared, for their relative size, to the largest and the smallest body in our firmament. The question at once occurs, Is Satan still so far from the World that with all its incomprehensible spaces it seems to him only as a point of light! To this question Professor Masson, in a personal letter, replies: "It is not necessary, either for poetical consistency or for the syntax of the passage, to suppose that Milton meant to produce the exact optical effect, as witnessed by Satan himself. . . . This World of ours, in proportion to the Empyrean [Heaven?] from which it hangs is but as "a star of smallest magnitude close by the moon." This idea seems to be confirmed by iii. 422, 423, where Milton, resuming the story, says, 'A *globe* far off it seemed; now seems,'" etc.

BOOK III

1–55. APOSTROPHE TO LIGHT

This passage, though in harmony with the sentiment, is an interruption to the narrative, and is usually censured as an artistic defect. Addison and Masson, however, raise points in Milton's defence; and the lyric beauty of the lines is such that few critics would like to strike them out of the poem. The most serious objection is that the poet intrudes himself and his misfortunes, his transient personal interests, upon the interests of a World and eternity; but perhaps his view of what man is in the estimation of God may have made it seem right for him to do this. It was not a mere accident in God's great plan that John Milton became blind.

1. *Offspring of Heaven,* etc. Light is reverently conceived of either as an attribute of Christ, the first-born of Heaven, or of God in his eternal essence (*Rev.* xxi. 23). In our World light is only the "first of things" (vii. 244), a far lower conception.

7, 8. *Or hear'st thou rather,* a classicism for "Art thou rather called?" Milton's third suggestion, based upon *Job* xxxviii. 19, is that the origin of light is one of God's secrets purposely hidden from human knowledge.

9. *Before the heavens,* the visible intra-mundane heavens (*Gen.* i. 3).

11. *The rising world of waters.* "Rising" means "being created." Until the third day of creation the earth's surface was all of waters.

17. *Other notes,* etc. Whatever this may mean, it is not a pretence to superiority in genius to him "whom universal Nature did lament," only a difference in inspiration, in purpose, and in mood. Neither is it likely that Milton is thinking of the insignificant hymn of about a dozen lines *"In Praise of Night"* (our star-lit Night) attributed to the mythic Orpheus, but rather of the pathetic story of this Tracian singer who sought his wife in the world of shades, "drew iron tears down Pluto's cheek," and led outward to the verge of day "his half-regained Eurydice." Milton's modesty, aside from his claim to supremacy in his subject and his divine guidance, is evident from ix. 41–47.

21. *Thee I revisit safe.* Safe, because at every step he had the guidance of his "celestial patroness" who, as we have seen, directed him by the Word of God.

25, 26. *Drop serene . . . dim suffusion.* "Two phrases from the medical science of Milton's day. *Gutta serena,* literally 'drop serene,' was that form of total blindness which left the eyes perfectly clear, without spot or blemish. Such was Milton's" (see *Sonnet* xxii.).—*Masson.* "Suffusio = cataract."—*Bohn.*

27. *Muses.* He did not disparage classical poetry; to him it was all "sacred," though not equal to that of the Hebrew Scriptures.

30. *Flowery brooks,* Kedron and Siloa. The latter must have had precious memories for the poet as the water in which a blind man, at the command of Jesus, washed and received his sight.

32. *Nightly,* either in his natural or his poetic dreams. Compare vii. 29; ix. 22; and *Job* xxxv. 10.

35. *Thamyris,* a Thracian mentioned by Homer (*Il.* ii. 595), who relates his presumption in challenging the Muses to a contest of song, and his punishment in being deprived by them of sight, voice, and skill in music. He is said to have written on the wars of the Titans with the gods and on the creation of the World.

Mæonides, Homer; so called either from being the son of Mæon, or from being a native of Mæonia, a name of ancient Lydia.—*Clar. Press.*

36. "*Tiresias,* the blind prophet of Thebes, is a great character in the legends and dramas of the Greeks; *Phineus,* a blind king and prophet, is made by some a Thracian, by others an Arcadian."—*Masson.* The Latin *vates* was used to designate both poets and prophets.

38. *Wakeful bird.* Nature's ideal of sweetness in song seems to be realized in the nightingale, which sings in darkness. The ideal bard, as these examples indicate, is made after the same model and shut out from the active world by blindness. Milton seems to have thought himself divinely set apart by unmistakable indications for the task upon which he is engaged. Such a conviction is of itself an inspiration.

44. *Human face divine. Gen.* i, 27.

56–415. A DIVINE CONSULTATION

A council opposed to that of the infernal kakistocracy is now in session. Critics who despise theology find this part of the poem tiresome, but Addison justly remarks: "He [Milton] has represented the abstruse doctrines of predestination, free-will, and grace, as also the great points of incarnation and redemption (which naturally grow up in a poem that treats of the Fall of Man) with great energy of expression, and in a clearer and stronger light than I ever met with in any other writer." The passage now to be considered is in fact compacted of hundreds of scriptural texts, easily discovered with the aid of the *Christian Doctrine* and a *Concordance*. Though the work has been done, these pages must not be cumbered with a multitude of references that would be profitless to most readers.

57. *Pure Empyrean* (ἐμπύριος, in, or on, fire), the highest Heaven where the pure element of fire was supposed to subsist. St. Augustine speaks of that upper fire as "tranquil, pure, harmless, eternal, in contrast with earthly fire which is turbid, smoky, corruptible, and corrupting" (*De Civ. Dei* xxii. 12). This highest Heaven Milton believes to have been in existence long before the Creation of the World, or even that it may have been eternal, though not necessarily so (*Christ. Doct.* vii.).

58. *Above all highth.* We may think of the throne as at the zenith of the Heavenly dome, but the conception dare not be too materialistic.

61. *Stars,* a scriptural designation of the angels (*Job* xxxviii. 7). They receive benediction from God as the planets receive light from the sun.

71. *Coasting.* "Sailing along the coast," seeking a place for attack, as the Spanish Armada sailed along the coast of England.

75. *Without firmament.* There is no transpicuous body of air resting upon the landscape; mists conceal it and storms rage over it.

78, 79. For the manner in which God sees through all time and for a Platonic conception of God's way of speaking, consult St. Augustine (*De Civ. Dei* xi. 21; xvi. 6).

95. *Pledge.* "The tree of knowledge of good and evil was . . . a pledge, as it were, a memorial of obedience" (*Christ. Doct.* x.).

96. *Faithless progeny.* "Even such as were not then born are judged and condemned in them (*Gen.* iii. 16, etc.), so that without doubt they also sinned in them and at the same time with them" (*Christ. Doct.* xi.).

102. For a discussion of God's sovereignty as related to man's freedom see *Christ. Doct.* iii.

108. "Many there be that complain of Providence for suffering Adam to transgress. Foolish tongues! When God gave him reason he gave him freedom to choose, for reason is but choosing; he had else been a mere artificial Adam."—*Areopagitica.*

125. *Till they enthrall themselves.* In the Fall they lost their original freedom, so that reason no longer holds sway (*Rom.* vii. 15).

135. *Ambrosial fragrance.* Fragrance of smell pervades the atmosphere of love and here accompanies the promise of mercy. What an affluence of rich odors—flowers and fruit, incense and spices—there is about the bride and her beloved in Solomon's *Song*! The coming of Raphael, the angel of Love, to Paradise has similar associations (v. 286–294).

136. *Elect,* "in the sense of beloved or excellent" (*Christ. Doct.* ix.).

137. *Sense of new joy,* etc. The rapture of the Bride in the presence of her Beloved.

147. *Innumerable,* not reducible to earthly numbers, or verse.

153–155. The intercession of Abraham for Sodom is the basis of these lines (*Gen.* xviii. 25).

156–166. The intercession of Moses for the Israelites (*Num.* xiv. 12–19) proceeds on the argument that if God's peculiar people are destroyed, the Egyptians will hear of it and rejoice and question the power of God to perform his promises and oaths.

184. *Elect above the rest.* God's calling is either general or special. His special calling is that whereby he, at the time which he thinks proper, invites particular individuals (in preference to others), elect as well as reprobate, more frequently and with a more marked call than others. Abraham, the Israelites, and Paul are given as instances (*Christ. Doct.* xvii.).

195. *Umpire.* Conscience is the moral faculty common to the whole race of men and is to be appealed to in judgment (*Rom.* ii. 14–16).

216. *Charity so dear.* Only divine love could reach so high (*Rom.* v. 7).

218. *Silence was in Heaven.* This suggests *Rev.* viii. 1 to the commentators; and indeed the poet and the seer are apparently describing the same event. In the *Apocalypse* the silence follows the opening of the seals, which may be understood as a disclosure of man's destiny such as has just been made by the Almighty. It precedes the offering of incense upon the golden altar before the throne—an act which Milton connects with the intercession of the Messiah for the penitent of mankind both before and after the Fall (xi. 17–44).

258. *By thee raised.* "Having triumphed over death and laid aside the form of a servant, he was exalted by God the Father to a state of immortality and of the highest glory, partly by his own merits and partly by the gift of the Father" (*Christ. Doct.* xvi.).

303–322. This passage closely follows *Philip.* ii. 6–10, containing the same argument with a few additions from other parts of the Scripture.

322. "This placing Hell in the centre of the earth was probably a slip of memory on the part of Milton."—*Keightley.* The numerous charges of forgetfulness by this commentator convict him of utter ignorance of the poet's mental habits. Milton does not here put Hell in the centre of the earth, and he manifests everywhere a memory, a caution, and a regard for the truth worthy of his transcendent intellect.

353. *Amarant* (ἀμάραντος, unfading). "Pliny asserts of this flower that, though gathered, it keeps its beauty, and even when it has faded, it recovers its beauty by being sprinkled with water."—*Hume.* The amaranth is the emblem of *Humility,* with which those are crowned who possess the kingdom of Heaven (*Matt.* v. 3). As pride precedes and causes destruc-

tion (*Prov.* xvi. 18), so humility brings riches, honor, and life (*Prov.* xxii. 4.). The grace is characteristic of children (*Matt.* xviii. 2–4) and may, therefore, fitly be regarded as the crown of perpetual youth. It is commended by the apostles as an ornament better than braided hair or costly pearls, and of great price in the sight of God (1 *Tim.* ii. 9; ἀμαράντινος, 1 *Pet.* iii. 3, 4).

355. *For man's offence to Heaven removed.* When at the Fall pride took possession of man's natural heart, humility became an exotic.

357. *Shading the Fount of Life.* The Fount of Life is the Redeemer (*John* iv. 10). Here the flower, though elsewhere but an herb, becomes a tree, so far does his humiliation or condescension surpass that of any other, angel or man. The word "shading" delicately suggests the sorrow which his humiliation cost the Son of God.

358. *River of Bliss,* etc. The Elysian flowers are the graces, of which Humility is chief, covered with benediction by Christ's words on the Mount (*Matt.* v. 3–11).

360. *With these,* the Elysian flowers, representing all the spiritual graces.

363. *Sea of jasper,* the same as the "sea of glass mingled with fire" (*Rev.* xv. 2). The most valued jasper, says Dr. Gill, "is green spotted with red or purple." The scene, then, recalls that at the dedication of Solomon's temple, when the glory of Jehovah filled the house and the people bowed themselves upon the pavement and offered sacrifices (2 *Chron.* vii. 1–6). The purple roses are substituted for the bleeding victims and the jasper pavement for the greensward dyed with blood. These "sacrifices of thanksgiving" are the realities corresponding to those grosser sacrifices required in the law of Moses.

365. *Then crowned again.* "Before honor is humility." God gives "grace to the humble."

367. *Like quivers,* because from those harps are drawn the psalms and hymns which may be used against spiritual foes (*Ps.* xlv. 5; *Rev.* xv. 2).

398–402. A similar pæan of victory is found in *Rev.* xv. 1–4.

413–415. *My song . . . my harp.* "These expressions suggest that, though the passage which they conclude may be read as Milton's report of a choral hymn of the angels, Milton himself joins the chorus."—*Masson.* More judicious is the same writer's comment on v. 202–204: "In the Greek choruses, though many are singing, the singular pronoun is used."

416–497. THE LIMBO OF VANITY

The outside of the World is put by the poet to a use that has puzzled commentators and drawn words of severe criticism. Addison, Landor, and others condemn the mixture of allegory and fact, while Masson, who seldom disapproves, speaks of the passage as "extraordinary." But Milton did not invent this Limbo. In the Middle Ages three Limbos were recognized—the *Limbus Patrum,* the *Limbus Infantum,* and the *Limbus Fatuorum.* The senile, the infantile, and the imbecile are outside the borders of the reasonable world; so are the wicked and impenitent. Though Milton did not believe in any intermediate state of activity of the soul as separated from the body between death and the Resurrection, yet he admits the propriety of speaking of the dead as in two distinct spiritual states: "That spiritual state in which the souls as well as the bodies of the arising saints previously [*i.e.,* before the Resurrection] abode might not improperly be called Paradise" (*Christ. Doct.* iii.). We have then two Paradises for the dead—one for the righteous, apparently within Heaven itself; the other, grimly called the Paradise of Fools, on the reverse side of the World in Chaos.

418. *Opacous globe.* The boundary between Chaos and the World and the barrier set by Jehovah to the sea (*Job* xxxviii. II).

420. *Luminous inferior orbs.* "The spheres of the pre-Copernican system."—*Masson.* It would seem just as reasonable to say, The heavenly bodies as we know them.

424. *Dark, waste,* etc. At the entrance to Hades (*Odys.* xi. 14–22) Ulysses found the land and the people of the Cimmerians enveloped

> "In eternal cloud
> And darkness. Never does the glorious sun
> Look on them with his rays, when he goes up
> Into the starry sky, nor when again
> He sinks from heaven to earth. Unwholesome night
> O'erhangs the wretched race."

Critics have recognized the resemblance of this to *Job* iii. 3–9.

429. *Glimmering,* as at the entrance to Virgil's Hades. Old age is the natural entrance to Hades, and hence we find the characteristics of the place corresponding to those attributed by the Preacher to the closing period of life (*Eccl.* xii. 2–6).

431. *Vulture,* in allusion to that which fed upon the liver of Prometheus. The *Imaus* (now Altai) range separated the nomadic from the settled Tartars, and in more ancient times divided Scythia, the country of which Prometheus was king.

434. *Lambs or yeanling kids.* Like the liver of the giant these symbolize the desires and appetites, the springs of movement and action, which fail in age.

437. *Plains of Sericana.* The vast sterile spaces known as the desert of

Cobi symbolize the barrenness in pleasure of unregenerate old age.

439. *Cany wagons.* Recent travellers through this region still mention the light bamboo wagons bearing sails and driven by the wind. Like the grasshopper (*Eccl.* xii. 5) they represent the trifles that are burdensome to the old.

443. *Living or lifeless.* Outside of the sphere of light and reason already wander in their natural lifetime those of whom the aged in their mental imbecility are typical.

448. *All who in vain things,* etc. This account of Limbo has the same relation to the poem as the book of *Ecclesiastes* has to the Bible and the passage in the *Æneid* vi. 268–308 has to that epic. From these two sources have also come most of the suggestions needed by Milton, though he has supplemented them with illustrations of folly found in sacred history and parable and in profane myths.

455. *Unaccomplished works of Nature,* etc. This Limbo at the entrance of Hades, like the land of the Cimmerians around the Palus Mæotis (Μαιῶτις, apparently from μαιεύω), is a sort of borderland to Life receiving its waste and imperfect physical as well as intellectual products. "The rubbish heap of the universe" it has been called.

459. *Not in the neighboring moon.* "Milton here alludes to and corrects Ariosto (*Orlando Furioso* xxxiv. 70) who makes Astolfo ascend, under St. John's guidance, to the moon."—*Clar. Press.* More likely the allusion is to the old astrologic teaching that the moon causes madness and disorders of the brain and reason—a doctrine that has given us such words as lunacy, moonstruck, etc.

461. *Translated saints,* etc. The moon is a fitter symbol of reason than of folly (note on v. 416), and hence may be taken as the Elysium of the wise and just, while its "argent fields" are the meadows of white asphodel, where the faithful rest as in the bosom of Abraham.

466. *Babel.* The object of the builders was human glory (*Gen.* xi. 4; *Luke* xiv. 28–30).

471. *Empedocles* (ἔμπεδος + κλέος, lasting glory), a Sicilian philosopher who flourished B.C. 444. The volcano, by throwing out one of his sandals, revealed the manner of his death. He is typical of the few who brave hardships and death itself for honor among men.

473. *Cleombrotus* (κλέος + ἄμβροτος, glory immortal), an Academic philosopher of Ambracia, in Epirus. After reading the *Phædo* of Plato he killed himself. He typifies those who seek escape from the hardships of life and the fear of death by suicide.

474. *Embryos.* Those who, convinced of the truth of Christianity, are deterred by the fear of man from professing it (*John* xii. 42, 43).

Idiots. In contrast with the embryos, those who having the outward semblance lack the inward knowledge of Christianity (*Rom.* ii. 28, 29).

Eremites. Those who put the light under a bushel (*Matt.* v. 14–16).

Friars. In contrast with the hermits, those whose religion consists in externals, who wear it as a cloak for selfishness.

475. *White, black, and grey.* Carmelites, Dominicans, and Franciscans.

476. *Pilgrims. Luke* xxiv. 5, 25.

479. "Alluding to the old superstition that if a man were buried in a friar's habit he never came into Hell."—*Clar. Press.* Compare *Matt.* xxii. 11–13; *Zech.* xiii. 4.

481–483. Milton uses the language of the Ptolemaic system as modified by Alphonso of Castile in which the Earth was the centre of the Universe, and the ten spheres revolved about the Earth, carrying the heavenly bodies with them. The connection in which this reference stands forbids the belief that the poet meant to give his approval to the correctness of the system.

Planets seven. The seven planetary spheres, beginning with the lowest, were those of the Moon, Mercury, Venus, the Sun, Mars, Jupiter, and Saturn.

The Fixed. The eighth sphere was that of the fixed stars.

482. *Crystalline Sphere.* "To account for the very slow change called the 'precession of the equinoxes,' it had been necessary to imagine a ninth sphere, called the 'Crystalline Sphere,' beyond that of the Fixed Stars; and finally, for further reasons, it had been necessary to suppose all enclosed in a tenth sphere called the 'Primum Mobile,' or 'First Moved.'"—*Masson.*

484. *Saint Peter.* In *Christ. Doct.* xxix., Milton argues at some length that not to Peter exclusively or in a higher sense than to the other apostles were the keys of the Kingdom of Heaven committed, and that therefore the authority derived from him by the Roman pontiffs is without foundation. Fools above all men are those who are so easily deceived in matters of the highest importance (2 *Thess.* ii. 11).

487. *Cross wind,* the whirlwind of judgment which those who sow the wind (vanity) are to reap (*Hos.* viii. 7; *Prov.* xxii. 8).

496. *Few. Matt.* vii. 14; *Æn.* vi. 744. The use of the words "long after" indicates that the "few" especially referred to are such as here and there saw and withstood the stupendous fraud of mediæval ecclesiasticism, the last conspicuous folly on a continental scale.

498–539. THE GATE OF HEAVEN

The gate of Solomon's temple and the gates of the new Jerusalem supply many features of this description. As in them, every feature is the embodiment of some spiritual truth.

505. *Kingly palace-gate.* The gate to the Kingdom of Heaven is Righteousness (*Ps.* cxviii. 19, 20). The temple at Jerusalem was sometimes called a palace (1 *Chron.* xxix. 1, 19), and, built under divine instruction (2 *Chron.* iii. 3), became to men the visible symbol of Heaven.

506. *Diamond and gold.* It is everlasting and incorruptible—thieves cannot break through and rust cannot corrupt. The two pillars at the entrance to Solomon's temple were named Jachin and Boaz—stability and strength.

507. *Sparkling orient gems.* The gates of the new Jerusalem are of pearls (*Rev.* xxi. 21). To those who enter it is like the coming of day, and the Sun of Righteousness arises with healing in his wings (*Mal.* iv. 2).

510. *The stairs were such,* etc. *Gen.* xxviii. 10–22. Jacob named the place where he dreamed Bethel, the house of God, and spoke of it as the gate of Heaven. It is a necessary conclusion that he took the ladder as a stairway leading up to the gate.

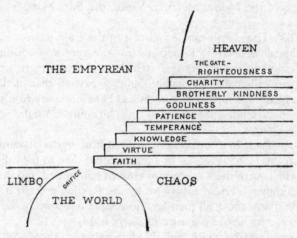

516. *Mysteriously was meant.* The one transcendent mystery of our religion is the incarnation of Christ (*Christ. Doct.* xiv.). The poet probably means that each of the steps implies a virtue found in perfection only in Christ. The chain binding the World to Heaven (ii. 1005, see note) on a nearer approach resolves itself into a stairway, the steps of which are faith, virtue, knowledge, temperance, patience, godliness, brotherly kindness, and charity, and lead by a sure way "into the everlasting kingdom of our Lord and Saviour Jesus Christ" (2 *Pet.* i. 5–12).

518. *A bright sea.* These were the waters under the threshold of Ezekiel's temple (*Ezek.* xlvii. 1–5). The "argument" to this book speaks of them as "the waters above the firmament." They are, therefore, on the border of this World, and to cross them means to go out of the World.

They are thus clearly distinguished as the waters of death.

520. *Sailing arrived.* Most of those who came from earth to Heaven passed through the river of Death, sustained by God's angels in the passage (*Luke* xvi. 22).

522. *Rapt in a chariot.* A few, as Elijah, were translated, borne over the river of Death without touching its waters (2 *Kings* ii. 11, 12).

524. *To aggravate,* etc. The way of righteousness is clearly seen and deliberately rejected (2 *Pet.* ii. 21).

529. *Wider,* etc. The enlargement of the width of the opening beyond the extent of the Promised Land along the whole eastern frontier of which the Jordan (river of Judgment), the conventional emblem of death, flows is probably intended to express symbolically the fact that before Satan entered the World death was not a necessity in passing from Earth to the heavenly Canaan.

539. *Such as bound the ocean wave. Job* xxxviii. 9–20. The continent of Heaven forms its shore and the empyreal air rests upon it.

540–742. TRUTH AND HYPOCRISY

The interior of the World, particularly the Sun, is now described. The light of the Sun typifies Truth, whose effect upon a corrupt spirit is to engender falsehood and hypocrisy. The mysticism is unmistakable.

540. *On the lower stair.* This stair is Faith, which devils have in common with saints; the devils also believe and tremble (*James* ii. 19).

543–553. *As when a scout,* etc. The comparison is an allusion to the adventures of Æneas after his landing near Carthage, city of the Pœni (whence *punica fides, i.e.,* bad faith, treachery). Driven ashore by a dark and perilous storm and having wandered through an uncultivated land, in the morning he ascended a high hill and was affected with wonder at his first view of the rising city with its massive and beautiful structures (*Æn.* i. 419–438). The quality of Satan's faith is thus suggested.

556. *Above the circling canopy.* The conical shadow cast by the opaque earth reaches not near the point whence Satan views the World. Material objects do not interfere with the view from the lofty stand-point of Faith.

557. *From eastern point,* etc. When Satan entered the World Libra was in the east and Aries in the west. According to tradition the World was created in the spring-time; the sun was therefore in Aries (x. 329) and with that constellation beyond the western horizon at Satan's entrance. It follows that the time was soon after sunset.

558. *Fleecy star that bears Andromeda.* When Aries is in the west, Andromeda lies above it. Andromeda (ἀνήρ + μήδεα, Human Care)

represents the anxiety and weariness accumulated during the day and borne away by sleep, typified in the "fleecy star" (compare "dewy-feathered Sleep," *Il Penseroso,* 146). Aries descending in the west takes with it the cares of the day as night comes on inducing sleep. The "Atlantic seas" symbolize the troubled scenes of human life. Doubtless the words also have some reference to the Lamb of God, the bearer of all human sin and care (*John* i. 29; 1 *Pet.* v. 7).

562. *World's first region.* At this hour the zenith was occupied by the Milky Way which marks the path taken by the Fiend. The description of the Milky Way by Ovid (*Met.* i. 167–177) furnishes many of the objects mentioned as lying along Satan's course.

564. *Oblique.* The Galaxy extends transversely across the heavens and furnishes a suitable highway for Satan, who always seeks crooked courses. Ovid declares it to be the way of the gods to the palace of Jupiter.

568. *Hesperian gardens.* The stars are the true Hesperides, or islands of the evening, from which toil and care are absent. Home joys flourish under their genial light.

572. *Likest Heaven.* Because it is a symbol of the Divine Law (*Ps.* xix.) which is an "example and shadow of heavenly things" (*Heb.* viii. 5). The poet seems to have the nineteenth Psalm in mind throughout his whole description of the sun.

574. *But up or down,* etc. The phrase "hard to tell," as well as the various kinds of motion described, points to *Prov.* xxx. 18, 19, which mentions as hard to understand the way of an eagle through the air, the way of a serpent on a rock, and the way of a ship on the sea. The serpent moves by undulations up and down; the eagle flies in a spiral with the sun, sometimes central, sometimes eccentric; the ship moves from side to side to escape the force of adverse winds. Satan's crooked course may have resembled any or all of these (compare ix. 510–518, 631–633).

583. *Magnetic beam.* The attractiveness of the light is matched by that of God's law (*Ps.* xix. 10). There is abundant evidence that the spiritual conception proceeds *pari passu* with the natural.

586. *Shoots invisible virtue,* etc. *Ps.* xix. 6. The classical epithet of the sun-god is Ἕκατος, the far-shooting.

588. *A spot,* etc. Satan seeking information from the angel of the Sun is like the murderous Herod consulting the sacred oracles to find the birthplace of the second Adam (*Matt.* ii. 4–6).

596. *If stone,* etc. Milton combines the stones in Aaron's breastplate with those in the foundation of the New Jerusalem, thus bringing together the beginning and the end of the Divine Word. Carbuncle is mentioned in the first but not in the second; chrysolite in the second but not in the first. These two kinds, red and gold, are pre-eminently the colors of light.

600. *That stone,* etc. The Spirit of the Lord, acting through the Word, converts the soul (*Ps.* xix. 7, 12). The "philosopher's stone" which was to transmute all baser metals into gold was no more eagerly sought by the studious alchemists than a means of restoring the human heart to purity was by the moralists. Gifts, sacrifices, and carnal ordinances were vain to satisfy the conscience (*Heb.* ix. 9, 10).

603. *Bind volatile Hermes.* In physical science this means to solidify quicksilver; in mental science, the power of synthesis.

Call up unbound, etc. "Proteus, in legend the sea-god whom it was almost impossible to fix in his nature or real shape, so many disguises could he assume, stands here for the elementary matter or 'prime substance' of the alchemists."—*Masson.* In mental science this represents the power of analysis. The meaning of the whole is that with all their powers of analysis and synthesis men have failed to devise that which will purify a defiled conscience.

607. *Elixir pure . . . potable gold.* The *elixir vitæ* and the *aurum potabile* were sought after as means to secure perpetual youth and health. The Word of God is a cordial "rejoicing the heart" (*Ps.* xix. 8); it converts the soul (*Ps.* xix. 7), and even in the unfriendly atmosphere of earth produces glorious effects by its wondrous alchemy (*Ps.* xix. 12, 13).

614. *Undazzled,* because he has not the vision to see the truth in its power (*Ps.* cxix. 18; *Job* xxxviii. 15).

616. *As when his beams,* etc. 1 *John* i. 5–7. At the sun the rays are everywhere vertical as they are on the earth's equator at noon. Within the temple of Jove on Mount Lycæus (λύκη, light) no shadows were projected from the bodies of animals. The whole of Peloponnesus might be seen from this mountain (*Pausanias* viii. 28).

620. *Sharpened his visual ray. Ps.* xix. 8.

625. *Tiar,* the crown of oriental kings. Phœbus, the sun-god, has a crown of rays (Ovid, *Met.* ii. 40, 41). "The prudent are crowned with knowledge."

630. *Glad was the spirit,* etc. Truth and hypocrisy meet here as when the wise men from the East met Herod. The cruel king was glad to meet the sages, and deceitfully professed devotion to Christ in order to accomplish his murderous purpose (*Matt.* ii. 1–8).

636. *A stripling cherub,* Cupid in the borrowed form which he often assumed in order to deceive and destroy (*Æn.* i. 670–711). The flowing hair, the coronet, the youth, the grace, the many-colored plumes, all belong to Cupid. Compare *Faerie Queene* II. viii. 5, 6.

645. *Drew not nigh unheard.* Hypocrites are fond of proclaiming their zeal (*Matt.* vi. 2).

648. URIEL (God's Light) is prominent as an archangel in 2 *Esdras.* In the natural world he is the angel of *Light;* in the moral world, the angel

of *Truth*. Of the angels Milton says (*Christ. Doct.* ix.): "Seven of these in particular are described as traversing the earth in the execution of their ministry. *Zech.* iv. 10, 'those seven are the eyes of Jehovah which run to and fro through the whole earth.' *Rev.* v. 6, 'which are the seven Spirits of God sent forth into all the earth.' See also i. 4 and iv. 5."

657. *Interpreter.* The light enables men to see the works which declare the glory of God. The sun is therefore the chief interpreter (*Ps.* xix. 1–4).

658. *All his Sons attend.* When the light of God's truth comes among men, few heed its message; in Heaven all obey gladly—witness the joy at the first dawn of Creation (*Job* xxxviii. 7, 24).

666. *From quires of Cherubim.* As a lover of wisdom this was his proper resort.

667. *Brightest Seraph.* The designation of Uriel, though some question it, is exact. As an angel of light he is a Seraph; as the angel of the chief orb of light he is the brightest of his class; and because his orb is the ruler of the day, by divine appointment (*Gen.* i. 16) he is an archangel.

671. *That I may find him,* etc. The pretence of Herod by which the Magi were temporarily deceived.

686. *Suspicion sleeps,* etc. Suspicion (Subtilty, *Prov.* i. 4) is the Argus set as a watch-dog at the gate of Wisdom's house (see *Odys.* xvii. 292). The original hundred-eyed Argus (surnamed Panoptes, All-seeing) was lulled to sleep, it is said, by Mercury with the music of his flute.

697. *Merits praise.* The Queen of Sheba is praised (*Matt.* xii. 42) for having come in person, not satisfied with report, to hear the wisdom of Solomon.

709. *Came to a heap.* A heap in Scripture means a ruin (*Isa.* xxv. 2). It stands as an intermediate step between Chaos and order. It is the material collected for the building.

711. *Infinitude confined.* When the Almighty "set a compass on the face of the depth" (*Prov.* viii. 27).

712. *Second bidding.* The first brought Silence, the second Light. In the spiritual sense the first is necessary to the second.

716. *Quintessence.* "Aristotle supposed besides the four elements a fifth essence out of which the ethereal bodies were formed, and of which the motion was orbicular."—*Clar. Press.* This quintessence is *Light* (vii. 244).

721. *The rest,* etc. The materials not needed for the interior were made into a wall to protect the treasures of Creation.

726. *Moon.* Uriel fully describes the manner in which the World is lighted—information of the first importance to this spirit of spoliation and murder.

734. *Those lofty shades,* etc. Like Hezekiah showing his treasures to the emissaries of Babylon (*Isa.* xxxix. 2). Uriel exposes to the covetous spirit

the most precious things within his charge. The shades were intended for secrecy and careful concealment.

736. *Bowing low.* Satan for once does reverence to Truth. Uriel is accustomed to such honor in Heaven, where all respect the truth and act in accordance with it. Nothing is here which ought to shock even M. Taine's democratic soul.

742. *Niphates* (Νιφάτης, quasi Νιφετώδης, snowy), now Nimroud Tagh, is a lofty mountain range in Armenia and the northern boundary of Eden (Assyria). Armenia is mentioned in the Bible only as the country to which the murderers of Sennacherib, king of Assyria, fled (*Isa.* xxxvii. 38). Satan selects the murderers' refuge.

BOOK IV

1–130. SATAN THE DESTROYER

Satan on the border of Assyria (Eden) manifests the emotions of one who is about to take an innocent life. The temper and feelings of many murderers spoken of in the Scriptures are attributed to him.

1. *O for that warning voice,* etc. The wish has a partial fulfilment in the visit of Raphael, the angel of *Rev.* viii. 13, who brings a warning. The poet's prayer, however, seems to be for the more specific and stirring alarm of *Rev.* xii. 12.

3. *Second rout.* The first was in the expulsion from Heaven, as narrated in the sixth book.

13. *Not rejoicing.* Compare *Il.* vii. 216. Herod Antipas, the slayer of John the Baptist, was "sorry" when asked to kill the prophet, though heartily desiring the death (*Matt.* xiv. 9).

18. *Horror and doubt,* etc. "Horror" is the revulsion of nature from the crime; "doubt" is the fear of consequences. Both elements entered into the hesitation of Herod and Pilate (*Mark* vi. 20, 26; *John* xix. 8, 12). Thus Hell was at once within them and round about them.

32. *O thou,* etc. Edward Phillips, Milton's nephew, tells us that the six lines beginning here were at first intended by the poet as the opening of Lucifer's part in the tragedy to be called *Adam Unparadised*.

41. *Matchless,* etc. Paul (Saul), while persecuting and slaying Christians, was engaged in a like insane contest (*Acts* xxvi. 14).

48. *How due,* etc. The owner of the vineyard (*Matt.* xxi. 34–41) who sent at the proper season to collect his fruits typifies God who seeks for gratitude from his creatures. Satan is like the husbandmen who killed the messengers from their lord, and intended after slaying his son to seize the inheritance and escape the tribute.

63. *Drawn to his part,* etc. When the rebel Absalom stole the hearts of the Israelites from his father, many of the best and bravest, either from love to the rightful monarch or from outward connections, adhered to

David (2 *Sam.* xv. 6, 15).

67. *What to accuse,* etc. David's great love for his children gave Absalom the opportunity for concocting rebellion, and that rebellion produced a Shimei who cursed the good king (2 *Sam.* xviii. 5; xvi. 5–13).

76. *A lower deep,* etc. Under his curse the first murderer cried out, "My punishment is greater than I can bear," yet sevenfold vengeance was to overtake the slayer of Cain, and seventy-seven-fold the slayer of his descendant, the murderer Lamech (*Gen.* iv. 15, 24).

79. *O then at last relent.* Addressed by Satan to himself, and not, as Keightley thinks, to God.

82. *Disdain . . . shame.* Herod could not endure the humiliation of breaking his oath and the fear of ridicule when the question of killing John was decided (*Matt.* xiv. 9; *Il.* xxii. 99–108).

88. *Under what torments,* etc. Even while Herod was being worshipped as a god he was smitten for his impiety with a loathsome disease (*Acts* xii. 21–23).

93–99. Compare this with the history of Absalom, especially the last lines with 2 *Sam.* xvi. 21, 22.

103. *This knows my Punisher,* etc. The law of Moses permitted no satisfaction for the life of a murderer (*Num.* xxxv. 31). Achilles contemptuously refused to make a compact with Hector (*Il.* xxii. 260–267).

108. *With hope farewell fear.* The murderous Moloch has lost both hope and fear (ii. 45–50).

112. *More than half.* "By reigning in Hell and the World and leaving to God only Heaven."—*Clar. Press.*

115. *Thrice changed,* etc. Probably in allusion to Lycaon (λύκη, light) who was changed into a wolf for his cruelty. The name Lycaon is suggestive of that "angel of light" into which the ravenous Satan had been transformed.

120. *Outward calm,* etc. The sheep's clothing worn by moral wolves (*Matt.* vii. 15–20).

128. *Fierce.* Like the murderous spirits in *Matt.* viii. 28 and *Mark* v. 2–5.

131–171. SATAN IN EDEN

Satan is now within the direct influence of Paradise. The garden has not only (1) the natural features of *Gen.* ii. but also the marks and qualities of (2) God's Holy Mountain, (3) the Congregation of the Faithful, and (4) the Bride of Christ. All these, indeed, are but different forms of expression for the same thing. For the allegorical interpretations of Paradise in the early church see St. Augustine, *De Civ. Dei* xiii. 21.

132. *Eden,* in Hebrew, means Pleasantness or Joy, and is synonymous

with Asshur (Assyria).

Paradise is a Persian word whose meaning is contained in the epithet here joined with it.

133. *Enclosure* here is not the same as the "wall" below, but the whole mount of Paradise considered as a feature in the landscape. "Ezekiel xxviii. 13, 14 appears to have led to the notion that the garden was on the summit of a hill, as described by Dante and Ariosto."—*Clar. Press.*

135. *Wilderness.* The approach to the dwelling-place of the Bride in the Song is through a wilderness (*Cant.* iii. 6; viii. 5).

Hairy. The Latin *coma* and the Greek κόμη are used to designate the foliage of trees.

139. *Cedar,* etc. Cedars and firs are among the trees "in the garden of God" (*Ezek.* xxxi. 8). The cedar, the fir, and the pine are trees of God's planting for his servants in the wilderness (*Isa.* xli. 19). The good man is symbolized by the palm and the cedar (*Ps.* xcii. 12).

140. *As the ranks ascend.* The trees outside of the wall, but a part of the general enclosure, represent those righteous men who, obeying the voice of conscience and following the light of nature, served God without the fuller revelation of his love in the Redeemer.

142. *Higher than their tops.* Christ taught that the least in the Kingdom of Heaven is greater than the greatest saint outside (*Matt.* xi. 11; xiii. 17).

143. *Verdurous wall.* The Bride in the Song (*Cant.* iv. 12) is spoken of as "a garden enclosed;" and the house of Israel is described as a vineyard on a very fruitful hill and enclosed with a hedge. Both are typical of the church of God.

147. *Goodliest trees,* etc. Emblematical of true disciples who bear much fruit and gladden the heart of the Saviour (*John* xv. 8, 11).

155. *Vernal delight.* It is always Spring when the Beloved meets the Bride. "The winter is past, the rain is over and gone" (*Cant.* ii. 11–13).

156. *Gentle gales,* etc. The south wind, wafting the odors of Paradise, whispers to Satan yet at a distance of its loveliness and wealth (*Cant.* iv. 13–16).

159. *As when to them who sail,* etc. Keightley thinks that the poet here imagines an impossibility: "When a vessel going to India has passed Mozambique, the coast of Arabia is due north of her, and at an immense distance, with a portion of the east coast of Africa interposed." But perhaps the voyage is not to India; it may be through the gulf of Aden (Eden) to the town of the same name, before the Christian era an important commercial point in the trade between Europe and Asia. In passing through the gulf the ship's crew might enjoy the spicy odors wafted out to sea from Arabia Felix.

168. *Than Asmodeus,* etc. "The commentators unanimously condemn the semi-burlesque ending of a beautiful passage."—*Clar. Press.* But con-

sider the poet's object. The odor of prosperity from Paradise came to Satan as the odor of fish comes to a cormorant (196), stimulating the appetite instead of nauseating. The material wealth and comfort which crown the industry of a Christian community are attractive even to those who cannot endure the spiritual conditions. Many follow Christ for "loaves and fishes" rather than for the "bread of life" (*John* vi. 26, 27).

170. *Tobit's son.* Masson's summary of the points in the story is brief and clear. "In the book of Tobit the evil spirit Asmodeus, in love with a Jewess named Sara, living in the Median city of Ecbatane, destroys her husbands in succession, till at last, after her betrothal to Tobias, the son of Tobit, he is foiled. Instructed by the archangel Raphael, Tobias burns the heart and liver of a fish, 'the which smell when the evil spirit had smelled, he fled into the utmost parts of Egypt, and the angel bound him.'"

172–392. SATAN ON THE TREE OF LIFE

In Paradise there are three very distinctly marked localities—the Entrance, the Bower with its surroundings, and the neighborhood of the trees of Life and of Knowledge. These localities correspond to the three parts of the human soul—the Intellect, the Sensibilities, and the Will. The last is the seat of Authority. There is also such a seat in the church (*Matt.* xxiii. 2), and Satan assumes it in mounting the Tree of Life.

175. *Brake,* etc. A hedge is at the foot of the hill as a wall is about its top. When Jehovah descended upon Mount Sinai to declare his law, bounds were set about the mount so that neither man nor beast might touch it (*Exod.* xix. 12, 13). The requisites for citizenship on Mount Zion are given in *Psalm xv.*

181. *At one slight bound,* etc. He despises both Law and Gospel.

183. *As when a prowling wolf,* etc. *Il.* xii. 299–306; *John* x. 12.

188. *Or as a thief,* etc. *John* x. 1; *Matt.* xxiv. 43.

193. In one of his prose pamphlets Milton says that it is the scent of gain that attracts hireling teachers into the church. To get rid of such hirelings he favored the abolition of compulsory church rates.

194. *On the Tree of Life,* etc. Its elevation and central position put it in the place of Authority. Hirelings assume the highest seats and most vital offices in the church, namely, those of instruction and rule. Instruction is the life of the soul (*Prov.* iv. 13); and when the people are not fed with spiritual truth, they starve and become morally rotten (*Lycidas* 113–129).

196. *Like a cormorant.* The cormorant *(corvus marinus)* is a sea-bird that lives entirely on fish. Christian ministers are "fishers of men" (*Matt.* iv. 19); they take men to save them; while false teachers, like the cormorant, take them to devour them.

199 *Only used for prospect,* etc. "This passage has puzzled all commentators. What use *could* Satan have made of the tree? He was immortal already."—*Clar. Press.* The answer is easy when Satan's attitude is considered. He is like those hypocrites who have seized places of power and influence in spiritual affairs for material advantage. The holding of a sacred office and even the preaching of the Gospel from mercenary motives will not insure salvation (*Matt.* xxiii; vii. 21–23).

203. *Perverts best things.* "Godliness is gain" is changed to "Gain is godliness" (1 *Tim.* vi. 5, 6).

210. *Eden stretched her line,* etc. How positive the poet is in fixing the site of Paradise, which has been variously assigned to every quarter of the globe! How does he reach such definite knowledge? In the first place he gets from the prophet Daniel (xi. 45) the site of the "Holy Mountain" on whose summit Paradise was planted at the spot where Seleucia, the capital of the Grecian conquests in Upper Asia, afterwards arose on the banks of the Tigris. Then he is apparently justified by Ezekiel (xxxi.) in regarding Eden as synonymous with Assyria. Telassar is supposed to be, like Assyria, derived from Asshur (Happy). For a time the western boundary of the Assyrian empire, under the Macedonian dynasty (*Dan.* viii. 9), was Palestine. On the eastern border of the ancient land of Israel was Auran or Hauran (the modern name of Bashan). This point of measurement is evidently selected by Milton because of *Ps.* lxviii. 15, "The hill of God is as the hill of Bashan; an high hill as the hill of Bashan." The line is stretched from the high hill of God on the east, across a once fertile almost perfectly level plain, to a similar hill of Bashan on the west.

219. *Ambrosial fruit.* Ambrosia was the food of the gods and the support of their immortality. Such fruit is still furnished from heaven to heirs of the celestial Paradise (*John* vi. 27–65).

223. *A river large,* etc. The river is the Tigris (ix. 71) on which Paradise was situated at the point where Seleucia was subsequently built, and where the Euphrates and the Tigris were formerly joined by a channel uniting the two. The Tigris at several places in its course falls into subterranean caverns and disappears, reappearing again many miles farther on. It gets its name from the swiftness of its waters.

233. *Four main streams,* etc. *Gen.* ii. 10–14.

241. *Not nice Art,* etc. The spiritual graces are now the result of much attention and discipline, developing here and there in frequented spots under careful culture and training; in Paradise they flourished spontaneously and universally, in retirement (shade) as well as in publicity (sunlight).

248–256. *Wept odorous gums,* etc. These features of the Garden are all found in the garden of the Song. The "odorous gums" (myrrh) represent Pity (*Cant.* v. 5); "balm" is Sympathy; the "fruit of golden rind" seems to be Love (*Cant.* ii. 3, 4).

257. *Another side,* etc. Some thirty lines, beginning here, present features of the landscape that correspond to parts in the head of the Bride.

258. *The mantling vine,* etc. "The hair of thine head [is] like purple" (*Cant.* vii. 5).

261. *Or in a lake,* etc. "Thine eyes [are] like the fish pools in Heshbon" (*Cant.* vii. 4). The myrtle wreath was given of old to bloodless victors, and fitly adorns the brows of those who conquer by love. The lake crowned with myrtle typifies the eyes of the Bride full of gentleness— "Thou hast doves' eyes within thy locks."

266. *Universal Pan.* Pan (Health) is the god of shepherds and of music and the dance, like the Lover in the Song (*Cant.* i. 7; ii. 8–13). Of the head the tongue is the tuneful member, and in perfect health is full of joyful eloquence and poetry.

269. *Enna,* whence Prosperpina, the daughter of Ceres, was carried off by Dis, or Pluto, was in the centre of Sicily in a region of corn-fields. See Ovid, *Met.* v. 341, etc.

273. *Daphne,* etc. The famous Castalian spring was on Mount Parnassus in Greece; but the one here meant was near Apollo's sacred grove of Daphne not far from Antioch.

275. *Nyseian isle.* The name Nysa was applied to several places sacred to Bacchus. Milton's "Nyseian isle" is supposed to be an island in Lake Tritonis, about the middle of the northern coast of Africa, where the river Triton flows from the lake. In the common legend Bacchus is brought up secretly at Nysa to avoid the wrath of Juno; here it is to avoid the wrath of Rhea, Saturn's wife and Jupiter's step-mother.—*Masson.*

281. Todd quotes from Heylin's *Microcosmus,* published 1627: "The hill of Amara is a day's journey high: on the toppe whereof are 34 pallaces, in which the younger sons of the emperor are continually enclosed to avoid sedition." The four places mentioned are noted for very different features, and, judged from comparisons in the Song, are intended to furnish an analogy to the Cheeks, Brows, Nose, and Lips of the Bride in their perfect proportions and beauty. The possible remoteness of the lips from the heart and the danger of mistaking the one for the other are set forth in the opposition between Mount Amara and true Paradise (*Matt.* xv. 8).

289. *Erect . . . native,* etc. *Eccl.* vii. 29. "Native" is opposed to borrowed. Their majesty is not due to dress; their righteousness is their own (*Ps.* viii. 5–8).

293. *Sanctitude severe and pure.* By the former of these he means Justice—that virtue which decides with strict fairness between man and man; by the second Honesty, which decides with like fairness between self and others. Here truly we have the foundation of "authority in man."

299. *He for God only,* etc. The relation and distinction of the sexes are set forth in 1 *Cor.* xi. 3–15 and 1 *Tim.* ii. 8–14. Observe that Satan beholds the indications of supremacy and subjection from his seat on the Tree of Life, the place of authority and government.

311. The coyness of the Bride and her "amorous delay" appear in the Song of Songs. She hides from view that she may hear the voice of her Lover calling her forth; she seems reluctant that the sweet urgency of love may compel her (*Cant.* ii. 14; i. 4).

325. *Under a tuft of shade,* etc. The fifteen lines beginning here are based upon *Cant.* ii. 3–6, where the Bride banquets with her Beloved. The shade probably signifies a temporary relaxation of authority in the tenderness and perfect equality of love.

340. *About them frisking played,* etc. In the Holy Mountain the fiercest animals were in subjection (*Isa.* xi. 6–9). Like them, the bodily instincts in the spiritual analogue were at first under the control of reason. Both animals and instincts now too often spurn control.

354. *Ocean Isles.* Apparently the Azores named in line 592.

Ascending scale. Easily suggested by the rising of Libra as the sun went down with Aries. But the whole heaven is conceived of as a balance with its fulcrum on the Tree of Life, the highest point in Paradise.

361. *Not spirits,* etc. *Ps.* viii. 5.

366. *Ah! gentle pair,* etc. The plot of Satan against the first Adam and his consort is a parallel to that against the second Adam and his band of disciples. Satan entered Judas and was thus able to observe the most tender intercourse at the last Supper; through the traitor a league ("covenant") was made with the mortal enemy; this enemy brought out all his dignitaries to seize the victims; and state reasons were advanced to justify the seizure (see *Luke* xxii. 3, 5, 52 and *John* xi. 47–52). Compare also the devices of the tempter, *Prov.* i. 10–14.

393–535. ON HOLY GROUND

Satan descends from his lofty seat of authority to the earth and mingles with the lower animals, entering the body now of one, then of another. In so doing he assumes the character of Bacchus, the wine-god, whose chariot—a chariot denotes rapture—is drawn by wild beasts and who himself enters the bodies of lions and other fierce, cruel, and deceitful creatures. This idea may have been suggested to the poet by the fact that when the traitor Iscariot had received the sop dipped in wine Satan entered into him and hurried him to the execution of his fiendish design (*John* xiii. 26, 27). The scene probably signifies that Satan has here determined to make his approach to man through the animal instincts and appetites.

402. *A lion.* When Bacchus assisted the gods in their war against the giants he assumed for the occasion the form of a lion.

403. *A tiger.* Bacchus is fabled to have conquered India, the haunt of the tiger, and sometimes rides in a chariot drawn by tigers.

404. *Two gentle fawns.* Bacchus is sculptured by the ancient artists with a *nebris,* or fawn skin, thrown over his shoulders.

410. *Turned him all ear,* etc. Satan became all ear, or all attention with his ear, to absorb "new utterance," other than that of expressive gesture, look, and attitude, namely, that of articulate speech, to which up to this moment he had been a stranger.

424. *By the Tree of Life.* The Tree of Life and the Tree of Knowledge were both in the midst of the Garden and hence near together (*Gen.* ii. 9). The intimate relation of volition and obedience is easily recognized. In prose Milton gives a somewhat more materialistic conception to the Tree of Life and the Tree of Knowledge.

440. *For whom,* etc. 1 *Cor.* xi. 8, 9.

449. *That day I oft remember,* etc. Masson, overlooking the symbolism of the passage, is puzzled by the "apparent inconsistency between this and the thread of time given in the action of the poem." Eve expresses the sentiment of the Bride in the Song, "We will remember thy love more than wine" (*Cant.* i. 4).

451. *Under a shade on flowers.* The Bride was born under the apple-tree (*Cant.* viii. 5). Eve, like the Bride, is supported by the graces. Adam, as the surroundings of his birth show, also has some of them, but the virtues are in larger proportion (viii. 254).

454. *From a cave,* etc. The nymph Echo was fabled to live in a cave near the river Cephisus. In giving the story of Echo and Narcissus, Ovid tells of a lake of pure water surrounded by grass, unruffled by shepherds, or goats, or flocks of any kind, or birds, or wild animals, or the fallen branches of trees (*Met.* iii. 394–412). The story of Echo is interwoven with that of Narcissus, and her fate is essentially like his.

466. *Pined with vain desire.* In the loneliness of her maidenhood Eve surrenders herself to reflection, as Adam on his first awakening gave himself to reason and speculation (viii. 261 *et seq.*), and with like unsatisfactory results.

475. *Mother of human race. Gen.* iii. 20; *Gal.* iv. 26.

478. *Under a platane.* Virgil applies the epithet "sterile" to the platane (*Georg.* ii. 70). Horace calls the tree *cælebs* (*Odes* II. xv. 4). It signifies, then, that Eve found Adam unwedded.

481. *Return fair Eve,* etc. *Cant.* vi. 13; *Gen.* ii. 23. The Song contains most of the elements found in about twenty lines beginning at this point.

500. *As Jupiter on Juno smiles,* etc. As the blue sky looks upon the earth

between the showers of Spring. The special favor of Heaven is frequently spoken of under the figure of descending showers.

505. *Sight hateful,* etc. The story of Bacchus is interwoven by Ovid with that of Jupiter and Juno. In the amours of Jupiter with Semele, the mother of Bacchus, she extorted from her lover a promise to visit her as he visited Juno. He came in storm and lightning, she perished in the flame and descended to Erebus. The love which is health and joy to Eve consumes Satan with rage and jealousy.

509. *Fierce desire.* Bacchus sometimes takes the form of a kid and thus evinces his lustful nature. His foster-mother, Amalthea, was a goat, and is represented in the sky by the constellation Capella.

515. *Knowledge forbidden!* Bacchus is one of the light-bearing deities of the ancients. Not only was his statue sculptured with a torch (the symbol of knowledge) in his hand, but his worshippers bore torches at festivals in his honor. The Dionysia, or theatrical exhibitions, in which Æschylus, Sophocles, and Euripides distinguished themselves at Athens, were established in honor of Bacchus.

530. *A chance but chance,* etc. A wandering Spirit of Heaven unemployed and, therefore, ready for gossip with the devil, thirsty at a fountain, and with appetite for the wine-god's garrulous beverage, or drowsy in retirement, and therefore incautious of its utterances would be a very remote contingency.

The story of the evil spirit in the guise of Bacchus is written in the heavens among the constellations. In the northern sky is Auriga, the charioteer, having his head wreathed with ivy like the wine-god's. In his bosom, over his heart, he fondles a goat whose heart is the bright star, Capella. Below her are two kids, her offspring. On the head of the charioteer is the foot of the Camelopard, whose haughty step and lofty head denote Pride. Behind are lynxes (ounces), bears, lions, and a dragon.

A larger use is made of the episode of Jupiter and Juno in the fourteenth *Iliad* than would appear from the single mention of their names. A number of delicate touches, here and there, are traceable to this origin. It is an intermediate link between the mythological story of Bacchus and the story of the Lover and the Bride in the Song. From the last named, as the notes indicate, are drawn the principal sentiments and acts ascribed to the human pair.

536–597. THE WARNING

The spirit of Truth warns the spirit of Wisdom of Satan's presence, as the Word of God perpetually warns the Church. The warning is directed to that part of Paradise which symbolizes the head or intelligence (1 *Cor.*

x. 15). The entrance to Paradise is through the intellect or reason, thence to the heart, and thence to the will. Satan precisely reverses this order.

536. *Proud step.* In this consists the Fiend's likeness to the camelopard.

537. *Sly circumspection.* The lynx is extremely sharp-sighted with regard to things nigh at hand.

542. *Eastern gate.* Keightley is confident that Milton here committed an oversight and that he did not mean the inner side of the eastern gate. But compare ll. 782–784.

543. *Rock of alabaster,* etc. The rock is analogous to the white forehead of the human countenance, within which is the seat of the intellect. "Brow of alabaster" is a phrase so common as to be trite.

549. GABRIEL (Man of God) is mentioned by Daniel and Luke. He is the spirit of Heavenly Wisdom, with the loftier attributes of Homer's Pallas Athene and the heroes and demigods whom she rules. His characteristics are those of the wise and prudent man depicted in the book of *Proverbs.* His clear and accurate reasoning fits him to be the appointed judge of Paradise. Beelzebub is his corrupted counterpart among the fallen hosts.

551. *Heroic games.* As bodily training improves physical strength and agility, so the discipline of noble thoughts improves the spiritual graces and virtues.

553. *Celestial armory.* The Bride with all her tenderness and grace has an arsenal from which she draws spiritual weapons against her foes (*Cant.* iv. 4).

556. *On a sunbeam.* In contrast with the crookedness of Satan's course, Uriel's was direct, neither up nor down, to the right hand nor to the left (*Prov.* iv. 18).

As a shooting-star. This seems to be derived from *Il.* iv. 75–77, though in Homer the warning is carried by the spirit of Wisdom instead of to it. Pallas

> "In haste
> Shot from the Olympian summits, like a star
> Sent by the crafty Saturn's son, to warn
> The seamen or some mighty host in arms—
> A radiant meteor casting sparkles round."

560. *Impetuous winds.* Attention has been called to Satan's transformation into Auriga, who bears the Goat in his bosom. The ancient navigators had observed that the constellation of the She-goat and the Kids (*Capella* and *Hædi*) brought stormy and rainy weather, and they were therefore regarded as inauspicious for mariners and dangerous for ships. Hence the name αἴξ, applied to the constellation of the She-goat, has

also the meaning of "a tempest."

561. *By lot,* etc. This does not mean that chance controlled the selection; the lot was a direct appeal to the decision of God (*Prov.* xvi. 33).

576. *Winged warrior.* The epithet "winged" may be derived from *Dan.* ix. 21. The power of Wisdom in war is declared in *Eccl.* ix. 13–18. The goddess Athene, who represented Wisdom to the Greeks, was noted for her warlike temper and strength.

581. *Since meridian hour,* etc. Wisdom and Folly cannot be entertained together. Satan's entrance to Paradise had prevented the coming of good spirits from Heaven.

588. *By morrow dawning,* etc. Probably because night is the time when evil manifests itself (*Prov.* iv. 16).

592. *Beneath the Azores.* The Azores (Azor or Açor, a hawk) are directly west of Paradise and nearly 90° distant, so that when the sun had passed these islands it had set in Paradise. The hawk denotes vigilance; the descent of the sun marks the time for a change of sentinels and a strengthened guard.

Prime orb. The Sun is so called because it is the most important body in our firmament. Masson takes the "Prime Orb" to mean the Primum Mobile; but why should the poet withdraw our thoughts from the two bodies on which they have long been fixed, the Sun and the Earth?

596. *Purple and gold.* Promising a fair day on the morrow (*Matt.* xvi. 2).

598–775. AT THE BOWER

The foregoing scene was enacted in that part of Paradise which represents the head; this is enacted in that which represents the heart. Naturally the passion of Love controls the choice of sentiment. Hints continue to be furnished by the relations of the Lover and the Bride, of Christ and the Church, and of Jupiter and Juno. But the story of Cupid and Psyche is blended with them, and invests the whole with its dreamy charm.

598. *Evening* is the time devoted to sentiment and tenderness. The present description harmonizes in general with Virgil's account of the night when Dido was kept awake by her unfortunate passion for Æneas (*Æn.* iv. 522–528).

602. *Wakeful nightingale.* The nightingale (Φιλομήλα, fond of apples) is the bird of Love. Compare with the Greek name, "Comfort me with apples," etc.—*Cant.* ii. 3–5.

605. *Hesperus* is the planet of Love (viii. 519), and leads forth the stars representing the saints with their pure influence; while the Moon, the symbol of Wisdom, rules majestically over all (*Dan.* xii. 3; *Cant.* vi. 10).

614. *Dew of sleep.* Compare note on v. 56.

626. *Yon flowery arbors.* The Lover is found at noon in the paths made by the footsteps of the flocks or in the shepherds' tents (*Cant.* i. 7, 8). The shepherds' tents are Milton's "arbors," and the foot-paths of the flocks his "alleys."

630. *Those blossoms,* etc. "Blossoms" and "gums" represent gifts of love and pity coming from Christian benevolence (*Acts* iv. 32–37. See note on l. 248).

635. *Author and disposer.* The relation of husband to wife is constantly used to symbolize the relation of Christ to the Church. Here Adam is called the "author and disposer" in allusion perhaps to *Heb.* xii. 2.

639. *With thee conversing,* etc. Todd refers to *Gen.* xxix. 20. It is relevant to this to say that in the vale where Cupid had his palace there was perpetual spring.

641. *Sweet is the breath of morn,* etc. *Cant.* ii. 10–13.

649. *Gems of heaven.* The pair are supposed as yet to know nothing of the true nature of the stars, and the æsthetical Eve is impressed chiefly with their beauty. God's saints, who are compared to the stars, are also called his jewels (*Mal.* iii. 17).

650. *Neither breath of morn,* etc. When Cupid deserted Psyche, she roamed through the world in fruitless search of him, often in despair vainly endeavoring to destroy herself. The pain and the despair of the Bride in a similar plight are told in *Cant.* v. 6–8.

660. This line has been much criticised. Landor, apparently forgetting that Eve was formed from the rib of Adam, objects to calling her the daughter of man. The epithet "accomplished" has been censured for its frigidity, but it identifies Eve with Pandora whom the gods endowed with all their gifts.

665. *Lest total darkness,* etc. The saints keep truth aglow upon the earth, and thus prevent spiritual darkness from regaining sway. Their lavish deeds of love and intercessions deliver men from spiritual death. Their example, instruction, and influence prepare for Christ the Sun of Righteousness.

677. *Millions,* etc. Mount Zion (Paradise) entertains "an innumerable company of angels."

681. *Echoing hill or thicket,* i.e., publicly or privately, as God is worshipped by men. Public devotion, of which the tribes going up to Jerusalem were a type, is where the utterance of one finds an echo in many hearts. Saints delight to speak of God's kingdom and talk of his power (*Ps.* cxlv. 10, 11). Milton believed it the special office of some angels to be present at religious assemblies (*Christ. Doct.* ix.). Praise from the thicket typifies devotion in the family.

687. *Harmonic number.* The number needed for a full chorus.

688. *Divide the night,* etc. In Cupid's palace Psyche was regaled with music by invisible performers. The festival seasons of Israel were celebrated with songs in the night (*Isa.* xxx. 29).

689. *Hand in hand,* etc. The Bride leads her Lover to the Bower, her home (*Cant.* viii. 2). The home of Love is in the heart, and the Bower is the heart of Paradise.

694. *Laurel and myrtle.* Laurel was used to crown blood-stained, myrtle to crown bloodless victors; hence they stand for the moral qualities of Courage and Kindness.

696. *Acanthus,* etc. The acanthus, on account of the beautiful form of its dark and shining leaves, was used as a model in architecture for the capitals of Corinthian columns. It may typify Fortitude, while the yielding and flexible shrubs with which it is joined represent Gentleness.

698. *Iris all hues,* etc. These flowers symbolize the Affections; those "under foot" the Desires; the former flourish, the latter are kept in subjection. Adam and Eve have been compared to Jupiter and Juno. The flowers here mentioned reproduce the colors—the rainbow hues, the purple, and the white—with which the couch of the god and the goddess were surrounded, when they were overshadowed by a golden cloud (*Il.* xiv. 342–348). Pope long ago recognized a part of this resemblance between Homer and Milton.

702. *More colored,* etc. Alluding to the house of costliest stones built by Solomon for his wife, Pharaoh's daughter (1 *Kings* vii. 8–12). Christ preferred the glory of the flowers to that of Solomon (*Matt.* vi. 28, 29).

703. *Other creatures here,* etc. Love can exist only among reasonable beings.

705. *In shadier bower,* etc. Pan and Sylvanus are Joy and Sorrow; the Nymphs and Fauns are the more violent emotions of Grief and Mirth. Pan was fond of sunshine in the mountains and pastures and was the favorite of Bacchus; and his entrance means the coming of Joy. Sylvanus was old and carried about with him a cypress, the symbol of mourning, and his approach threatens Sorrow. The Nymphs (νύβω, to cover, or veil) represent the more demonstrative emotions of Grief (compare note on ii. 789). The Fauns are round-faced, frolicsome beings and represent Mirth. Joy and Sorrow, Mirth and Grief, all visit the heart, the former two more permanent, the latter more transient guests (*Prov.* xiv. 10).

709. *Flowers, garlands,* etc. Thoughtful readers will find in this the same meaning as in *Cant.* vii. 13. The simplicity of this bridal couch contrasts strongly with the luxurious tapestry, fine linen and perfumes of the bed of the "strange woman" (*Prov.* vii. 16, 17).

712. *Genial angel.* Milton has been censured for self-contradiction here and in viii. 485, where he represents Eve as brought to Adam by her Maker. But there is no contradiction. Milton shows (*Christ. Doct.* v.)

from *Hosea* xii. 3, 4 that God and Angel are sometimes interchangeable terms. The "genial Angel" is Love, and "God is Love;" hence where God is there Love is also. In one place prominence is given to the spiritual attraction, in the other to the divine ordinance in the marriage relation.

716. *Unwiser son,* Epimetheus, because he did not share his brother's distrust of the gift of the gods and became the unfortunate husband of Pandora.

719. *Authentic* (αὐθέντης, an absolute master) means that the fire referred to was Jove's to command as a sole and special prerogative.

720. *At their shady lodge.* The praise offered came from the heart.

738. *Which God likes best.* Milton was strongly opposed to formalism in religion, and took in their strict sense such passages as *Matt.* vi. 7, 8.

740. *Troublesome disguises.* Bodily attire is suggestive of the far more reprehensible disguises which sin has caused men to wear over their thoughts and feelings. The absolute sincerity of the state of innocence is here expressed.

751. *Sole propriety.* The ownership of husband and wife in each other is the only ownership that was provided for in Paradise; and in the early church there was a strong tendency to return to this paradisaic condition (*Acts* iv. 32–37).

755. *Founded in reason,* etc. Descriptive of "wedded love," and not of "relations." In his works on Divorce Milton insists on the difference between those unions made by God and founded in reason and love, and those alliances formed "under the influence of some evil genius," and "pregnant with dishonor, with misery, with hatred, and with calamity."

759. *Unbefitting holiest place.* "Marriage is honorable in itself and prohibited to no order of men; wherefore the Papists act contrary to religion in excluding the ministers of the church from this rite" (*Christ. Doct.* x.).

762. *Present or past,* etc. From the practice of the patriarchs Milton drew the inference that polygamy is right and lawful. This is by far the most serious error to be found in his writings; and it is difficult to conceive how a man so sternly pure in thought and act could defend so disgusting a dogma.

763. *Here Love,* etc. The story of Cupid shines through the narrative, but here is a direct reference to the winged god with his golden and flower-tipped shafts.

768. *Mixed dance,* etc. The orgies with which Cotytto, the goddess of licentiousness, was worshipped at Corinth. One aim of St. Paul's letters was to bring about pure relations between the sexes among the Corinthian Christians.

773. *Showered roses,* etc. The "bright golden cloud" over Jupiter and Juno shed upon them "its drops of glistening dew" (*Il.* xiv. 351).

776–1015. WISDOM AND FOLLY

The influences set in motion culminate in the discovery and arrest of Satan, his trial before Gabriel, and his expulsion from Paradise. The Homeric treatment of Pallas Athene, her favorites, and their triumphs over brute force and folly is largely drawn upon in the scene. The antitheses of Wisdom and Folly in the book of *Proverbs* are still more freely used to set forth the antagonism between Gabriel and Satan.

776. *Now had Night measured,* etc. "Prosaically it was nine o'clock in the evening, but the clock here is that vast astronomical clock, of which the great circle of the starry heavens is the dial-plate, and the earth's shadow the moving hour-hand."—*Masson.* The ancients divided the night into four watches; the time here indicated is the beginning of the second watch, which, with the third, was the time of special danger from insidious foes (*Luke* xii. 38, 39).

778. *Ivory Port.* As the alabaster rock over the gate corresponds to the human forehead, so the gate itself is the lips whose changeful hues are like those of the ivory (*Faerie Queene* II. ix. 41). This suggests the "ivory palaces" of *Ps.* xlv. 8, and also the two gates of Sleep, one of horn, the other of ivory, through which the shades pass (*Æn.* vi. 893–896). The true shades pass through the gate of horn, as the soul escapes through the lips in the paleness of death; the false shades pass through the gate of ivory as dreams, when the lips have the hues of healthful slumber.

781. *Gabriel to his next in power.* Pallas (Minerva, Wisdom) had among the Homeric heroes two favorites, Ulysses and Diomed. Ulysses (note on i. 81) serves as a model for Beelzebub, while Diomed (Divinely Counselled) is in some respects a model for Gabriel and has his second in command, Sthenelus (σθένος, strength) as Gabriel has his second Uzziel (Strength of God). Wisdom and Strength are constant companions in Scripture, but Wisdom is always the superior (*Eccl.* ix. 16).

782. UZZIEL . . . *south,* etc. This puts Uzziel (Strength) on the right hand of Paradise, where he belongs, and Gabriel on the left. "The Hebrews, in speaking of the quarters of the world, imagine themselves turned with the face to the East, the back to the West, the right hand to the South, and the left hand to the North" (Cruden's *Concordance*).

784. *Circuit . . . flame,* etc. *Zech.* ii. 5. "Gabriel breaks his company of angels into two divisions by the order, 'Right wheel' and 'Left wheel' (the Latin equivalent for which was, 'Wheel to the spear,' 'Wheel to the shield,' the right hand of course being the spear hand and the left holding the shield)."—*Masson.*

788. ITHURIEL *and* ZEPHON. Ithuriel (ith-Uriel, a servant of Uriel, or Truth) is *Memory.* Zephon (Searcher, the name of the North wind) is *Conscience.* Memory, bearing the Law of God, and Conscience are both

searchers of the heart (*Heb.* iv. 12; *Prov.* xx. 27).

796. *Hither bring.* To the place of judgment where Wisdom sits as magistrate (*Prov.* viii. 15, 16).

798. *Dazzling the moon.* Because armed with the Law of God, superior to all human reason (*Exod.* xxxiv. 29–35).

800. *Squat like a toad.* It is the bloated appearance and the (supposed) venom of the toad that makes it an emblem of the tempter. St. Augustine says that knowledge without charity (1 *Cor.* viii. 1) is what puffs up the demons.

810. *Ithuriel . . . touched,* etc. The spear is the divine command with which, as in the temptation of Christ, the devil is unmasked, discomfited, and finally put to flight. Tertullian says: "Let some one be brought forward here at the foot of your judgment seat, who, it is agreed, is possessed of a demon. When commanded by any Christian to speak, that spirit shall as truly declare itself a demon as elsewhere falsely a god" (*Apol.* i. 23). A test for spirits is given 1 *John* iv. 1–3.

814–827. *As when a spark,* etc. The ideas of this passage may be traced in *Isa.* xxix.—the intrusion of a secret plotter (15), the unconsciousness of the victim (10), the discovery of the scorner (20), and the emotion of the imperilled sleeper when awaked (9, 22). The comparison has its basis in 3–7. First comes a threat of war (like the "rumored war" of the poet); then a "familiar spirit" speaking from the ground (like Satan in the form of a toad); then a mass with the characteristics of dust and chaff (like powder, which has the appearance of the one and the inflammability of the other); then a sudden, instantaneous change (like the explosion); then thunder, earthquake, and flame (like the earth-shaking and the blaze attending the explosion); and lastly, the general effect as of "a dream of a night vision" (compare v. 30–35).

829. *Sitting where ye durst not soar.* When all the angels yet held their thrones through love to God, condemning Law and rebuking Conscience could not reach them. Satan had truly been far above the possible flight of Ithuriel and Zephon. Law and Conscience are a terror to evil-doers, and fear is a lower motive to obedience than love (1 *John* iv. 18).

844. *Cherub.* The idea of *knowledge* contained in the word *conscience* makes Milton call Zephon a cherub.

845. *Severe in youthful beauty.* Innocence, or an undefiled conscience, belongs particularly to children. The rebuke of the Lord seems to have come to the negligent Eli more effectively through the youthful Samuel than through the "man of God" (1 *Sam.* ii. and iii.).

847–849. Patrick Hume pointed out that this is almost a literal translation of *Persius* iii. 35–38.

852. *Best with the best,* etc. It is more honorable to contend with the

master than with the servant. In like spirit Goliath "disdained" the boy-ish David.

858. *Like a proud steed.* The goddess Athene, Gabriel's classical dupli-cate, is a manager of horses, one of her titles being Hippeia. She directed the construction of the Trojan horse, acted as the charioteer of Diomed, the horse-tamer (*Il.* v. 837–841), conducted that warrior and Ulysses in stealing the horses of Rhesus from the Trojan camp at night (*Il.* x. 498–501), and presented to Bellerophon in a dream a magic bridle with which to control the flying steed Pegasus. The reining signifies the restraint which Wisdom enables Conscience to place on the tongue of the guilty one. Athene and her favorites are also distinguished by their power of self-restraint under provocation (*Il.* iv. 22, 23; 401, 402).

862. *Western point.* According to the Hebrew way of fixing direction this would be behind the back (note on l. 782). Compare the rebuke of Christ to the Tempter, *Luke* iv. 8, etc.

863. *Squadron.* The spirit of Wisdom is a spirit of order. The Greeks, conducted by Athene, marched to battle in "serried phalanxes," with unbroken ranks, and in silent obedience to the command of their lead-ers; while the Trojans, ruled by Mars, rushed forward with disorder, tumult, shouting, and clamoring in many languages (*Il.* iv. 427–438).

866. *I hear the tread,* etc. Others have noticed the resemblance of this speech to that of the wise Nestor at the return of Ulysses and Diomed from the Trojan camp with the horses of Rhesus ('Ρῆσος > ῥῆσις, a saying, a speaking). Restraint upon the tongue is thus symbolized (*James* iii. 2–5).

868. *Through the shade.* Gabriel's vision is like that of the owl-eyed Athene.

871. *Fierce demeanor. Luke* ix. 42. Athene encourages Diomed to resist "the fiery, frantic Mars" (*Il.* v. 829–838). Her anger on this occasion sug-gests the "stern regard" with which Gabriel addresses Satan.

885. *Contemptuous,* etc. Like a fool Satan begins his defence by despis-ing the wholesome rebuke of Wisdom (*Prov.* i. 7, 30). To him obedience and submission are folly. "It is an abomination to fools to depart from evil" (*Prov.* xiii. 19).

903. *Disdainfully, half smiling.* The irony with which Wisdom mocks those who despise her counsels and reproofs (*Prov.* i. 26; *Job* xii. 2).

912. *Presumptuous.* Many points in this description of Satan remind us of Thersites, the typical fool of the *Iliad* (ii. 217–219):

> "Squint-eyed, with one lame foot, and on his back
> A lump, and shoulders curving towards the chest;
> His head was sharp, and over it the hairs
> Were thinly scattered."

Compare this with the description of him who goes under the name of the fool, the scorner, and the wicked person in *Proverbs*. For the squinting we have *Matt.* vi. 22, 23; for the lameness, *Prov.* xxvi. 7; for the humped shoulders and narrow chest of crouching timidity, *Prov.* xxviii. 1; for the sharpness of the head signifying lack of capacity, *Prov.* xiv. 6, etc.; for the thinness of the hair implying inability to conceal the lack, *Eccl.* x. 3 etc. Satan manifests all these characteristics in the present colloquy.

914. *Scourge that wisdom.* The scourge is the reward of folly (*Prov.* xxvi. 3). Thersites was chastised by Ulysses (*Il.* ii. 265, 266).

920. *Courageous chief,* etc. Athene had great capacity for endurance, and taunted Aphrodite, when slightly wounded by Diomed, with her fear of pain (*Il.* v. 418–425).

924. *Frowning.* The scorner rewards his reprover with hate (*Prov.* ix. 8).

928. *Blasting volleyed thunder.* The special antagonist of Gabriel in the war in Heaven was Moloch (Mars), but the spirit of Satan was in all his hosts, and Gabriel may therefore be said to have encountered Satan himself. The thunder by which Moloch was overcome in that celestial struggle was not Gabriel's usual weapon (the spear), which is sober rebuke and would have been despised by the ferocious antagonist (*Prov.* xxiii. 9). Of the Olympic deities only Athene (besides Jove) was allowed to wield the thunderbolt. To overcome Mars on the plain of Troy, she struck him with a stone, and then ridiculed him by comparing him to an unruly boy whom his mother had been chastising (*Il.* xxi. 400–414). This gives a hint of what is meant by the thunder. It is that scathing laughter of unerring Wisdom at the folly of spirits with faculties for intelligence (*Ps.* ii. 4; *Prov.* i. 26).

931. *Inexperience.* For the age and experience of Wisdom see *Prov.* viii. 22–31.

941. *Though for possession,* etc. Though to get possession we may have to try what you and your gay legions (called "gay" because of Gabriel's iron) can do to prevent it.

948. *To say and straight unsay. Prov.* xxvi. 7. Satan's failure to give a consistent account of himself constitutes one point of likeness to the lame Thersites.

953. *Army of fiends,* etc. The army is apostrophized in the four lines beginning here. Could their faithfulness to their leader, or his to them, absolve them from their prior obligation to the rightful Ruler of all? They had renounced allegiance to a legitimate sovereign to accept the military despotism of a usurper. A pretence of faithfulness with such disloyalty is the second inconsistency of Satan.

959. *Fawned and cringed.* To obey God from love is freedom; to cringe to him from fear is slavery. Satan had reversed the rule of common-sense.

His fawning and cringing rendered him as deformed in spirit as the hump-backed and narrow-chested Thersites was in body.

965. *To the infernal Pit,* etc. It is a fit task for the spirit of Wisdom to seal up the devil and prevent his deceiving the nations, as in *Rev.* xx. 1–3.

969. *Waxing more in rage.* Like the insane and ferocious demon of *Mark* v. 2–4.

976. *In progress,* etc. A "progress" is a journey in state of the sovereign through his realm. In England it was sometimes greatly oppressive, as the places visited were required to defray the expenses, frequently very extravagant, of entertainment. *Star-paved* is not a meaningless epithet. The stars symbolize the angelic glory, and Satan taunts the angels with their submission to a Ruler who tramples upon their honor, as an Eastern despot rides over the pavement of his prostrate subjects.

978. *Turned fiery red.* The middle watches of the night are past and the rays of the coming dawn are beginning to brighten the East and gradually the whole horizon to the northern and southern points. This change is accompanied by a spiritual change in the angelic guardians who redden with anger and shame under Satan's insolence.

980. *As when a field,* etc. A field of ripened wheat tossed by winds is liable to scatter its seeds upon the ground and leave the heads but empty chaff; so a wise man swayed by gusts of passion is in danger of becoming as light-headed as a fool.

987. *Teneriff or Atlas.* The peak of Teneriff has been thought by some to be identical with the Atlas of Homer. Apparently, whether a giant or a mountain, Atlas supporting the world figured forth the ancient idea of the Will. Self-will, which is the essence of Satan's character (note on i. 82), here becomes reckless wilfulness in withstanding both Gabriel's rebuke and his irony and suggests the comparison to Mount Atlas.

989. *Horror plumed.* The goddess of Wisdom bore the head of the Gorgon Medusa upon her shield and turned men into stone with its horror. The old fable means that through Care (note on ii. 611), Wisdom drives men mad (*Acts* xxvi. 24). Horror (Gorgon) upon the helmet of Satan signifies that his folly had ended in "mischievous madness" (*Eccl.* x. 13).

990. *What seemed,* etc. "A hesitating touch that spoils the picture. Milton was apparently struck with the material nature he had assigned to these spiritual beings."—*Clar. Press.* How could this be remedied by any description of Satan's *armor?* "The intentional vagueness of such description is so effective because it stirs but does not satisfy the imagination. It rouses a sense of the mysterious and indescribable."—*Cambridge ed.* There is a better reason: Milton is setting forth the condition of the superlative fool who is "wise in his own conceit" (*Prov.* xxvi. 12). Satan

seems to himself to have abundant means of intellectual attack and defence, but his logic is as incoherent as vapor.

994. *Had gone to wrack,* etc. The account of this expulsion never loses sight of that of the deaf, dumb, and lunatic spirit with whom the disciples wrought in vain while the Master was on the Mount of Transfiguration. At the Master's approach the spirit became alarmed and extremely violent and was afterwards, on account of its stubbornness, referred to as a mountain. When Christ cast him out, it was thought at first that the extruded demon had killed his victim in the going. Christ subsequently taught his disciples that not pride and anger but humility and prayer are the conditions of successful exorcism (*Matt.* xvii. 14–21; *Mark* ix. 14–29; *Luke* ix. 37–42).

997. *Golden scales. Il.* viii. 69; xxii. 209; *Æn.* xii. 725. There is much balancing of one thing against another in the *Proverbs:* the spirit of Wisdom is preeminently one that weighs and ponders. The significance of Libra between Astræa and Scorpio is well worth possessing. On one side of the Balance is the Scorpion, the symbol of death; on the other side is the Virgin with a quill in one hand and a sheaf of wheat in the other, probably identical with the incomparable virgin Athene, the spirit of intelligence and life. The issues of death and life are dependent upon a proper weighing.

999. *Wherein all things,* etc. *Isa.* xl. 12–15; *Prov.* xxi. 2; xxiv. 12. Earth is balanced with air to show the lightness and insignificance of material good.

1002. *Two weights.* Two successive verses in *Prov.* xxvi. "Answer not a fool according to his folly, lest thou also be like unto him," is the weight in favor of "parting"; "Answer a fool according to his folly, lest he be wise in his own conceit," is in favor of "fight." The decision is easy, for two fools are worse than one. Hence Gabriel does not reply to Satan's taunts. In Homer, Æneas declares the unprofitableness of brawls and scolding (*Il.* xx. 242–255).

1011. *Read thy lot.* Satan's advantage was in fighting; Gabriel's in parting; the decision was in favor of the latter.

BOOK V

1–135. A DREAM AND ITS INTERPRETATION

Natural and moral darkness have vanished together, and the strange experience of Eve now seems to her like a painful dream. A part of the story of Cupid and Psyche is made the basis of her vision. Adam uses some of Spenser's poetical philosophy to interpret it.

2. *Orient pearl.* Aurora sometimes appears in art as a nymph crowned with flowers, with a star above her head, standing in a chariot drawn by winged horses, while in one hand she holds a torch, and with the other scatters roses, as illustrative of the flowers springing from the dew, which the poets describe as diffused from the eyes of the goddess in liquid pearls. *Faerie Queene* IV. v. 45.

6. *Aurora's fan.* The name Aurora is thought to be allied to *aura,* and the corresponding Greek name Eos to ἄω (to blow), so that the goddess represents not so much the light as the cool air of the dawn.

13. *Hung over her enamoured.* Doubtless suggested by a scene in the story of Cupid and Psyche, which, in turn, in much of its sentiment resembles the Song of Songs.

16. *Zephyrus on Flora breathes,* soft as the west wind in Spring. Zephyrus transported Psyche in her sleep to the enchanted palace of Cupid.

22. *Citron.* Virgil (*Georg.* ii.) speaks of the citron as an antidote to witchcraft and poison. It is thought by some to be the "apple" of *Cant.* ii. 3–5.

31. *Have dreamed,* etc. Like the Bride in *Cant.* v. 2, and the sleeper in *Isa.* xxix.

38. *Why sleepest,* etc. Cupid disturbs the slumber of his victims (*Æn.* iv. 529–531).

43. *Sets off the face of things.* "An expression worthier of Addison than of Milton."—*Landor.* But it gives exactly the intended idea of artificial effect.

45. *Whom to behold but thee,* etc. The beauty of Psyche was so great that

people crowded from all parts to gaze upon her charms, erected altars to her and neglected the worship of Venus.

50. *Alone I passed.* The Bride in the Song, Psyche in the myth, and Queen Dido (*Æn.* iv. 68–73) are represented as having wandered in dreams far in fruitless search of the lost lover.

55. *One shaped and winged,* etc. As Eve looked upon the fruit, the desire to partake of it was formed, and this desire is represented in the winged spirit standing by the tree. To Eve at this stage Satan appears as he appeared to Uriel, in the likeness of Cupid.

56. *His dewy locks distilled ambrosia,* etc. "My head is filled with dew, and my locks with the drops of the night," pleads he who tempted forth the Bride upon her perilous search. Dew is representative of sleep. When Eve says that her tempter's locks were dewy, she means that the influence of his presence was to cause drowsiness. Sleep, like food and drink, renews the strength of the body; and before the Fall these were sufficient to keep it from decay and consequently immortal. Sleep, and sometimes Night as the bringer of Sleep, like the food of the blessed, are therefore called "ambrosial" (l. 642).

58. *O fair plant,* etc. Expressive of the reaching out of Cupid (Desire).

65. *O fruit divine,* etc. Expressive of the satisfaction of Desire (*Prov.* xiii. 19; ix. 17).

72. *Good communicated,* etc. This truth is illustrated in Christ's miracle of feeding the five thousand (*Matt.* xiv. 16–20).

78. *Thyself a goddess. Gen.* iii. 5. The guerdon promised to Psyche and finally conferred upon her was immortality and life with the gods.

86. *Up to the clouds,* etc. Psyche was raised into the air by holding fast to Cupid in his flight.

95. *Dearer half.* The ideal love of the husband for the wife is represented in Christ's love and self-devotion for the Church (*Eph.* v. 25).

102. *Reason as chief.* Spenser describes the human frame as the dwelling-place and domain of Alma, who represents Reason (*Faerie Queene* II. xi. 2).

> "But in a body which doth freely yeeld
>   His partes to Reasons rule obedient,
> And letteth her that ought the scepter weeld,
>   All happy peace and goodly government
> Is settled there in sure establishment.
>   There Alma, like a virgin queen most bright,
>   Doth flourish all in beautie excellent."

Fancy next. In the same house is one called Phantastes living in a chamber painted with

"Infinite shapes of things dispersed thin"

and full of flies buzzing about (*Faerie Queene* II. ix. 42):

"All those were idle thoughts and fantasies
Desires, dreams, opinions unsound,
Shewes, visions, soothsayes and prophesies;
And all that fained is, as leasings, tales and lies."

106. *Joining or disjoining.* In a syllogism whose conclusion is affirmative the major and the minor term are said to be joined; when the conclusion is negative, they are disjoined.

117. Evil enters the mind whenever one is tempted; Christ was tempted in all points as we are, yet without sin (*Heb.* iv. 15).

123. *That wont to be,* etc. *Cant.* vi. 10. The cheerfulness and serenity of the righteous is often compared to the brightness of the morning (2 *Sam.* xxiii. 4).

128. *Kept for thee in store.* As for the Bride (*Cant.* vii. 13) and for the Church (*John* xiv. 1–3).

131. *Wiped them with her hair,* etc. The woman whose tears of penitence fell on the feet of Jesus wiped them with the hairs of her head (*Luke* vii. 38). Her tears were also dried by the gracious tenderness of Jesus, who forgave her sins and bade her go in peace.

136–208. THE MORNING HYMN

This passage is recognized as one of the most signal examples in literature of beauty and harmony in writing. The plan of the hymn is taken from *Ps.* cxlviii., but sentiments are added from other portions of the Bible.

137. *Under shady arborous roof.* From the recesses of the heart. The sun shining into the Bower symbolizes the entrance of truth into the heart of the faithful (2 *Cor.* iv. 6).

142. *Discovering . . . all the East.* The East is the source of light and the reputed home of the wise (1 *Kings* iv. 30). The entrance of Divine light into the soul improves even the natural understanding (*Ps.* cxix. 98–100).

146. *Various style.* The frequent admonition to "sing unto the Lord a new song," seems to Milton inconsistent with prescribed forms of worship.

149. *Unmeditated.* Their rapturous thoughts naturally flow into expression; meditation is not needed where the Holy Spirit vouchsafes his inspiration (*Matt.* x. 19, 20).

165. *Rev.* i. 8. The whole song of praise is addressed to the Messiah, for it cannot be said of God himself, as in l. 161, that the angels behold him.

166. *Fairest of stars,* etc. When the Sun is in Aries, the constellation of the Harp, with Lyra (or Vega) a beautiful star of the first magnitude, is almost directly overhead at daybreak. It must have occurred to the poet, in imitation of the psalmist, to appeal to the harp at the beginning of his song of praise (*Ps.* cviii. 2, and often). The absence of an earthly instrument of music is thus supplied by this noble introduction of the constellation; and the poet is acquitted of the twofold blunder of trying to make Venus do double duty, both here and as one of the "five other wandering fires," and serve in one night as both evening and morning star.

171. *Eye and soul.* "The sun is called *mundi oculus* by Ovid (*Met.* iv. 228), and *mundi animus* by Pliny."—*Newton.*

173. *When thou climb'st,* etc. These are designated times for worship (*Ps.* lv. 17).

176. *Fixed in their orb,* etc. Adam and Eve are not yet so advanced as to adopt the Ptolemaic theory of the universe; they are only taking appearances.

178. *Mystic dance.* The mystic philosophy of antiquity found in the sacred dances of the Greeks a resemblance to the courses of the stars. According to some of the Fathers, the angels are always dancing, and the glorious company of the apostles is really a chorus of dancers (*Encyc. Brit.* vi. 800). Compare ll. 618–627 and *Ps.* cxlix. 3. The *Pitt Press* ed. has a useful note on this point.

180. *Air and ye elements.* The four elements in the order of their creation in the six days' work are Air, Water, Earth, and Fire. They were the first things made after the boundaries of the world were fixed, and hence "the eldest birth of Nature's womb."

182. *Perpetual circle.* Newton refers to Cicero (*De Nat. Deorum* ii. 33): "Et cum quatuor sint genera corporum, vicissitudine eorum mundi continuata natura est. Nam ex terrâ, aqua; ex aquâ, oritur aer; ex aere, aether; deinde retrorsum vicissim ex aethere, aer; inde aqua; ex aquâ, terra infima."

202. For the use of the singular pronoun consult note on iii. 413–415.

209–307. THE MISSION OF RAPHAEL

The ejaculation of the poet (iv. 1–8) and the prayer of Adam and Eve for help in the impending evil are answered from Heaven by sending Raphael to Paradise.

216. To *wed her elm.* The figure is classical, being found in Horace

(*Epod.* ii. 9), Virgil (*Georg.* ii. 367), and Ovid (*Met.* xiv. 669).

221. RAPHAEL (God's Health) personifies *Love* and unites in himself
the pure qualities of Mercury and Juno, as Belial unites their impure
qualities. Juno was the bride of Jove in heaven; Mercury was his confi-
dant and messenger in his erotic intrigues with the fair ones of earth.
The *sociable* quality belongs to Mercury (*Il.* xxiv. 334, 335).

224. *Stir.* Raphael as the angel of Love is, like Mercury, a spirit of
peace, annoyed by tumult, and therefore sent to quiet the disturbance
made by Satan.

229. *Half this day*, etc. The angels who visited Abraham came at noon
and seem to have departed at evening (*Gen.* xviii. 1–5, and xix. 1). *Exod.*
xxxiii. 11.

237. *Warn him,* etc. See note on iv. 556.

246. *Fulfilled all justice.* Themis, or Justice, warned Atlas of the
approaching theft of his golden fruit (*Met.* iv. 643).

247. *Nor delayed the saint.* Compare the promptness of Mercury when
sent to Priam (*Il.* xxiv. 340–342):

> "And hastily beneath his feet he bound
> The fair, ambrosial, golden sandals worn
> To bear him over ocean like the wind
> And o'er the boundless land."

249. *Ardors.* This word prepares the way for the comparison of
Raphael to the Phœnix, that rose in youthful freshness from the flames
of its own funeral pyre.

251. *Flew through the midst,* etc. Identifying Raphael with the angel of
Rev. viii. 13.

254. *The gate self-opened.* Compare the descent of Juno (*Il.* v. 749–751;
viii. 393–395):

> "The gate of Heaven
> Opened before them of its own accord—
> Gates guarded by the Hours, on whom the care
> Of the great heaven and of Olympus rests,
> To open or to close the wall of cloud."

The wall of Heaven resembles our sky resting, like a hollow hemi-
sphere, upon our flat earth, never stopping or delaying progress from
place to place, but rolling outward, as any approach, to let them through.

260. *With cedars crowned,* etc. Combine *Ezek.* xxxi. 8 with *Isa.* ii. 2.

261. *As when . . . the glass,* etc. As the telescope assists the natural vision,
so the power of Love sharpens the spiritual sense. Its revealing power is

declared in the Scripture, and we know its jealousy and watchfulness. Hence the large eyes of Juno and her use of the sleepless Argus to watch her rivals.

264. *Or pilot,* etc. As the island of Delos or of Samos appears among the Cyclades to the practised eye of a pilot, so the Earth appears among the stars to Raphael. Delos was abhorred by Juno, because it gave shelter to her rival Latona; Samos was favored by her, because a temple was there erected in her honor. Presiding over marriage and birth, Juno was the foe of Latona (Death). To Raphael the Earth is either a Delos or a Samos, as man's lapse or steadfastness will make it an abode of Death or of Life.

269. *Polar winds,* etc. Implying cold such as Mercury found on Mount Atlas (*Æn.* iv. 246–255). Divine Love can neither be chilled nor diverted from its object.

272. *A phœnix,* etc. See note on l. 249. The Phœnix, according to Herodotus, resembles an eagle in outline and size. It was said to go from Arabia once every five hundred years, to deposit the ashes of the preceding Phœnix, or its own ashes, in the temple of the Sun at Thebes, in upper Egypt. The rabbins have thought that there is a reference to this Arabian bird in *Ps.* ciii. 5, and in *Job* xxxix. It is renewed in youth after long periods of time, and is a good emblem of the transformation and renewal wrought by Divine Love in the heart. As bearing upon this it may be noticed that the version of 1881 has the word "eagle" in *Rev.* viii. 13, instead of the "angel" of the version of 1611.

There is some relationship between this fabulous bird and the tutor of Achilles, the aged Phœnix, who remained unmarried and thought of himself as transformed again into a beardless youth (*Il.* ix. 445–448). The Phœnix and Mercury are associated in *Il.* xxiv. 314–321, where Jove's eagle is sent ahead of Mercury on the mission of pity and help to Priam. The mission of Raphael, that of Mercury and the eagle, and that of the Phœnix to the temple of the Sun are all missions of pity, as symbolized by the egg of myrrh which the Phœnix bears.

275. *On the eastern cliff.* Divine Love is not a mere sentiment, but goes through the intellect before it reaches the heart, its final destination.

279. *O'er his breast,* etc. In Raphael's attire the breast-covering is "righteousness"; the girdle is "truth" as represented in the divine promises; the shoes are the "preparation of the gospel of peace" (*Eph.* vi. 14, 15). We have a parallel to this in Homer's account of the robing of Juno (*Il.* xiv. 178–189). The cloak about her shoulders was the work of Pallas Athene and represented the wisdom of that goddess; Raphael's broad shoulders are a mark of wisdom. Juno borrowed the cestus or girdle of Venus,

> "Embroidered, many-colored and instinct
> With every winning charm—with love, desire,
> Dalliance and gentle speech—that stealthily
> O'ercomes the purpose of the wisest mind."

Like this many-colored zone was that of Raphael with colors "dipt in Heaven." The "shapely sandals" on Juno's feet are matched by the "feathered mail" shading the feet of Raphael. The errand of Juno so attired was to make peace in the distracted household of Oceanus; that of Raphael, to bring peace to Paradise.

285. *Like Maia's son,* etc. In resembling Juno he resembles Mercury, for the two have much in common. Mercury stole Jove's sceptre, Juno attempted to rule the world by putting her spouse to sleep; Mercury stole the cestus of Venus, Juno borrowed it; both are alike in "fleetness like the wind."

286. *Heavenly fragrance. Ps.* xlv. 7, 8. The oil with which Juno anointed herself "perfumed the air of earth and heaven" (*Il.* xiv. 170–174).

287. *Straight knew him.* The angel of Love is easily distinguished (1 *Cor.* viii. 3).

289. *In honor rise.* Expressing their sense of Love's dignity. The gods assembled in the halls of Jupiter started from their seats when Juno came among them (*Il.* xv. 85, 86).

291. *Glittering tents.* The tents, the field, the odors, the wilderness, the spices are all features of the Garden in the *Song.* The sense of "wilderness" is given not as meaning a dreary desolate region, but a fertile spot waiting for the hand of Art to reduce it to order.

308–560. THE HOSPITALITY

The hospitality of Abraham and Manoah in sacred story and of Alcinous in classic legend is here imitated. Possibly the name Alcinous (Strong-minded) may have suggested the introduction of philosophy at the table.

310. *Morn risen on mid-noon.* This figure, which has been universally applauded as a stroke of the highest genius, is partly anticipated in the *Hymn on the Nativity,* 83. The Phœnix was the son of Eos, or the Dawn.

311. *Some great behest.* Abraham and Manoah inferred that their angelic visitants had some message for them. Compare *Gen.* xviii. and *Judg.* xiii. for various features of this meeting and interview.

321–323. Eve's meaning, which some have strangely misunderstood, is that the earth, inspired of God, brings forth fruit that is best eaten fresh from the stalk, though abundantly, in small excess over immediate needs, but furnishes beforehand in larger amounts that which improves by storing and drying, to be gathered and laid up. Paradise allows no hoarding for display, or in distrust of future supplies. The law is illustrated in the giving of manna (*Exod.* xvi. 16–32).

334. *What order,* etc. True hospitality in natural or spiritual things stimulates appetite, and emulates the example of Christ in keeping the best until last (*John.* ii. 10).

339. *In India East or West,* etc. The East Indies are the native country of the Fig; the West Indies and neighboring parts of the continent of the Orange, the Hesperian fruit of iv. 250. The "middle shore" is usually understood to mean the coast of the Mediterranean, but that involves some difficulties and we must probably include all between the East and the West Indies. Pontus, according to Pliny, is the native place of the Cherry, which was brought thence into Italy by Lucullus. Others of our common fruits are found wild in Pontus, giving it the surname of Euxinus (Hospitable). The Pomegranate *(Punicum granatum)* has its home on the Punic coast.

341. *Alcinous. Odys.* vii. 114–131. In the garden of this hospitable king Mercury was honored with libations, and the gods appeared visibly at the feasts.

344. *For drink,* etc. The drinks are those of *Cant.* v. 1; the *must* being sweet wine that does not intoxicate, the *meaths* a drink of honey, and the *creams* the milk.

350. *Our primitive great sire.* The title applies to Abraham, "the father of the faithful," no less than to Adam, and rounds out the resemblance between Abraham's reception of his angelic visitors and Adam's reception of Raphael.

354. *More solemn,* etc. The great and wealthy Solomon had all this tedious pomp, these horses and liveried servants, when he offered hospitality to the Queen of Sheba (2 *Chron.* ix. ; 1 *Kings* iv.). The beauty of the lily, for which God cares, is beyond all the glory of human art and splendor.

361. *Native of Heaven,* etc. Here is an uncertainty like that of Æneas before his goddess-mother Venus (*Æn.* i. 327, 328); of Alcinous before Ulysses (*Odys.* vii. 199); and of Manoah before the angel. It is the privilege of the hospitable to entertain angels "unawares" (*Heb.* xiii. 2).

371. *Virtue.* The commentators are puzzled to know why Raphael is here called Virtue and afterwards (viii. 249) a Power. In the received version of the Scriptures the word "virtue" is used to translate both ἀρετὴ and δύναμις, and is therefore a wider term including "power." The special reason for using here the title Virtue is that in the garden of Alcinous, before Ulysses was invited to partake of the banquet, he did

homage to the queen, the revered Arete (Virtue), and wore a garment made by her.

378. *Pomona* (*pomum,* an apple), among the Romans a goddess presiding over fruit-trees. The Bride (*Cant.* viii. 5) was brought up under the apple-tree.

380. *Undecked, save with herself.* The Bride is adorned with jewels, lilies, and purple, which, however, are only the beauties of her own person, the well-turned joints, the fair complexion, and the dark mass of hair.

381. *Fairest goddess,* etc. The three who contended for the prize of beauty on Mount Ida were Juno, Minerva, and Venus, of whom the last was adjudged the most beautiful.

388. *Mother of mankind,* etc. The salutation resembles that to Sarah (*Gen.* xviii. 9, 10), that to Manoah's wife (*Judg.* xiii. 3), and that to the virgin Mary (*Luke* i. 28–31).

391. *Raised of grassy turf,* etc. The bounteous supply placed on the table is an offering to the Lord, as in the case of Manoah, and the table becomes an altar for the gift. It is therefore made according to the direction given for altars (*Exod.* xx. 24).

395. *A while discourse,* etc. In discoursing with the angel of Peace, the givers of the feast observed the injunction of *Matt.* v. 23, 24. Before feasting in the garden of Alcinous, libations were poured to Mercury.

406. *May of purest spirits,* etc. A cautious interpretation of the statement that "man did eat angels' food."

410. *Every lower faculty,* etc. "Spirit being the more exalted substance virtually and essentially contains within itself the inferior one; as the spiritual and rational faculty contains the corporeal—that is, the sentient and vegetative faculty" (*Christ. Doct.* vii.). The senses are mentioned in an order corresponding to the intimacy of the knowledge which they impart. We hear of things remote through the testimony of others; we see things in our presence; the smell attracts or repels us; the touch requires contact; the taste gives us inner experience.

412, 413. These terms are as applicable to spiritual as to physical processes. Concoction corresponds to mature deliberation; digestion to analysis; assimilation to synthesis, which passes from the concrete to the abstract and turns corporeal into incorporeal.

416. *The grosser feeds the purer.* The philosophy resembles that of *Æn.* vi. 724–727. It is impossible to believe that Milton intended this speech of Raphael to be understood in any literal sense, and therefore, though without great confidence, I venture the following explanation: The universe is a living unit, like man, and contains Body, Life, Intellect, and Love, of which in each case the lower nourishes and sustains the higher. The moon possibly symbolizes the body of wisdom attainable by human reason under present conditions, and the vapor on its face the doubts and

uncertainties pertaining to such conditions. The sun may appear to Raphael as an emblem of Love, which is friendly to Life and augmented in the increase of life, and therefore spoken of as supping with the Ocean, the source and symbol of Life. Raphael's partial identification with Juno is the chief basis of this explanation.

429. *Mellifluous dews,* etc. The poet describes the giving of the manna, which is called "angels' food" (*Ps.* lxxviii. 25) and which appeared on the ground after the dew had evaporated (*Exod.* xvi. 13, 14, 31).

433. *Think not I shall be nice.* "A dinner of herbs where love is" satisfies an uncorrupted appetite (*Prov.* xv. 17), but the heaven-sent manna did not content the murmuring Israelites (*Numb.* xxi. 5).

434. *Nor seemingly,* etc. Raphael says to Tobias: "All these days I did appear unto you; but I did neither eat nor drink, but ye did see a vision" (*Tobit* xii. 19).

436. *Keen dispatch,* etc. The offerings of Manoah were consumed by fire.

439. *Nor wonder,* etc. The transmuting power of Love is probably in the poet's mind (*Rom.* xii. 1, 2).

443. *Eve ministered,* etc. Eve here assumes the duties of Hebe's office, one of which was to prepare the chariot of Juno (*Il.* v. 722), and another to act as cup-bearer to the gods. The two functions are allied (note on iv. 396). The Bride acts as cup-bearer (*Cant.* viii. 2).

447. *Sons of God. Gen.* vi. 2. See note on xi. 622.

461. *Now know I well,* etc. Manoah knew by the consumption of his sacrifice that an angel had been present and had made him an object of special favor (*Judg.* xiii. 21–23).

467. *Yet what compare!* A thought in the mind of one who sat at table with Jesus (*Luke* xiv. 15).

469. *From whom all things proceed.* To sustain a similar statement Milton elsewhere quotes *Rom.* xi. 36. He argues that matter is an emanation from God and discusses the whole subject in *Christ. Doct.* vii.

478. *Till body up to spirit work.* Commentators have found in this passage a kind of materialism, inasmuch as it makes body change into spirit; but the poet at the same time just as strongly affirms the reverse, that body is originally derived from spirit. "Neither is it more incredible that a bodily power should issue from a spiritual substance than that what is spiritual should arise from body; which, nevertheless, we believe will be the case at the Resurrection" (*Christ. Doct.* vii.). 1 *Cor.* xv. 44.

479. *So from the root,* etc. St. Paul's analogue for illustrating the change from the natural to the spiritual body, but extended more into particulars.

482. *Spirits odorous breathes.* To Milton spirit begins with etherealized matter and not with thinking substance. The powers of vitality, sensibility, and reason must be added to spirit, and, except perhaps in the case of

the infinite God, are incapable of separate existence.

484. *Vital . . . animal . . . intellectual.* Milton regards these as functions of man and not the separable parts of which man is composed. "Man is a living being, intrinsically and properly one and indivisible, not composed or separable, not according to the common opinion made up and framed of two distinct and different natures, as of soul and body—but the whole man is soul and the soul man, that is to say, a body or substance, individual, animated, sensitive, and rational" (*Christ. Doct.* vii.). He maintains that at death men go out of existence and remain so until the Resurrection.

488. *Discursive or intuitive.* "An old distinction with psychologists. Discursive reason, or Understanding, they say, is that which arrives at knowledge gradually by searching, comparing, distinguishing, etc.; Intuitive Reason is immediate insight or perception of what *must* be true necessarily. But there is great debate as to the validity of the distinction."—*Masson.*

491. *Wonder not then,* etc. In the time of Christ it seems to have been accepted that spirits would not eat human food, and on one occasion use was made of the notion to overcome the unbelief of the disciples (*Luke* xxiv. 37–43).

497. A belief expressed by St. Augustine, *De Civ. Dei* xiii. 23.

503. *Whose progeny,* etc. Adam is at once the son of God and the progenitor of the human race (*Luke* iii. 38).

509. *Scale of nature,* etc. "Scale" (*scala,* a ladder) suggests the ladder which Jacob saw at Bethel (*Gen.* xxviii. 12). Jacob's ladder reached from earth to heaven, Adam's from matter to spirit, which, properly taken, means from earth to heaven.

519. *Son of Heaven and Earth.* The designation is founded on the twofold origin of man, the spiritual and the material (*Eccl.* xii. 7).

527–541. The freedom of the human will is fully discussed in the third chapter of the *Christian Doctrine.*

547. *Cherubic songs,* etc. The preference here expressed doubtless has its basis in 1 *Cor.* xiii. 1, 2, where the superiority of Love (Raphael) over all wisdom and eloquence, human or angelic, is strongly affirmed.

548. *Nor knew I not,* etc. I knew (had the consciousness) that I was created free both to choose and to act.

557. *Worthy of sacred silence,* a translation of Horace's *sacro digna silentio.* But the motive for the thought is found in *Rev.* viii. 1, which tells of a silence in Heaven just before the revelation of the history of rebellion against God. Observe (l. 562) that Raphael makes a "short pause" before beginning his narrative.

558. *We have yet large day.* After Ulysses has spoken long, Alcinous asks for a further account of the Grecian heroes at Troy and says encouragingly:

> "A night immeasurably long
> Is yet before us. Let us have thy tale
> Of wonders. I could listen till the break
> Of hallowed morning, if thou canst endure
> So long to speak of hardships thou hast borne."

561–657. ENTHRONEMENT OF THE MESSIAH

Raphael's narrative opens with the enthronement of the Son of God over the angels, the stupendous event which marks the true chronological beginning of the poem. Resistance to the new beneficent reign was the form in which Evil originated; and the history of Evil is the subject of the whole narrative.

564. *Sad task and hard.* Ulysses and Æneas preface their narratives with a declaration of the unwelcomeness and difficulty of the task (*Odys.* ix. 12; *Æn.* ii. 3).

565. *The invisible exploits,* etc. This single caution should have prevented the stupid blunders of critics who charge the most careful, consistent, and philosophical of poets with confounding matter and spirit. Milton's representations of spiritual activity have everywhere the support of such authorities as Homer, Virgil, Spenser, and the Sacred Writers.

569. *The secrets of another world,* etc. Virgil intimates that to reveal the secrets of the spirit world is unlawful (*Æn.* vi. 266). Euripides makes the offence of Tantalus to have consisted in not restraining his tongue—in divulging the secrets of the gods (*Orest.* 10). Paul, when caught up into Paradise, "heard unspeakable words which it is not lawful for a man to utter" (2 *Cor.* xii. 4). *Matt.* xiii. 11; 1 *Cor.* ii. 7–16).

573. This was Christ's avowed method of presenting spiritual truth (*John* vi. 63, and elsewhere).

578. *Heavens . . . roll . . . earth . . . rests,* etc. Raphael did not in beginning his narrative care to announce a startling theory of the universe. He conformed his language to the appearance of things and thus justified the method of the Sacred Writers (*Eccl.* i. 4, 5). When afterwards the question was distinctly raised, the same speaker proposed the Copernican theory.

583. *Heaven's great year.* "The years of the right hand of the Most High" (*Ps.* lxxvii. 10) may be noteworthy either for their number or their length. Plato's great year of the fixed stars is 25,920 years, and, according to some writers, equalled the life of the Phœnix (Vir. *Eclog.* iv. 5, 12).

587. *Hierarchs.* Since all believers are "priests unto God" (*Rev.* i. 6), all their leaders are properly called "hierarchs."

589. *Standards and gonfalons.* In the standard the streamer is commonly fixed to the upright staff, in the gonfalon to a horizontal cross-piece. The first is used probably as in the case of the Israelites (*Numb.* ii.). to distinguish the tribes; the second, on account of its prominence in religious processions, to mark those distinguished as the Levites were in the camp of Israel.

594. *In orbs,* etc. Compare the scene described in *Dan.* vii. 9–14.

601. *Thrones, Dominations,* etc. Corresponding to the titles under the government of Babylon when a conspiracy was formed against the advancement of Daniel, the first president (Throne). *Dan.* vi. 1–7.

617. *All seemed,* etc. No loyalty could be more obsequious than that tendered to Darius whom it was proposed for thirty days to raise to godhead.

622. *Mazes intricate,* etc. The rejoicing of Wisdom in the presence of God (compare vii. 10–12 with *Prov.* viii. 30). This play of Wisdom is seen both in the courses of the stars and in the Word of God (*Ps.* xix.), and is hard to understand to those not specially enlightened (2 *Pet.* iii. 15–17).

631. *Desirous.* The longing for fellowship joined with love was manifested by Jesus at the Last Supper (*Luke* xxii. 15).

In circles, a more exact translation than our "round about" (κύκλῳ, *Rev.* vii. 11).

633. *Rubied nectar,* Homer's νέκταρ ἐρυθρὸν (*Il.* xix. 38) and the wine of *Matt.* xxvi. 29.

636. *On flowers reposed,* etc. The angels are sustained by divine grace and in turn manifest graces in themselves (see note on iii. 358).

642. *Ambrosial night. Il.* ii. 57. Sleep, like food and drink, restores the wasted vigor of the human body. Among the immortals the supply is always equal to the waste. Sleep is one of the means to this immortality.

646. *Roseate dews.* The slumber was like that of Jupiter and Juno with "glistering dews" falling upon them from a golden cloud (*Il.* xiv. 351). The scene is one for the angel of Love to describe.

648. *Wider far,* etc. The courts of God at Jerusalem were three: the inner for the Levites, the second for the children of Israel, and the outer for the Gentiles. But his courts are wherever true spiritual devotion is rendered (*John* iv. 21–23).

651. *In bands and files.* These correspond to families and fellowships on earth and are the natural outgrowth of affection. God approves and blesses such unions of aims and desires (*Matt.* xviii. 19, 20).

652. *By living streams,* etc. *Rev.* vii. 17. Israel abiding in tents along the rivers may have furnished a model for this scene. The wizard Balaam found the Israelites too many to be numbered (*Num.* xxiii. 10; xxiv. 5, 6). The houses in which the gods slept were made by Vulcan.

655. *Fanned with cool winds.* Care deprives the lost of slumber, but these cool winds signify the dispersion of care and sorrow (*Rev.* vii. 17; xxi. 3, 4).

658–802. THE CONSPIRACY

A conspiracy of rulers and kings against Jehovah and his Anointed is connected with the Messiah's exaltation (*Ps.* ii.) and with his crucifixion (*Matt.* xxvii. 1, 2). The conspiracy against Daniel is not forgotten, and secret consultations between Agamemnon and Ulysses are imitated.

659. *He of the first,* etc. The other two "presidents" in Babylon were jealous of Daniel's prestige (*Dan.* vi. 4), and the high-priest was the chief conspirator against Christ (*John* xviii. 13, 14).

671. *Next subordinate.* Beelzebub. The relation of the two may be understood from the notes on i. 81 and 82. It is the relation of the Will to the Reason, of the chief to the councillor.

673–685. *Companion dear,* etc. A relation very similar to that between Satan and Beelzebub existed between Agamemnon (ἄγαν + μέμνων , the Very Resolute, or Steadfast) and Ulysses (compare *Il.* iv. 339–361, etc.).

689. *The quarters of the North.* As the Hebrews reckoned direction, the north was on the left hand, and fitly, therefore, the locality of the enemy (*Ezek.* xxxviii. 15). "By the title of the 'North' in Holy Writ the devil is used to be designated, who with the thought to bind up the hearts of the nations with the iciness of insensibility, said, 'I will sit also upon the mount of the covenant in the sides of the north.' And he is 'stretched over the empty place,' because he has possession of the hearts that are not filled with the grace of the love of God" (*Gregory the Great on Job* xxvi. 7).

696. *He together calls,* etc. The tail of the great Dragon "drew the third part of the stars of Heaven" (*Rev.* xii. 4). Beelzebub performs this office in harmony with *Isa.* ix. 15.

697. *Or several.* After Ulysses had gone among the Grecian host and persuaded now one, now another, he addressed the whole army together. Temptation may assail either in public or in private.

703. *Ambiguous words,* etc. Beelzebub resembles Ulysses in this (*Æn.* ii. 98, 99). The warrior commonly wore a cloak which he cast off when he acted his real nature. The Greeks obeyed him when, bearing the royal sceptre, he addressed them in the name of Agamemnon (*Il.* ii. 183–186).

708. *As the morning star.* Pallas distinguished her other favorite, Diomed, with similar glory (*Il.* v. 4–6):

> "Upon his head
> And shield she caused a constant flame to play,
> Like to the autumnal star that shines in heaven
> Most brightly when new bathed in ocean's tides."

Homer's "autumnal star" is Sirius, which in early autumn rises before the sun. Christ calls himself "the bright and morning star," meaning that he is the hope of the world. In his exalted expectation the king of Babylon is compared to Lucifer, "the son of the morning." In sublime anticipation, when the foundations of the earth were laid, "the morning stars sang together." In all these passages the star is the symbol of hope. Beelzebub was elated with hope in the new enterprise of his chief, and by like false hopes one-third of the heavenly host were allured and deceived.

721. *Nearly it now concerns,* etc. Like the heavenly irony in view of the building of the tower of Babel (*Gen.* xi. 4–7).

726. *Let us advise,* etc. Landor says of this: "Such expressions of derision are very ill applied and derogate much from the majesty of the Father. We may well imagine that very different thoughts occupied the Divine Mind." But Landor's ideal God probably differs in many respects from the God of Revelation. Is not ridicule the proper reward of folly? Do we not instinctively laugh at a conspicuous lack of common-sense? Why should God appoint one method for us and another for himself in punishing folly? The humiliation and shame which men feel when they have erred is the effect of the scourge of this divine irony. The Greeks smiled at the discomfiture of Thersites. Athene laughed at the overthrow of the blustering Mars.

734. *Lightning divine.* I am disposed to regard "lightning" as a noun, notwithstanding the form "light'ning" of the first edition. It is the reflection, or rather the visible expression, of the mind of the Father that is thus set forth. Lightning, as we have seen (note on iv. 928), is the symbol of the laughter of Wisdom at the folly of her foes, and is both a weapon and a trophy of her triumph. There was lightning in the face of the angel who had overcome the prince of Persia (*Dan.* x. 6) and in that of the angel who had released our Lord from his tomb (*Matt.* xxviii. 3).

745. *As the stars,* etc. The stars are spoken of under the figure of an army, and a numerous army is also compared to the drops of dew (*Deut.* iv. 19; 2 *Sam.* xvii. 12).

749. *Seraphim and Potentates and Thrones.* Some have undertaken to make out for Milton a ninefold angelic hierarchy, like Dante's, but with little success. Milton's threefold superior division is, I think, taken from 1 *Cor.* xiii. 13. The inner circle about the throne of God is devoted to Love, and on it dwell the Seraphim who are said to love most. The next circle

is given to Hope, and on it are the Potentates, for hope gives strength and courage (*Ps.* cxix. 81; *Rom.* viii. 24). The outer circle is that of Faith and is assigned to the Thrones, because Faith justifies, like one sitting on a throne of judgment. Where Faith, Hope, and Love are, there grow the nine fruits of the Spirit (*Gal.* v. 22, 23). Love, Joy, and Peace characterize the three degrees of Seraphim; Patience, Kindness, and Goodness (the elements of Hope—*Rom.* xv. 4), the three degrees of Potentates; Faithfulness, Meekness, and Self-control, the three degrees of Thrones. But these divisions are not mutually exclusive; a Seraph may also be one of the Potentates or Thrones. Satan and his adherents had already put themselves beyond the outermost circle of Faith, and had forsaken their allegiance.

751. *All thy dominion.* This is coextensive with the earth, including the sea. The proportion fully stated is as follows: The possessions of one man are to the dominions of the race as the dominions of the race are to the kingdoms of the Blessed. Such a proportion is implied in the question, "What shall it profit a man if he gain the whole world and lose his own soul?"

757. *A mount raised on a mount.* In imitation of the "Mountain of the Congregation" described in *Isa.* ii. 2, 3, and *Mic.* iv. 1, 2. There is also, perhaps, an allusion to the exploits of the Giants who piled Ossa upon Pelion, in order to scale the heavens in the contest with the gods.

758. *With pyramids and towers.* Ovid's description of the palace of the Sun is imitated, as at the beginning of Book II.

760. *Lucifer* (Light-bringer), though commonly applied to the morning-star, more fitly designates the sun, as apparently it does here.

770. *Calumnious art,* etc. The calumny consists in representing their beneficent Ruler as a tyrant, the art in so skilfully perverting the divine decree as to give color of truth to the representation.

774. *Merely titular,* empty of significance, since all authority is vested in the Messiah.

783. *Too much to one,* etc. Such was the feeling of those who questioned the authority of Christ and drew from him the parable of the wicked husbandmen who abused the servants and killed the son of the lord of the vineyard (*Luke* xx. 1–14).

792. *Orders and degrees.* In the kingdom of Heaven, says Milton in a melodious period, "they undoubtedly that by their labors, counsels, and prayers have been earnest for the common good of religion and their country shall receive above the inferior orders of the blessed the regal addition of principalities, legions, and thrones into their glorious titles."

799. *Much less for this,* etc. We cannot acknowledge his right to impose laws upon us; much less, because he has done this, can we admit his claim to worship and adoration; we will not obey, much less worship him.

802. *To govern, not to serve.* Satan sees greatness in authority; Christ in service (*Matt.* xx. 25–27; *Luke* xix. 14).

803–907. APOSTASY AND FAITH

Like Enoch and Noah in the antediluvian world and Lot in Sodom, one arises in the midst of the general godlessness to testify against it. He appears, like Antipas the "faithful martyr" at Pergamos (*Rev.* ii. 13), at the very seat of Satan.

805. ABDIEL (Servant of God) is the angel of *Faith.* He has many points in common with the Homeric Vulcan, who among the angry gods advised submission to Jupiter (*Il.* i. 571–583), forged the thunderbolts, and was a most obsequious servant. Vulcan also wrought invincible shields for Hercules, Achilles, and Æneas; Faith performs the same office for the Christian (*Eph.* vi. 16).

807. *In a flame of zeal,* etc. Vulcan, as the god of Fire, was sent by Juno to oppose with his flames the angry current of the river Xanthus roused against Achilles (*Il.* xxi. 136, 235, 324; *Rev.* xii. 15). His association with fire explains the classing of Abdiel with the Seraphim.

832–838. The thought closely follows *Heb.* i., to which other parts of Abdiel's speech also point.

843. *One of our number. Heb.* ii. 11. Keightley supposes the meaning to be that the Son by becoming king over angels lowered himself to their nature, and thus, in effect, raised them to his. Others, admitting this to be the obvious sense, object *Heb.* ii. 16. The latter passage, however, has not prevented theologians from believing that before his incarnation the Messiah existed in the angelic nature. St. Augustine remarks: "God appeared again to Abraham at the oak of Mamre in three men, who, it is not to be doubted, were angels, although some think that one of them was Christ, and assert that he was visible before he put on flesh" (*De Civ. Dei* xvi. 29). This should be compared with *Dan.* iii. 25.

846. *Hasten to appease,* etc. *Ps.* ii. 12.

850. *Out of season . . . singular . . . rash.* The appeals of Faith affect different minds differently. Felix found the message unseasonable (*Acts* xxiv. 25); some reject it because of unpopularity (*John* xii. 42); others because of fear (*John* ix. 22).

856. *Who saw,* etc. An attack upon the first article of faith. *Heb.* xi. 3.

860. *Self-begot, self-raised,* etc. He means that Time and Chance concurred in their production, as Saturn and Ops were the progenitors of the gods.

864. *Our puissance,* etc. *Ps.* xii. 4. In direct opposition to the spirit of Faith, which ascribes all power to God (*Acts* iii. 12, 16).

869. *Beseeching or besieging.* Possibly in allusion to the mock worship paid to Christ by the soldiers (*Matt.* xxvii. 27–30).

872. *As the sound of waters.* "Their voice roareth like the sea" was said of the Northern army arrayed against the daughter of Zion (*Jer.* vi. 22, 23). The figure sustains the allusion to the contest between Vulcan and the roaring Xanthus (*Il.* xxi. 325, 365).

880–894. *Contagion spread.* The apostates are the evil spirits of 2 *Pet.* ii. and *Jude.* Jude likens them to those engaged in Korah's rebellion, to which we here find unmistakable allusions (*Num.* xvi. 16–50).

898. *Unmoved, unshaken,* etc. These words are carefully chosen and signify that Faith is opposed (1) to Unbelief, (2) to Doubt, (3) to Wavering, (4) to Fear. Of these Unbelief is the farthest and Fear the slightest remove from Faith; the adjectives are, therefore, in the order of a climax which is continued in the nouns, Loyalty, Love, and Zeal.

901. *Nor number, nor example,* etc. The evil spirits of Peter and Jude are associated with the destruction of Sodom and Gomorrah (2 *Pet.* ii. 6–8; *Jude* 7). Abdiel's experience is like Lot's.

905. *Nor of violence,* etc. The superiority of the faithful to all sorts of physical torture and violence has been proved in all ages (*Heb.* xi. 36, 37).

BOOK VI

1–43. THE REWARD OF FAITH

LIKE THE faithful ones of earth, Abdiel escapes from his peril among the enemies of God and receives divine approval for his steadfastness.

1, 2. *All night,* etc. He was protected a whole night, like Daniel, from the mouths of lions, and escaped, like Lot, through the plain to the mountain of safety.

3. *Circling hours.* The Hours (Ὧραι, Seasons) were originally understood as divisions not of the day but of the year; and they were twelve in number, corresponding to the twelve signs of the zodiac. Commentators on *Gen.* xlix. have pointed out a connection between the twelve signs and the twelve sons of Jacob. In *Rev.* xxi. 12, the names of the twelve tribes are written on the twelve gates of the new Jerusalem, and at those gates are likewise twelve angels whom, in all probability, Milton regarded as impersonations of the Hours. The venerable Bede substituted the names of the twelve Apostles for those of the heathen signs of the zodiac.

4. *There is a cave,* etc. Lot dwelt in a cave of the mountain while God was destroying Sodom; Moses was hidden in a "cleft of the rock" on Mount Sinai, while the glory of God passed by (*Exod.* xxxiii. 22). Others of the sacred writers speak of hiding from the terrible glory of God in "clefts of the rock" (1 *Kings* xix. 9–13; *Isa.* ii. 19–21). The glory which is unbearable to men and from which they need to be hidden is the beatific day of Heaven, but even there the angelic nature gratefully receives the shade. Moreover, the difference between Heaven and Earth is emphasized in that here man must retire into the cave, there the glory retires.

10. "*Obsequious,* obedient, doing its duty, cf. 783; now a depricatory word, implying servile."—*Pitt Press.* But is not the word intended to set forth the contrast between the ruling majesty of Light and the subordinate function of Darkness?

12. *Went forth the Morn,* etc. If Night retires as a servant, Day comes as a conquering ruler. In Homer the Morn is arrayed in "saffron robes."

16. *Embattled squadrons.* In the morning Elisha (one of the faithful embraced in *Heb.* xi. 32) by special illumination saw himself guarded against the foes who had gathered in the night (2 *Kings* vi. 17).

19. *War in procinct.* "The Roman soldiers standing ready to give battle were 'in procinctu,' girded."—*Clar. Press.*

20. *Already known,* etc. The king of Israel learned from Elisha the movement of the Syrians before the messengers came and verified the prophet's word (2 *Kings* vi. 8–12).

26. *High applauded.* The "good report" obtained by the faithful (*Heb.* xi. 2, 39).

29. *Servant of God, well done!* etc. The reward of the faithful (*Matt.* xxv. 21).

32. *In word mightier than they in arms.* The Word of God, which Abdiel maintained, is "sharper than a two-edged sword" (*Heb.* iv. 12).

44–110. THE MARCH TO BATTLE

The rebellion is against the divine decree, and therefore Michael's army contains the defenders of the Law while Satan's contains its enemies. The forces approach each other like the Greeks and Trojans moving to battle.

44. MICHAEL (Who is like God?) is the spirit of Justice. In *Jude* (9) he appears as the antagonist of Satan, contending about the body of Moses, the Lawgiver. He resembles Achilles, the son of Thetis (Law), the greatest warrior of the *Iliad*. Landor thinks that the "archangel is here commanded to do what God gave him not strength to do." This is an error of the same nature as that corrected in the note on i. 170.

45. *In military prowess next.* In the Grecian host the strongest warrior after Achilles was Ajax, the war-hero; but since "Wisdom is better than weapons of war" (*Eccl.* ix. 18), Gabriel here fitly holds the second place.

49. *Equal in number.* These military saints, led by the spirit of the Law, are to inflict upon the rebels the penalties for transgression. Every violation of the Law has its appropriate penalty (*Heb.* ii. 2).

56. *Clouds began,* etc. The scene resembles Sinai on the morning of the day when God descended to communicate the Law to Moses (*Exod.* xix. 16–18). The clouds veil from the eyes of finite beings the unendurable terror of God's wrath, and the smoke binds up the flashes of anger that seem trying to get free and consume the disobedient.

60. TRUMPET. The first of the trumpets mentioned in *Rev.* viii. The trumpet, the loudness and the terror all accompanied the giving of the

Law on Sinai (*Exod*. xix. 16).

62. *Quadrate* Masson understands to mean "a cubic mass." The Latin *quadratus agmen* means an army marching in regular order of battle in the form of a parallelogram.

63–69. The union (*Il*. iii. 9), the noiseless obedience to leaders (*Il*. iv. 427–432), the heroic ardor (μένεα πνείοντες), and the firmness under the leadership of Neptune (*Il*. xiii. 130–133) manifested by the Greeks before Troy are all here attributed to the marching angels. Similar union, order, wisdom, obedience, and firmness are enjoined upon Christians (*Eph*. iv. 1–16).

73. *As when the total kind,* etc. Probably with chief reference to *Rev.* xix. 17.

79. *Far in the horizon,* etc. The enemies of Israel fill the whole "breadth of the land" at their coming (*Isa*. viii. 8; *Rev*. xx. 8, 9).

83. *Shields various.* The Trojan army, unlike the Grecian, was composed of many different nations and languages, and fought less unitedly than the Greeks. Here the loyal army has but one kind of shield—Faith; while the apostates put their trust in various things—Force, Cunning, Valor, etc. (*Isa*. x. 12, 13).

85. *Banded powers,* etc. The word "banded" directs us to *Ezek*. xxxviii., where the army of Gog with "all his bands" is preparing to burst "like a storm" upon Israel. In fact this particular prophecy contains the entire basis for the distinction in physical aspect between the battles of the three days.

99. *High in the midst,* etc. Another view reminding us of Satan's resemblance to the Rutulian leader, Turnus (*Æn*. vii. 783, 784). The epithet "godlike" (Θεοειδής) is applied by Homer to Paris, Hector, Sarpedon, and other favorites of Apollo.

101. *Idol* (εἴδωλον), image. The reason for speaking of Satan as the image or likeness of divine majesty will be seen in the note on l. 301.

102. "*Flaming* would be properly of Seraphim, but perhaps Milton thought that the Seraphim of Isaiah were the Cherubim of Ezekiel."—*Keightley*. How lightly this critic tosses aside the supposed erudition of Milton! As the sun among clouds, so is Satan among the Cherubim; and as the dark masses are brightened by its beams, so under Satan's influence the Cherubim which have no light in themselves become "flaming."

103. *Then lighted,* etc. Hector, though using a chariot to bear him from place to place, was accustomed to fight on foot (*Il*. v. 494; vi. 103).

109. *Haughty strides,* etc. So the godlike Paris advanced in front of the Trojan line when moving to battle (*Il*. iii. 16–22). In like manner Goliath defied the armies of Israel; the epithet "towering" strongly suggests the Philistine giant.

111–201. ABDIEL'S SINGLE COMBAT WITH SATAN

This combat unites features of that between the scrupulously truthful Menelaus and the perfidious Paris, and that between David and Goliath, suggesting at the same time others of the faithful worthies named in *Heb.* xi.—Samson, Gideon, Elijah, and the prophets.

114. *O heaven!* etc. Apparently a general feeling towards the divinely beautiful but cowardly and treacherous Paris (*Il.* iii. 39, etc.). Such emotion is the sign of a faithful spirit (*Rev.* ii. 2; 1 *Sam.* xvii. 26).

118. *To sight unconquerable.* So Goliath seemed to the men of Israel, except David, and so the Anakim to the spies, except Caleb and Joshua.

120. *Whose reason I have tried,* etc. Menelaus tried the effect of an embassy upon the Trojans and afterwards the effect of force (*Il.* iii. 205, 351). David, having heard the blasphemy of Goliath, put him on a level with the brutish lion and bear, to be dealt with only by force. Samson, too, by means of a riddle upon a lion which he had slain, vanquished the Philistines intellectually before he did it physically (*Judg.* xiv. 18, 19).

128. *Half-way,* etc. David met Goliath between the armies of Israel and Philistia (1 *Sam.* xvii. 48); Menelaus met Paris between those of Troy and Greece (*Il.* iii. 340–342).

137. *Out of smallest things,* etc. David killed Goliath with a smooth stone from the brook and revived Israel's faith in God, illustrating the truth of John the Baptist's declaration that out of "these stones" God could "raise up children unto Abraham" (*Matt.* iii. 9).

139. *Or with solitary hand,* etc. Illustrated by the fate of Sennacherib under the hand of the destroying angel (2 *Kings* xix. 35).

147. *My sect,* etc. The "*followers*" of them who through faith inherit promises" (*Heb.* vi. 12).

152. *Seditious angel.* Involving the charge brought by Ahab against Elijah—"Art thou he that troubleth Israel?"

161. *Some plume.* After the combat Menelaus bore away "the helmet with the horse-hair crest" that belonged to Paris (*Il.* iii. 369). David brought away from the conflict with Goliath the head of the giant, presumably with the helmet (1 *Sam.* xvii. 54).

168. *The minstrelsy,* etc. The minstrelsy of David more than once put to flight the evil spirit in Saul (1 *Sam.* xvi. 14–23). For the next line compare the taunt of Goliath, "Am not I a Philistine and ye servants to Saul?"

183. *Reign thou in Hell,* etc. *Ps.* lv. 15. David's threat consigned Goliath to the same fate—"I will smite thee and take thine head from thee."

188. *On thy impious crest.* Faith strikes at the seat of reason and intelligence. David smote Goliath on the forehead. Menelaus smote Paris on the head, but his weapon failed him (*Il.* iii. 361–363).

189. *He lifted high.* Menelaus commonly prayed to Jove before striking

a blow (*Il*. iii. 351–354, etc.). David met Goliath in the name of God. Christ taught the need of divine aid for casting out devils (*Matt*. xvii. 21).

190. *Swift with tempest*. Abdiel's classical counterpart, Vulcan (note on v. 805), forger of Jove's thunderbolts, sometimes used his own terrible fires in battle. When Juno summoned him to the conflict at Troy, she gave him a tempest of the winds to consume the foe, "heads and armor," with a fiery torrent (*Il*. xxi. 335, 336). Elijah brought fire from heaven upon his enemies (2 *Kings* i. 9–14).

193. *Ten paces huge*, etc. Hector recoiled and fell on his knee when struck by Diomed on his triple helmet, the gift of Apollo (*Il*. xi. 350–356). The third captain sent by Ahaziah to arrest Elijah sank to his knees in supplication. Satan does involuntary homage to Faith (*James* ii. 19).

197. *A mountain*, etc. The evil spirit who the disciples could not cast out was spoken of by Christ as a mountain that a little faith might remove into the sea (*Matt*. xvii. 18–20). Compare *Faerie Queene* I. xi. 54.

200. *Ours joy filled*, etc. As in the armies of Israel, when the huge bulk of Goliath lay lifeless upon the ground (1 *Sam*. xvii. 52).

202–405. MICHAEL'S ENCOUNTER WITH SATAN

The ensuing conflict resembles the contest of the Greeks and Trojans over the dead body of Patroclus, whom Achilles finally comes upon the field to avenge. It is the contest referred to in *Jude*, where Michael is said to have disputed with the devil about the body of Moses, and is elsewhere designated as a contest between the Letter and the Spirit of the Law.

202. *Archangel* TRUMPET. The second sounding, that of *Rev*. viii. 8. For the shouting compare *Josh*. vi. 20 and *Judg*. vii. 20–24.

207. *Now storming fury rose*, etc. Some of the noises of battle are referred to in *Job* xxxix. 23–25; but Homer's descriptions are more direct and complete (*Il*. iv. 440–451). Milton's critics invariably select this passage to show how the poet has confused matter and spirit. But it must be interpreted in view of *Ezek*. xxxviii. 9, upon which it is based. There is a "war of elements" in which ethereal forces contend; there are arrows of heat and cold, spears of light and shields of darkness, chariots of cloud and steeds of fire. There is also spiritual warfare—the "clamor" of contradiction, the clashing of "arms on armor" in intellectual attack and defence, the "brazen chariots" of transporting passions which such contests generate.

215. *Under fiery cope*. Compare the fighting over the corpse of Patroclus (*Il*. xvii. 366–377).

217. *Heaven resounded*, etc. As when the gods took part in the strife

before Troy (*Il.* xx. 56–58).

221. *The least of whom,* etc. The angels under Michael were the defenders of the Law. Since its least portion has a greater validity than the whole course of nature, the good angels may be said to be armed with the momentum of all the elements (*Matt.* v. 18).

223. *How much more,* etc. It does not follow that because he who breaks one part of the Law is guilty of the whole, therefore he who breaks all the parts is no more guilty. The meaning is that every part of the Law is defended with the force of the whole.

230. *Each divided legion,* etc. The spirit of Gadara is spoken of in the same breath as one and many. "What is thy name? And he said Legion" (*Luke* viii. 30). He was a spirit of uncleanness that found the body of swine an acceptable refuge and embraced all the various forms of vice allied in kinship of defilement.

234. *To turn the sway of battle* is to change defence into attack, as Jesus invariably did when assailed by his enemies.

236. *The ridges* are the ranks of the host.—*Clar. Press.* The ranks are opened by drawing aside the shields, to throw weapons in attack; closed by bringing together the shields in defence.

240. *Deeds of eternal fame,* etc. Those who do and teach the Law are "called great in the kingdom of Heaven" (*Matt.* v. 19; *Ps.* cxix. 96).

245. *In even scale,* etc. When Hector was about to encounter Achilles for the last time, Jove weighed the destinies of the two warriors and showed the immediate death of Hector (*Il.* xxii. 209–213).

247. *Prodigious power,* etc. After the death of Patroclus, and before the coming of Achilles to avenge him, Hector was the most powerful warrior on the field of Troy and struck terror even into Ajax and Menelaus. Besides, the Greeks were compelled to fight in darkness and invisible to one another (*Il.* xvii. 565–647). Such darkness is hinted at, as an essential part of this scene, in the expression, "fighting seraphim confused." Moral darkness comes whenever the devil has unusual power, as at the time when Christ was arrested (*Luke* xxii. 53).

250. *Felled squadrons at once.* Jupiter declared that if all the Trojans, without the aid of the gods, were ranged against Achilles, they could not resist him even "for a little while" (*Il.* xx. 26, 27). Michael wields "the sword of the Spirit." When the Spirit came upon Samson, with the jaw-bone of an ass he slew a thousand Philistines (*Judg.* xv. 14–16).

251. *Two-handed sway.* In allusion, probably, to the fact that the tables of the Law filled Moses' two hands (*Deut.* ix. 15).

255. *Tenfold adamant.* Satan opposes the letter of the Law to its spirit; the pride of such a nature is almost invincible (*Matt.* xix. 16–26).

258. *Glad,* etc. The feeling of Achilles when he saw Hector approaching (*Il.* xx. 423, 424).

260. *Captive dragged in chains.* Satan was led captive by Christ (*Eph.* iv. 8). Achilles frowned when about to fight with Hector (*Il.* xx. 428; xxii. 260, 312) and afterwards dragged him dead at his chariot wheels.

275. *Evil go with thee,* etc. Compare the curse upon Simon Magus, who wished to buy the Holy Ghost with money (*Acts* viii. 18–20).

282. *Nor think thou,* etc. The constant reply to the threats of Achilles is that he is terrible only with words. From several instances take *Il.* xxii. 279–282:

> "Godlike Achilles, thou hast missed thy mark;
> Nor hast thou learned my doom from Jupiter,
> As thou pretendest. Thou art glib of tongue,
> And cunningly thou orderest thy speech
> In hope that I who hear thee may forget
> My might and valor."

293. *Meanwhile,* etc. Those who despise the Law (Moses) are certain also to despise the Gospel (Christ) (*John* v. 45–47).

297. *For who, though with,* etc. Three vigorous similes fall short of expressing the tumult of the battle when Hector and Neptune (like Achilles, a representative of retributive justice) led the opposing hosts of Troy and Greece into conflict (*Il.* xiv. 394–399).

301. *Likest gods they seemed,* etc. The apparent equality established by the poet between Michael and Satan may be understood, if we recall what they represent. When Patroclus was slain, Hector stripped from him the armor of Achilles and afterwards wore it himself, so that Vulcan was called upon to forge a new suit for the Grecian hero. This illustrates the meaning exactly. The Law is divine in letter and spirit, but the letter may be used to oppose its true intent, as the devil used the Scripture in tempting Christ and as the Jews used it to condemn the only perfectly obedient One to death (*John* xix. 7). Thus Satan withstood Michael in armor belonging of right to the saint himself.

304. *Swords.* Neptune, the avenger, has "a sword of fearful length and flashing blade like lightning" (*Il.* xiv. 385, 386). The sword of the Spirit encounters a two-edged sword (*Heb.* iv. 12). This is perhaps the dilemmas with which Jesus was frequently assailed by his enemies and with which he attacked them in turn. Several of them are given in *Luke* xx.

305. *Shields.* The Word of God (compared to the sun in *Ps.* xix.) is a means of defence as well as of attack and is so used by sinners as well as by saints.

311. *Nature's concord* is produced by the operation of law: to oppose the Law to itself would be a return to Chaos.

316. *With next to Almighty arm.* God gave the Law and he alone can

abrogate it in letter or in spirit. But the victory of Christ delivered men from the bondage of the letter into the freedom of the spirit (2 *Cor.* iii. 6).

320. *The sword of Michael,* etc. The presence of the Spirit gave temper to the sword of Michael, and effect to the words of Peter on the day of Pentecost, else the miracle of Christ's resurrection would have had no more power than other miracles. The gift of the Spirit enabled the Apostles to address every man in his own tongue in a more intimate sense than is usually supposed; it enabled them to show men their own hearts and to make their own thoughts act the part of accusers.

322. *Neither keen nor solid,* etc. The first of these words is often applied to wit or wisdom, the second to stupidity or ignorance. Peter first refuted the slander and enlightened the ignorance of his hearers, and then charged upon them the guilt of having murdered Christ (*Acts* ii. 12, 13, 36).

327. *Then Satan first knew pain,* etc. When the multitudes had heard Peter, "they were pricked in their heart." No such feeling seems ever before to have resulted from the preaching of the Gospel.

329. *Discontinuous wound.* The sword of the Spirit "divides asunder the soul and spirit, the joints and marrow, and is a discerner of the thoughts and intents of the heart" (*Heb.* iv. 12). The account of the wound inflicted by Michael is apparently based on this verse.

332. *Nectarous humor.* When Mars was wounded as Satan here is, he hurried groaning and bleeding to the skies (*Il.* v. 856–871). Tears, instead of blood, are the sign of a wounded spirit. The "nectarous humor" of angels corresponds to the tears of men, the word "nectarous" bearing the analogy to the *saltness* of tears, because of the preserving quality of salt. Compare note on v. 56.

335. *Forthwith,* etc. *Il.* xiv. 424–431.

344. *Soon he healed.* Pæan healed Mars after he was wounded by Diomed (*Il.* v. 899–901), just as flattery restores the spirit wounded by rebuke. The chariots of Hector and Satan probably signify nearly the same thing as the ministrations of Pæan—the support furnished by the favorable public opinion of their adherents.

350. *All heart they live,* etc. The *Clar. Press* quotes what Pliny says of God (*Nat. Hist.* ii. 5): "Quacunque in parte, totus est sensus, totus visus, totus auditus, totus animæ, totus animi, totus sui." If the devil is in the heart ever so little, he is there with all his faculties (*Matt.* xiii. 13–15); and likewise if faith is there in ever so small a measure, it is there with all its saving efficacy (*Matt.* xvii. 20).

355–357. *Gabriel . . . Moloch.* The encounter between Gabriel and Moloch, like the encounters between Pallas, or her favorite Diomed, and Mars, illustrates the superiority of Wisdom to brute Force (*Eccl.* ix. 18). The wisdom of the proto-martyr Stephen "cut to the heart" the murderers of Christ, so that they stopped their ears, cried with a loud voice, ran upon the spiritual victor and took his life (*Acts* vi. 11–14; vii. 54–57). But Moloch (Mars) was defeated in the contest with Stephen no less than in the contest with Diomed (*Il.* v. 859–861) or the present encounter with Gabriel.

363–365. *Uriel and Raphael . . . Adrammelech and Asmadai.* The former two we have already met. Adrammelech (2 *Kings* xvii. 31) was one of the foreign gods brought into Samaria with those who settled there after the captivity of the ten tribes. Asmadai is the evil spirit whom Raphael drove, as narrated in the book of Tobit, into the uttermost parts of Egypt. These contests may be understood by comparing them with those between Phœbus and Neptune, between Mercury and Latona, and between Juno and Diana. In the first, the light of the sun, with all that it implies, is opposed to the darkness of the shadow of death, and the light wins. In the second, the peaceful activity of Mercury, god of the useful arts, is opposed to the absolute inertness of Latona (Death). In the third, the wedded love of Juno is opposed to the virgin indifference of Diana (*Il.* xx. 70–72). Uriel wins as Phœbus does. Raphael, as we have seen, unites the qualities of Mercury and Juno, and his victory over Asmadai, therefore, means a conquest over both inertness and indifference.

369–371. *Abdiel . . . Ariel,* etc. Compare the deeds of Menelaus (*Il.* xvii. 61–81, 109). These additional exploits of Abdiel suggest *Heb.* xi. 33, 34, where Faith is said to have "stopped the mouths of lions, quenched the violence of fire." Ariel (Lion of God) is a name applied to Jerusalem (*Isa.* xxix. 1) and stands for the Jewish people; Arioch (Lion-like) probably represents the nations akin to the Jews, and Ramiel the Gentiles.

These victories of the angels are paralleled on earth in the conquests won by the apostles in their preaching. After Philip's testimony on both sides of Jerusalem, to the Samaritans on the north and the Ethiopian on the south, came Paul's and Peter's to the Gentiles. Beginning at Jerusalem and extending to the neighboring nations, they finally proclaimed the Gospel to all men (*Acts* viii. 5–8, 26–39; ix. 20–31).

375. *Contented with their fame,* etc. Such fame was that of Dorcas and Cornelius (*Acts* ix. 39; x. 4).

386–393. This passage has its basis in *Ps.* lxxvi.

406–523. THE FIRST NIGHT COUNCIL

Stripped of its allegorical cloak, the question before the apostates is by what means to resist and quench the Holy Spirit who caused them pain and wrought all their discomfiture. The plan devised is an invention which, literally understood, would mean the gunpowder and cannon used in earthly wars, and which in spiritual effect is analogous to that of intoxicants upon men. In those who use it, it produces forgetfulness of pain (*Prov.* xxxi. 6, 7), and their drunken laughter is discomfiting to all lovers of order and sobriety. Figures drawn from drunkenness applied to spiritual conditions are very common in the Scriptures.

412. *Placed in guard their watch.* The Trojans kept watch after their success over the Greeks deserted by Achilles (*Il.* viii. 553–565). Christ enjoins watchfulness upon his followers, and lights up the dark future for them with the "cherubic fires" of prophecy (*Matt.* xxiv.).

416. *Council.* Agamemnon called a council after his defeat by the Trojans (*Il.* ix. 9–12).

418. *Known in arms.* The address of Teucer to his men in adversity is purposely imitated (Hor. *Odes* I. vii. 30–32). The introduction of Teucer's sentiments foreshadows a change in Satan's war policy.

425. *Powerfullest.* In an important sense this is true, notwithstanding the overthrow of the third day. They had resisted the Holy Spirit, but his function is not to take vengeance.

432. *As soon contemned.* Thus doing "despite unto the Spirit of Grace" (*Heb.* x. 29).

438. *More valid arms,* etc. Resistance to the Spirit is hardening. Apparently the more violent weapons are satire and ridicule, such as the Pharisees used when they drew from Jesus a warning against blasphemy of the Holy Ghost (*Mark* iii. 22–30; *Matt.* xii. 24–37).

442. *If other hidden cause,* etc. The Pharisees who had been warned against blasphemy sought after a sign, apparently that they might exercise their ingenuity in bringing discredit upon it (*Matt.* xii. 38).

447. Nisroch (Great Eagle) was the god of the Ninevites (2 *Kings* xix. 37), and corresponds to the Aquilo, or Boreas, of the ancients, who is referred to by Milton in the verses *On the Death of a Fair Infant* (8–12). The deity is associated with robbery and violence, as appears in the "boisterous rape" of Aquilo and in the character of the Ninevites (*Nah.* iii. 1; *Jon.* iii. 8). Nisroch represents *Selfishness,* which is condemned in the Scriptures under the name of Adultery, the word being used in the spiritual sense of loving self more than God. Christ charges this sin upon those who had spoken against the Holy Ghost, and warns them by the example of Nineveh, which had repented at the preaching of Jonah (*Matt.* xii. 39, 41). Nisroch is the "prime of principalities," whether we consider the size and strength of the eagle, the importance of Nineveh, or the antagonism of selfishness to the first great commandment.

449. *Sore toiled.* A reminiscence of *Il.* x. 471, where the Thracians, from the country of Boreas, are said to have slept after battle "overpowered with toil." Compare the condition of those who tried to entangle Jesus in his talk (*Matt.* xxii. 46).

450. *Cloudy in aspect.* The gloominess of the god is duplicated in his

worshipper, Sennacherib, whose army had been annihilated at one stroke by the angel of the Lord (Michael?).

456. *For what avails,* etc. The strength of Nisroch is subdued by spiritual pain, as the strong man armed and defending his house is overcome and spoiled by a stronger (*Matt.* xii. 29).

459. *Sense of pleasure,* etc. What Nisroch contemplates as not undesirable is the condition described by St. Paul as "past feeling" (*Eph.* iv. 19).

462. *Pain is perfect misery,* etc. Selfishness demands personal comfort and convenience; hence pain is an efficient weapon against it. Pain is much less effective against Ambition, by which, as in Satan, it is even despised.

469. *With look composed.* This contrasts with the disturbed countenance of Nisroch. Satan nevertheless proposes a course to satisfy Selfishness; it is to meet the sober demands of righteousness with contempt and ridicule.

475. *Plant, fruit, flower ambrosial.* From the distillation of these men get the fiery essence of alcohol, the intoxicating principle of all spirituous liquors. There is a moral as well as a physical drunkenness, where the natural instincts and appetites, released from the control of reason, exercise themselves as in beasts; and in both Nineveh and Babylon the two seem to be united and to constitute the conspicuous vice of those wicked cities. It is with the spiritual intoxication of so-called Pleasure that Satan proposes to quell the pain of spiritual wounding. A remarkable passage in prophecy (see note on l. 574) associates the drunkenness and degradation of Nineveh with what seems a description of cannon.

482. *In their dark nativity,* etc. Venus, or Aphrodite (ἀφρός, foam), the goddess of Pleasure, was born of foam *(spuma)* on the bosom of the sea.

484. *Hollow engines,* etc. The description is so ordered as to harmonize with what the Bible says of the human throat through which, with its vocal organs, evil thoughts are uttered and which may become "an open sepulchre" (*Rom.* iii. 13).

485. *With touch of fire.* Perhaps the fire of temptation whose instrument is the tongue (*James* iii. 6).

487. *From far,* etc. The epithet of Apollo (Ἕκατος, the far-shooter) is again called into service. Apollo was an archer and incited Pandarus to shoot at Menelaus after his victory over Paris. What suggestions of lust in this collocation of names and things! Pandarus (from whose name comes *pander*) uses a bow made of goats' horns to avenge the humiliation of Paris, the paramour of Helen and favorite of Venus (*Il.* iv. 105–126). Paris himself was formidable only with the bow, likewise made of horn; and he wounded in the foot both Diomed and Achilles, killing the latter. Homer particularly describes the noise of the bow of Pandarus, but Milton follows a stanza in Spenser (*Faerie Queene* I. vii. 13).

490. *Disarmed the Thunderer.* When Paris with his arrows had wounded

Diomed, he exulted in his foe's discomfiture with a laugh (*Il.* xi. 378). The war-horse, whose "neck is clothed with thunder," neighs, as if laughing in scorn, at the sound of battle. Thunder, then, both here and elsewhere, symbolizes laughter. The laughter of worldlings, pleasure-seekers, and drunkards is the base counterfeit of Wisdom's terrible laughter at the folly of sin.

493. *Meanwhile revive,* etc. Compare the words of the archer, Teucer (Hor. *Odes* I. vii. 25–29).

501. *In future days,* etc. A similar prophecy is found in *Il.* xii. 34, 35; and, when analyzed, the doings of Apollo (Destroyer) and Neptune (Death) in breaking down the Grecian wall very much resemble those of the inventors of cannon in breaking down fortifications and making the use of ordinary armor ridiculous.

511. *The originals of nature,* etc. Corresponding in man to the Appetites, needful for sustaining and propagating life. In the same line of interpretation the "sulphurous and nitrous foam" represents the instincts of Desire and Aversion.

517. *Mineral and stone.* Milton calls these the "entrails" of the earth, and the entrails or bowels in man are often spoken of as the seat of the Sensibilities. The unregenerate heart is hard and cruel (*Rom.* ii. 5).

519. *Incentive reed.* See note on l. 485.

520. *Pernicious* (*perniciosus, per + neco,* to kill outright), destructive. The obvious sense is that the reeds, being touched to fire and ignited, become destructive when applied to the powder in the cannon. The tongue in man, first "set on fire of Hell," in turn "sets on fire the course of nature."

521. *Conscious Night.* Night is *confederate* and aids in the mischievous design.

524–670. THE SECOND DAY'S BATTLE

The virulence of the conflict hastens the doom of the apostates, as the sinfulness of men will hasten the last Judgment. The antediluvians, the cities of the Plain, and Jerusalem are all cited as illustrations of the condition of things just before the conclusion of the world's history.

526. The *matin* TRUMPET. The third sounding of *Rev.* viii. A morning trumpet sounding in the glow of a ruddy dawn announces the struggle that brings the catastrophe of judgment (*Ezek.* vii. 6, 7, 10, 14). It is like the divine threat before the Deluge (*Gen.* vi. 3).

527. *Golden panoply,* etc. "The whole armor of God" without a stain (*Eph.* vi. 11–17).

529. *Light armed.* The watchers wear armor which is less than the panoply—only a helmet and a breastplate (1 *Thess.* v. 6–8). The word

scour conveys the idea of a more careful search than a survey from the hill-tops. These watchmen and scouts carry the light of truth to the remotest parts of the world (*Matt.* xxiv. 14; *Mark* xvi. 15). This is one of the preliminaries to the end.

535. Zophiel (Spy of God) corresponds to the Iris of the *Iliad* in her office of messenger, in her tempest-like fleetness, and in the warning which she bears (*Il.* ii. 790–797). Both Homer and Milton make Iris not so much the rainbow as the morning and the evening red, the former foretelling foul, the latter fair weather. Zophiel is the spirit of *Zeal* and comes from the Cherubim to signify that he is directed by Knowledge, not like the zealous Jews (*Rom.* x. 2), or like Iris reproaching Pallas, calling her "as shameless as a hound" (*Il.* viii. 423).

539. *So thick a cloud.* The armies to come in the last days against Israel are "like a cloud" (*Ezek.* xxxviii. 9, 16). Compare *Il.* iv. 274. The form of the announcement fits the messenger.

546. *Rattling storm of arrows.* Consistent with the idea of a hail-storm. The arrows of Apollo rattled in his quiver when he came in anger to send a pestilence among the Greeks (*Il.* i. 46). St. Chrysostom in a homily on *Eph.* vi. 14–17 says that "Satan's fiery darts are doubts, evil desires, and sharp sorrows."

553. *Training,* etc. While Pandarus was bending his bow, the Trojans about him held up their shields to conceal the perfidious preparation (*Il.* iv. 113–115). Teucer, the Grecian archer, hid behind the shield of Ajax while fixing his arrows to the bow (*Il.* viii. 266–277).

558. *Vanguard,* etc. The irony and equivocation of this speech is usually regarded as a wholly unnecessary and not very successful attempt at humor on the part of Milton. But it is essential. The aim is to describe the action not of artillery but of wit. Literal cannon, Milton knew as well as we do, would be an absurdity in angelic warfare, but he has warned us distinctly enough (v. 571–574) that material images are employed to shadow forth the invisible operations of spirits. The noise of the cannon is analogous to laughter, but even that is not ultimate with the poet whose aim is rather to describe the mood here of those who laugh, and presently the confusion of those who are laughed at. Since the wit is Satanic, it need not be of the highest order.

572. *A triple mounted row,* etc. The Thracians who came from the country of Boreas ranged their arms in triple rows (*Il.* x. 473). Bacchus, the lustful god, who was also specially worshipped in Thrace, had in his train the Satyrs, a drunken, gluttonous, and lascivious rabble. The three kinds of animal appetite seem to be symbolized in these triple-based rows of gaping mouths.

574. *Hollowed bodies,* etc. There is a remarkable parallel between this parenthetical clause and the prophecy of *Nah.* ii. 2–4. The hollowed bod-

ies ("the emptiers have emptied them out"), the branches lopt ("marred their vine branches"), and the fir trees ("the fir trees shall be terribly shaken") are associated with other features in the same passage that are repeated here.

579. *A seraph,* etc. Bacchus had in his train a multitude of frantic devotees bearing thyrsi—reeds with pine cones at the point, often lighted so as to make torches. The seraphs are doubtless these Bacchæ who inflamed the lust of the Satyrs.

586. *Whose roar,* etc. Apparently one of the forms Milton gives his favorite myth—the story of Orpheus, who represents the original harmony of nature, torn in pieces by the frantic rage of the devotees of Bacchus.

588. *Disgorging foul,* etc. *Matt.* xv. 18–20. The vomit of the cannon is analogous to the loud laughter and filthy jesting of sensualists, which it is not only impossible to meet with reason but a shame even to listen to. The purer the spirit the more offensive and intolerable is the stench of such utterances.

592. *None on their feet,* etc. Spenser's Orgoglio delivered blows like those of a cannon-ball which would have "overthrown a stony towre" (*Faerie Queene* I. vii. 12). The Red-Cross Knight was unarmed when attacked by Orgoglio, "and lightly lept from underneath the blow," though overpowered by the mere wind of it. The use of arms is, of course, to convict and expel the apostates; but what can seriousness avail against satire and ridicule? Ridicule cannot touch virtue itself; but vain efforts to compel drunkards to sobriety may easily become ridiculous (*Matt.* vii. 6).

600. *If on they rushed,* etc. The situation was substantially the same as when Israel tried to punish the shameful deed of Gibeah and were beaten on two successive days by the slingers of Benjamin (*Judg.* xx.).

603. *To their foes a laughter.* Paris, when he had wounded Diomed, sprung from his ambush with laughter, and this laughter of the archers seems to have been particularly annoying and confusing (*Il.* xi. 378–406).

609. *Why come not on,* etc. Like the taunt of Hector, when Diomed, fearing the thunder of Jupiter, fled before him (*Il.* viii. 160–166). Whenever Jupiter helped the Trojans with his thunder, the Greeks were discomfited and driven.

614. *As they would dance.* Meriones, dodging the spear of Æneas, is ridiculed by the latter as a dancer (*Il.* xvi. 617, 618). The Satyrs, who represent the satisfaction of the animal appetites, are pre-eminently dancing creatures (*Isa.* xiii. 21).

619. *Result* (*re* + *saltare,* to dance again) has a double meaning, like "open front," "composition," and "proposals." The speech that follows also bristles with puns.

620. *Belial.* The promotion of this spirit of idleness and sensuality into prominence guarantees the meaning of the whole scene. It points to the conflict at Gibeah (*Judg.* xix. to xxi.). The outrage upon nature by the sons of Belial, its unanimous condemnation throughout eleven tribes of Israel, the left-handed slingers in defence, the repulse of Israel of whom thousands were "destroyed down to the ground," the inspiration from Heaven to renewed attack, the ambush, the final victory that came from a prior annihilation of all partners and means in lust and debauchery, the purifying flames that obliterated the defiled city, the threatened extinction of a whole tribe, and its preservation by union with the virgins of Jabesh, form a logically connected series of incidents by which Milton has certainly been guided in this part of his narrative.

629. *Highthened,* etc. Like Hector and the Trojans after their first success in battle with the favor of Jove (*Il.* viii. 538–554).

635. *Rage prompted them.* After Diomed was wounded by Paris, Ulysses sustained the fight almost alone against the Trojans, like

> "A wild boar issuing forth
> From a deep thicket, whetting the white tusks
> Within his crooked jaws; they press around
> And hear his gnashings, yet beware to come
> Too nigh the terrible animal."

The picture of rage is perfect (*Il.* xi. 414–418). The boastings of Hector in anticipation of a victory over Diomed kindled the anger of Juno, so that she shuddered till Olympus quaked (*Il.* viii. 198–200).

639. *Their arms away they threw.* The disciples, when "the abomination of desolation" appeared, fled, unencumbered, as quickly as possible, to the mountains (*Matt.* xxiv. 15–20). The time comes when the filthiness of the wicked becomes intolerable, the Holy Spirit departs, and widespread disasters ensue.

640. *For earth,* etc. Canaan, often a type of heaven, is "a land of hills and valleys" (*Deut.* xi. 11). A derived meaning probably is that heaven has distinctions corresponding to our nations on earth.

644. *Seated hills.* The nations are sometimes spoken of as hills or mountains (*Isa.* xli. 15). Convulsions and calamities among the nations belong to the closing scenes of the world's history (*Matt.* xxiv. 7). They are the antidote to pleasure-seeking and ungodly mirth.

646. *Amaze,* etc. The feeling of the Benjamites when they saw their polluted city (Gibeah=Hill) ascending in smoke to heaven (*Judg.* xx. 40–42). Other cities beside Gibeah seem to have been destroyed.

652. *Under the weight,* etc. In the war of the Gods with the Giants (following that of the Gods with the Titans) mountains were piled upon the

earth-born monster Typhœus who, like the cannon of the devils, cast forth smoke and flame.

656. *Their armor helped,* etc. The degraded habits of debauchees are a source of real suffering when the means of gratifying their passions are destroyed.

662. *The rest in imitation,* etc. It was by a *ruse de guerre* that Israel won an advantage over Benjamin, and Milton may have intended the mountains as a fit response and superior in ingenuity to Satan's stratagem. At all events, the contest seems to have reached the stage of mutual deception (*Matt.* xxiv. 23, 24).

666. *In dismal shade.* A state in which one cannot recognize his friends, because of mutual suspicion and treachery (*Matt.* xxiv. 10, 11). The succeeding lines are based on *Matt.* xxiv. 21, 22.

671–745. THE SECOND NIGHT COUNCIL

The corruption, violence, and falsehood of the last days of earth lose themselves in a night (*Matt.* xxiv. 29) which is terminated by Christ's second coming. Of the time of the end even the Son of God professes himself ignorant (*Mark* xiii. 32); hence a formal authorization of judgment is needed. Vice is expelled from heaven, as it will be from earth, after doing its greatest possible mischief.

673. *Consulting on the sum of things.* The crisis point in the moral history of all creation has been reached; the war between good and evil has attained its greatest intensity, and a disclosure of the divine purpose is required.

685. *Two days.* The earthly warfare against evil is likewise divided into three parts (*Rev.* xi. 14).

690. *Equal in their creation,* etc. Those who engaged in the fierce battles at Gibeah were brethren; the advantage seemed to lie with the more ingenious strategy. All human contests are between those of the same blood; the angelic strife was no exception to the rule of equality.

695. *What war can do.* The conflicts of the last times will break all ties of humanity, country, and kinship (*Matt.* x. 21, 35–37).

698. *Dangerous to the main.* "Main" here signifies the mainland or continent. As the mountains of heaven are analogous to the nations or municipalities on earth, the whole continent corresponds to the race of mankind. There is danger that the fighting in heaven may ruin the whole continent, as on earth there is danger that the tribulation of the last times, if allowed to continue, may destroy the whole race of men (*Matt.* xxiv. 22).

711. *Ascend my chariot.* "Who maketh the clouds his chariot" (*Ps.* civ.

3). The Son of Man comes in the clouds of heaven to judgment (*Matt.* xxiv. 30).

712. *Shake Heaven's basis. Matt.* xxiv. 29; *Heb.* xii. 26. In the war with the giants, Olympus shook under the immortal feet of angry Jove (Hesiod: *Theog.*) The next thirty lines are based upon familiar passages of Scripture.

746–912. THE THIRD DAY'S JUDGMENT

The remainder of the book describes the scenes of judgment and vengeance for which we have been prepared by the events of the second day. Scriptural accounts of the judgment are followed.

746. *O'er his sceptre bowing.* The Son is submissive to the Father even in the divine process of taking vengeance (1 *Cor.* xv. 27).

748. *Sacred morn* is Homeric (*Il.* xi. 84), but there is a special fitness in calling the morning of the judgment-day sacred, for it is pre-eminently "the day of the Lord" (*Joel* ii. 1, etc.). Compare also *Matt.* xxiv. 27.

749. WHIRLWIND SOUND. This, I think, is intended as the fourth sounding of the trumpet mentioned in *Rev.* viii. 12. It is the sound described in *Ezek.* i. 24 as "like the noise of great waters, as the voice of the Almighty, the voice of speech, as the noise of a host." The judgment scenes of the Bible are generally announced by the sounding of a trumpet (*Joel* ii. 1; *Matt.* xxiv. 31). To the loyal it was the voice of a trumpet summoning them to victory; to the apostates it was the sound of a whirlwind announcing overthrow. Those who sow the wind shall reap the whirlwind (*Hos.* viii. 7).

750–759. This passage is taken almost entire from the first chapter of *Ezekiel.*

761. *Radiant Urim.* "Urim" means lights, or flashing jewels.—*Masson.* Ezekiel (i. 27) describes the attire of the Son of Man: "From the appearance of his loins even upward and from the appearance of his loins even downward, I saw as it were the appearance of fire and it had brightness round about." It is the same as the "vesture dipped in blood" (*Rev.* xix. 13) and the "dyed garments" (*Isa.* lxiii. 1–3) of the Messiah when about to take vengeance on his enemies.

762. *Victory sat eagle-winged. Ps.* xcviii. 1. The eagle is the bird of Jove, typifies his might and presages his triumph. See note on i. 197.

764. *Three-bolted thunder.* Suggestive of the trident of avenging Neptune. The thunder was a reply at all points to the Satanic imitation, which had also this triple nature.

776. *His sign in Heaven. Matt.* xxiv. 30. The sign is by some supposed to be the Cross, but the Cross is not so spoken of in the Bible. On the

other hand, the Rainbow is called a sign both by sacred (*Gen.* ix. 13) and by profane (*Il.* xi. 27, 28) writers; besides, the Rainbow is part of the scene in the preceding lines, while the Cross is not.

780. *His way prepared. Isa.* xl. 3–5; *Luke* iii. 4. When Neptune came to battle against the Trojans, a way was smoothed for him over the waves (*Il.* xiii. 29, 30).

784. *With fresh flowerets,* etc. One of the incidents when the Messiah comes with vengeance (*Isa.* xxxv. 1, 2, 4).

787. *Hope conceiving from despair.* When Troy was burning, its remaining defenders fought with the feeling that "The only safety to the conquered is to hope for no safety" (*Æn.* ii. 354).

789. *What signs avail?* Like the brethren of Dives, they are not turned from their rebellion by a scene analogous to the Resurrection (*Luke* xvi. 31).

791. *Hardened more,* etc. The raising of Lazarus, so far from convincing the enemies of Jesus, only made them more bitter (*John* xi. 53; xii. 10, 17–19).

795. *At length prevail,* etc. The alternatives considered by the priests who plotted against Christ were either to destroy him or to perish in the expected ruin of the Jewish nation (*John* xi. 50).

801. *Stand still,* etc. Like the other speeches of the Divine Being, this contains the very language as well as the sentiment of Scripture, and the basal texts need no pointing out.

823. *Nor other strife,* etc. Men are to be judged by the *deeds* done in the body (2 *Cor.* v. 10), and not by their wisdom or opinions. Perhaps this fact suggested to the poet the idea of a contest lowered to the plane of physical strength.

824. *Into terror changed,* etc. The Angel in the pillar of cloud stood between Israelites and Egyptians, giving light to the former and spreading darkness over the latter (*Exod.* xiv. 19–24).

827. *The Four spread out,* etc. *Ezek.* i. 24. If, as has been supposed, the Four represent the four evangelists, then their prominence in this judgment scene is most fitting, for "the word that I have spoken the same shall judge him in the last day" (*John* xii. 48).

832. *Gloomy as night.* To his foes the coming of the Messiah is like the coming of Neptune (Death) in the form of Calchas (Darkener?) against the Trojans (*Il.* xiii. 44, 45). Night is metaphorically put for death in *John* ix. 4.

834. *The steadfast Empyrean shook.* The title of Neptune is "Shaker of the Shores," and when he moves, the earth trembles (*Il.* xiii. 18, 19). The things shaken are subject to death or decay (*Heb.* xii. 27); the throne is unshaken, because it endures forever (*Heb.* i. 8–12; *Ezek.* xxxviii. 19).

835. *Full soon,* etc. Inspired by Neptune, Idomeneus the Cretan, bran-

dishing two spears, ran against the Trojans, like the lightning of Jove (*Il.* xiii. 241–244).

838. *Plagues.* Corresponding to the "seven last plagues" of *Rev.* xv. and xvi. Compare *Hab.* iii. 5; *Ezek.* xxxviii. 22.

844. *Tempestuous fell,* etc. The Four are the evangelists; the Word of God is like a tempest with arrows for rain (*Ps.* xviii. 13, 14).

848. *Every eye glared lightning.* The "burning coals" of *Ezek.* i. 13 seem to be taken by Milton for the eyes of the "living creatures," and from these fires "went forth lightning."

850. *Withered all their strength.* The figure is apparently an allusion to the cursing of the barren fig-tree (*Matt.* xxi. 19). The words beginning at "withered" and ending at "fallen" mark the successive stages of decay—the leaves fade, the sap forsakes the branches, the trunk dries, the life is gone, rot begins and the tree falls (*Jude* 12).

853. *Yet half his strength,* etc. When Jesus withered the fig-tree with his curse, he declared the power of faith to work still greater wonders.

860. *Crystal wall,* etc. *Rev.* vi. 14. The wall is like our horizon. When a part of the sky is hidden by a storm, the horizon wall seems to be broken and rolled inward. When the Trojans fled from Achilles into their city, the gates were thrown wide open and Apollo came to meet and rescue them (*Il.* xxi. 537–539).

863. *Strook them with horror.* The sight before them was the realm of death, which is abhorrent even to the gods, but not the worst of evils. Physical death, terrible as it is, is often preferred to mental anguish, and men seek it (*Rev.* ix. 6).

867. *The unsufferable noise,* etc. Analogous to the crash of the final ruin of heaven and earth (2 *Pet.* iii. 10). Delos would have fled and, like all other places, refused shelter to Latona in her pangs, but it had been moored by the will of Jupiter.

871. *Nine days they fell.* Describing the fall of the Titans, Hesiod says: "A brazen anvil descending from heaven nine nights and days, on the tenth would come to earth; and again, a brazen anvil descending from earth nine nights and days, on the tenth would come to Tartarus." In the Bible a millstone is commonly used to denote rapid descent through waters (*Luke* xvii. 2; *Exod.* xv. 5; *Rev.* xviii. 21). The idea of a nine days' fall probably has its basis in the Ptolemaic conception (much more ancient than Ptolemy) of nine heavens, furnishing nine natural stages of descent. There are indications that the seven angels with the "seven last plagues," the angel announcing the fall of Babylon and the angel summoning the birds of prey (*Rev.* xvi.–xix.) are arranged in harmony with the same plan.

Confounded Chaos roared. Chaos is the sea of elements which on the final day "shall melt with fervent heat" (2 *Pet.* iii. 10–12). At the fall of Babylon the sea is profoundly agitated (*Rev.* xviii. 17–19).

874. *Encumbered,* etc. The spirits of vengeance and destruction that follow the Messiah's army are said to be glutted and drunken with the flesh and blood of the dead (*Ezek.* xxxix. 19; *Rev.* xix. 21). In like manner Chaos, the realm of natural death, is encumbered with too great a burden of the dead (*Jer.* vii. 32).

875. *Yawning received them whole.* In the destruction of Korah the earth swallowed all his company and all their goods (*Num.* xvi. 31–33).

878. *Repaired her mural breach.* So "the earth closed upon" Korah's company and the waters of the Red Sea upon Pharaoh's host. The heavenly horizon is now clear from all appearance of cloud or storm.

Professor William C. Wilkinson asks for an explanation of the change from the masculine pronoun referring to heaven in l. 783 to the feminine here. I venture this: In the former instance Heaven is personified—Uranus looks cheerfully upon Gæa beneath who smiles back in answer. In this line heaven is conceived of as a city with walls and is treated, according to the rule of Latin grammar, as a feminine. The two are not the same; the former is the upper, or sky, portion; the latter the lower, or earth, portion of the quadrature the poet calls heaven. See diagram of Milton's Universe in "A General Survey."

893. *Measuring things in Heaven,* etc. The account is given, after the manner of Christ, in the guise of a parable (*Matt.* xiii. 35). There are still, as of yore, those who do not know how to interpret a parable. I cannot claim to have unravelled all of the complicated allegory of this book, but only to have indicated its leading lessons. If the story has been spoiled of its charm for truculent boyhood, perhaps it may seem somewhat worthier of study by mature minds.

909. *Let it profit,* etc. The admonition of Jesus, after he had spoken his parables, was, "He that hath ears to hear, let him hear" (*Matt.* xiii. 9, 43).

BOOK VII

1–39. POETIC INSPIRATION

THIS DIGRESSION from the thread of the story treats of the several kinds of Poetic Inspiration. That kind which Milton claims for himself comes from heaven and has its source in Spiritual Joy. Earthly inspiration comes from Sorrow—

"Our sweetest songs are those that tell of saddest thought;"

its Pegasus is the offspring of Neptune (Vengeance) and Medusa (Care), and rises skyward from a fountain of tears. The daughters of Memory haunt this fountain. Of these Calliope (the Fair-faced, though the lexicons say the Sweet-voiced), the Melancholy of *Il Penseroso,* is at the close of the passage put in contrast with Milton's Urania. The third and lowest kind of inspiration is that into which Bacchus enters, equally hostile to the lofty Joy of heaven and the decent Sorrow of earth.

1. *Descend,* etc. Raphael has just communicated to Adam that warning of the Apocalyptic angel who "flew through the midst of Heaven" and cried "Woe, woe, woe, to the inhabiters of the earth!" This invocation then means more than a change in the subject-matter of the poem from celestial to terrestrial themes; it divides the whole action into two widely different parts.

2. *If rightly . . . called.* The name might imply that the earth is not and never was her congenial dwelling-place.

4. *Pegasean wing.* Compare note on ii. 930. The leading of Urania conducted the poet far above the heights of the clouds, above the reach of Sorrow and Care.

5. *The meaning, not the name.* Poetic art without feeling is but a name without significance; when the song expresses the feeling, we have the meaning, or the inspiring divinity herself. Spiritual Joy is the inspiration of celestial song.

10. *Wisdom thy sister,* etc. *Prov.* viii. affirms the intimacy of Wisdom and Joy (30, 31), their priority to hills and fountains, and therefore to Helicon and Hippocrene (24, 25), their employment of "witty inventions" (12), probably understood by the poet as the measures of sacred song. The phrase of Wisdom "playing" *(Vulgate, "ludens")* before God is accepted by Milton in his *Tetrachordon,* and what conception of greater dignity could it imply than the music of poetic numbers? Thus the Spirit of Song existed before the World and was the delight of God himself. Compare Hesiod, *Theog.* 51.

12. *Up led by thee,* etc. Milton, like Paul, was caught up by his delight in spiritual truth into the third heaven and heard unutterable words (v. 569, 570).

15. "*Thy tempering,* tempered by thee, *i.e.,* made to suit the breathing of 'an earthly guest.'"—*Verity.*

17. *As once Bellerophon,* etc. *Il.* vi. 201. Those who are exalted to spiritual privileges, as were Paul and Milton, are exposed to spiritual pride and the errors connected therewith. St. Paul recognized this danger, and credited his "thorn in the flesh" with keeping him humble in a way less disastrous than that in which the gadfly stinging Pegasus humbled Bellerophon.

24. *More safe I sing,* etc. Naturally because men are better acquainted with the earth and better able to understand it (*John* iii. 12). But there was the new danger that his earthly sufferings would cloud and destroy the accuracy of his spiritual vision.

29. *Nightly or when morn,* etc. "Johnson, on the authority of Richardson's *Life* (1734), relates that Milton 'would sometimes lie awake whole nights . . . and on a sudden his poetical faculty would rush upon him with an *impetus,* and his daughter was immediately called to secure what came.'"—*Verity.* I am suspicious of all such traditions, for they are contradicted by the result—the existence of a poem with a logical coherence and exactness at the furthest possible remove from sudden visions and irresistible impulses. Night and morn are mentioned because they are scripturally designated as times of spiritual visitation (*Job* xxxv. 10; *Ps.* xxx. 5). Inspiration may come during either sleep or wakefulness; or, as St. Paul expresses it, either in the body or out of the body (2 *Cor.* xii. 2).

32. *Drive far off,* etc. Hor. *Odes* III. i. 1–4. "The dissonance of Bacchus" is "the song of drunkards" referred to in *Ps.* lxix. 12. In Milton's time the bard had reason to pray for such deliverance.

33. *The race of that wild rout,* etc. The descendants of the rabble who destroyed Orpheus. Both the name and the history of Orpheus (Ὀρφνός, Darkness, or Ὀρφανός, The Bereaved) connect him with Sorrow. Wine is an antidote to Sorrow (*Prov.* xxxi. 6, 7); and accordingly Orpheus, the sweet, melancholy singer, with whom shadowy trees and

gloomy rocks were in sympathy, and who moved Pluto to tears, is torn in pieces by the wild and cruel devotees of Bacchus.

34. *In Rhodope.* Melancholy is pale, and her representative is Calliope (Fair-face); but wine flushes the countenance, and hence Orpheus is destroyed in Rhodope (Red-face).

36. *Nor could the muse,* etc. Even sorrow is not sacred and cannot move to pity among the savage devotees of Bacchus (*Ps.* lxix.).

39. *Thou art heavenly, she an empty dream.* The dream between Joy and Sorrow in origin and duration is beautifully set forth in *Isa.* li. 11.

40–130. DIVINE REVELATION

The nature and the object of Revelation, as suggested by various expressions of Scripture, are set forth in this passage.

41. *The affable archangel.* Raphael has been called "the sociable spirit," because, like Mercury, he delights to consort with men; now he is "the affable," because, like the same deity, he is distinguished for his eloquence (Hor. *Odes* I. x. 1).

52. *Admiration* (wonder). The thing that puzzled Adam, the origin of evil, the appearance of the great red dragon in Heaven (*Rev.* xii. 3), has puzzled the world ever since.

62. *How the world,* etc. As the first thing found in the Scriptures, this is presumably the first thing a perfect man would wish to have revealed.

72. *Divine Interpreter.* Mercury is called "interpres divum" (*Æn.* iv. 378).

84. *Deign to descend,* etc. Adam argues that as the higher has been freely given, the lower will not be withheld. Paul also reasons thus (*Rom.* viii. 32).

86. *How first began.* To Adam's mind creation was a necessity (viii. 278); the inquiry is only about the method and the motive. Naturally the larger features are specified—heaven, earth, and the intervening space.

91. *Holy rest,* etc. The seventh day of the creative week was hallowed because God rested then; hence the poet assumes that all God's resting-time is holy. The contrast between God's eternity and the earth's lateness is impressively set forth in *Ps.* xc.

95. *Secrets,* etc. For a reference to the secrets of creation see *Matt.* xiii. 35 and *Rom.* xvi. 25.

99. *Suspense in heaven,* etc. The interest of the narrative is such as to take away consciousness of the flight of time. Possibly those Scriptures which speak of the sun's standing still may be understood in this way.

103. *Unapparent Deep.* Chaos is called "unapparent" either to distinguish it from the visible earthly ocean, or, as others suggested, in allusion

to the darkness which covers the chaotic Deep.

115. *What thou canst attain,* etc. The end of Revelation, as stated in 2 *Tim.* iii. 15–17, is to make "wise unto salvation." The seraph Raphael (Love) is the very spirit of revelation and has the same commission as had the inspired writers.

126. *Knowledge is as food,* etc. The figure is found in *Job* xv. 2 and 1 *Cor.* viii. 1.

131–191. MOTIVE OF THE CREATION

A proposition of Milton's *Christian Doctrine* is: "Creation is that act whereby God the Father produced everything that exists by his Word and Spirit—that is, by his will, for the manifestation of the glory of his power and goodness." For proof are cited *Gen.* i. 31; *Ps.* xix. 1; *Rom.* i. 20, etc. The immediate motive here assigned is to repair the loss caused by Satan's apostasy.

131. *Lucifer.* The mention of Satan by this name suggests Babylon. The fall of Babylon, the redemption of the world, and the song of triumph on Mount Zion are joined together in *Rev.* xiv. 1–8.

139. *At least our envious foe,* etc. Our adversary at least, perhaps also others, has been mistaken with regard to the number of the faithful. Satan's envy and ambition were foiled because his adherents were not in a majority.

147. *Number sufficient,* etc. The rebellious were to the faithful as the one steward who hid his lord's money was to the two who used it. It was easy for the one who employed well the ten talents to use also the additional talent of the unfaithful steward (*Matt.* xxv. 28–31). Heaven is now partitioned on this principle; the heritage of the apostates is given to the faithful.

150. *Lest his heart,* etc. The creation of a new heaven and a new earth follows the general judgment (2 *Pet.* iii. 13). The principle of judgment, which is also that of restoration, is to take benefits from those who misuse them and give them to a nation bringing forth the fruits thereof (*Matt.* xxi. 43).

154. *In a moment,* etc. So the world is to be new created at the last day (1 *Cor.* xv. 52).

162. *Inhabit lax,* etc. Substantially the command given to the descendants of Noah after the Deluge, disobedience to which resulted in the confusion of tongues at Babel (*Gen.* ix. 1, 7; xi. 4–9).

169. *Nor vacuous the space.* Milton takes several pages of his *Christian Doctrine* to prove that the world was not made of nothing, but of something, and that something was God himself. It need not be said that the reasoning is inconclusive.

176. *Immediate are the acts,* etc. This explanation harmonizes the passages that represent the creation as instantaneous with those that represent it as consisting of six different acts and extending through six successive days. The absurdity of the attempt to make Milton responsible for modern mistaken notions of a creation in six literal days is here very evident. He does not take *Gen.* i. literally, and he does not expect to be taken literally himself. Readers of Milton are not enemies of science; those who oppose reason and investigation know as little of Milton as they do of science. Besides, it is dishonest to deny that the impression which *Gen.* i. gives to uninstructed minds is that the creation occupied just six days. The issue cannot be disguised in any such fashion.

192–242. PRELIMINARIES OF CREATION

Many passages descriptive of the creation are found in the Bible, and from these Milton gathered the particulars now presented.

194. *Girt with omnipotence,* etc. The girdle strengthens the body, and in *Rev.* i. 13 one like the Son of Man appears "girt with a golden girdle."

197. *About his chariot,* etc. The poetical account of creation in *Ps.* civ. represents the Messiah as covered with light, riding on a chariot of clouds, and walking upon the wings of the wind. The light becomes the seraphs of Milton; the clouds the cherubs; and the winds are the winged spirits. Besides, the seraphs are potentates; the cherubs, thrones; and the winged spirits, virtues.

210. *On heavenly ground,* etc. The assailants of Heaven had sunk through the ocean of Chaos, as the Egyptians sank in the Red Sea; and Chaos was casting up the inert earth of its bottom, as the dead bodies of the Egyptians were cast up by the winds and waves. Chaos also symbolizes Time and its ruinous forces, overturning and destroying everything not as high and as firmly fixed as heaven.

214. *And surging waves.* Newton and Keightley prefer "in" to "and." But it was the winds *and* waves acting together that turned up the sands, and not either of them alone.

215. *With the centre mix the pole.* Heaven, being a hemisphere, has but one pole, at the zenith.

225. *Golden compasses.* "He set a compass upon the face of the depth." They are taken from God's treasuries of wisdom (*Prov.* viii. 27, 21, 22).

227. *This universe,* etc. The mistakes of many make it necessary to call attention to the fact that it is not our earth which is here outlined by the sweep of the golden compasses, but the whole stellar universe.

232. *Thus God,* etc. The earth, speaking according to appearances, was

at the centre, where one foot of the golden compasses stood, and the heaven was limited by the circumference around which the other foot swept. In fact, however, there were as yet no heaven and no earth; they were "without form and void," and only their respective places were marked.

236. *Vital virtue,* etc. The Spirit is the life-giving and life-sustaining power. Body as well as soul is purified by its presence (1 *Cor.* vi. 9–11).

239. *Then founded,* etc. "Spirit" is the subject of all these verbs. Like things were brought together and unlike things were separated, so that there was no longer a chaotic mixture of earth, water, and air, but each so-called element found its own place. Collections of earth and water were formed into globes and the air was spun out between them. The full meaning of the poet may best be gathered from a comparison of his model, Ovid (*Met.* i. 21–31).

243–550. THE SIX DAYS OF CREATION

Besides the first of *Genesis,* many hints for the account of creation are derived from *Ps.* civ., *Job* xxxviii., and other Scriptures, as well as from the first book of Ovid's *Metamorphoses.*

243–260. THE FIRST DAY.

245. *Sprung from the Deep,* etc. This is a fair inference from the statement that there was an evening and a morning and from *Job* xxxviii. 12.

247. *Sphered in a radiant cloud,* etc. A pillar of cloud and fire led the Israelites in their journeys, showing that light may be diffused from such a source. This was a "tabernacle" or temporary abode, as distinguished from the sun, the permanent "house" or home of light.

253–256. *Nor passed uncelebrated,* etc. *Job* xxxviii. 7. The birth of Apollo and Diana was celebrated by the attendant goddesses with a shout.

261–275. THE SECOND DAY.

268. *The waters underneath,* etc. Milton seems to conceive of the waters above the firmament as something like the Crystalline Sphere of the Ptolemaic system, lying outside of the heavenly bodies. These waters, forming the border of the World, also stand for what we call the river of Death (iii. 518).

271. *Misrule of Chaos far removed,* etc. The establishment of the waters above the firmament is perhaps referred to in the expression, "He

strengthened the fountains of the Deep." This expression, occurring as it does in the midst of others relating to the framing of the World, may very well suggest to the poet the idea that the waters above the firmament may have something important to do with the stability of the earth.

276–338. THE THIRD DAY.

295. *As armies,* etc. A celebrated passage in Homer (*Il.* iv. 422–428) compares an army rushing to battle to ocean billows. The reversal of the figure in this place is significant, because it represents the waters as obeying their Lord as perfectly as if they had intelligence and understood the command.

299. *With torrent rapture,* etc. Waters are apparently spoken of in *Ps.* lxv. 13, where it is said, "They shout for joy, they also sing."

321. *The smelling gourd.* No doubt the ivy, which is so closely associated with wine and with the leaves and berries of which Bacchus was crowned. The word which the King James translators rendered "gourd" is "hedera" (ivy) in several Latin translations. Bees gathered honey from the flowers and an oil seems to have been made of the berry. These facts may have suggested to Milton the epithet "smelling," and they also clearly connect the gourd with the oil that makes a man's face to shine (*Ps.* civ. 15).

Corny, bearing corn, and perhaps having a hard horn-like nature. From this comes the "bread which strengthened man's heart."

323. *Bush with frizzled hair,* etc. It is common to speak of leaves as the *coma,* or hair, of trees. "Implicit" is not "tangled," but "folded in." The figure is reversed in the "bushy locks" of *Cant.* v. 11.

328. *With borders,* etc. *Rev.* xxii. 2. A feature common to earth and heaven. Raphael admires it as Mercury does the bower of Calypso (*Odys.* v. 73, 74).

335. *Ere it was in the earth.* Milton here follows the received (but incorrect) translation of *Gen.* ii. 5, which should be, "And no plant of the field was as yet in the earth." This criticism by Keightley is confirmed by the Revised Version of the Scriptures.

339–386. THE FOURTH DAY.

355. *Unlightsome first.* Genesis makes a clear distinction between the creation of the "lights" and the putting of them into the firmament "to give light."

358. *Sowed with stars,* etc. The word "star" is derived from a root meaning to strew or sprinkle; hence some take its meaning to be "that which is strewn or sowed" (*Isa.* li. 16).

361. *Made porous,* etc. The houses of Menelaus (*Odys.* iv. 72) and Alcinous (*Odys.* vii. 87) compared in splendor to the sun and moon, and the palace of Jupiter have many rooms filled with furniture of gold, silver, brass, and ivory.

364. *Hither as to their fountain,* etc. Milton is probably working upon the psalmist's conception of the sun as a bridegroom (*Ps.* xix. 5). The light received by the planets is like the joy diffused by the bridegroom's presence among his friends (*Matt.* ix. 15; *John* iii. 29, 30). The first of these citations illustrates the relation of Christ as a bridegroom to his disciples in general, the second his relation to John the Baptist in particular. As the morning star heralds the coming of the sun, John heralded the coming of Christ. His light, too, like that of the planets, increased from his nearness to Christ, the Sun, though it seemed to diminish.

370. *Glorious lamp.* The Latin *lampas* signifies both a wedding torch and the sun (Stat. S. vi. viii. 59; Virg. *Æn.* iii. 637).

372. *Jocund to run,* etc. *Ps.* xix. 5, 6. Masson and Verity explain "his longitude" to mean the sun's "path from east to west." This is inconsistent with the statement that the Pleiades dance before him, because when the sun is in Aries (as is all along assumed, *e.g.* x. 329) the Pleiades rise after him. I am forced, therefore, to the conclusion that "his longitude" means the sun's annual circuit or path in the opposite direction, from west to east, now the ecliptic.

382. *Dividual,* divided or shared.—*Masson.* Compare Ovid, *Met.* iii. 682, where "dividua" is used in the sense of "divisible," referring to the phases of the moon.

387–448. THE FIFTH DAY.

402. *In sculls,* etc. Some fishes are gregarious, like those taken in the sea of Galilee (*Luke* v. 4–7); others live singly, like that which swallowed Jonah, amid the sea-weed (*Jon.* ii. 5).

405. *Groves of coral.* As Paradise had some trees for food and others for beauty and pleasure, so the sea has algæ for food and coral groves for enjoyment.

408. *Their food,* etc. Observe that the word "prey" is avoided; before the Fall vegetable food was the only kind for man or beast (*Gen.* i. 30).

409. *On smooth* (water), etc. Dolphins and seals are known for their sports in calm waters. Dolphins are called "bended" from their rounded backs—"Tergo dolphina recurvo" (Ovid, *Fasti* ii. 113).

417. *Tepid caves and fens and shores.* The places where the first eggs were hatched without animal heat serve to classify the birds; nocturnal birds come from the dark caves, waterfowl from fens, and land birds from the shores.

421. *Summed their pens,* completed their plumage.—*Masson.* "*Summed;* preened."—*Verity.* A term of falconry applied to a hawk when his feathers have grown to their full strength.—*Clar. Press.*

422. *Under a cloud in prospect.* The earth seemed to be shaded by a cloud, so numerous were the birds in the air.

435. *Nightingale. Odys.* xix. 518. The transformation of Philomela into a nightingale is excelled by few myths in favor with the poets, especially with Milton (see note on iv. 602).

438. *The swan,* etc. This is a good representative of the waterfowls, and, like most of the other birds mentioned in the passage, has a well-known poetical legend connected with it and figures among the constellations.

443. *Cock whose clarion,* etc. In Greek the cock is called ἀλέκτωρ, the sleepless.

444. *Other whose gay train,* etc. The peacock is associated with the story of Argus and his hundred eyes. *Job* xxxix. 13.

449–550. THE SIXTH DAY.

457. *The wild beast.* The distinction between wild and tame animals is broadly made both in *Gen.* i. and *Ps.* civ. In the latter the haunts of the wild animals are designated.

461. *Those rare,* etc. The same principle prevailed in stocking the earth after the Flood (*Gen.* vii. 2).

463. *Clods now calved.* The Latin *brutus,* first applied to the heavy, unwieldy earth, has come to be the generic name for the stupid, unreasoning animals. Their origin shows their nature, and the clod is a symbol of their low, brutish life (*Eccl.* iii. 21).

464. *The tawny lion,* etc. The manner of his birth suggests the lion's most characteristic act—lying in wait and suddenly springing upon his prey (*Job* xxxviii. 40). His reputed strength makes it proper that he should be named first of the wild beasts.

467. *As the mole.* The lynx (ounce), the leopard (libbard), and the tiger are all beasts of the cat kind, noted for their slyness, and with eyes better suited for night than day (*Ps.* civ. 20). They differ from the lion in that while he is usually found in the open country, they prefer forests and cover. Hence they are compared to the mole.

469. *The swift stag,* or roebuck, an animal of the deer kind, is frequently mentioned in the Bible for its fleetness.

471. *Behemoth. Job* xl. "Behemoth here is the elephant; in *Job* it is the hippopotamus of the Nile."—*Clar. Press.* No; so far as Milton goes, his description is an exact copy of Job's. The description does not fit either the elephant or the hippopotamus, and there is no need that it should.

Behemoth is "the biggest born of earth;" the leviathan exceeds him, but he is in the sea. The creature has a slothful habit, and Milton contrasts him with the stag.

473. *As plants.* Flocks and olive plants serve to designate the same thing, viz., families of children, in *Ps.* cvii. 41 and cxxviii. 3. The white fleece and the peaceful disposition of the sheep are analogous to the white flowers of the olive and the peace it symbolizes.

476. *Those waved,* etc. The butterfly is taken as a type of the insect world. To the Greeks it was an emblem of the immortal soul (having the same name ψυχή) by reason of its passing through a kind of death in its chrysalis state and coming to a nobler resurrection. The beautiful story of Cupid and Psyche is based on this notion.

480. *These as a line,* etc. Under "worm" are included serpents and whatever moves by convolutions without the aid of limbs. For the winged serpent see *Isa.* xiv. 29.

485. *Parsimonious emmet,* etc. *Prov.* vi. 6–8. The ants labor together and provide for themselves without a "guide, overseer, or ruler," and thus are a model for a republic.

490. *The female bee,* etc. The critics innocently follow one of their number, certainly not a naturalist, who originated the comment that "the working-bees are *males*. The drone here meant is the queen bee." Information on this point is cheap. Milton elsewhere sees in the beehive the model of an aristocracy.

495. *The serpent,* etc. The serpents of Laocoon had manes and other features here mentioned (*Æn.* ii. 206). Serpents are innocuous under the Messiah (*Isa.* xi. 8, 9).

499–514. *Now Heaven,* etc. With slight changes the thought is that of Ovid, *Met.* i. 71–88.

516–548. *Therefore the Omnipotent,* etc. The first two chapters of Genesis furnish all the leading thoughts of this passage. Add *Ps.* viii. 6–8 and *Ezek.* xxxi. 9, 10.

551–640. THE SABBATH

554. *Thence to behold,* etc. The view of his work which the Creator takes when it is completed (*Gen.* i. 31) is beautifully conceived of by Milton as a comparison of the material product with the intellectual model. No correction was needed; the agreement was perfect; the work was "very good."

558. *Acclamation. Psalms* xxiv., civ., and several others associate the most ardent praise with a review of the creative power of God.

575. *Led to God's eternal house,* etc. The Saviour at Jerusalem, when he received the hosannas of the multitude, was on the way to the temple (*Matt.* xxi. 9–12).

577. *A broad and ample road,* etc. "But when they [the blessed gods] go to feast and festival, then they move right up the steep ascent and mount the top of the dome of Heaven."—Plato's *Phædrus.* Compare *Prov.* iv. 18 and Ovid, *Met.* i. 168–171.

588. *He also went,* etc. Though God rules in Heaven, he dwells at the same time with him that is of a contrite spirit (*Isa.* lvii. 15).

594. *The harp,* etc. These musical instruments are generally those of *Ps.* cl. The pipe is associated with the solemnity spoken of in *Isa.* xxx. 29.

596. *Organs of sweet stop* are wind instruments; *sounds on fret* are stringed instruments. The *Clar. Press* says that "frets" are the divisions by which the strings of a guitar or violin are lengthened or shortened at will. Masson says about the same.

619. *The clear hyaline,* etc. "Hyaline (like galaxy in line 579) is followed immediately by its translation."—*Clar. Press.*

620. *Almost immense. Job* xxxviii. 18 and *Hab.* iii. 6 show that though God may measure the earth (that is, the whole world), man cannot.

621. *Every star perhaps,* etc. The plurality of worlds is suggested by *Heb.* xi. 3, 12.

636. *Face of things,* visible appearance of things. The expression conveys the idea that the angel is describing only external appearances, and therefore scientific accuracy is not to be expected. Adam's questions afterwards show that he understood the angel in this way. Such a method enables the poet to do as he has done—to mention those features of the creation which principally strike the human sense or imagination.

BOOK VIII

1–178. THE PLAN OF THE UNIVERSE

"The discourse on astronomy in this book (extending down to line 178) is interesting mainly," says Verity, "as a proof that Milton was acquainted with the teaching of Copernicus." If so, its interest is small indeed. Proof to the contrary, namely, that Milton, a graduate of Cambridge, of reputation as a scholar, a friend of Galileo, could reach advanced years without a knowledge of the Copernican system would truly be interesting, if not astounding. The value of the passage consists rather in its philosophy of the relation of man to the visible universe.

1–4. In the first edition of *Paradise Lost,* when it was in ten books instead of twelve, and the seventh and eighth were united, there was at this place the single line, "To whom thus Adam gratefully replied." In the second edition it appeared as it now stands.

3. *Thought him still speaking.* Agamemnon awoke from a dream, "The heavenly voice still sounding in his ears" (*Il.* ii. 41). Compare *Odys.* xiii. 1, 2.

5. *What thanks,* etc. Alcinous richly rewarded Ulysses at the close of his long narrative.

25. *I oft admire* (*i.e.,* wonder). This can be explained on the ground that Adam represents the race, while he is also an individual. The order of the universe is one of the most difficult problems that the race has undertaken to solve, but Adam as an individual has for the first time had the question suggested to him by the words of the angel.

27. *Disproportion,* subordinating the magnificent heavens to the little earth.

34. *Served by more noble,* etc. Human order requires the less to serve the greater (*Luke* xxii. 25–27).

37. *Incorporeal speed.* If the heavenly bodies make a daily revolution about the earth, their speed is like that of spirit rather than that of

399

matter. The poet probably has in mind the fleetness of time which these
bodies mark by their movements.

40. *Which Eve perceiving.* Taine and a few others have no perception of
the delicacy of this arrangement. They would have had Eve remain and
give her opinion on the order of the universe, the end of man, and the
relations between the sexes. These critics are in too much of a hurry.
Some eight days later Eve is found ready enough to express herself on
the subject of the divine economy and the rights of woman.

44. *Among her fruits and flowers,* etc. *Cant.* iv. 13, 14. These represent her
household duties to which godly women attend with conscientious care.
Venus (Aphrodite), whom Eve here resembles, was a goddess of fruits and
flowers (the rose and the myrtle). Where her delicate feet touched the
earth of Cyprus, the grass sprung beneath them (Hes. *Theog.* 188).

48. *Yet went she not,* etc. The ability of women to understand subjects
which they are forbidden to discuss in public is implied in the direction
to ask their husbands at home (1 *Cor.* xiv. 35). The perception and deli-
cacy of Eve took away the need of any law or precept in Paradise.

57. *Not words alone,* etc. Milk and honey represent the wisdom and ten-
derness coming from the lips of the lover (*Cant.* iv. 11).

60. *Not unattended,* etc. Love attended on Venus and beautiful Desire
followed her (*Theog.* 101).

66. *Heaven is as the book of God,* etc. The controlling idea of *Ps.* xix.
The instructions which the heavens were intended to convey may be
learned equally well whether the heaven moves or the earth.

74. *To be scanned,* etc. "Scan" is used in the sense of "criticise," "find
fault with." The secrets of God are used, as in several chapters of the
book of Job, to teach man humility by showing him how little he knows.
The effect of even pretended knowledge of the heavens is illustrated in
the case of the Chaldean astronomers (*Isa.* xlvii. 10–13).

77. *Left to their disputes.* Bacon says (*Advancement of Learning,* ii.): "As
for the vertical point (of natural philosophy) 'Opus quod operatur Deus
a principis usque ad finem' (*Eccl.* iii. 11), we know not whether man's
inquiry can attain unto it." In the Vulgate (here quoted) the words
immediately preceding are, "Mundum tradidit disputationi eorum."—
Clar. Press.

78. *His laughter,* etc. Landor objects: "I cannot well entertain the notion
of the Creator's risible faculties. Milton here carries his anthropomor-
phism much further than the poem (which needed a good deal of it)
required." But compare *Isa.* xliv. 24, 25.

81. *Contrive to save appearances.* Bacon in his essay on *Superstition* tells of
"astronomers which did feign eccentrics and epicycles and such engines
of orbs, to save the phenomena, though they knew there were no such
things."

85. *By thy reasoning,* etc. The human tendency is to judge from size and physical splendor (1 *Sam*. xvi. 7; 1 *Cor.* i. 26–29).

105. *Lodged in a small partition.* The insignificance of the earth in the structure of the universe is declared in various Scripture passages (*Isa.* xl. 12–28). "The globular bodies of the stars greatly exceeded the magnitude of the earth, which now to me appeared so small, that I was grieved, to see our empire contracted, as it were, into a very point" (Cicero, *Som. Scip.*).

107. *The swiftness,* etc. "Those eternal fires which you call constellations and stars, and which being globular and round are animated with divine spirit and complete their cycles and revolutions with amazing rapidity" (*Som. Scip.*).

113. *Distance inexpressible,* etc. Hence it is used to measure the love of God to man (*Ps.* ciii. 11).

121. *If it presume.* The psalm that contains the glowing description of God's creation contains also a prayer against presumption (*Ps.* xix. 13).

122. *What if,* etc. It can make no practical difference to man whether the earth or the sun is the physical centre of the universe.

128. *In six,* etc. The Moon, Mercury, Venus, Mars, Jupiter, Saturn.

130. *Three different motions* (1) The daily rotation of the earth on its axis, (2) the annual orbit round the sun, (3) the libration or oscillation of the axis itself.—*Masson*. These motions mark out respectively the days, years, and seasons of *Gen.* i. 14.

131. *Which else,* etc. "Within this [the Primum Mobile] are contained seven other spheres that turn round backward, that is, in a contrary direction to that of the heaven" (Cicero, *Som. Scip.*).

134. *Rhomb* (ῥόμβος, wheel). Of the Primum Mobile Cicero continues: "In this sphere reside the original principles of those endless revolutions which the planets perform."

140. *What if that light,* etc. Galileo had correctly surmised that the faint light observed on the dark part of the crescent moon is caused by light reflected from the earth.

145. *Her spots,* etc. This conjecture has been proved to be erroneous.

149. *With their attendant moons.* "A reference to Galileo's discovery that Jupiter and Saturn have satellites," say the commentators. But Jupiter and Saturn are not suns, and therefore this may be a speculation reaching beyond the solar system.

153. *For such vast room,* etc. This reasoning is supported by *Isa.* xlv. 18, which would seem to apply to other bodies as well as to the earth.

162. *Flaming road.* The *Clar. Press* says that *flaming* is used as an epithet of road, though meant of the sun. This loses the force of the figure. The journey of the sun's chariot is made with such speed that the wheels raise fire instead of dust along their course.

164. *Spinning sleeps.* In contrast with the fiery speed of the sun, the earth might turn on its axis so slowly as to appear not to turn at all, or, in poetic language, to sleep; the horses of the sun would have to rush along with furious speed, those of the earth might "pace" leisurely and accomplish the same end.

179–354. THE CREATION OF MAN

The origin of man, his relation to the universe and to the divine Creator are now treated in the same philosophical vein as marks the discussion of the plan of the World just ended.

180–185. *How fully,* etc. The angel relieved Adam of the necessity of going through the long and dreary course of Ecclesiastes, and taught him at the beginning that wisdom which the Preacher reached only after a lifetime of experiment and disappointment (*Eccl.* i. 13–18).

190. *Warned or by experience taught.* The Preacher was taught by experience, Adam by warning.

199. *A lower flight,* etc. This must not be understood as something of less dignity, only as something nearer at hand. Man is the most important of God's works, and self-knowledge is recognized as the most valuable of all.

212. *Fruits of palm-tree,* etc. The Bride in the Song is like a palm-tree whose fruit combines the virtues of grapes (wine) and apples (bread) (*Cant.* vii. 7, 8). Adam's delight in the angel resembles that of the two disciples in the wonderful Stranger who told them divine truth on the way to Emmaus (*Luke.* xxiv. 25–32).

214. *They satiate,* etc. The words of God, such as the angel speaks, are compared to honey for sweetness (*Ps.* cxix. 103). But honey satiates and hunger follows the eating, while spiritual food affords perpetual nourishment.

218. *Nor are thy lips ungraceful,* etc. The first Adam also has the qualities which belong pre-eminently to the second Adam (*Ps.* xlv. 1, 2).

222. *Speaking or mute,* etc. While the first Adam "loved righteousness" and bore the image of God, there was the same reason for giving honor to him as afterwards to the second Adam. The "smell of myrrh and aloes and cassia" coming out of the "ivory palaces" symbolizes the wisdom and eloquence issuing from the lips of the holy man (*Ps.* xlv. 7–9) and the kings' daughters and the queen in gold of Ophir represent the graces of elegant form and motion. The poet translates into plainer language the psalmist's highly imaginative description.

229. *I that day was absent,* etc. "An extremely ingenious idea," says Masson, "permitting the introduction of Adam's own story of what he

recollects of his creation." Addison also quotes this as a "shining passage." But it is more than a mere artistic device; it sets forth a profound truth. It is not enough, though pertinent, to say that Raphael in his likeness to Mercury, who guided the dead to the shades below, might be expected to visit Hades. The absence of Raphael from the world at the creation of man is demanded by the fact that not until man became aware of God's love to him did he begin to love God; and this, it would seem, could not take place until after Eve was brought to Adam by the "genial angel" (1 *John* iv. 10, 19, 20).

232. *Squared in full legion.* A legion of spirits is apparently representative of a man's full capacity, the whole power of the soul (*Mark* v. 9; one legion for each of twelve disciples, *Matt.* xxvi. 53). A legion of angels under the command of Raphael means love of God with the whole heart (as enjoined *Matt.* xxii. 37, 38) and, as here, a corresponding hatred of evil (*Ps.* xcvii. 10).

236. *Destruction with creation,* etc. Suggested by *Gen.* vi. 6, 7, and *Matt.* xiii. 25–30.

238. *But us he sends,* etc. Whether or not Milton's Deity is a selfish tyrant, as critics declare, he is the Deity of nature and of Revelation. Compare *Heb.* i. 6–14 and *Luke* xvii. 7–10.

240. *Fast we found,* etc. Because man was made upright and the whole creation was "very good." For the noises in Hell see *Æn.* vi. 552–558 and *Matt.* xxv. 30.

246. *Ere Sabbath-evening.* So that the judgment "very good" could be pronounced at the completion of the work.

253. *As new waked,* etc. Though created on the evening of the sixth day, Adam did not awake to consciousness until the morning of the seventh. His resemblance to Christ continues in the manner of his awaking to life. Compare *Ps.* cx. 3: "The people shall be willing in the day of thy power [the sabbath?], in the beauties of holiness [Adam rests on the 'flowery herb'] from the womb of the morning [Adam is both born and waked from sleep]: thou hast the dew of thy youth [the 'balmy sweat' covering Adam]."

255. *Soon dried,* etc. The drowsiness, symbolized by the dew, is quickly dispelled upon awaking (compare note on v. 56, 57).

257. *Straight toward heaven,* etc. "Man not only sees but considers and looks up at that which he sees, and hence he alone of animals is rightly called ἄνθρωπος." Plato's *Cratylus.* "*Coelum* tueri jussit, et erectos ad sidera tollere" (Ovid, *Met.* i. 85, 86) *Eccl.* iii. 21.

261. *About me round,* etc. The enumeration includes some of the most important objects mentioned in *Ps.* civ., all of which manifest the power and godhead of the Creator (*Rom.* i. 20).

270. *But who I was,* etc. These are something like the questions which

St. Paul answered for the Athenians (*Acts* xvii. 28).

271. *To speak I tried,* etc. This does not agree with our scientific view of the origin of language, but harmonizes with the miracles of Christ in giving speech to the dumb (*Matt.* ix. 33; xii. 22) and with the gift of tongues at Pentecost (*Acts* ii. 4).

273–283. *"Thou sun," said I,* etc. The fruitless search of man's reason after God is thus begun. Compare *Job* xi. 7–9; *Acts* xvii. 27, 28.

286. *On a green shady bank,* etc. A view of God's works is followed by meditation upon them. Meditation is sober and fitted for the shade; it is also glad, and hence is pursued among flowers (*Ps.* civ. 34).

287. *There gentle sleep,* etc. The meditation was "at eventide," like Isaac's (*Gen.* xxiv. 63), and the sleep was that of the night following the sabbath. Having had no experience of falling asleep, Adam thought he was again passing into the nonentity whence he came.

292. *At my head a dream,* etc. Scripture furnishes instances of dreams used by God to convey to men a knowledge of his will (*Job* xxxiii. 15, 16). Among the Gentiles also dreams were regarded as messengers of Jove.

302. *Smooth sliding without step.* The transfer from the outside world to Paradise is like the change from a state of nature to a state of grace, as gentle and invisible as the motion of a breeze (*John* iii. 8).

308. *Sudden appetite,* etc. Adam, like Peter at Joppa when hungry and in a trance, saw what was actually taking place. The vision was afterwards explained (*Acts* x. and xi.).

345. *The same of fish,* etc. The conspicuous omission of fish among the animals to which Adam gave name and their inclusion with those over which dominion was given is the reason of this sentence (compare *Gen.* i. 28 with ii. 19).

350. *Approaching two and two,* etc. As when the beasts came to Noah in the ark. The obeisance is the sign of fealty to man's overlordship in nature and the awe of his superior endowments (*Gen.* ix. 2).

353. *Such knowledge,* etc. The knowledge was such as enabled him to name the animals "according to their properties" and resembled that given to Solomon in a dream (1 *Kings* iii. 12; iv. 33).

355–520. THE CREATION OF WOMAN

356. *Presumed,* because God knows human needs without asking (*Matt.* vi. 8).

357. *O, by what name,* etc. Adam named the creatures that had passed before him from his perception of their nature, but the attributes of God

are infinite and make him incomprehensible, so that he cannot be named as we name things that we know.

368. *As with a smile,* etc. The sign of God's complaisance, as when Solomon prayed for wisdom (1 *Kings* iii. 10).

369. *Is not the earth,* etc. Adam thrice rejected the lower animals for companionship, as Peter afterwards thrice rejected them for food (*Acts* x. 10–16).

383. *Among unequals,* etc. Even among men friendship can exist only with equals—it does not exist between master and servant (*John* xv. 15).

387. *The one intense,* etc. "The stretched (intense) musical string cannot make harmony with one that is slack (remiss)."—*Clar. Press.* Compare the principle illustrated in the command not to "plough with an ox and an ass together" (*Deut.* xxii. 10).

392. *They rejoice,* etc. In *Gen.* i. 21, 25 the different species are separated from one another with great particularity. There is no suggestion of evolution.

397. *Worse than,* etc. The difference between man and beast is the greatest of all.

399. *A nice and subtle happiness,* etc. Adam seems fastidious in asking for more after receiving so much. The whole world is not an acceptable gift without a companion to share his pleasures. Compare the Preacher's account of the solitary man (*Eccl.* iv. 8).

419. *No need that thou,* etc. Compare this with what is said on the generation of the Son in the *Christian Doctrine.*

421. *Through all numbers absolute* (omnibus numeris absolutus) perhaps in explanation of the fact noticed in the *Christian Doctrine* that Elohim, a Hebrew name of the Deity, is a plural.

423. *Single imperfection,* etc. Neither man nor woman alone is complete (1 *Cor.* xi. 11, 12). Not only conjugal love, however, but parental, filial, and fraternal is essential to completeness. The term "amity" extends the relations of dependence even beyond the family.

439. *Hast rightly named,* etc. Adam had applied to them the term "brute" and thus shown his knowledge of their heavy, immobile, earthly nature. Besides, his reasoning had proved his self-knowledge, his free will, his likeness to God, and his difference from the brute.

444. *Be so minded still.* A momentous piece of advice in view of the future abandonment of men to beastly lusts and habits (*Rom.* i. 24).

448. *Fit and meet.* The two words of nearly identical meaning are used, probably, to signify that Adam chose a companion neither below nor above himself; the choice was neither an unworthy nor an ambitious one.

458. *Sleep.* This marks the close of the eighth day, after which Eve was made (*Gen.* ii. 21).

460. *Open left the cell,* etc. This is like the usual interpretation of *Num.* xxiv. 4, 16; where Balaam, overpowered by the spirit of prophecy, is said to have had his eyes open. In the vision Adam saw Eve, his own future bride, and Balaam saw Israel symbolizing the church of God and Bride of Christ.

465. *Opened my left side,* etc. "Some divines hold the rib to have been taken from the left side."—*Clar. Press.* The idea certainly has a poetic fitness so great that if the opposite had been asserted we should surmise a mistake.

478. *She disappeared,* etc. The stories of Admetus and Alcestis and of Orpheus and Eurydice seem partly involved in this appearance and disappearance of Eve in a dream. In both cases love "strong as death" followed the lost one to the world of shades. Orpheus recovered his wife from Pluto on condition of not looking back while leading her out of Hades, but on the very verge of day (waking) he turned (reflected) and lost her. In *Sonnet* xviii. Milton likens himself to Admetus in the loss of his own wife and in having her restored for a brief time to his fancy in a dream.

482. *Adorned,* etc. Like Pandora, the *all-gifted.* For what follows see *Gen.* ii. 22 and *Cant.* viii. 2.

488. *Grace was in all,* etc. The description suits Homer's account of the large-eyed, imperial Juno, and also Solomon's picture of the Bride whose grace is set forth in *Cant.* vii. 1, and whose eyes are compared to the fish-pools in Heshbon, which in their deep repose reflect the sky.

494. *Nor enviest.* Pandora was given to man to injure him, not so Eve (*Prov.* xviii. 22).

500. *Divinely brought,* etc. *Prov.* xix. 14. When Rebekah was brought into the presence of Isaac she covered her face with a veil (*Gen.* xxiv. 65).

503. *That would be wooed,* etc. *Cant.* i. 4. Eve had no veil but her hair (iv. 304) and this may explain her turning away like the Shulamite.

510. *To the nuptial bower.* Isaac brought Rebekah into his mother's tent (*Gen.* xxiv. 67).

512. *Constellations,* etc. The meaning of the benign stellar influence is beautifully given in the last stanza of Spenser's *Epithalamion.* Compare *Gen.* xxiv. 60.

514. *Gratulation,* etc. The relatives of Rebekah, when they dismissed her from home to be the wife of Isaac, "blessed her." Both heaven and earth were to be blessed in the marriage, but the nations of the earth (hills) are specially mentioned (*Gen.* xxvi. 4).

517. *Flung rose, flung odors. Cant.* iv. 16. "Rose" (Lat. ros) is used, I think, in the sense of *dew.* The fresh northern "gales" dispersed the dew; the mild southern "airs" diffused the odors.

521–653. THE PHILOSOPHY OF LOVE

533. *Beauty's powerful glance.* Even in the sinless state the Lover confesses that his heart is "ravished" by the glance of the Bride (*Cant.* iv. 9).

554. *Authority and Reason,* etc. In the decision of Paris, Beauty in the person of Venus took precedence of Authority and Reason in the persons of Juno and Minerva. Solomon subordinated both the interests of his kingdom and his own reputation for wisdom to his devotion to his wives.

560. *With contracted brow.* This expresses disapproval of sentiments that, chivalric though they be, prepare the way for a fall like that of Solomon (1 *Kings* xi. 9).

571. *Ofttimes nothing profits more,* etc. Masson calls this "a very Miltonic sentiment," but it is just as truly a Pauline sentiment (*Rom.* xii. 3). Nothing deprives men of their own self-respect and the respect of others so soon as effeminacy or subjection to a woman. Paris and the contempt visited upon him prove this. The "sobriety" commended by the apostle has in it a large element of dignity and self-respect.

587. *Attractive, human, rational.* The corresponding virtues are modesty, kindness, and sobriety, commended as the true glory of woman (1 *Tim.* ii. 9, 10). Adam should love what God loves.

591. *Scale,* ladder; the elevating power of love is declared in 1 *John* iv. 12.

595. *Half abashed.* Adam perceives his sentiments to be unworthy of his manhood.

600. *Those graceful acts,* etc. The graceful acts mixed with love and compliance corresponds to the "chaste conversation coupled with fear" which is calculated to win the love and confidence of husbands (1 *Pet.* iii. 1, 2).

605. *Harmony,* etc. Harmony in sentiment is essential to love. In the palace of Cupid, Psyche was constantly regaled with music by invisible musicians.

611. *Approve the best,* etc. Since the Fall men are too often compelled to say with Medea of the same passion (Ovid, *Met.* vii. 19–21):

> "Aliudque Cupido
> Mens aliud suadet. Video meliora, proboque;
> Deteriora sequor."

619. *Love's proper hue.* The innocent question about love among the heavenly spirits, touching as it did the very heart of Raphael, the Heavenly Love of the poem's first drafts, caused the archangel to blush

and to reveal himself as Venus revealed herself to her son (*Æn*. i. 402–405):

> "Avertens rosea cervice refulsit,
> Ambrosiaeque comae divinum vertice odorem
> Spiravere; pedes vestis defluxit ad imos;
> Et vera incessu patuit dea."

621. *Without love no happiness.* After answering the question of the Sadducees about marriage in Heaven, Jesus announced the great principle that love to God and man brings one near to the kingdom of heaven (*Mark* xii. 28–34).

627. *Total they mix,* etc. Christ prayed that his disciples might be one. Christ and the believer are spoken of as each containing the other. Adam accepted the familiar idea that spirits do not communicate by words of human speech, and suggested looks, smiles and touch as their means of expressing love. Raphael assures him that the expression instead of being more restricted is more complete than on earth.

631. *Beyond the Earth's green Cape,* etc. The sun has passed Cape Verd and the Cape Verd Islands, which lie from 60° to 70° west of the site of Paradise. Raphael therefore spent with Adam as much time as the three angels passed with Abraham—from noon to near sunset. The great and fertile narratives of the angelic rebellion and the creation of the World had been finished and the discussion had continued to the verge of what was profitable—the mission of Raphael was fulfilled by the exhaustion of the subject. The language contains an allusion to Juno's mission "to the far end of the green earth" (*Il*. xiv. 200–205).

633. *Be strong* is the English equivalent of the classical *vale*.

651. *Oft return.* An adaptation rather than an exact use of conventional forms, which belong to intercourse of equals. The only possible place for Adam to meet the angel was in Paradise.

653. *Adam to his bower. Gen.* xviii. 33. The lesson of instruction and warning was taken to heart.

BOOK IX

1–47. EPIC SUBJECTS

NEARING THE catastrophe, the poet again stops to glance forward and backward and to compare his subject with others that have been or might have been chosen.

2. *As with his friend.* The visits of God and the angels were not discontinued altogether, but confined to a few choice spirits of the race (*Exod.* xxxiii. 11; *Deut.* xxxiv. 10).

13. *More heroic,* etc. His subject is The Wrath of God, which includes all the elements found in the anger of Achilles (insulted Law), the rage of Turnus (despised Love), the ire of Neptune (defied Vengeance), and the indignation of Juno (offended Majesty).

24. *Unpremeditated.* Milton professes to be speaking under the guidance of the Holy Spirit who needs not human thinking (*Matt.* x. 19, 20). The ideas derived from the Sacred Scriptures are so lofty and poetical as to turn without effort into verse.

26. *Long choosing,* etc. On this Masson says: "The subject of Paradise Lost had first occurred to him about 1640; but 'long choosing' among other subjects had followed; and not till 1658, when he was fifty years of age, had he seriously begun." The alternate subject that had occurred to his mind was The Wars of Arthur and the Knights of the Round Table. Of this subject from the realm of chivalry he gives an estimate in the following lines.

29. *To dissect,* etc. One feature of chivalry—a useless expenditure of courage and life and therefore tedious as leading to no end.

33. *Races and games,* etc. Another feature of chivalry—contests of strength and skill in the tournaments of the Middle Ages.

37. *Marshalled feasts,* etc. A third feature of chivalry. "*Sewers,* those who ushered in the meals and arranged them on the tables; *seneschals,* house-stewards."—*Masson.*

39. *Artifice or office mean.* In all this display there is nothing that suggests greatness of soul, demands heroism, or may not be done by the most ignoble.

43. *Sufficient,* etc. The matter of my verse, with its universal and eternal significance, is enough to give it properly the name of a heroic poem and its actors the name of heroes.

44. *Unless an age too late,* etc. The ideas that the race is degenerating, and that a cold climate and the burden of years are unfriendly to poetry are familiar to all.

48–191. SATAN'S RETURN

At his first entrance into Paradise Satan had come as against Job in the temper of a murderer. The second time he comes more as an adulterer to corrupt (*Job* i. 13–19; ii. 7).

50. *Short arbiter.* The adulterer avoids the day and even the twilight (*Job* xxiv. 13–17).

54. *Improved,* etc. The devil's professed friendship is worse than his open enmity.

63. *Seven continued nights.* These nights, being twenty-four hours long, cover the space of a week. If the day when the sons of God present themselves before him is the sabbath, the most natural supposition, then the period of Satan's absence is the same as that between the two temptations of Job (*Job* i. 6; ii. 1). The number seven is inwoven with the history of Apollo. White swans flew seven times around Delos before he was born. He was surnamed Ἑβδομαγενής from being born on the seventh day of May.

64. *Thrice the equinoctial,* etc. This is the "going to and fro in the earth and the walking up and down in it" referred to in *Job* i. 7 and ii. 2.

69. *There was a place,* etc. Satan's first assault was directly upon the Will (the Tree of Life), the second was indirectly through the physical nature (the Fountain).

76. *Sea he had searched and land,* etc. The course here designated is nearly all over rivers and other bodies of water, only short stretches of land lying between. Corruption follows his track over the waters as by infection of the blood it makes its way through the natural body (*Job* ii. 7). The names in the passage confirm this interpretation. The Arctic and the Antarctic regions were, as Satan went, on the right hand and the left from Eden. In the other direction the course is from Orontes (ὁράω, to see), the eyes, to Ganges, also called Padda (foot), because the Brahmins in their legends make the river to flow from the foot of Vishnu. The trail is over all, from right to left, from head to foot.

86. *The serpent subtlest,* etc. *Gen.* iii. 1. The serpent's subtlety is like

innocent artifices and tricks of men, misleading the unwary but making the wise more vigilant. It is the play of wisdom, strengthening itself by exercise. But this very thing is dangerously like deception that has injury and evil for its object. "That proud and envious angel . . . chose the serpent, because, being slippery and moving in tortuous windings, it was suitable for his purpose" (*De Civ. Dei* xiv. 11).

95. *Doubt might beget,* etc. What would cause suspicion if seen in other animals would be carelessly passed as an innocent sleight in the serpent.

107. *As God in Heaven is centre,* etc. This is the key to Satan's admiration of the earth; it is more consonant with the aspirations of a selfish and ambitious spirit, which would be ministered unto without returning anything but influence. Satan's idea of divinity is to receive from all without giving. It is pure selfishness. Bacon connects these ideas: "It is a poor centre of a man's actions, himself. It is right earth; for that only stands fast upon his own centre; whereas all things that have affinity with the heavens move upon the centre of another, which they benefit."

125. *Unless by mastering,* etc. Satan's love of the world transforms him into Mammon who cannot endure divided rule with the Almighty, much less brook subjection (*Luke* xvi. 13).

139. *Before had been contriving,* etc. The planning of the world prior to its creation is hinted in *Job* xxviii. 27 and *Prov.* viii. 22. The thought, however, is half distasteful to Satan because it would imply foreknowledge of events in God.

145. *Spent of old,* etc. John the Baptist rebuked the Pharisees and Sadducees for thinking that the power to raise up children to Abraham (faithful servants of God) was spent (*Matt.* iii. 9).

159. *Glide obscure.* Satan meditates deceit, of which the serpent is the nearest type, his sly habits are the best concealment, and his mazy folds the best defence.

163. *O foul descent,* etc. Thus the King of Babylon at the moment of his highest exaltation was reduced to a beast, driven away from the dwellings of men, and endowed with the heart of a brute (*Dan.* iv. 28–33).

179–185. *Through each thicket,* etc. Hedges are the hiding places of serpents (*Eccl.* x. 8). The serpent of Cadmus lived in a cave in the midst of an ancient wood untamed by the axe and near a thicket (virgis ac vimine densis). Its labyrinthine folds are also noted (Ovid, *Met.* iii. 28–44).

192–384. THE SEPARATION OF EVE FROM ADAM

St. Paul teaches that the devil has a special advantage over husbands and wives who are separated from each other (1 *Cor.* vii. 5). Such a separation here takes place before the temptation of the first pair.

194. *All things that breathe. Ps.* cl. 6. Everything that is fragrant, for the praise is silent, ascending like incense.

195. *Earth's great altar.* In *Rev.* vi. 9 the souls of the martyrs are said to cry from under the altar as Abel's blood cried from the earth. The place of the dead is under the earth. After the Fall the ascending fumes invoke vengeance rather than blessing.

198. *Joined,* etc. Incense and song, the silent praise of the heart and the vocal praise of the lips, are united in the worship of God. The grace before meat here precedes a larger feast for the higher nature (*Matt.* xiv. 19).

214. *Let us divide,* etc. Eve selects for each work becoming to the sex. To Adam with his strength is assigned the training of the weak wood-bine and ivy; to Eve with her grace the direction of the rose and the myrtle.

218. *Spring of roses.* A rose-bush, or a collection of bushes, as *sprung* from the ground.

232. *For nothing lovelier,* etc. This sentiment has given the critics an opportunity to hint that Milton, again as elsewhere defending his own domestic economy, relegates woman to the drudgery of inferior duties. But the language clearly points to *Prov.* xxxi. 27, 28, 23.

239. *Smiles,* etc. Even the meritorious activity of the "virtuous woman" is not quite the ideal for Paradise. The lover feeding among the lilies (*Cant.* v. 13; vi. 3) in talk sweetened by caresses, and strengthened by the smiles of the Bride for duties that are pleasures—he enjoys the perfection of existence.

242. *Not to irksome toil,* etc. Labor with sweat of the face was a curse coming from the Fall.

261. *Whether his first design,* etc. Either of these things would, if accomplished, soon involve the other, for human love cannot truly exist without divine, nor divine without human (1 *John* iv. 8).

270. *Virgin majesty,* the self-assertion becoming to her as a virgin in distinction from the submission befitting her as a wife. The virgin goddess, Diana, aspired to leadership (compare her epithet Ἡγεμόνη), and Eve's likeness to her is declared in the comparison of the woman to one "of Delia's train" (l. 387).

273. *Offspring of Heaven and Earth,* etc. This form of address is that of Juno when she is incensed at Jupiter: Αἰνότατε Κρονίδη, Most dread Saturnius (*Il.* iv. 25). Saturn, or Cronus, was the son of Uranus (Heaven) and Gæa (Earth); and the patronymic as well as the epithet is therefore exactly translated in the line.

276. *Overheard,* etc. This touch, from Sarah in the tent-door (*Gen.* xviii. 10), shows how completely Milton exhausts the stories he uses. Observe also how delicately, by the phrase, "just then returned," Eve guards herself against a suspicion of eavesdropping.

288. *How found they harbor,* etc. Still in the manner of the angry Juno to her lord: ποῖον τὸν μῦθον ἔειπες;—What word hast thou uttered?

292. *From sin and blame entire.* The Horatian expression "integer vitae scelerisque purus" coincides with such Scriptures as *John* v. 14 and *Job* ii. 9, where wholeness or integrity consists in freedom from guilt.

294. *To avoid the attempt,* etc. The offence to spiritual dignity involved in temptation is clearly seen from *Job* ii. 10; *Matt.* iv. 7, etc.

309. *Influence of thy look,* etc. Another touch of chivalry in Adam. Womanly praise is the reward of manly virtue, and *vice versa* (1 *Sam.* xviii. 6, 7; *Prov.* xxxi. 28).

318. *Domestic Adam.* Adam is the typical husband, jealous for the honor and safety of his family (2 *Cor.* xi. 2, 3).

337. *Let us not then suspect,* etc. Eve mistakes her self-confidence for confidence in God. It is, however, the height of presumption to assert that unless God's plan suits man's desire that plan is a mistake.

342. *Fervently,* etc. Adam was strongly wrought upon by Eve's suggestion of imperfection in God. His reply is in substance that of Job to his wife.

359. *Firm we subsist,* etc. Eve's suggestion that human happiness is frail is answered by the Scriptural truth that man was made upright.

371. *Securer,* in their own estimation. The thought is that when both are together they may feel secure against temptation and hence be more easily surprised than when separated and expecting their enemy.

372. *Thy stay not free,* etc. The heart is with its desires, and a compulsory stay would create the loathing of imprisonment.

377. *Though last.* This is usually understood as the repetition of a cheap slander against womankind in general, but it is only a hint of the process of self-justification which precedes wrong-doing by man or woman.

382. *Nor much expect,* etc. This shows how utterly unprepared, notwithstanding her protests, Eve was to meet Satan and how thoroughly she was imbued with self-confidence.

385–531. THE MUTUAL APPROACH OF EVE AND THE SERPENT

The temper of Eve takes her to that part of the Garden where she is most likely to meet the Serpent, who in turn lies in wait for her. She manifests the haughtiness of spirit that precedes a fall.

387. *Like a wood-nymph,* etc. This suits Daphne, who was a wood-nymph, both a mountain and a tree nymph (Oread and Dryad), and a virgin attendant of Delia (Diana).

389. *In gait surpassed,* etc. Diana ("Αρτεμις, the Spotless) is the goddess of virginity. Eve in her self-confidence has a virgin mind; she has a con-

sciousness of her own perfections surpassing that of Diana herself, and manifests it by her lofty gait and "goddess-like deport."

390. *Though not,* etc. Diana's implements gave her sway over the lives of animals: Eve's only over the destiny of plants.

392. *Guiltless of fire.* The introduction of fire among men by Prometheus made the gods their enemies. Fire was necessary to make the implements of Pales and Pomona, but not those of Eve.

393. *Pales or Pomona.* The first of these carries a sickle, the second a pruning-knife. The time for pruning is winter or early spring, before the trees blossom and Pomona yields to Vertumnus, the power that changes flowers to fruit.

395. *Ceres in her prime,* etc. At the April festival of Ceres, celebrated before the bladed grain began to ear, the goddess carried a basket, and in this Eve's likeness to her consists. Eve, then, was equipped with a pruning-knife, or sickle, and a basket.

408. *Such ambush,* etc. *Prov.* i. 10–13. The object of the ambush is murder *or* robbery; hence Milton did not write "and" instead of "or," as Keightley thought he should have written. Eve might have been intercepted and murdered, or she might have been, as she actually was, sent back ruined, like one robbed of his wealth.

420. *By fountain,* etc. Daphne, the pattern for Eve in the present scene, is associated with springs and streams of water.

425. *Veiled,* etc. Fragrance, or incense, accompanies worship and symbolizes it. Goddess-like Eve enjoys the fragrance as a sort of dumb worship.

427. *Oft stooping,* etc. The goddess repays her worshippers with condescension and honor.

435. *Stateliest covert,* etc. The trees named are all evergreens, like the cypresses in the famous grove of "Daphne by Orontes." They are fit surroundings in their stateliness for the proud woman in the midst of them.

437. *Thick-woven arborets.* These supply the place of the bushes of laurel (δάφναι) from which the grove of Daphne got its name.

439. *Spot more delicious,* etc. The virgin goddess, Diana, is associated by name with the first two of these gardens and by qualities of person and character also with the third (*Faerie Queene* III. vi. 16 *et seq.*; *Odys.* vi. 102 *et seq.* The description of the Bride in *Cant.* vi., especially the virgin companions and the epithet "undefiled," fits Artemis).

444. *The person more,* etc. A place so suggestive of honor and exaltation would naturally please an ambitious spirit; but the admiration for Eve has its foundation in the story of Apollo's passion for the wood-nymph Daphne (the victor's laurel) (*Met.* i. 452 *et seq.*).

445. *As one who long,* etc. The grove of Daphne was the summer resort

of the citizens of Antioch. The rural scenes suggest the "simplicity" of Eve before she was corrupted by the Serpent (2 *Cor.* xi. 3).

450. *The smell of grain,* etc. The sense of smell soonest distinguishes between purity and corruption. Apollo's conquest of Python (πύθω, to rot, decay) seems to have been closely followed by his passion for the Arcadian nymph Daphne.

458. *Angelic but more soft,* etc. Conveying the idea that she resembled a goddess, a kind of being for whom there is no provision in Milton's celestial economy.

461. *With rapine sweet,* etc. Still in allusion to the passion for Daphne. The story that Mercury once stole away his quiver from Apollo (Hor. *Odes* I. x. 9–12) probably has its foundation in the same myth.

483. *Whose higher intellectual,* etc. To one bent on deceit Adam's intellect was a serious obstacle to success (1 *Tim.* ii. 14). Adam's physical strength equalled or even excelled Samson's, and overmastering the lion (*Judg.* xiv. 6) could easily cope with the serpent in which Satan was hidden.

490. *Not terrible,* etc. To the tempter physical beauty is well known as a powerful auxiliary. Of itself it is often an incentive to pride and ambition.

498. *Circular base,* etc. This serpent combines features belonging to the serpents that destroyed Laocoon with features belonging to the serpent of Cadmus (*Æn.* ii. 204–208: *Met.* iii. 32–43).

505. *That in Illyria,* etc. The transformation of Cadmus and his wife Hermione (usually called Harmonia) into serpents is described by Ovid (*Met.* iv. 563–604).

506. *Or the god in Epidaurus.* Æsculapius, the god of medicine, was transformed into a serpent in "Epidaurus abounding in vines" (*Il.* ii. 561).

507. *Nor to which transformed,* etc. Olympias was the mother of Alexander the Great, and Jove was reputed to be the father of both Alexander and Scipio. Satan comes in the insinuating power of Music, Wine, and Flattery, symbolized in the three myths just cited.

517. *Curled many a wanton lure.* Like the serpent in the wine-cup (*Prov.* xxiii. 31).

518. *She busied,* etc. A person usefully employed is less easily tempted than an idler (1 *Tim.* v. 13).

521. *Duteous at her call,* etc. The ideal state in God's "holy mountain" is when all the beasts of the earth live in harmony and follow the leading of a child (*Isa.* xi. 6). The lower animals obeyed the call of Eve better than the herd of Circe (men turned by the sorceress into swine) obeyed their mistress.

529. *Serpent tongue organic,* etc. "Either he actually used the serpent's tongue as an instrument of speech (although 'not made' for it, 749), or he caused a voice to sound by impression of the air."—*Verity.*

532–779. THE TEMPTATION

The methods and power of flattery are skilfully displayed in this scene.

532. *Sovran mistress,* etc. The address to Eve resembles that of Ulysses to the daughter of Alcinous in her likeness to Diana. The resemblance is such as might come from expressing the effect of the same personal qualities upon the same admirer under different circumstances.

538. *Fairest resemblance,* etc. The image of Diana fell down, it was fabled, from her father Jupiter and she was worshipped by all the world (*Acts* xix. 27, 35).

543. *These beasts among.* As goddess of the chase Diana was associated with wild beasts. It is with profound significance that Paul speaks of encountering "beasts at Ephesus," where Diana was worshipped (1 *Cor.* xv. 32).

549. *His proem tuned,* etc. This figure from music fits the foregoing allusion to the transformation of Cadmus and Hermione. The music is from the voice of the flatterer.

558. *The latter I demur,* etc. The beasts of the field often act as if they were governed by reason, and thus become means of instruction to the more highly endowed race of men (*Job* xii. 7; *Prov.* vi. 6).

568. *Empress,* etc. Compare the titles and expressions of admiration applied by Ulysses to Nausicaa, the daughter of Alcinous; they are such as would befit Diana, the "resplendent" moon-goddess and empress of the night.

576. *A goodly tree far distant.* Ulysses tells Nausicaa of a goodly palm which he had seen in Delos by the altar of Apollo (*Odys.* vi. 162–167). The tree is remote from beasts because of their lack of capacity; they are below the desire for knowledge.

581. *Sweetest fennel,* etc. Newton leads the critics to Pliny (*Nat. His.* xix. 9): *feniculum anguibus gratissimum.* Serpents were also supposed to suck the teats of ewes and goats. Fennel is from the Latin *foenum* (hay), the special food of oxen, as milk is of the young of animals. The fruit of knowledge is contrasted with the food of dulness and ignorance and the tree appears "to be desired to make one wise."

585. *Those fair apples.* The apple symbolizes Desire (*Cant.* ii. 5). It was an apple that Discord threw among the gods with the cry, Ἡ καλὴ λαβέτω, "Let the fair one take me!" Thence arose the dispute between Juno, Minerva and Venus. The last-named became possessor of the golden apple and brought on the Trojan war with its countless miseries, even as Lust always produces wars and fightings.

591. *Thy utmost reach or Adam's.* Only beings endowed with reason, like man, or such as have gradually acquired reason, like the serpent, are capable of attaining to the knowledge of good and evil; other animals are below it.

595–608. *To pluck and eat,* etc. King Solomon also tested all pleasure, tried wisdom and knowledge, and finally abandoned himself to female charms (*Eccl.* ii. 3, 10; 1 *Kings* xi. 4).

612. *Universal Dame,* lady of the universe. A larger title than even "queen of heaven."

615. *Thy overpraising,* etc. The serpent professed that the fruit had conferred upon him the power of reason; the overpraising of Eve raised a question as to his possession of reason, and hence as to the virtue of the fruit.

622. *Hanging incorruptible,* etc. The fruits of knowledge continue to hang waiting for later generations to pluck them. Men will reach out for them when prepared to receive them (1 *Cor.* iii. 2; *Heb.* v. 12–14).

625. *Wily adder.* Serpent, snake, adder, is a regular progression downward; an adder is poisonous. (*Prov.* xxiii. 32).

627. *Beyond a row of myrtles,* etc. This should have admonished Eve that the tree was beyond honor and even safety.

631. *Swiftly rolled in tangles,* etc. The methods of the tempter in entangling the unwary are thus symbolized (*Matt.* xxii. 15).

634. *As when a wandering fire,* etc. The critics have been severe upon Milton's physics. But the poet is not so much describing the *ignis fatuus* (foolish fire) as giving external form to the idea of Lust.

638. *Some evil spirit,* etc. See *Chambers's Encyc.* art. *Ignis Fatuus.*

641. *To bogs and mires,* etc. The lusts of men lead them into temptation and snares and finally drown them in destruction and perdition (1 *Tim.* vi. 9).

644. *Our credulous mother.* She is the first of the "silly women" led captive by the devil and her own lusts (2 *Tim.* iii. 6).

653. *Sole daughter of his voice.* "A literal rendering of a Hebrew phrase which implies 'a voice from heaven.'"—*Verity.* As Minerva came from the head of Jove, so the command came forth armed with a threat and potent in divine omniscience.

667. *New part puts on.* He assumes the role of an orator defending liberty and human rights; he wavers between affected sympathy with the wronged and indignation at the oppressor. But it is all hypocrisy, like the words and gestures of an actor who does not feel what he expresses.

670. *Some orator,* etc. The language is general, but the particular orator in mind is probably that Tertullus who accused Paul before Felix. This orator hurried through his preface and continued in a passion that distorted all the facts of Paul's case (*Acts* xxiv. 1–9).

680. *Mother of science!* The serpent professes to have received knowledge from the Tree, but not that only; what he had received, active within him, had been productive of more and enabled him to criticise the actions of the Deity himself.

692. *Will God,* etc. God commends wisdom to man and confers it

upon those who seek it (*James* i. 5). Persistency and determination in seeking are praiseworthy.

702. "The fear of God resting on faith in his justice removes the fear of death, since death implies that he is unjust."—*Clar. Press.*

711. *Proportion meet,* etc. *Ps.* viii. gives man an intermediate place between angels and brutes, below the one, above the other.

716. *What are gods,* etc. The idea that the food eaten by the gods is all that makes them different from men is a perversion of such truths as *John* iv. 14; vi. 48–51.

718. *The gods are first,* etc. Satan denies the causative agency of God or the gods, removing the foundation of the true faith and substituting the pagan creed, that all things, even the gods, were the offspring of heaven and earth (i. 509 *et seq.*).

722. *If they all things,* etc. The argument is, If the gods made everything, why did they provide for their own circumvention by putting the forbidden fruit where it is? Or, if without law there is no transgression, why was law made? (*Rom.* vii. 7–13).

735. *On the fruit she gazed,* etc. She was in the same danger as those who look upon the wine when it is red, or those who listen to the song of the Sirens. Bacchus and the Sirens are nearly related.

739. *Hour of noon.* The time for rest and refreshment.

748. *Gave elocution,* etc. Knowledge is prerequisite to speech.

756. *For good unknown,* etc. The almost necessary course of Eve's reflection upon the problem before her—What is meant by death and by knowing good and evil?

771. *Author unsuspect.* "Author" is explained as meaning "adviser." So generous a counsellor, Eve reasons, is beyond suspicion.

780–833. EVE'S TRANSGRESSION

782. *Earth . . . Nature,* etc. The inanimate creation shivered with earthquake; all life from its seat (Eve=Living) to the lowest forms was disturbed and excited out of its appointed equable flow.

784. *Back to the thicket,* etc. Like adulterers and murderers ever since (*Job* xxiv. 13–18).

793. *As with wine,* etc. The pleasure-seeking woman of Babylon held a cup filled with wine, the blood of saints and martyrs, and was drinking death as Eve was eating it (*Rev.* xvii. 6).

799. *My early care,* etc. "I will seek it yet again," say those who have tasted the wine of Pleasure (*Prov.* xxiii. 35; *Isa.* v. 11).

805. *Though others envy,* etc. Eve's meaning seems to be: The gods themselves owe their superior wisdom to eating of the tree of

Knowledge; it is not something inherent in them which they can confer as being above it. On this account, to preserve their superiority, they forbid the fruit to man and are envious of him. The serpent is different from the gods in this, and therefore, next to the fruit itself, I owe most to the serpent's experience and guidance.

810. *Though secret she retire.* Wisdom is something to be sought after; her treasures are hidden (*Job* xxviii. 12–17; *Prov.* ii. 4).

813. *Other care perhaps,* etc. Pagans could so conceive of their gods (1 *Kings* xviii. 27).

821. *To add what wants,* etc. Eve's treachery was like that of Samson's wives; they used their knowledge to the injury of their husband, causing anger and estrangement. After the infidelity of his first wife the indignant Samson was offered her younger and fairer sister (*Judg.* xiv. and xv.).

834–989. THE TEMPTATION OF ADAM

835. *Low reverence done,* etc. This does not imply gross idolatry, as some have supposed, but only that Eve mistakenly imagines herself to have found true wisdom and pays it proper respect (*Prov.* iv. 8).

842. *As reapers,* etc. A return to rural associations to remind us of the simplicity that precedes the knowing of good and evil. The end of knowledge is "to give subtilty to the simple." The crown represents the praise given by the husband to the faithful wife (*Prov.* xxxi. 28)

845. *The faltering measure,* etc. Eve had failed to meet her engagement and gave anxiety to her husband, even as the Corinthian church, by its failure in liberality, caused anxiety to Paul, who had espoused it (2 *Cor.* xi. 2–9).

852. *New gathered,* etc. Knowledge is more attractive when new and fresh, before it becomes common (*Eccl.* i. 8–10).

854. *Prologue and apology.* The prologue comes before a piece of acting in explanation, and the apologue follows in deprecation of harsh judgment. The words imply a lack of genuineness in Eve's behavior.

855. *Bland words at will,* etc. Eve comes with the "impudent face" and "flattering" words of the "strange woman." "At will" indicates that there was no confusion produced by her consciousness of dishonesty.

867–875. *The Serpent wise,* etc. The success of transgressors is a temptation to others; and the pride of pleasure-seekers, like the arrogance of affected godhead, is the strongest inducement to follow their example (*Ps.* lxxiii. 2–9).

881. *Thou therefore also taste,* etc. The flattery of the "strange woman" has slain "many strong men" (*Prov.* xii. 26). Adam is a little farther on (1060) compared to Samson and to Hercules in a breath. This offer of the fruit

coming from the intoxicated Eve and finally covering Adam with shame
(1054–1059) is like the offering of the robe from Deianira, daughter of
Œneus ('Οινέυς, όινος, wine) or Bacchus. The poison of the serpent
entered Adam no less than the poison of the Hydra, transfused through the
blood of Nessus that soaked the robe, entered Hercules. Through the influ-
ence of Jupiter, Hercules did reach godhead, and received as his wife Hebe
instead of the jealous Deianira.

887. *Distemper flushing.* Shame, the "promotion of fools," is beginning
to manifest itself in the blushes on her face.

892. *From his slack hand,* etc. He does not praise her, for only "a
woman that feareth the Lord shall be praised."

896. *O fairest,* etc. The lamentation over Eve fitly imitates that of the
prophet over Israel, "the daughter of my people" (*Lam.* iv. 1–16). Like
that favored nation she is fairer than the fairest, most precious and most
beautiful objects in nature, and comparable only to objects of the imag-
ination, but suddenly lost, defaced ("their visage is blacker than a coal"),
robbed of innocence (implied in the comparison to Sodom), devoted to
calamity and death as the result of her iniquities.

911. *Should God create,* etc. The feeling of Moses when God proposed
to him to destroy Israel and to make of him a mightier nation (*Num.* xiv.
11–19).

918. *Recomforted,* etc. Man's ability to draw strength from despair is
illustrated in the case of King David at the death of his child (2 *Sam.* xii.
20–23).

921. *Bold deed,* etc. It was rebellion and usurpation to disobey God and
aspire to divinity.

930. *Profaned first,* etc. After the holy place in the temple at Jerusalem
was profaned by the "abomination of desolation," God abandoned it to
destruction.

938. *Nor can I think,* etc. The Jews were accustomed to harden them-
selves in iniquity with the reflection that they were Abraham's children,
though denying Abraham's works of faith (*Matt.* iii. 9).

952. *With thee,* etc. The feeling of Moses when Israel was threatened
with extinction for idolatry (*Exod.* xxxii. 32). Compare also Paul (*Rom.*
ix. 3).

967. *One heart,* etc. Adam's resolution to die with Eve proved the two
one in heart as well as in flesh (1 *Cor.* vi. 16).

971. *One guilt,* etc. The Fall is always spoken of as one act, never as
two. Eve represents the element of desire in transgression; Adam the ele-
ment of volition. This idea is figured forth in the union of the sons of
God with the daughters of men, giving birth to those giants in crime
before the Flood. It also appears in the forms of the evil spirits—the front
of man and the back of woman making their heads (*Rev.* ix. 7, 8).

980. *Oblige thee with a fact,* bind thee to me with a deed. Others say, "make thee guilty," but this does not fit so well the alternative "deserted."

990–1045. COMPLETION OF THE SIN

990. *She embraced him,* etc. The story of Samson and in general of the victims of the "strange woman" appears in this and many following incidents.

1000. *Earth trembled,* etc. This travail of Nature attends the birth of sin (*James* i. 15); but sin is continually being born, and therefore "the whole creation groaneth and travaileth in pain together until now" (*Rom.* viii. 22).

1003. *At completing.* Compare note on l. 971. It is always Adam's sin that is spoken of as having produced the Fall (*Rom.* v. 19).

1008. *As with new wine,* etc. The wine mingled by Wisdom and that mingled by Lust (*Prov.* ix. 2, 5; xxiii. 30) have sometimes been mistaken for each other (*Acts* ii. 13; *Eph.* v. 18).

1013. *Carnal desire inflaming,* etc. The effect of the wine of Lust (*Prov.* xxiii. 33). Peter mentions lasciviousness first among the sins that the carnal mind falls into. Allied sins go with it (1 *Pet.* iv. 3). Bacchus unites drunkenness and lasciviousness.

1017. *Exact of taste,* etc. Taste is the faculty of nice discrimination and, intellectually considered, ranks very high. Carnal taste is much lower, and it is to this that Eve ministers.

1020. *I the praise yield thee,* etc. Hebe, the cup-bearer of the gods, bore the epithet "revered" (*Il.* iv. 2) and distributed nectar which stimulated mirth among the immortals.

1024. *If such pleasure,* etc. The lusts of the flesh would now cause Adam to break ten commandments as soon as one. Compare note on x. 16.

1029. *Never did thy beauty,* etc. This speech resembles that of Jupiter to Juno (*Il.* xiv. 313–328), when she arranged to beguile him, in order that he might not be aware of the activity of Neptune upon the earth.

1037. *To a shady bank,* etc. Jupiter had a special marriage chamber framed by Vulcan, but when suddenly smitten with passion at sight of Juno, did not lead her thither (*Il.* xiv. 338). Adam's marriage chamber was the Bower of Paradise (the heart), and the fact that the two did not repair thither proves an absence of true love from the carnal enjoyment.

1039. *Flowers were the couch,* etc. When Jupiter embraced Juno (*Il.* xiv. 347–349),

"Underneath the pair
The sacred Earth threw up her freshest herbs—

The dewy lotus and the crocus flower,
And thick and soft the hyacinth."

1043. *Mutual guilt,* etc. "Mutual" is used in its true sense of "reciprocal," "given and received." The reaction of the will and the desires upon each other is in the poet's mind.

1044. *Till dewy sleep,* etc. Over Jupiter and Juno "a bright golden cloud gathered and shed its drops of glistening dew" (*Il.* xiv. 350, 351). Jupiter was presently overpowered by Sleep and Neptune wrought dismay upon earth unchecked. Samson slept on the knees of Delilah, until she had sheared off his locks and made him weak (*Judg.* xvi. 19).

1046–1189. SHAME AND ITS EFFECTS

The consciousness of shame and the means to hide it—clothing for the body and falsehood for the soul—are the topics of these lines.

1049. *Grosser sleep.* Their natural slumber was "airy light," but this was like the "deep sleep" of Samson, who was unaware of what he was losing in his slumbers.

1053. *Eyes how opened,* etc. Samson lost his eyes in consequence of his last debauch with Delilah (*Judg.* xvi. 20, 21). But the darkening of his eyes seems to have been the opening of his mind to his own degradation.

1054. *Innocence that as a veil,* etc. In her dreams the Bride was deprived of her veil (*Cant.* v. 7), and the nature of her experience connects it with that of the drunken man in *Prov.* xxiii. 35.

1060. *Herculean Samson.* See note on l. 881. The Nessus shirt of Hercules is in its effects like the rags of shame hanging on Adam. Blistering and maddening, the one affected the body, the other the mind.

1074. *Leaves us naked,* etc. The condition of the Israelites after their idolatry. The rags of shame, guilt, falsehood, and apostasy took the place of the washed garments that had clothed them before. Their ornaments were made into the molten calf (*Exod.* xxxii. 2, 3, 25).

1079. *The last of evils.* Shame *follows* the commission of any kind of sin and is the final reward of evil doers (*Dan.* xii. 2).

1083. *Will dazzle now,* etc. After the idolatry of the Israelites, when Moses came a second time from Sinai with the tables of the Law, his face shone, the people were afraid of him and he put a veil over his face (*Exod.* xxxiv. 29–35).

1085. *In solitude live savage,* etc. Like the Cacus (κακός, bad) whom Virgil describes as a half-man, living in a cave inaccessible to the rays of the sun (*Æn.* viii. 194, 195). He was the enemy of Evander (εὐ ανήρ, good man), and his haunt was lit up and himself destroyed by Hercules.

1091. *But let us now,* etc. The coming of shame made it necessary for man to disguise himself, even before the gaze of his fellows and partners in guilt.

1100. *Not that kind,* etc. There is a modesty which is like shame in its external manifestations, which shrinks from praise, and which has no relationship whatever with the shame of transgressors. Between modesty and shame, though they may even sometimes bear the same name, there is a difference as wide as that between the fruitful and the fruitless fig-tree.

1102. *To Indians known.* The part of India referred to, besides being the home of the banyan, or Indian fig, has been noted from early times for its manufacture of cotton, woollen, and silk fabrics for clothing, so that the place is permanently associated with the making of "those troublesome disguises that we wear."

1105. *Daughters grow,* etc. Clothing was invented to cover shame and often symbolizes the disguise of falsehood invented to cover guilt. The growth of the banyan with its numerous stems about the main trunk, and the advancement in clothing from those first fig-leaves to the sumptuous robes of later times, are analogous to the growth of falsehood where many lies are required to support the first concealment of departure from rectitude.

1108. *The Indian herdsman,* etc. The reference is, I think, to a particular Indian herdsman, Bacchus, the tamer and yoker of the wild animals of India. Wine has a direct relation to dress (*Prov.* xxiii. 21). Bacchus and his revellers delight in masks—covering every part of the face except the eyes. These masquerades afford to lust and crime their best opportunities—they mark the extreme of that sensuality which had only begun to manifest itself in Adam and Eve—a few fig-leaves to a whole forest.

1111. *Broad as Amazonian targe.* Milton is credited by some of the commentators with having described the banyan-tree accurately except that he makes the leaves too large. But the leaves of the banyan are heart-shaped, and five or six inches across. Besides, an Amazonian targe is not broad, is less than a half shield, and performs its office so poorly that Amazons in battle were commonly wounded in the breast. This is, no doubt, what led Milton to make the comparison—the insufficiency of the shield and of the leaves for covering, with a hint at the effeminacy implied in the word "aprons." The leaves had to be sewed together before they would cover the shame, as falsehoods are patched together to cover a crime.

1116. *Columbus found the American.* Physical nakedness with guilt in the heart had reduced them to the savage state, and God's first mercy is to clothe them. Though clothing is used to disguise man from his fellows, the want of it in a guilty state is unendurable.

1119. *As they thought,* etc. Spiritual nakedness and guilt are often unsuspected by their subjects (*Rev.* iii. 17).

1128. *Both in subjection now,* etc. They are in the degraded and weakened condition of men in the country of the Amazons, where women rule. The myth of the Amazons finds its realization, if not in political, then in spiritual history (*Isa.* iii. 12).

1131. *From thus distempered breast.* Adam was degraded from his place as guide and superior of Eve, and hence his anger. Jupiter's anger at the guile of Juno, after their slumber on Mount Ida, expressed itself in a speech much like this of Adam (*Il.* xv. 14–33).

1144. *What words,* etc. An exact translation of the phrase in which the irritated Juno was accustomed to address her spouse (*Il.* i. 552; iv. 25).

1153. *Was I to have never,* etc. Prudence would have kept her there, but desire led her away. That which before the Fall should have been accomplished by love was afterwards fixed by a law (*Gen.* iii. 16).

1162. *Then first incensed.* Jupiter was incensed at the chiding of Juno (*Il.* i. 560; xv. 13).

1168. *Now upbraided.* By the suffering consequent upon transgression the Desires are turned back in their tracks and become accusers of the too indulgent Will (*Rom.* ii. 15). The Tempter has turned Accuser.

1170. *What could I more?* The Will is often right when the Desires are wrong and need restraint (*Rom.* vii. 18–21). Originally the Desires were also right and became subject to vanity not willingly (*Rom.* viii. 20). Satan's work at Eve's ear in the Bower was to corrupt the Desires, which before the Fall were free.

1188. *The fruitless hours,* etc. Those who have fallen into such a snare must humble themselves and seek forgiveness. Without this the time is fruitlessly spent (*Prov.* vi. 1–11).

BOOK X

1–84. IMMEDIATE CONSEQUENCES OF
THE FALL— IN HEAVEN

1. *Heinous and despiteful act.* Like the sowing of tares among the wheat (*Matt.* xiii. 24–28).

5. *Was known in Heaven.* By the fruits of sin in the lives of Adam and Eve to the angels, but by direct inspection of the heart to God.

16. *Manifold in sin.* "For what sin can be named which was not included in this one act? It comprehended at once distrust in divine veracity, and a proportionate credulity in the assurances of Satan; unbelief; ingratitude; disobedience; gluttony; in the man excessive uxoriousness, in the woman a want of proper regard for her husband, in both an insensibility to the welfare of their offspring, and that offspring the whole human race; parricide, theft, invasion of the rights of others, sacrilege, deceit, presumption in aspiring to divine attributes, fraud in the means employed to attain the object, pride and arrogance" (*Christ. Doct.* xi.). In confirmation Milton quotes *Eccl.* vii. 29 and *James* ii. 10.

18. *The angelic guards ascended.* The guards were commanded by Gabriel (Wisdom), who sat in the place of judgment and delighted to dwell with men in their primitive innocence (*Prov.* viii. 15, 16, 31). Ovid says (*Met.* i. 150) that Astræa (see note on iv. 997) was the last of the immortals to leave earth on account of its vices and miseries. The angels were "mute and sad," like Pallas under the arbitrary decisions of Jove (*Il.* viii. 457–460).

22. *Displeased all were,* etc. The angels were grieved at the quarrel between Adam and Eve as the gods were at the quarrel between Jupiter and Juno (*Il.* i. 570).

27. *The ethereal people ran.* The Greeks ran together to an assembly at the call of Ulysses (*Il.* ii. 208), and again to receive tidings of the adventures of Ulysses and Diomed, returned from the Trojan camp (*Il.* x. 542).

The running in these cases signifies eagerness for the communications of Wisdom (*Prov.* ii. 1–5).

37. *Could not prevent,* etc. They were striving against invincible Fate, for the word of God had already gone forth that Satan would prevail. The power of all the gods and goddesses availed nothing against "all-disposing Jove" (*Il.* viii. 20–22). In the New Testament it is frequently stated that things were done to fulfil the word of God spoken by the prophet.

43. *No decree,* etc. God had foretold the fall of Man, and it would inevitably occur, though not by influence of the foreknowledge or prophecy.

64. *On the Son blazed,* etc., as on the mount of Transfiguration (*Mark* ix. 3). The glorification of the Son of God in the presence of Moses and Elijah, representatives of the Law, may symbolize this very thing—the Messiah's authority to judge transgressors leniently, yet in full satisfaction of the Law.

80. *Attendance none shall need,* etc. The Messiah, coming for judgment and salvation, says: "Of the people there was none with me" (*Isa.* lxiii. 3; compare "ethereal people," l. 27). The object of judgment was to produce conviction of sin, a spiritual result which could not have been seen by the angels. The flight of Satan was evidence of his consciousness of guilt. The serpent, being a brute, was incapable of such consciousness. Neglect of the distinction between Satan and the serpent has made the passage obscure to certain minds.

85–228. JUDGMENT ON EARTH

86. *Him Thrones and Powers,* etc. The Messiah is not only superior to all other authority and power, but he unites all the various powers in himself. This idea controls in the description of the judgment seat of the Ancient of Days in *Dan.* vii.

88. *To Heaven-gate.* The place of judgment, whence the roads diverge to Heaven and to Hell.

90. *The speed of gods,* etc. The Messiah is at the same instant in the gate, the place of judgment, and on earth in the presence of man.

95. *The evening cool,* etc. *Gen.* iii. 8, 9. Landor objects to the idea that the wrath of the Messiah, having had time to cool, was now less violent. But it gives a divine sanction to the apostolic injunction, "Let not the sun go down upon your wrath," and is not inconsistent with Scriptural representations of God.

109. *Eve more loath,* etc. Two reasons may be suggested for this: first, that Eve was the guiltier of the two, as may be gathered from 1 *Tim.* ii.

14; and, second, that representing the element of Desire in wrong-doing, she in her sin rather than Adam in his showed spiritual estrangement from God.

129. *Whose failing,* etc. It is the duty of the husband to give his life for the wife (*Eph.* v. 25), concealing her faults and bearing her punishment.

142. *Her doing seemed,* etc. This is investing her with the essential function of divinity. God only by his actions can determine right and wrong, and none can call him to account, or say to him, "What doest thou?"

148. *Resign thy manhood.* Manhood embraces the prerogative of ruling, and Adam loses his manhood by allowing the woman to rule, just as Solomon lost his kingdom through subjection to his wives (1 *Kings* xi. 11).

165. *Unable to transfer,* etc. The serpent, being mute, was unable to shift the blame upon Satan, the prime offender.

168. *Justly then accursed,* etc. Not the serpent only, but the whole brute creation vitiated in nature felt the effects of the Fall and lay under the curse (*Rom.* viii. 22).

173. *In mysterious terms.* Christ taught in parables which were often misunderstood by those who heard (*Matt.* xiii. 11–13). The disciples, however, were intended to understand, and Adam also, after his repentance, had the meaning of the curse explained (xii. 375–385).

175–228. These lines are *Gen.* iii. 14–21 and certain explanatory passages turned into blank-verse.

229–409. HADES—THE BRIDGE OF SIN AND DEATH

The Creator in the beginning established a connection between the World and Heaven by a stairway of the Virtues (iii. 516, note); the Fall made a new connection with Hell out of the Vices of men and devils.

231. *In counterview.* This implies opposition. The fear of Death restrains Sin; the power of Sin to corrupt limits the rage of Death.

232. *Outrageous* is perhaps suggested by Nebuchadnezzar's furnace heated sevenfold and destructive even beyond its proper confines (*Dan.* iii. 22; *Rev.* ix. 2).

243. *Methinks I feel,* etc. Like Hecate, the goddess of witchcraft, "lured by the smell of infant blood," Sin is attracted to the death of Innocence (compare ii. 662–665 and notes).

249. *Thou my shade,* etc. Death follows Sin, as Nemesis, daughter of the Night (Hesiod, *Theog.* 223), followed those who had fallen under the displeasure of the gods.

252. *Lest the difficulty,* etc. The possibility of a failure in Satan's enterprise, even after its apparent accomplishment, is hinted at in *Gen.* iii. 22.

256. *To found a path,* etc. This seems to be "the street of the great city which spiritually is called Sodom and Egypt" (*Rev.* xi. 8). Sin has been identified both with the scarlet woman who represents "that great city which reigneth over the kings of the earth" (*Rev.* xvii. 18) and with the strange woman who presides over the way to Hell (*Prov.* vii. 27). Sin's part in the road is hinted at in the name Sodom given to the city; Death's part in the name Egypt.

258. *A monument* is a reminder, a memorial, such as the tower of Babel was intended for. The memorial of Babylon consists of the lives of slaughtered innocents, whose blood cries continually to Heaven for vengeance (*Rev.* vi. 9–11; xvii. 6; xvi. 19).

267. *Such a scent,* etc. This conception of Death unites the dog and the vulture, both of which feed upon the carcasses of the slain. Jove's gryphons, or eagles, are similar, and are consequently called "winged hounds" (Æsch., *Prom. Vinct.* 803, 1022). Their function is to prey upon the wicked not after but before bodily death. They represent guilt, "which, though in its primary sense it is an imputation by God to us, yet is also, as it were, a commencement or prelude of death dwelling in us, by which we are held as by a bond, and rendered subject to condemnation and punishment." (*Christ. Doct.* xii.).

273. *As when a flock,* etc. Matt. xxiv. 28; *Rev.* xix. 17.

277. *Scent of living carcasses.* Guilt pollutes the sinner while living, so that the "mind and conscience is defiled" (*Tit.* i. 15). The pollution of guilt exhales the evil odor that attracts the Avenger.

279. *Grim Feature.* The Greek Nemesis (νέμω, to distribute that which is due, as "the wages of sin") was a personification of the righteous anger of the gods, and the epithet is therefore exact. Death is not a creature, but a something (Feature) that "is not and yet is" (*Rev.* xvii. 8).

283. *Anarchy of Chaos.* From the events of Time—the acts of lawless men—the bridge of Sin and Death is built, the record is made which consigns men to everlasting punishment. Among these events Sin and Death are separated for a while, but they come together at last.

286. *Solid or slimy,* etc. The easiest reference is to the materials used in building the tower of Babel—brick for stone and slime for mortar (*Gen.* xi. 3). But perhaps a reference to the "abominations and filthiness" in the hand of the scarlet woman (*Rev.* xvii. 4) would come nearer the poet's meaning.

289. *As when two polar winds,* etc. A wind symbolizes Sin in *Isa.* lxiv. 6 and the terrors of Death in *Job* xxx. 15. The former is a hot blast from the south, the latter a cold one from the north.

290. *Cronian Sea.* "Pliny (*Natural History* iv. 16) says that the sea one day's sail from Thule is frozen and is called Cronian."—*Clar. Press.*

Cronian is from Cronus (Time). The use of the name confirms the fore-going notes.

294. *Mace petrific,* etc. The mace of Death is the trident of Neptune. The mace is the weapon of priests who are not permitted to bear the sword; and the word "petrific," like the subsequent word "pontifical," points to the successors of St. Peter as somehow aiding in the construc-tion of this portentous bridge.

296. *As Delos,* etc. Delos was raised to the surface of the sea and made firm by order of Neptune. The liquid part of the bridge material is frozen into stone-like solidity by the Gorgon look of Death.

298. *With asphaltic slime.* This feature connects the valley of Death (compare "shoaling," l. 288) with the vale of Siddim, where there were slime-pits (*Gen.* xiv. 10), and where, too, the horror of destruction turned Lot's wife into a pillar of salt.

299. *Roots of Hell.* 1 Tim. vi. 10. The power of the scarlet woman over the nations of the earth is obtained through her merchandise (*Rev.* xviii. 11–17).

304. *A passage broad,* etc. Matt. vii. 13; *Æn.* vi. 126.

306. *From Susa,* etc. "Shushan the palace" is an Old Testament desig-nation. The city bore the epithet "Memnonian," which suggests the darkness of Death, for Memnon is called by Hesiod (*Theog.* 986) king of the Ethiopians. The Memnonium of Thebes has been believed to be a tomb. Neptune, too, had his magnificent palace at Ægæ under the sea (*Il.* xiii. 21; *Odys.* v. 381).

311. *And scourged,* etc. "The Greeks who, in the bridging of the sacred Hellespont, saw the beginning of a long career of audacious impiety, gradually transformed the fastenings with which the passage was finally secured into fetters and scourges, with which the barbarian in his mad-ness had thought to chastise the aggression of the rebellious stream."— *Class. Dict.* Death bears "a whip of scorpions," and Neptune also has his scourges.

313. *Pontifical.* The title "pontiff," established by Numa, was afterwards assumed by the Roman emperors and used finally as a sacred designation of the pope. The epithet is further evidence of Milton's identification of Rome with the spiritual Babylon, whose fall is like that of a great mill-stone ("pendent rock") into the sea (*Rev.* xviii. 21).

315. *To the self-same place,* etc. The Limbo of Vanity. The beginning of the way of sin is in foolishness (*Eccl.* x. 13). Those void of understanding enter the strange woman's house, which "is the way to Hell" (*Prov.* vii. 27).

320. *In little space,* etc. Near the road leading from Earth to Heaven is the house of Sin, which Hell, reaching out with a long arm, had inter-posed so as to draw men away from Heaven into her own broad road (*Prov.* vii. 12–15). This interpretation requires "interposed" to be a verb,

the predicate of "Hell," and not a passive participle. Masson inclines to the same grammatical construction, though he does not seem to take quite the same meaning from the clause.

323. *Three several ways.* There is a passage downward to Earth, a stairway upward to the right leading to Heaven, a bridge downward to the left leading to Hell. Here Sin begins her allurements, having her house on the corner of the street (*Prov.* vii. 8). One of the names of the sorceress Hecate at the entrance to the lower world is Trivia (*Æn.* vi. 13).

328. *Betwixt the Centaur and the Scorpion,* etc. The time was near daybreak, the twilight for which the adulterer waits (*Job* xxiv. 15–17). His highest object (zenith) was to avoid shame and punishment, represented in Centaurus and Scorpio.

336. *Saw their shame,* etc. The sin of the Israelites made them naked to their shame among their enemies (*Exod.* xxxii. 25).

351. *Stupendious bridge.* The emotion at the works of Sin and Death surpasses ordinary wonder. St. John "wondered with great admiration." The pure wonder with horror, the depraved with pleasure (*Rev.* xvii. 6, 8; xiii. 3).

362. *Though distant,* etc. The power of sorcery is here described. Egyptian sorcerers by their enchantments called up frogs upon the land of Egypt (*Exod.* viii. 7). The three frog-like spirits of *Rev.* xvi. 13 appear to represent Satan, Sin and Death, and the miracles attributed to them emanate from their sorcerous power.

371. *Portentous bridge.* "Portentous" involves the idea of presaging calamities, causing fear in those subject to death (*Heb.* ii. 15).

381. *His quadrature,* etc. The term "quadrature" seems to have been universally misunderstood. Lexicographers have invented the new definition of "a quadrate, a square." Commentators agree in taking it to signify a square or cubic form, though everywhere else the word has a different and well-understood sense. The moon is in her quadratures when half her disc is illuminated; at the close of the second book Heaven is compared to the moon; and the two passages together confirm the contention that the "quadrature" of Heaven is of the shape of a half moon. Sin can therefore depreciate Heaven by speaking of it as a mere hemisphere in contrast with the perfect sphere of the World.

389. *Near Heaven's door.* Bunyan saw a way to Hell even from the gate of Heaven.

395. *Them to acquaint,* etc. When the Philistines were successful over Israel and Saul and his sons fell by their own hands on the battlefield of Mount Gilboa, the victors published it "in the house of their idols and among the people." Not only did they proclaim their victory, but placed trophies of it—the armor and body of Saul—in the house of Ashtaroth (the stars) and on the wall of Beth-shan (house of ivory—probably rep-

resentative of the sky). The trophies of Satan's victory over Adam, king of a larger Israel, are likewise hung in the sky, when Sin and Death take possession thereof (1 *Sam.* xxxi. 9, 10; 2 *Sam.* i. 20).

404. *Plenipotent on earth.* The devil gives power to death (*Heb.* ii. 14) and the dragon to the terrible beast of Revelation (*Rev.* xiii. 2, 4).

410–584. CONSEQUENCES OF THE FALL—IN HELL

The scene is changed back to Pandemonium and the action is analogous to events in the history of the real and the spiritual Babylon.

412. *Spreading their bane,* etc. Newton thinks that Milton here adapts to his own use Ovid's journey of Envy to Athens (*Met.* ii. 793 *et seq.*). The approach of Death sickens all nature; and it is the malign influence of the planet Earth that smites the neighboring planets with eclipse and pales the glory of the far-off stars.

415. *Causey* signifies a road paved with stone. The bridges of Xerxes were really causeways against which the angry Hellespont roared and finally broke them down.

419. *Wide open and unguarded.* So Cyrus and his Persians found the gates of Babylon on the night when the city was taken.

427. *These kept their watch,* etc. There was no armed force to resist Cyrus until he came to the palace, where Belshazzar (Nabunahid) was feasting his lords while the Medes were taking the city (*Dan.* v.). Anxiety and fear entered the palace on account of the handwriting on the wall.

431. *As when the Tartar,* etc. The Tartar retreats from that region known to biblical writers as Meshech, and the Bactrian Sophi from that known as Tubal, the one lying northwest, the other east, of the Caspian Sea. The tribes of these regions are the prophetic Gog and Magog, who, after their descent upon the land of God's people, retire to the mountainous region of the Caucasus, easy of defence.

435. *The realm of Aladule.* Aladule was the last king of Armenia before its conquest by the Turks. The retreat of the Sophi left deserted the country eastward of his kingdom around the Caspian Sea; the retreat of the Tartars was from the western side of the sea. Fear drew the population of Hell about its capital, as the tribes were drawn from both sides of the Caspian to the mountains. Fear paralyzes the arms of the sinner, so that for the time evil exists in the heart rather than the act. The fear of punishment to come with the reappearance of Satan paralyzed Hell.

442. *In show plebeian,* etc. Fear of the consequences of his crime was doubtless the reason for his assumed humility. The expectation of judgment had quelled the old spirit of boasting (*Heb.* x. 27).

444. *Plutonian hall.* "Plutonian" is from Plutus, the god of wealth. Like

Belshazzar's capital, with its vessels of gold and silver from the temple of Jerusalem, Pandemonium held the spoils of Paradise.

448. *Saw unseen,* etc. The helmet of Pluto rendered its wearer invisible. Regaining confidence among his helpers and on his imperial throne, Satan presently manifested himself in his true form, flashing star-like from a cloud, as Apollo did in his temple at Delphi (*Hom. Hymn*).

458. *Congratulant.* The throng of representative spirits did homage by shouting; the peers, in virtue of their equality, approached him on terms of intimacy (*Isa.* xiv. 9).

471. *Unreal,* because it is the place of nonentity, chance and death.

476. *The untractable Abyss.* The "chasm" or "gulf" in front of Hell-gates.

In the womb, etc. Among the storm-tossed atoms in the elemental war.

478. *Fiercely opposed,* etc. This has been regarded as a lie of Satan's, but it can be so taken only by assigning more importance to the words of the old Anarch than to the obstacles actually encountered.

480. *Protesting fate supreme.* An allusion to *Luke* xvi. 26.

488. *Worth your laughter!* When God is angry with his people, their "enemies laugh among themselves" (*Ps.* lxxx. 6).

508. *A dismal universal hiss,* etc. "The triumphing of the wicked is short." "The viper's tongue shall slay him" (*Job* xx. 5, 16).

511. *His visage drawn,* etc. The process of the metamorphosis is copied from Ovid's story of the transformation of Cadmus into a dragon (*Met.* iv. 563–603).

518. *Hiss for hiss.* While following Ovid Milton does not forget the scene in Belshazzar's palace. The handwriting on the wall that interrupted the festivities produced a change in Belshazzar, first in his countenance, then in the joints (*arma*) of his loins, then in his knees smiting together (intertwining), then in his descent to the very dust because of fear, then also in his voice, which, expressing his terror, must have been strongly aspirated, like the hiss of serpents. Similar changes must have come over Belshazzar's lords and princes.

520. *His bold riot.* The word "riot" can hardly be understood except from the scene in Belshazzar's palace with its noise, drunkenness and blasphemy (*Dan.* v. 3–9).

523. *Complicated monsters,* etc. The king had a hurried conference with the magicians, astrologers, Chaldeans, and soothsayers, probably the lowest orders in the kingdom, but none could interpret the writing or escape the general terror.

524. *Scorpion and asp,* etc. The different grades of authorities in Babylon seem to be represented by the kinds of serpents in about this order: sheriffs, captains, judges, princes, governors, counsellors (lawyers), and treasurers. The epithet "drear" applied to "elops" is perfectly intel-

ligible on this explanation. The counsellors are "drear," because mute in the crisis (*Dan.* iii. 3). An instance where dignitaries are compared directly to serpents is found in *Isa.* xiv. 28, 29.

526. *Not so thick,* etc. Gorgon in the myths is the storm-cloud, its blood is rain, and the serpents formed are streams of water. Of the islands named Ophiusa Rhodes is the most noted in fable and song. It was first inhabited (according to *Diod. Sic.* and *Strabo*) by the Telchines who were styled Ὑιοὶ Θαλάσσης, Sons of the Sea, and were powerful enchanters able to "summon at pleasure clouds, rain, hail, and snow." The fable evidently hints at the numerous streams that water the island and here symbolize the transformed devils. When men are in terror their hearts are said to melt and become like water (*Josh.* vii. 5). It is fear, then, that transforms the evil spirits and humbles them in the dust.

530. *In the Pythian vale,* etc. Python (from πύθω, to rot) suggests the moral stench that envelops the name of the wicked (*Prov.* x. 7).

540. *Horrid sympathy. Met.* iv. 594, 598. The humiliation, torment, and sorrow of Babylon spread to the kings, merchants, sailors, and all who had commerce with her. Their riches vanished when the great city bought their merchandise no more (*Rev.* xviii.).

548. *A grove hard by,* etc. *Met.* iv. 600. As water causes seeds or dry roots to grow (*Job* xiv. 8, 9), so fear and humiliation have their proper growth of real or affected penitence (2 *Cor.* vii. 10). When the Pharisees and the Sadducees came to receive baptism from John, he addressed them as a "generation of vipers" and admonished them to "bring forth fruits meet for repentance" (*Matt.* iii. 7, 8).

551. *The bait of Eve.* The tree of Knowledge promised godhead and brought death. This is also the effect of false repentance, or, to use Milton's word and the language of Babylon, of penance. Compare *Col.* ii. 23.

553. *Imagining for one,* etc. The system of penance, established by a corrupt hierarchy, demanded abstinence from almost everything that makes life tolerable (*Tim.* iv. 1–4). Christ himself was censured for his eating and drinking (*Matt.* xi. 19).

557. *To delude them.* The Pharisees had a complete system of penance, fasts, tithes, and slavish observances for their painful devotion to which Christ called them fools.

559. *Thicker than the snaky locks,* etc. *Isa.* xiv. 11. Megaera (μεγαίρω, to grudge) is one of the Furies and seemingly personates Envy. The evil spirits grudge men even God's natural gifts and induce them foolishly to deny themselves all innocent enjoyments.

561. *Fruitage fair to sight.* The system of penance varnishes over a corrupt life, but does not remove the corruption. The tree brings forth fruit after its own kind, which looks well enough externally, but is corrupt within (*Matt.* xxiii. 25, 27).

Like that which grew, etc. *Deut.* xxxii. 32, 33. "The story of the Dead Sea apples, or apples of Sodom, fair outside but full of ashes within, had its origin in the fact that there is in that region an apple-like fruit which explodes on pressure."—*Masson.* Josephus, by telling the story, gives it sufficient dignity for this poem.

563. *Not the touch but taste deceived.* Notwithstanding the contrary opinion of Masson and others, I gather from this language that the fruit of the infernal vale deceived the taste as well as the touch and was swallowed, but only to be ejected again (*Job* xx. 14, 15).

566. *Chewed bitter ashes,* etc. Ashes are the residuum when a fire has burned out; dregs, when the wine has been drawn off. When the fire of lust has gone down, and the exhilaration of pleasure has passed off, there remain remorse and despair. Repentance to salvation is something "not to be repented of" and brings forgiveness and peace; but remorse is hateful.

575. *Yearly enjoined, some say,* etc. Corresponding, perhaps, to the remembrance of sins made very year in the celebration of the Passover, which lasted seven days (*Exod.* xii.; *Heb.* x. 3).

579. *Purchase.* Alluding to the ransom which the Redeemer paid to release the world (from the devil's possession, as some say) (*Matt.* xx. 28; 1 *Tim.* ii. 6).

581. *Ophion with Eurynome,* etc. The myth is quoted to suggest, I think, the full possession of the Antediluvian world gained by the devil through Eve and her descendants, "the daughters of men." Saturn (Time) and Ops (Wealth) dispossessed them after the Deluge by means (1) of shortened lives on earth, and (2) the prosperity divinely conferred upon the good and the calamities visited upon the evil. Thus the world was governed in the interests of righteousness before the Law (Dictæan Jove) was born.

585–719. CONSEQUENCES—ON EARTH

Changes on a large scale in the physical condition of the World are caused by the entrance of Death. These produce a necessity for subsequent changes in human life to correspond.

587. *Once actual, now in body,* etc. A distinction is made between the sinful act and the innate, continual propensity to sin, which, as Milton observes (*Christ. Doct.* ix.), "is called in Scripture 'the old man and the body of sin,' *Rom.* vi. 6; *Eph.* iv. 22; *Col.* iii. 9."

589. *Not mounted yet,* etc. *Rev.* vi. 8. The sense is that though death would follow Adam, yet complete possession was still a long way off. After the Deluge the term of human life was greatly diminished.

591. *All-conquering Death.* The epithet would apply as well to the beast, which, as we have seen, Milton takes for Death (*Rev.* xiii. 7).

598. *Alike is Hell,* etc. He does not respect anything, however excellent or evil, so as to spare it. He is an enemy to the bad as well as the good.

601. *Unhide-bound corpse.* Paul speaks of the body of death (*Rom.* vii. 24). The beast in *Dan.* vii. 23, like that of *Revelation* identified with Milton's Death, is one that "shall devour the whole earth" (*Hab.* ii. 5).

603. *On these herbs,* etc. Death fed on them at least as soon as man began to take them for food, and they were given for this purpose after the Fall (*Gen.* iii. 18). Before the Fall only the fruit of trees was given, and not even vegetable death was required for man's sustenance. Animals were given for food only after the Deluge (*Gen.* ix. 2, 3), but for clothing and sacrifice we know that they were killed before.

606. *The scythe of Time.* The ancient Saturn (Cronus, Time) was armed with a scythe or sickle. In the *Apocalypse* there appears "one like the Son of Man" having a sickle and reaping the earth. An angel with a sickle likewise appears gathering "the clusters of the vine of the earth" (*Rev.* xiv. 16, 19). The sickle is in all these cases probably the same, though what it gathers may be either preserved or destroyed.

610. *Betook them several ways.* Sin could reside only in man, while Death could as yet attack only the lower creation.

616. *See with what heat,* etc. Landor has censured Milton for attributing "much of the foulest language" in the poem to the Almighty, and others have concurred in the censure. But Sin and Death are called "dogs," first, because dogs actually devour the flesh and blood of the dead (1 *Kings* xxi. 23, 24); and, secondly, because they symbolize the power of death (*Ps.* xxii. 15–20). The eagle, or vulture, also noted for feasting upon dead bodies, has been called the "winged hound of Jove," just as Sin and Death are called God's hell-hounds. These vultures are properly mentioned with strong abhorrence. They are not God's creatures.

620. *Impute folly,* etc. To expect the recovery of anything left in the hands of Death seems unreasonable. Sarah laughed when, though as good as dead for this purpose, she was promised a son (*Gen.* xviii. 12–15); Christ was derided when he said that the dead maiden was only sleeping (*Matt.* ix. 24). When Paul spoke of the Resurrection the Athenians mocked (*Acts* xvii. 32).

630. *Draff and filth.* Corruption cannot inherit incorruption; and death swallows up the corruption, leaving the spiritual body to be raised in purity and immortality (1 *Cor.* xv. 35–54).

632. *Crammed and gorged,* etc. The fowls are "filled with flesh" in the great final battle with the Word (*Rev.* xix. 21).

647. "The new Heaven and Earth are to *rise* from the conflagration (2 *Pet*. iii. 12, 13) or to *descend* (*Rev*. xxi. 2)"—*Clar. Press.*

649. *Calling forth by name,* etc. God calls the host of heaven, whether stars or angels, by their names (*Ps*. cxlvii. 4; *Isa*. xl. 26). It matters not here whether separate beings have charge of the heavenly bodies, or whether the latter are obedient of their own accord.

653. *Cold and heat scarce tolerable.* Ovid, *Met*. i. 119, 120; *Ps*. cxlvii. 17, etc.

656. *To the blanc moon.* The paleness of the moon indicated superfluous moisture in the air, and her "office," therefore, was to deluge the earth with rain. Lunar influence was supposed to cause madness.

657. *To the other five,* etc. Planetary influence seems to be assumed in *Ps*. cxxi. 6 and *Judg*. v. 20. The planets (including Sun and Moon) gave name to the days of the week, and their influence produced the different temperaments—Jovial, Saturnine, Mercurial, etc. All of the aspects here specified, and not merely a few of them, as has been held, are of "noxious efficacy."

661. *Taught the fixed,* etc. Virgil (*Georg*. 1.) mentions the Kids, the Dragon and Arcturus, as tempestuous in their rising. The Pleiades were favorable to mariners and their "sweet influence" is referred to in *Job* xxxviii. 31.

668. *Some say,* etc. Since before the Fall the equator is supposed to have coincided with the ecliptic, it follows that one or the other circle must have altered its position. If the Ptolemaic system were true, the ecliptic must have been moved; if the Copernican, the equator.—*Keightley.* Compare *Ps*. ix. 6.

673. *To Taurus,* etc. Leaving out Aries on the equatorial line, where the Sun now moved, the enumeration includes the rest of the signs in the northern hemisphere, and with Capricornus in the extreme south marks out the limits of the seasons. "*Atlantic sisters;* the seven daughters of Atlas, the Pleiades; seven stars in the constellation Taurus. *Spartan twins;* Gemini, *i.e.,* Castor and Pollux, sons of Leda, wife of Tyndareus, king of Sparta."—*Clar. Press.*

678. *Else had the spring,* etc. In the Golden Age spring was perpetual; but with the Silver Age came the four seasons (*Met*. i. 107–118).

685. *Forbid the snow,* etc. Masson understands "forbid" to mean "would have prevented from coming to." Estotiland, an old name for Greenland, was regarded as the most northern land in the world, while the island south of Magellan was the most southern. The idea is that but for the fall of man snow would have been kept from the earth. This is a favorite fancy with poets, perhaps justified by *Job* xxxviii. 22, 23.

688. *Thyestean banquet,* etc. In the banquet the father, Thyestes, was caused unwittingly to devour the flesh of his murdered children, and

"the sun, it is said, at the sight of this horrible deed checked his chariot in the midst of his course." The eating of the forbidden fruit was a Thyestean banquet, for in it Adam was devouring his descendants, who by his act became the prey of Death. That heavenly bodies are affected by crimes on earth is shown at the crucifixion of Christ, when "the sun was darkened."

696. *Norumbega* is a province "coinciding with the present New England and part of New York;" *Samoieda* is in the northeastern part of Siberia. The cold here is intenser than in the same latitudes elsewhere, and hence they may represent those "mountains of brass" between which God's artillery is kept. The four winds from this "brazen dungeon" between Norumbega and Samoieda very likely are intended to take the place of those four chariots coming from between two mountains of brass in *Zech.* vi. 1–8. They are equipped with God's artillery, snow and hail (*Job* xxxviii. 22, 23).

701. *With adverse blasts,* etc. *Job* xxxvii. 9; *Zech.* ix. 14. The noise of the whirlwind is associated with the roaring of lions, and hence the whirlwinds of the south are said to come from Sierra Leone, the Lion Mountains. The sun is in the constellation Leo during the extreme heat of summer. Lions and heat are also brought together in *Job* iv. 9–11.

704. *The Levant and the Ponent,* etc. "Eurus and Zephyr, called also Levant and Ponent (rising and settling) are the east and west winds."— *Clar. Press.* "Sirocco (ventus Syrus) blows from the southeast, and Libecchio (ventus Libycus) from the southwest."—*Keightley*. The east wind in Scriptural lands is exceedingly dry and parching (*Gen.* xli. 6). The Sirocco, or Simoom, is supposed to have destroyed Sennacherib's host (2 *Kings* xix. 7). Libecchio may have been one of the winds encountered by Paul in his voyage to Rome and by Jonah in his flight to Tarshish. Zephyrus is put by Virgil among the noxious winds (*Æn.* i. 131).

713. *Fled him,* etc. Fear takes the place of the original servitude (*Gen.* ix. 2).

720–1006. HUMAN DESPAIR

The weight of the divine judgment, the prospect of inevitable death, and the wretchedness caused by domestic discord lead Eve (like Job's wife) to the proposal of suicide.

720–728. *O miserable of happy!* Compare lament of Job when his prosperity was changed into adversity (*Job* xxix. 2, 20; xxxi. 33).

728, 729. William Lauder in 1750 professed to have found these lines in the *Adamus Exul,* a very rare work of Grotius, and ll. 616, 617 of this book in a work by a certain Jacobus Masenius. It has been pointed out that Lauder himself dishonestly made Latin out of the English for the purpose of convicting Milton of "plagiarism." See note on i. 261.

730. *Increase and multiply.* The result of the command given in *Gen.* i. 28 is described in *Gen.* vi. The injunction was repeated after the Deluge, as if, in view of experience, it might seem doubtful whether the race ought to be propagated (*Gen.* ix. 1, 7).

741. *Heavy though in their place.* The weight of things is the measure of the force which draws them to the centre of the earth. At the centre all weight is lost, but the curses of posterity lose nothing of their heaviness when they find their proper centre in Adam.

751. *Thy terms too hard,* etc. Adam's spirit is that of the unprofitable servant and deserves his rebuke and punishment (*Matt.* xxv. 24–30). The temper of Job was different (*Job* i. 21; ii. 10).

764. *Not thy election,* etc. What one does by necessity he feels less responsibility for than what he does by free will. God acted under no necessity when he created man (*James* i. 18).

778. *My mother's lap.* The goddess Terra had the surname of Magna Mater among the ancients.

784. *Lest that pure breath,* etc. The doubt of the Preacher comes to torment Adam (*Eccl.* iii. 20, 21; xii. 7). Milton did not accept the idea of an immortality of the soul apart from the body and prior to the Resurrection. It was the heathen, not the Christian, idea of immortality that tormented Adam.

786. *Then in the grave,* etc. Milton interprets the expression "spirits that are in prison" (1 *Pet.* iii. 19) as descriptive of the state of the dead, and equivalent to *in sepulchro,* in the grave (*Christ. Doct.* xiii.).

792. *All of me then shall die.* Chap. xiii. of the *Christ. Doct.* is devoted to the proof of this proposition: "Inasmuch, then, as the whole man is uniformly said to consist of body, spirit, and soul (whatever may be the distinct provinces severally assigned to these divisions), I shall show first that the whole man dies, and secondly, that each component part suffers privation of life."

806. *By which all causes,* etc. Newton finds here one of the axioms of scholastic philosophy, "Omne efficiens agit secundum vires recipientis, non suas."

816. *Incorporate both.* The meaning is that as both reside in the same body (*Rom.* vii. 24) so death will last while he lasts, and both may be eternal.

822. *Ah, why should all,* etc. To reconcile the principle of punishing the children for the sins of the father with the just principle of making every man suffer for his own sin Milton says: "It is a principle uniformly acted upon in the Divine proceedings, and recognized by all nations and under

all religions from the earliest period, that the penalty incurred by the violation of things sacred (and such was the tree of knowledge of good and evil) attaches not only to the criminal himself, but to the whole of his posterity, who thus become accursed and obnoxious to punishment" (*Christ. Doct.* xi.).

825–856. We need hardly look outside of Job's lament for a single thought of this passage.

861. *With other echo,* etc. In the days of his health and prosperity the words of Job had an echo of blessings instead of curses (*Job* xxix. 11–13).

864. *Desolate* is used as of a woman forsaken by her husband. Adam, being "incensed" at Eve, was spiritually estranged, however near.

871. *Thy inward fraud.* The serpent was the subtlest beast of the field, and the evil woman is "subtile of heart" (*Prov.* vii. 10). Jupiter charges Juno with like dishonest subtlety (*Il.* xv. 14). Female beauty as a mask in these cases covers moral ugliness.

875. *Wandering vanity,* etc. The characteristic of a good housewife is "keeping at home" and of a bad one "wandering about from house to house" (*Tit.* ii. 5; 1 *Tim.* v. 13) and frequenting the most public places (*Prov.* ix. 14).

885. *Crooked by nature,* etc. The rib becomes to the angry husband a symbol of woman's character, its crookedness of her wandering disposition, and its origin from the left side of her tendency to evil (1 *Tim.* v. 13, 15). The supernumerary rib would incline man to wrong while it remained either in his body or by his side. The rib being altogether removed, *i.e.,* the woman and the need of her, man would have remained upright.

888. *Oh, why did God,* etc. Critics have noted the resemblance of this to a passage in Euripides (*Hippolytus,* 616). Certain utterances of St. Paul advising against marriage give additional point to the question (1 *Cor.* vii.).

890. *Spirits masculine.* There is no distinction of sex in Heaven (*Matt.* xxii. 30).

891. *Fair defect,* etc. Created to meet a want of man's nature, she is taken as the representative of a defect (*Gen.* ii. 18).

896. *Disturbances,* etc. The history of Israel furnishes many instances of disaster in the government wrought by feminine intrigue. Solomon's wives, Jezebel, Athaliah, and Ahab's daughters at once occur to the mind.

901. *Whom he wishes,* etc. Merab, Saul's eldest daughter, after being promised to David, was withheld from him and given to an obscure man (1 *Sam.* xviii. 19). The fact that Michal, a younger daughter of Saul, who loved David, was soon after given to him indicates that Merab herself may have been unwilling to form the alliance. Michal was afterwards taken from David and given to another (1 *Sam.* xxv. 44).

904. *Or his happiest choice,* etc. This may have been the reason why Elkanah had two wives who were unfriendly to each other (1 *Sam.* i. 5–8). The "household peace" of Jacob, Elkanah, and David was much disturbed by the plural marriages of those men.

920. *This uttermost distress,* etc. The threatened separation brings up considerations that are found in 1 *Cor.* vii. 12, 15, 26.

921. *Forlorn of thee,* etc. After the rupture between Psyche and Cupid, she became the slave of Venus, who tormented her. The fact is prosaically expressed in *Gen.* iii. 16, "Thy desire shall be to thy husband."

929. *Than thyself more miserable,* etc. This may be inferred from the language of the divine judgment, "I will greatly multiply thy sorrow."

931. *I against God and thee. Luke* xv. 18. Eve in preferring the serpent's advice to Adam's was committing the worst sin that a woman can commit against her husband.

936. *Me sole cause,* etc. It is a mark of the true penitent that he takes blame upon himself instead of casting it upon others (2 *Sam.* xxiv. 17). Helen of Troy, beholding the evils resulting from her crime against her husband, wishes that she might have perished before these things had happened (*Il.* iii. 173–175; vi. 344–348).

943. *Reconcilement.* The estrangement of husband and wife, the consequent temptation by the devil, and the subsequent reconciliation are all suggested to the poet by the same passage (1 *Cor.* vii. 5–11).

947. *Unwary and too desirous,* etc. Like the reply of Christ to the sons of Zebedee: "Ye know not what ye ask" (*Matt.* xx. 22). All the disciples, before the actual test, thought themselves willing to die for their Master (*Matt.* xxvi. 35).

950. *Bear thine own first.* Only one who is himself without sin can become a sacrifice for the sins of others (*Heb.* vii. 26, 27).

968. *How little weight,* etc. The value put upon words of idle wanderers, like Eve, may be gathered from the fact that Paul calls them "tattlers" (1 *Tim.* v. 13).

974. *Will not hide,* etc. Eve here expresses the sentiments of the Stoics. The sum of man's duty, they said, is to subdue his passions of joy and sorrow, hope and fear, and even pity. A wise man, moreover, may justly and reasonably withdraw from life, whenever he finds it expedient. The apathy proposed by the Stoics would relieve the extremes of human life and suicide would end them.

979. *Care of our descent,* etc. Paul gives as a reason for celibacy the additional carefulness for the things of this world and the "trouble in the flesh" which the married state produces (1 *Cor.* vii. 32, 28).

984. *This cursed world,* etc. *Eccl.* ix. 3. The curse upon the world, the sorrow of human life and a return to dust are all parts of the divine judgment.

1001. *Let us seek death.* Psyche sought death after her separation from Cupid; Dido committed suicide upon the loss of Æneas; Job's wife proposed death to her husband as a means of escaping from life's trials and sufferings.

1004. *Have the power of many ways,* etc. Spenser's *Despayre* gave wide choice to the Red-Cross Knight:

> "Then gan the villein him to overcraw,
> And brought unto him swords, ropes, poison, fire,
> And all that might him to perdition draw;
> And bad him choose what death he would desire;
> For death was dew to him that had provokt God's ire."

1006. *Destruction with destruction,* etc. Eve proposes to do what was really accomplished by Christ, who by death destroyed him that had the power of death (*Heb.* ii. 14).

1007–1104. THE BIRTH OF HOPE

The argument against suicide naturally attacks the Despair that counsels self-destruction. Despair yields to Hope drawn from the words of God; Hope leads to the consideration of Art and of the use of Fire, its principal agent. Experience of God's mercy leads to penitence and humiliation.

1010. *Nothing swayed.* Like the great sufferer Job, when advised to destroy himself (*Job* ii. 10).

1014. *Something more sublime,* etc. The wise man of the Stoics was said to be king of circumstances and superior to life itself in daring upon occasion to take it from himself. Christ manifested this sublimity in laying down his life for men. The same superiority to life and pleasure is demanded of Christ's followers (*Matt.* x. 39).

1018. *Anguish and regret,* etc. Judas destroyed himself in such a frame of mind and he was a lover of wealth (*Matt.* xxvii. 5). He contrasts with those martyrs for Christ who "loved not their lives unto death" (*Rev.* xii. 11).

1026. *Contumacy,* etc. The contumacious are punished with severer strokes, while those who accept God's discipline with patience receive favor (*Rom.* ii. 4, 5).

1038. *So our foe shall scape,* etc. Satan is a foe put within man's power, and if he escape, Adam's life, on the principle of 1 *Kings* xx. 39–42, must answer.

1043. *Savors of rancor,* etc. God's mercy, forbearance and goodness are often thus met (*Rom*. ii. 5–8). Adam sees God's *long-suffering* in the postponement of their punishment; his *forbearance* in the exaction of less than they deserve; his *goodness* in the supply of their wants.

1060. *Much more if we pray,* etc. Prayer envinces a wish to be reconciled with God, and friendship justly expects more than enmity (*Matt*. vi. 30–33).

1065. *Show us in this mountain.* From Mount Carmel Elijah's servant first saw indications of the coming storm of wind and rain (1 *Kings* xviii. 41–45). Disorders in the moral world and approaching judgments are first observed from the spiritual height of the church.

1067. *Which bids us seek,* etc. Nature of herself no longer furnishes either food or shelter for man, and the necessity forces a resort to *Art*.

1069. *Diurnal star,* etc. The sun is meant here, as also in 2 *Pet*. i. 19. The fires of Vesta were kindled from the sun, probably by means of mirrors.

1072. *Or by collision,* etc. The idea seems to be that as friction reduces rock to dust, so attrition may grind air into the finer element of fire. "Nubes mediocriter collisae fulgurationes faciunt; efficiunt majore impetu pulsae fulmina" (Seneca, *Quaes. Nat*. I. 1).

1075. *Tine the slant lightning.* "Tine" here seems to have a double use. Its meaning (A. S. *tynan, teonan,* to vex, irritate, incense) is to kindle; but it is also applied as a noun to the prongs of a fork, and hence suggests the "forked lightning."

1078. *Such fire to use,* etc. According to the legend, Prometheus gave man fire and taught him to use it. But Prometheus, as has been seen, sometimes represents Satan; and Satan may in a sense be said to have given fire to man—namely, by causing such a condition of things as to render it necessary. According to Milton, however, only the evil came from Satan, while the remedy came from God. For the treachery of mankind in betraying Prometheus Jupiter gave them as a reward a remedy against the evils of old age, but here the remedy comes in view of man's renunciation of Satan by repentance.

1086. *To the place repairing,* etc. The union of justice and mercy is thus set forth; they meet in the same place and that place is God's judgment seat (*Ps*. lxxxv. 10).

1092. *Sorrow unfeigned,* etc. It was like the sorrow, repentance and faith of Nineveh that drew compassion from God (*Jon*. iii. 5–10) or like that of the returning prodigal.

BOOK XI

1–71. PRAYER ACCEPTED

3. *Prevenient grace,* etc. The grace of God comes, even before it is sought, inducing the heart to prayer and supplication (*Isa.* lxv. 24).

8. *Their port,* etc. In the very act of humbling themselves they are exalted (*Luke* xviii. 11–14).

12. *Deucalion and chaste Pyrrha,* etc. The mention of these two at this point is eminently fit. Deucalion was the son of Prometheus and Clymene; Pyrrha the daughter of Epimetheus and Pandora. With the Fall has come the knowledge of fire, as described at the close of the preceding book; and Adam and Eve have passed into a second state, which is an outgrowth of the first. But the meaning is also that as Noah and his wife, the ancestors of all the postdiluvians, offered sacrifices and entered into a new covenant with God, so Adam and Eve, the first heads of the race, entered into new relations with God after the Fall. Deucalion and Pyrrha before the shrine of Themis (Justice); Noah and his wife before their altar (*Gen.* viii. 20–22) and Adam and Eve in the place of judgment stood in the same relation to all after generations.

15. *Nor missed the way,* etc. Prayers not granted by the gods were said to be dispersed by the winds (*Æn.* xi. 795). Adam and Eve had complied with the conditions of effective prayer (1 *Pet.* iii. 7; *Matt.* xviii. 19).

17. *Dimensionless.* Sincere prayer in the fewest words makes its way from the closet through closed doors to the ear of the Almighty (*Matt.* vi. 6–8). *Rev.* viii. 3, 4.

22. *What first-fruits,* etc. The joy of the Son, his intercession for transgressors, and the fruits of redemption are brought together in *Isa.* liii. 11, 12. The next thirty lines are made up principally of Scripture texts.

57. *Two fair gifts,* etc. St. Paul designates the gifts that come through Christ (who restores the endowments of Eden) as Righteousness and Eternal Life (*Rom.* v. 17–21).

67. *Synod,* etc. The following speech of the Almighty, formed upon *Gen.* iii. 22–24, is addressed to the angels and implies their presence. Themis summoned the gods to a council prior to the final exploit of Achilles (*Il.* xx. 4).

72–262. THE DESCENT OF MICHAEL

As the angel of Divine Love (Raphael) had been sent to warn Adam of his danger from Satan, so the angel of Justice (Michael) is here commissioned to execute the penalty for disobedience.

72. *The Son gave signal,* etc. Michael directed the sounding of the trumpet in vi. 202, while here the Son directs it. The change is significant. The apostate angels were delivered into the hands of Justice without mercy; but fallen and penitent man is delivered to Justice indeed (for Michael is chosen to execute the sentence), yet under the control of the great Intercessor. "A voice from the four horns of the golden altar which is before God" (*Rev.* ix. 13)—whence Christ has just interceded for Adam—directs some of the trumpets in St. John's vision.

73. *He blew his trumpet,* etc. The first of the trumpets of doom to be sounded in the history of this world and the fifth of the whole series (*Rev.* viii. 13; ix. 1).

74. *Heard in Oreb,* etc. The second of the trumpets having reference to man (*Exod.* xix. 16–19) and the sixth of the series (*Rev.* ix. 13).

76. *To sound at general doom.* The third trumpet on earth and the last of the Apocalyptic vision (*Matt.* xxiv. 31; 1 *Cor.* xv. 52; *Rev.* xi. 15).

77. *Filled all the regions.* The trumpet at Sinai was heard throughout the camp of Israel (*Exod.* xix. 16; xx. 18). The last trumpet to gather the elect together shall be heard throughout the earth (*Matt.* xxiv. 31).

80. *In fellowships,* etc. The Israelites abiding in their tents by families, as Balaam saw them in his prophetic trance, furnish the original of this picture (*Num.* xxiv. 5, 6). "Families" is too suggestive of carnal union—hence "fellowships" is used.

93. *Lest therefore,* etc. The disobedience of the Fall came from no hostility of the human will towards God; the subsequent penitence was proof of that; but man's fickleness might suffer a change to voluntary hostility, and, as in the case of the devils, make the evil condition unchangeable (*Gen.* iii. 22, 23). For the significance of the Tree of Life see remarks on iv. 172–392.

100. *Cherubim. Gen.* iii. 24. Like the select three hundred of Gideon (Destroyer) with their trumpets, their flaming lamps and the sword of the Lord for their battle-cry (*Judg.* vii. 20–22), these are chosen for courage, vigilance, and power of inspiring panic or fear.

105. *Without remorse.* Michael (see notes in Book VI.) has many points of likeness to Achilles. The present phrase is an exact translation of the name Achilles (α ἴλεος, without pity). The spirit of Justice must not be swayed by human sympathy.

108. *Yet, lest they faint,* etc. Compare the prayer of the penitent and the answer of the Judge, *Jer.* x. 24 and xlvi. 28.

114. *What shall come,* etc. The angel of *Rev.* x., by Milton identified with Michael, had a revelation of the future to communicate to St. John. Compare *Rev.* i. 1.

123. *Lest Paradise,* etc. The Church of God was entered by evil spirits and made a den of corruption in the time of Christ (*Matt.* xxi. 13) and before the Reformation.

129. *Like a double Janus,* etc. *Ezek.* x. 21, 12. Janus, though usually represented with two faces, is sometimes represented with four and is then called *Quadrifrons.* He had charge of the gates of Heaven, and hence all gates (januae) on earth were called after him and supposed to be under his care. He presided over the opening of the day under the title of Matutinus, and his two faces probably represented morning and evening. He also ruled the opening of the year, the first month being named after him, and then his four faces represented the seasons.

131. *Argus* was the hundred-eyed guardian appointed by the jealousy of Juno to watch her rival Io. According to some versions of the fable, Hermes charmed him to sleep with a shepherd's pipe, or with the caduceus, before killing him. Argus with all his hundred eyes might be lulled to sleep, but not so "he that keepeth Israel" (*Ps.* cxxi. 4).

135. *Leucothea* (White Goddess) is apparently the white morning mist (*Gen.* ii. 6). In *Odys.* v. she supplies Ulysses with a veil of "heavenly woof."

143. *But that from us,* etc. The second part of faith is to believe that God "is a rewarder of them that diligently seek him" (*Heb.* xi. 6).

159. *Eve rightly called,* etc. The name Eve is not given in the Bible to the woman until after the Fall and the Divine judgment, as if to signify a recovery of spiritual life to the race of mankind through her seed.

167. *Infinite in pardon,* etc. His pardon is as large as the iniquities of men, and they are infinite (*Isa.* xl. 2).

172. *To labor,* etc. Having fallen into temptation through her idle wanderings, Eve in her penitence thinks first of correcting her idleness (1 Tim. v. 14).

181. *Fate subscribed not.* The decree for removal had already gone forth (*Gen.* iii. 23).

183. *On bird, beast, air.* In these things the ancients were accustomed to look for their auguries, the Jews apparently agreeing with the Gentiles.

185. *The bird of Jove,* etc. *Il.* viii. 247. The bird of Jove is the eagle; the

birds of gayest plume I take to be doves, which have feathers of silver and gold (*Ps.* lxviii. 13).

194. *By these mute signs,* etc. The eagle hasting to the prey is a figure of the fleetness of human life (*Job* ix. 26); the lion hunting his food is a symbol of the wrath of God against human transgression (*Job* x. 16). Both are alike signs of approaching dissolution.

204. *Darkness ere day's mid-course,* etc. In the Scriptures Moses and Elijah regularly represent the power of Law and Justice. Michael impersonates the same power, and in his coming is like those saints at the transfiguration of Christ. The radiant persons of Moses, Elijah, and Jesus, and the bright cloud that encompassed them, have their corresponding features in the account of Michael's descent.

209. *A sky of jasper* is one covered with cloud streaked with morning red, perhaps like the cloud in the Transfiguration.

211. *Doubt and carnal fear,* etc. The disciples before a similar spectacle were fearful, puzzled, and heavy with sleep (*Luke* ix. 32–34).

213–222. Compare *Gen.* xxxii. and 2 *Kings* vi. 13–17.

227. *Of us will soon determine.* It was a common belief that to behold one of these supernatural visitants meant death to the beholder. Indications of this belief are found in *Gen.* xxxii. 30; *Judg.* xiii. 22, etc.

229. *Yonder blazing cloud,* etc. *Matt.* xvii. 5. The mighty angel of the *Apocalypse,* whom Milton identifies with Michael, was clothed with a cloud, and also set "his right foot upon the sea and his left foot on the earth" with that majestic "gait" which impresses Adam.

233. *Yet not terrible,* etc. Neptune, the death-god, is noted for his majestic strides and Michael has much of the sternness of this avenging deity. He chastises the erring, but "whom the Lord loveth he chasteneth," and Michael has, therefore, also some characteristics of Raphael, the angel of Love.

239. *Not in his shape celestial,* etc. John describes him in his celestial shape, but Jacob wrestles with him in his human shape (*Gen.* xxxii. 24).

241. *Military vest.* He is the leader of the heavenly armies in the *Apocalypse.*

242. *Livelier than Melibœan.* Melibœa, a city of Thessaly, was famous for a fish which was used in dyeing purple. *Sarra* is Tyre. Sar was the name of the shell-fish from which the celebrated Tyrian purple was made.

244. *In time of truce.* War and peace are suggested in turn by the appearance of Michael. The vesture was purple, the royal color of peace, and the bloody stain of war; the helmet was there, but "unbuckled"; the sword was there, but sheathed; and the spear was used as a sceptre.

Iris had dipt, etc. Ἴρις is the word translated "rainbow" in *Rev.* x. 1. The Iris of Milton, Homer, and the Bible is red, and not many-colored as the translation "rainbow" would imply.

245. *His starry helm,* etc. The helmet of saints is salvation (*Eph.* vi. 17), or "the hope of salvation" (1 *Thess.* v. 8). The morning-star is the symbol of hope in Homer, Milton, and the Bible. The helmet of Achilles "glittered like a star" (*Il.* xix. 381).

Prime in manhood, etc. Though "Moses was a hundred and twenty years old when he died, his eye was not dim nor his natural force abated" (*Deut.* xxxiv. 7). The vigor and undecaying strength of the law is transferred to the lawgiver (*Heb.* i. 11, 12).

247. *As in a glistering zodiac.* Raphael's belt was like a starry zone. There the stars were the divine promises; here they probably are the divine threatenings, though in both cases the girdle is Truth (*Eph.* vi. 14).

249. *Adam bowed low,* etc. This is the homage which man, when penitent, pays to Divine Justice. On the other hand, Justice would cease to be itself if it bowed or yielded to the weakness of man. The Law is exacting; every point must be fulfilled (*Matt.* v. 17).

258. *Redeem thee quite,* etc. Adam, like other men, is exposed to the effects of the original sin, but nothing further. If he were now to keep the Divine Law perfectly, he might be redeemed from death, for the man who doeth the things in the law shall live by them (*Rom.* x. 5; *Luke* x. 27, 28). Perhaps the translation of Enoch and Elijah may exemplify this truth.

263–369. EFFECT OF THE SENTENCE

The conviction of the guilty pair and judgment in general terms came on the preceding evening from the Messiah; the specific sentence for immediate execution is here announced by Michael.

265. *Eve who unseen,* etc. Compare the well-known passage, *Jer.* xxxi. 15, which expresses sorrow for exile from Jerusalem, and therefore is a fit model for Eve's lament on being exiled from Paradise.

270. *Thee, native soil,* etc. To these things Eve had attached herself as a child is attached to a parent. The walks and shades symbolize the guidance and protection which a parent exercises over a child. Parental care is a type of Divine Providence, and therefore the walks and shades are a "fit haunt of gods" (*Ps.* ciii. 13).

273. *O flowers,* etc. To the flowers Eve herself is as a mother training her children from infancy. The graces of humility and docility appropriate to children are found in perfection only in the kingdom of God (*Matt.* xviii. 1–4). The duties of a mother to her offspring are typified in the attentions of Eve to her flowers—training in morality and instruction in the Word of God.

280. *Thee, lastly, nuptial bower,* etc. This touches the conjugal, as the former part of the lament touched the filial and parental affections that are satisfied in a perfect home. In the relation of husband and wife there is a descent from communion on the high plane of mutual love to the lower plane of authority and obedience.

287. *Lament not, Eve,* etc. In her reluctance to depart from Paradise Eve is like Lot's wife, who looked longingly back to the home upon which the judgments of God were descending (*Gen.* xix. 26; *Luke* xvii. 31–33).

292. *Where he abides,* etc. Andromache, after being deprived by Achilles of parents, brothers, and home, finds all made up to her in Hector (*Il.* vi. 413–430).

296. *Whether among,* etc. Michael is called "one of the chief princes," "the great prince," and the commander of the heavenly armies (*Dan.* x. 13; xii. 1; *Rev.* xii. 7).

307. *If by prayer,* etc. Compare the experience of David, 2 *Sam.* xii. 16, 22, 23.

318. *Place by place,* etc. The patriarchs were accustomed to mark the places of God's appearance to them with memorial stones (*Gen.* xii. 7, and often).

340. *Surmise not then,* etc. Compare the reply to the woman of Samaria to correct her ideas as to the proper place for worship (*John* iv. 20–23).

343. *Thy capital,* etc. The sign of Adam's headship of the race. The tribes of men would go up to Paradise as the Israelites went to Jerusalem (*Ps.* cxxii. 4).

345. *To celebrate and reverence thee,* etc. Had Adam remained steadfast he would have received some of the reverence now given to the second Adam as the head of the human race. But the first Adam is deprived of his headship and, like every other man, must now look to Christ as his head and the head of mankind (1 *Cor.* xi. 3).

357. *To show thee,* etc. An angel revealed the future to Daniel and to St. John (*Dan.* x. 14; *Rev.* x. 6, 7).

362. *Moderation,* etc. Paul recommended moderation and showed by his own example how to practise it (*Philip.* iv. 5, 11, 12). "Medio tutissimus ibis" (Ovid, *Met.* ii. 137).

365. *Endure they mortal passage,* etc. *Matt.* x. 22. The patience here recommended works experience and experience the hope which sustains man in the hour of death.

366. *Ascend this hill,* etc. We are not permitted to forget the scene upon the mount of Transfiguration, where the Second Adam met Moses and Elijah, like Michael, representatives of the Law. The disciples, like Eve, had their eyes drenched with sleep (*Luke* ix. 32), but they saw as in a vision what was going on (*Matt.* xvii. 9).

370–465. THE MASQUE OF DEATH—FIRST ACT

In the draught of a tragedy on the subject of this poem Milton provides for showing Adam a "mask of all the evils of this life and world." This, with a prologue describing the theatre, is exhibited before Adam in the remainder of the present book.

371. *Safe guide.* Moses, the lawgiver, was the guide of God's people to the rest of Canaan.

378. *Of Paradise the highest,* etc. The idea of a material hill of such a height must be dismissed. Adam was in the spirit, as Ezekiel (viii. 3) and John (*Rev.* i. 10) were on other occasions. What Adam saw was presented to him in a picture, as the visions of Daniel were presented to that prophet. But could not Adam have seen the western hemisphere as well as the eastern from such a hill? I answer, no; because it is impossible to form a picture of two opposite sides of the world, or of any other object, from the same spot. Hence Adam beholds the opposite side of the world "in spirit."

382. *For different cause,* etc. Michael gave the prospect to the first Adam to show him what he had lost; Satan to the Second Adam to show him what he might win. The seats of empire would remind Adam of his lost headship of the race.

388. *Seat of Cathaian Can.* Genghis Khan, the Mongolian conqueror, came from the north of China, and his capital city, Cambalu, or Cambaluc, was in the sixteenth and seventeenth centuries supposed to be somewhere north of China, but it is now known to have been on the site of Pekin ("Paquin").

389. *Samarchand,* on a branch of the Oxus, was the first capital of Tamerlane's empire.

391. *Great Mogul.* The first Great Mogul, or emperor of Delhi after the Mongolian conquest of Hindoostan, was a great-grandson of Tamerlane.

392. *The golden Chersonese* (Aurea Chersonesus) was the ancient name of Farther India, including the peninsula of Malacca.

394. *In Hispahan.* In the latter part of the seventeenth century the population of the city was estimated at from 600,000 to 1,000,000.

395. *In Moscow.* Muscovy and Turkey in Europe were formerly reckoned as parts of Asia.

397. *Negus* in Ethiopic signifies king, and is therefore a title, like Pharaoh, Sultan, Shah, etc.—*Keightley.* The most northern port of Abyssinia on the Red Sea is Ercoco (Arkecko).—*Masson.*

398. *The less maritime kings.* The lesser kingdoms on the African coast. The first four are on the eastern coast, the next two on the western.

402. *Or thence,* etc. The reader is supposed to be sufficiently acquainted

with the earth not to be misled by the loose form of this enumeration.

403. *Almanzor,* "the victorious," Caliph of Bagdad, reigned from 754 to 775; his conquests extended over the northwest and a great part of the north coast of Africa.

407. *Rich Mexico,* etc. The riches of Mexico consisted largely in silver, those of Peru in gold.

410. *Guiana.* "Sir Walter Raleigh's last voyage was to Guiana, for the discovery of a gold-mine which he asserted to be there. Wonderful traditions had been current of a golden city, El Dorado, in the interior."— *Clar. Press.*

Milton's enumeration is remarkable no less for what it omits than for what it includes. We observe that the empires and kingdoms are those of modern times, that they are famous for producing and amassing silver, gold, silks, ivory, and precious stones, and that they are barbarous or semi-barbarous, no enlightened Christian kingdom being included. Rome is not an exception, for Rome is the very seat of worldliness and Mammonism. The kingdoms of Britain, Germany, Holland, and Scandinavia are regarded as kingdoms of Christ and therefore not properly included in this enumeration. Hence also the Holy Land is passed over in silence. Whether France would be included under the sway of Rome it would be difficult to decide.

414. *Euphrasy and rue.* Euphrasy (εὐφρασία) means delight, mirth; rue is a bitter herb. This purgation corresponds in part to that of the book which the angel gave to John, sweet and bitter together (*Rev.* x. 10)— preparing him to receive a disclosure of the world's history. It may mean that by the discipline of life men are prepared to receive wisdom.

416. *Well of life,* etc. *Ps.* xxxvi. 9. Spiritual truth comes to men by three agencies, Moses, the Prophets, and Christ, all brought together on the mount of Transfiguration.

432. *An altar* was used *as a landmark* by Jacob and Laban (*Gen.* xxxi. 45–54).

434. *A sweaty reaper.* This uncleanliness violates the decency of worship (*Matt.* vi. 17; *Exod.* xl. 30–33).

436. *Unculled.* The wrong was not in offering green ears, for such an offering was afterwards commanded (*Lev.* ii. 14), but in the neglect to offer only the full and perfect.

437. *More meek.* Because he observed the proprieties of worship violated by the other.

445. *Into the midriff.* Cain killed Abel treacherously, probably as Joab killed Abner and Amasa (compare *Gen.* iv. 8 with 2 *Sam.* iii. 27; xx. 9, 10).

453. *He also moved.* Christ and the angels are not indifferent to the sufferings of the righteous (*Isa.* lxiii. 9; *John* xi. 35). The spirit of Justice is quickly "moved" by wrong-doing.

466–554. THE SECOND ACT

469. *Grim cave.* Caves were used in ancient times as burial places (*Gen.* xxiii. 17, 19). Under the sea, between Tenedos and Imbrus, Neptune had a cave where he kept his horses (*Il.* xiii. 32, 33). The entrance to Hades is the mouth of a cave (*Æn.* vi. 237).

470. *More terrible,* etc. Seneca says, "Pompa mortis magis terret, quam mors ipsa."

472. *By fire, flood, famine,* etc. Compare *Æn.* vi. 273–289, where Virgil gives an account of the forms of evil that dwell about the entrance to the cave of Orcus.

476. *The inabstinence of Eve.* Eve, as has been seen, represents the element of Desire in the moral nature, and it is giving loose reins to desire that produces intemperance, with its train of evils.

485. The three lines beginning here were not in the first edition of the poem.

487. *Marasmus,* consumption.

492. *Oft invoked,* etc. *Rev.* ix. 6.

494. *Sight so deform,* etc. The spectacle of the mutilated Deiphobus in Hades caused Æneas to weep. Deiphobus, too, got his deformity through his alliance with Grecian Helen after the death of Paris (*Æn.* vi. 495–539).

496. *Though not of woman born.* Neither was Æneas born of woman, but of the goddess Venus. No element of unmanly tenderness was needed in Adam's nature to account for his tears at the wretchedness which he saw. The second Adam, born of a woman, wept over the restlessness and misery of Jerusalem (*Luke* xix. 41, 42).

502. *Better end here unborn.* A natural reflection for the man upon beholding the scenes which, when God saw, caused him to repent that he had made the race (*Gen.* vi. 6). For what follows see *Job* iii. 20, 21, 10–13).

511–524. The questions of these lines are propounded and answered in *Rom.* i. 22–27.

531. *By temperance taught.* As indulgence of appetite shortens the years of men and causes suffering (*Prov.* v. 9–11), so self-restraint lengthens life and increases comfort (*Prov.* iii. 2, 16, etc.). Since appetite is strongest in youth, obedience to parents means self-restraint, and long life is the reward for such obedience. A worldling no less than a Christian may practise the abstinence and receive the benefit.

535. *Like ripe fruit. Job* v. 26. Newton refers to Cicero (*De Senectute,* xix.): "Et quasi poma ex arboribus, cruda si sint vi avelluntur; si matura et cocta, decidunt; sic vitam adolescentibus vis aufert, senibus maturitas."

538. *This is old age,* etc. A description of old age in *Eccl.* xii. may have suggested some of these ideas to Milton.

544. *A melancholy damp,* etc. The clouds returning after the rain, hiding the stars and weighing down the spirits (*Eccl.* xii. 2, 3) are probably the basis of these lines.

553. *Nor love thy life nor hate,* etc. Commentators quote *Martial* x. 47: "Summum nec metuas diem, nec optes," and Horace, *Odes* I. ix. 9: "Permitte divis cetera."

555–636. THE THIRD ACT

556. *A spacious plain.* "The tents of wickedness" have often become congregated on plains, as on the plain of Shinar, or Babylon (*Gen.* xi. 2), the plain of the Dead Sea (*Gen.* xix. 28, 29), and the Roman Campania.

557. *Tents of various hue.* Milton in describing the doings of Cain's descendants follows the account in *Gen.* iv. 20–22. The "herds of cattle" belong to Jabal's family, the instruments of music to Jubal's.

561. *His volant touch,* etc. The *Clar. Press* quotes Professor Taylor's opinion that the pregnant meaning of this passage can be fully appreciated only by a musician. "All other poets but Milton and Shakespeare make blunders about music, they never." The musician's touch moves back and forth over the keys as if a spirit were among the harmonic relations.

571. *First his own tools,* etc. Tubal-Cain in many respects resembles Vulcan, the worker of metals in mythology. The latter, when visited by Thetis in behalf of Achilles, has his implements—the anvil, the sledge, and the pincers—about him (*Il.* xviii. 476). The first object of the art in which he is engaged is *Use,* the second *Ornament.* Accordingly, we find Vulcan united in marriage to the most beautiful of women, Charis (Grace) (*Il.* xviii. 382), or even Venus, the goddess of beauty. The poetical mind of Milton thus saw a larger meaning in the biblical statement that "the sister of Tubal-Cain was Naamah" (The Beautiful).

574. *On the hither side,* etc. The human pair descended from the Garden on the eastern side and lived among the hills between Eden and the table-land of Persia (*Gen.* iii. 24). Cain removed still farther to the east (*Gen.* iv. 16).

577. *Just men,* etc. They are called "the sons of God"; and this implies that they are blameless, harmless, and without rebuke (*Phil.* ii. 15), and led by the Spirit of God (*Rom.* viii. 14).

582. *A bevy of fair women,* etc. The wanton women who rule the rulers of Zion are described in *Isa.* iii. 12, etc.

590. *Nuptial torch,* etc. As in the cities on the shield of Achilles (*Il.* xviii. 490–496).

591. *Hymen then first invoked,* etc. Probably based on *Gen.* iv. 26, "Then began men to call upon the name of the Lord." Of course, the usual interpretation of this difficult clause would forbid such a use of it; but the rabbins take it to mean that at this time men began to practise idolatry. Milton's idea would agree with this and the context in *Genesis* would suit it perfectly.

595. *Attached the heart,* etc. Peaceful scenes are attractive to the natural heart, and special divine grace is needed to deliver man from the seductions of pleasure.

605. *Created as thou art,* etc. Holiness and not pleasure is the end of man (1 *Pet.* i. 14–16).

614. *Seemed of goddesses,* etc. Helen of Troy was declared even by the aged senators of the city to be "like in feature to the deathless goddesses" (*Il.* iii. 158).

618. *Bred only,* etc. They are not trained intellectually to be the companions and helpers of men, woman's true sphere, but to gratify the lower nature by means of bodily attractions and accomplishments.

622. *The Sons of God.* "Keightley observes that Milton has at different times adopted each of the three hypotheses as to the 'sons of God' in *Gen.* vi. 2 (cp. v. 447; xi. 622, and *Par. Reg.* ii. 179)."—*Clar. Press.* But in the first case Milton denies that the sons of God (if they were angels) could have been guilty of the lust described; in the second he affirms that the sons of God were men; and in the third he represents the evil spirits as inspiring the men in their lusts. There is no inconsistency.

625. *Atheists* confirms the interpretation of l. 591. It also suggests 2 *Cor.* vi. 14.

Now swim in joy, etc. The flood of woe that comes from such marriages is fitly symbolized by the deluge that drowned the world. The alliances of the Israelites with the daughters of Moab had a similar issue (*Num.* xxv. 1–6).

632. *Man's woe,* etc. "Todd points out this 'ungallant jingle' and quotes contemporary writers to show that this derivation of 'woman' is not Milton's invention."—*Clar. Press.*

634. *Effeminate slackness,* etc. Such effeminacy is condemned in *Prov.* xxxi. 3 and *Isa.* iii. 12.

637–712. THE FOURTH ACT

639. *Towns and rural works.* Newton saw the resemblance of the various parts of this vision to the scenes on the shield of Achilles, but he does not seem to have suspected the reason for it in the identity of Michael and Achilles.

642. *Giants of mighty bone,* etc. Gen. vi. 4. Instead of giants, gods were among the warriors graven on the shield (*Il.* xviii. 518, 519).

647. *A herd of beeves,* etc. *Il.* xviii. 523–540. A scene like this must have occurred (for Lot was rich in flocks and herds) in the first recorded battle (*Gen.* xiv. 12–16).

655. *Others to a city,* etc. Sieges follow warfare in the field, for it was the prior experience of war that taught men to fortify their cities. Compare the siege of Rabbath Ammon, one of the severest described in the Bible (2 *Sam.* xi.).

660. *In other part,* etc. *Il.* xviii. 497–508. The city gates were the place of council to the Hebrews, as the agora was to the Greeks and the forum to the Latins.

664. *In factious opposition,* etc. The old men and the young (warriors) gave different counsels according to their respective natures, as afterwards to Rehoboam (1 *Kings* xiii. 1–16). Enoch, at the age of 365, stood between the old and the young and advised a course of moderation and justice (*Jude* 14, 15).

669. *Exploded,* etc. Like the Sodomites, they hissed their disapprobation, but both Enoch and Lot were delivered by divine interposition (*Gen.* xix. 9, 10).

676. *Death's ministers, not men.* The expression points to *Il.* xviii. 535–540.

687. *Prodigious births,* etc. Lust leads to inner discord, eventuating in actual wars in the flesh (*James* iv. 1, 2).

691. *To overcome in battle,* etc. This applies to the Fourth, or Heroic, Age of Hesiod, in which Jupiter "made the divine brood of heroes, better and braver than the third or brazen race" (*Works and Days,* 157).

713–901. THE CATASTROPHE

714. *Jollity and game,* etc. This agrees with Christ's picture of the time (*Matt.* xxiv. 38).

718. *Civil broils.* Contentions and wounds without cause are the natural sequence of tarrying too long at the wine (*Prov.* xxiii. 29, 30).

719. *A reverend sire,* etc. At the age of 600 Noah condemned the world in building the ark (*Heb.* xi. 7).

728. *From the mountain,* etc. The ark was to be made "of gopher wood" (*Gen.* vi. 14); and as the Hebrew means "pitch," Milton took the wood to be a species of pine.

738. *The South-wind,* etc. Ovid in describing Deucalion's flood says, "Madidis Notus evolat alis."

740. *The hills to their supply,* etc. The meaning is that the hills added their waters to the supply of the clouds. The warm South wind melted the snow that lay on the hills and weighted the clouds still more heavily with vapor, or began to fill the valleys from the overflowing brooks and torrents. The use of the word "dusk" is easily understood from a comparison of *Job* vi. 16, where snow waters are said to be "blackish."

747. *Rode tilting,* etc. Gen. vii. 18; *Met.* i. 287–303. Milton doubtless added the feature from Ovid, in order to suggest that the only shelter from divine wrath is that divinely appointed—Jesus Christ, the ark of safety (1 *Pet.* iii. 20, 21).

758. *Till gently reared,* etc. Daniel, too, was overcome with sorrow at the vision of the future and lost all strength, until the angel in the form of a man touched and strengthened him (*Dan.* x. 14–19).

767. *The burden of many ages.* This burden was borne by the second Adam, the true head of the race (*Isa.* liii. 4). Daniel, faint and sick with sorrow at the revelation of the future, felt the burden of all the sins of Jerusalem (*Dan.* viii. 27; ix. 2–19).

768. *Gaining birth abortive.* These evils to come, by being foretold to Adam, are brought forth before their time.

772. *Evil he may be sure,* etc. Matt. vi. 34. The impossibility of finding out the future and the certainty of evil to come to all who live is the burden of *Ecclesiastes.*

784. *Peace to corrupt.* The state of things before the Flood was one of peace (*Matt.* xxiv. 38) and corruption (*Gen.* vi. 12).

789–798. *First seen in acts,* etc. For the basis of this description see *Dan.* xi. 9–32.

802. *Practise how,* etc. The Jews at the time of Christ were subject to the Romans and paying them tribute; and the days of Noah were like those of Christ (*Matt.* xxiv. 37–39).

805. *That temperance may be tried.* Intemperance is the fault of the faithless servant who falls under the condemnation of his master (*Matt.* xxiv. 49) and was the special sin of the Antediluvians.

829. *Then shall this Mount,* etc. The opinion of Luther on this point became the popular one: "Paradise shut at first by the sin of man has since been so utterly wasted and overwhelmed by the Flood that no trace of it remains." The fate of Paradise is like that of Jerusalem whose temple was utterly swept away by the flood of Roman invasion (*Matt.* xxiv. 2; *Dan.* ix. 26).

831. *Pushed by the horned flood.* The river gods were usually represented with horns (Virgil, *Georg.* iv. 371). A horned he-goat was to Daniel a symbol of the Grecian power that came against the Holy Land (*Dan.* viii. 21–25).

833. *The great river,* the Hiddekel, or Tigris, flowed under the mount of Paradise (*Dan.* x. 4). "Probably the Euphrates is meant" (*Gen.* xv. 18).—*Verity.*

835. *The haunt of seals,* etc. "The wild beasts of the islands" (*Isa.* xiii. 22, etc.) are so called probably because of their amphibious nature.

840. *Hull.* "A ship is said to hull when all her sails are taken down and she floats to and fro."—*Richardson.*

842. *Keen north wind,* etc. The Deluge lasted about a year (*Gen.* vii. 11; viii. 14), and after the one hundred and fifty days during which the waters "prevailed," winter came on and the cold began to straiten the breadth of the waters (*Job* xxxvii. 10).

844. *And the clear sun,* etc. The waters fell during the early winter until the mountain tops were seen (*Gen.* viii. 5). From that time on—the beginning of the tenth month, corresponding to about our first of January—the sun grew gradually stronger and aided in removing the waters. Possibly the expression "watery glass" is used by Milton to signify that the waters were frozen and that the ark was held by the ice for several months above Mount Ararat.

855–864. *A raven flies,* etc. *Gen.* viii. 6–20. The raven and the dove probably symbolize the motives of Selfishness and Love. Love brings men back into the kingdom of God when Selfishness, which ought to conduce to the same end, fails.

865. *In the cloud a bow,* etc. *Gen.* ix. 13–17. Even the pagans knew the rainbow as a "sign" (*Il.* xi. 27, 28).

874. *Far less I now lament,* etc. God also had esteemed more highly the one righteous man whom he saved than the whole ungodly world which he destroyed (2 *Pet.* ii. 5; *Ps.* xxxvii. 16).

878–901. *His anger to forget.* Noah's sacrifice, with the reverence and worship that prompted it, turned away God's anger. The basis of these lines is mainly in *Genesis.*

BOOK XII

1–104. THE ORIGIN OF SLAVERY

1–5. These lines were not in the first edition, but were added when the work was divided into twelve books.

4–9. The effect of the divine revelation upon Adam was like that of a similar revelation upon Daniel (*Dan.* x. 15, 16).

11. *I will relate,* etc. The angel with Daniel likewise abandoned the method of instruction which he had at first used—the method of visions setting forth the truth by symbolical figures—and resorted to plain narrative, "I will show thee that which is noted in the Scripture of truth" (*Dan.* x. 21). This parallel furnishes an overwhelming refutation of Addison's criticism (*Spectator,* 309): "To give my opinion freely, I think that the exhibiting part of the history of mankind in vision, and part in narrative, is as if a history-painter should put in colors one-half of his subject and write down the remaining part of it."

14–20. The remembrance of Divine judgments was temporarily effective, as it was afterwards upon the Israelites (*Judg.* ii. 7; *Deut.* viii.).

23. *By families,* etc. *Gen.* x. 5, 20, 31, 32. The organization of society was patriarchal.

25. *Not content,* etc. Nimrod's ambition was like Abimelech's (*Judg.* ix, 1, 2). Fraternal equality is the proper relation of men to each other, but in establishing kingship Nimrod and Abimelech destroyed this equality.

29. *Law of nature.* The law of nature is to be governed, as in the patriarchal state, by the oldest and wisest, but the law of monarchy frequently assigns the superiority to the most ignoble. This is the moral of Jotham's parable (*Judg.* ix. 8–15).

34. *As in despite of Heaven,* etc. The expression, "a mighty hunter before the Lord," has received the two explanations here offered by Milton: one that Nimrod blasphemously defied the Almighty, and the other that he pretended to derive his sovereignty from Heaven and to reign *jure divino.*

36. *From rebellion,* etc. The name Nimrod was supposed to mean "rebellious." Though he taxes men with rebellion, he is himself a rebel against the authority of nature and God.

40. *From Eden towards the west,* etc. *Gen.* xi. 2. That Nimrod was the founder of Babel is stated in *Gen.* x. 10; and yet Masson strangely remarks that "commentators find no authority in the Bible for connecting Nimrod with the building of the tower of Babel."

42. *The mouth of Hell.* Babylon is the harlot whose "house is the way to Hell" (*Prov.* vii. 27). Babylon often does service for Rome, which is not far from Lake Avernus, reputed to be the mouth of Hell (*Faerie Queene* I. v. 31). It seems to have been a common thing among the Reformers of the sixteenth century to refer to Rome as the mouth of Hell.

52. *In derision,* etc. Milton takes the words of God in *Gen.* xi. 6 to be ironical.

63. *A various spirit,* etc. The Confusion of Tongues typifies the alienation of spirit which sprung up among the builders. A spirit of variance or faction came among those over whom Abimelech ruled (*Judg.* ix. 23). Opposed to this is the Spirit of Unity, which on the day of Pentecost, pervading the disciples of Christ, enabled them to address those of diferent speech, every one in his own tongue.

64. *O execrable son,* etc. Abimelech, who usurped kingly power after destroying all his brethren except Jotham, was cursed by that brother and afterwards by his own subjects (*Judg.* ix. 10, 27). In consequence of the curse, discord arose among the supporters of Abimelech, and his sovereignty soon came to naught. Jotham's parable would, doubtless, profoundly impress an ardent republican like Milton.

69. *Man over man,* etc. God expressly reserved the right of life and death over man when he gave it over animals (*Gen.* ix. 5, 6). When the Israelites asked a king, God regarded it as a refusal of his own authority (1 *Sam.* viii. 7; *Matt.* xxiii. 8–10).

73. *To God his tower,* etc. The later kings of Babylon repeated this attempt, when they commanded their subjects to worship images and refrain from the worship of God (*Dan.* iii. 4–6; vi. 6–9). The spiritual Babylon has the same ambition (2 *Thess.* ii. 4).

76. *Where thin air,* etc. The fate of aspiring leaders who fight against God seems to be desertion (*Acts* v. 36–39). The thin air of the upper regions accurately symbolizes the ever-decreasing number of adherents as tyranny becomes more exacting. The force of Adam's question then is, By what means will this tyrant overcome the ever-increasing tendency to desert?

79. *Justly thou abhorr'st,* etc. Nimrod, like Abimelech, probably gained his throne by slaughter and deceit, and is therefore to be abhorred (*Ps.* v. 6).

86. *Reason,* etc. Compare the opening sentences of *The Tenure of Kings and Magistrates.*

94. *As undeservedly,* etc. They have as little right to enslave man's body as the passions have to enslave his soul; hence the tyrants are in turn punished for their oppression (*Judg.* ii. 11–18).

97. *Decline so low from virtue,* etc. Virtue seems to be used here in the sense of courage. Nations sometimes become so cowardly and so lose their manliness that slavery fits them best. Witness the history of the Gibeonites (*Josh.* ix. 22–27).

101. *Irreverent son,* etc. *Gen.* ix. 20–27. The Gibeonites were descended from Canaan, the son of Ham.

105–284. THE INTRODUCTION OF LAW

114. *This side Euphrates,* etc. The eastern side, on which Paradise was situated (*Josh.* xxiv. 2, 14).

117. *While yet the patriarch,* etc. According to the chronology of *Gen.* xi. Noah survived the Flood 350 years, and Abraham was born 292 years after the Flood. The two were therefore contemporary for fifty-eight years.

128. *I see him,* etc. A distinction between the angel from whom the prophecy comes and the man to whom it comes; to the angel the future is as the present.

140. *Things by their names,* etc. The angel, after the example of the sacred writers, gives names to places by anticipation (compare *Gen.* xii. 8 and xxviii. 19).

144. *Double-founted stream.* The streams that make up the Jordan come from springs on the two sides of Anti-Lebanon. "Jordan" means "River of Judgment."

158. *Disgorging at seven mouths,* etc. Egypt is presently (l. 191) called the "river-dragon." The great dragon of the *Apocalypse* has seven heads and casts out of its mouth water as a flood (*Rev.* xii. 3, 15). Egypt, as well as Sodom and Babylon, is a type of the hostility organized against the people of God (*Rev.* xi. 8).

194. *More hardened after thaw,* etc. The metaphor of fear melting the heart is common in Scripture, and is applied particularly to Egypt in *Isa.* xix. 1. Pharaoh's heart was hardened and melted again and again.

220. *Inglorious life with servitude,* etc. Achilles expresses his preference for servitude on earth to a kingdom in Hades (*Odys.* xi. 488–491):

> "Noble Ulysses, speak not thou of death,
>   As if thou couldst console me. I would be

> A laborer on earth and serve for hire
> Some man of mean estate who makes scant cheer
> Rather than reign o'er all who have gone down
> To death."

224. *Found their government,* etc. The senate here referred to are the "elders" of the people, appointed to rule and judge among them (*Exod.* xviii. 13–26). The elders and tribal officers are often mentioned in the later history.

231. *Civil justice.* These laws are contained in *Exod.* xx.–xxiii., and were formally accepted by the people and their rulers (*Exod.* xxiv. 7). The *religious rites* were given in a more private way to Moses himself and are contained in *Exod.* xxv.–xxxi.

240. *Mediator. Deut.* v. 5; *Gal.* iii. 19. Christ is a better mediator than Moses (*Heb.* viii. 6).

250. *Of cedar,* etc. 1 *Kings* vi. 15–23. Inasmuch as the Bible declares the *ark* to have been made of "shittim wood," Keightley here again convicts Milton of error. But the ark and the sanctuary were not the same, and as cedar was used in building the temple, Milton was probably right. The ark was kept in the tabernacle as afterwards in the temple (*Exod.* xl. 21).

255. *Seven lamps,* etc. *Exod.* xxv. 31–37. "Josephus says that the seven lamps signified the seven planets, and that therefore the lamps stood slopewise to express the obliquity of the zodiac."—*Clar. Press.* But we have better authority than Josephus; for the seven candlesticks seen by John, the seven stars and the seven angels of the churches are all identified with one another (*Rev.* i. 20).

271. *Enlightener,* etc. The commandment or law of the Lord enlightens the eyes (*Ps.* xix. 8). It is a school-master to bring men to Christ (*Gal.* iii. 24).

274. *Eyes true opening,* etc. *Ps.* cxix. 18. Like Simeon, Adam rejoiced when he saw the Saviour (*Luke* ii. 30).

285–465. THE REVELATION OF GRACE

307. *Therefore shall not Moses,* etc. *Deut.* xxiv. 4; *Num.* xx. 12. The act that caused the exclusion of Moses from the Promised Land shows that he was not superior to the Law, but a servant to it, as he is designated in *Heb.* iii. 5.

310. *But Joshua,* etc. *Acts* vii. 45; *Heb.* iv. 8. The rest of Canaan symbolizes the final rest of the Christian (*Heb.* iv.). Jesus is like Joshua in conquering the foes of God's people, leading them in safety and establishing them in the Promised Land.

353. *First among the priests,* etc. I quote Masson on this passage: "In con-

sequence of a struggle for the high-priesthood between two rivals [Jason and Menelaus, 2 *Macc.* v.], Antiochus Epiphanes, King of Syria, was able to come to Jerusalem, where he plundered and polluted the Temple, and put the Maccabees to death (B.C. 173); the kingly power and the high-priesthood were united in Aristobulus, eldest son of the high-priest, John Hyrcanus (B.C. 107), and the native dynasty was abolished by Pompey (B.C. 61) who appointed Antipater, the Idumaean, to the government. Antipater's son Herod, in whose reign Christ was born, became king of Judaea B.C. 38."

372. *With such joy surcharged,* etc. With like gladness Abraham saw the day of Christ (*John* viii. 56); and Simeon was affected with joy that became painful in its intensity (*Luke* ii. 28–32).

377. *My steadiest toughts,* etc. Adam had been like the prophets and righteous men who desired to see the day of Christ, but died without the sight (*Matt.* xiii. 17).

383. *Needs must the Serpent,* etc. He in the person of Herod and the Jews did in fact expect it when they were troubled at the birth of Christ (*Matt.* ii. 3).

389. *With more strength,* etc. Christ taught Peter that he had no need of human strength and that victory won by such means was not permanent (*Matt.* xxvi. 52, 53).

432. *Fix far deeper,* etc. The fate of the devil is to be tormented with the beast (Death) and the false prophet (Sin) forever (*Rev.* xx. 10); Christ suffered from death only temporarily, and the subjection of his disciples to the same is also temporary. When this is accomplished, Satan shall be bruised under the feet, first of Jesus, then of his disciples (1 *Cor.* xv. 25; *Rom.* xvi. 20).

442. *In the profluent stream.* Milton defines baptism as the sacrament "wherein the bodies of believers who engage themselves to pureness of life, are immersed in running water (in profluentem aquam)."—*Christ. Doct.* xxviii.

466–551. CHRISTIAN LIBERTY

467. *At the world's great period.* The second Angel that appeared to John in the vision of the trumpets likewise announced the end of the world (*Rev.* x. 6, 7).

480. *What will betide,* etc. The question was anticipated and answered by the Saviour before his departure from the world (*John* xvi. 1–4).

501. *Speak all tongues,* etc. *Acts* ii. 4–6. The meaning here goes far deeper than the mere possession of philological knowledge. The Spirit of Truth speaks to a man in the language of his own heart, so that he cannot fail to understand.

508. *Wolves shall succeed,* etc. *Acts* xx. 29, 30. The wolves are those who, denying the power of Christianity in their own hearts, use it for earthly gain and self-aggrandizement.

515. *Names, places, and titles,* etc. The very things forbidden by Christ (*Matt.* xxiii. 1–13). Milton boldly expresses his judgment about these matters in a number of his prose pamphlets. The "power of the keys" given to Peter (*Matt.* xvi. 19) and afterwards to all the disciples (*John* xx. 23) was in later times appropriated by the hierarchy, or rather by the Antichrist, of whose power the Roman pontiff is the representative.

521. *Spiritual laws by carnal,* etc. Thus Jesus denied the jurisdiction of Pilate over him (*John* xix. 11), but the poet is thinking also of a later attempt to force the conscience of Christians through the exercise of civil power by spiritual authorities.

525. *Force the Spirit,* etc. Milton says of those who use compulsion in matters of faith that "instead of forcing the Christian, they force the Holy Ghost; and against the wise forewarning of Gameliel, fight against God."

531. *Heavy persecution,* etc. Shadowed forth in the war made by the beast of the Pit (Death) against God's two Witnesses (*Rev.* xi. 7), which are probably Truth and Liberty (*John* viii. 32).

534. *In outward rites,* etc. Thus exposing to shame the dead bodies of the two Witnesses. Sodom and Egypt are the recognized foes of Truth and Freedom (2 *Pet.* ii. 1–6; *Exod.* xx. 2); but no less really at Jerusalem, "where our Lord was crucified," and especially at Rome, within whose jurisdiction the crime of crimes was accomplished, have God's two Witnesses been abused and mocked (*Rev.* xi. 8–10).

540. *Respiration,* etc. *Rev.* xi. 11. Critics find here a threat of Milton at his political enemies; but the passage is only the natural terminus of the poem. The vision of the trumpets reaches its culmination in the last times when God's two Witnesses revive, strike terror into their foes, and rise publicly to heaven in a cloud to form a part of the retinue of the Messiah coming to Judgment. Is St. John also aiming at the English royalists, or is divine wisom here declaring the consequence of a tendency perpetual in our nature?

552–587. THE SUM OF WISDOM

554. *Measured this transient,* etc. The Angel of the *Apocalypse* stood with one foot on the sea and one on the land and solemnly declared the end of time after the sounding of the seventh trumpet (*Rev.* x. 2–7). The angel likewise gave John a reed with which to measure the temple of God, that is, to comprehend the history of the church (*Rev.* xi. 1).

555. *Beyond is all abyss.* Paul speaks of the "deep things of God" which

human eyes have not seen and human hearts have not conceived (1 *Cor.* ii. 9–11).

557. *Greatly instructed,* etc. To instruct and comfort is the office of the Spirit; and he, like Michael, does it through the word of Truth (*John* xiv. 16, 17).

559. *What this vessel,* etc. Christ measured his revelation to his disciples by what they could bear (*John* xvi. 12; 2 *Cor.* iv. 6, 7).

576. *Though all the stars,* etc. *Eccl.* xii. 13. The wisdom that consists in the fear of the Lord is preferred to that which consists in the knowledge of natural science (*Job* xxviii. 28). Love is also put above all mysteries and all knowledge (1 *Cor.* xiii. 2).

587. *Paradise within,* etc. The peace and joy of Heaven constitute this inner Paradise (*John* xiv. 27).

588–649. THE EXIT

588. *Let us descend,* etc. Like the disciples on the mount of Transfiguration, Adam had found it pleasant to be in a state of spiritual exaltation, instructed by the spirit of Justice in the ways of Providence, but the desire to remain so could not be gratified (*Matt.* xvii. 9; *Luke* ix. 37).

589. *The hour precise,* etc. Adam, promised salvation, in the presence of Michael is like the ancient Priam (Redeemed) with a ransom in the presence of his natural foe Achilles. Priam had placated Achilles, had received food from him, and was persuaded to compose himself to sleep in the enemy's camp; but Achilles could not have protected the old king after the break of day. Hence Mercury (Peace) roused the old man and hurried him homeward. Lot could not have been safe in Sodom or Adam in Paradise when the ministers of justice began their work. The departure of Priam from the Grecian camp, of Lot from Sodom, of the disciples from the mount with Moses and Elijah, and of Adam from Paradise seems to have been taken in the morning. The spirit of Justice is punctual; and this led Christ, when referring to his own reception of the stroke of Justice due to our sins, to speak so frequently of his "hour" (*Luke* xxii. 53).

591. *By me encamped,* etc. The guards whom Hermes had put to sleep while Priam was in the Grecian camp would have detained Priam had he remained a little longer.

594. *We may no longer stay.* Christ only, when the time for the execution of justice came, was prepared to meet it. Peter attempted to stay or defeat justice (*Matt.* xxvi. 54).

595. *With gentle dreams,* etc. This implies that the interview with Michael ended in the early morning.

597. *Thou at season fit,* etc. What the three disciples saw upon the mount was not to be revealed until after Christ's resurrection (*Matt.* xvii. 9). Daniel's vision was also sealed for a time (*Dan.* xii. 9).

607. *Adam to the bower,* etc. Eve's resting in the Bower signifies that the peace which a contemplation of the Redeemer brings to the mind descends also into the heart and comforts it (*Phil.* iv. 7). Like the Bride in the Song, though Eve slept, yet her heart was awake and ready to admit the Beloved (*Cant.* v. 2).

626. *From the other hill,* etc. This hill represents the Law, as the hill from which Adam had just descended represents Grace (*Gal.* iv. 25, 26). The two sons of Abraham, Isaac and Ishmael, typify the same things, and, like Law and Grace, are both of holy original. Ishmael, whose hand was against every man (*Gen.* xvi. 12) typifies the Law, and his descendants lived about Mount Sinai.

629. *As evening mist,* etc. This is apparently the "mist of darkness" (2 *Pet.* ii. 17) reserved for those who forsake the liberty that is in Christ, and the same as the veil upon the heart of such as turn to Moses instead of Christ, the Law instead of the Gospel (2 *Cor.* iii. 12–17).

631. *At the laborer's heel,* etc. The laborer typifies those who, depending upon their own righteousness, seek justification by the Law. The peril is as great as that of a man trying to cross a marsh in the mist and darkness of night, and one who encounters it is in danger of missing his home in heaven.

634. *As a comet,* etc. The comet portends famine, war, and pestilence, such as follows when God's Spirit of Truth and Grace is resisted and rejected (*Rev.* xi. 6). These are God's means of punishment (2 *Sam.* xxiv. 13–16).

635. *The Libyan air adust,* etc. The deadly Simoom or Sirocco is meant.

637. *In either hand,* etc. Addison pointed out that this is from *Gen.* xix. 16.

639. *Down the cliff,* etc. The mountain which was aflame with the Law could not be touched by man or beast (*Exod.* xix. 12, 13).

644. *Dreadful faces,* etc. The terror of the scene was like that which Abraham saw towards Sodom (*Gen.* xix. 28) and the Israelites towards Sinai (*Exod.* xix. 18).

645. *Some natural tears,* etc. The feeling was like that of Æneas and his companions when they left the plain where Troy, now in ashes, had recently stood (*Æn.* iii. 10–12). Æneas was also accompanied in his wanderings by the gods.

648, 649. *They, hand in hand,* etc. Disproportionate attention has been given the last two lines on account of Addison's suggestion that they might have been omitted. The question, like so many other puzzles of the poem, can be answered by a reference to the Scripture passage which

Milton was developing or by which at least he was guided. The prophetic vision with which Adam was favored was much like the last one of the prophet Daniel relating to the end of the world, and the human pair are dismissed with a reminiscence of the dismissal of the prophet: "Go thou thy way till the end be; for thou shalt rest, and stand in thy lot at the end of the days."

FICTION

FLATLAND: A ROMANCE OF MANY DIMENSIONS, Edwin A. Abbott. 96pp. 0-486-27263-X

SHORT STORIES, Louisa May Alcott. 64pp. 0-486-29063-8

WINESBURG, OHIO, Sherwood Anderson. 160pp. 0-486-28269-4

PERSUASION, Jane Austen. 224pp. 0-486-29555-9

PRIDE AND PREJUDICE, Jane Austen. 272pp. 0-486-28473-5

SENSE AND SENSIBILITY, Jane Austen. 272pp. 0-486-29049-2

LOOKING BACKWARD, Edward Bellamy. 160pp. 0-486-29038-7

BEOWULF, Beowulf (trans. by R. K. Gordon). 64pp. 0-486-27264-8

CIVIL WAR STORIES, Ambrose Bierce. 128pp. 0-486-28038-1

WUTHERING HEIGHTS, Emily Brontë. 256pp. 0-486-29256-8

THE THIRTY-NINE STEPS, John Buchan. 96pp. 0-486-28201-5

TARZAN OF THE APES, Edgar Rice Burroughs. 224pp. (Not available in Europe or United Kingdom.) 0-486-29570-2

ALICE'S ADVENTURES IN WONDERLAND, Lewis Carroll. 96pp. 0-486-27543-4

THROUGH THE LOOKING-GLASS, Lewis Carroll. 128pp. 0-486-40878-7

MY ÁNTONIA, Willa Cather. 176pp. 0-486-28240-6

O PIONEERS!, Willa Cather. 128pp. 0-486-27785-2

FIVE GREAT SHORT STORIES, Anton Chekhov. 96pp. 0-486-26463-7

TALES OF CONJURE AND THE COLOR LINE, Charles Waddell Chesnutt. 128pp. 0-486-40426-9

FAVORITE FATHER BROWN STORIES, G. K. Chesterton. 96pp. 0-486-27545-0

THE AWAKENING, Kate Chopin. 128pp. 0-486-27786-0

A PAIR OF SILK STOCKINGS AND OTHER STORIES, Kate Chopin. 64pp. 0-486-29264-9

HEART OF DARKNESS, Joseph Conrad. 80pp. 0-486-26464-5

LORD JIM, Joseph Conrad. 256pp. 0-486-40650-4

THE SECRET SHARER AND OTHER STORIES, Joseph Conrad. 128pp. 0-486-27546-9

THE "LITTLE REGIMENT" AND OTHER CIVIL WAR STORIES, Stephen Crane. 80pp. 0-486-29557-5

THE OPEN BOAT AND OTHER STORIES, Stephen Crane. 128pp. 0-486-27547-7

THE RED BADGE OF COURAGE, Stephen Crane. 112pp. 0-486-26465-3

MOLL FLANDERS, Daniel Defoe. 256pp. 0-486-29093-X

ROBINSON CRUSOE, Daniel Defoe. 288pp. 0-486-40427-7

A CHRISTMAS CAROL, Charles Dickens. 80pp. 0-486-26865-9

THE CRICKET ON THE HEARTH AND OTHER CHRISTMAS STORIES, Charles Dickens. 128pp. 0-486-28039-X

A TALE OF TWO CITIES, Charles Dickens. 304pp. 0-486-40651-2

THE DOUBLE, Fyodor Dostoyevsky. 128pp. 0-486-29572-9

THE GAMBLER, Fyodor Dostoyevsky. 112pp. 0-486-29081-6

NOTES FROM THE UNDERGROUND, Fyodor Dostoyevsky. 96pp. 0-486-27053-X

THE ADVENTURE OF THE DANCING MEN AND OTHER STORIES, Sir Arthur Conan Doyle. 80pp. 0-486-29558-3

THE HOUND OF THE BASKERVILLES, Arthur Conan Doyle. 128pp. 0-486-28214-7

THE LOST WORLD, Arthur Conan Doyle. 176pp. 0-486-40060-3

DOVER · THRIFT · EDITIONS

FICTION

A JOURNAL OF THE PLAGUE YEAR, Daniel Defoe. 192pp. 0-486-41919-3

SIX GREAT SHERLOCK HOLMES STORIES, Sir Arthur Conan Doyle. 112pp. 0-486-27055-6

SHORT STORIES, Theodore Dreiser. 112pp. 0-486-28215-5

SILAS MARNER, George Eliot. 160pp. 0-486-29246-0

JOSEPH ANDREWS, Henry Fielding. 288pp. 0-486-41588-0

THIS SIDE OF PARADISE, F. Scott Fitzgerald. 208pp. 0-486-28999-0

"THE DIAMOND AS BIG AS THE RITZ" AND OTHER STORIES, F. Scott Fitzgerald. 0-486-29991-0

MADAME BOVARY, Gustave Flaubert. 256pp. 0-486-29257-6

THE REVOLT OF "MOTHER" AND OTHER STORIES, Mary E. Wilkins Freeman. 128pp. 0-486-40428-5

A ROOM WITH A VIEW, E. M. Forster. 176pp. (Available in U.S. only.) 0-486-28467-0

WHERE ANGELS FEAR TO TREAD, E. M. Forster. 128pp. (Available in U.S. only.) 0-486-27791-7

THE IMMORALIST, André Gide. 112pp. (Available in U.S. only.) 0-486-29237-1

HERLAND, Charlotte Perkins Gilman. 128pp. 0-486-40429-3

"THE YELLOW WALLPAPER" AND OTHER STORIES, Charlotte Perkins Gilman. 80pp. 0-486-29857-4

THE OVERCOAT AND OTHER STORIES, Nikolai Gogol. 112pp. 0-486-27057-2

CHELKASH AND OTHER STORIES, Maxim Gorky. 64pp. 0-486-40652-0

GREAT GHOST STORIES, John Grafton (ed.). 112pp. 0-486-27270-2

DETECTION BY GASLIGHT, Douglas G. Greene (ed.). 272pp. 0-486-29928-7

THE MABINOGION, Lady Charlotte E. Guest. 192pp. 0-486-29541-9

"THE FIDDLER OF THE REELS" AND OTHER SHORT STORIES, Thomas Hardy. 80pp. 0-486-29960-0

THE LUCK OF ROARING CAMP AND OTHER STORIES, Bret Harte. 96pp. 0-486-27271-0

THE HOUSE OF THE SEVEN GABLES, Nathaniel Hawthorne. 272pp. 0-486-40882-5

THE SCARLET LETTER, Nathaniel Hawthorne. 192pp. 0-486-28048-9

YOUNG GOODMAN BROWN AND OTHER STORIES, Nathaniel Hawthorne. 128pp. 0-486-27060-2

THE GIFT OF THE MAGI AND OTHER SHORT STORIES, O. Henry. 96pp. 0-486-27061-0

THE ASPERN PAPERS, Henry James. 112pp. 0-486-41922-3

THE BEAST IN THE JUNGLE AND OTHER STORIES, Henry James. 128pp. 0-486-27552-3

DAISY MILLER, Henry James. 64pp. 0-486-28773-4

THE TURN OF THE SCREW, Henry James. 96pp. 0-486-26684-2

WASHINGTON SQUARE, Henry James. 176pp. 0-486-40431-5

THE COUNTRY OF THE POINTED FIRS, Sarah Orne Jewett. 96pp. 0-486-28196-5

THE AUTOBIOGRAPHY OF AN EX-COLORED MAN, James Weldon Johnson. 112pp. 0-486-28512-X

DUBLINERS, James Joyce. 160pp. 0-486-26870-5

A PORTRAIT OF THE ARTIST AS A YOUNG MAN, James Joyce. 192pp. 0-486-28050-0

THE METAMORPHOSIS AND OTHER STORIES, Franz Kafka. 96pp. 0-486-29030-1

THE MAN WHO WOULD BE KING AND OTHER STORIES, Rudyard Kipling. 128pp. 0-486-28051-9

YOU KNOW ME AL, Ring Lardner. 128pp. 0-486-28513-8

SELECTED SHORT STORIES, D. H. Lawrence. 128pp. 0-486-27794-1

THE CALL OF THE WILD, Jack London. 64pp. 0-486-26472-6

FIVE GREAT SHORT STORIES, Jack London. 96pp. 0-486-27063-7

THE SEA-WOLF, Jack London. 248pp. 0-486-41108-7

WHITE FANG, Jack London. 160pp. 0-486-26968-X

DEATH IN VENICE, Thomas Mann. 96pp. (Available in U.S. only.) 0-486-28714-9

THE NECKLACE AND OTHER SHORT STORIES, Guy de Maupassant. 128pp. 0-486-27064-5

BARTLEBY AND BENITO CERENO, Herman Melville. 112pp. 0-486-26473-4

THE OIL JAR AND OTHER STORIES, Luigi Pirandello. 96pp. 0-486-28459-X

THE GOLD-BUG AND OTHER TALES, Edgar Allan Poe. 128pp. 0-486-26875-6

TALES OF TERROR AND DETECTION, Edgar Allan Poe. 96pp. 0-486-28744-0

DOVER·THRIFT·EDITIONS

FICTION

THE QUEEN OF SPADES AND OTHER STORIES, Alexander Pushkin. 128pp. 0-486-28054-3

THE STORY OF AN AFRICAN FARM, Olive Schreiner. 256pp. 0-486-40165-0

FRANKENSTEIN, Mary Shelley. 176pp. 0-486-28211-2

THE JUNGLE, Upton Sinclair. 320pp. (Available in U.S. only.) 0-486-41923-1

THREE LIVES, Gertrude Stein. 176pp. (Available in U.S. only.) 0-486-28059-4

THE BODY SNATCHER AND OTHER TALES, Robert Louis Stevenson. 80pp. 0-486-41924-X

THE STRANGE CASE OF DR. JEKYLL AND MR. HYDE, Robert Louis Stevenson. 64pp. 0-486-26688-5

TREASURE ISLAND, Robert Louis Stevenson. 160pp. 0-486-27559-0

GULLIVER'S TRAVELS, Jonathan Swift. 240pp. 0-486-29273-8

THE KREUTZER SONATA AND OTHER SHORT STORIES, Leo Tolstoy. 144pp. 0-486-27805-0

THE WARDEN, Anthony Trollope. 176pp. 0-486-40076-X

FATHERS AND SONS, Ivan Turgenev. 176pp. 0-486-0073-5

ADVENTURES OF HUCKLEBERRY FINN, Mark Twain. 224pp. 0-486-28061-6

THE ADVENTURES OF TOM SAWYER, Mark Twain. 192pp. 0-486-40077-8

THE MYSTERIOUS STRANGER AND OTHER STORIES, Mark Twain. 128pp. 0-486-27069-6

HUMOROUS STORIES AND SKETCHES, Mark Twain. 80pp. 0-486-29279-7

AROUND THE WORLD IN EIGHTY DAYS, Jules Verne. 160pp. 0-486-41111-7

CANDIDE, Voltaire (François-Marie Arouet). 112pp. 0-486-26689-3

GREAT SHORT STORIES BY AMERICAN WOMEN, Candace Ward (ed.). 192pp. 0-486-28776-9

"THE COUNTRY OF THE BLIND" AND OTHER SCIENCE-FICTION STORIES, H. G. Wells. 160pp. (Not available in Europe or United Kingdom.) 0-486-29569-9

THE ISLAND OF DR. MOREAU, H. G. Wells. 112pp. (Not available in Europe or United Kingdom.) 0-486-29027-1

THE INVISIBLE MAN, H. G. Wells. 112pp. (Not available in Europe or United Kingdom.) 0-486-27071-8

THE TIME MACHINE, H. G. Wells. 80pp. (Not available in Europe or United Kingdom.) 0-486-28472-7

THE WAR OF THE WORLDS, H. G. Wells. 160pp. (Not available in Europe or United Kingdom.) 0-486-29506-0

ETHAN FROME, Edith Wharton. 96pp. 0-486-26690-7

SHORT STORIES, Edith Wharton. 128pp. 0-486-28235-X

THE AGE OF INNOCENCE, Edith Wharton. 288pp. 0-486-29803-5

THE PICTURE OF DORIAN GRAY, Oscar Wilde. 192pp. 0-486-27807-7

JACOB'S ROOM, Virginia Woolf. 144pp. (Not available in Europe or United Kingdom.) 0-486-40109-X

MONDAY OR TUESDAY: Eight Stories, Virginia Woolf. 64pp. (Not available in Europe or United Kingdom.) 0-486-29453-6

NONFICTION

POETICS, Aristotle. 64pp. 0-486-29577-X

POLITICS, Aristotle. 368pp. 0-486-41424-8

NICOMACHEAN ETHICS, Aristotle. 256pp. 0-486-40096-4

MEDITATIONS, Marcus Aurelius. 128pp. 0-486-29823-X

THE LAND OF LITTLE RAIN, Mary Austin. 96pp. 0-486-29037-9

THE DEVIL'S DICTIONARY, Ambrose Bierce. 144pp. 0-486-27542-6

THE ANALECTS, Confucius. 128pp. 0-486-28484-0

CONFESSIONS OF AN ENGLISH OPIUM EATER, Thomas De Quincey. 80pp. 0-486-28742-4

THE SOULS OF BLACK FOLK, W. E. B. Du Bois. 176pp. 0-486-28041-1